BLUE GUIDE

SICILY

Ellen Grady

Edited and with additional information by
Michael Metcalfe

Somerset Books • London

Eighth edition 2012

Published by Blue Guides Limited, a Somerset Books Company
Winchester House, Deane Gate Avenue, Taunton, Somerset TA1 2UH
www.blueguides.com
'Blue Guide' is a registered trademark.

ISBN 978–1–905131–54–9

A CIP catalogue record of this book is available from the British Library.

Distributed in the United States of America by
W.W. Norton & Company, Inc.
500 Fifth Avenue, New York, NY 10110.

The editor and publisher have made reasonable efforts to ensure the accuracy of all the
information in *Blue Guide Sicily*; however, they can accept no responsibility for any loss,
injury or inconvenience sustained by any traveller as a result of information or advice
contained in the guide.

Statement of editorial independence: Blue Guides, their authors and editors, are prohibited
from accepting payment from any restaurant, hotel, gallery or other establishment for its
inclusion in this guide, or on www.blueguides.com, or for a more favourable mention than
would otherwise have been made.

The first edition of *Blue Guide Sicily* was published in 1975, compiled by Alta Macadam.
Subsequent editions have been by Alta Macadam (2nd–5th), Ellen Grady (5th–7th)
and Ellen Grady with contributions from Michael Metcalfe (present edition).

Your views on this book would be much appreciated. We welcome not only specific
comments, suggestions or corrections, but any more general views you may have: how this
book enhanced your visit, how it could have been more helpful. Blue Guides authors and
editorial and production team work hard to bring you what we hope are the best-researched
and best-presented cultural, historical and academic guide books in the English language.
Please write to us by email (editorial@blueguides.com), via the comments page on our website
(www.blueguides.com) or at the address given above. We will be happy to acknowledge
useful contributions in the next edition, and to offer a free copy of one of our titles.

Editor-in-chief: Annabel Barber
Editors of this edition: Michael Metcalfe, Annabel Barber

Maps; Dimap Bt and © Blue Guides Ltd
Line drawings: Michael Mansell RIBA & Gabriella Juhász; Site plans: Imre Bába

Ellen Grady wishes to thank all the Pro Loco and tourist offices of Sicily, Grazia Barbagallo
Mazza, Beatrice Basile, Fabio Bonaccorsi, Salvo Buffa, Rosario Cassaro, Laura Cassataro, Enzo
Castagna, Claudio Castiglione, Carmelo Chiaramonte, Salvatore Cucuzza Silvestri, Tony
D'Aiello, Franco D'Angelo, Primo David, Damiano Ferraro, Michele Gallo, Maria Costanza
Lentini, Tania Lo Cicero, Alta Macadam, Carmelo Mangano, Vincenza Muscia, Lorenzo Nigro,
Margherita Perricone, Emilia Poli Marchese, Diana and Giacomo Mazza, Franco Purpura,
Antonio Scalisi, the Touring Club Italiano, Sebastiano Tusa, the Whitaker Foundation and
Roger Wilson. And to all those who helped her so much in the past, sadly no longer with us:
Santi Correnti, Pino Di Cristina, Marcello La Greca, Carmelo Paci and Bruno Ragonese.

Michael Metcalfe would like to thank Annalisa Amico, Marcello Baglioni, Paul Beston,
Giacomo Biondi, Maria Grazia Branciforti, Francesca Buscemi, Jeremy Dummett, Marco
Falzone, Pietro Militello, Jonathan Prag, Francesco Privitera, Santo Privitera, Dario Puglisi,
Emanuela Santaniello and Lavinia Sole. Above all, he would like to thank Simona Todaro and
Sara Metcalfe for their time, company and understanding.

Grateful thanks are also due to Andrew J. Clark, Charles Freeman, Joseph Kling,
Nigel McGilchrist and George Rohrmann; and especially to Tony Spawforth, whose
Complete Greek Temples (Thames & Hudson, 2006) is an excellent resource.

Photo editing and pre-press: Hadley Kincade
Cover image: Detail from the mosaic of the Ten Girls, in the Villa del Casale at Piazza Armerina
©EmmePi, Europe/Alamy/Profimedia–Red Dot. Frontispiece: Detail of carving from the cloister
of Monreale cathedral ©istockphoto.com/Roberto Gennaro; 'Welcome' mosaic from Morgantina,
photo: Annabel Barber. Interior photographs by Giacomo Mazza: pp. 54, 145, 213, 298, 425;
Tom Howells: pp. 267, 270, 322, 331; William Hocker: p. 89; Walter Lo Cascio: p. 118 (Walter
Lo Cascio, Via XX Settembre 60, 93100 Caltanissetta); Annabel Barber: pp. 252, 259, 269, 341;
Alinari Archives, Florence: pp. 128, 238, 277, 317, 337, 359, 441; ©Aliena/Dreamstime.com:
p. 18; ©imagebroker/Alamy/Profimedia–Red Dot: p. 27; ©luigi nifosi/Shutterstock: pp. 36, 305;
©Melvyn Longhurst/Alamy/Profimedia–Red Dot: p. 74; ©funkyfood London–Paul Williams/
Alamy/Profimedia–Red Dot: pp. 76, 293; Museo Mandralisca, Cefalù/Giraudon/The Bridgeman
Art Library. p. 93; dreamstime: p. 125; ©istockphoto.com/Stefano Corso: p. 131; ©istockphoto.
com/photovideostock: p. 137; ©QCumber/Alamy/Profimedia–Red Dot: p. 158; Photo Scala,
Florence 2005: p. 168; ©istockphoto.com/ilbusca: p. 183; 1990, Photo Scala, Florence, courtesy
of the Ministero Bene e Att. Culturali: pp. 193, 194; ©EmmePi Travel/Alamy/Profimedia–Red
Dot: p. 234; The Art Archive/Archaeological Museum Syracuse/Gianni dagli Orti: p. 275;
Boerescu/Shutterstock: p. 343; ©Hemis/Alamy/Profimedia–Red Dot: pp. 376, 462; ©Christophe
Boisvieux/Corbis/Profimedia–Red Dot: p. 388; Martin Polhack/Shutterstock: p. 394;
©CuboImages Srl/Alamy/Profimedia–Red Dot: p. 404; ©Iconotec/Alamy/Profimedia–Red Dot:
p. 409; ©Stapleton Collection/Corbis/Profimedia–Red Dot: p. 443.

Every effort has been made to contact the copyright owners of material reproduced in this
guide. We would be pleased to hear from any copyright owners we have been unable to reach.

Material prepared for press by Anikó Kuzmich
Printed in Hungary by Dürer Nyomda Kft, Gyula.

CONTENTS

THE GUIDE

PRACTICAL INFORMATION

MAPS & PLANS

HISTORICAL SKETCH

by Charles Freeman and Ellen Grady

Sicily lies at the crossroads of the Mediterranean. The Italian mainland is very close, separated by the narrow Straits of Messina, while the coast of North Africa is only some 250km away, a day's sailing in good conditions. Anyone passing across the Mediterranean would be likely to make landfall in Sicily, which historically gave it immense strategic value. The island's fertility also attracted settlement, with the result that periods of prosperity were interspersed with violent conflict over resources. Sicily today is a palimpsest of earlier civilisations, their remains jostling alongside each other against the backdrop of extraordinary natural beauty.

There are traces of human settlement from the Palaeolithic age (35,000–9000 BC), with the Upper Palaeolithic (18,000–9000) especially rich in sites. These show a population able to exploit a variety of habitats along with the development of burial rituals, decorative artefacts, mostly in stone, and cave art. The art is concentrated in a group of caves on Levanzo and around Monte Pellegrino in the northwest of the island, with the focus mainly on animals, predominantly horses, oxen and deer. In the Mesolithic period (9000–6000 BC) there was more exploitation of the sea, with the result that some communities became settled on the coast. However, it was red deer which were the main source of food and hides: their bones make up 70 percent of remains on some sites. Settled agriculture, which in Sicily dates from c. 6000–5500 BC, appears to have been an imported change. The remains of corn, sheep and goats are found for the first time in this period. Pottery, known as Stentinello ware, from a Neolithic site near Syracuse, has impressed or incised decoration and from about 5500 is painted, copying styles from Italy. A particularly important trade until about 2500 was in obsidian from the Aeolian island of Lipari, a volcanic stone which can be easily cut and shaped to make tools.

The first extensive contact with the wider Mediterranean comes in the Mycenaean age (1600–1150 BC). The Mycenaean strongholds were in the Greek Peloponnese and their chieftains were successful traders, whose presence in Sicily reached its height in about 1400 BC. This is the first time that Sicily can be placed within a far-flung trading complex, with evidence of routes which stretched as far east as Rhodes and Cyprus. A harbour site such as Thapsos, near modern Syracuse, certainly grew prosperous on trade. Mycenaean civilisation disintegrated after 1200, and Sicily, like many other parts of the Mediterranean, retreated into isolation. The island's primary contact for the next three centuries was with Italy.

Sicans, Sicels, Ausonians and Elymians

Greek historians provide some details of the inhabitants of Sicily before the 8th century. Thucydides, writing in the 5th century BC, speaks of a native people of Sicily known as the Sicans, who were pushed into the southern and western parts of the island by newcomers from Italy, the Sicels (hence 'Sicilia'), who settled in the eastern region. Thucydides gives a date for the 'invasion' of some three centuries before the first Greek settlement (i.e. about 1050), but other Greek sources suggest it was much earlier, well before the Trojan War, so perhaps 1300–1250. There is some archaeological and linguistic evidence to support the arrival of newcomers from Italy in the 13th century BC, with another group known as the Ausonians, named after their mythical founder Auson, arriving from central Italy perhaps in the 11th century. A third people, the Elymians, whom Thucydides tells us were refugees from Troy, are recorded as having settled in the west of Sicily.

Phoenicians and Greeks

In the 8th century Mediterranean trade began to revive. The Phoenicians, the biblical Canaanites, from the ancient cities of the Levantine coast, are normally seen as the pioneers, probing into the western Mediterranean in search of metals with which to pay their overlords, the Assyrians. They gave confidence to the Greeks who began following the same routes. Naxos was the first Sicilian landfall for those aiming to sail round the toe of Italy from the east and it was here that settlers from Chalcis in Euboea established a base in 734. A small fertile valley gave them the means to settle and the native population appears to have been dispersed. This became the usual practice as a mass of other Greek migrants followed the Chalcidians. The Corinthians settled the best harbour of the coast, Syracuse, the very next year, while Euboeans who had earlier settled at Cumae on the west coast of Italy, then took over the harbour at Zancle (later Messina) to protect their route to Italy. So quite quickly the better harbours were taken and settlements founded. Excavations at Megara Hyblaea show how temples and an agora (a market place) on a native Greek model were planned into the early settlement. With the best sites on the east coast taken, Greeks moved along the southern coast of Sicily to found Gela (688) and Akragas (Agrigento; 580). The Sicel communities were broken up, their populations dispersed or absorbed. The Greek colonisation of Sicily was so successful that grain was soon being exported back to Greece and across to Italy and Africa. Pottery from Athens, Sparta and Corinth is found on Sicilian sites and coinage appears quite early, in the last half of the 6th century. Settlements developed into cities with large temples and other public buildings. They sent competitors to the Olympic games and, with plenty of fertile pasture for horses, were especially successful in chariot racing.

Yet there was trouble brewing. The Phoenicians had established their own settlements, notably Carthage on the coast of north Africa, and in Spain, which was rich in metal resources, and it was inevitable that there would be settlements on Sicily itself. At first these were no more than staging posts concentrated in the west. The most successful Phoenician site was Motya, a small island off the west coast (modern Mozia). It was close to Carthage, defensible (with a perimeter wall 2500m) and enjoyed good relationships with the native Elymian population. The earliest occupation dates from the late 8th century but by the 7th century there is evidence of industrial activity, in iron and dyes, and the population may have reached 16,000 in the 6th century. It was now that the Persian empire absorbed the Phoenician cities of the Levant, and gradually the western settlements developed their own independent empire under the control of Carthage.

The Carthaginians

Conflict between Carthaginians and Greeks was perhaps inevitable. The first clashes were over sites outside Sicily as the Carthaginians tried to exclude outsiders from the western Mediterranean. In 514, a Spartan, Doreius, attempted to challenge Carthage's growing power by making a Greek settlement within Carthaginian territory in Sicily, but he was driven out. The Greek cities began mobilising themselves in resistance. It became increasingly common for strong leaders, so-called tyrants, to emerge as rulers of the Greeks. One such was Gelon of Gela (491–477) who decided to make Syracuse his capital by transferring half his own city's population there. In 480 he won a spectacular victory at Himera, which led to the Carthaginians being subdued for the next 70 years. In 453 the Greeks then faced another threat, from a Hellenised Sicel, Ducetius. His Sicel League defeated several Greek cities until he was overcome in 451.

In 431 a major war broke out between Athens and Sparta, the Peloponnesian War. One of Sparta's allies, Corinth, still had close ties with its colony Syracuse, and the wealth of Sicily made it an important prize. The Athenians saw their chance to exploit local tensions when the city of Segesta appealed to them for support in their war against Selinunte. Athens sent a major expedition to the island but the size of the fleet aroused suspicions in Syracuse. Suspecting that Athenian ambitions encompassed more than just tiny Selinunte, the Syracusans called on Spartan military expertise and Corinthian naval support and destroyed the Athenian fleet. The historian Thucydides has left a harrowing account of the debacle, with the few Athenian survivors being herded off to work in Syracuse's stone quarries. However, Syracuse was also weakened. The Carthaginians saw their chance of taking revenge for Himera, and in 405 moved from their western enclave to capture Akragas and Gela. It was this crisis which saw the emergence of Syracuse's most successful tyrant, Dionysius I (*see box on p. 344*).

On Dionysius' death, his son Dionysius II became the new ruler of Syracuse. He was a failure. Despite a visit from the Athenian philosopher Plato to school him in the art of good government, the empire collapsed into anarchy. The smaller Greek cities broke away under their own tyrants, who fought among themselves as well as against the Carthaginians. Things became so desperate that the Syracusans sent back to their mother city Corinth to ask for help in restoring order. The man sent was Timoleon. He deposed Dionysius II in 344, but then had to face a siege of Syracuse by a resurgent Carthaginian empire. Only an outbreak of plague saved the city from capture. Timoleon finally defeated the Carthaginians at the Crimissus River in 341. He regained control of the smaller Greek cities, and brought about a short lived but significant period of prosperity. On his death, however, anarchy returned as different groups fought each other for power over Greek Sicily. This was the pattern for the next 70 years. A war leader would emerge, have a few years of success, and then be killed or lose control. So one Agathocles came to power as 'general with full powers' in Syracuse in 319 and took on the Carthaginians in a campaign which included an expedition to Africa itself but which ended in his defeat both there and in Sicily. He was forced to sue for peace and was assassinated in 289. One of his few achievements had been to marry a stepdaughter of the new Greek ruler of Egypt, Ptolemy I, and by doing so, bring Sicily into the wider Hellenistic world. From now on Sicilian tyrants tended to ape their colleagues in the eastern Mediterranean by taking on the trappings of kingship, including a cult of the ruler, courts and a royal family. The most influential legacy of Agathocles was largely unexpected. His mercenary force from Italy, the so-called Mamertines (in their native language 'sons of the war god Mamers', the Oscan equivalent of Mars), exploited the anarchy after his death to seize the city of Messana (later Messina), the former Greek city of Zancle, and use it as a base for plundering northeastern Sicily. A new tyrant of Syracuse, Hieron II, who like Agathocles presented himself as royalty, defeated them in 265, whereupon the Mamertines called on the Carthaginians for help. The Carthaginians did send a small garrison but the next year the Mamertines went further and appealed to Italy's most successful military power, the city of Rome. It was to be a decision which would change history.

The Romans

The Romans decided to launch an expedition to Sicily. The threat of Roman incursion brought the Carthaginians and Hieron into alliance against them but the Romans defeated their united forces, whereupon Hieron sought an alliance with Rome. It was granted and Hieron became one of the most successful of the Sicilian tyrant-kings. By supplying the Roman armies with grain, he was able to keep his kingdom and status intact, and was able to stand by and watch the protracted and debilitating war which Rome waged against the Carthaginians (the First Punic War 264–241 BC).

One of Rome's first successes in Sicily was the capture of Akragas, which had been held by a Carthaginian garrison. However, it became clear that Rome—then without a navy—could never defeat Carthage unless it acquired one. There are few better examples of Rome's resilience than the story of how she became a naval power and, despite many setbacks and some major defeats, finally crushed the Carthaginians in a naval victory off the Aegadian islands in 241. Carthaginian control of western Sicily, which had lasted many centuries, was brought to an end. The Carthaginians were still not finally defeated, however. In 218 a brilliant leader emerged: Hannibal. Seeking revenge on Rome, he invaded Italy from Spain. Then, in 215, Hieron II of Syracuse died. Syracuse was still an independent state: not wanting to fall under Roman control, she appealed to Carthage for support. Realising how crucially important it would be to regain Sicily as a base for supplies, Hannibal granted it, and sent troops. The Roman counterattack was swift, and they captured Syracuse in 212 (their victory retarded by the brilliant defence techniques masterminded by the great scientist Archimedes). The Roman general Marcellus freighted such rich booty back in triumph to Rome that Roman conservatives talked of the corruption of their city by the decadence of the Greek East.

Sicily, 'the nurse at whose breast the Roman people is fed' as Cicero was to put it, proved to be vital to Rome for a steady supply of grain to the growing city and the

Roman armies. Also an important strategic base, it was Rome's first overseas province and was ruled through a praetor, an elected magistrate with military powers. Hieron had instituted a tax in grain and it was comparatively easy for the Romans to divert this to themselves. Sicily would prove to be a well-behaved province: administration was light and cities were given a high degree of independence. By the 2nd century BC there was once again great prosperity on the island. Though the old hilltop cities went into decline, it was because their inhabitants were moving down to take advantage of the new security and opportunities for grain production on lower land. Estates grew large and slaves were brought in *en masse* from Rome's new conquests in the East. Their treatment by the new owners appears to have been brutal, however, and between c. 135–132 and c. 104–100, there were major slave revolts (*see box on p. 250*) which took hard fighting to suppress. Oppression of a very different kind came at the hands of corrupt governors, the most notorious of whom was Verres (73–71; *see box on p. 189*). Archaeology suggests that nonetheless the underlying prosperity of the province continued without interruption.

The island could not escape the civil wars which tore Rome apart in the second half of the 1st century BC. When Julius Caesar confronted the ageing general Pompey in Italy in 49, he won over Sicily by promising the Sicilians 'Latin rights', privileges which in earlier times had been given to favoured cities (and which gave access to full Roman citizenship). In the short term it worked (Pompey was defeated in 48) but after Caesar's own assassination in 44, the son of Pompey, Sextus, seized Sicily and withheld the grain supply from Rome. The Sicilians unwisely collaborated with him and when Caesar's great-nephew, Octavian, retook the island, he dealt ruthlessly with any city which did not immediately surrender. The entire population of one, Tauromenium (Taormina), was deported and others lost their Latin rights. Octavian (known, from 27 BC, as Augustus, and the first Roman emperor) established several colonies of former Roman soldiers in the province, to enforce better control, and took large tracts of land as imperial estates.

As the Roman empire expanded, the role of Sicily as a source of grain was diminished and Egypt and the North African provinces became major suppliers. A 1st-century AD mosaic of corn-growing provinces in Ostia, the port of the city of Rome, shows symbols of Sicily alongside those of Egypt, Africa and Spain. No legions needed to be stationed on the island and there is only one isolated reference to banditry, in the 260s. Mount Etna and Syracuse have occasional mentions as tourist attractions. Sicilians seem to have played little part in imperial administrations, but the archaeological evidence is of general prosperity: well-endowed towns with theatres, baths and aqueducts. One source even lists two Sicilian towns, Catania and Syracuse, as thirteenth and fourteenth in a list of celebrated cities of the empire, while the villa at Piazza Armerina shows just how sophisticated life was for the elite in the 4th century.

The Byzantine period

So life continued until the Western empire began to disintegrate in the 5th century. In 429, the Vandals under their leader Gaiseric took North Africa and began raiding the prosperous coastal towns of Sicily. In 486 he was finally able to take control of the whole island, which he sold eight years later to Odoacer, ruler of Italy following the deposition of the last Western emperor. In 535, a counter-attack by the Eastern, now Byzantine, empire, under its general Belisarius, ended with Sicily becoming part of the empire itself. By now Sicily was heavily Christianised, and papal estates had succeeded the older imperial ones. More letters survive from Pope Gregory the Great (590–604) about his Sicilian estates than about all the others put together.

The Arabs

When Sicily was captured for Byzantium by Belisarius, Syracuse became the main city on the island. The Byzantines introduced the manufacture of silk, by planting mulberries on the hills behind Messina, particularly subject to the *maestrale* wind from the northwest, cold and salty, which deposits a fine layer of salt on the leaves of the trees: the resulting thread of silk, after the silk-worms have eaten these leaves, is stronger. But the island's economy, based only on silk and wheat, began to flag, and the population was dramatically decreasing, due to poor farming methods and bouts of famine. When the Arabs landed at Mazara del Vallo in AD 827, called in by the Byzantine governor Euphemius (who was seeking assistance in his rebellion against the Byzantine emperor), they were fulfilling a long-held dream. Within 50 years they had taken over governance of the whole island, and were to prove far-sighted and intelligent rulers. They brought with them skilled craftsmen, both Jewish and Muslim. Jewish Berbers from Morocco settled in Syracuse, where they became acclaimed weavers. In Piazza Armerina and Messina their goldsmiths became renowned in the art of making wire from gold mixed with a little copper, which was exported for making filigree jewellery. Arab farmers revolutionised agriculture by introducing terracing, irrigation and water-storage tanks. They planted new crops, ranging from rice, cotton, sugar-cane, pistachios, apricots, peaches and citrus, to roses and jasmine for the perfume industry, indigo, and groves of mulberry trees to feed the silk-worms and intensify production. The island was divided into three administrative districts: Val Demone, Val di Mazara and Val di Noto, each governed by a *cadi*, who reported to an emir in Palermo. Numerous settlers came from North Africa and Spain to swell the population, and by the 10th century Sicily was one of the most prosperous countries in Europe and Palermo was one of the great centres of scholarship and art, surpassed only by Constantinople, and rivalling Cordoba and Cairo for the number of mosques, gardens and fountains. The Arabs called this country *Balad es-Siqilliah*, 'Land of the Sicels'.

The Normans

The Normans probably set their sights on Sicily around 1035, but they too had to wait for the right moment, and theirs too would prove to be an extremely long-drawn-out conquest. The Normans' greatest strength was in their mercenary troops, the most respected and feared in Europe. Their moment came in 1060, when the *cadi* Ibn at-Thumnah of Catania fell foul of Ibn al-Hawwas of Agrigento. He summoned the armies of Robert Guiscard and Roger de Hauteville to fight for him; they won that battle, the *cadi* was killed, and the Normans hung onto their spoils. Not only this; they kept fighting. In the same year Roger took Messina; by 1091 the whole island was under his control.

Despite their ruthlessness in battle, the Normans proved willing to adapt to the Arab, Jewish, Greek and Latin traditions which already existed on the island, and different religions and customs were respected. The first Sicilian Parliament met at Mazara del Vallo in 1097. Count Roger was never crowned king, although he is usually known as Roger I of Sicily. In 1099 Pope Urban II named him great-count of Calabria and Sicily, and apostolic legate. This prerogative was to prove of fundamental importance for the future of Sicily, because it meant that the ruler had the right to name the prelates in his territory—in practice, total power. When his son Roger II was crowned in 1130, it was his own archbishop who did it, and not the pope. He was probably the wealthiest ruler in Europe, and his court in Palermo the most opulent. Meanwhile Messina flourished as a supply base for the Crusaders.

Norman domination, with its architecture showing a strongly Oriental influence, has left many magnificent buildings, of which the churches are its most celebrated achievement today. The interiors of Cefalù and Monreale cathedrals and of the Cappella Palatina in Palermo all have exquisite mosaic decoration.

The Swabians, Angevins, Aragonese and Bourbons

The Norman dynasty did not last long; in 1194 the crown was claimed by Emperor Henry VI of Swabia in the name of his wife Constance (daughter of Roger II), and the last of the Hautevilles were put to death. Henry died young and was succeeded in 1198 by his baby son Frederick II of Hohenstaufen, a great king ('Stupor Mundi' or 'Wonder of the World') whose reign was troubled by a prolonged struggle with the Papacy. His court in Palermo, drawing on Islamic, Jewish and Christian cultures, was famous for its splendour and learning. Unlike his predecessors, Frederick did not endow monasteries or build cathedrals; he devoted his building energies to creating a line of fortifications running from Germany to southern Italy and Sicily. Castles dominated the cities in this area and fortresses were erected at strategic points inland. The Swabian line ended with the beheading of Conradin in 1268.

Charles of Anjou, brother of Louis IX of France, had the backing of the (French) pope, and was invested with the crown of Sicily and Naples, thus beginning the hated Angevin rule. The famous revolt of 1282, known as the Sicilian Vespers (*see p. 69*), brought an end to that unhappy period, and the Sicilians called Peter of Aragon, renowned for his sense of justice and good government, to be their king. He agreed, on condition that after his death Sicily and Aragon would be ruled as separate kingdoms. This did not come to pass, and in the course of time Sicily lost her independence and became a province of Aragon and then of Spain as a whole, to be ruled by a series of viceroys for the Spanish and then the Bourbon kings. One of these kings, Alfonso the Magnanimous, founded the University of Catania in 1434, the first in Sicily. Rebellions, famine, unrest and epidemics mark the 15th century, and in 1492 when Muslims and Jews were expelled from Spain's dominions by Ferdinand and Isabella, they were expelled from Sicily too (a quarter of all Jews in the Italian peninsula lived in Sicily), and the Inquisition was installed in Palermo.

Architecture and painting in the early 15th century were much influenced by Catalan masters, as can be seen from the south porch of the cathedral and at Palazzo Abatellis in Palermo. Matteo Carnelivari was the most important architect working in Palermo at this time. The Renaissance sculptor Francesco Laurana came to work in Palermo in the middle of the 15th century. Another influential sculptor in the second half of the same century was Domenico Gagini; his style was continued into the following century by his son Antonello and his vast progeny. If the dramatic 15th-century fresco of the *Triumph of Death* (now in the Palazzo Abatellis Regional Gallery of Palermo) is by a Sicilian master, it is the most important Sicilian painting of this period. The most famous artist of the late 15th century is Antonello da Messina, whose introduction of the technique of oil painting, which he probably learned in the Netherlands, dramatically altered the history of Western art.

The Counter-Reformation and Baroque

Because of its position on the Straits, Messina was in closer contact with the mainland than other towns in Sicily, and during the 16th century artists from Florence and Rome often travelled there, attracted by its political and social importance. Sculptors were particularly welcome, as civic administrations endeavoured to beautify their towns with flamboyant 'urban furniture'. When the young monk Giovanni Angelo Montorsoli arrived from Florence in 1547, he introduced Tuscan Mannerism with his Orion fountain (*see p. 428*), a work which proved immensely influential. This was the period of the Counter-Reformation, when lavish churches and convents were being erected all over the island in response to the Protestant threat. It was also an age of increased insecurity, as Turkish pirates continually harried ships and coasts. The brilliant victory of the Christians over the Muslims of Mohammed Ali at Lepanto in 1571 did little to solve this particular problem; and in the interior of the island brigands and bandits were making life difficult for farmers and travellers.

From the mid-17th to the end of the 18th centuries numerous splendid Baroque churches were erected in Palermo, many of them by the local architect Giacomo Amato, and the interiors were lavishly decorated with coloured marble, mosaic inlay and stuccoes. Giacomo Serpotta was a great master of this art, while Pietro Novelli of Monreale was the most outstanding of the 17th-century Sicilian painters. But it is in eastern Sicily where we find the finest examples of the so-called Sicilian Baroque (*see p. 296*). The eruption of Mount Etna in 1669, followed by the earthquake of 1693, meant that first Catania, and then most of the other towns, had to be completely rebuilt. Beauty emerged defiantly from tragedy. Architects, sculptors, master-masons, stucco-moulders, wood-carvers and painters were suddenly in great demand, and their art flourished.

In 1713, after the Treaty of Utrecht which concluded the War of the Spanish Succession, Spanish rule in Sicily ended. The island was assigned first to Savoy, then to Austria, and finally to the Bourbons of Naples, who would hold it as part of the Kingdom of the Two Sicilies until 1860.

Revolution and Unification

When Napoleon failed to invade Sicily in 1806, the British took control for a short time, and established a constitution (though it never received sufficient backing to be effective). Disaffection with the Bourbons, whose inept rule left so many Sicilians impoverished and disenfranchised, led to revolution in 1848. Though the rebels were savagely crushed, the revolutionary spirit refused to die, and in 1860 Garibaldi led an attack against the Bourbons which paved the way for Italian Unification. Unification worked better for the north of Italy than for Sicily, who found the rule of the Piedmontese statesman Camillo Cavour unsympathetic, and felt that northern Italian cities were being favoured over southern. What is certain is that the economic position of Sicily remained a long way behind that of the rest of Italy. With the collapse of the sulphur industry, a blight which attacked the silkworms making it impossible for them to spin their cocoons, and the phylloxera outbreak which destroyed the vineyards, almost a million and a half Sicilians (almost half the population at the time) chose to emigrate, to the Americas and to Australia, between 1895 and 1910.

The twentieth century

Despite economic hardship, the early 20th century was the golden age of Art Nouveau. The inspired work of Ernesto Basile and Francesco Fichera made this style fashionable throughout Sicily: as a centre of Art Nouveau architecture, Palermo is surpassed in Italy only by Turin and Milan. The carefree, wealthy middle class of Palermo, gravitating around the Florio financial empire, were flitting from their beautiful new homes to one lovely theatre after another, and to the fashionable bathing resort of Mondello, in a city which had only one hospital, and a rather forbidding one at that; while thousands of people were living in extreme poverty, in crowded slums hidden behind the attractive main streets. After the disastrous earthquake which felled Messina in December 1908, the economy of the whole island suffered. Rebuilding was by no means complete when the Second World War broke out. The geographical position of Sicily meant that the Allies chose the island for their first important attack on Hitler in Europe, Operation Husky in 1943. In 1944 civil war broke out on the island, with many islanders calling for independence. The statute for autonomous government was approved by Rome in 1946 and the first modern Sicilian parliament was elected in 1947. No economic miracle has been performed however, and even now thousands of Sicilians are still forced to emigrate in search of work.

The Mafia

The Mafia probably began as a kind of defence mechanism, or insurance policy, against the suffocating and insensitive governments of the 18th and 19th centuries. It provided immediate justice for those who had been wronged. A senior person was chosen in each community to solve controversies, he was paid in kind and his decisions were final. Everything regarding this system was protected by close secret (*omertà*), which even torture or death could not reveal. The method was certainly favoured by the aristocracy of the island, who saw it as a way of maintaining control over the people, through the offices of much-feared local agents. Shopkeepers, farmers, craftsmen, practically all categories, were invited to make regular 'offerings', or provide free services, to these individuals, in order to avoid dire consequences, but also to be sure of protection. It became an ingrained custom, called *mafia* only after the Unification of Italy in 1860: *mafia* is a Piedmontese word; on the island it has always been known as *Cosa Nostra*, 'Our Thing'.

After the Second World War, thanks to the collusion between politics and the Mafia, the phenomenon became much worse. Giovanni Falcone, the magistrate who investigated the Mafia and was assassinated in 1992, estimated that there were more than 5,000 'men of honour' in Sicily, chosen after a rigorous selection process. He saw these men as true professionals of crime, who obeyed strict rules. Through the rigid 'protection' system they have controlled Sicilian business transactions for many years.

In the 1980s a number of people in key positions, including magistrates, journalists, trade unionists, politicians, and members of the police force who stood up to the Mafia, were killed by the organisation. But things began to change in the following decade. In 1991 a courageous group of shopkeepers and tradesmen in Capo d'Orlando formed an association and stood up in court against their extortionists, and their example has been followed by other Sicilians. 1992 was the year in which the *Mani Pulite* ('Clean Hands') judicial investigations began, which exposed the link between corrupt politicians, kick-backs and extortion. Many well-known political figures did not survive the scandal. In 1993 the arrest of Totò Riina, the acknowledged *capo dei capi*, after more than 20 years 'in hiding' in Palermo, closely followed by the capture outside Catania of Nitto Santapaola, local boss in that city since 1982, and more recently by that of Bernardo Provenzano (the elderly boss had been 'in hiding' for over 40 years) was greeted, with some scepticism, as a step in the right direction. Giovanni Brusca, who detonated the bomb which killed Giovanni Falcone, was arrested in 1996. In 1997 many bosses were condemned (and most of them were sentenced to life imprisonment) for their part in the murder of Falcone. Meanwhile, a group of stalwart magistrates in Palermo continues the struggle against the power of the Mafia; in spite of meagre resources, they never give up.

THE PROVINCE OF PALERMO

Palermo province is geologically the oldest part of Sicily, with serrated, spectacular mountains of Dolomitic limestone, fertile valleys and a beautiful coastline. The picturesque old city of Palermo, once a glittering mecca of mosques, fountains and gardens, a seat of knowledge and culture without equal, is still a fascinating place, and the province contains many small towns, some of great historical importance such as Piana degli Albanesi, Castelbuono, Caccamo (with Sicily's largest castle) and Cefalù, while others are noted for their architecture; the opulent 18th-century villas of Bagheria, for example, are world-famous. The great 17th-century musicians and composers Francesco, Alessandro and Domenico Scarlatti were all born in Palermo.

PALERMO

The city of Palermo (*map p. 542, B1*), capital of the province and of the Sicilian region as a whole, stands on a bay at the foot of Mt Pellegrino, a headland described by Goethe as the loveliest he had ever seen. It is the fifth largest city in Italy, with a population of c. 660,000, and has a superb climate. Its most important monuments come from the medieval period of Arab and Norman rule, the Baroque era under the Spanish and the 19th century when Palermo was an established part of the Grand Tour. The outstanding archaeological museum has an important collection of ancient artefacts. Monuments of world-class significance include the remains of Norman buildings with their characteristic Arab-style red domes, and the glorious mosaics in the Norman palaces and churches. Modern Palermo is a busy port, but while the city has expanded far beyond its ancient boundaries, most of the monuments are to be found in the historic centre.

Sea levels were higher in antiquity. The original Phoenician settlement, established c. 750 BC, was on a promontory bounded by two rivers. This settlement later became the basis for the Arab al-Kasr, the Cassaro or castle, the heavily fortified inner city. As the waters receded, a lower city developed nearer the port, the *halisah* or Kalsa, where the Arab emir had his palace. The Normans chose the inner city as their base and built the Palazzo dei Normanni on an existing Arab fort at the highest end. The city is divided into four quarters by Corso Vittorio Emanuele and Via Maqueda. Originally the higher section of the Corso was called the Cassaro. Under the Normans, the paved section of it between the palace and the cathedral became Via Marmorea and under the Spanish it was Via Toledo. The two roads cross at Quattro Canti. In the 19th and 20th centuries the city expanded northwards, from Piazza Verdi along the Viale della Libertà.

In central Palermo very few street names are written up, even though they all have an official name on the maps. In the Jewish Quarter (Giudecca), roughly corresponding to the area just south of Sant'Agostino, you will notice that the signs are written in Italian, Arabic and Hebrew, underlining the cosmopolitan character of old Palermo.

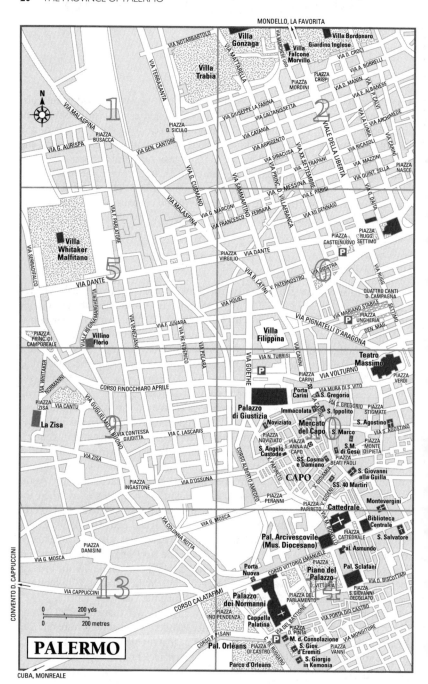

MONDELLO, LA FAVORITA

CONVENTO D. CAPPUCCINI

CUBA, MONREALE

PALERMO

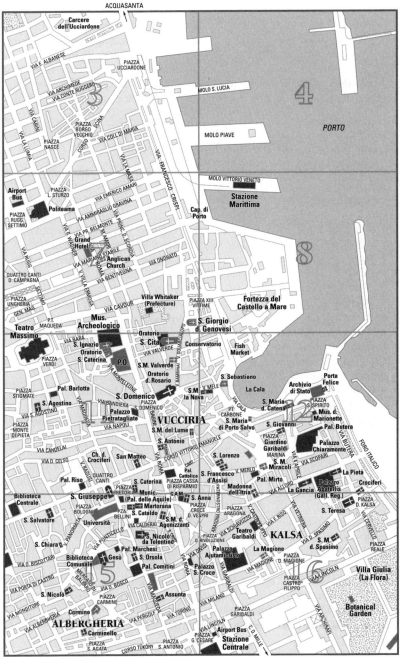

Palermo remains an exotic destination. The city's setting in a sheltered bay, the Conca d'Oro, has impressed many visitors over the centuries, including Goethe, Swinburne and Maupassant, all of whom left glowing accounts of their travels. There is a distinctly North African feel to the city, with its street markets, gardens and promenades filled with palm trees. While the Baroque predominates, there is a profusion of different architectural styles reflecting the city's multicultural past, including an elegant opera house.

TEN THINGS TO DO IN PALERMO

La Martorana, the cathedral, Palazzo dei Normanni and the Cappella Palatina, the archaeological museum, Palazzo Abatellis, Villa Whitaker Malfitano and Monreale are the must-see sights of Palermo. Here are ten others, less well-known.

1. A friendly jostle, elbow-to-elbow, for the breakfast ritual at the Bar Massaro (Via Basile 24, near the main University on Viale delle Scienze; *beyond map 5*).
2. Pay your respects to Rosalia, patron saint of the city, in her cave home near the top of Mt Pellegrino. Elegant in her dress of gold, she sleeps, while you marvel at the collection of ex-votos.
3. Palermo's insouciant blend of sacred and profane can be experienced by a stroll through the raucous Ballarò street market, with its colourful mountains of fish, fruit and vegetables; step into the Gesù and blink at the equally voluptuous Baroque splendour (*map 15*). A similar contrast is found by walking though the Capo stalls, groaning with produce, and then popping into the church of the Immacolata (*map 10*).
4. Browse for curios in Piazza Peranni (*map 10*), and don't be afraid to haggle.
5. If in season, don't miss an opera at the Teatro Massimo (*map 11*).
6. Lunch should consist of an *arancina bomba* at the Bar Touring at Via Lincoln 18 (*map 16*), followed by a healthy constitutional in the Villa Giulia park, which is conveniently opposite, and the Botanical Garden close by.
7. Find time for a surprising puppet show at Mimmo Cuticchio's little theatre in Via Bara dell'Olivella (*map 11*), and watch those wooden paladins spring to life—and fight to the death.
8. Among the marvels of the Loggia, in Via Valverde (*map 11*), the most astonishing is the oratory of Santa Cita, with its exuberant stuccoes by Serpotta, justly described as the Birth and Death of Baroque.
9. Of all the gardens of Palermo, that of San Giovanni degli Eremiti (*map 14*) is the most romantic.
10. In the evening, try some Palermo-style street food 'nni Francu u vastiddaru (Corso Vittorio Emanuele 102; *map 12*), where the eclectic Franco prepares delectable sandwiches using chick-pea fritters, octopus, lamb intestines, beef spleen and ricotta, as his forebears have been doing since the founding of the city.

HISTORY OF PALERMO

Traces of Palaeolithic settlements have been found in grottoes on Mt Pellegrino. The great fertility of the Conca d'Oro, the plain behind the bay, has supported the inhabitants of Palermo throughout her history. A Phoenician colony was founded here c.750 BC, which was known to the Greeks as Panormos ('all harbour', in other words a reliably safe anchorage, on account of its superb natural harbour). It became an important Carthaginian centre, hotly disputed during the First Punic War, and not finally acquired by Rome until 254 BC. It became a *municipium*, and after 20 BC, a flourishing *colonia*. After the invasions of the Vandals and Ostrogoths it was conquered for the Byzantine emperors in 535 and remained in their possession until 831, when the Arabs captured it after a prolonged resistance. Under Muslim rule it became capital of an emirate (and named *al-Madinah*: 'the city') rivalling Cordoba and Cairo in oriental splendour, as 'the city of a thousand mosques'; the luxuriant gardens and fountains of the city enchanted travellers. It became an important trading-post and cosmopolitan centre which showed tolerance towards Christians and Jews.

Taken by Robert Guiscard and his brother Roger de Hauteville (who became Count of Sicily) in 1072, it again enjoyed prosperity under Roger's son King Roger II (1130–54), and became the centre of trade between Europe and Asia. Under the brilliant reign of Emperor Frederick II of Hohenstaufen (1198–1250), the city became famous throughout Europe for its learning and magnificence.

The famous rebellion of the Sicilian Vespers (*see p. 69*) put an end to the misrule of Charles of Anjou in 1282. During the long period of the increasingly tyrannical Spanish domination which followed, the city gradually declined. Under the terms of the Treaty of Utrecht (1713) Sicily was allotted to Vittorio Amedeo of Savoy, who was, however, forced to exchange it for Sardinia (1718), ceding Sicily to the Neapolitan Bourbons. Under their rule the island fared little better, though Ferdinand IV established his court at Palermo in 1799 during the French occupation of Naples, and during the 18th century, Palermo was the largest town in Italy after Naples. The island was granted a temporary constitution in 1811 while under British protection (1806–15). The city rebelled against misgovernment in 1820, 1848, and in April 1860. On 27th May 1860 Garibaldi and the 'Thousand' made a triumphant entry into the city. Much of the centre of Palermo was badly damaged during air raids during the Second World War, but is now undergoing extensive and careful renovation.

QUATTRO CANTI & PIAZZA PRETORIA

The centre of the city is marked by the monumental crossroads known as the **Quattro Canti** (*map 11*), at the central intersection of the four main streets (now Corso Vittorio

Emanuele and Via Maqueda), and named Piazza Vigliena after the Duke of Vigliena, Spanish viceroy in 1611. It is now a confined and congested road junction, often called Teatro del Sole, Theatre of the Sun, because during the course of a day the sun illuminates each of the four corners in turn. The decorative façades bear fountains with statues of the Four Seasons, four Spanish kings of Sicily, and the four patron saints of Palermo, Cristina, Ninfa, Oliva and Agata. On Corso Vittorio Emanuele, the Porta Nuova can be seen in one direction (southwest) and the sea in the other (northeast), beyond Porta Felice. From Via Maqueda, there is a vista of the hills surrounding the Conca d'Oro.

The Fountain of Shame

A few steps along Via Maqueda to the southeast, Piazza Pretoria (*map 11*) is almost entirely occupied by a High Renaissance fountain (1554–55), designed by Francesco Camilliani, and later (1573) assembled and enlarged here by his son Camillo and Michelangelo Naccherino. The rivalry between Palermo and Messina, both of which through the centuries have struggled to emerge as the foremost city on the island, can be read in the history of this fountain. Messina was the first to supply its citizens with water from a nearby river by means of a modern aqueduct in 1547. A beautiful fountain, designed by a follower of Michelangelo, was commissioned in celebration of the event and situated beside the cathedral (*see p. 428*). The Senate of Palermo, loth to be outdone, then purchased the enormous fountain which had originally been designed by Camilliani for the gardens of the Tuscan villa of Peter of Toledo, father-in-law by his daughter Eleanor to Cosimo de' Medici. Vasari was a great admirer of the fountain, which introduced the High Renaissance Mannerist style to Palermo. Occupying almost the whole of the piazza, the great basin is decorated with some 50 statues of monsters, harpies, sirens and tritons. Also copied from Messina was the idea of representing the four rivers, in this case the Oreto, Papireto, Kemonia and Gabriele. Instead of Orion, the figure on the summit was made to represent the Genius of Palermo (*see below*). Unfortunately for the city government, the nude and semi-clad white Carrara marble sculptures from Florence did not win the full approval of the pious citizens of Palermo, who dubbed the new arrival the 'Fontana della Vergogna', or Fountain of Shame.

Palazzo delle Aquile and Santa Caterina

Palazzo delle Aquile, named after the eagles which decorate its exterior, but sometimes also referred to as Palazzo Pretorio, is the Town Hall (*open Tues–Fri 9.30–5.30, Sat 9.30–1, tickets available at the GAM, Galleria d'Arte Moderna in Piazza Croce dei Vespri, map 15; T: 091 8431605*). Sadly in need of repair, especially inside, it was built in 1470, enlarged in the 16th century, and over-restored in 1874. The façade is surmounted by a 17th-century statue of St Rosalia. This was formerly the seat of the Senate, which governed the city from the 14th century until 1816, senators being nominated from the local aristocracy. In the atrium is a Baroque portal by Paolo Amato and a Roman funerary monument with statues of a husband and wife. At the foot of the 19th-century staircase stands part of a 16th-century **fountain of the Genius of Palermo**, one of a number of allegorical statues in the city with the figure of a young king with an old face, personifying Civic Rule, entangled in a serpent biting his chest, representing Wisdom, sometimes with a dog at his feet, for Loyalty, or a lion, for Strength, and an eagle on his shoulder, representing the Empire. On the first floor, the assembly room, which has a 16th-century painted wooden ceiling, is covered with numerous inscriptions relating to events which have taken place there. The other rooms, including that of the mayor, were decorated in 1870 by Giuseppe Damiani Almeyda and contain mementoes of Garibaldi and Napoleon.

The east side of the piazza is closed by the flank and dome of the 16th-century church of **Santa Caterina** (*open 9.30–1, summer also afternoons Mon–Sat 3–7; Info: T: 338 4512011, 338 7228775*). The interior, especially the choir, is an elaborate example of Sicilian Baroque, with striking effects of early 18th-century sculptural decoration and marble veneering. In the right transept is a marble statue of St Catherine by Antonello Gagini (1534). The frescoes in the cupola are by Vito d'Anna (1751).

San Giuseppe dei Teatini

Across Via Maqueda is the side of the church of **San Giuseppe dei Teatini** (*map 11–15; open Mon–Sat 7.30–12 & 5.30–8; T: 091 331239*). The upper church, built by Giacomo Besio of Genoa, was the scene of two popular assemblies called by Giuseppe d'Alessi during the revolt of 1647 against the Spanish governors. In the lavish Baroque interior, in addition to the 14 monolithic columns in the nave, eight colossal columns of grey marble support the well-proportioned central dome. The frescoes of the nave roof are copies of the originals by Filippo Tancredi; those in the dome are by Borremans; the stuccoes are outstandingly good. The two large angels holding the stoups on either side of the entrance are by Marabitti. In the fourth south chapel, with handsome marble decoration, is a statue of the Madonna by the Gagini school, while in the south transept, beneath the altarpiece (*St Andrew of Avellino* by Sebastiano Conca), is a charming frieze of child musicians, and the altar has a bas-relief of a Madonna amidst angels, both by Federico Siragusa (1800). In the choir vault are fine reliefs with full-length figures by Procopio Serpotta. In the chapels flanking the choir are (right) a Crucifix by Fra' Umile da Petralia and (left) reliefs by Filippo Pennino, and an 18th-century statue of St Joseph. In the north transept, above an altar of marble mosaic (probably late 17th century), is a painting of St Cajetan (Gaetano) by Pietro Novelli. St Cajetan (1480–1547) founded the Theatine order in response to a perceived lack of monastic spirit among the clergy.

Next to the church is the former convent of the Theatines, now occupied by the **university**. The small **Geological Museum** founded here in the early 19th century by the Theatine Giorgio Gemmellaro is now at Corso Tüköry 131 (*beyond map 15; Museo Geologico; open 1 Oct–31 May Mon–Sat 9–1; T: 091 7041051*). It has a collection of fossils, local rocks, and a woman's skeleton, known as Thea, from the Upper Palaeolithic era.

PIAZZA BELLINI & LA MARTORANA

Adjoining Piazza Pretoria is Piazza Bellini (*map 15*), dominated by the Romanesque campanile of La Martorana and the three red domes of San Cataldo, raised above part of the east wall of the Roman city and surrounded by trees. Also facing the square is the small Teatro Bellini, originally designed for operettas but gutted by fire in 1964 and now partly occupied by a pizzeria. It risks being transformed into a condominium.

La Martorana

La Martorana or Santa Maria dell'Ammiraglio (*open 9–1 & 3.30–5.30; Sun and holidays 9–1; T: 091 6161692*) was founded c. 1143 by George of Antioch, a Syrian of the Greek Orthodox faith who served as admiral of the fleet and first minister under Roger II. It was presented in 1433 to a Benedictine convent founded in the 12th century by Eloisa, wife of Goffredo Martorana. The Sicilian Parliament met here after the Sicilian Vespers. Since 1935 it has shared cathedral status with San Demetrio in Piana degli Albanesi, a small town of Albanian origin in the province, and services are conducted here according to the Greek Orthodox rite. Outside, the Norman structure survives on the north and south sides, although a Baroque façade was inserted in 1588 on the north side when the Norman narthex was demolished and the atrium covered.

The present entrance is beneath the 12th-century **campanile**, which survived the alterations (only its red dome is missing). Inside, the central Greek-cross plan of the tiny original church can still be detected, despite the Baroque alterations at the west end and the lengthening of the chancel in 1683.

The original mosaic decoration remains on and around the **central cupola (1)**; it is possible to climb up for a closer view. The mosaics, probably by Greek craftsmen from Constantinople, were completed between 1143 and 1151: Christ and four Archangels

LA MARTORANA

■ Norman
▨ Norman (destroyed)
▨ Baroque

1 Central cupola (*Christ and the Archangels*)
2 South apse (*St Anne*)
3 North apse (*St Joachim*)
4 Baroque chapel
5 *George of Antioch at the Feet of the Virgin*
6 *King Roger Crowned by Christ*
7 Arab door

West end

Campanile

10 yards
10 metres

Twelfth-century mosaic panel from La Martorana, showing Roger II crowned by Christ.

are depicted in the dome and, in Arabic lettering, a quotation from a Byzantine hymn. Around the drum are prophets and the Evangelists. The *Annunciation* is depicted on the triumphal arch. Beyond, in the **south apse (2)**, is St Anne and in the **north apse (3)** St Joachim, the parents of the Virgin. In the side vaults are the four Evangelists, the *Nativity* and the *Dormition of the Virgin*.

The **Baroque-style chapel (4)** beyond the place of the central apse was frescoed by Antonino Grano. Above the lapis lazuli tabernacle is a fine altarpiece of the *Ascension* (1533) by Vincenzo da Pavia. It was painted shortly after he returned from Rome to Sicily with Polidoro da Caravaggio. The balustrades in front of the apses and the mosaic floor, with its delicate designs in tones of pink and blue, are also Norman.

At the west end are two further original mosaic panels (restored; set in Baroque frames) from the destroyed portico: on the north side, **George of Antioch at the Feet of the Virgin (5)**, and, on the south side, **King Roger Crowned by Christ (6)**, a rare portrait of Roger II of Sicily. The Baroque vault frescoes illustrating episodes from the life of St Benedict, using brilliant, harmonious colours, were carried out by Willem Borremans (1714), his first work in Sicily, with the collaboration here and there of Olivio Sozzi and Gaetano Lazzara. During recent restoration, along the side walls, gilded bronze grilles were revealed, after being hidden by wooden panels for centuries. They allowed the Benedictine nuns, a cloistered order, to follow Mass without being seen.

In the embrasure of the south portal is a 12th-century **carved wooden door (7)**, of Arab workmanship.

Southeast of the church some arches survive of the cloister of the 12th-century **Casa Martorana**, the Benedictine convent founded by Eloisa Martorana. The convent has disappeared, but the marzipan fruits which used to be made by the nuns here, immortalised by the name *frutti di martorana* and one of Sicily's most famous products, are still produced by numerous confectioners all over the island.

San Cataldo

Next to La Martorana, directly opposite its campanile, is the church of **San Cataldo** (*open 9.30–12.30 & 3-6*). It was founded by Maio of Bari, William I's chancellor, and because of his assassination in 1160 the interior was never decorated. After 1787 it served as a post office and was restored in 1885. The fine exterior has blind arcading round the windows and crenellations at the top of the wall. Three small red domes with little windows rise in the centre. The simple plan of the interior has three aisles ending in apses and three domes high up above the central aisle. The beautiful old capitals are all different. The original mosaic floor and lattice windows survive.

ON & AROUND CORSO VITTORIO EMANUELE

The busy Corso Vittorio Emanuele (*map 12–14*), the main street of the city, has had several names in the past: it was Tarek el-kasr in Arab times, meaning 'Way to the Castle', and Via Toledo under the Spanish, named after one of their viceroys.

Piazza Bologni to Piazza San Giovanni Decollato

On the left-hand side after Quattro Canti (heading southwest away from the port), the Corso passes the somewhat decrepit but nevertheless handsome **Piazza Bologni**, with a statue of Charles V by Scipione Li Volsi (1630). The statue is the butt of local jokes about the meaning of the emperor's outstretched hand, suggesting for example that he is indicating the height of the city's tide of litter. To the right is the ample prospect of Palazzo Villafranca (Giovanni Battista Vaccarini), now belonging to the Church, and used for art exhibitions. From the far end of the piazza, beside the neglected Palazzo Ugo delle Favare with its attractive balconies, a detour down the interesting old **Via Panormita** on the right (*map 15*) takes in the Piazzetta Speciale where the Palazzo Speciale has an 18th-century staircase in its pretty courtyard, and there is a small café. Further on is Piazza Santa Chiara where the church, with a splendid interior, is often used for concerts. Numerous immigrants, especially from Senegal, have settled in this part of the city. Via dei Biscottari continues, with a view left down Via Benfratelli to the 14th-century tower of San Nicolò, and passes under a massive arch to emerge in Piazza San Giovanni Decollato beside the impressive **Palazzo Sclafani** (*map 14*), built by Matteo Sclafani in 1330. Part of the original façade has attractive lava-stone decoration around the windows. The fine 14th-century portal has sculptures by Bonaiuto da Pisa, who probably came to Palermo with traders from his native city. Opposite is the **ruined church of San Giovanni Decollato**, with a huge Morton Bay fig tree growing through its façade.

Piazza Bologni to Piazza della Cattedrale

Facing Piazza Bologni, across the Corso, is the façade of **Palazzo Riso** (1784), the grandest of all the buildings designed by the pre-eminent Neoclassical architect Giuseppe Venanzio Marvuglia, now the seat of the Museo d'Arte Contemporanea della Sicilia (*open Tues–Sun 10–8, Thur and Fri 10–10; T: 091 320532, www.palazzoriso.it, NB: No lift*), and the venue for exhibitions of modern art. Notice the wooden herons, turkeys and pigeons on the balcony railings. Further west along the Corso is the church of **San Salvatore** (*map 15; open 9.30–12.30 & 3–5; closed Tues; 1st and 3rd Sun of month open 10.30–1; T: 091 323392*), built in 1682 by Paolo Amato on a preceding Norman church and abbey where, according to legend, the daughter of Roger II, Constance de Hauteville, was abbess when on 27th January 1186 she was forced to renounce her vows and marry Henry VI, son of Frederick Barbarossa, for reasons of political expediency. Even the pope (Urban III) refused to officiate at the union of this unlikely pair, who were wedded in Milan by the patriarch of Aquileia, who was promptly excommunicated for his defiance of papal wishes. Eight years later Constance gave birth to Frederick II of Hohenstaufen. Bombed during the Second World War, the oval interior with its marvellous stuccoes by Serpotta has been well restored.

On the opposite side of the Corso the narrow Via Montevergini leads to the ex-church of **Montevergini** (*map 10; now the Atelier Nuovo Montevergini theatre; open Wed–Sun 7pm–2am; T: 091 6124514*), with a lovely façade by Andrea Palma and a little campanile with an onion-shaped dome decorated with early 18th-century tiles, beside an 18th-century loggia for the nuns. After deconsecration in 1866 it became a school for artisans, then the seat of the Fascist party, and was later used (until 1955) as a law court. The trial of Gaspare Pisciotta, who in 1950 murdered his brother-in-law, the famous bandit Salvatore Giuliano, took place here. In the interior there are vault frescoes by Borremans, and a Neoclassical sanctuary decorated by Emanuele Cordona, with frescoes by Giuseppe Velasco.

Further along the Corso (no. 429) is the **Biblioteca Centrale della Regione Siciliana** (*map 14; open Mon–Fri 8.30–7, Sat 8.30–1.30; T: 091 7077642*), which occupies the former Jesuit college and is entered by the portal of the adjacent church of Santa Maria della Grotta. It owns over 500,000 volumes and many ancient manuscripts (particularly of the 15th and 16th centuries). Just beyond is **Piazza della Cattedrale**, with the elaborate flank of the cathedral on the opposite side of a garden enclosed by a balustrade bearing statues of saints.

THE CATHEDRAL

The cathedral (*map 14; open Mon–Sat 9–5.30, in Nov–Feb 9.30–1; Sun and holidays 7.30–1.30 & 4–7; no visits during services; T: 091 334373, 329 3977513, www.cattedrale.palermo.it*), dedicated to the Assumption of the Virgin, is a building of many styles not too skilfully blended, but remains a striking edifice with golden-coloured stone and sharp contrasts of light and shade. The present church, on the site of an older basilica which did duty as a mosque in the 9th century, was founded in 1185 by Walter of the Mill, an Englishman who came to Palermo as tutor to the young William II and later became archbishop of Palermo. Known locally as Gualtiero Offamiglio, he accumulated such a powerful following that the king responded by creating a new city at Monreale, and making Walter its archbishop. Not to be outdone, Walter rebuilt the existing cathedral to underline his position.

Exterior of the cathedral

Work on the fabric continued for many centuries and in the 15th century much of the exterior acquired a Catalan Gothic style. The incongruous dome was added by Ferdinando Fuga in 1781–1801. The façade, turned towards the southwest on Via Matteo Bonello, is a fine example of local Gothic craftsmanship (13th–14th centuries). The doorway dates from 1352. Two powerful Gothic arches span the road to a Norman tower, transformed into the campanile in the 19th century. The east end, with three intricately-decorated apses and two towers matching those at the west end, is almost entirely original 12th-century work. The usual entrance is from the garden (with its statue of St Rosalia) through the great south porch, a splendid Catalan Gothic work by Antonio Gambara (1426). In the tympanum there is a delicate relief of the Redeemer between the Archangel Gabriel and Mary. Beneath is a frieze of saints in polychrome relief. The remarkable painted intarsia decoration above the three arches, which probably dates from 1296, was discovered during recent restoration work. It represents the Tree of Life in a complicated geometric composition showing Islamic influence. The twelve roundels are decorated with a great variety of symbolic animals, including fish, cockerels, serpents, crabs, mice, camels, lions, wolves, bears, peacocks, dragons, doves and owls, as well as fruit and flowers and human figures. Intended to be 'read' from left to right, the last roundel seems to represent the sun with the head of Christ in the centre. Beneath the porch, the column on the left, probably preserved from the earlier mosque, is inscribed with a passage from the Koran. The fine wooden doors are by Francesco Miranda (1432).

Interior of the cathedral

The interior is relatively plain, 18th-century restoration having removed the majority of the decorative artwork. However, there is much to see.

Royal tombs

The first two chapels of the south aisle (*open Mon–Sat 9.30–1.30 & 2.30–5.30, possible combined ticket with crypt, treasury and Diocesan Museum*) enclose six royal tombs: the porphyry sarcophagus of **Frederick II of Hohenstaufen (1)** (d. 1250), Holy Roman Emperor and King of Sicily, and the sarcophagus of **Constance of Aragon (2)** (d. 1222), Frederick's dearly loved first wife, a Roman work with a frieze showing a lion hunt. The tomb of **Henry VI (3)** (d. 1197), Holy Roman Emperor, son of Frederick Barbarossa, and father of Frederick II of Hohenstaufen. Beneath mosaic canopies against the back wall are two further tombs: of **Roger II (4)**, the first king of Sicily (d. 1154), who was crowned in this cathedral in 1130, and his daughter **Constance de Hauteville (5)** (d. 1198; *see p. 29*). Later Aragonese burials are, on the left that of **Duke William of Athens (6)** (d. 1338), son of Frederick II of Aragon, and (in Frederick II's sarcophagus) Peter II (d. 1342), King of Sicily. The smooth porphyry sarcophagi are almost certainly Imperial Roman in workmanship, because the quarries of this type of stone were already exhausted in the Middle Ages. It is not known how they came to be here in Palermo.

Nave and south side

In the nave are **statues of saints** from a high reredos (25m) by Antonello Gagini and his family, who worked on it for over 64 years. Known as the Tribuna, this masterpiece was dismantled arbitrarily in the 18th century. Now models of the work, and some fragments of it, are on view in the Diocesan Museum. The canopied **stoup (7)** is of 1557. The other **stoup (8)** is attributed to Domenico Gagini, damaged but of fine workmanship.

In the fourth south chapel **(9)** is an **altarpiece by Pietro Novelli**; notice also, in the sixth chapel **(10)**, **reliquary urns of saints of Palermo**, and, used as an altar frontal, the tomb slab of St Cosmas, a Sicilian bishop martyred in 1160; the seventh chapel **(11)** has a fine marble altar (1713).

In the south transept **(12)** there is an altarpiece by Giuseppe Velasco and, above the altar, a bas-relief of the *Dormition of the Virgin* by Antonello Gagini (1535).

In the **Chapel of St Rosalia (13)** is a 17th-century silver coffer containing the relics of the saint (*see p. 68*); the reliefs on the walls are 19th-century, while the choir-stalls date from 1466. The meridian line on the floor, 22m long, was made by Father

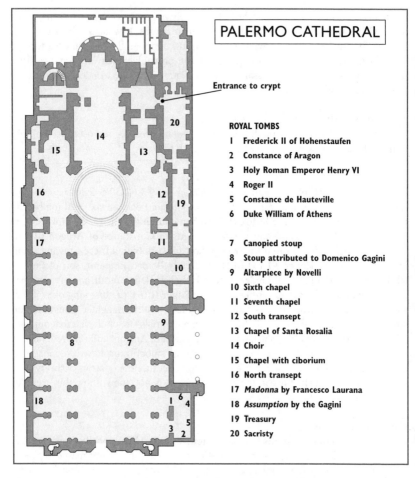

PALERMO CATHEDRAL

Entrance to crypt

ROYAL TOMBS

1 Frederick II of Hohenstaufen
2 Constance of Aragon
3 Holy Roman Emperor Henry VI
4 Roger II
5 Constance de Hauteville
6 Duke William of Athens

7 Canopied stoup
8 Stoup attributed to Domenico Gagini
9 Altarpiece by Novelli
10 Sixth chapel
11 Seventh chapel
12 South transept
13 Chapel of Santa Rosalia
14 Choir
15 Chapel with ciborium
16 North transept
17 *Madonna* by Francesco Laurana
18 *Assumption* by the Gagini
19 Treasury
20 Sacristy

Giuseppe Piazzi, priest, mathematician and astronomer, in 1801. The light coming through the tiny hole in the dome on the right at midday indicates the zodiac sign for the time of year.

The choir and north side

The left end of the **choir (14)** has a *Resurrection of Christ* on the altar, high reliefs, and (in niches) statues of the Apostles, all fragments of Antonello Gagini's reredos. The chapel north of the choir **(15)** houses a large domed ciborium in lapis lazuli (1663), and the funerary monument of Bishop Sanseverino (1793).

In the north transept **(16)**, at the foot of an early 14th-century wooden Crucifix donated by Manfredi Chiaramonte, are marble statues of mourners by Gaspare Serpotta and Gaspare Guercio. On the altar are fine reliefs with scenes of the Passion by Fazio and Vincenzo Gagini.

In the seventh north chapel (**17**) there is a statue of the Madonna by Francesco Laurana and his school. The second north chapel (**18**) has an *Assumption* and three reliefs by the Gagini, also once part of the high altar.

Treasury, sacristy and crypt

The **treasury** (**19**) (*open Mon–Sat 9.30–1.30 & 2.30–5.30, possible combined ticket with royal tombs and Diocesan Museum*) contains the extraordinary crown of Constance of Aragon (first wife of Frederick II), made by local craftsmen c. 1210, in fine gold filigree set with semi-precious stones, and found in her tomb in the 18th century. Also displayed here are the contents of some of the other royal tombs, 18th- and 19th-century copes, chalices and altar frontals.

Beyond the treasury is the **sacristy** (**20**), which has two fine portals by Vincenzo Gagini (1568), and the entrance to the **crypt**, where 23 tombs are preserved, many of them Roman sarcophagi (all of them numbered and labelled in Italian). The tomb (no. 12) of Archbishop Giovanni Paternò (d. 1511) has a very fine effigy by Antonello Gagini, whose patron he was, resting on a Greek sarcophagus. The tomb (no. 16) of the founder of the cathedral, Archbishop Walter (d. 1190), has a beautiful red, green and gold mosaic border. No. 7 is a large Roman sarcophagus with a scene of the coronation of a poet with the nine Muses and Apollo. The tomb of Frederick of Antioch (d. 1305; no. 9) has a Gothic effigy of the warrior semi-recumbent, with his helmet at his feet and sword by his side.

Museo Diocesano

Across the busy Via Matteo Bonello, the Palazzo Arcivescovile (Archbishop's Palace), with a portal of 1460 which survived the 18th-century rebuilding, houses the Diocesan Museum (*map 14; open Tues–Sun 9.30–1.30, Sat 10–6, closed Mon, possible combined ticket with restricted parts of cathedral; T: 091 6077111, www.museodiocesanopa.it*). Here a large and important collection of marble and mosaic fragments from the cathedral and other churches destroyed during the Second World War, together with splendid paintings of the 11th–18th centuries, are displayed to the best advantage, there is also an interesting bookshop.

On the ground floor are 15th-century frescoes, a 12th-century mosaic from the cathedral, and Vincenzo da Pavia's *St Conus the Hermit and St Anthony Abbot* (1550). In the basement the museum's superb collection of sculpture is displayed, with several examples of the works of the Gagini family, as well as works in stucco. On the ground floor again, in the north wing, 16th- and 17th-century paintings chart the movement from Mannerism to *Caravaggismo*, with one room entirely dedicated to works by Pietro Novelli. On the first floor are 13 galleries, including the *alcova del cardinale* (cardinal's bedroom); the Sala Azzurra (Blue Room), decorated with 19th-century chinoiseries; the Sala Verde (Green Room), once used by the nuns of St Clare, with a beautiful floor painted with flowers.

Perhaps the crowning glory of the museum is the Cappella Borremans, with a series of joyful, colourful religious allegories painted as frescoes on every available surface; commissioned from Willem Borremans by Archbishop Matteo Basile in 1733.

On the other side of Via Bonello is the **Loggia dell'Incoronazione**, erected in the 16th–17th centuries using recuperated columns and capitals. It takes its name from the tradition that the kings used to show themselves to the people here after their coronation. Behind is the Cappella dell'Incoronata, a Norman building partly destroyed in 1860. Close to the cathedral, at Via Pietro Novelli 3, is **Palazzo Asmundo** (*open Tues–Sat 9–1; T: 091 6519022; www.palazzoasmundo.it*). Built in 1615, it contains beautifully frescoed salons (by Gioacchino Martorana, 1764) that give an insight into the lives of the Sicilian nobility. The Wunderkammer collections include paintings, wooden trousseau-chests, coins, postcards, old maps, water-colours, French and Neapolitan porcelain, majolica tiles and a unique set of census bricks inscribed with details of the donor; they were walled into churches, convents and institutions. There is also a very pleasant cafeteria.

Villa Bonanno (Piazza Vittoria)

Piazza Vittoria, or Piano del Palazzo (*map 14*), is occupied by **Villa Bonanno**, a public garden thick with palm trees, many of which were unfortunately killed by the red borer, a beetle that was accidentally introduced into Sicily in the 1990s. The piazza has been used throughout Palermo's history for public celebrations. Partially protected by a roof are some remains of three **Roman houses** (*open 9–5.30 winter, 9–6.30 summer; Sun and holidays 9.30–1.30*), the only buildings of this period so far found in the city, one a substantial villa with mosaics including the Hunt of Alexander, possibly copied from a work by Philoxenos of Eritrea, a Greek painter of the 4th century BC. It is comparable with the famous mosaic of the Battle of Alexander and Darius in the House of the Faun in Pompeii. Building A is of a later date, probably 2nd century BC. The garden adjoins **Piazza del Parlamento**, with a monument to Philip V of Bourbon, at the foot of the Palazzo dei Normanni. Spanning the Corso is the **Porta Nuova**, a triumphal gateway with a conical top celebrating Charles V's Tunisian victory (1535).

PALAZZO DEI NORMANNI & THE CAPPELLA PALATINA

Map 14. Open Mon–Sat 8.15–5.45, last tickets at 5; Sun and holidays 8.15–1, last tickets at 12.15; closed Easter Mon, 25 April, 1 May, 15 July, 4 Sept, 26 Dec; no access to the hall of parliament, Sala d'Ercole, Tues, Wed and Thur; T: 091 6262833, www.federicosecondo.org). The Norman Palace, or Palazzo Reale, stands in the highest part of the old city. At the north end of the long façade (1616) is the massive Torre Pisana, part of the Norman palace, which houses the Museo della Specola (*entrance from Piazza del Parlamento 1, guided visits only from Mon–Fri at 9 and 10.30, Sat 9, 10.15, 11.30, lots of stairs and no lift, to book visit, T: 091 233247, 091 233243, www.astropa.unipa.it*), with the instruments used by Father Giuseppe Piazzi, the first director of the astronomical observatory founded here in 1786, including his famous Ramsden Circle, 1.5m in diameter, by means of which he discovered the first asteroid, Ceres, in 1801. You will also find three telescopes which belonged to the great-grandfather of Giuseppe Tomasi di Lampedusa, a keen amateur astronomer. The view over Palermo from the tower is exceptional.

The visitors' entrance is at the back, from Piazza Indipendenza; this is reached by steps down from the south side of the façade to the busy Via del Bastione, which skirts the great wall of the palace. From the bastions a ramp leads up to the back entrance. Here a monumental **staircase** (**A**; 1735) leads up to a loggia overlooking a fine **courtyard** (**B**; 1600). Set into the wall of the loggia is a **pillar** (**C**) with an inscription in Greek, Latin and Arabic, relating to a water-clock built for Roger II in 1142, probably in Fez, Morocco.

Cappella Palatina

Beneath the portico of seven columns (six of which are of Egyptian granite) with modern mosaics, is the side entrance to the Cappella Palatina (*open as palace, but closed Sun and holidays 9.45–11.15 for services, and for weddings. NB: Binoculars are useful to view the painted ceiling*), a jewel of Arab-Norman art commenced by Roger II in the 1130s and consecrated in 1140. The interior is famous for its wonderful mosaics, some of the finest works of their kind in the world. They were commissioned by Roger II to follow a carefully-planned design intended to celebrate his monarchy, and the subjects seem to have been chosen with particular reference to the Holy Spirit and the theology of light. *Ego eimai to phos tou kosmou*, 'I am the light of the world', is the message in Greek shown by the figure of Christ Pantocrator in the central apse. In fact, although much space is dedicated to Sts Peter and Paul and the life of Christ, no mention is made of their martyrdom; the stories culminate with their triumph. There were 50 windows (later blocked) designed to illuminate at all times of the day the stories told on the walls. Throughout the chapel the texts written in three languages, Latin, Arabic and Greek, show that the king was addressing all the subjects in his multi-ethnic kingdom. The earliest and finest mosaics are in the east part of the chapel and are thought to have been the work of Byzantine Greeks. Here the splendour of the mosaics is increased by the use of silver as well as gold tesserae.

The light changes constantly so the chapel should, if possible, be visited at different times of the day. It takes the form of a small aisled basilica, with a raised choir and a cupola above the central bay, it demonstrates the perfection of this style of architecture. Every detail of the decoration is exquisite. The ten antique columns of the nave are of granite and cipollino marble; the unique ceiling (dated 1143) is of Fatimid workmanship, with splendid *muqarnas* in carved and painted cedarwood from Lebanon, in rich and varied designs; no saints and angels here, but musicians and dancing-girls, banquets at court with servants pouring wine for the guests, warriors and hunters, picnics under the trees (later ecclesiastical authorities added haloes to the figures in order to transform the decoration into a representation of a Christian paradise). The ambo and **paschal candlestick** (**D**) are good examples of the richest Norman marble decoration. The figure wearing a crown at the foot of the candlestick is a rare portrait of Roger, looking like Mr Punch as he supports the seated Christ. The floor and dadoes are made of white marble inlaid with red, green and gold patterns, all different, combining in a delightful harmony of colour and design with the glittering mosaics on a gold ground above. Here too the finest available materials were used, red porphyry and green serpentine alternating with rare stones from all over the known world.

In the **cupola of the sanctuary** (**E**) is *Christ Surrounded by Angels and Archangels*; on the drum, David, Solomon, Zachariah and St John the Baptist; on the pendentives, the Evangelists. On the triumphal arch, the *Annunciation* is depicted. Above the **south apse** (**F**) is the *Nativity*; on the upper part of the south wall, *Joseph's Dream* and the *Flight into Egypt*; on the nave arch, *Presentation in the Temple*; in the middle of the south wall, *Baptism*, *Transfiguration* and the *Raising of Lazarus*; and on the lower part of the south wall, *Entry into Jerusalem*. On the lower part of the north wall, five bishops of the Greek Church (among the best preserved mosaic figures in the building), and, on the arch, three female saints. Above the **north apse** (**G**) are a *Madonna and Child* and St John the Baptist. In the **main apse** (**H**) is the solemn, stern *Christ Pantocrator*, above a late 18th-century mosaic of the Virgin.

The mosaics in the nave were probably the last to be carried out (c. 1154–66); they illustrate the Book of Genesis, in two tiers of scenes between the clerestory windows and in the spandrels of the arches. The cycle begins in the upper tier of the right wall nearest to the sanctuary, showing the first seven days of the Creation up to the Creation of Eve. The sequence continues in the upper tier of the left wall (beginning at the

Creation of the Sun, Moon and Stars: from the mosaic cycle in the nave of the Cappella Palatina.

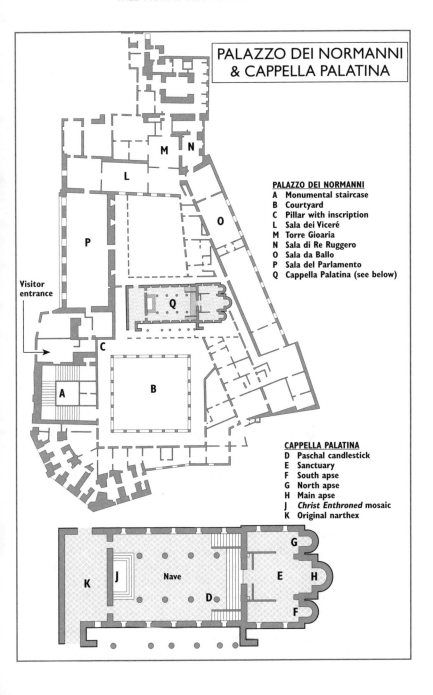

PALAZZO DEI NORMANNI & CAPPELLA PALATINA

PALAZZO DEI NORMANNI
A Monumental staircase
B Courtyard
C Pillar with inscription
L Sala dei Viceré
M Torre Gioaria
N Sala di Re Ruggero
O Sala da Ballo
P Sala del Parlamento
Q Cappella Palatina (see below)

Visitor entrance

CAPPELLA PALATINA
D Paschal candlestick
E Sanctuary
F South apse
G North apse
H Main apse
J *Christ Enthroned* mosaic
K Original narthex

Nave

entrance end) with the *Fall* up to the *Building of the Ark* (striking in its similarity to a Viking longship). The lower tier of the right wall (from the apse end) illustrates the *Flood* up to the *Hospitality of Lot*, and continues in the lower tier of the left wall (entrance end) with the *Destruction of Sodom* and continues up to *Jacob's Dream* and *Jacob Wrestling with the Angel*, which is the last scene in the sequence (nearest to the sanctuary).

In the aisles are scenes from the lives of Sts Peter and Paul, also executed after the mosaics in the sanctuary, possibly by local artists. The sequence begins at the east end of the right aisle with *Saul Leaving Jerusalem for Damascus* and the last scene in this aisle shows *St Peter's Escape from Prison*. The cycle continues at the entrance end of the left aisle with *Sts Peter and John Healing the Lame Man at the Temple Gate*, and the last scene in this aisle, nearest to the sanctuary, shows the *Fall of Simon Magus*.

Above the recomposed Norman throne on a dais at the west end is a 15th-century mosaic of **Christ Enthroned between Sts Peter and Paul (J)**. The original **narthex (K)**, now the baptistery with a mosaic font, has two beautifully carved mosaic doorways with bronze doors. The sacristy and treasury are usually closed.

The royal apartments

The staircase leads up to the top floor of the palace and the former royal apartments, largely decorated in the 19th century. The **Sala dei Viceré (L)** has a series of portraits of viceroys from 1754 to 1837. The **Torre Gioaria (M)** (from the Arabic *al-johara*, the pearl, meaning the heart of the building), or Tower of the Winds (for the weather-vane which once stood on the top), preserves part of the Norman construction, with four columns. The most interesting room is the so-called **Sala di Re Ruggero (N)** (King Roger's Room), with delightful mosaics probably dating between 1160 and 1170 (and thus actually from the time of William I), including centaurs, birds, palm trees, lions and leopards. In the vault are heraldic beasts. The floor and the lower parts of the walls, with marble and mosaic decoration, all survive intact, and there is a beautiful table from Naples, made of a slice of fossilised wood. The **Sala da Ballo (O)** (ballroom) has a fine view over the piazza to the sea.

Other parts of the palace are not shown when in use (*usually Tues, Wed, Thur, ask at the ticket office*), including the Sala del Parlamento, or Sala d'Ercole, decorated by Giuseppe Velasco, where the Regional Assembly meets. There is no access to the vaulted armoury, treasure-chamber and dungeons, surviving from the Norman period.

Around the palace

Across Corso Re Ruggero is **Palazzo d'Orléans** (*map 14*), now the seat of the president of the Sicilian Region. This was the residence of the exiled Louis-Philippe d'Orléans (1773–1850), eldest son of the Duke d'Orléans and the last king of France, at the time of his marriage in 1809 to Marie-Amélie, daughter of Ferdinand IV of the Two Sicilies. Their son Ferdinand-Philippe (1810–42) was born here in the following year. The beautiful gardens, Parco d'Orléans, full of birds, were laid out in 1797 (*open Mon–Fri 9–1 & 3–6; Sat, Sun and holidays 9–1; T: 091 6965038*).

In Piazza della Pinta is the little **Oratorio della Compagnia della Madonna della**

Consolazione (San Mercurio). The stucco decoration in the interior has recently been attributed, as an early work, to Giacomo Serpotta. Via dei Benedettini leads from here to the church of **San Giovanni degli Eremiti**, (*open Tues–Sun 9–7, Mon 9–1.45; T: 091 6515019*), symbol of the city and perhaps the most romantic building of Norman Palermo, thanks to its small, carefully-tended and luxuriant garden. It was built by Roger II in 1132–48, and has now been deconsecrated. Paths lead up through the beautiful groves, with splendid palm trees, cactus and flowering jasmine, overshadowed by five charming red domes, the tallest one crowning the campanile of the little church. In the bare interior, the nave is surmounted by two domes divided by an arch (pierced by a window). At the east end are three apses and three smaller domes, the one on the left part of the campanile.

To the right is an older structure, probably a mosque, consisting of a rectangular hall with cross vaulting and once divided by a row of pillars. Adjoining this (seen from the right of the entrance to the church) is a portico of five arches, whose inner wall is now the right wall of the church, and an open courtyard. The little cloister of the late 13th century has twin columns bearing pointed arches which surround a delightfully peaceful part of the garden.

THE ALBERGHERIA DISTRICT

The **church of Gesù** (*map 15; open Mon–Sat 6.30–1 & 4–7, Sun and holidays 6.30–12.30 & 5–6.30, T: 091 580655 & 091 332313*), also known as Casa Professa, was the first church to be erected in Sicily by the Jesuits (1564–1633). The sturdy tower (with a Catalan window) of the 15th-century Palazzo Marchesi, in Piazza dei Santissimi 40 Martiri, forms the base of its campanile. The palace garden is sometimes open.

The splendid interior was beautifully decorated in the 17th and 18th centuries with colourful inlaid marble and sculptures (especially good in the nave chapels, 1665–91; the lovely 18th-century Andronico organ is out of order, although fortunately intact). The entrance wall inside has very fine 18th-century sculptural decoration. In the right aisle, the second chapel has paintings of two saints (St Philip of Argirò and St Paul the Hermit) by Pietro Novelli, and the fourth chapel has a statue of the Madonna by the Gagini school. The presbytery also has remarkably good marble decoration. Also accessible is the crypt and the charming Oratorio del Sabato.

Beside the church is the fine Baroque atrium of the Casa Professa, now partly occupied by the town library, **Biblioteca Comunale** (*open Mon–Fri 9–1; Tues, Wed, Thur also 3.30–5.30; T: 091 7407571*), founded in 1760. It has over 330,000 volumes, and more than 1,000 incunabula and manuscripts.

Around Piazza Ballarò

Piazza Ballarò is the scene of the noisy, colourful daily market known since the Arab period as the **Mercato di Ballarò** (*map 15; from the Arabic suq al-Bahlara, when Bahlara was a village near Monreale where the merchants lived, and the fruit and vegetables were brought into town through the nearby Porta Sant'Agata*). This is part of the Quartiere dell'Albergheria, one of the poorest districts in the city, which was devastated by bombing in 1943. Beyond, the church tower of **San Nicolò** can be seen, once part of the 14th-century town fortifications, which can be visited (*Via Nunzio Nasi 18, open Tues and Sat 9.30–12.30; Info: www.leviedisicilia.com*).

Via Ballarò continues left through the market to Piazza del Carmine, with more stalls, above which towers the fantastic dome of the church of the **Carmine** (*open Mon–Sat 8.30–1.30, no visits during Mass*) with its telamones and colourful majolica tiles (rebuilt 1681). The sumptuous Latin-cross interior, a central nave and two aisles divided by columns, contains on the first south altar a portrait of St Andrew Corsini by Pietro Novelli; on the fourth, a statue of St Catherine by Antonello Gagini; and on the fifth, a *Madonna* by the Gagini school. The altars in the transepts are by Giuseppe and Giacomo Serpotta (1683–84), and the paintings (in the sanctuary) by Tommaso de Vigilia (late 15th century). From the left aisle you can reach the charming 14th-century cloister. Since 1219 the church preserves a thorn from the crown of Jesus, shown to the faithful on the Fridays of Lent and 3rd May. The door to the left of the passage to the cloister leads to the sacristy, with a 14th-century wooden Crucifix.

Via Musco and Via Mugnosi lead to the church of the **Carminello** (*open Sun and holidays 10.30–1; T: 329 2950170*) at Via Porta Sant'Agata 5, built in 1605 and decorated with stuccoes at the end of the 17th century and the beginning of the 18th. Those on the entrance wall have recently been attributed to Procopio Serpotta.

Palazzo Comitini to San Matteo
Palazzo Comitini, on the corner of Via del Bosco and Via Maqueda (*map 15; open Mon–Fri 9–1, T: 091 6628260*) by Nicolò Palma (1771), seat of the Province of Palermo. The 18th-century Rococo interior has lovely frescoed ceilings, Murano chandeliers and decorative mirrors. On the opposite side of Via Maqueda (to the right) is the long façade (mid-18th century) of Palazzo Santa Croce. Just beyond is the **Assunta** (*open 9–12 & 4–6.30, Sat and Sun 9–12*), a convent-church built in 1625–28 through the generosity of the Moncada family. The small interior is glowing white, richly decorated in the 18th century with stuccoes by Giacomo Serpotta (perhaps assisted by his son Procopio) at the very height of his skill—notice in particular the high altar and the angels. The lovely swirling vault frescoes are by Filippo Tancredi, the altarpieces by Borremans. The inlaid marble floor dates from 1638.

Returning towards the Quattro Canti, Via Maqueda passes, next to Palazzo Comitini, the church of **Sant'Orsola** (*open 9–1*), built in 1662. The interior was redecorated in the late 18th century. The two last chapels on either side of the nave contain stuccoes by Giacomo Serpotta (1692) and (in the left chapel) an altarpiece of *St Jerome* by one of the Zoppi di Gangi. A fine painting of the *Madonna and Child* (as Salvator Mundi) by Pietro Novelli is kept in the sacristy.

Further on, on the opposite side of the road, is the church of **San Nicolò da Tolentino** (*open 9–12 & 4.30–6.30, July–Sept mornings only; T: 091 6163013*), in the centre of a district where Jews lived freely from the 9th century onwards. However, Ferdinand of Spain expelled them from the city in 1492, and the synagogue here was destroyed and replaced by this church in 1609. The two altarpieces in the transepts are by Pietro Novelli. The convent houses the city archives.

Just beyond, **Via dei Calderai**, the picturesque 'Street of the Tinkers', diverges right from Via Roma. It leads to Via Giovanni da Procida where the church of Santa Maria degli Agonizzanti is situated (*closed for repairs*). East from the Quattro Canti, Corso Vittorio Emanuele leads towards the sea. A short way along on the left is the sturdy Baroque church of **San Matteo** (*open Tues–Sat 9–1, Sun and holidays 9.30–12; T: 091 334833*). It was begun in 1633 by Mariano Smiriglio, and contains lovely stucco work by Giacomo Serpotta and frescoes by Vito d'Anna (1754).

EAST OF QUATTRO CANTI

Beyond Via Roma, the narrow Via Paternostro (with numerous shops where luggage is sold or repaired) curves right towards the attractive piazza in front of the 13th-century church of **San Francesco d'Assisi** (*map 12; open Mon–Fri 9–5, Sat 9–11; T: 091 6162819, 091 582370*). The façade has a beautiful portal with three friezes of zig-zag ornamentation (1302) and a lovely rose window.

The church was damaged by an earthquake in 1823 and again during air raids in 1943, after which it was restored. The Franciscan nave of 1255–77 is flanked by beautiful chapels added in the 14th–15th centuries. Eight statues by Giacomo Serpotta (1723) decorate the inside portal and nave. Above the door is a fine sculpted arch of 1465. In the second chapel in the south aisle there is an altarpiece of *St George and the Dragon* in high relief and carved roundels by Antonello Gagini (1526); in the third chapel there is a *Madonna* attributed to Antonio Gagini flanked by 15th-century statues of saints. The Gothic fourth chapel contains a beautiful 15th-century *Madonna* by a Catalan sculptor and the sarcophagus of Elisabetta Omodei (1498) attributed to Domenico Gagini. Beyond the side door and another Gothic chapel is the sixth chapel with three bas-reliefs by Ignazio Marabitti (including the altar frontal). The seventh chapel has interesting 14th-century lava-stone decoration on the arches.

The chapel to the right of the sanctuary has a fine polychrome marble intarsia decoration (17th–18th century; carefully restored after war damage). The eight figures of Sicilian saints are by Giovanni Battista Ragusa (1717). The altarpiece of the *Immacolata* in mosaic is to a design by Vito d'Anna and below is an elaborate marble altar frontal. The sanctuary has fine 16th-century carved and inlaid choir stalls. The chapel to the left of the sanctuary has intricate marble decoration and an 18th-century wooden statue of St Francis. The eighth north chapel once had a bust of St John in polychrome terracotta, attributed to Antonello Gagini. It has been replaced by a cast (the original is in the Diocesan Museum; *see p. 33*). The four statuettes of the *Virtues* are attributed to Pietro da Bonitate. By the door into the sacristy there is a tomb-effigy of the young warrior Antonio Speciale attributed to Domenico Gagini (1477) with a touching inscription above it. The fifth chapel has a 14th-century portal with zig-zag ornamentation and remains of early frescoes. The arch of the fourth chapel, the Cappella Mastrantonio, is a superb piece by Francesco Laurana and Pietro da Bonitate (1468), the earliest important Renaissance work in Sicily. On the left wall of the chapel, the *Madonna and Saints* has been attributed to Vincenzo da Pavia. In the second chapel a highly venerated silver statue of the Immaculate Virgin (1647) is hidden by a curtain, and the remains of a fresco of St Francis is on the left wall. In the first chapel (light on the right), with a fine 16th-century portal, is a *Madonna and Child with St John*, by Domenico Gagini (with a beautiful base), and a relief of the Madonna.

To the left of the church is the **Oratorio di San Lorenzo**, entrance at Via Imma-colatella 5 (*open 10–6; T: 091 6118168*). The interior, designed by Giacomo Amato, is decorated with stuccoes illustrating the lives of St Lawrence and St Francis, perhaps the masterpiece of Giacomo Serpotta (1699–1707). Ten symbolic statues, eight viva-cious little reliefs, and the *Martyrdom of St Lawrence* situated above the door, the whole encircled by a throng of joyous cherubs, make up a well-balanced and animated com-position. The modelling of the male figures above the windows is especially skilful. The *Nativity*, by Caravaggio (1609; his last known work, painted for this church), was stolen from the altar in 1969 and has never been recovered.

Palazzo Mirto

At no. 2 Via Merlo, an 18th-century gateway leads into **Palazzo Mirto** (*map 12; open 9–5.30; Sat, Sun and holidays 9–1, possible combined ticket with Palazzo Abatellis and Ora-torio Bianchi; T: 091 6164731*). The main façade on Via Lungarini, with a double row of balconies, dates from 1793. The residence of the Lanza-Filangeri family since the early 17th century, it was donated by them, together with its contents, to the region of Sicily in 1982. The well-kept interior is interesting as a typical example of a princely residence in Palermo, with 18th- and 19th-century decorations, including a little 'Chi-nese' room with a leather floor. The contents include furniture (mostly 18th and 19th century), Capodimonte porcelain and Murano glass. On the ground floor, near the delightful stables (1812), the funerary stelae of Giambattista and Elisabetta Mellerio (1814), two of Antonio Canova's finest works, are displayed (hopefully temporarily, they need a more suitable setting), purchased by the region of Sicily in 1978 to prevent them being exported.

Beyond, opposite Palazzo Rostagno is the Renaissance church of **Santa Maria dei Miracoli** of 1547. The church was once on the harbour front, and its loggia was used by merchants (now a small theatre, the Teatro Libero).

Piazza Marina and La Cala

Santa Maria dei Miracoli overlooks **Piazza Marina** (*map 12*), once a shallow inlet of the sea. Here 16th-century Aragonese weddings and victories were celebrated by jousting. Later, in the proximity of two prisons (the Vicaria and that of the Inquisition), public executions were held here: condemned prisoners were burned alive, or hung, drawn and quartered. The centre is occupied by the Giardino Garibaldi, with fine palms and enormous old Morton Bay figs, *Ficus magnoloides*, one of which, before recent pruning, was the largest tree in Europe; they are now home to a colourful and garrulous colony of ring-necked parakeets.

At the seaward end of Piazza Marina is **Palazzo Chiaramonte** (*open Tues–Sat 9–1 & 2.30–6.30, Sun 10–2; T: 091 6253892*), known as Lo Steri (i.e. *hosterium*, or fortified palace), begun in 1307 by the powerful Chiaramonte family on a Norman glass factory, and finished in 1380. The exterior, though deprived of its battlements, retains several of its original windows. Warned by her spies, Queen Blanche of Navarre in 1412 fled from the palace in the middle of the night, in order to escape her would-be wooer Count Bernardo Cabrera. In 1535 Charles V convened the Sicilian parliament here, after which it became the palace of the Spanish viceroys. From 1605–1782 it was the seat of the Inquisition; some graffiti, restored and displayed in the Sala delle Armi, provide a fascinating historical record of the persecutions. Occupied by the law courts from 1799 until 1972, the building was restored in 1984 by the university to serve as the rectorate. The Sala Magna has a wooden ceiling (with a serious termite problem) painted by Simone da Corleone and Cecco di Naro (1377–80), illustrating 32 different episodes of chivalry, courtly love and legend. Also on display is Renato Guttuso's most famous painting, the *Vucciria*, illustrating shoppers and merchandise in the sensual confusion of the daily food market, which he donated to the university in 1974.

In the notorious **Carcere dei Penitenziati** next door, the Inquisition prison, hundreds of people accused of heresy or witchcraft underwent atrocious torture, as commanded by Torquemada. One of them was a friar from Racalmuto, Diego La Matina (his story is told by Leonardo Sciascia in *Morte dell'Inquisitore*), who in 1656, during a particularly gruelling interrogation, managed to kill his inquisitor with his handcuffs. After that he was tied to a chair for months before being burnt at the stake, while his tormentor was proposed to the Vatican as a saint and martyr. Recently, by using new materials and techniques, the graffiti (some in English and German) and the drawings which entirely covered the walls of the cells have been recuperated. The old prison will house the Museum of the Inquisition, to be dedicated to Diego La Matina, though at the time of writing it was still on the drawing-board.

Beyond the last side of the square is **La Cala**, now an elegant yachting harbour surrounded by a promenade. It is all that remains of the Phoenician port which once extended far into the old town. On the corner by the Corso is the church of **San Giovanni dei Napoletani** (1526–1617; *open for services*). The elegant interior has a magnificent 17th-century organ by Raffaele La Valle, a choir-loft decorated with 15 panels, perhaps the work of Vincenzo da Pavia, and a *St John the Baptist* by a Zoppo di Gangi.

On the opposite side of the Corso is the late 15th-century church of **Santa Maria della Catena** (*open Mon–Fri 9–12; T: 091 321528*), probably the work of Matteo Carnelivari (1502–34). Its name, *catena* (chain), probably refers to the chain that used to close the old port: it stretched from this bank across the harbour to Castello a Mare. There is also a legend that three innocent people were condemned in 1391 and as custom demanded, were sent to spend the night in this church in prayer; as they prayed their chains dropped from them and they were spared. A flight of steps leads up to the three-arched porch, which, with its two corner-pilasters, provides an ingenious combination of Gothic and Renaissance styles. The delicate carving of the three doorways is attributed to Vincenzo Gagini. The elegant interior has been beautifully restored. In the first south chapel, under a 16th-century canopy, is a lovely 14th-century fresco of the *Madonna and Child*, discovered in the 1980s. The four statues are by the Gagini school. In the second chapel is a late 15th-century relief of the *Madonna and Child with Angels* from the church of San Nicolò alla Calza. In a chapel with a 16th-century relief are frescoes by Olivio Sozzi. The sanctuary is particularly beautiful, with elaborate Gothic decoration and double columns.

In the corner of the square is the outstanding **Fontana del Garraffo** (Paolo Amato, 1698), a sumptuous piece of Baroque street-furnishing surrounded by a little garden. The slender little figure on the top represents *Abundance Chasing Away the Hydra Monster*.

The lower end of the Corso, the *Cassaro Morto*, was virtually destroyed by bombing raids in 1943; the **Fontana del Cavallo Marino**, with a seahorse by Ignazio Marabitti, is now surrounded by palm trees. The reconstructed **Porta Felice** (1582–1637) has no arch between the two monumental pillars to allow the tall *vara* (or 'float') of St Rosalia to pass through it on her feast day. The long 17th-century façade of Palazzo Butera stands above the terraced *Mura delle Cattive*, or 'Wall of the Bad Women' (*open Mon–Sat 10–7*). The name may refer to a time when women caught in adultery were exposed to public ridicule. Alternatively, it may refer to the widows who, for reasons of decorum, could not take their *passeggiata* with other ladies along the Foro Italico, so they passed the time here in malicious gossip. The busy, broad **Foro Italico**, which runs outside the walls, offers a splendid view of Mt Pellegrino, and a large public garden has been created on the seafront.

Museo Internazionale delle Marionette

At Piazzetta Antonio Pasqualino 5 (a turning off Via Butera) is the Museo Internazionale delle Marionette Antonio Pasqualino (*open Mon–Sat 9–1, Sun 10–1, July–Aug also afternoons 2.30–6.30, closed Sun and holidays; T: 091 328060; www.museomarionettepalermo. it*) founded in 1975. There is a complete collection of puppets from Sicily and Naples, as well as from Africa, the New Hebrides, Vietnam, Korea, Burma, China, and India (particularly Rajasthan), shadow puppets from Malaysia, Cambodia, and Indonesia, and Professor Jingles' Punch and Judy Theatre from England, all beautifully displayed.

Santa Maria della Pietà

Via Butera continues (past a plaque on a wing of Palazzo Butera recording Goethe's stay here in an inn on this site in 1787) to Via Torremuzza and the church of Santa Maria della Pietà (*map 12; open Mon–Sat 8–1 & 4–7; T: 091 6165266*), with a splendid Baroque façade by Giacomo Amato (1678–84). The interior is a particularly striking example of local Baroque architecture. The delightful vestibule has stuccoes by Procopio Serpotta and frescoes by Borremans: it supports a splendid nuns' choir. Four choir-screens in gilded wood decorate the nave. The fresco in the vault is by Antonino Grano (1708). The first south altar has a painting of Dominican saints by Antonio and Francesco Manno, and the second, a *Madonna of the Rosary* by Olivio Sozzi. The high altar has a tabernacle in lapis lazuli. The third north altar has a *Pietà* (in the beautiful original frame) by Vincenzo da Pavia and the second, *St Dominic* by Olivio Sozzi.

OPRA DEI PUPI

Sicily has long been famous for its puppet theatres, known as the *opra dei pupi*. In the 19th century, at the height of their popularity, the most important puppet theatres on the island were in Palermo, Trapani, Syracuse, Caltagirone, Acireale and Catania. In the 1960s, puppet theatres languished and many closed down, but recently there has been a revival of this traditional entertainment. The puppets, which vary in size from Palermo (small, with jointed knees) to Catania (large, even 30kg, stiff legs), are made of wood, with shiny armour. The puppeteer, who stands on a wooden platform just above the stage, manoeuvres them by using quite heavy iron bars. However cumbersome they may look offstage, they immediately come to life when brought into the scene, and swagger into position with great panache. The plays focus on chivalric episodes in the lives of the paladins of Charlemagne's court, portrayed through the various heroic deeds of Orlando, Rinaldo, Astolfo and others who challenge the Saracens. The key moment in every play is the battle, enacted in the traditional style, with much foot stamping, blood spurting, heads rolling, corpses piling up on both sides of the stage (Christians on one side, Muslims on the other), even the occasional dragon or wizard putting in an appearance. Garibaldi is also a source of inspiration for the *pupari*, as is King Arthur of the Round Table. The Sicilian puppet theatre has been declared a Masterpiece of Intangible Heritage by UNESCO.

La Gancia

The church of **La Gancia**, or Santa Maria degli Angeli, entered by the side door (*map 12; open Mon–Fri 9–5, Sat 9–1, Sun and holidays 10–12.30; T: 091 6165221*), has a fine exterior of the 15th century. In the interior, the wooden ceiling and 17th-century organ (no longer in use) date from the transformation begun in 1672. In the second south chapel are Antonello Crescenzio's, *Madonna with Sts Catherine and Agatha* (signed and dated 1528) and Pietro Novelli's (attributed), *Holy Family*; in the fourth chapel: Antonello Gagini's (attributed), seated *Madonna* (the head of the Christ Child is modern); in the fifth and sixth chapels, inlaid marble panels with scenes of the Flight into Egypt: outside is a pulpit made up of fragments of sculpture by the Gagini. The chapel to the right of the choir has fine marble decoration and stuccoes by Giacomo Serpotta. On the choir piers are two delicately carved *Annunciations* attributed to Antonello Gagini. In the chapel to the left of the choir are more stuccoes by Serpotta, and a *Marriage of the Virgin* by Vincenzo da Pavia. North transept: on the wall (high up), *St Francis* by a Zoppo di Gangi. North aisle: in the sixth chapel are two beautiful reliefs (one of the *Descent into Limbo*) by Antonello Gagini; in the third chapel, Pietro Novelli's *St Peter of Alcantara*, and in the second, Vincenzo da Pavia's *Nativity*.

The adjoining **convent** is famous in the annals of the revolution of 4th April 1860 against Neapolitan rule. The convent bell gave the signal to the insurgents; Francesco

Riso, their leader, was mortally wounded, 13 were captured and shot while two hid for five days in the vaults of the church under the corpses of their companions, before escaping through the *Buca della Salvezza*, a hole they dug through the wall next to Palazzo Abatellis, while three housewives pretended to quarrel in order to distract the Bourbon troops.

Via Alloro, a narrow medieval street with some old palaces, only now recovering from Second World War bombing, continues back from the church of La Gancia towards the centre of the city. On the right is the church of the **Madonna dell'Itria dei Cocchieri** (*open Sat 3.30–6, Sun for Mass at 11; T: 091 6165848*), once the seat of the confraternity of coachmen. Built in 1596, it has a crypt with 18th-century frescoes.

PALAZZO ABATELLIS (GALLERIA REGIONALE)

Map 12. Via Alloro 4. Open Tues–Fri 9–5.30; Sat, Sun and holidays 9–1; closed Mon; possible combined ticket with Palazzo Mirto and Oratorio Bianchi; T: 091 6230011.
Palazzo Abatellis was designed in 1490–95 by Matteo Carnelivari, Nicolò Grisafi and several other architects and master-builders for Francesco Abatellis, appointed 'master-pilot' (or admiral) of Sicily by the Spaniards, in a style combining elements of the Renaissance with late Catalan Gothic. The façade is unusual and interesting, especially the square portal, formed of slender wooden poles tied together by writhing serpents, forming a trellis carved in stone. Above it is the coat of arms of Francesco Abatellis, a griffon wearing the crown of a count. Although he married twice, Abatellis died without issue, so he left the palace to the Benedictine nuns, who later passed it to the Dominican order, which held it from 1526 until 1943, when it was damaged by bombs. It had been much altered internally, and was freely restored in 1954 as the home of the Galleria Regionale della Sicilia. This is a superb collection of Sicilian sculpture and paintings, well documented and beautifully arranged, and recently much enlarged. The 16th-century monastery church of the Portulano, used by the Dominican nuns, is also open to the public, after having been completely cleared, showing to advantage its beautiful architecture and an altarpiece by Vincenzo da Pavia of *Christ at the Column*, together with other works by the same artist. This gallery is used for temporary exhibitions.

Ground floor
A doorway of original design leads out to the courtyard and the portico, with a collection of medieval fragmentary sculptures. Steps to the left lead up to the loggia, dedicated to Islamic stone carvings. The ground floor is devoted principally to sculpture.

Room I contains wooden beams and window- and door-frames from the Martorana convent (now demolished), which stood next to the church of the same name; they are remarkable for the typical 12th-century geometric designs.

Room II The former chapel is dominated by a famous large fresco of the *Triumph of Death*, detached from Palazzo Sclafani. Dating from c. 1449, it is of uncertain attribution, thought by some scholars to be a Sicilian work and by others to be by Pisanello or his school. Death is portrayed as an archer on a spectral horse, killing the contented and successful (right) with his arrows, while the unhappy, sick and aged (left), among whom are the painter and a pupil, pray in vain for release. The painting has provided inspiration for several artists, among them Pablo Picasso (*Guernica*).

Room IIA displays a collection of softly luminous panel paintings from the churches of Santa Cita and San Giacomo La Marina by Vincenzo da Pavia, who spent the last part of his life in Palermo. Particularly worthy of note are the *Deposition*, and the perfectly balanced *Presentation at the Temple*.

Room III: A corridor containing Islamic majolica lustre-ware, known as *loza dorada*, including a magnificent pale ivory and gold-coloured vase of Hispano-Moresque type (13th–14th century) from a church in Mazara del Vallo, thought to come from Malaga, and three splendid dishes manufactured in Manises, leads to three rooms devoted to late 15th- and early 16th-century sculpture.

Room IV: Works by Francesco Laurana, principally a bust of Eleonora of Aragon (1475), his masterpiece. Eleonora, daughter of Ferdinand I of Naples, married Ercole d'Este, Duke of Ferrara, gave him three children, and presided over a particularly rich period in that city's history.

Room V: Devoted to the Gaginis; particularly notable are a marble statuette of the Madonna and Child, the Tabernacle of the Ansalone, the *Madonna of the Good Rest* (1528), and the head of a young boy, all by Antonello Gagini.

Room VI: Contains architectural fragments by the Gaginis and their school, including the capitals from the church of the Annunziata in Palermo, destroyed by a bombing raid in 1943, some painted panels of typical medieval *droleries* from the church of Sant'Agostino in Trapani, and fragments from a ceiling in Palazzo Chiaramonte in Palermo, painted by Cecco di Naro and Simone da Corleone in 1377–80, with scenes from the Bible and of knightly chivalry.

First floor

The first floor is reached by a staircase from the courtyard. It contains the Picture Gallery (Pinacoteca), with its representative series of Sicilian paintings, most of which are from the churches and convents of Palermo, including 13th–14th-century works, still in the Byzantine manner, and later works showing the influence of various schools (Umbrian, Sienese, Catalan and Flemish).

Room VII: A delicate Byzantine mosaic of the Madonna, a painted 13th-century Crucifix, and other early works.

Room VIIA illustrates through a series of panel paintings the arrival in Sicily of works from Tuscany and Liguria, thanks to the commercial ties linking Palermo with Pisa and Genoa in the 14th century.

Room VIII: Paintings of the late 14th and early 15th centuries from Tuscany and Liguria, including a splendid polyptych by an unknown master from Siena, the *Madonna Enthroned between Sts Catherine of Alexandria, Paul, Peter and Dominic*, together with other triptychs and polyptychs by Sicilian masters,

including several *Coronations of the Virgin* by the same unknown artist, and works by the Master of the Trapani Polyptych.
Room IX: A large gallery, often called the 'Room of the Crucifixes', dominated by two splendid early 15th-century wooden Crucifixes painted in tempera on both sides, one by the Master of Galatina and the other by Pietro Ruzzolone. On the walls are detached frescoes by Tommaso de Vigilia, and the magnificent Gothic-style *Corleone Polyptych*, still intact with its original wooden panelling, from the monastery of San Salvatore in Corleone.
Room X: Precious works by Antonello da Messina, including the stunning little panel-painting universally considered to be his masterpiece, the *Virgin Annunciate* (1474), and *Sts Gregory, Augustine and Jerome*, parts of a missing polyptych, probably painted in 1473. Notice also here, the lovely Catalan Gothic processional banner from Tusa.
Room XA: *Angel* and *Virgin Annunciate*, two early 16th-century panel-paintings by Johannes de Matta.
Room XI: Late 15th-century paintings and frescoes by Tommaso de Vigilia, a Crucifix by Pietro Ruzzolone and works by Riccardo Quartararo, notably *Sts Peter and Paul* (1494) and *Coronation of the Virgin*. Notice the rich, dark colours used by Quartararo, and his sense of balanced design; behind the array of saints and martyrs assembled for the coronation ceremony, the bright wings of the angels indicate God on high, looking down from his mandorla in the sky. The upper half of the chapel overlooks the *Triumph of Death* (*see above*).
Room XII: Another mandorla here, with Antonello Crescenzio's dazzling *Assumption of the Virgin*, with angel musicians

and cherubim. Other 16th-century works include Andrea da Salerno's *Sts John the Baptist and John the Evangelist* and Antonello Crescenzio's copy (1538) of Raphael's *Spasimo* (*see p. 50*).
Room XIII: A number of 15th and 16th-century Flemish works, most notably, by Mabuse, the Malvagna Triptych (after 1511) of the *Virgin and Child between Sts Catherine and Barbara* (on the outside, *Adam and Eve*), a painting of extraordinary detail. Also two paintings, *Nativity* and *Flight into Egypt* by Vincenzo da Pavia, and a copy of Jan Van Scorel's *Mary Magdalene*.
Room XIV: Mannerist-style paintings by the Tuscan-Roman school of the 16th century.
Room XV: More works by Vincenzo da Pavia, to be compared with the earlier ones in Room XIII. These works date from after his Roman sojourn, where he was strongly influenced by Polidoro da Caravaggio.
Room XVI: Displayed here are the most important Mannerist paintings of the museum, in the style of Michelangelo. Two works by Giorgio Vasari, one by Polidoro da Caravaggio, one by Girolamo Muziano, and one by Marco Pino.
Room XVII (Quadreria): A tiny gallery which leads through to the new wing. Paintings are hung in the old-fashioned way, crowding the walls under a painted wooden ceiling. Not only religious subjects, but also landscapes, still-lifes, interiors and portraits, mostly from the aristocratic homes of Sicily, in a fascinating sequence.
Sala Verde: The new wing displays works on two floors. The first-floor Sala Verde (Green Room) was designed to show to advantage the huge canvases

of Sicilian late Mannerist art. During the Counter-Reformation, large, lavish altarpieces were much in demand for churches and convents. Notice the luminous paintings by Vincenzo da Pavia and Giuseppe Alvino, or the mesmerising diagonal flow of the *Adoration of the Magi* by Pietro d'Asaro. A charming pastoral scene by Pietro d'Asaro has also been included in this section. Highlight of the collection is a glittering monstrance in gold, silver-gilt, enamel and diamonds known as the *Sfera d'Oro* (Golden Sphere), a masterpiece by the silversmith Leonardo Montalbano, who was commissioned to make it in 1640 by Anna Graffeo, Duchess of Majno, forced to enter a convent after the death of her husband and sons. She gave the craftsman all her jewellery to use as his materials. Stolen from the museum in 1870, it was recovered in 300 pieces, because the thieves had smashed it for the gold and precious stones. It proved impossible to repair until recently, when the parts were joined using a laser, the first time the technique was used in this way.

Sala Rossa: The second-floor Red Room is dedicated to the works of artists influenced by Caravaggio, including Pietro Novelli, Van Dyck, Andrea Vaccaro, Cesare Fracanzano, Matthias Stom, Luca Giordano, Mattia Preti and Agostino Scilla, all excellently displayed.

THE KALSA DISTRICT

The Quartiere della Kalsa (*map 16*) was almost flattened by 1943 bombing raids, and has only recently been restored. From the seaward end of Via Alloro, Via Torremuzza leads past the church of the Crociferi or San Mattia, by Giacomo Amato. Further on is the façade (1686–1706) of the church of **Santa Teresa alla Kalsa** (*open 8–11 & 4.30–6, closed Thur morning; T: 091 617658*), also by Amato, and one of his best works. In the interior, the first south chapel contains Giovanni Odazzi's *Holy Family* (1720); and the second has Ignazio Marabitti's marble *Crucifixion* (1780–81). The high altarpiece is by Gaspare Serenario (1746) and the two statues of female saints in the sanctuary are by Giacomo Serpotta. The first north altarpiece is by Sebastiano Conca and the second is by Willem Borremans (1722).

The church faces **Piazza della Kalsa** (from the Arabic *el-halisa*, 'the elect'). This was one of the oldest parts of the city, fortified by the Arabs in 938, with its own walls and defensive castle. The stately 17th-century Oratorio dei Bianchi (*open Tues–Fri 9–12, possible combined ticket with Palazzo Abatellis and Palazzo Mirto; T: 091 6230039*) incorporating the church of Victory, built over one of the gates of the Kalsa citadel, has been restored. The ground floor displays sculptures recuperated from churches in the neighbourhood destroyed by the 1943 bombs, and the first floor, reached by a magnificent staircase, is used as an exhibition venue.

Villa Giulia and the Botanical Garden

Via Niccolò Cervello ends at Viale Lincoln across which is the entrance to **Villa Giulia** (*open 8–8*) or La Flora, a delightful garden laid out in 1777, with beautiful trees (the tallest in Palermo) and flowers, much admired by Goethe in 1787. In the centre are four niches in the Pompeian style, and a sundial fountain; towards the sea is another statue of the *Genius of Palermo*, by Marabitti. The **Botanical Garden** (*open Nov–Feb Mon–Sat 9–5, Sun and holidays 9–2; May–Aug 9–8 daily; Sept and April 9–7 daily; March and Oct 9–6 daily; last tickets 30mins before closing; T: 091 6238241; entrance through side gate*) adjoining the Villa is one of the loveliest in Europe. The entrance pavilion was built in Greek Doric style in 1789 by Léon Dufourny; Venanzio Marvuglia worked on the decoration and added the side wings. The garden was laid out by the noted botanist Filippo Parlatore, who was born in Palermo. Opened to the public in 1795, it has ficus trees, bamboo, various palms, lotus trees, bananas, frangipane, and many other plants from all over the world, a lovely circular lily pond, and the Serra Carolina, a beautiful 19th-century greenhouse. The exotic character of the garden is enhanced by a colony of ring-necked parakeets, nesting in the hollow trunks of the poplar trees along the avenues.

Santa Maria dello Spasimo

From beside the church of Santa Teresa, Via Santa Teresa and Via dello Spasimo lead away from the sea through the Kalsa district to the former church and convent of Santa Maria dello Spasimo (*open 9am–11.45pm; T: 091 6161486*), beautifully restored as a cultural centre for exhibitions, concerts and theatre performances. Founded in 1509, the church and convent were never completed, as the area was taken over by the Spanish viceroy as part of a general plan to strengthen the city's defences. In 1573 the convent was sold to the Senate and the church was used as a theatre after 1582, and again at the end of the 17th century. Part of the convent became an isolation hospital for plague victims in 1624, and in the 19th and 20th centuries it was used as a general hospital. Over the centuries the buildings have been adapted as warehouses, a deposit for the snow brought down from the mountains for making ice cream, and as storage for the débris after the bombardments of the Second World War. After the hospital was finally closed in 1986, restoration work began.

Beyond the 16th-century cloister is the church (roofless except for the beautiful Gothic apse vault), which has been made safe, leaving a few trees growing in the nave. In 1516 Raphael was commissioned to paint for this church an altarpiece of *Jesus Falling Beneath the Cross*. It came to be known as *Lo Spasimo di Sicilia*. After an adventurous journey, during which, according to Vasari, the painting was lost at sea in a shipwreck, but subsequently discovered on the shore near Genoa, it was finally installed here in 1520, the year Raphael died. The Spanish viceroy presented it to Philip IV of Spain in 1661 and it is now in the Prado in Madrid. Several copies were made of the painting (one made by Antonello Crescenzio in 1538 can be seen in Palazzo Abatellis), and some experts believe that the original may now be in the Prefecture of Catania, because a switch was accidentally made at some unknown date. The original frame is by Antonello Gagini. Beyond the church is a little public garden on the bastions, and another chapel used for exhibitions.

Piazza Magione

Just beyond Lo Spasimo is **Piazza Magione**. In the centre, between two agaves, is a small memorial plaque to Giovanni Falcone, who was born in this district in 1939. It was set up by the city of Palermo in 1995, 'in gratitude and admiration' for this courageous magistrate, assassinated by the Mafia in 1992. At the beginning of Via Castrofilippo is the little **Teatro Garibaldi** (*T: 091 6114255*), built in 1861 on what was the garden of the Magione, and visited by Garibaldi himself in 1862. Also on this side of the piazza is the fine Norman apse of the **church of La Magione** (*open Tues–Sat 9–1.30 & 2.30–7; Sun and holidays 9–1.30; T:091 6170596, www.basilicalamagione.diocesipa. it*), which stands in majestic isolation, painstakingly restored after the 1943 bombing raids. A precious example of Arab-Norman architecture, it was founded for the Cistercians by Matteo d'Aiello before 1151 as the church of the Trinity, but transferred to the Teutonic Knights in 1193 by Emperor Henry VI as their mansion, from which it takes its name. The interesting façade has three handsome and very unusual doorways. The beautiful tall interior has a fine apse decorated with twelve small columns. Above the 14th-century stone altar hangs a painted Crucifix. The contents include a statue of Christ and also a *Madonna and Child* by the Gagini school, a 15th-century marble triptych, and a tabernacle of 1528. The custodian will show you the charming little Cistercian cloister of c. 1190 around a garden; one walk with twin columns and carved capitals has survived. A room off the cloister contains a detached 15th-century fresco of the *Crucifixion* with its sinopia. Outside is a delightful garden and a monumental 17th-century gateway on Via Magione.

Via Magione leads to **Via Garibaldi**, typical Palermo, a dilapidated street with some handsome palaces and opulent balconies. Here at no. 23 is Palazzo Ajutamicristo, built by Matteo Carnelivari in 1490, with Catalan Gothic elements. Charles V was entertained here on his return from Tunis in 1535. Via Garibaldi, and its continuation south, Corso dei Mille, mark the route followed by Garibaldi on his entry into the city. At the north end is **Piazza della Rivoluzione**, the scene of the outbreak of the rebellion of 1848, inspired by Giuseppe La Masa and mercilessly crushed by the Bourbon troops; even today people use the expression *un quarantotto*, a 'forty-eight', to mean a total disaster. A fountain here portrays the *Genius of Palermo* (*see p. 24*).

The Gallery of Modern Art

Piazza della Croce dei Vespri (*map 15–16*) is named after the graves of many French victims of the Sicilian Vespers, marked in 1737 by a cross. Two sides of the piazza are occupied by the fine 18th-century **Palazzo Valguarnera-Ganci**, still owned by the family. Visconti used the sumptuous Salone degli Specchi as the setting for the scene of the great ball in his film *The Leopard*, based on the novel by Giuseppe Tomasi di Lampedusa (*see p. 207*). Nearby is the church of **Sant'Anna**, with a fine Baroque façade begun in 1726 by Giovanni Biagio Amico, with sculptures by Giacomo Pennino and Ignazio Marabitti, on designs by Giacomo Serpotta. The interior dates from 1606–36, with frescoes in the south transept by Filippo Tancredi.

The enormous, long-abandoned convent next door now houses the splendid GAM, **Galleria di Arte Moderna E. Restivo** (*map 15; open Tues–Sun 9.30–6.30; last tickets 1hr before closing, cafeteria and bookshop; T: 091 8431605, www.galleriadartemodernapalermo.*

it), with 19th- and 20th-century works, mostly by artists from Sicily and southern Italy, and worth a visit in its own right for the beauty of the 29 galleries. Particularly impressive are the sculptures by Mario Rutelli and Benedetto Civiletti, and the sections dedicated to Michele Catti, Francesco Lojacono, Antonino Leto, Ettore De Maria Bergler, Renato Guttuso, Pippo Rizzo and Giuseppe Sciuti. Don't miss the outstanding works by Onofrio Tomaselli (Gallery IX), Domenico Morelli and Antonio Mancini (Gallery XI), and the huge canvas by Corrado Cagli on the landing between the first and second floors.

SAN DOMENICO, THE VUCCIRIA & LA LOGGIA

The church of Sant'Antonio on Via Roma (*map 11*) occupies the highest point of the eastern part of the old city. The 14th-century campanile, which once used to summon the citizens to assembly, was lowered in height at the end of the 16th century, and the church reconstructed after the earthquake of 1823 in the medieval style of the original. Opposite the church, at no. 258, is Palermo's drama theatre, **Teatro Biondo** (*open for visits Sun 10–12; T: 091 7434341, www.teatrobiondo.it*). Beside the church of Sant'Antonio, steps lead down into the maze of small streets around Piazza Caracciolo and Piazza Garraffello, the scene of a busy daily market known as the **Vucciria**, one of the most colourful sights in the city. All kinds of produce is sold on the streets here, including fish. In Piazza Garraffello is Palazzo Lo Mazzarino, where the father of the famous Cardinal Mazarin was born in 1576. The market extends along Via dei Cassari passing the 18th-century church of Santa Maria del Lume, designed by Salvatore Marvuglia. From Piazza Garraffello Via Materassai leads to Piazza San Giacomo La Marina and the 16th-century church of **Santa Maria la Nova** (*map 11–12; open Mon–Sat 9–12 & 5–6.30; T: 091 326597*) with a Catalan Gothic porch (the upper storey was added in the 19th century in neo-Gothic style). The fine interior contains stuccoes in the presbytery and 18th-century paintings.

Close by, towards the sea, you can see the well-sited late Renaissance façade of **San Sebastiano** (*T: 091 326597 to book visit, possible Sat 4.30–6*). Inside are 18th-century polychrome marble altars, stuccoes by Giacomo Serpotta (1692) and 18th-century frescoes.

San Domenico

In the centre of Piazza San Domenico (*map 11*) rises the column of the Immaculate Virgin by Giovanni Amico (1724–27). The large **church of San Domenico** (*open 9–11, Sat and Sun also 5–7; T: 091 329588*), rebuilt in 1640, has an imposing façade of 1726 in grey and golden brown. Since the middle of the last century the church has served as a burial-place for illustrious Sicilians. In the third south chapel is a very fine statue of St Joseph by Antonio Gagini. The sixth chapel has a painting of St Vincent Ferrer by Giuseppe Velasquez (1787). The beautiful altarpiece of St Dominic in the south transept is by Filippo Paladini, and on the left wall there is a monument to Giovanni Ramondetta by Giacomo Serpotta and Gerardo Scudo (1691). In the chapel to the right of the sanctuary is a fine bas-relief of St Catherine attributed to Antonello Gagini, a Neoclassical monument by Benedetto de Lisi (1864), a small *Pietà* in high relief by Antonello Gagini and a pretty little stoup. One of the organs dates from 1781; beneath the one on the right is a small funerary stele (1848) of the poetess Giuseppina Turrisi Colonna by Valerio Villareale. The sanctuary has 18th-century choir-stalls. The chapel to the left of the sanctuary has Gaginesque reliefs and the tomb of Ruggero Settimo (1778–1863), who convened the Sicilian parliament in this church in 1848. On either side of the altarpiece by Vincenzo da Pavia in the north transept, are funerary monuments by Ignazio Marabitti. A bust of the painter Pietro Novelli is in the north aisle. In the fourth north chapel is an altarpiece of St Raymond, using his cloak as a sail, attributed to Filippo Paladini, while in the third chapel is a statue of St Catherine by Antonello Gagini (1527), with reliefs on the base, and on the right, a statue of St Barbara by his school. The second chapel has a terracotta statue of St Catherine of Siena, and the first an altarpiece by Andrea Carreca da Trapani. The fragmentary 14th-century cloister, which was part of the first church built on this site by the Dominicans, can only be visited by prior arrangement.

Next to the church is a small but well-arranged museum dedicated to the Unification of Italy, the **Museo del Risorgimento** (*open Mon–Fri 10–12; T: 091 582774, www. storiapatria.it*), with documents and memorabilia relating to this dramatic period of the history of Palermo. You will find Garibaldi's favourite chair, his crutches, cigar, swords, and slippers. Portraits and marble busts portray the principal exponents, both of the 1848 rebellion and of the battles of 1860 against the Bourbons, which would result in Italy becoming one nation, 'from Trento to Pantelleria', as Garibaldi said. The central salon has monumental bronze statues, of Garibaldi on horseback by Vincenzo Ragusa, Francesco Crispi and Ruggero Settimo (*see p. 61*). The museum also houses a fine library on the Risorgimento.

La Loggia and its churches

NB: The ticket office for all the churches of La Loggia is in Via Valverde, next to the church of Santa Cita; same opening times for all: Mon–Sat 9–1; T: 091 8431605, www.tesoridellaloggia.it.

Behind the church of San Domenico, in an area often called La Loggia because at its centre was the loggia of the merchants and bankers of Genoa, there are still many jewellery shops. Via Bambinai continues as Via Squarcialupo, the large church on the left being **Santa Cita** or Santa Zita (*map 11*), rebuilt in 1586–1603, and badly bombed in 1943. It was first built in the early 14th century by a merchant from Lucca (hence the dedication to the 13th-century St Zita, long-suffering patroness of domestic servants, who was born there) together with a hospital for Tuscan merchants. In the 16th century the Dominicans, who had acquired the church, allowed wealthy families to bury their dead here, thus ensuring an income for their convent and permitting the creation of the lavish funerary chapels. The interior contains fine but war-damaged sculptures by Antonello Gagini (1517–27). In the apse behind the altar is a marble tabernacle surrounded by a magnificent arch, both superbly carved. The splendid altarpiece is

Street urchin of Palermo, immortalised by Giacomo Serpotta in the late 17th century.

a panel-painting by Filippo Paladini of St Agnes of Montepulciano (1603). In the second chapel to the left of the choir is the sarcophagus of Antonio Scirotta, also by Gagini; and more sculptures by the same artist are in the second chapel (Platamone) to the right of the choir. The Chapel of the Rosary has refined polychrome marble decoration (1696–1722) and sculpted reliefs by Gioacchino Vitaliano. The crypt under the chapel of the Lanza family is now open to the public; it has an altarpiece of inlaid marble, and a sculpture by Giorgio da Milano.

Adjoining the left side of the church is the **Oratorio del Rosario di Santa Cita**, reconstructed in the early 17th century, approached through a little garden and loggia. The stucco decoration of the exquisite interior is one of Giacomo Serpotta's masterpieces: between 1685 and 1688 he worked on the nave and in 1717 on the apse. On the entrance wall there is an elaborate representation of the *Battle of Lepanto*, which commemorates the victory over the Turks in which the Christian fleet was protected by the Madonna of the Rosary (the confraternity of the Rosary had been founded just before the battle in 1571). On the two side walls are New Testament scenes in high relief representing the 15 Mysteries of the Rosary between numerous seated allegorical statues. The decorative frames and stucco drapes are supported by hundreds of mischievous cherubs, for which Serpotta used the street urchins of Palermo as models. The altarpiece of the *Madonna of the Rosary* (1702) is by Carlo Maratta. The ebony benches with mother-of-pearl inlay are of 1702, while the beautiful inlaid marble floor is decorated with eight-pointed stars, symbol of the Madonna.

In Via Bambinai is the **Oratorio del Rosario di San Domenico**. The interior is dominated by the masterful blue-and-red altarpiece by Van Dyck, representing the *Virgin of the Rosary with St Dominic and the Patronesses of Palermo*. The artist painted it in Genoa in 1628, having left Palermo because of the plague. The wall paintings of the *Mysteries* are by Novelli (who was particularly influenced by Van Dyck), Lo Verde, Matthias Stom, Luca Giordano and Borremans. Giacomo Serpotta's graceful stuccoes (1720), elegant society ladies representing various allegorical virtues, display amazing skill. The black and white ceramic floor is also well preserved.

In the handsome Piazza Cavalieri di Malta, the church of **Santa Maria di Valverde** was built in 1635 by Mariano Smiriglio. It has a grey marble side portal, and a campanile rebuilt in 1723. The sumptuous Baroque interior (1694–1716), decorated with polychrome inlaid marble, was designed by Paolo Amato and Andrea Palma. On the high altar is an 18th-century wooden statue of the Madonna of the Rosary and a fine canvas of the *Madonna of Carmel*, painted for this church by Pietro Novelli in 1642. The Virgin and Child are pictured holding the sacred scapular of the Carmelite Order; to the left, St Teresa of Avila is about to receive from a cherub the emblematic burning arrow of her calling. The vault fresco and those on the walls of the choir are by Antonino Grano, while the large one over the choir is by Olivio Sozzi (1750). The church has four highly elaborate altars, of which the most important is that of St Lucy (*see box on p. 333*), whose cult was strong in Palermo. The lovely 15th-century statue of the saint, by an anonymous sculptor, has been replaced here, after being thought lost for more than a century. Dignified and solemn, Lucy is wearing a blue dress.

Nearly opposite Santa Cita is the fine 14th-century doorway of the Conservatorio di Musica. Close by is the isolated 15th-century church of **San Giorgio dei Genovesi** (*map 7*), restructured for the Genoese merchants by Giorgio di Faccio in 1576–91, and intended to be an indication of their wealth and influence (at the time they were the most powerful bankers and merchants in Sicily and the Kingdom of Naples). It has a sturdy, Renaissance façade with a newly-restored portal. The interior, with nave and aisles, is also in the purest Renaissance style. Marble tomb-slabs (17th and 18th centuries) cover the floor of the nave. Notice the freshly restored paintings by Luca Giordano (*Madonna of the Rosary*), Bernardo Castello, Filippo Paladini (*St Luke Painting the Madonna*) and Palma Giovane (*Martyrdom of St George* and *Baptism of Christ*).

Beyond lies **Piazza delle Tredici Vittime**, where an obelisk commemorates 13 republicans shot by the Bourbons on 14th April 1860. A huge steel stele, 30m high, was set up here in 1989 to commemorate victims of the struggle against the Mafia. A fence protects recent excavations of 10th-century Arab buildings, and part of the Norman fortifications of the city (restored in the 16th century), known as **Castello a Mare** (*map 8; open Tues–Sat 9–5.30, Mon Sun and holidays 9–1; T: 335 227009*).

In Via Cavour, on the other side of Piazza XIII Vittime, is **Villa Whitaker** (1885; *map 7*), surrounded by a garden. This was one of two properties in Palermo owned by the Whitaker brothers. It is now used by the Prefecture.

Around Sant'Ignazio

In front of Piazza San Domenico, across Via Roma, the narrow Via Monteleone leads up behind the remarkable Art Deco **Post Office** (1933) to, at no. 50, the **Oratorio di Santa Caterina d'Alessandria** (*temporarily closed*). The oratory has been owned by the Knights of the Holy Sepulchre of Jerusalem since 1946. The interior has fine stuccoes by Procopio Serpotta (1719–26), two paintings by Zoppo di Gangi, and a *Madonna and Child* by Vincenzo da Pavia, above a bench inlaid with ivory and mother-of-pearl. The polychrome marble floor dates from 1730.

The church of **Sant'Ignazio all'Olivella** (*map 11; open 9–10 & 5–6; Sat, Sun and holidays 9.30–12.30; T: 091 586867*), begun in 1598, has a fine 17th-century façade. The beautiful interior has a barrel vault designed by Venanzio Marvuglia (1772) with frescoes by Antonio Manno (1790). In the first south chapel is Filippo Paladini's *St Mary of Egypt*; the second chapel has beautiful 17th-century inlaid marble decorations. In the south transept is an altarpiece by Filippo Paladini. The painting of the *Trinity* over the main altar is by Sebastiano Conca, and in the sanctuary are two statues by Ignazio Marabitti. In the left transept is an interesting altarpiece, of unusual design, of the *Martyrdom of St Ignatius* by Filippo Paladini (1613). The fifth north chapel was sumptuously decorated in 1622 and has an altarpiece of *St Philip Neri* by Sebastiano Conca (1740) and two statues by Giovanni Battista Ragusa. The third north chapel is also elaborately decorated, with polychrome marble and semi-precious stones and an altar frontal in relief. The small fresco of the *Pietà* in the vault is by Pietro Novelli, who also painted the altarpiece of the Archangel Gabriel in the first chapel.

The narrow **Via Bara all'Olivella**, in front of the museum and the church of Sant' Ignazio, is one of the liveliest streets in Palermo, with craft shops, cafés, traditional restaurants and a puppet theatre.

MUSEO ARCHEOLOGICO REGIONALE SALINAS

Map 7–11. Open Mon 8.30–1, Tues–Sat 8.30–6.45, Sun and holidays 9–1.30; T: 091 6116805. NB: At the time of writing the museum was in a lengthy phase of reorganisation. Some collections may therefore eventually be moved to a different position in the building.
Palermo's archaeological museum, housed in a former monastery, is one of the finest museums in Italy, illustrating the history of western Sicily from prehistoric times to the Roman era. It was founded in the early 19th century by the university. Since then it has acquired a wide range of objects, including the important Casuccini collection, the most representative display of Etruscan antiquities outside Tuscany. It also houses finds from excavations in the western part of the island, notably those of Selinunte.

Ground floor

In the centre of the Small Cloister (**1**) is a triton from a 16th-century fountain.
Rooms 3–4: Contain Egyptian and Punic sculpture, including two Phoenician sarcophagi of the 5th century BC found near Palermo, and the *Pietra di Palermo*, a slab of black diorite with a hieroglyphic inscription recording the delivery of 40 shiploads of cedarwood to Pharaoh Snefru (c. 2700 BC), which has proved invaluable in dating ancient Egyptian history; three pieces from the same stele are in the museums of London, Cairo and Berlin.
Room 5 (Large Cloister): In the centre is a papyrus pool. In the arcades (**a**) are Roman fragments: in niches *Zeus*

Enthroned (**b**) from Solunto, a pseudo-acrolithic statue of the 4th century BC, and a colossal statue of emperor Claudius (**c**) in a similar pose. Here also is an interesting funerary stele with three portrait busts (40–30 BC).
Rooms 6–9: Finds from Selinunte, and a splendid cornice of lion-head waterspouts from the Doric Temple of Victory at Himera (5th century BC), discovered by Pirro Marconi in 1929–30.
Room 10: The famous metopes of Selinunte. These sculpted panels once decorated the friezes of the temples at Selinunte, and they show the development in the skill of the local sculptors from the early 6th to the end of the

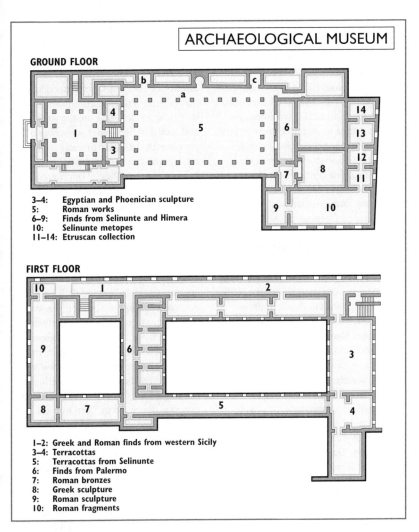

ARCHAEOLOGICAL MUSEUM

GROUND FLOOR

3–4:   Egyptian and Phoenician sculpture
5:      Roman works
6–9:   Finds from Selinunte and Himera
10:     Selinunte metopes
11–14: Etruscan collection

FIRST FLOOR

1–2: Greek and Roman finds from western Sicily
3–4: Terracottas
5:    Terracottas from Selinunte
6:    Finds from Palermo
7:    Roman bronzes
8:    Greek sculpture
9:    Roman sculpture
10:   Roman fragments

5th centuries BC. On either side of the entrance are three delicate female heads and fragmentary reliefs from Temple E. Beneath the windows are six small Archaic metopes, sculptured in low relief, from an early 6th-century temple, perhaps destroyed by the people of Selinunte themselves to repair their citadel, in the time of Dionysius the Elder (397–392 BC). They represent scenes with Demeter and Persephone (one with a quadriga), three deities, a winged sphinx, the *Rape of Europa*, and *Herakles and the Cretan Bull*. Facing the windows is a reconstruction, incorporating original fragments, of a frieze and cornice with three triglyphs and three stunning Archaic metopes from Temple C (early 6th century), representing *Apollo on his Quadriga*; *Perseus, protected by Athena, beheading the Gorgon*; and *Herakles punishing the Cercopes*, thieves who had attempted to steal his weapons, so he transformed them into monkeys. Also on this wall are parts of two metopes from Temple F, with scenes from the *Gigantomachia* (5th century BC). Opposite the entrance, four splendid Classical metopes from temple E (early 5th century) show *Herakles Fighting an Amazon*, the *Wedding of Zeus and Hera*, the *Punishment of Actaeon*, who is attacked by dogs in the presence of Artemis, and *Athena overcoming a Titan*.

Rooms 11–14: The Casuccini collection of Etruscan antiquities from Chiusi. Particularly interesting are the urns and tombs in high relief, a number of panels with delicately carved bas-reliefs (many with traces of painting), and a magnificent oinochoe of bucchero ware (6th century BC) portraying the story of Perseus and Medusa, perhaps the finest vase of its kind in existence.

First floor (reached from the Small Cloister)

Rooms 1– 2 (North Gallery): Greek and Roman finds from sites in western Sicily, arranged topographically. Selinunte, Lilybaeum, Randazzo, the Aeolian Islands and Marsala are especially well represented. Between the cases, containing vases, terracottas, and bronzes, are sepulchral stelae from Marsala painted with portraits of the deceased, and sections of lead water-pipes, showing junction points and stop-cocks from the Cornelian aqueduct at Termini Imerese.

Rooms 3–4: Terracotta figures, mainly from Gela, Himera, and Palazzolo Acreide, and a 5th-century kylix fished from the sea off Termini Imerese.

Room 5 (South Gallery): Displays some of the 12,000 terracotta votive figures found in the Sanctuary of Demeter at Selinunte, which can be seen to demonstrate chronology through the evolution of their design.

Room 6 (West Gallery): Contains some of the more important recent finds from sites in Palermo (fine vases).

Room 7: Large Roman bronzes. The ram is a superb sculpture dating from the 3rd century BC, probably modelled on an original by Lysippus (or even the work of Lysippus himself) and formerly one of a pair. Until 1448 they were above the portal of the Castello Maniace in Syracuse; in the 18th century they were admired by Jean Houel and Goethe in the Royal Palace in Palermo. The second ram was destroyed in 1848 by a cannon shot. The very fine *Herakles Fighting a Stag* is a Roman copy of a 3rd-century BC original which decorated a fountain at Pompeii, and was donated to the museum by Francesco I of Bourbon, as his personal inauguration gift.

Room 8: Devoted to Greek sculpture: in the centre is a *Satyr Filling a Drinking Cup*, a Roman copy from Torre del Greco of a Praxitelean original. Further items displayed here are a portrait of Aristotle, a Roman copy of an original of c. 330 BC, beautiful 5th-century reliefs and stelae, and a fragment of the frieze of the Parthenon.

Room 9: Roman sculpture: reliefs of Vestal Virgins, and *Mithras Killing the Bull*, a 2nd-century sarcophagus. On the floor a mosaic pavement (3rd century AD). **Room 10**: Roman fragments on the

landing at the head of the stairs. Nearby is a small chapel (*usually closed*), which is part of the 17th-century convent.

Second floor

This floor, with a superb collection of Greek vases, surrounds the Large Cloister. At the top of the stairs to the right is the short gallery with proto-Corinthian pottery of the 7th century BC. The Long Gallery has a splendid series of Attic **black-figure vases** (580–460 BC). Among the lekythoi with figures on a white ground is one (second central case) showing the Sacrifice of Iphigenia, signed by Douris, one of the more prolific Greek vase-painters; it has been calculated that he probably made 10,000 vases in the course of his life. In the fifth central case is a red-figure stamnos with *Herakles and the Hydra* (480–460 BC). In the room at the end (right) **red-figure vases** are displayed, including a hydra with the *Judgement of Paris*, and a bell-shaped krater with Dionysiac scenes. Another room displays mosaic floors (1st century BC–4th century AD), mostly from Piazza Vittoria in Palermo.

The **wall-paintings** here include five from the 1st century BC from Solunto and a fragment (1st century AD) from Pompeii. The room at the end of the next long corridor contains Italiot vases (4th–3th century BC), many with reliefs and traces of painting from Puglia, Campania and Sicily.

The last long gallery contains the collection of **prehistoric and Early Bronze-Age material** which comes mainly from northwest Sicily. Here are displayed casts of the fine incised drawings (late Palaeolithic) of masked figures and animals from Cave B at Addaura on Monte Pellegrino (*see p. 66*). Nearby are the bones of elephants, rhinoceros and hippopotami found in Via Villafranca, Palermo, in the so-called Grotta dei Giganti, Cave of the Giants.

SANT'AGOSTINO & THE CAPO DISTRICT

From the Quattro Canti, Via Maqueda runs gradually uphill to the north, passing the Capo quarter (*map 10*), a large bombed site whose ruined buildings were cleared in 1981. Plans for this district, which is owned by the Church, are uncertain. On its far side is Via Sant'Agostino, home to the Mercato del Capo, a businesslike street-market for cloth, clothes and household goods, full of life and not unlike the souks in Damascus or Cairo.

Sant'Agostino

Beyond the market, on the right, hidden by traders' stalls, is the church of Sant'Agostino (*map 10; open Mon–Sat 7.30–12 & 4–6, Sun and holidays mornings only; T: 091 584632*). The unusual tall side portal is attributed to Domenico Gagini. The beautiful façade, on Via Maestri dell'Acqua, has a late 13th-century portal decorated with a lava-stone mosaic and a 14th-century rose window.

The interior, consisting of a single massive nave, was decorated with gilded stuccoes by Giacomo Serpotta and assistants from 1711, with numerous cherubs, statues and lunettes over the side altars. The first altar on the right has a panel painting by Simon de Worbrecht (16th century) of Blessed William of Aquitaine; the second altar, a 17th-century *Flight into Egypt*; the fourth altar, by Antonino Grano (17th century), *St Nicholas of Tolentino*; beyond the passage of the right entrance is the chapel of the Madonna del Soccorso, with a bas-relief of the Eternal Father. Left of the high altar is the chapel of the Crucifix, with a precious 17th-century reliquary. The fourth altar on the left-hand side has a painting by Giuseppe Salerno (Zoppo di Gangi) of St Thomas of Villanova and stories from his life. To the left of the second altar is a monument to Francesco Medici, with his bust (1774; surmounted by a cockerel) by Ignazio Marabitti. The 16th-century cloister, with tall pulvins above its capitals, surrounds a little garden. The fine Gothic entrance to the chapter house was exposed here in 1962 and restored.

The Mercato del Capo and its district

Via Sant'Agostino then widens and continues uphill to the next crossroads at the centre of the Mercato del Capo, the heart of the maze of narrow streets making up the Capo district. Via Porta Carini, with stalls selling fish, fruit and vegetables, leads to **Sant'Ippolito Martire** (1583), with a façade of 1728. A chapel off the south aisle contains numerous ex-votos, and in the north aisle is a damaged 14th-century Byzantine fresco of the Madonna. The 18th-century paintings include the high altarpiece of the *Martyrdom of St Hippolytus* by Gaspare Serenario.

Opposite is the church of the **Immacolata Concezione** (*open 9–12.30, Sat also 4–6*) built in 1612. The interior, one of the most beautiful in the city, was elaborately decorated during the 17th century with paintings, sculptures, singing galleries, inlaid marble altars and a sumptuous organ. On the gilded stucco ceiling is a fresco by Olivio Sozzi. At the end of the street is the **Porta Carini**, the only one of the three gateways to have survived at the northern limit of the old city, though it was reconstructed in 1782.

From the crossroads of the Mercato del Capo, Via Cappuccinella continues through the food market and Piazza Sant'Anna al Capo, in a very rundown area of the city. In Via Quattro Coronati (right) is the little church of the **Quattro Coronati** built in 1674. At the next crossroads, Via Matteo Bonello and Via del Noviziato lead right to the church of the **Noviziato dei Gesuiti**, Santo Stanislao (*temporarily closed*), in the area behind the law courts. Built in 1591, the interior preserves some fine 18th-century stuccoes and inlaid marble decoration, as well as an effigy of St Stanislaus by Giacomo Pennino (1725).

In the other direction, Via Matteo Bonello leads to the picturesque church of **Sant'Angelo Custode** (on the corner of Via dei Carrettieri), preceded by an outside stair. It dates from the early 18th century. To the west is the wide and busy Via Papireto across which is **Piazza Peranni**, where Palermo's famous flea market for antiques and bric-à-brac, the Mercato delle Pulci, is held.

Via Carrettieri returns down to the Mercato del Capo in Via Beati Paoli, which leads right to **Piazza Beati Paoli**, named after a much-feared secret society which operated in this area in the 17th century. The church of **Santi Cosma e Damiano** was built after the plague of 1575 and that of **Santa Maria di Gesù** was founded in 1660 (it contains a large 18th-century vault fresco). Via Beati Paoli continues past the church of San Giovanni alla Guilla, rebuilt in 1669 and badly damaged in World War II. On the right Vicolo Tortorici leads into Piazza Santi 40 Martiri with the church of **Santi Quaranta Martiri alla Guilla** (*open Sun 9–1; T: 339 1588692*), founded by some Pisan nobles in 1605 and rebuilt in 1725. It contains splendid frescoes by Willem Borremans. The word *guilla* derives from the Arabic *wadi*, or river, meaning the church was built on the banks of the River Papireto.

THE NINETEENTH-CENTURY CITY

Piazza Verdi (*map 11*), laid out at the end of the 19th century, is one of the more central squares in the city. It is dominated by the opera house, **Teatro Massimo** (*open Tues–Sun 10–3, last tour 2.30; no visits during rehearsals; T: 091 6053267, www.teatromassimo.it*), by Giovanni Battista and his son Ernesto Basile from 1875–97, a huge Corinthian-style structure. Among the historic late 19th-century opera theatres in Europe, its stage is exceeded in size only by those of the Paris and the Vienna opera houses. It was inaugurated in 1897 with Verdi's *Falstaff*. In the piazza in front of the theatre are two decorative little kiosks which used to be the ticket offices, also designed by Basile. From the piazza, Via Maqueda continues north by **Via Ruggero Settimo** (map 7), a street named after the much-loved patriot Ruggero Settimo, president of a short-lived independent Sicily in 1848, proclaimed in defiance of the Bourbons. The road is lined with clothes shops as far as the enormous double Piazza Ruggero Settimo and Piazza Castelnuovo (*map 6*), home to the **Politeama Garibaldi**. This 'Pompeian' structure (completed in 1874, by Giuseppe Damiani Almeyda) is crowned by a bronze quadriga by Mario Rutelli and is now used mostly for concerts, although originally designed to accommodate the circus.

Via Dante (*map 6*) leads west out of Piazza Castelnuovo. Once very fashionable, there are several delightful Art Nouveau houses along its length, and it ends by the parks of Villa Serradifalco and Villa Whitaker Malfitano (*see p. 64*). To the east, in Via Roma (*map 7*), is the **Grand Hotel et des Palmes** (formerly Palazzo Ingham). Richard Wagner stayed here in 1882 with his family and completed *Parsifal*. The building was modified in 1907 by Ernesto Basile. Close by (opposite) is the **Anglican church** of the Holy Cross (*open Wed 10–12*), commissioned by Joseph Whitaker in 1872, a perfect example of Victorian Arts and Crafts in the heart of Palermo. **Viale della Libertà** (*map 2*), a wide avenue laid out in 1860, with trees and attractive Art Nouveau houses, leads north. Beyond the two squares Mordini and Crispi, the road narrows. On the left it passes a statue of Garibaldi in a garden recently renamed after the magistrate Giovanni Falcone and his wife Francesca Morvillo, both assassinated by the Mafia in 1992.

Opposite is the larger **Giardino Inglese**, a delightful 19th-century public garden, now terribly neglected. It is bordered on the far side by Via Generale Dalla Chiesa which commemorates General Carlo Alberto Dalla Chiesa, prefect of the province and a *carabiniere*, who was assassinated by the Mafia here in 1982 (plaque), along with his wife and chauffeur, after just five months in office.

Further east towards the sea is the **Ucciardone** (*map 3*), built as a prison by the Bourbons in 1837–60, and now a maximum security jail, near the modern port of Palermo. At Via Cristoforo Colombo 134 is the **Museo del Mare** (*Environs map; open Tues–Sun 9.30–12.30; T: 091 361309*), a very interesting collection of objects relating to the sea, from fishing to shipbuilding—there are historical photos, model ships, cannons and an exhibition on lighthouses.

Villa Trabia to Piazza Vittorio Veneto

West of Viale Libertà is **Villa Trabia** (*map 1*), seat of the Lanza di Trabia family, an elegant 18th-century building (now used as local government offices), with beautiful gardens open to the public (*open 8–6, entrance from Via Salinas*).

Across Via Notarbartolo, Viale della Libertà passes (left; no. 52) the head office of the Banco di Sicilia with the **Museo d'Arte e Archeologia della Fondazione Mormino** (*Environs map; open Mon–Fri 9–1 & 3–5, Sat morning only, closed Sun, holidays and Aug; T: 091 7792724, www.fondazionebancodisicilia.it*), which contains archaeological material from excavations financed by the bank: a precious collection of Greek vases; Sicilian pottery dating from 15th–19th centuries; prints, maps and watercolours; and numismatic and philatelic collections (that representing the Kingdom of the Two Sicilies is unique in the world). Thanks to donations, two new galleries have been opened in the museum; one dedicated to the Futurist artist Pippo Rizzo from Corleone, and the other to 19th-century painters including De Nittis, Boldini, Sciuti, Morelli, Lojacono, Leto and many others. Some of the bank's collections will eventually be transferred to the historic Palazzo Branciforte (Via Maqueda 323), where a beautiful new setting, Museo Mormino (*www.museomormino.it*) was being prepared at the time of writing.

Viale della Libertà ends in the circular **Piazza Vittorio Veneto**, with its marble *Nike* monument to Liberty. From here Via d'Artigliera (right) leads to Piazza dei Leoni at the south entrance (c. 4km from the Quattro Canti) to La Favorita park (*described on p. 66*).

LA ZISA & THE WEST OF TOWN

The palace of La Zisa, now home to the Museo d'Arte Islamica (*map 9; open Tues–Sun and holidays 9–1.15 & 2–6.15, Mon mornings only; T: 091 6520269*), takes its name from the Arabic *al-aziz* meaning magnificent. It is the most important secular monument of Arab-Norman architecture to survive in Sicily, and is purely Islamic in inspiration.

The fine exterior has a symmetrical design, although the double-light windows on the upper floors were all destroyed in the 17th century by the Sandoval family, who set up their coat-of-arms on the façade and altered the portico. In King William's day the sandstone was faced with plaster decorated in a red and white design. The small pond outside, formerly part of the gardens, collected the water from the fountain in the ground-floor hall, which was fed by a nearby Roman aqueduct. A damaged inscription in Kufic letters at the top of the east façade has not yet been deciphered.

HISTORY OF LA ZISA

La Zisa was one of a group of palaces built by the Norman kings in their private park of Genoard (used as a hunting reserve) on the outskirts of Palermo. It was begun by William I c. 1164–65 and completed by his son. The palace is known to have been used by Frederick II, but it was already in disrepair in the late 13th century. It was fortified by the Chiaramontes in the 14th century. By the 16th century it was in a ruined state and was drastically reconstructed by the Spanish Sandoval family, who owned it from 1635 to 1806. It was expropriated by the Sicilian government in 1955, but then abandoned until part of the upper floors collapsed in 1971. After years of neglect, a remarkable restoration programme was begun in 1974 and it was finally opened to the public in 1990. The structure had to be consolidated throughout, but the astonishing architecture has been preserved. As a finishing touch, the magnificent gardens were imaginatively re-created, with lily ponds, fountains and walks, but unfortunately they were then totally neglected and are now ruined.

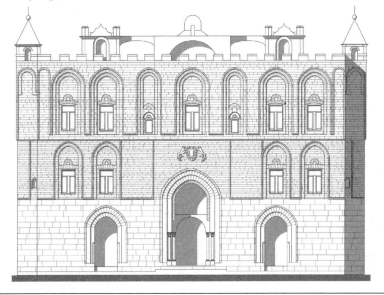

Interior of La Zisa

The beautiful interior of the palace is on three floors. The exceptionally thick outer walls (1.9m on the ground floor), the original small windows and a system of air vents kept the palace protected from the extremes of hot and cold. The rooms were all vaulted: the square rooms with cross vaults and the oblong rooms with barrel vaults.

Amphorae were used in the construction of the vaults to take the weight of the foundations of the floors above. Some of the vaults have had to be reconstructed in reinforced concrete. The pavements (very few of the original ones remain) were of tiles laid in a herring-bone pattern, except for the ground-floor hall, which was in marble. The miniature stalactite vaults (known as *muqarnas*) which decorate niches in some of the rooms and the recesses of many of the windows are borrowed from Arab architectural styles.

On the ground floor are explanatory plans and a display illustrating the history of the building. A model in Plexiglass shows the parts where it had to be reconstructed and where iron girders have been inserted to reinforce the building. The small chambers here were originally service rooms or for the use of court dignitaries. The splendid central hall, used for entertainments, has niches with stalactite vaults. Around the walls runs a mosaic frieze which expands into three ornamental circles in the central recess.

The Norman mosaics (which recall those in King Roger's Room in the Royal Palace; *see p. 38*), show Byzantine, Islamic, and even Frankish influences. A fountain gushed from the opening surmounted by the imperial eagle in mosaic and flowed down a runnel towards the entrance to be collected in the fish pond outside. A majolica floor survives here and the faded frescoes were added in the 17th century. The little columns have beautiful capitals. On the inner side of the entrance arch is a damaged 12th-century inscription in large stucco letters.

Two symmetrical staircases led up to the first floor (replaced by modern iron stairways). Here the living-rooms are connected by a corridor along the west front. Numerous fine vaults survive, and a series of air vents (*see above*). Medieval Egyptian objects, including metalwork, ceramics and wooden lattice work, which served as windows, are displayed in some of the rooms, as well as amphorae found in the vaulting. On the top floor is a remarkable central hall with columns and water channels, which was originally an open atrium surrounded by loggias, used in the summer. The small rooms on either side were probably a harem.

Around La Zisa

To the north of the Zisa, in Via dei Normanni, is the church of Gesù, Maria e Santo Stefano which incorporates a Norman chapel built at the same time as the palace. In Piazza Zisa is the 17th-century church of the Annunziata, with Sandoval family funerary monuments.

Villa Whitaker Malfitano and Villino Florio

From the Zisa, Via Whitaker and Via Serradifalco lead north to **Villa Whitaker Malfitano** (*map 5; open 9–1, closed Sun and holidays, guided visits only, last tickets 12.30; T: 091 6820522*) at Via Dante 167. Built for Joseph (Pip) and Tina Whitaker by Ignazio Greco in 1887, the house became the centre of English society in Palermo at the beginning of the 20th century. The Whitakers were visited by Edward VII in 1907 and by George V and Queen Mary in 1925. Pip Whitaker, descendant of the famous Marsala wine merchants, was owner and excavator of Mozia and the house was left by his daughter on her death in 1971 to the Joseph Whitaker Foundation. The furnishings, Sicilian,

French and English, are superb. It is surrounded by a magnificent park of rare trees and plants collected by the owners, an orangery and an orchid nursery.

To the south of Villa Whitaker Malfitano, at Viale Regina Margherita 38, is the **Villino Florio** (*open Tues–Sat 9–1, garden only*), one of Ernesto Basile's best works (1889), perfect Art Nouveau in style down to the smallest detail, and furnished by Ducrot. It has been carefully restored after a fire in 1962, and is used by the Regione Siciliana.

Convento dei Cappucini

South of La Zisa, at Via Cappuccini 1, is the **Convento dei Cappuccini** (*beyond map 13 and Environs map; open 9–1 & 3–6, Sun and holidays mornings only; T: 091 6524156, 329 4150462*), famous for its catacombs. Here, the bodies of priests and friars, aristocrats and wealthy citizens—adults as well as children—were dried by the Capuchins, dressed in their best finery, and hung up in full view along the underground passages. There are still more than 2,000 bodies here, including that of Rosalia Lombardo, a little girl who died in 1920 and was embalmed by Alfredo Salafia, who died immediately afterwards and was thought to have taken the secret of her perfect conservation to his grave—until in 2010 the manuscript in which he described his technique was discovered and published. Among the famous people buried in the **cemetery behind the monastery** is the great writer Giuseppe Tomasi di Lampedusa, in the family vault.

OUTSKIRTS OF PALERMO

The Punic necropolis and La Cuba

Outside Porta Nuova (*map 14*), Corso Calatafimi begins, which leads to Monreale. On the left is a huge charitable institute built in 1735–38 by Casimiro Agretta; the church façade (1772–76) is by Marvuglia. On the corner is a fountain of 1630, the only one to survive of the many which used to line the road. Opposite is the vast Albergo dei Poveri, an intimidating building (1746–72) by Orazio Furetto, built as the Poor House, recently restored and now used for important exhibitions. Beyond the Albergo dei Poveri are a series of barracks including (on the left, c. 1 km from Porta Nuova) the Caserma Tüköry (no. 100), where excavations since 1989 have revealed part of a huge **Punic necropolis** (*entrance from La Cuba*), with tombs dating from the 6th century BC. Here, separated from the barracks by a wall with a charming modern mural, is **La Cuba** (*Environs map; open Tues–Sat 9–6.30; Mon, Sun and holidays 9–1; T: 091 590299*), a Norman palace built by William II (1180) in imitation of the Zisa. The name Cuba comes from the Arabic *kubbeh*, meaning dome. A copy of the Arabic inscription at the top of the outer wall and a model of the Cuba are displayed in a restored stable block. The building is now roofless and a few trees grow inside the walls. In one part are remains of a hall with miniature stalactite vaults, delicate reliefs, and a small cupola decorated with stuccoes. It was once surrounded by water, today replaced by a little garden.

Still further along Corso Calatafimi, opposite a department store and behind no. 575, a short road leads right to the remains of the now derelict 17th-century Villa Di

Napoli. Here is the entrance to the **Cubula** (*closed*), a little pavilion with its characteristic red dome, built by William I. Once surrounded by a fishpond, it is the only survivor of the many which used to decorate his private park in this area.

THE NORTHERN OUTSKIRTS & MONTE PELLEGRINO

La Favorita

La Favorita's extensive area of woods and formal gardens lies at the foot of Monte Pellegrino. The public park (nearly 3km long), is crossed by a one-way road system, and contains a hippodrome and other sports facilities. The main entrance, Porta dei Leoni (c. 7km from Quattro Canti), is at the north end. The park began life as a royal estate, bought by Ferdinand of Bourbon in 1799 and laid out by him according to the taste of the times, adapting a dainty villa in Viale Duca degli Abruzzi as his residence with Queen Maria Carolina from 1799–1802 during their enforced exile from Naples under Napoleon. The estate was officially named 'La Favorita' by the king after Maria Carolina's death in 1814, when he contracted a morganatic marriage with the beautiful widow Lucia Migliaccio, his 'favourite' since 1812.

The **Palazzina Cinese** (*open Tues–Sat 9.30–5.30, Sun and holidays 9–1; T 091 7071408, 328 3605848, www.casinacinesepalermo.it*) is a charming Chinese-style building, re-designed for the royal couple by Venanzio Marvuglia. It consists of a basement with the ballroom and three floors, terminating in a pagoda. The first floor, with its walls covered with painted silk, a triumph of *trompe l'oeil*, was for receptions. The dining-table is provided with a central mechanism connecting it to the kitchen below, so dishes could be sent up and down as necessary, avoiding the presence of servants. The bathroom has a large oval tub of marble sunk into the floor. On the second floor is the king's bedroom, with a baldachin supported by eight white marble pillars, while Maria Carolina's Neoclassical bedroom is on the third floor together with two guest rooms, one in Turkish style, and the other recalling Pompeii.

The **Museo Etnografico Siciliano Pitrè** (*closed for repairs*) next door, was founded in 1909 by Giuseppe Pitrè. The museum illustrates Sicilian life through its customs, costumes, popular arts (such as painted carts and ex-votos), musical instruments, implements and typical everyday objects.

Monte Pellegrino

Between the Mondello road and the sea is Monte Pellegrino (606m), described by Goethe as the most beautiful headland in the world: it rises sharply on all sides except the south. The rock, in places covered with trees and cacti, has a remarkable golden colour. It is almost certainly the ancient *Heirkte*, the headland that was occupied by Hamilcar Barca in the First Punic War and defended for three years (247–244 BC) against the Romans. The Arabs called it *Gebel Grin*, hence the modern name Pellegrino; however, the peregrine falcon, *Falco pellegrino* in Italian, still nests on the headland, as it always has. In the Addaura Caves (*no access*) on the northern slopes prehistoric rock carvings were discovered in 1952. The incised human and animal figures date

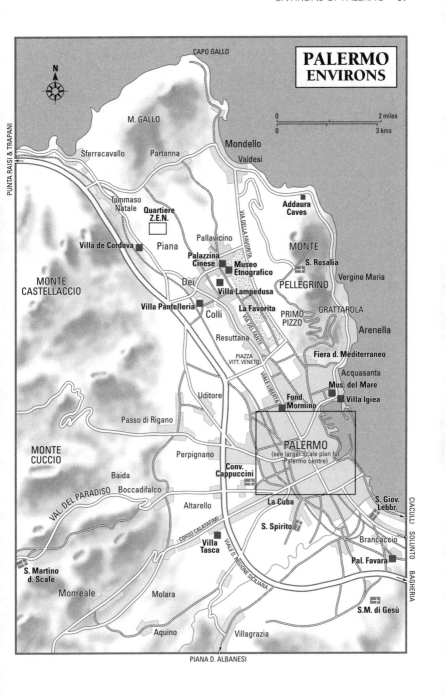

**PALERMO
ENVIRONS**

N

0   2 miles
0   3 kms

CAPO GALLO

M. GALLO

Mondello

PUNTA RAISI & TRAPANI

Sferracavallo   Partanna

Valdesi

Tommaso
Natale   Quartiere
Z.E.N.

Addaura
Caves

VIA DELLA FAVORITA

Villa de Cordova

Piana

Pallavicino

MONTE

Palazzina
Cinese   Museo
Etnografico

S. Rosalia

Vergine Maria

MONTE
CASTELLACCIO

Dei

Villa Lampedusa

PELLEGRINO

Villa Pantelleria   Colli

La Favorita

PRIMO
PIZZO

GRATTAROLA

Resuttana

VIA DEI FANTE

Arenella

PIAZZA
VITT. VENETO

Fiera d. Mediterraneo

Acquasanta

Uditore

VIALE LIBERTÀ

Fond.
Mormino

Mus. del Mare

Villa Igiea

Passo di Rigano

PALERMO
(see larger scale plan for
Palermo centre)

MONTE
CUCCIO

Perpignano

Conv.
Cappuccini

VIAL DEL PARADISO

Baida

Boccadifalco

Altarello

La Cuba

S. Giov.
Lebbr.

CIACULLI

CORSO CALATAFIMI

S. Spirito

SOLUNTO

Villa
Tasca

Brancaccio

Pal. Favara

BAGHERIA

S. Martino
d. Scale

VIALE D. REGIONE SICILIANA

Monreale

Molara

S.M. di Gesù

Aquino   Villagrazia

PIANA D. ALBANESI

from the Upper Palaeolithic period: they include an exceptionally interesting scene of uncertain significance with 17 human figures, some with animal masks, who appear to be carrying out a cruel ritual or dance. Plaster casts of the carvings can be seen in the archaeological museum (*see p. 59*). Recent exploration of several caves in this area has revealed imprints in red ochre of hands, also dating to the Upper Palaeolithic.

Sanctuary of Santa Rosalia

The most direct approach to Mt Pellegrino from Palermo is from Piazza Generale Cascino, near the fair and exhibition ground (Fiera del Mediterraneo). From here Via Pietro Bonanno ascends to the sanctuary of St Rosalia, crossing and recrossing the shorter footpath used by pilgrims making the annual pilgrimage on 3–4 September (often barefoot or on their knees). A flight of steps zig-zags up the Scala Vecchia (17th century) between the Primo Pizzo (344m; left) and the Pizzo Grattarola (276m). The terrace of the rosy-pink Castello Utveggio (built as a hotel in 1932, now used as a congress venue), provides the best view of Palermo.

A small group of buildings marks the Santuario di Santa Rosalia, at 428m, a cavern converted into a chapel in 1625 (*open summer 7.30–8, winter 7.30–6, T: 091 540326*). It contains a statue of the saint by Gregorio Tedeschi, and a bas-relief of her coronation, by Nunzio La Mattina. The water trickling down the walls is held to be miraculous and is carefully captured by Futuristic-looking metal conduits. The outer part of the cave is filled with an extraordinary variety of ex-votos.

Rosalia, daughter of Duke Sinibald and niece of William II, lived here as a hermit until her death in 1166. She is supposed to have appeared to a hunter on Mt Pellegrino in 1624 to show him the cave where her remains were, since she had never received a Christian burial. When found, her relics were carried in procession through Palermo and a terrible plague, then raging in the town, miraculously ceased. She was declared patron saint of Palermo and the annual procession in her honour (14–15 July), with a tall and elaborate float drawn through the streets by oxen, became a famous spectacle.

A steep road on the farther side of the adjoining convent climbs up to the summit, from which there is a wonderful panorama extending from Ustica and the Aeolian Islands to Etna. Another road from the sanctuary leads to a colossal 19th-century statue of St Rosalia by Benedetto de Lisi, high on the cliff edge.

Mondello

From the north end of the Parco della Favorita, a road runs through the suburb of Pallavicino and beneath the western slope of Mt Pellegrino, finally reaching the shore and the numerous elegant little seaside villas of Mondello, a sandy beach extending for 2km from Mt Pellegrino to Mt Gallo; a noted bathing resort, created by Donna Franca Florio for the amusement of her guests. The opulent Art Nouveau-style restaurant, the Charleston (1910), which overhangs the water, was originally the bathing establishment from which society ladies could discreetly lower themselves into the sea. The surrounding garden city was laid out between 1892 and 1910. There are hundreds of beach cabins which block the view, and devour much of the narrow beach, but Mondello still has plenty of devoted patrons who vie to pay a lot of money each year for them. At the north end is the old fishing-village of Mondello, with a medieval tower. To the south is Valdesi, from where Lungomare Cristoforo Colombo returns towards the centre of Palermo following the rocky coast at the foot of Mt Pellegrino. Inland from Mondello is Partanna and, above the promontory, the dramatically beautiful Capo Gallo (527m) rises vertically from the sea (now a nature reserve).

THE FLORIO FAMILY

If Palermo in the 1890s was a capital city of the Belle Epoque, and if Mondello was the most fashionable bathing resort in the world, credit is certainly due to the Florio family. In 1893, when Ignazio Florio married Donna Franca Jacona di San Giuliano, the most beautiful and fascinating woman in Sicily, he owned the Aegadian Islands with the tuna fisheries, the Marsala wine company, and a fleet of 99 merchant ships. In 1906 his nephew Vincenzo launched the Targa Florio, a gruelling motor-race on the hair-raising roads of the Madonie Mountains, which still takes place today (for veteran cars only; *www.girodisicilia.com*). Donna Franca's home in Palermo was a magnet for poets, artists, royalty and heads of state, while her Cartier jewellery was envied by Britain's Queen Mary. Although not untouched by personal tragedy, the Florios glittered on the social horizon of Palermo until well into the 1920s.

THE SOUTHERN DISTRICTS

Santo Spirito and the Sicilian Vespers

From the station Corso Tüköry (*map 15*) leads west to Porta Sant'Agata (follow the signs for Policlinico/Ospedale). Here Via del Vespro forks left; beyond the Policlinico and just across the railway are the flower stalls and stonemasons' yards outside the cemetery of Sant'Orsola, in the midst of which is the church of Santo Spirito or dei Vespri (*Environs map; open 8–1.30; T: 091 422691*). This fine Norman church (1173–78) was founded by Archbishop Gualtiero Offamiglio (Walter of the Mill; *see p. 30*). It has an attractive exterior with arches and bands of lava-stone and lattice-work windows. The interior has a painted wooden ceiling and a painted wooden 15th-century Crucifix.

On 31st March 1282 at the hour of vespers, a French soldier offended a young Sicilian bride in front of this church by shoving his hands up her skirt and down her bodice, to see whether she was concealing a dagger on her husband's behalf (Sicilians had been forbidden to carry weapons): her husband retaliated by strangling the soldier and the crowd immediately showed their sympathy by killing the other French soldiers present. Their action sparked off a rebellion against the Angevin overlords and by the next morning some 2,000 Frenchmen had been killed. The revolt spread to the rest of the island and in the following centuries the famous 'Sicilian Vespers' came to symbolise the pride of the Sicilians and their struggle for independence from foreign rule. The revolt also had important consequences on the course of European history, as from this time onwards the political power of Charles of Anjou, who had the support of the papacy, dwindled and he lost his ambition to create an empire.

San Giovanni dei Lebbrosi and Ciaculli

From Porta Garibaldi near the station, **Corso dei Mille** (*map 16*) leads south to the Oreto; this ancient thoroughfare was used by Garibaldi and his men when they entered the city in 1860. Just across the river is the Ponte dell'Ammiraglio, a fine bridge built by George of Antioch in 1113, and extremely well preserved. Since the river has been diverted it is now surrounded by a derelict garden and busy roads. Here the first skirmish between the Garibaldini and the Bourbon troops took place on 27th May 1860. On the left of the Corso, hidden behind crumbling edifices (and now approached from Via Salvatore Cappello 38), is **San Giovanni dei Lebbrosi** (*Environs map; open Mon–Sat 9.30–11 & 4–5, mornings only on Tues; T: 091 475024*), one of the oldest Norman churches in Sicily. Traditionally thought to have been founded by Roger I in 1072, it was more probably erected at the time of Roger II, when a leper hospital was built here.

A short way beyond is Piazza Scaffa. Via Brancaccio leads south through its unattractive suburb. Via Conte Federico continues to the Castello del Maredolce or **Palazzo Favara** (*entrance from Vicolo Castellaccio, open for special events; T: 333 1531785, www. castellodimaredolce.it*) which, although almost totally engulfed by apartment blocks, has been miraculously saved and partly restored. The palace, once surrounded on three sides by an artificial lake, was built as a pleasure-palace by Emir Jafar in the late 10th century, restored by Roger II, then used in the 12th century as a prison and in the 13th century as a barracks; after serving as a hospice, in the 18th century it was relegated to the status of farm warehouses. Its form was almost completely obliterated by illegal constructions and demolitions, but serious attempts are now being made to recuperate the emir's palace, with its gardens and lake (where the water has already begun to flow again), in order to create a large public park including the Baroque church of San Ciro at the foot of Monte Grifone, and the so-called Caves of the Giants, at present inaccessible.

A road leads from here to the suburb of **Ciaculli**, where a large estate once owned by the Mafia boss Michele Greco was confiscated by the state and is now farmed by a group of young people; the area is famed for its late-ripening tangerines, *mandarino tardivo di Ciaculli*, a Slow Food praesidium. A house in the centre of the grove, built illegally, will be transformed into a social centre with a theatre. Greco, known as *il Papa* (the Pope), was found guilty of some 100 murders and died in prison. The vegetation and landscape of the park is typical of the Conca d'Oro which once surrounded Palermo.

MONREALE

On the mountain slopes behind Palermo, overlooking the Conca d'Oro, Monreale is the site of one of the most superb churches in the world and certainly the most important

Norman building in Sicily, with wonderful mosaics (*map p. 542, B1 and Environs map*).

The town of Monreale in fact grew up around William II's great duomo (*open 8–6; roof terrace and north transept 9.30–12 & 3.30–5.30; T: 091 6404413*), dedicated to the Madonna and called Santa Maria la Nuova, alluding to a new archbishopric created in her honour. Begun c. 1174, and already near to completion by 1182, it was the last and most beautiful of the Norman churches in Sicily, built as much for political as for religious motives, an immensely impressive structure high on the hill above Palermo. It is one of the architectural wonders of the Middle Ages. The usual entrance is in Piazza Vittorio Emanuele, with its Triton fountain by Mario Rutelli.

CONSTRUCTION OF THE CATHEDRAL

William II needed to create a new archbishopric and ensure the sympathy of its new incumbent in order to counterbalance the power of his former tutor, the English archbishop of Palermo, Walter of the Mill, who was supported by the papacy. By handing over the cathedral to the Cluniac Benedictines, the king made a clever move: the abbot was automatically an archbishop in rank and his appointment needed no further approval, either from the pope or from the clerics in Sicily, and the French monks had no sympathy for Walter, or for the Vatican. The King justified the enormous expenditure by telling of a dream he had while sleeping under a carob tree during a hunting expedition. The Madonna told him to dig under the tree and use the treasure he would find there to build her a great church. It is estimated that the mosaics were made with 2200kg of pure gold. Hundreds of the finest craftsmen from Constantinople were employed to expedite the work. The monolithic granite columns came from a pagan temple or temples, the stone being northern European in origin, and some of them have been sawn in half, perhaps to complete a set from a number of damaged columns. The slender marble columns in the cloisters are believed by some scholars to have been brought here by the Benedictine monks from the sunken Roman city of *Baia*, near Naples. There they may once have formed the portico of a villa: some, especially on the east side, show traces of having spent years under the sea, the marble bored in places by a type of mussel known as the sea-date (*Lithophaga mytiloides*). Baia, being subject to a volcanic phenomenon which causes the area to rise and sink alternately, may have been easily accessible at that time. The columns with their capitals do not fit the arches they support; perhaps a last-minute adaptation was made by the architects in order to allow for their use.

Exterior of the cathedral

The façade, facing the adjoining Piazza Guglielmo, flanked by two square towers (one incomplete) and approached by an 18th-century porch, has a fine portal with a beautiful bronze door signed by Bonanno da Pisa (1186). The splendid apses, decorated with

MONREALE CATHEDRAL: WEST FRONT

interlacing arches of limestone and lava-stone, can be seen from Via del Arcivescovado. The entrance is beneath the portico along the north side built in 1547–69 by Gian Domenico and Fazio Gagini, complete with benches. Here the portal has a mosaic frieze and a wonderful bronze door by Barisano da Trani (1179).

Interior of the cathedral

The interior (102m by 40m), remarkably simple in design but glittering with golden and coloured mosaics covering a surface of over 6400m square, gives an immediate impression of majesty and splendour. Similar in concept to the Cappella Palatina in Palermo, the design is carried out on a much greater scale. Beyond the rectangular crossing, surmounted by a high lantern, with shallow transepts, is a deep presbytery with three apses, recalling the plan of Cluniac abbey churches. The stilted arches in the nave are carried on 18 slender columns with composite capitals, of Roman origin, all of granite except the first on the south side, which is of cipollino marble and represents the archbishop. The ceiling of the nave was restored after a fire in 1811, and then restored again in the 1980s when the 19th-century timber proved to be full of termites; that of the choir bears the stamp of Arab workmanship.

The mosaics

The magnificent series of mosaics tell in pictures the Old and New Testaments (*NB: Coin-operated lights are essential to see the exquisite details; binoculars are useful*). It is not known whether only Greek, or local craftsmen trained by Byzantine artists, were involved in this remarkable project, and the exact date of its completion is uncertain (thought to be around 1182). The large scenes chosen to illustrate the theme of Christ's Ascension and the Assumption of the Virgin fit an overall scheme designed to celebrate the Norman monarchy and to emphasize its affinity with Jerusalem. Under the rich decoration of the upper walls runs an elegant marble and mosaic dado in the Arab style.

Nave: Above the arcade the Genesis cycle begins in a double tier, starting with the upper row at the eastern end of the south side with the Creation and continuing round

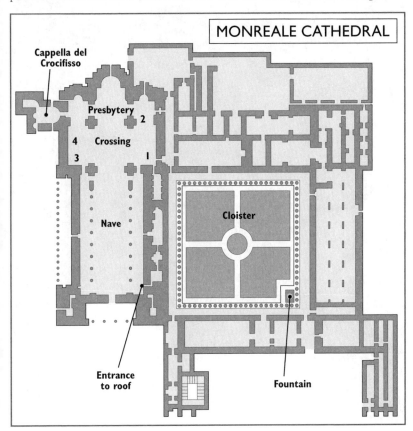

Christ Pantocrator, from the main apse of Monreale cathedral.

the western wall and along the northern side to end (on the lower tier) with *Jacob's Dream* and *Jacob Wrestling with the Angel*.

Crossing and transepts: The story of Christ is illustrated from the *Nativity* to the *Passion*. The piers in the transept are covered on all sides with tiers of saints.

Aisles: The Ministry of Christ.

Presbytery: On either side are scenes from the lives of Sts Peter and Paul, whose figures are represented in the side apses. In the main apse is the mighty half-length figure of Christ Pantocrator, with a solemn and rather severe expression on his face. Below is the enthroned Madonna, with angels and apostles, and lower still, on either side of the east window, figures of saints including Thomas Becket, made within ten years of his martyrdom; Henry II of England was William II's father-in-law. Above the original royal throne (left) *William II Receives the Crown from Christ*; above the episcopal throne (right) *William Offers the Cathedral to the Virgin*. The floor of marble mosaic dates in its present form from 1559, but that of the transepts is the original 12th-century paving.

Transepts

The **south transept** contains the porphyry sarcophagus of William I (**1**; d. 1166) and that of William II (**2**; d. 1190) in white marble (1575). Here is the Cappella di San Benedetto (1569), with a relief of the saint by Marabitti (1760). The **north transept** (*admission fee*) to the left of the choir conserves the tombs (**3**) of Margaret, Roger and Henry, the wife and sons of William I, and an inscription (**4**) recording the resting-place (1270) of the body of St Louis when on its way back from Tunis; his heart remains buried here. The Cappella del Crocifisso and treasury are accessed from the Diocesan Museum.

In the southwestern corner of the nave is the **entrance to the roof** (*admission fee*) which provides wide views of the Conca d'Oro and the coast. Stairs (180 steps) and walkways lead across the roof above the cloisters and round the apses of the cathedral.

The cathedral cloister

On the south side of the church is the lovely cloister, the Chiostro dei Benedettini (*open Tues–Sat 9–6.30, Mon, Sun and holidays 9–1; T: 091 6404403*), a masterpiece of 12th-century art, with Arab-Norman arches borne by 228 twin columns, with carved Romanesque capitals, of which very few are alike. Many of the columns are also decorated with mosaics or reliefs. They are the work of five master craftsmen, each of whom made some of the capitals, assisted by several apprentices, but only one capital is signed. A prolific confusion prevails of birds, animals, monsters, plants and people, representing religious scenes, mythology, Christian symbolism, and even the sacrifice of a bull to Mithras. The monks grew fruit trees in the enclosure (or *hortus conclusus*): trees symbolising Paradise—date-palms, olives, figs and pomegranates. In the southwest corner, a stylised palm tree in a little enclosure of its own forms a charming fountain, used by the monks to wash their hands before entering the refectory; the symbolism of the various elements here alludes to the rite of baptism.

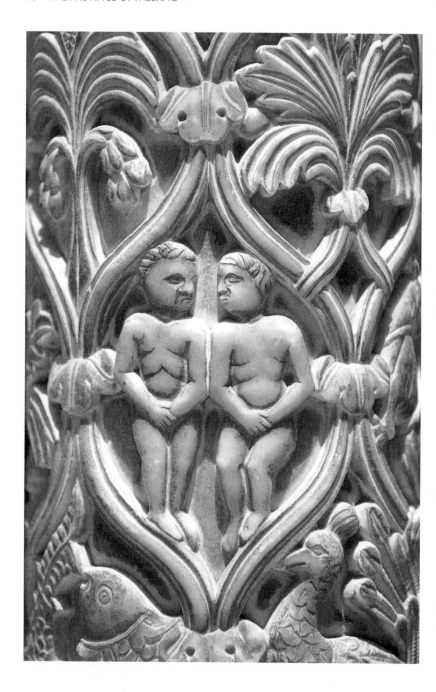

The Diocesan Museum

This sparkling museum displays many exceptional works of art never before shown in public, and also gives the opportunity of admiring the cathedral, both inside and out, from some unexpected angles. Situated in the old seminary next to the Archbishop's Palace, the Museo Diocesano (*entrance from Via Arcivescovado; open 9–1 & 2.30–6.30; T: 091 6419001, www.museodiocesanomonreale.it*), houses on three floors a collection of religious art dating from the 13th–19th centuries, consisting of paintings, embroidered silk vestments, tapestries, religious articles in gold, silver and coral, and sculptures in wood, terracotta and stone.

Ground floor

The entrance corridor, flanked with a series of stone sculptures, including the so-called sarcophagus of William, leads into the San Placido gallery with a surprising view of the cloister from the window at the far end. Dominating the gallery is a large tapestry representing the *Dream of William*, the symbol of the museum, showing William II asleep under the carob tree, while cherubs play with the gold coins he will use to build this great church. On the walls are showcases designed to recall the side altars of a church, each one displaying an altarpiece of various types, for example the precious, delicate *Madonna with the Christ Child* in ceramic by Andrea Della Robbia. Chronological order is not followed here, because this room was the only one large enough to hold some of the huge 17th- and 18th-century altarpieces, such as the *Last Supper* by Giuseppe Patania.

First floor

There are two galleries on this floor, both offering splendid views over the Gulf of Palermo. Room 1, from where you can also see the interior of the cathedral and the mosaics, is dedicated to the earliest works of art, which go back to the Norman period. Of particular interest is the *Madonna Hodegetria* icon, full of symbolic significance, where the Madonna wearing a blue dress (humanity) and a purple robe (divinity), is gently supporting the tiny, but surprisingly adult, red-robed (the colour of the Passion) Christ Child, who is offering His mother a rose (sweetness and thorns) with His right hand, and holding a scroll (I am the Light of the World) in His left. From this room you reach the richly-decorated, *horror-vacui* Baroque Cappella del Crocifisso inside the cathedral, commissioned by Archbishop Juan Roano in the late 17th century, and displaying together all the works of art commissioned by the Spanish prelate, in the space he intended for them, together with some others which found their way there later. Notice in particular the painted stucco altarpiece of *St Mary of the Woods*, and Vito d'Anna's impressive *Madonna*. Room 2, allowing a splendid view of the exterior of the apses with their marvellous intarsia decoration in coloured stone, displays art works of the 16th and 17th centuries, and is dominated by Pietro Novelli's masterpiece, the *Guardian An-*

Detail of Adam and Eve, shown ashamed of their nakedness and attempting to cover it, in the cloister of Monreale cathedral (12th century).

gel. Once seen and never forgotten, textures and colours are perfectly rendered in this mesmerising painting. The Archangel Raphael, with swan's wings, attired in swirling silk robes of saffron and scarlet, is showing Heaven to his charge, a little boy dressed in dark green. The arms of the angel divide the canvas diagonally, from the face of a cherub in the upper left corner to that of the child in the lower right.

Second floor
On the second floor are two large communicating galleries. The first is dedicated to a private collection donated by Salvatore Renda Pitti. Part of the room, which looks out over the cloister, displays a series of priestly robes and religious objects commissioned by the archbishops through the centuries, accompanied by explanatory panels. The second gallery, housed in a room with a beautiful barrel-vaulted, coffered ceiling commissioned by Archbishop Domenico Gaspare Lancia di Brolo in the late 19th century, displays an interesting selection of the more recent works of art. A separate section here shows items of popular devotion, such as ex-votos and humble carvings and paintings.

The town
A cool and shady public garden, called **Belvedere**, with lovely trees and views, is entered on the right of the façade of the new convent (1747), now a school. The restored 18th-century **Town Hall** occupies part of the Norman royal palace (remnants of which can be seen from behind). In the council chamber is a *Madonna with Two Saints* (in terracotta), attributed to Antonello Gagini (1528), and an *Adoration of the Shepherds*, by Matthias Stom (17th century). Behind is Via Arcivescovado, from which the magnificent exterior of the east end of the cathedral can be seen. The choir school here incorporates some arches and windows of the Norman palace.

Also entered from the Belvedere is the **Galleria d'Arte Moderna Sciortino** (*open Mon–Sat 8–1; Tues, Thur and Sat also 3–6; Sun and holidays 9–1; T: 091 6405443*), a rich collection donated to the town of paintings, drawings, sculptures and ceramics by contemporary artists, including Greco, Guttuso, Pirandello, De Chirico, De Pisis, Schifano, Morandi, and an *Adoration of the Shepherds* by Matthias Stom.

The little town also possesses some fine Baroque churches. The **Chiesa del Monte** in Via Umberto contains stuccoes by Serpotta and his school, and the *Madonna of the Constellation* by Orazio Ferraro (1612). Higher up is the **Collegiata**, with large 18th-century paintings in the nave by Marco Benefial, and an exquisite wood and tortoise-shell *Crucifixion* (16th century; on the high altar). On the external wall of the apse is an outstanding panel of majolica tiles, showing the *Crucifixion* with Monreale in the background; it is probably the work of Giuseppe Mariani (early 18th century).

In Piazza Vaglica is the 18th-century Collegio di Maria, close to the church of the **Santissima Trinità**, with a very elegant interior, and, in Via Venero, the church of **San Castrense**, the patron saint of Monreale, a pretty 18th-century building with stuccoes by the school of Serpotta and an altarpiece by the Florentine sculptor Antonio Novelli (1602). High above Monreale is the 19th-century church of **Madonna delle Croci**, with a fine view.

SAN MARTINO DELLE SCALE

The road between Monreale and San Martino delle Scale ascends to Portella San Martino, where a path climbs up through a pinewood to (c. 20mins) the **Castellaccio** (766m; *temporarily closed*), the southwestern summit of Mt Cuccio and a splendid viewpoint. The castle was a fortified monastery built by William II as a hospice for the convent of Monreale. Towards the end of the 18th century it was abandoned and fell into ruin until in 1899 it was purchased by the Club Alpino Siciliano.

San Martino delle Scale (500m) is a hill resort in pinewoods. The huge Benedictine **Abbey of San Martino** (*open 8.30–12.30 & 4–6, Sun and holidays 9–11.30 & 5–7; T: 091 418104, www.abbaziadisanmartino.it*), possibly founded by St Gregory the Great in the 6th century, was destroyed by the Arabs in 820, rebuilt after 1347 by Archbishop Emanuele Spinola and the Benedictine Angelo Sisinio, and enlarged c. 1762 by Venanzio Marvuglia. It is now occupied by the Abadir, a fine-arts academy and restoration laboratory. The church, dating from 1561–95 (with part of the 14th-century masonry in the north wall) contains choir stalls (1591–97) carved by Nunzio Ferraro and Giovanbattista Vigilante from Naples. *St Benedict* and the *Madonna with Sts Benedict and Scholastica* are both by Pietro Novelli. Six altarpieces here are by one of the artists known as Zoppo di Gangi (a particularly interesting one shows the *Seven Archangels*, each with his symbol: Uriel (Light and Fire) a lamp; Michael (Justice) a sword; Gabriel (Messenger) a lily sceptre; Jehudiel (Prizes and Pestilences) a crown; Raphael (Healer and Guardian) a child; above them, on a cloud, are blue-dressed Barachiel (Blessings) a book, and, dressed in red, Sealtiel (Grace) a vase of flowers. There is also a portrait of *St Martin* by Filippo Paladini. The sacristy contains vestments of the 16th–18th centuries and paintings attributed to Annibale Carracci and Guercino, and a fine reliquary. The carved doorway into the claustral part of the convent dates from the 15th century, and nearby is a stoup dated 1396.

At the foot of the bell-tower is a statuary group of *St Martin and the Beggar*, by Marabitti. A statue (1728) of St Benedict, by Giuseppe Pampillonia, surmounts the fountain in the main cloister (1612; altered and enlarged in the 18th century). The Oreto fountain is by Marabitti (1784). The refectory ceiling (*Daniel in the Lions' Den*) was frescoed by Pietro Novelli. A small museum shows paintings, church silverware, embroidered altar-cloths and vestments, and coral. A gallery of paintings on the subject of St Benedict, covering all the most important pictorial styles, *Nel nome di Benedetto*, occupies the ex-library of the convent, and forms part of the so-called 'Museo Diffuso' of Figurative Arts created by the towns of the upper Belice valley (*www.mirabileartificio.it*).

BAGHERIA & THE RUINS OF SOLUNTO

Bagheria (*map p. 542, B1*) is a country town famous for its 18th-century Baroque villas set amidst lemon groves and vineyards. It was the birthplace of the artist Renato Guttuso, and also of the Oscar-winning film-maker Giuseppe Tornatore, author and director of *Cinema Paradiso* (1989). Suffocated by uncontrolled building in the last 40 years, which has encroached on the gardens and parks of the villas, the town now hardly lives up to the old Sicilian proverb: '*Baaria, sciuri ppi la via*', ('in Bagheria the flowers grow on the streets'). Many of the villas are neglected. Only two of them, Villa Cattolica and Villa Palagonia, are now usually open to visitors. The gardens of Villa San Cataldo are open on Sundays.

The conspicuous Villa Cattolica, a fine building of c. 1737, houses the **Museo Guttuso** (*open winter 9–1 & 2.30–7, summer 9.30–2 & 3–7.30, closed Mon; T: 091 943902, www.museoguttuso.com*), which has a large collection of paintings by Renato Guttuso and other contemporary artists. Guttuso's bright blue marble tomb by Giacomo Manzù is in the garden. Near the villa, beyond a railway crossing (right), is the start of the long Corso Butera, which passes the lovely Palazzo Inguaggiato attributed to Andrea Giganti (1770), before reaching the piazza in front of the 18th-century **Chiesa Madre** (*open 7.30–12 & 4.30–8; T: 091 963750*); the frescoes were carried out by Guttuso in 1923. Villa Butera is visible at the far end of the Corso, built in 1658 by Giuseppe Branciforte (façade of 1769).

In front of the Chiesa Madre is the beginning of Corso Umberto, which ends at Piazza Garibaldi beside (left) a garden gate (guarded by two monsters) of **Villa Palagonia** (*open 9–1 & 4–7; T: 091 932088*). The garden, and vestibule and hall on the first floor are open. The beautiful building was erected in 1705 by Francesco Gravina, Prince of Palagonia (and his architect Tommaso Maria Napoli). His eccentric grandson Ferdinando Gravina Alliata lived in rooms decorated in a bizarre fashion, including the hall with its ceiling covered with mirrors set at strange angles (now very damaged) and its walls encased in marble with busts of ladies and gentlemen. The oval vestibule has frescoes of four labours of Hercules. The villa is famous for the grotesque statues of monsters, dwarves, and strange animals on the garden wall by Ferdinando. At the time these carved figures were not to everyone's taste; when Goethe visited the villa in 1787 he was appalled by them. Their effect is now diminished by the houses built just outside the wall. Opposite is the entrance gate to the avenue which leads up to Villa Valguarnera (*not visible from here; closed to the public*). Built by Tommaso Napoli c. 1713–37, this is the most handsome of the Bagheria villas. The statues above the parapet are by Marabitti.

At Via Cherubini 12 is a modern art museum, **Museo Osservatorio dell'Arte Contemporanea in Sicilia** (*open Tues–Sat 5–8.30, closed Sun, Mon and holidays; T: 091 968020, www.museum-bagheria.it*) dedicated to Sicilian artists of today, including Consagra, Fiume, Guttuso and Caruso. Off Via IV Novembre is Villa Trabia (mid-18th century), perhaps by Nicolò Palma, with a façade of 1890. It is surrounded by a neglected park. Near the railway station is the early 18th-century Villa Cutò, and a little further on is Villa San Cataldo, which received a neo-Gothic facelift in the early 19th century.

The frescoed salons of the 18th-century Villa Aragona Cutò, just outside town at Via Consolare 105, house a poignant museum dedicated to toys and wax figures, the **Museo del Giocattolo e delle Cere Pietro Piraino** (*open Tues–Fri 9–1 & 3–6.30, Sat Sun and holidays mornings only; T: 091 943801, www.museodelgiocattolo.org*), including a remarkably complete collection of French clockwork figures, made in the 19th century by the Gaultier brothers. The villa is also used for exhibitions.

Solunto

The solitary ruins of Solunto (*map p. 542, B1; open 9–5.30, Sun and holidays 9–1; T: 091 904557*) are in a beautiful position on the slopes of Mt Catalfano (374m) overlooking the sea, and close to Santa Flavia. The ancient town of *Solus* is thought to have replaced a Phoenician settlement of the same name in the vicinity (perhaps at Cozzo Cannita, where traces of walls have been found), which was destroyed in 397 BC by Dionysius of Syracuse. Solus was built in the 4th century BC on an interesting grid plan similar to the urban layout of some Hellenistic sites in Asia Minor. It fell to the Romans, who named it *Soluntum*, in 254 BC and had been abandoned by the beginning of the 3rd century AD. It was discovered in 1825 and much of the site still remains to be excavated.

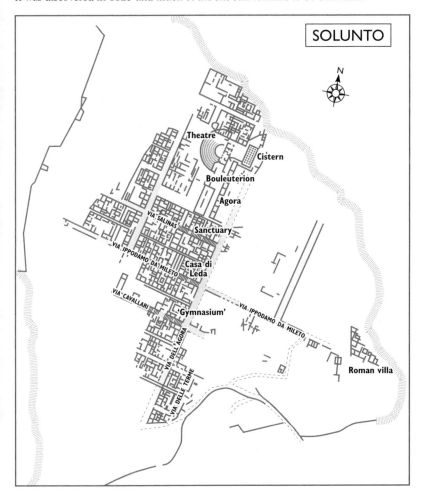

The entrance is through Padiglione A of the Antiquarium, an introduction to the site with plans and descriptions, illustrated by Hellenistic capitals, statues and architectural fragments. A Roman road, beside terraces of prickly pear, mounts the side of the hill past Via delle Terme (with the remains of baths) and curves round to the right into the wide Via dell'Agora. This, the main street, traverses the town to the cliff edge overlooking the sea; it is crossed at regular intervals by side streets with considerable remains of houses on the hillside above. Beyond Via Ciauri and Via Perez is the stepped Via Cavallari (named after the 19th-century excavator here), on which are some of the columns and the architrave of the so-called gymnasium (restored in 1866), in fact a large private house. This short stretch of Via dell'Agora is also beautifully paved in brick.

The next stepped road, Via Ippodamo da Mileto (named after the great 5th-century BC town planner Hippodamus of Miletus, who was known for his cities arranged in a grid pattern; he has no other connection to Solunto), links the main hill to another small hill towards the sea. Here on the slope of the hill above is the so-called Casa di Leda on three levels: above four small shops on Via dell'Agora is an oblong cistern and courtyard with a fountain off which are rooms with mosaic and tiled floors and traces of red wall-paintings. Further up Via Ippodamo da Mileto stand the remains of other interesting houses.

Back on Via dell'Agora, beyond a large sanctuary (on the corner of Via Salinas), the road widens out into the large agora with brick paving in front of nine rectangular exedrae along the back wall, thought to have been used as shelters for the public. On the hillside above are traces of the theatre and a small bouleuterion probably used for council meetings. The hillside higher up may have been the site of the acropolis. Via dell'Agora next passes a huge public cistern, still filled with water, part of a complex system of storage tanks (many vestiges of which are still visible), made necessary by the lack of spring water in the area.

Before leaving the site you pass through Padiglione B of the Antiquarium, displaying the latest archaeological finds, descriptions of funerary practices, arts and crafts of ancient Solunto, and objects pertaining to the city, recovered from the seabed off Porticello.

On the edge of the cliff, looking towards Cape Zafferano, in Via Bagnera is a small **Roman villa** with mosaics and wall-paintings. The view along the coast towards Cefalù, of the Aeolian Islands and Etna, is magnificent. In the foreground are the medieval castle of Solanto and the bay of Fondachello with the villas of Casteldaccia amid luxuriant vegetation on the slopes behind.

At the foot of Mt Catalfano a few lemon groves survive but the area is becoming increasingly developed with up-market holiday homes, as can be seen especially around the **fishing-village of Porticello**. A thriving fish market still opens here very early in the morning.

Cape Zafferano is an isolated crag of dolomitic limestone, of great geological interest. On the cape grow dwarf palms and (flowering in the spring) wild orchids, and on the sandy beach at its foot the loggerhead turtle returned to nest in 2011, after many years of absence.

THE EAST OF THE PROVINCE

TERMINI IMERESE

Termini Imerese (*map p. 542, C2*), consisting of an upper and lower town, is built on the slopes of a hill, and has a commercial port. *Thermae Himerenses* received its name from the two neighbouring Greek cities of *Thermae* and *Himera*. After the sack of Himera (*see p. 87*) in 409 BC by the Carthaginians, the inhabitants of the destroyed city were resettled in Thermae. In 307 BC it was ruled by Agathocles (361–289 BC), a native of the town and the most ferocious of the Greek tyrants of Syracuse. Its most prosperous period followed the Roman conquest. The thermal mineral waters were praised by Pindar. Outside the town are conspicuous remains of a Roman aqueduct built in the 2nd century AD to bring water from a spring 7km away. In the upper town there is a spacious main square, with an old-fashioned men's club. From the belvedere behind the duomo there is a good view of the coast and the port.

Exploring Termini Imerese

The 17th-century **duomo** (*open 9–12 & 3.30–8.30, closed Fri*) has a façade dating from 1912. The four statues of saints are copies of the originals, now removed inside. Beneath the tower (right) is a fragment of a Roman cornice. The interior, with huge columns and capitals, contains sculptures by Giuliano Mancino and Bartolomeo Berrettaro, including a statue of the Madonna, bas-reliefs, and the four statues of saints (1504–06) from the façade. The chapel also has two 17th-century funerary monuments. In the sanctuary is a Crucifix, painted on both sides, by Pietro Ruzzolone (1484). In the chapel to the left of the choir are reliefs by Marabitti and Federico Siragusa. In the fourth chapel of the south aisle is a marble oval relief of *Our Lady of the Bridge*, by Ignazio Marabitti.

Palazzo Comunale (the Town Hall) was also built in the 17th century and is approached by an outside staircase. Just out of the piazza, in Via Cicerone, is the important, well-displayed **Museo Civico Baldassare Romano** (*open Tues–Sat 9–1 & 4–6.30, Sun and holidays 9–1; T: 091 81228550*), founded in 1873. On the ground floor are prehistoric finds from Termini; vases from Himera; coins; Roman capitals, sculptures, inscriptions, and glassware. The last room contains Arab-Norman material and a Renaissance doorway. On the first floor is a chapel frescoed in the 15th century by Nicolò da Pettineo, paintings (16th–19th century), a natural history collection, and the plaster gallery of local sculptor Filippo Sgarlata. The museum incorporates the little church of **Santa Maria della Misericordia** (1600), entirely decorated with stuccoes of the Serpotta school, with a beautiful triptych (*Madonna with Sts John and Michael*), ascribed to Gaspare da Pesaro (1453). There is also a garden containing architectural fragments.

In Via Mazzini, which leads out of Piazza Duomo, is the church of **Santa Croce al Monte**, containing 16th and 17th-century Sicilian paintings. Viale Iannelli leads west from Piazza Duomo to the 14th-century church of **Santa Caterina**, with 15th-century frescoes illustrating the life of the saint, probably by the local artists Nicolò and Giacomo Graffeo; they have been beautifully restored.

In Villa Palmeri, the public gardens laid out in 1845, are remains of a Roman public building, known as the **Curia**, dating from the 2nd century AD. From the gardens Via dell'Anfiteatro leads to the sparse ruins of the **Roman amphitheatre** (1st century AD).

From behind the duomo there is a good view down to the pretty blue-tiled dome of the church of the **Annunziata**. A road winds down from here to the lower town and, on the site of the Roman baths, the Grand Hotel delle Terme (*see p. 112*), begun in 1890 to a design by Giuseppe Damiani Almeyda. The thermal waters (43°C) still in use here provide natural steam baths and bathing pools.

CACCAMO

Caccamo (*map p. 542, C2*) is a little town of ancient origins in a fine position above olive groves in the hills. There is a tradition that the Carthaginians took refuge here after their defeat at Himera in 480 BC, after their general Hamilcar had committed suicide by throwing himself on the funeral pyre of his dead soldiers, and most of his army had been taken prisoner.

The impressive 12th-century **castle** (*open 9–5*), the largest in Sicily, stands at the entrance to the town. It was one of the major Norman strongholds on the island, and, never captured, it remained the residence of the dukes of Caccamo until the 20th century. Here in 1160, Matthew Bonellus organised a revolt of the barons against William I (the Bad); after the failure of the rebellion, Bonellus was captured and taken to Palermo, where he was hamstrung, blinded and imprisoned. The castle was enlarged by the Chiaramontes in the 14th century, and was sold to the region of Sicily in 1963 by the De Spuches family. The main tower was 70m high but toppled in an earthquake in the 19th century. The empty interior has been heavily restored.

From the main road (Corso Umberto) steps and narrow streets lead down to **Piazza Duomo**, an attractive and unusual square on two levels, with a marvellous view over the valley. Above the raised terrace, with a balustrade decorated with four statues of the town's patron saints, is the 17th-century **Monte di Pietà** (the pawnbrokers; the palace now houses the tourist offices and exhibitions) flanked by the façades of two churches. On the left is the Oratorio del Santissimo Sacramento, while that on the right is dedicated to the Souls in Purgatory. It contains charming gilded stuccoes in the sanctuary and the custodian will show the crypt below, also beautifully decorated with stuccoes, containing the crumbling, fully-clothed mummified skeletons of past inhabitants.

The duomo

The duomo (*ring if locked*) has a fine 17th-century façade. Founded in 1090, it was altered in 1477 and 1614. There is a lovely relief (1660) of St George by Gaspare Guercio above the door. The tall campanile was built above a 14th-century tower of the castle.

In the interior, St George (the patron saint) features in a number of fine works of art. In the right aisle is a 15th-century triptych and a charming processional statue of the saint with his dragon. In the south transept the architrave of the door into the sacristy has delicate carvings of the Madonna and Child with angels and Sts Peter and Paul attributed to Francesco Laurana. The roundels of the *Annunciation* and relief of the Madonna and Child are by the Gagini school. The rich treasury and sacristy are also shown on request. They contain 16th–19th century church silver, a precious collection of vestments and Flemish paintings. In the chapel to the right of the sanctuary is a *Madonna and Child* sculpted by the Gagini school. By the main altar is an unusual font (1466) with four large heads, perhaps representing Matthew, Mark, Luke and John. In the sanctuary are two polychrome wooden statues: *St John the Baptist* by Antonino Siragusa (1532) and *St Lucy* (16th century). An exquisite silver processional statuette of St Rosalia is also kept here. On the main altar are three very fine alabaster carvings (16th–18th century).

In the north transept are two painted terracotta sculptures: a *Madonna and Child* by the Gagini school and a *Pietà* group by the early 15th century Sienese school. The altar here has 16th and 17th century reliquary busts and an early 18th-century Neoclassical carved and gilded altar frontal. In the left aisle an altar decorated with inlaid marble has a 14th-century painted Crucifix, and the first altarpiece, depicting the *Miracle of St Isidore* is a stunning painting by Matthias Stom. A sedan chair and armour belonging to the De Spuches family are also kept in this aisle.

There are good views of the castle from the old streets behind the duomo. In the other direction, Via Cartagine leads to the deconsecrated church of San Francesco and, beyond, the church of **Santissima Annunziata**, its Baroque façade flanked by two earlier towers. Inside is a carved 16th-century organ case, and the sanctuary has stuccoes by the Serpotta school. The church of **San Benedetto alla Badia** (1615) was attached to a former Benedictine convent. The charming interior has a splendid majolica tiled floor in the nave and choir, once attributed to Nicolò Sarzana but now thought to date from before 1701. There are also fine wrought-iron grilles. The two graceful female figures in stucco on either side of the sanctuary are by the school of Serpotta.

Santa Maria degli Angeli (1497; *ring at the convent*) has a fine *Madonna and Child* over the door. Inside its original wooden trussed ceiling is preserved (with 15th-century paintings of Dominican saints) and a statue of the Madonna by Antonello Gagini.

ALIA & ROCCAPALUMBA

Some 30km southeast of Caccamo, **Alia** (*map p. 542, C2–C3*) is a remote town founded by the Arabs, surrounded by spectacular hills and wheat-fields. Later, under Spanish rule, it became the seat of the Santa Croce barons, who built their palace next to the church of Madonna delle Grazie (1639). At the moment the economy is depressed and the once-flourishing town is suffering from depopulation. Well-kept and picturesque nevertheless, Alia has a small ethno-anthropological collection housed in the Biblioteca Comunale, the public library in Via San Giuseppe (*open Mon–Sat 9–1; T: 091 8882108*).

Not far from the town (4km), in a dramatic isolated sandstone outcrop, is a group of caves called **Grotte di Gurfa** (*if closed, T: Romy Travel 091 8219412, 348 2477205, 389 9916756*), entirely carved out by hand during ancient times, and successively used as dwellings. The caves include a mysterious tholos, 16m high. Some scholars date the complex to the Copper Age, about 5,000 years ago, when it would have been either a sanctuary to a divinity or a burial site. An inscription in Phoenician has recently been discovered close to the entrance of one of the caves. However, other scholars refute these conjectures, claiming the caves to be no older than Norman, and the 'Phoenician inscription' to be accidental scratches in the soft rock.

Roccapalumba

The town of Roccapalumba (*map p. 542, C2*), on the opposite side of the River Torto with respect to Alia, was founded in 1630 by the Ansalone family at the foot of an enormous, isolated rock—the Rock of the Doves—which is the meaning of the name. The settlement must be much older, because the sanctuary church of the Madonna della Luce, partly built into the rock, is one of the oldest Norman churches of the territory, dating back to the 11th century. The miraculous image of the Madonna inside the church is said to have appeared suddenly to protect some travellers assailed by bandits as they were going through the pass. Roccapalumba is known as the *paese delle stelle*, the village of the stars, because the clear air and low light interference allow good observations of the stars at all times of the year. The Parco Astronomico at Borgo Regalgioffoli (*to request a visit, T: Pro Loco 091 8215207 or Tourist Office 091 8215523*) has two observatories and a planetarium.

HIMERA

Near a large industrial area including a power station and a once-important car factory, which occupies the low coastal plain east of Termini Imerese, is the site of Himera (*map p. 542, C2*), close to the Buonfornello motorway exit (if coming from the Palermo direction, take the exit for Catania and the Buonfornello exit appears nearly immediately) and on the bank of the River Grande (or Imera Settentrionale), but very poorly signposted. On the right of the road, just across the busy railway line are the remains of a temple. Above the road is a conspicuous modern museum, below the site of the ancient city.

The site

The remains of Himera (*open 9–6, Sun and holidays 9–1*) occupy two areas, divided by the main road. On the north side of the road are the ruins of a peripteral **Doric temple**, probably built around 470 BC. It measured 22m by 55m and had 14 columns at the sides and six in front. The cella had a pronaos and opisthodomos in antis. This is the only building which remains here of a sanctuary probably dedicated to Athena. It is still known as the Temple of Victory, although some scholars no longer believe it was built to celebrate the victory of 480 BC over the Carthaginians. In any case it seems to have been burnt and destroyed by the Carthaginians in 409 BC. Only the basement and lower part of the columns and part of the cella walls survive. In the Middle Ages the site was built over and it was only rediscovered in 1823 and excavated by Pirro Marconi in 1929–30, when the splendid lion-head water-spouts from the cornice were taken to the archaeological museum in Palermo.

HISTORY OF HIMERA

Himera was a colony of Zancle (Messina), founded in 648 BC near the mouth of the Himera river, and at the head of the valley which provided access to the interior of the island. It was the westernmost Greek colony on the north coast of Sicily, and probable birthplace of the lyric poet Stesichorus (born c. 630 BC), famed in antiquity for his innovative treatment of traditional myths. In 480 BC Terillus, the tyrant of Himera, called on the Carthaginians to help him against his enemies, resulting in a great battle outside the city between the Carthaginians and the combined armies of Agrigento and Syracuse, reported by Herodotus as one reason why the Sicilians couldn't aid their fellow Greeks during the great Persian invasion. The Greek alliance won a decisive victory. The Carthaginian leader Hamilcar (not to be confused with Hannibal's father) reportedly spent the battle attempting to seek favourable omens from his religious sacrifices, then threw himself into a fire and was burnt to nothing when he saw that the battle had been lost.

In the last decade of the 5th century, the Carthaginians returned in force, and in 409 Himera bore the brunt of an attack which almost destroyed Greek power in Sicily and ushered in a new age of tyrants at Syracuse. This time, Greek collective defence failed utterly and Diodorus Siculus describes the heroic and desperate defence of Himera. Eventually the Greeks tried to evacuate the city, but lacked enough ships. Half the population was evacuated while the remainder fought on, scanning the horizon for their salvation, but after a few days, when the evacuation fleet finally came into view, the defences were breached and the Carthaginians poured in, bringing enslavement and slaughter on a huge scale to the city, which never recovered. The fugitive survivors founded the new city of Thermae (Termini Imerese) to the east (*see p. 83*).

In 2008 work on the railway line brought to light the **western necropolis** (no access), with over 9,500 intact tombs dating from the mid-7th to the end of the 5th century BC. Hundreds of burials were of new-born children, who had been placed in jars together with their terracotta feeding-bottles. The Greek warriors who took part in the epic battles of 480 and 409 BC were buried in collective tombs containing up to 59 bodies, all young men killed with lances. A particularly interesting detail is that in many cases they were buried together with their horses. The other two necropoleis discovered so far lie to the east and south of the city, and are also currently closed to the public.

Off the main road, just beyond, a byroad (south; *signposted*) leads up to the museum and the areas of the city excavated since 1963. The **Antiquarium** (*open 9–6.30, Sun and holidays 9–1.30; T: 091 8140128*) is a striking modern building, and there are good plans and descriptions of the site. The first section displays finds from the temples in the sacred area on the hilltop, including a votive deposit with fragments of metopes. The second section has material from the city and necropoleis, including ceramics, architectural fragments and votive statues. There is also a third section devoted to finds from recent excavations in the surrounding territory, including Cefalù and Caltavuturo. The highlight of the collection is the gold libation vessel from Caltavuturo, the phiale-mesomphalos, recently returned from the Metropolitan Museum of New York. The name means 'offering-dish with a belly-button in the middle', because a deep indentation—the *omphalos*—in the bottom of the bowl enabled it to be balanced on the fingers without touching the rim. This rare example weighs 982.4g and is made of solid gold, with a *repoussé* ornamentation consisting of four concentric circles of honey bees, acorns, lotus blossoms and beech nuts on a ground of gold granules, with vine tendrils and bunches of grapes on the smooth central omphalos. An inscription in Greek has enabled scholars to date the vessel to the late 4th/early 3rd centuries BC. It is very similar to another dish in the Metropolitan Museum, to the point that they could have been made by the same craftsman, but the other dish is inscribed in Phoenician.

Just above the museum are **excavations of part of the city**. Steps continue up to a plateau on the edge of the hill overlooking the plain towards the sea. The spectacular view extends along the coast as far as Solunto. In the other direction you can see the village of Gratteri, nestling in the Madonie Mountains. This path follows an ancient street bordered on either side by houses that have been partially excavated. On the plateau, in the area known as the Quartiere Nord, entire city blocks have been uncovered, in which there is a sanctuary with a temenos enclosing the bases of an altar and four temples (7th–5th centuries BC). The rest of the blocks consist of housing. These houses, from the archaic period, were assigned regular plots of land (16m by 16m), but some dwellings were built over two or even four such plots.

CEFALÙ

Cefalù (*map p. 542, C1–D1*), with its stunning Norman cathedral and ruins of an ancient acropolis on the rock above the city, is a very picturesque small town with a lovely beach. The old city is still medieval in character, with many enticing shops, restaurants and cafés along its well-kept cobbled streets.

HISTORY OF CEFALÙ

Founded at the end of the 5th or early 4th century BC, the name *Kephaloidion* comes from the head-like shape of the rock which towers above the town. In 307 BC the town was taken by Agathocles of Syracuse. In 857 it was conquered by the Arabs. In 1131 Roger II rebuilt the town, and constructed the magnificent cathedral which became head of a powerful bishopric. In the 1920s the necromancer Aleister Crowley lived near Cefalù, transforming a cottage into the Temple of Thelema ('Do as thou wilt, shall be thy creed') and scandalising the locals to the point where he was arrested, found guilty of immoral behaviour, and expelled from Italy.

View of Cefalù across the water, with the Kephaloidion rock beetling upwards above and behind it.

Exploring Cefalù

At the beginning of **Corso Ruggero**, the main street of the town, in Piazza Garibaldi, on the right, is the sandstone façade of Maria Santissima della Catena (1780; *closed*) preceded by a high portico with three statues. On the right of the façade are a few large blocks from the old walls (late 5th century BC) on the site of Porta Terra, the main entrance to the old town. The Corso continues past (right) Vicolo dei Saraceni (signposted for the Tempio di Diana, beyond which begins a path up to the acropolis) and then runs slightly downhill. On the left is the **Osterio Magno**, once King Roger's palace and now used for exhibitions, with a fine 13th-century triple window high up on its façade and (in Via Amendola) windows decorated with black lava-stone.

On the left are a series of nine picturesque, straight, parallel streets which lead downhill to Corso Vittorio Emanuele, with a view of the sea beyond. They possibly reflect the grid plan of the ancient city. The Corso continues past the tall, plain façade of the 16th-century church of the Annunziata. To the right opens the little piazza in front of the 15th-century **church of the Purgatorio** (or Santo Stefano Protomartire). Inside is the tomb of Baron Mandralisca (*see p. 92*).

The duomo

Further along the Corso on the right, the piazza planted with palm trees leads up to the splendid duomo (*open 8–7*). The setting is dramatic, with the formidable rock rising

CEFALÙ DUOMO: WEST FRONT

immediately behind it and the small town at its feet. Begun by Roger II in 1131, and intended as his burial-place, it was still unfinished at the time of his death in 1154. His successors lost interest in the project and it was not consecrated until 1267; Frederick II of Hohenstaufen even removed the royal porphyry tombs—officially for safety—and took them to Palermo, but to carry out this scandalous act he waited until the bishop was away on a mission in the East. Excavations during restoration work have revealed Roman remains on this site. The church is preceded by a raised terrace, part of the original Norman design, surrounded by a balustrade with statues. The soaring façade is flanked by two massive, subtly different bell-towers with fine windows. Above the narthex built by Ambrogio da Como in 1471 is a double row of blind arcades. The beautiful exterior of the south side and transept is visible from Via Passafiume.

Interior of the duomo

The basilican interior has 16 ancient columns with Roman capitals, probably from the Temple of Diana (*see p. 94*), supporting Arab-Norman arches. The open timber roof of the nave bears traces of painting (1263). The 72 contemporary stained-glass windows high up in the nave are the work of Michele Canzoneri, and represent episodes from the Old and New Testaments. In the north aisle is a statue of the Madonna by Antonello Gagini, in honey-coloured stone. In the sanctuary is a 15th-century painted Crucifix attributed to Tommaso de Vigilia.

The presbytery is decorated with exquisite **mosaics**—the best preserved and the earliest of their kind in Sicily—on a background of dusky gold, symbolic of divinity. They were carried out for Roger II in a careful decorative scheme, reflecting Byzantine models, but much more free and spontaneous than anything seen before from those workshops. The king probably intended them to line the whole interior of the building. It is thought that they are the work of Greek craftsmen, summoned from Constantinople by Roger himself. In the apse is the splendid colossal figure of **Christ Pantocrator** holding an open book with the Greek and Latin biblical text from John 8:12 ('I am the Light of the World: he that followeth me shall not walk in darkness'), a masterpiece.

On the curved apse wall below are three tiers of figures: the Virgin in prayer between four archangels (dressed as Byzantine dignitaries; holding loaves of bread symbolising Salvation), and the Apostles in the two lower registers, quite informal in their stance, as if we had suddenly interrupted their conversation. In the vault are angels and seraphim and on the walls below are (left) prophets, deacon-martyrs, and Latin bishop-saints, and (right) prophets, warrior-saints, and Greek patriarchs and theologians. An inscription beneath the window states that the mosaics of the apse were completed in 1148. The soft folds of the robes, the gentle expressions, the marvellous texture and subtle colour of the angels' wings, are certainly the work of very accomplished artists.

The south aisle and transepts were stripped of their Baroque decoration in the 1970s, in order to restore the building as far as possible to its Norman aspect. As a result, one of the twin world-famous 16th-century organs by Raffaele La Valle was lost without trace, perhaps stolen on commission. Such drastic intervention has been the subject of much heated discussion (and is now forbidden), but the achieved effect of light and space is breathtaking. On the left pilaster of the sanctuary, high up in a niche, is a statue of the annunciatory angel. In the Neoclassical chapel to the left of the sanctuary is an elaborate 18th-century silver altar.

The cloister

An alley leads along the north side of the church to the entrance to the cloister (*open 10–1 & 3–6, Sun T: 338 8175498 to confirm visit*) with the remains of a portico of twin columns with carved capitals, including Noah's Ark (no. 5) and the Trinacria symbol supporting pointed Arab-Norman arches, at present undergoing a careful recuperation. This closed rectangular space was intended to favour meditation. Starting mid-way along the south side and heading east, the capitals, of which there were originally 70, represented Genesis, then the Song of Songs, followed by the Gospels and the Apocalypse.

Piazza Duomo

In Piazza Duomo is Palazzo Maria, with medieval traces, and the 17th-century Oratorio del Santissimo Sacramento beside the Neoclassical Palazzo Legambi. Opposite is Palazzo Vescovile (1793), next to the 17th-century seminary with a hanging garden. Opposite the duomo is the former monastery of Santa Caterina, extensively restored as the town hall a few years ago by the architect Gae Aulenti.

Museo Mandralisca

From Piazza Duomo, Via Mandralisca leads down to the Museo Mandralisca (*open 9–7, Aug 9–11pm; T: 0921 421547, www.fondazionemandralisca.it*). The palace cellars, containing huge terracotta jars for storing oil, can be seen from the road. Enrico Pirajno, Baron Mandralisca (1809–64), once lived here and he left his remarkable collection to the city as a museum (now run by a private foundation). The baron was a member of the first Italian parliament and he took a special interest in natural history and archaeology (participating in excavations on Lipari and near Cefalù). He also endowed a local school.

On the ground floor is a mosaic from Cefalù (1st century BC). On the first floor is a famous vase from Lipari showing a vendor of tuna fish (4th century BC; *pictured on p. 168*); a numismatic collection dating from the Greek period up to the 19th century, with about 400 pieces, particularly notable for its coins from Lipari, Cefalù and Syracuse; and a collection of paintings. In Room 3 is the famous **Portrait of a Man by Antonello da Messina** (c. 1465–72), the jewel of the collection and one of the most striking portraits of the Italian Renaissance. Mandralisca apparently bought this small painting from a pharmacy in Lipari, where he discovered it in use as part of a cupboard door. The sitter, with his enigmatic smile, has never been identified. The influence of the Flemish school of painting is evident in this exquisite work, here displayed to great advantage. Recently discovered in the cellars of the museum, and carefully restored, is another masterpiece: *St John the Baptist* by Giovanni Antonio Sogliani, perhaps purchased by the baron during a visit to Florence in 1861. Notice the subtle colouring, the gentle expression of the saint, the clever depiction of his red silk mantle in this painting, which almost certainly formed part of a much larger work—the Crucifix is cut off at the top, and the saint's left hand is not entirely visible.

Also displayed here is a sarcophagus in the form of an Ionic temple which dates from the 2nd century BC. Other rooms hold Mandralisca's remarkable collection of some 20,000 shells and also archaeological material, including Italiot vases from Lipari (320–300 BC) and a well-preserved kylix.

The second floor contains more archaeological finds, and miscellaneous objects including a 19th-century dinner service, arms, reliquaries, paintings (*Madonna and Child* attributed to Antonello de Saliba), and an ornithological collection. Mandralisca's important library, which has been expanded, is also accessible.

The port and the Rocca

Corso Ruggero ends at Via Porpora, which leads right to a restored square tower in a gap between the houses. Outside the tiny postern gate a fine stretch of the megalithic

Portrait of a Man by Antonello da Messina.

walls (5th century BC) built onto the rock can be seen. In the other direction Via Carlo Ortolani di Bordonaro leads past (right) Piazza Francesco Crispi with the church of the Madonna del Cammino. Modern steps lead up to a 17th-century bastion (Capo Marchiafava) where a 14th-century fountain has been placed (good view). Via Ortolani continues down towards the sea and ends beside a terrace overlooking the little port, with picturesque old houses on the seafront.

From here Via Vittorio Emanuele leads back past the church of the Badiola (12th–17th centuries), next to its convent (the old portal survives on the corner of Via Porto Salvo). Opposite is the 16th-century **Porta Pescara**, with a lovely Gothic arch through which the sea can be seen. It is now used to display fishermen's tackle and nets. Beyond, on the right, wide steps curving down past a few trees lead to the **Lavatoio**, a picturesque medieval wash-house, where a spring of slightly salty water (the tears of Daphnis; *see below*) was converted into a laundry by the Arabs and was still in daily use until quite recently. At the south end of Via Vittorio Emanuele is the newly-restored Opera House (*T: 0921 925011*).

From Corso Ruggero and Vicolo dei Saraceni, steps and a path lead up (in c. 1hr) to the **Rocca**, the summit (278m) of which commands a wonderful view. According to legend, the rock is the head of the shepherd Daphnis. He so loved the nymph Nomia that he promised to be faithful to her, on pain of being blinded. Chimaera then enticed him into the woods, gave him wine and seduced him. Nomia accordingly blinded him, and Hermes, on the orders of Hera, to whom Nomia was dear, turned him into stone. His bitter tears at his folly are said to form the spring that supplies the Lavatoio. On the top of the Rocca is the so-called **Temple of Diana**, with walls made out of huge polygonal blocks and a carved architrave over the entrance. It was probably a sacred edifice built in the 5th–4th century BC over an earlier cistern. Stretches of castellated walls can also be seen here as well as numerous cisterns and ovens, but only vague traces remain of the original castle.

THE MADONIE MOUNTAINS

The Madonie Mountains (*map p. 542, C2–D2*) lie between the Imera Settentrionale river to the west and the Pollina to the east. The Pizzo Carbonara (1979m) is the second highest mountain on the island (after Etna). The area of some 40,000 hectares is protected as a nature reserve known as the Parco Naturale Regionale delle Madonie. The vegetation in the upland plains and mountains includes beech, enormous holly trees some 14m high and centuries old, manna ash (manna is still extracted from the bark in the Pollina and Castelbuono area), chestnuts, oaks, poplars, ilexes, cork trees and ancient olives. A rare species of fir, *Abies nebrodensis*, only found here, distinguished by the terminal twigs on the branches which form a neat cross, was saved from extinction in 1969. Apart from these extensive woods the landscape has spectacular rock formations, pastureland where sheep and cattle are grazed, and small hill towns of great interest. For more information on the flora and fauna of the Madonie, visit the museum in Castelbuono.

Gibilmanna

The sanctuary of Gibilmanna (*map p. 542, D2*) is in a beautiful position looking towards the sea, on the slopes of the Pizzo Sant'Angelo (1081m), with woods of olives, cork oaks, pines and chestnuts. The name is derived from the Arabic *gebel*, meaning mountain, and manna, which was extracted from the manna ash trees in the locality and used for medicinal purposes. There was a sanctuary here founded by the Benedictines in the 6th century; in 1535 it became a Capuchin convent, and it is still a famous centre of pilgrimage. The sanctuary (*open 7.30–1 & 3.15–7.30; T: 0921 421835*), rebuilt in the 17th century, has been altered many times and its external appearance dates from the 20th century. The exquisitely carved altarpiece was made by the Gagini family.

The Museum of the Franciscan Presence in Sicily (*open 10.30–12.30 & 3.30–6.30, tickets at the sanctuary library; T: 0921 420883*) preserves works of art from convents and churches in this area of the island. These include 16th–18th-century paintings, church vestments, statuettes (in wax and wood), ex-votos, a rare early 18th-century wooden organ with cane pipes, and an ethnographical collection illustrating monastic life. It is also possible to visit the catacombs. An astronomical observatory (1952) stands on the nearby Cozzo Timpa Rossa (1006m).

Gratteri

A little hill town facing west, Gratteri (*map p. 542, C2*) provides a fine distant view along the coast. The churches (*often closed*) are the 19th-century Nuova Matrice, containing four thorns from the Crown of Jesus and a fragment of the True Cross, and the Matrice Vecchia, dedicated to the Archangel Michael, built in the 14th century. It has a separate bell-tower with seven bronze bells, one of them dated 1390. Beautiful crochet-work is still made here by the women.

Isnello

Isnello (*map p. 542, C2–D2*) is a pleasant little town built along a long rock which gives the town its name, the Rocca dell'Asinello, with the ruins of the castle at one end. The **Chiesa Madre** has 16th-century frescoes by Antonino Ferraro, 17th-century stuccoes by Giuseppe Li Volsi, and a carved wooden choir and organ-loft dating from the early 17th century. A marble ciborium is attributed to Domenico Gagini (1492). The *Deposition* is by Giuseppe Salerno. The little church of **San Michele** has an important painted wooden ceiling, a wooden Crucifix by Fra' Umile da Petralia, a painting of *Martyrs* by Giuseppe Salerno, and a 15th-century fresco of St Leonard. The church of the Rosario (*closed*) contains a painting of the *Madonna of the Rosary* attributed to the Flemish school. The church of the **Annunziata** contains a *Nativity* by Giuseppe Salerno, while the organ, still in use, is by Antonino La Valle.

Steps lead up from the piazza by the Chiesa Madre to the church of **Santa Maria Maggiore** (*key at Via Purgatorio 4*) near the ruins of the castle, and beneath a rock called the Grotta Grande. It has a pretty bell-tower. The charming interior has a decorative organ-loft over the entrance, and a late 15th- or early 16th-century Crucifix, unusual in its iconography and painted on both sides, hangs from the centre of the nave ceiling. Above the main altar is a *Madonna and Child* of the Gagini school (1547). There is also a charming little statue of the Madonna as a baby, lovingly preserved in a glass case. The quality of the lace, crochet, embroidery and filet made by the local women is renowned.

Collesano

The spectacular little medieval town of Collesano (*map p. 542, C2*) has several inter-esting churches including the **Chiesa Madre** (Basilica San Pietro), which contains a painted Crucifix of 1555, an organ dated 1627 by Antonino La Valle, a fine carved tab-ernacle of 1489 by Donatello Gagini, and a *Madonna with Angels* by Giuseppe Salerno. The frescoes (1624) are the work of Gaspare Vazano. In **Santa Maria la Vecchia** (1140) is a statue of the *Madonna* by Antonello Gagini. At Corso Vittorio Emanuele 3 is the wonderfully informative **Museo Targa Florio** (*open 9.30–12.30 & 3.30–7, closed Mon and Thur afternoons; T: 0921 664684, www.museotargaflorio.it*), dedicated to the oldest motor race in the world (*see p. 69*). The pottery made in Collesano is unusual and in-teresting, both for the shapes of the vases and the colours.

CASTELBUONO

An ancient town of warm rose-coloured stone and mellow old brick, whose rooftops are animated by jackdaws and swifts, Castelbuono (*map p. 542, D2*) basks at the foot of its spectacular castle, in a fold of hills covered with forests of manna ash and chestnuts. Of Byzantine origins, it became the seat of the Ventimiglia princes of Geraci in the 14th century, and the medieval structure of the centre is still intact.

The Matrice Vecchia and the castle

The main road leads up past a 16th-century fountain with bas-reliefs and a statue of Venus to Piazza Margherita, with another 16th-century fountain. Here the **Matrice Vecchia** of 1350 is preceded by a loggia. It contains a marble ciborium attributed to Giorgio da Milano (late 15th century), a huge polyptych on the high altar attributed to Pietro Ruzzolone, and statues and frescoes of the 16th century. The crypt has frescoes of the Passion of Christ. Also in the piazza is a building owned by the Ventimiglia fam-ily in the 14th–16th century and used as a prison from the 18th century up to 1965. Exhibitions are now held here and it has a local tourist office.

The ancient street continues uphill past the Town Hall to the castle (*open 8.30–2 & 2.30–8; T: 0921 671211*) built by the Ventimiglia family in 1316 and exceptionally well restored. The castle is said to have both a ghost, that of Queen Constance Chiaramonte (14th century), whose footsteps can be heard running through the rooms on the first Tuesday of every month, and a secret passage which unites the castle to the mauso-leum of the Ventimiglias. Off the courtyard is the chapel of St Anne (c. 1683) with white stucco cherubs on a gold ground by the Serpotta school. The skull of the saint is preserved here in a 16th-century silver urn, and the chapel possesses a treasury. The castle also houses the Civic Art Gallery (contemporary artists) and a small museum of country life and the extraction of manna. Behind the castle the terrace has a view of the Madonie and the little hill town of Geraci Siculo.

The Matrice Nuova and San Francesco

From the Matrice Vecchia a road (signposted) leads up to a piazza with palm trees and a memorial surrounded by cannon used in the First World War. Here is the **Matrice Nuova**, begun at the beginning of the 17th century (and rebuilt in 1830). It contains a painted Crucifix attributed to Pietro Ruzzolone, stucco altars, and a 16th-century triptych. Another road leads up from the right of the Matrice Nuova to the church of **San Francesco**, which has a pretty white and gold interior decorated in the 18th century, with an organ and monks' choir above the entrance. It also has decorative chandeliers and charming little confessionals dating from 1910. Off the right side of the sanctuary, entered through a lovely late 15th-century doorway carved by the school of Laurana, is a pretty octagonal chapel with twisted columns. Here are the tombs of the Ventimiglia family, including one dated 1543 and one 1687, and somewhere, apparently, the secret passage to the castle. The two 15th-century frescoes were detached from the Franciscan convent. The attractive 18th-century cloister of the convent (*under repair; delayed by new archaeological discoveries*) is entered between two marble columns left of the church façade.

Museo Minà Palumbo

At Via Roma 52 the former convent of Santa Venera now houses the Museo Minà Palumbo (*open 9–1 & 3–7, 4–8 in summer; T: 0921 671895, www.museominapalumbo.it*). It is named after the naturalist Francesco Minà Palumbo, a native of Castelbuono. His collections, which he carefully catalogued, provide a fascinating documentation of the Madonie. The exhibits include fossils, a botanical and natural history section, minerals, archaeological finds (including prehistoric material), examples of glass produced here from the late 16th to the end of the 18th centuries, and examples of paper produced in the town between 1822 and 1846. There is also an interesting display illustrating the extraction of manna (used for medicinal purposes as a mild laxative, especially for babies, and also as a sweetener in cakes) from the trunks of manna ash trees in the area. Castelbuono and Pollina are the only places in the world where manna is still produced.

THE SOUTHERN MADONIE

Sclafani Bagni and Caltavuturo

Sclafani Bagni (*map p. 542, C2*) is a small remote fortress-village on a precipitous crag with superb views. The name derives from *Esculapii fanum*, that is temple or sacred place of Asclepius, God of healing. The medieval town gate bears the coat of arms of the Sclafani (Matteo Sclafani, count of the town in 1330, constructed its defences). Higher up the Chiesa Madre or Santa Maria Assunta (*open Mon, Wed, Fri 2–6*) contains a splendid sarcophagus, in white Greek marble, with Bacchic scenes, two statues (the Madonna and St Peter) by the school of Gagini, an organ by Antonino La Valle (1615), and a processional statue of the Ecce Homo, made of *papier mâché*, the work of Fra' Umile da Petralia. Above, steps lead up to the scant remains of the Norman castle, with an excellent view.

In the lower part of the town is the church of San Giacomo on the edge of the hillside, with charming stuccoes in the interior in very poor condition. The church of San

Filippo contains a worn but pretty tiled floor, a 17th-century wooden processional Crucifix in a tabernacle, and two curious statues of waxed canvas (1901), much venerated locally.

Caltavuturo means 'Rock of the Vulture', and its ancient fortress on a crag (*map p. 542, C2*) was of great strategic importance from earliest times, bringing considerable fortune; the accidental discovery in 1980 of a solid gold libation bowl (now in the Antiquarium of Himera; *see p. 88*), bears witness to this. Together with Sclafani, Caltavuturo protected Himera on the coast against attacks from the interior; for the Arabs it was fundamental. By the 16th century it had lost its importance and the population moved down to a lower, more comfortable position on the mountainside. During World War Two it was a German base, and suffered heavy bombing attacks in 1943.

Very picturesque, many streets are narrow and cobbled, or consist of steep steps. Via Dante leads into the tiny Piazza Madre Chiesa, with the Chiesa Madre dedicated to Sts Peter and Paul, built in 1582. Inside there is a sad-faced *Our Lady of the Snows* by Francesco Laurana, in white marble; interesting for her unusual curled hair-style, and the masterful rendering of the folds of her mantle. Also in this church is the case (unfortunately the pipes are missing) of a rare organ by Raffaele La Valle. The church of Santissimo Salvatore (12th century) is the oldest church in Caltavuturo, and shows strong Byzantine-Arab traditions; it also served as a watch-tower. I Mannari, on the steep mountainside, are a series of tiny gardens and sheep-pens, each surrounded by a low stone wall, and united by stairs; here and there are tiny cottages. They give an idea of how difficult life was in the past for these farmers.

Polizzi Generosa

Beautifully positioned at the head of the Imera valley, Polizzi Generosa (*map p. 542, C2–D2*) is a delightful little town which received its name 'Generosa' from Frederick II in 1234. It once boasted 76 churches within its walls, and many of them now belong to local confraternities (who have the keys). From the small Piazza Umberto, where all the main roads converge, Via Cardinale Rampolla leads up to the **Chiesa Madre**, with a charming 16th-century porch and two very worn statues of St Peter and St Paul. A Gothic portal has been exposed beside the Renaissance doorway. In the right aisle is a painting of the *Madonna of the Rosary* by Giuseppe Salerno. At the end of the aisle, a chapel on the right (closed by a grille) contains some particularly fine sculptures, including the sarcophagus of Beato Gandolfo da Binasco (recomposed) by Domenico Gagini; reliefs by the Berrettaro family, and a fragment of the *Last Supper* by Domenico Gagini and his workshop. In the sanctuary, but very high up, is a precious large triptych, the *Madonna Enthroned amidst Angels* and recently attributed to Rogier Van der Weyden (early 16th century). It is one of the loveliest paintings in Sicily. Painted on Flemish oak and still in its original frame, it shows the Madonna with Sts Catherine and Barbara, all wearing rich scarlet silk gowns, accompanied by angel musicians.

Beside the Chiesa Madre is **San Gandolfo la Povera** (1622), with a high altarpiece of St Gandulph by Giuseppe Salerno. The road continues up to the church of San Francesco, founded in 1303, now used as a concert hall. On the left is **Piazza Castello** with the ruins of the so-called castle of Queen Blanche of Navarre (11th century). In the walled garden of Baron Casalpietro, two fir trees belonging to the endemic species *Abies nebrodensis* survive; there are very few of them left in the world. A little museum of the Madonie, **Museo Ambientalistico Madonita**—MAM (*open 8–8; T: 0921 641811, www. mam.pa.it*) at Corso Agliata 102 illustrates the local natural history (especially rocks and fossils dating to 200 million years ago).

Below San Francesco is the church of San Nicolò de Franchis (*locked*), founded in 1167 by Peter of Toulouse. Nearby is **Santa Margherita** (or the Badia Vecchia), a 15th-century church. It has delicate white and gold stucco decoration. The barrel vault and sanctuary have 19th-century pictorial decorations, including a copy of Leonardo's *Last Supper*.

Another road from Piazza Umberto leads up to the remains of the circular **Torre di Leo**, named after a family who purchased it in 1240, next to the church of San Pancrazio dei Greci, which contains a painting by one of the Zoppi di Gangi. From the terrace there is an impressive view of the mountains.

The main street of the little town, Corso Garibaldi, also starts in Piazza Umberto. It leads past the centrally-planned church of San Girolamo by Angelo Italia. Next to it is the former **Collegio dei Gesuiti** (*open 10–1 & 3.30–6.30; T: 0921 551613*), a large building now occupied by the Town Hall, the civic library and a museum in two sections, one devoted to archaeological finds from the area, and the other to ancient toys. The fine interior courtyard has loggias on two levels and a single balcony on the top storey. In the morning visitors are allowed up to the top storey where an open balcony has a fine view over the roofs of the town (and the ruined church of the Commenda below).

The Corso continues past a flight of steps (right) which lead up to the large Palazzo Carpinello with a long, low façade, and ends at a terrace known as the **Belvedere**, which has a magnificent panorama: the Palermo–Catania motorway is reduced to a winding stream in the distant valley below, while to the east rise the Madonie Mountains. The ancient church of Santa Maria Lo Piano, seat of the Teutonic Knights, contains 17th-century paintings. Via Malatacca leads down from the Corso towards **Sant'Antonio Abate**, which has a red Islamic dome crowning its bell-tower (once a minaret) and also contains a painting by one of the Zoppi di Gangi. One-storey Arab-style houses can be seen in this quarter.

Petralia Sottana

Petralia Sottana (*map p. 542, D2*) sits on a hillside enclosed by the mountains. The attractive Corso Paolo Agliata passes Santa Maria della Fontana (16th–17th century) and the 18th-century church of San Francesco before reaching Piazza Umberto (with a view of the Imera Valley). The Chiesa Madre, which has a lovely bell-tower, was rebuilt in the 17th century. It contains a fine sculpted altarpiece of 1501 and a 17th-century statue of the *Madonna and Child*. Above the town, on the road for Petralia Soprana, is the church and convent of the Santissima Trinità, with a marble altarpiece by Gian Domenico Gagini (1542). The women here still weave the brightly coloured rag rugs called *pezzane* or *frazzate*.

Petralia Soprana

Occupying a beautiful position on a hillside (1147m) above pinewoods, Petralia Soprana (*map p. 542, D2*) is one of the most interesting and well-preserved little towns in the interior of the island, and the highest in the province. *Petra* was important in the Roman era, and in 1062 it passed into the hands of Roger I. During the 19th and early 20th centuries rock-salt mines were in operation here, one of which is still in use. The exteriors of the attractive old stone houses have not been covered with plaster as in numerous other Sicilian towns.

In the central Piazza del Popolo is a large war memorial, and the neo-Gothic Town Hall (1896). Via Generale Medici leads up past (left) the lovely façade of San Giovanni Evangelista (1770; *closed*) to **Piazza Fra' Umile**, with a bust commemorating Fra' Umile da Petralia, the local sculptor, famous for his Crucifixes which adorn many churches in Sicily. On the right is the 18th-century Oratorio delle Anime del Purgatorio with a very worn portal. Further up is Piazza dei Quattro Cannoli with a pretty 18th-century fountain and palace.

Beyond on the right a wide flight of steps leads down to the **duomo**, consecrated in 1497, which has a delightful 18th-century portico. At one end is a squat tower and at the other is the 15th-century campanile with a two-light window in which two quaint statues of St Peter and St Paul have been placed. The gilded and white stucco decoration in the interior was carried out in 1859. On the north side the first altar has a fine painted statue of the *Madonna and Child*, and the fourth altar a marble statue of the *Madonna*. The fifth has a high relief of the *Pietà* with symbols of the Passion. In the chapel to the left of the sanctuary is an 18th-century gilded wooden altarpiece. The realistic Crucifix in the sanctuary was the first work of Fra' Umile da Petralia (c. 1624). The polychrome statues of St Peter and St Paul are by Gaetano Franzese (1764), and the large painting of their martyrdom is by Vincenzo Riolo. On the fifth south altar is a beautiful *Deposition*, attributed since its recent restoration to Pietro Novelli or the school of Ribera.

Above the duomo is the 18th-century domed circular church of San Salvatore (*closed*), which was built on the site of a Norman church. It contains 17th–18th-century statues.

From the other side of Piazza del Popolo, Via Loreto leads uphill past a pretty courtyard, several handsome palaces, and the 16th-century church of San Michele. The street ends in the piazza (paved with cobblestones) in front of the attractive church of **Santa Maria di Loreto**. The façade of 1750 is by local sculptors, and the two little spires on either side are decorated with coloured stones. It is preceded by a wrought-iron gate of 1881. The beautiful interior has a carved altarpiece attributed to Gian Domenico Gagini (with a *Madonna* attributed to Giacomo Mancini). It also contains paintings by Vincenzo Riolo, 18th–19th-century statues, and a fine sacristy of 1783. On the right a lane (Via Belvedere) leads out under an arch to a terrace beside the apse of the church, with an excellent vista which extends as far as Etna on a clear day.

On the edge of the hill, below Corso Umberto, is the church of **San Teodoro**, founded by Count Roger and rebuilt in 1759. An interesting sarcophagus decorated with animal carvings was discovered here in 1991.

Gangi

East of the Petralias, a few kilometres east of the boundary of the Madonie park, Gangi (*map p. 542, D2*) is a large town perched on a ridge in the middle of mountainous countryside (1011m). The town's medieval origins can still be appreciated in the street plan. At the top of the hill is the Palazzo Bongiorno, now the town hall, formerly the seat of the wealthiest family in the region, decorated with 18th-century frescoes by Gaspare Fumagalli. The town was the birthplace of Giuseppe Salerno, known as the Zoppo di Gangi (Cripple of Gangi), whose *Last Judgement* hangs in the church of San Nicolò (it is based on Michelangelo's *Last Judgement* in the Sistine Chapel), and also of his colleague Gaspare Vazano, also known as the Zoppo di Gangi. Attached to the castle is a Renaissance chapel attributed to the Gagini family (early 16th century).

THE WEST OF THE PROVINCE

Piana degli Albanesi

In Piana degli Albanesi (*map p. 542, B2*), the most interesting of the 15th-century Albanian colonies in Sicily, the inhabitants still use their native tongue, are Catholics of the Byzantine-Greek rite, and wear traditional costume for weddings and important festivals. Garibaldi planned the tactics that led to the capture of Palermo from here. Piana is known for its excellent bread, cheeses and huge *cannoli di ricotta*.

In the handsome main street, Via Giorgio Kastriota, is the cathedral of **San Demetrio** of 1498 (*usually open 10–12.30*). On the west wall is a 19th-century painting of St Nicholas by Andrea d'Antoni. On the north wall of the church is a small Byzantine *Madonna and Child*. The statues are attributed to Nicola Bagnasco, and the damaged apse frescoes are by Pietro Novelli. The iconostasis was decorated with paintings in 1975.

The main street leads uphill to the piazza beside the church of the Madonna Odigitria (1607), on a design by Pietro Novelli. Just out of the square is the church of **San Giorgio**, the oldest church in the town, built in 1495. Inside, on the right side is a mosaic by the local artist Tanina Cuccia (1984) and a painting of St Philip Neri by Giuseppe Patania. The iconostasis has 20th-century paintings. On the left side is a fresco of St Anthony Abbot by Antonio Novelli and a charming equestrian statue of St George, fully armed. Other churches of interest include **San Vito** (18th century, with statues) and **Santissima Annunziata** (1624; with a fresco by Pietro Novelli).

At Via Guzzetta 11, the old Oratorio San Filippo Neri has been converted into a library, cultural centre and the delightful **Museo Civico Nicola Barbato** (*open Tues, Thur, Sat 9.30–1 & 4–7; Wed, Fri 9.30–1; Sun 10–1; T:091 8575668, 091 8561006*), on two floors, with interesting sections displaying traditional costumes and 18th-century jewellery worn by the women of Piana.

A few kilometres south of the town is **Portella della Ginestra**, where there is a memorial to the peasants massacred here while celebrating a traditional May Day festival in 1947. Eleven people were killed and 59 wounded by outlaws led by Salvatore Giuliano from Montelepre. This was later understood as an attempt by right-wing activists, in collusion with the Mafia, to combat Communism and advocate independence for the island (both the right wing and the separatists had just lost votes in the local elections).

Southeast of the town is the **lake of Piana degli Albanesi**, a reservoir formed in 1923 by an impressive dam between Mt Kumeta (1200m) and Mt Maganoce (900m) across the River Belice, now a nature reserve (Oasi di Piana degli Albanesi), a good place to observe migrating duck.

Monte Jato

West of Piana, **San Giuseppe Jato** (*map p. 542, A2*) is fast becoming one of the more interesting destinations for curious and adventurous visitors. Excavations on Mt Jato carried out over the past 30 years by the University of Zürich have unearthed remains of the ancient city called *Iaitas* by the Romans, which flourished from the 4th century BC until it was destroyed by Frederick II in the 13th century. The area now has 21 marked trails, of various levels of difficulty, for trekkers and ramblers, using for the most part ancient and medieval paths and bridle-tracks, which had all but disappeared from sight and from memory. The trails offer unforgettable glimpses of historic remains, wildlife, and the lovely countryside of the area. Descriptions of the walks and maps are available from the local tourist offices.

Outside the nearby village of **San Cipirello**, where in Via Roma there is a small museum (*open 9–1, closed Sun and holidays*) dedicated to the site and displaying unusual statues found at the theatre there, a road leads up through lovely countryside to the **archaeological area** on top of the hill. The best-preserved remains date from the Hellenistic period. From the entrance gate it is a walk of about 20mins to the top of the hill with the theatre (late 4th century BC, reconstructed in the 1st century AD), which could seat 4,000, a temple of Aphrodite (c. 550 BC), and a large villa on two floors with a peristyle and 25 rooms. The agora has also been partially uncovered. There are splendid views from this isolated spot.

Partinico, Borgetto and Montelepre

Partinico (*map p. 542, A1*) is an agricultural town associated with the name of Danilo Dolci (1924–97), a philanthropist from Trieste who dedicated his life to opposing the Mafia using non-violent methods. In Piazza Duomo is a fountain of 1716. The Biblioteca Comunale (town library) nearby has a museum (*open Mon–Fri 9–12.30 & 4–6.30*) with finds from Monte Jato and Rocca d'Entella, and a local ethnographical collection, with an oil press and wine cellars. From the duomo, Corso dei Mille leads past a Neoclassical bandstand (1875) to the 17th-century church of San Leonardo, with works by the school of Novelli. Opposite is the church of the Carmine (1634).

Not far from Partinico is **Borgetto**, a small farming community where the women are famous for their very particular home-made macaroni. The hill town of **Montelepre** is famous for its associations with Salvatore Giuliano, the unwilling bandit. He used his mule to carry black-market flour to the village; when apprehended, he shot a *carabiniere*. He reigned over a large part of the province for seven years before he was murdered here in 1950 by his brother-in-law, Gaspare Pisciotta, at the age of 27. His body was shown to the press in a courtyard in Castelvetrano with the story that he had been tracked down and killed there by the Carabinieri. He remained a mythical figure in the imagination of many Sicilians until 1960, when his connection with the Mafia and local police was revealed, as well as his presumed part in the massacre of peasants at Portella della Ginestra (*see previous page*).

Carini and Terrasini

A lovely town that gives its name to the gulf here, **Carini** (*map p. 542, A1*) has interesting stalactite caverns in the outskirts, and the fine 16th-century Castello La Grua Talamanca (*open 9–1 & 4–8, closed Mon; ask at Tourist Office, T: 091 8611339*), one of the most beautiful in Sicily. The castle is remembered for the tragic story of the Baronissa di Carini, who in 1563 was murdered by her own father when he believed she had a lover.

Beyond the airport at Punta Raisi and Mt Pecoraro is the lovely Gulf of Castellammare, which stretches away to Capo San Vito, the mountains behind providing a striking backdrop. It is a popular area for holiday homes, but the countryside is still beautiful, with olive and citrus groves. **Terrasini** (*map p. 542, A1*) is now a holiday resort, with a particularly good civic museum on the Lungomare Peppino Impastato, the Museo Civico Palazzo D'Aumale (*open 9–1.30 & 2.30–7; T: 091 8683327*), with an archaeological section consisting of objects found on dives in and around shipwrecks (with explanations of how the ships were built, how the amphorae were stacked on board, etc), fishing techniques and ex-votos. On the first floor is an excellent natural history section, including geology and palaeontology, with a collection of fossils. The museum also displays a fine collection of hand-painted Sicilian carts.

THE SOUTH OF THE PROVINCE

Belmonte Mezzagno to Ficuzza

Between Bagheria and Piana degli Albanesi, **Belmonte Mezzagno** (*map p. 542, B1*) was founded in 1752 and has a scenographic church built in 1776, dominating the valley of the Eleuterio (the ancient *Eleutheros*) below, densely inhabited, but with some remaining persimmon plantations. Above the plain is the ruined **castle of Misilmeri**, which takes its name from the Arab *Menzil el-Emir* (dwelling of the Emir). Here in 1068 Count Roger de Hauteville defeated a large Muslim army, paving the way for Norman domination of Sicily.

At **Marineo** (*map p. 542, B2*) the picturesque Castello Beccadelli Bologna, built at the foot of the Montagnola as the residence of the aristocratic Bologna family by Matteo Carnelivari in 1559, now houses the Museo Regionale della Valle dell'Eleuterio (*open Tues–Sat 9–6.30, Sun and holidays 9–1; T: 091 8726491*), and besides offering stupendous views over the Eleuterio valley, houses a fine archaeological collection of objects found during recent digs in the surrounding area.

Further south, **Ficuzza** is a village dominated by the Palazzina Reale (*open 9–12.30 & 1.30–4; T: 091 8460108*), a handsome building in sandstone with numerous chimneys and two clocks, now used by the Azienda Forestale. It was built by Venanzio Marvuglia in 1803 as a hunting-lodge for the Bourbons, whose huge estate surrounded the lodge. Behind it extends the Bosco della Ficuzza, now a nature reserve, a splendid forest of oak, chestnut and ilex, among the most extensive and interesting wooded areas of its kind left on the island, noted for its fine trees, plants and wildlife. Although once much more extensive, it still covers some 4,000 hectares. Several rough roads and paths run through the woods, although much of it is fenced off for protection. Above the forest rises the Rocca Busambra (1613m), a huge spur of calcareous rock which dominates the plain for many kilometres around. Above the sheer rock face, its summit provides pastureland. Numerous birds nest here, including the golden eagle. The Gorgo del Drago, the source of the River Frattina, is a lush green oasis, with yellow and red rocks.

Cefalà Diana to Castronuovo di Sicilia

The town of **Cefalà Diana** (*map p. 542, B2*) has a unique Islamic bath-house, the Bagni di Cefalà (*open Mon–Sat 9–1; T: 091 8201184, call day before to make sure*), which dates back to the 10th–11th centuries and is considered to be the most interesting Arab building to survive on the island. The baths have a splendid barrel vault and a pretty arch with two capitals and columns at one end. The water bubbles up here at 38°C (it was diverted to Villafrati for 22 years and has only recently been restored), and now the spring and its course are protected as a nature reserve. The Kufic inscription on a frieze of tufa ('Of our lord prince the Emir two admirable baths') which runs around the top of the outside wall has virtually disappeared. The 13th-century castle is prominent on a rocky outcrop to the south, and very photogenic, with its crenellated battlements.

Ciminna, further east, has a number of interesting churches, including the Chiesa Madre with 17th-century stuccoes by Scipione and Francesco Li Volsi and a painting of St John the Baptist by the architect Paolo Amato, who was born here. The village was famously used as a location in Visconti's film *The Leopard* (1963).

The little hill town of **Mezzojuso**, *Menzil el-Jusuf*, Village of Joseph, has Arab origins. Settled by Albanians in the 15th century, it has two mother churches, side by side in the main square. The church of the Annunziata follows the Latin rite, while that of San Nicola holds Greek-Orthodox services. The Basilian monks of the convent behind the church specialise in restoring 16th-century books.

Vicari, above the fertile valley of the River San Leonardo, has a wonderfully romantic ruined castle, probably built by the Arabs, with views of extraordinary beauty. Count Roger wintered here after the battles of 1077. **Lercara Friddi** (*map p. 542, B3*), founded in 1605, with its attractive crumbling 18th-century churches, was once important for its sulphur mines. When the sulphur economy collapsed at the end of the 19th century, a thousand families emigrated to Venezuela and the USA, practically depopulating the town. In his compilation of Sicilian reflections *Words are Stones*, the writer Carlo Levi describes the mines and their working conditions here during a strike in 1951.

On the southern border of the province, on a hill overlooking the River Platani, is **Castronuovo di Sicilia** (*map p. 542, B3*), once a town of strategic importance, now in decline. Much reforestation has been taking place here in the last few years; the inhabitants are farmers and raise milk-cows: the *tuma persa* cheese made here has superb flavour, as does the bread. Many of the churches contain 18th-century stuccoes by Antonio da Messina, and the 15th-century Chiesa Madre has works by the Gagini family.

Some way further to the east at **Regaleali** (*map p. 542, C3*) is the famous wine estate of the Tasca d'Almerita family, on the southern border of the province (best reached from Vallelunga in the province of Caltanissetta). The cellars are open to the public (*open 10–11.30 & 3–6*) and wine and local produce can be purchased (*www.tascadalmerita.it*).

Prizzi to Contessa Entellina

To the west, the medieval town of **Prizzi** (*map p. 542, B3*) stands near the lake formed by damming the River Sosio, beneath curious outcrops of rock. Many of the old houses in the centre have been painted with bright murals. Excavations on the Montagna dei Cavalli in the vicinity have revealed 4th–3rd century BC remains, possibly the ancient city of *Hippana*, destroyed by the Romans during the First Punic War. The finds can be seen in the Museo Civico in Corso Umberto (*open 9–1, closed Mon*).

Bisacquino (*map p. 542, A3–B3*) was once an Arab citadel, then a medieval fortress-town. 'Moth-soft Besacquino [sic]' wrote Lawrence Durrell in his *Sicilian Carousel*, an apt description of this gentle place where time stands still. Yet the inhabitants know all about the passage of time: church clocks were still made here until recently. There is a Museo dell'Orologio da Torre, a museum of tower clocks (*T: 0918 351026*), in Corso Umberto. The bell-tower of the Chiesa Matrice is unique in Sicily because of its triangular shape.

Contessa Entellina (*map p. 542, A3*) is a charming mountain village that takes its first name from the Countess Caterina Cardona di Chiusa (who gave asylum to Albanian refugees in 1450) and its surname from Entella (a town of the Elymians which lies to the northwest on a high, isolated rock). On the extensive plateau, excavations of the ancient city, ravaged in the past by *tombaroli* (clandestine diggers), are in progress. So far the fortifications, part of the medieval fortress, and a building of 4th–3rd century BC have been identified. The necropolei lay at the foot of the hill. The archaeological area is always open; the museum is at Via I Maggio 1 (*open Mon–Sat 9–12; T: 091 8355554*).

Corleone

Corleone (*map p. 542, B2*) is a picturesque town of Arab origin nestled in the hillside, now surrounded by anonymous modern buildings. In recent years it has been notorious for its powerful Mafia gang, whose boss Totò Riina ruled Cosa Nostra for many years until his arrest in 1993, after more than 20 years 'in hiding' in Palermo.

A Lombard colony was established here by Frederick II in 1237. Traces of its importance as a medieval town can be seen in the old centre which preserves some fine palace doorways in its narrow streets, and numerous churches (over 100, because every important family felt the need for a personal church). The **Chiesa Madre** (*if closed, ring at the inconspicuous north door approached from the road on the left of the outside steps through a gate*) contains some interesting wooden statues (16th–17th centuries), wooden choir-stalls by Giovanni Battista Li Volsi, and paintings (on the transept altars) by Fra' Felice da Sambuca, and (first north chapel) Tommaso de Vigilia (*Adoration of the Magi*).

The **public gardens**, laid out in 1820, are well kept and the **Museo Civico Pippo**

Rizzo (*open Mon–Sat 9–1 & 3.30–7.30, Sun 9–1; T: 091 8463918*), which houses an interesting archaeological collection, is in Palazzo Provenzano.

THE ISLAND OF USTICA

Ustica, with some 1,400 inhabitants, lies a little over 50km northwest of Palermo (*map p. 542*). It is a small fertile island (just over 8.6km square), all that remains of a volcano, more than a million years old. The colours of Ustica are memorable; Antonio Gramsci, the prominent communist who was held prisoner here, remembered the 'impressive rainbows, and the extraordinary colours of the sea and the sky'. Ustica's highest hills rise to c. 240m above sea-level. The island was once covered with trees but few woods remain, the landscape now being dotted with wheatfields, vineyards, almond groves and orchards, with hedges of prickly pear. Capers and lentils are also produced. Ustica has interesting migratory birdlife, including the peregrine falcon, kestrels, storks, herons, razorbills and cormorants. The rocky shoreline has numerous grottoes; it is particularly remarkable for its numerous fish—grouper abound, as well as hake, red mullet, prawns, shrimps, lobsters and (in spring) swordfish—and for its seabed, hosting a great variety of seaweed, including the rare *laminaria*. In 1986 the first marine reserve in the Mediterranean was established around the island's coast, bringing renewed prosperity to the island. The reserve has now been extended to include the whole island. There is no source of water on Ustica apart from some of the caves, such as the Blue Grotto, but there is now a desalination plant. The pleasant little village above the port of Cala Santa Maria is well kept, and only crowded in the summer months. One road encircles the island, and mule tracks, ideal for trekking, wind through the interior.

HISTORY OF USTICA

The name Ustica, from the Latin *ustum* (burnt), derives from the colour of its black volcanic rock. It was inhabited in prehistoric times and in the Roman era. The Greeks called it *Osteodes* (the place of bones), in reference to the 6,000 mercenaries abandoned here by the Carthaginians when they rebelled after a pay dispute, at the time of the wars with Syracuse. Attacks of Barbary pirates defeated all attempts to colonise it in the Middle Ages. It remained deserted for many centuries until in 1762 it was repopulated from the Aeolian Islands and Naples by the Bourbons because of its strategic location on the trade route between Naples and Palermo. At the time three towers were constructed to defend the island.

The island was used as a place of exile and as a prison until 1961: Carlo and Nello Rosselli and Antonio Gramsci were held here as political prisoners under the Fascist regime. In September 1943 Italian and British officers met in secret on the island to discuss details of Italy's change of sides.

Exploring Ustica

The little village above the port of **Cala Santa Maria** was laid out on geometric lines by the Bourbons in the 18th century. A road winds up to the piazza (also reached by steps from the port). To the right of the church, Via Calvaria leads uphill to the Via Crucis, where on the left a path continues up to the Rocca della Falconiera, a defensive tower now used for exhibitions (the fort is also reached by car along a narrow road paved with pebbles). The tower is on the site of a 3rd-century BC settlement, also inhabited in Roman times. It has been excavated on three levels; the most conspicuous remains include a staircase and some 30 cisterns used to collect rainwater, and a number of tombs.

There are marvellous views above the lighthouse which marks the eastern tip of the island and the rocky point known as the **Punta Omo Morto**, a nesting-place for numerous birds. To the southwest of the lighthouse a necropolis of the 5th–6th centuries AD has been identified.

On the other side of the village the **Torre Santa Maria**, another Bourbon tower, once used as a prison, has been restored and is now the archaeological museum. The finds from the island, including Bronze-Age objects from the village at Faraglioni (*see below*) and underwater finds, are well displayed. Near the tower are remains of a 16th-century Benedictine convent and interesting old houses known as the *centro storico*, with stables built around courtyards, some of them carefully restored as homes by the local inhabitants.

On the northern tip of the island, at **Faraglioni**, excavations begun in 1989 unearthed a large prehistoric village (14th–13th centuries BC), probably settled from the Aeolian Islands, with some 300 houses built in stone. The defensive walls are among the best fortifications of this period to have been discovered in Italy.

On the west coast, between Cala Sidoti and Caletta, is the central zone of the **Riserva Naturale Marina** (*T: 091 6043111*), a protected area marked by red buoys where fishing is prohibited and boats have to keep offshore. Swimming is allowed only at the extreme northern and southern ends of the reserve (*limited access*). The aquarium here has an interesting display of Mediterranean sea plants and fish.

Above the bay is the Bourbon Torre dello Spalmatore, with fine vaulted rooms, owned by the marine reserve. Plans to use it as an aquarium and cultural centre seem to have fallen through. Just to the south is the lighthouse at Punta Cavazzi, which will become a scientific laboratory for marine research. A buoy in the sea here marks an underwater archaeological itinerary for skin-divers where a number of finds from various wrecks have been left *in situ* (*www.archeologiaviva.com*).

Ustica is much visited by divers and the marine reserve collaborates with the fishermen who live on the island to arrange boat trips for visitors. Ustica is now considered to be a world centre for diving and underwater observation. Underwater tours are organised and the waters are particularly rich in hidden caves and slopes.

PRACTICAL INFORMATION

• **By air:** Falcone Borsellino Airport is at Punta Raisi, 35km west of Palermo (*www. gesap.it*). Prestia e Comandè (*T: 091 586351, www.prestiaecomande.it*) runs regular coach services from the airport to the central railway station at Piazza Giulio Cesare (*map 16*), with stops along Via Emerico Amari (*map 7*) and on Via della Libertà (*map 2*). The service operates from 4am–11pm (Palermo–Airport) and 5am–midnight (Airport–Palermo); journey time 50mins; tickets can be bought on the bus. There is also the hourly Trinacria Express fast train connection to the central station (4.45am–9.40pm from Palermo and from 5.40am–5 past midnight from the airport), or the Metro. Taxis are expensive.

• **By rail:** Palermo Centrale (*www.trenitalia. com*) for all state railway services to Agrigento, Messina, Trapani, Catania, Caltanissetta and Enna. Baheria and Santa Flavia–Solunto, Termini Imerese and Cefalù are on the main Palermo–Messina line. The nearest station to Alia is Roccapalumba (5km from both towns).

• **By sea:** Siremar (*www.siremar.it*) runs ferries and hydrofoils to Ustica. Ustica Lines (*www. usticalines.it*) has hydrofoils connecting Palermo to Ustica (90mins) and to the Aeolian Islands. Boats for the Aeolian Islands also leave from Cefalù.

• **By car:** Parking is difficult in the centre of Palermo. Pay car parks (with parking attendant) are near Piazza Castelnuovo, the station and Via Stabile. Elsewhere there are blue-line areas, for which scratch-and-show tickets are purchased at tobacconists or newsagents and then displayed inside the windscreen. If you want to stay longer, you can leave two or three tickets at once. If your car is illegally parked and towed away, telephone the city police (Vigili Urbani, T: 091 6954111) or ask a taxi driver to help.

• **By bus** (in Palermo)
City buses tend to be overcrowded, infrequent and very slow because of the traffic. Tickets must be purchased at tobacconists or newsagents and stamped at automatic machines on board. There are two excellent mini-bus circular services, both of which pass many of the city's most important monuments.
Mini-buses
Linea Gialla (yellow): Railway station—Corso dei Mille—Orto Botanico—Kalsa—Via Alloro (Regional Art Gallery in Palazzo Abatellis) —Via Maqueda—Ballarò—Corso Tüköry—Santo Spirito—Via Oreto—railway station.
Linea Rossa (red): Via Alloro (Regional Art Gallery in Palazzo Abatellis) —Quattro Canti—Cassaro (Corso Vittorio Emanuele) —Cathedral—Via Papireto—Via Sant'Agostino—Via Maqueda—Vucciria—Cala—Piazza Marina—Via Alloro (Palazzo Abatellis).
For Monreale, buses 309 and 389 leave from Piazza Indipendenza (*map 14*; frequent service in 20–30mins).
The **Hop On-Hop Off City-Sightseeing Bus** is an unmistakable red bus starting from Piazza Castelnuovo (Politeama; *map 6*), following two routes 'A' and 'B' (*www.palermo. city-sightseeing.it*).
Palermo's **Metro** (*metropalermo.it*) was still under construction in some stretches at the time of writing, but when complete will connect the city to the airport in the west and to Bagheria and Altavilla Milicia in the east.

• **By bus** (in the province)
Palermo has a new bus station in Piazzetta Cairoli, on Corso dei Mille, c. 500m from the railway station (*beyond map 16*).
AST (*T: 091 6800011, www.aziendasicilianatrasporti.it*) from Palermo (Viale delle Scienze)

to Bagheria, Burgio, Carini, Castelbuono, Cefalà Diana, Corleone, Isnello, Lercara Friddi,
Monreale, Montelepre, Montevago, Partanna,
Partinico, Prizzi, San Cipirello, Solunto,
Termini Imerese, and Vicari. **Cuffaro** (*www.*
cuffaro.info) from Palermo railway station (Via
Balsamo) to Agrigento (2hrs), Canicattì, Comitini, Favara and Racalmuto. **Interbus/Segesta**
(*interbus.it*) to Syracuse (3hrs 15mins) and
Trapani (approx. 2hrs). Buses leave Palermo
from Via Balsamo and arrive at Piazzetta Cairoli. **Randazzo** (*www.autobusrandazzo.altervis-*
ta.org) runs from Via Rosario Gregorio (corner
of Via Balsamo, near the railway station) to
Caccamo (70mins) and Termini Imerese.
Russo Autoservizi (*www.russoautoservizi.it*)
runs from Piazza Marina (*map 12*) west along
the coast to Castellammare del Golfo and San
Vito Lo Capo. **SAIS Autolinee** (*www.saisau-*
tolinee.it) from Via Balsamo near the railway
station to a number of destinations on the
island including Caltagirone, Catania, Catania
Airport (2hrs 30mins), Enna, Gela, Messina
(2hrs 40mins), and Piazza Armerina. **Salemi
Autolinee** (*autoservizisalemi.it*) from the bus
station on Piazzetta Cairoli (*beyond map 16*)
to Campobello di Mazara, Castelvetrano,
Marsala and Mazara del Vallo.
• **Museums:** See www.museidicharme.it for
information on many of Palermo's smaller
museums: these are Orto Botanico, Museo
del Mare, Palazzo Asmundo, Fondazione
Whitaker, Fondazione Banca di Sicilia, Museo
del Risorgimento, Museo delle Marionette,
Museo Gemmellaro, Tre Secoli di Moda,
Museo della Specola and the Museo del
Giocattolo in Bagheria.

WHERE TO STAY

Alia (*map p. 542, C2–C3*)
€ Some houses in the town offer B&B accommodation to visitors as *paese-albergo*; T:

Municipio 091 8210911, or Sig. Zimbardo, 091
8214275, 329 3551756.
Bagheria (*map p. 542, B1*)
€ **Franco il Conte**. Friendly, modern establishment with garage, good restaurant, Count
Franco is quite a personality. Giuseppe Tornatore once stayed here. *Via Vallone de Spuches
29/31, T: 091 966815, www.dafrancoilconte.it.*
Caccamo (*map p. 542, C2*)
€ **Case Vacanze Margherita**. Run by
Giovanni Brancato, for accommodation in
local houses participating in the *paese-albergo*
scheme. *Viale Regina Siciliana, T: 091 8121384,
333 3317018.*
Cefalù *Map p. 542, C1–D1.*
€€–€€€ **Alberi del Paradiso**. Quiet, eco-
friendly hotel, hillside position southwest
of the town centre, lovely garden with small
pool and a spa in the old water-mill. Comfortable rooms and good restaurant, shuttle
service to the centre of Cefalù and the beach.
*Via dei Mulini 18–20, T: 0921 423900 (enquir-
ies), 0921 440596 (to book), www.alberidelpara-
diso.it.*
€€ **La Plumeria**. Restored palace in the
town centre, 10 beautiful rooms, good breakfasts. *Corso Ruggero 185, T: 0921 925897, www.
laplumeriahotel.it.*
€€ **Villa Gaia**. Close to the seafront and
medieval centre, friendly hotel with 12 rooms
and suites, breakfast on the terrace. *Via
Pintorno 101, T: 0921 420992, www.villagaia-
hotel.it.*
Corleone (*map p. 542, B2*)
€€ **Casa Mia**. Vineyard on a hillside northwest of town, producing the famous Principe
di Corleone wines. Comfortable rooms, restaurant, pool with whirlpool, children's play-
ground, tennis, mini-golf. *Contrada Malvello,
SP 4bis (between Corleone and Roccamena), T:
0918 462922, www.agriturismo-casamia.com.*
Ficuzza (*map p. 542, B2*)
€ **L'Antica Stazione**. What was once the rail-

way station is now a delightful place to stay, with 8 comfortable rooms, just right for naturalists and hikers. Foxes have been known to come into the restaurant (and who can blame them–it has an excellent reputation). *T: 0918 460000, www.anticastazione.it.*

Gangi (*map p. 542, D2*)

€€€ **Gangivecchio**. Beautiful converted Benedictine monastery, with comfortable rooms and good restaurant. The farm produces award-winning olive oil and runs highly recommended courses in Sicilian cookery for guests. *Contrada Gangi Vecchio, signed from Gangi (approx. 5km), T: 0921 644982, www. gangivecchio.org.*

Mondello (*map p. 542, B1*)

€€ **Villa Esperia**. Attractive Art Nouveau building a few blocks inland from the beach; 22 rooms with opulent beds; garden and good restaurant, *Via Margherita di Savoia 53, Valdesi, T: 091 6840717, www.hotelvillaesperia.it.*

Montelepre (*map p. 542, A1*)

€€ **Il Castello di Giuliano**. Modern castle owned by Giuliano's nephew in a panoramic position on the outskirts of this village, still nostalgic for the legendary bandit (*see p. 102*). 23 spacious rooms, good restaurant, especially for pizza in the evenings. Local wines. *Via Magistrato Pietro Merra 1, T: 091 8941006 (hotel) and 091 8784727 (restaurant), www. castellodigiuliano.it.*

Palermo (*map p. 542, B1*)

€€€ **Villa Igiea Hilton**. A beautiful Art Nouveau building at Acquasanta, 3km north of the city. Built as a sanatorium by Donna Franca Florio (*see p. 69*), it never functioned as such. With the help of the architect Ernesto Basile she transformed it into a luxurious hotel (inaugurated on 19th December 1900). The Salone Basile, now used for functions, is a masterpiece, with walls painted with sinuous murals by Ettore De Maria Bergler, and furniture by Vittorio Ducrot, who col-

laborated with Basile on more than one Art Nouveau interior. In the restaurant is a portrait of Donna Franca by Giovanni Boldini, criticised by her husband as too sensuous: the artist was forced to re-touch her neckline. She is wearing her Cartier pearls. 122 rooms and suites, restaurant, park, access to the sea, tennis courts, fitness centre and pool. *Salita Belmonte 43, T: 091 6312111, www.amthotels. com, hotelvillaigiea.com. Map p. 67.*

€€€ **Excelsior Hilton**. A delightful Belle-Epoque atmosphere, central position, 119 quiet rooms, excellent service and good restaurant. *Via Marchese Ugo 3, T: 091 7909001, amthotels.it/excelsiorpalermo. Map p. 20, 2.*

€€€ **Grand Hotel et des Palmes**. Richard Wagner famously finished Parsifal here, in this former palace of the Ingham-Whitaker family, transformed into a hotel in 1874 and now a little frayed at the edges. 172 rooms and suites, some are better than others. Good restaurant, popular with Italian politicians. *Via Roma 398 (Politeama), T: 091 6028111, grandhoteletdespalmes.com. Map p. 21, 7.*

€€€ **Centrale Palace**. A prestigious 19th-century hotel; rooftop terrace, 104 lovely rooms (quieter at the back away from the Via Maqueda, with wonderful views from the top floor), good penthouse restaurant. *Corso Vittorio Emanuele 327 (Cassaro), T: 091 336666, www.centralepalacehotel.it Map p. 21, 15.*

€€€ **Grand Hotel Piazza Borsa**. In medieval Palermo, three old palaces have been transformed into a comfortable hotel with 127 rooms and suites, restaurant (well-reputed), fitness centre. *Via dei Cartari 18 (San Francesco), T: 091 320075, www.piazzaborsa.it. Map p. 21, 11.*

€€ **Joli**. Charming little hotel, central position, old-style rooms. *Via Michele Amari 11 (Piazza Florio), T: 091 6111765/6, www. hoteljoli.com. Map p. 21, 7.*

€€ **Mezzanino del Gattopardo**. For Tomasi

di Lampedusa fans, architect-designed B&B on the mezzanine floor of the architect's own house, a 15th-century palace, 2 delightful rooms with private bath and terraces offering rooftop views over the city, excellent breakfasts, lots of books by Sicilian writers. *Via Alloro 145, T: 091 9762520, 333 4771703, www.bandbilmezzaninodelgattopardo.it. Map p. 21, 12.*

€€ **Palazzo Amari Bajardi**. Elegant B&B near the Vuccceria. *Via San Cristoforo 15 (Vucciria), T: 339 2099964, www.palazzoamaribajardi.it. Map p. 21, 15.*

€€ **Porta Felice**. 33 modern rooms and a good fitness centre with Turkish bath and sauna, in a completely restructured 18th-century palace close to the medieval quarter. No restaurant, breakfast is served on the terrace. *Via Butera 45 (Foro Italico), T: 091 6175678, www.hotelportafelice.it. Map p. 21, 12.*

€€ **Quattro Quarti**. A small aristocratic palace has been transformed into a lovely, elegant hotel, only 4 charming rooms, no restaurant. Very special. *Corso Vittorio Emanuele 376 (Cassaro), T: 091 583687, 347 8547209, www.quattroquarti.it. Map p. 21, 15.*

€–€€ **La Dimora del Genio**. Unusual B&B full of character, with frescoed ceilings, in the heart of Palermo. Very good breakfasts (the owner loves cooking). *Via Garibaldi 58 (Kalsa), T: 091 6166981, 347 6587664, www.ladimoradelgenio.it. Map p. 21, 16.*

€ **Posta**. Historic hotel in the centre, opposite the post office, much favoured in the past by actors and singers on tour, nice rooms and good service, run by the same family for nearly 100 years. Garage available. *Via Gagini 77 (Politeama), T: 091 587338, www.hotelpostapalermo.it. Map p. 21, 11.*

€ **Orientale**. Close to the railway station, quite a find, this little family-run hotel occupies part of the huge 18th-century palace built for Prince Alessandro Filangieri di Cutò,

and has been a hotel since 1890. Quaint, large rooms with smart new bathrooms and air conditioning. Excellent value. No restaurant. *Via Maqueda 26 (railway station), T: 091 6165727, 091 6163506, www.albergoorientale.191.it. Map p. 21, 15.*

€ **Vecchio Borgo**. 32 beautifully decorated rooms in a very old district of Palermo, near a colourful daily food market. *Via Quintino Sella 1–7, T: 091 6118330, www.hotelvecchioborgo.eu. Map p. 20, 2.*

Piana degli Albanesi *(map p. 542, B2)*

€€–€€€ **Masseria Rossella**. Eighteenth-century country villa surrounded by olive groves, with 9 rooms, frescoed ceilings, pool and private chapel, close to the Ficuzza woods and the Rocca Busambra. *Contrada Rossella, T: 091 8460012, www.masseria-rossella.com.*

Polizzi Generosa *(map p. 542, C2–D2)*

€€ **Antico Feudo San Giorgio**. A 19th-century farmhouse within the Madonie Park, south of Polizzi Generosa, producing organic wheat, olive oil, wines and vegetables; guests can help with harvesting. Accommodation in rooms or apartments, large pool, good restaurant. *Contrada San Giorgio, T: 0921 642613, 0921 600690, www.feudosangiorgio.it.*

Santa Flavia-Porticello *(map p. 542, B1)*

€€€ **Donna Concetta**. Small hotel in a lovely old building overlooking the fishing harbour of Porticello, once belonging to Luigi Pirandello's uncle; all the rooms and suites are different. Excellent restaurant and fitness/beauty centre. *Via Roma 113, T: 091 9390060, www.donnaconcetta.it.*

Sclafani Bagni *(map p. 542, C2)*

€€ **Case di Cardellino**. Farm with panoramic views of Piano Battaglia, with 10 lovely rooms in the converted medieval grain silos. Swimming pool. Marvellous home cooking. *Contrada Cardellino, at km 18.7 on the SS 120 between Cerda and Caltavuturo, T: 0921 541825, www.lecasedicardellino.it.*

Termini Imerese (*map p. 542, C2*)
€€ Grand Hotel delle Terme. In a good position for touring the area; 70 rooms and suites, spa, gym and excellent restaurant, in a lovely Art Nouveau building. *Piazza Terme 2, T: 091 8113557, www.grandhoteldelleterme.it.*

Ustica (*map p. 542, C1*)
€€ Clelia. Welcoming little hotel with 26 rooms, air conditioning and good restaurant, close to the central square. *Via Sindaco 1° 29, T: 091 8449039, www.hotelclelia.it.*
€ Hibiscus. For a quiet holiday, this farm producing lentils and wine offers self-catering accommodation in 4 air-conditioned cottages. There is a restaurant 10mins' walk away. *Contrada Tramontana, T: 091 8449179, 091 8449543, www.agriturismohibiscus.com.*

WHERE TO EAT

Bagheria (*map p. 542, B1*)
€€ Don Ciccio. ■ A popular, reasonably-priced family-run trattoria, born as a tavern in 1943. No menu, tablecloths, tourists or *antipasti*; traditional starter is a hard-boiled egg with a glass of *zibibbo*. Allow yourself to be guided through the range of fish or meat dishes; when in season, excellent bluefin tuna with mint, peas and tomato sauce, or tasty choices from the charcoal grill such as stuffed squid, lamb chops, local sausages, all accompanied by their own wines. Home-made pasta very good. Fantastic, happy atmosphere, worth a detour. Closed Wed, Sun, public holidays and Aug. *Viale del Cavaliere 87, T: 091 932442.*

Castelbuono (*map p. 542, D2*)
€€€ Nangalarruni. ■ Renowned in this part of the world, people come a long way to feast on wild mushrooms, delicious grills, home-made desserts. Excellent wines. Closed Wed. *Via delle Confraternite 10, T: 0921 671428.*

Castellana Sicula (*map p. 542, D2–D3*)
€€ Natura in Tavola. Long-lost recipes from the Sicilian tradition are prepared here, including *capretto a' sciusciarieddu* (kid with vegetables and eggs), wild mushrooms and herbs from the countryside, and sometimes even 'u cunigghiu, a preparation consisting of vegetables with anchovies, tuna and dried cod. *Via Battisti 7/9, T: 0921 642880.*

Cefalù (*map p. 542, C1–D1*)
€€€ La Brace. An elegant restaurant, Dutch-owned, with a vaguely exotic atmosphere. Delicious fish, very good Sicilian wine list. Closed Mon and lunchtime Tues. *Via XXV Novembre 10, T: 0921 423570.*
€€ Ostaria del Duomo. Carefully prepared Sicilian food, good wine list. Near cathedral. Closed Mon in winter. *Via Seminario 5, T: 0921 421838.*

Gratteri (*map p. 542, C2*)
€ Re Befè. Atmospheric restaurant in the Madonie Park, also functions as wine bar. Local food and wines at their best. *Via Alcide De Gasperi 14, T: 346 9441428.*

Mondello (*map p. 542, B1*)
€€€ Alle Terrazze. Opulent Art Nouveau pier jutting out over the sea, once the legendary Charleston (*see p. 68*), very expensive, good cuisine and wines of Sicily, with suitably professional service and Philippe Starck chairs. Closed Mon. *Viale Regina Elena, T: 091 6262903.*
€€€ Bye Bye Blues. Owner-chef Patrizia is always inventive. Fish dishes a speciality, but the vegetable *antipasti* are magnificent, too. Superb desserts. Good wine list and they make their own liqueurs. Closed Mon. *Via del Garofalo 23, T: 091 6841415.*

Monreale (*map p. 542, B1*)
€€ Bricco and Bracco. A restaurant for carnivores. No pasta, everything is based on meat, including some unusual cuts and local specialities, all expertly cooked and served.

Red wines only, from the best Sicilian vineyards. Closed Mon. *Via Benedetto D'Acquisto 13. T: 091 6417773.*

€ **Taverna del Pavone**. A short distance from the cathedral, tiny informal trattoria which serves good pasta, and delicious home-made almond parfait with hot chocolate sauce. Closed Mon. *Vicolo Pensato 18, T: 091 6406209.*

Palermo (*map p. 542, B1*)

€€€ **Osteria dei Vespri**. Right under Palazzo Ganci, where Visconti filmed the ballroom scenes of *The Leopard*, a tavern where you can sample exciting fusions of Sicilian and Parma cuisine. Extensive wine list including most Sicilian and Italian wines. Closed Sun. *Piazza Croce dei Vespri 6, T: 091 6171631. Map p. 21, 15–16.*

€€€ **La Dispensa dei Monsù**. Authentic Palermo cuisine, using local ingredients, accompanied by their own wines. Expensive, but worth it. Open evenings only, closed Sun. *Via Principe di Villafranca 59, T: 091 6090465. Map p. 20, 2.*

€€ **Il Maestro del Brodo**. One of the oldest restaurants in town, famous for beef stew with saffron—still excellent, but nowadays people flock here for the imaginative seafood dishes too. Desserts are nothing special, choose fruit. Opens only for lunch, closed Sun. *Via Pannieri 7 (Vucciria), T: 091 329523. Map p. 21, 11.*

€€ **Piccolo Napoli**. This delightful *trattoria* is a popular lunchtime venue for Palermitans; certainly worth a journey for those who appreciate perfectly cooked fish. Try the spaghetti in fish broth. Good list of Sicilian wines. Closed Sun and Aug. *Piazza Mulino a Vento 4 (Politeama), T: 091 320431. Map p. 21, 7.*

€ **Antica Trattoria del Monsù**. This little restaurant is famous for the authentic Palermo-style pizza, baked in a stone oven (also at lunchtime). *Closed Wed. Via Volturno 41, T: 091 327774. Map p. 20, 10.*

€ **Le Tre Sorelle**. Historic trattoria (opened in 1888 offering simple traditional Palermo food, such as *pasta con le sarde* (macaroni with sardines and wild fennel) or *macco di fave* (broad-bean potage), using fresh ingredients from the Capo market close by. Sicilian wines. Closed Sun evening. *Via Volturno 110 (Opera House), T: 091 585960. Map p. 20, 10.*

€ **Gli Amanti**. Elegant little place for light lunch, snacks, evening pizza, ideal in summer. *Piazzetta Colonna (corner Via Cavour, nr Politeama), T: 091 599976. Map p. 21, 7.*

€ **Bar Mazzara**. ■ Simple delicious food, cooked in front of you, and the best *cotoletta palermitana* (breaded grilled steak) in the city. Tomasi di Lampedusa wrote *The Leopard* here. Great sweets too (the self-service restaurant is over the pastry-shop). *Via Generale Magliocco 19, T: 091 321443. Map p. 20.6.*

€ **Antica Focacceria San Francesco**. Opened in 1834, for traditional Palermitan snacks and sandwiches: fragrant crunchy bread with *panelle* (chick-pea fritters), *meusa* (grilled beef spleen), *purpu* (boiled octopus), *stigghiole* (stuffed intestines of kid or lamb, seasoned and wound around a cane and grilled). The owners are fighting a long war against the Mafia; frequently threatened, they are taking a firm stand. Closed Tues. *Via Alessandro Paternostro 58, T: 091 320264. Map p. 21, 16.*

€ **Nino 'u Ballerino**. ■ One of the most famous *meusari* of Palermo, who serves his snacks and sandwiches with the speed and the grace of a dancer, as his family has been doing since 1802. Street food at its best, not to be missed. Open evenings 6–10. *Corso Finocchiaro Aprile 76. Map p. 20, 9.*

Petralia Sottana (*map p. 542, D2*)

€ **Pomieri**. Country restaurant renowned for grilled meats, very appetising, good value for money. Also doubles as a hotel. *Contrada Pomieri, T: 0921 649998.*

Piana degli Albanesi (*map p. 542, B2*)
€ **Argomesi**. An old converted stable in the countryside near Piana prepares organic food to traditional recipes, fresh home-made pasta, local cheese, meat and vegetables; grilled vegetables or lamb chops are particularly good. Desserts are traditional too, a choice between a *cannolo di ricotta* or *cassata*. *Strada Provinciale 5, Contrada Dingoli, T: 091 8561008.*

Polizzi Generosa (*map p. 542, D2*)
€€ **'U Bagghiu**. Traditional mountain fare, accompanied by local wines. Also pizza. Closed Tues evening. *Via Gagliardo 3, T: 0921 551111.*

San Giuseppe Jato (*map p. 542, A2*)
€€ **Da Totò**. Home-made tagliatelle, delicious desserts. Closed Fri evening. *Via Vittorio Emanuele 251, T: 091 8573344.*

Terrasini (*map p. 542, A1*)
€€€ **Il Bavaglino**. Tiny restaurant, the realm of Giuseppe Costa, a gifted chef. Traditional dishes with an innovative twist, and the use of unusual ingredients; good wine cellar. *Via Benedetto Saputo 20, T: 091 8682285.*

Ustica (*map p. 542, C1*)
€€€ **Baia del Sole**. In a panoramic position, a cosy trattoria serving delicious stuffed baked squid, and pasta with capers, aubergines, shrimps, basil and tomato. *Contrada Spalmatore (they will provide transport to/from restaurant if you call them first), T: 091 8449175.*

€€ **Mario**. Spaghetti with sea urchins and other superb pasta dishes, including one made with cuttle-fish ink, or soup made with the local lentils, indicated by Slow Food as one of Sicily's best products. Open summer only. *Piazza Umberto 21, T: 091 8449505.*

€€ **Schiticchio**. Close to the Town Hall, a *trattoria* offering an exciting array of dishes prepared with fresh local fish and vegetables. Sicilian wines. Open every day in summer. *Via Tre Mulini, T: 091 8449662.*

€€ **Giulia**. Booking essential. The restaurant is small and very famous. Chef Pina specialises in *cernia* (grouper), either marinated in lemon, or cooked with breadcrumbs, tomato, olive oil, lemon and garlic. *Via San Francesco 16, T: 091 8449039.*

LOCAL SPECIALITIES

Alia Bar Centrale, at Via Garibaldi 32, has *scattate*, biscuits made of almonds and cinnamon, unique to Alia.

Bagheria Bar Ester, in the centre at Via Palagonia 113, is famous for ice cream and exquisite *cannoli di ricotta*, while at Don Gino, Via Dante 66, they make the best espresso coffee in Sicily.

Bisacquino The unique crunchy biscuits, called *pane nero*, are made from roughly chopped and toasted almonds. Find them at the Caffé Prezioso.

Castelbuono Fiasconaro (*Piazza Margherita 10, www.fiasconaro.com*). The Fiasconaro brothers produce nougat, liqueurs and a very particular cake called *mannetto*, a light-textured sponge cake iced with manna, which served warm, is the ideal accompaniment for tea or hot chocolate. It keeps for weeks, so you can take it home. They also prepare the typical Milanese Christas cake, *panettone*, using sourdough brought back from Lombardy by their grandfather 60 years ago. In October 2007 Fiasconaro goodies were among the foodstuffs provided for the astronauts on the *Discovery*. Another confection unique to Castelbuono is *testa di turco*, a kind of blancmange with a layer of flaky pastry in the middle, sprinkled with chocolate and cinnamon; find it at the Antica Gelateria del Corso (*Corso Umberto 46*), where Antonio also makes marvellous almond cakes, ice cream, and chocolate-covered roasted almonds. For pure manna and home-made *salame* and sausage, go to Mario Puccio (*Contrada Santa Lucia*).

Castellana Sicula This village in the heart of the Madonie Mountains is famous for the sourdough bread baked at the Forno Librizzi (*Corso Mazzini 17*), and also for the exquisite hand-made chocolates filled with almond or pistachio paste sold by Pasticceria Feruzza (*Corso Mazzini 129*).

Cefalù Anchovies, in olive oil with capers or chillies, are prepared by the fishermen of Cefalù. You will easily find them. Ciccio (*Lungomare Cefalù, www.ciccioshoes.it*) makes sports shoes to measure; he made his name by making shoes for Formula 1 racing drivers.

Monreale As might be expected, there is an excellent school for mosaics in the town where young people learn the art. Examples can be purchased in Piazza Guglielmo II, or at the Laboratorio del Mosaico Cangemi (*Via Torres 28, www.mosaicimonreale.net*). Monreale pottery is also attractive; here they specialise in applying brightly-coloured glazed fruits and flowers to earthenware vases. Elisa Messina is a talented craftswoman (*Via Torres 32, www.elisamessina.it*). Excellent Monreale sourdough bread can be found at Antica Forneria Tusa (*Via Pietro Novelli 25, closed Sun afternoon*). All the Monreale DOC wines can be found at Azienda Agricola Principi di Spadafora (*Contrada Virzì, T: 091 514952, 091 6703322, www.spadafora.com. Call for appointment, possible every day except Sun*).

Palermo Il Laboratorio Italiano (*Via Principe di Villafranca 42*) is a good address for Sicilian pottery. Domus Artis (*Via Nino Basile 6, near Casa Professa*), is where Luigi Arini still makes exquisite religious articles using wax, silver and coral, as established by a Vatican ruling in 1566 which indicated the materials, colours and symbolism that artists and craftsmen could use. Pasticceria Cappello (*Via Colonna Rotta 68*), is famed for prize-winning cakes; the delectable *torta sette veli*, a glossy

black confection with seven different kinds of chocolate, was invented here. Scimone (*Via Miceli 18*) also sells good confectionery, ask for *dita d'apostolo* (Apostle's finger biscuits). I Peccatucci di Mamma Andrea (*Via Principe di Scordia 67, www.mammaandrea.it*) for homemade chocolates, pralines, jams and liqueurs. Massaro (*Via Basile 24; University*), for superb breakfast pastries, perhaps the best in town. Bar Alba (*Piazza Don Bosco 7/c; Stadium*) is worth a trip for its famous snacks, ice cream and pastries (closed Mon).

There are silversmiths at Piazza Meli (Cala), coppersmiths near Ponte dell'Ammiraglio, and tinkers in Via Calderai. The picturesque Via Bara all'Olivella (Opera House) is a hive of activity, where many craftsmen can be found (but don't eat in the *trattorie*). At no. 40, Antonio Cuticchio makes marionettes for his brother Mimmo, celebrated *puparu*, who has his puppet theatres close by (*at nos 48 & 95; he will show you them free of charge, Tues–Fri 10–1 & 4–7.30; plays presented usually Sat and Sun 6.30; T: 091 323400, www.figlidartecuticchio.com*). At no. 60 is a toymaker offering rocking-horses, model trains and dolls of wood or *papier mâché*, while at no. 74 you will find La Coppola Storta (the Twisted Cap; a reference to the way Mafia members don their headgear), where young people sell the cloth caps of various materials that they manufacture in a large building confiscated from the Mafia by the magistrates, and at no. 64 is a nice shop, Ceramica d'Arte, with pottery from Caltagirone.

The street markets of Palermo are justly famous, and should not be missed even by the most hurried visitor. The stalls are set up in the morning around 8 and stay open all day until around 7.30. The biggest are: Vucciria (Piazza Caracciolo), for produce (especially fish); Ballarò (Piazza Ballarò), for produce and household goods; Capo (Via Sant'Agostino), for clothes, cloth and shoes; Papireto (Piazza Peranni), for antiques and bric-à-brac, usually called *Mercato delle Pulci*, flea market. Lattarini (Piazza Borsa, Via Roma), the name derives from *suq al-attarin*, perfume market, but nowadays they sell cloth, ropes, knitting yarn, underwear, boots and army surplus gear. Another food market opens in the afternoon and evening in Corso Scinà. A weekly antique market is held on Sun morning in Piazza Marina.

Piana degli Albanesi Kalinikta (*Corso Kastriota 163*), is the place to come for the celebrated enormous *cannoli di ricotta*, but they make delicious ice cream and granita too. Lucito (*Via Presidente Costantini 3*), is a goldsmith specialising in perfect replicas of antique Sicilian jewellery.

Polizzi Generosa The speciality of the local confectioners is a pie made with fresh cheese, sugar, candied pumpkin, chocolate and cinnamon, called *sfoglio*. The classic address is Pasticceria Al Castello (*Piazza Castello 10, closed Wed*), or try L'Orlando (*Via Rampolla 1*).

San Giuseppe Jato Monreale DOC Merlot is produced here, on the Feotto dello Jato estate (*Contrada Feotto, www.feottodellojato.it*).

Sclafani Bagni For the DOC wines for which this area is so famous, you can visit the Tasca d'Almerita estate, Tenuta Regaleali in Contrada Regaleali (*call to request visit, closed Sat, Sun and holidays, T: 092 1544011, www.tascadalmerita.it*).

Ustica Ustica's historic coffee house is the Bar Centrale (*Piazza Umberto 8*), a popular meeting-place, justly famous for the fruit *granita*.

FESTIVALS & EVENTS

Bisacquino Good Friday, procession which slowly weaves its way through the streets, singing the Passion of Christ in Sicilian. The ceremony ends when one of the young men of the town is symbolically crucified.

Caccamo Palm Sunday, *'U Signuruzzu a cavaddu'*, little boys chosen for their good behaviour mime the entry of Jesus and the Apostles into Jerusalem (*Info: T: 091 8103207*).

Castelbuono 24 June, feast of the patron San Giovanni, with nocturnal banqueting on boiled potatoes and broad beans (*Info: T: 0921 671124*). Aug, *Arruccata di li Ventimiglia*, a historical pageant (*Info: T: 0921 643607*).

Cefalù 14 Aug, an evening procession of fishing boats, lit up with lanterns, goes from the harbour to Point Kalura and back for the *Madonna della Luce*. Sept, Sherbeth Festival, dedicated to ice cream, *granita* and sorbets (*Info: www.sherbethfestival.com*).

Collesano Easter, *Festa della Casazza*, when the life of Christ is re-enacted (*Info: www. madonielive.com*).

Gangi Palm Sunday, solemn Procession of the Confraternities of white-robed worshippers accompanied by drummers, visiting all the churches of the town (*Info: Municipio T: 0921 644076, www.pasquainsicilia.it*).

Gibilmanna 1st Sunday in Sept, pilgrimage.

Gratteri On the first Thur after Corpus Domini (June) a very ancient ceremony takes place, with much beating of drums, going back to the time when the young men used to go hunting wolves on that day. 8–9 Sept, feast of the patron St James (*Info: www.gratteri.org*).

Isnello 5–7 Sept, feast of the patron St Nicholas. 29 June, broad bean and boiled potato feast. 1 May, pancake feast (*Info: www. siciliainfesta.com*).

Mezzojuso Last Sun before Lent, *Il Mastro di Campo*, when the town inhabitants enact the story of Count Cabrera who, madly in love, tries to make away with Queen Blanche of Navarre. Cannons are fired, biscuits are thrown into the crowd, Garibaldi's soldiers intervene, then the actors offer wine, cheese and barbecued sausages to everybody (*Info: Pro Loco T: 0918 203892, www.prolocomezzojuso.it*).

Monreale Nov, *Settimana Musica Sacra*, a week dedicated to religious music, performed in the cathedral (*Info: www.settimanamusicasacra.it*).

Palermo 10–15 July, *Fistinu di Santa Rosalia*, with celebrations including theatre performances, concerts, fireworks and a street procession with the statue of St Rosalia on a huge cart drawn by oxen. 3–4 Sept, pilgrimage (with a torchlight procession) to the shrine of St Rosalia on Mt Pellegrino. Nov–Dec, *Festival di Morgana*, annual meeting at the Pasqualino Puppet Museum of the puppeteers of Sicily, with plays, music, and exhibitions (*Info: www.festivaldimorgana.it*).

Piana degli Albanesi Easter celebrations are very special here. On Good Friday and Easter Sunday women wear gorgeous traditional dress, ancient Albanian hymns are sung in the cathedral, there are readings from the Gospel in seven languages, then a colourful procession takes place, and the traditional red eggs are distributed (*Info: Pro Loco T: 091 8574504*).

Polizzi Generosa end Aug, hazelnut fair with parades of Sicilian carts and folk music (*Info: www.siciliainfesta.com*). 3rd Sun in Sept, feast of St Gandulph. 26 Dec, festivities when a huge bonfire is lit in front of the ruined church of La Commenda (*Info: www.polizzigenerosa.it*).

Prizzi Easter Sun, *L'Abballu dei Diavoli*, or Dance of the Devils. In the morning, Death, dressed in yellow and the Devils dressed in red and wearing metal masks, race through the streets trying to capture souls to send to Hell (the nearby inn). In the afternoon the Madonna meets her Son Jesus, and they and the Angels, who fight with swords, defeat the Devils and Good triumphs over Evil once again (*Info: www.comune.prizzi.pa.it*).

Sclafani Bagni Last Sun in June, procession of the Ecce Homo (*Info: www.siciliainfesta.com*).

Terrasini Easter Sat and Sun, *'A festa di li Schietti* is probably of pagan origin and means 'the feast of the Bachelors'. A young man who wants to prove his strength has to lift an orange tree weighing about 50kg with one hand, then parade it around the town on his shoulders until he reaches the home of the girl he admires, when the orange tree is raised again. If she is suitably impressed with his strength, she may decide to marry him (*Info: www.prolocoterrasini.it*).

Ustica June–July, *Rassegna Internazionale di Attività Subacquee* dedicated to underwater activities, with meetings, competitions and diving, including the chance to go down in an old-fashioned diving suit (*Info: www.riasustica.it*).

THE PROVINCE OF TRAPANI

Trapani (pron: Trápani) is the most important city on the west coast of the island and the capital of a province where the wide, open landscapes, full of light reflected off the sea, are picked out in white, straggling, flat-roofed villages; very North African in atmosphere. Selinunte and Segesta, two of the island's most exciting archaeological areas, form part of this province, as do the fascinating old cities of Erice, Mazara del Vallo, Marsala and Alcamo, and the beautiful offshore islands of Pantelleria, close to Tunisia, and the Aegadians: Favignana, Levanzo and Marettimo. The ancient industry of extracting salt from seawater evaporated in the salt pans is still an important part of the local economy and produces a quality of salt that matches the best in the world; local coral is still worked in Trapani and Sciacca. Other local products include excellent olive oil guaranteed by the DOP label, pickled olives, cheese and black bread, but the place of honour goes to the fine DOC wines, including the various Marsalas, the acclaimed Bianco d'Alcamo, and those from Pantelleria; the province of Trapani, in fact, contains more than half of the vineyards of Sicily and, after Bordeaux, is the second largest wine-producing district in Europe.

Harvesting salt from the Trapani lagoon, painstakingly trawling it from the water.

TRAPANI

The city of Trapani (*map p. 543, B1*) lies below the headland of Mt San Giuliano, with the Aegadian Islands close offshore. The old city occupies a scimitar-shaped promontory between the open sea to the north and the port and salt marshes to the south, although from inland the town is approached through extensive modern suburbs laid out on a regular chessboard pattern. The elegant shops in the traffic-free old town have inviting window displays, and the Corso is lined with interesting monumental buildings. The collection of decorative arts in the Pepoli Museum is one of the best on the island, and is particularly famous for its works in coral.

HISTORY OF TRAPANI

Drepana or *Drepanon*, meaning 'scythe' (legend has it that the goddess Demeter dropped her scythe into the sea while distractedly searching for her daughter Persephone, and it became the promontory of Trapani), was the earliest recorded settlement here, when it was the port of *Eryx* (modern Erice). It was raised to the status of a Carthaginian city when Hamilcar Barca brought down part of the population of Eryx in 260 BC, but it was captured for the Romans by Catulus only 19 years later, in 241 BC. Trapani acquired strategic importance as the maritime crossroads between Tunis, Anjou and Aragon in the 13th century. In 1270 King Theodore of Navarre died in Trapani of typhoid, contracted near Tunis while he was returning from the Crusades, and here on the 'Scoglio del Malconsiglio', a rock at the extreme end of the cape, John of Procida is supposed to have plotted the Sicilian Vespers with his confederates. Edward I of England, who also landed at Trapani on his return from the Crusades in 1272, received the news of his accession to the throne here. The city was particularly favoured by Peter of Aragon, who landed at Trapani as the saviour of Sicily in 1282 after the Sicilian Vespers, also by Charles V, and passed a relatively prosperous time under the Spanish Bourbons. The Bourbons of Naples were less popular, and Trapani took part in the 1848 rebellion with such fervour that the city was awarded the silver medal for valour after Unification. The city was heavily bombed during World War Two.

EXPLORING TRAPANI

Piazza Vittorio Veneto and Via Garibaldi

In the large Piazza Vittorio Emanuele (*map 3–4*), laid out in the mid-19th century, is a monument (1882) to King Vittorio Emanuele II by Giovanni Dupré, one of his last works. From here Viale Regina Margherita skirts the north side of Villa Margherita, a charming garden laid out in the late 19th century, to Piazza Vittorio Veneto (*map 3*), the administrative centre of the city, with early 20th-century buildings including the

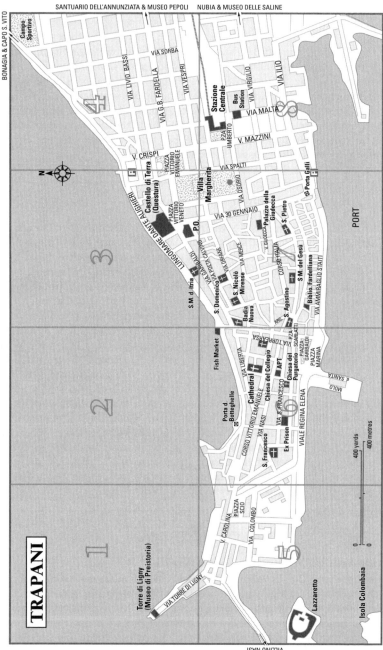

elegant Art Deco post office (1924). Close by is the Castello di Terra, a castle of ancient origin much reconstructed over the centuries and converted into a barracks in the 19th century. The outer walls now surround the modern police station (Questura). Streets to the north give access to the seafront, with a good view of the old town on the promontory.

Via Garibaldi leads towards the old centre past the 18th-century Palazzo Fardella Fontana, with an elaborate window above its portal, and the 18th-century Palazzo Riccio di Morana, decorated with stuccoes. The 17th-century church of **Santa Maria dell'Itria** (*map 3*) has a façade completed in 1745. Inside is a sculptural group of the *Holy Family* by Andrea Tipa. Beyond is the 19th-century red-brick Palazzo Staiti opposite the 18th-century Palazzo Milo.

Also on Via Garibaldi is the church of the **Carminello** (or San Giuseppe), with an 18th-century portal with bizarre twisted columns. It was built in 1699 and the statue in the apse of *Joseph and the Young Christ Child* is a charming 18th-century sculpture by Antonio Nolfo (an earlier version of the statue, used for processions, is kept in the sacristy). A wooden Crucifix in the church is attributed to Giacomo Tartaglio.

San Domenico and San Nicolò

The Salita San Domenico (with steps and cobbled paving) leads up to the church of **San Domenico** (*map 7; open 9–12 & 4–7; T: 0923 23362*), with a blind 14th-century rose-window. The interior contains a remarkable wooden Crucifix (thought to date from the 14th century) in an 18th-century chapel by Giovanni Biagio Amico in the left aisle. Near the entrance is a 15th-century fresco fragment. The sanctuary preserves the sarcophagus of Manfred, son of Frederick III of Aragon. A chapel behind has more recently-discovered fresco fragments of the 14th and 15th centuries. The Baroque frames, pulpit and organ (in good condition) bear witness to the wealth of the city in the 18th century, thanks to the importance of its salt and fishing industries.

Nearby, downhill to the south, is the church of **San Nicolò Mirense**, which has a little garden. Inside is a 16th-century marble tabernacle on the sanctuary wall and in the left transept a striking sculptural group of *Christ Between the Two Thieves*, a realistic 18th-century work in wood and *papier mâché* by a local sculptor. Via delle Arti and Via della Badia lead back to Via Garibaldi and the 17th-century façade of the **Badia Nuova** (or Santa Maria del Soccorso), with a fine interior decorated in pink and grey marble and elaborate organ lofts.

Via Torrearsa and the old Jewish district

From the Badia, Via Torrearsa leads right, past the 16th-century church of the Carmine, with a fine exterior with tall pilasters and a high cornice, to the seafront passing an attractive market building (1874; *map 6*). There is a fountain with a statue of Venus in the piazza. Via Torrearsa leads in the other direction to Palazzo Senatorio, used as municipal offices, built in 1672, which has an unusual façade with statues on the upper part.

Near the southern end of Via Torrearsa is the restored church of **Sant'Agostino** (*map 7*), with its 14th-century rose window and portal, now the Polo Espositivo

Sant'Agostino (*open summer Mon–Fri 4.30–7.30, Sat and Sun 9.30–12.30 & 4–8, winter 9.30–1 every day; T: 0923 869123, www.santagostinotrapani.it*) for exhibitions of religious art. The church, almost completely destroyed during the bombing raids of World War Two, was built for the Knights Templar by Roger II in 1118, close to their hospice for the assistance of Crusaders or pilgrims to Jerusalem. After a fire in 1425, the ceiling was replaced with an unusual series of painted wooden panels representing grotesque figures and allegories. The surviving ones are now partly in the local Pepoli Museum and partly in the Palazzo Abatellis gallery in Palermo.

The Saturn fountain here (a reference to the mythical foundation of the city by that god) is on the site of a 14th-century fountain. Nearby is the **Biblioteca Fardelliana** (*map 7; open 9–1.30 & 3–7.30, Sat 9–1, closed Sun and holidays; T: 0923 21506*), the prestigious civic library of the province, housed in the former church of San Giacomo, with a fine Mannerist façade. Opened to the public in 1830, it contains many important manuscripts, a collection of etchings, and some 118,000 volumes. Ask to see the Sala Fardella; its marble columns were brought here from the old church of St Roch, and in their turn they come from the great mosque of Arab Trapani. Originating in Tunis, they bear inscriptions from the Koran.

In the rebuilt district of San Pietro, back towards Villa Margherita, is **Santa Maria del Gesù** (*map 7; open Tues–Sat 8.30–12.30, Sun 6–8*), a church with a transitional 16th-century façade and a Renaissance south doorway in Catalan Gothic style bearing an *Annunciation*. The luminous, simple interior, golden in colour, contains a decorative niche with a very beautiful *Madonna and Child* in enamelled terracotta by Andrea della Robbia, under a marble baldachin by Antonello Gagini.

Further east in the former **Jewish district**, is the unusual Palazzo della Giudecca, usually called 'Lo Spedaletto', with an embossed tower, rusticated walls and 16th-century windows recalling the highly decorated plateresque style of Castile.

Along Corso Vittorio Emanuele

The broad, handsome Corso Vittorio Emanuele (*map 6*) leads west from Via Torrearsa towards the end of the promontory. On the right is the **Chiesa del Collegio dei Gesuiti**, built c. 1614–40 and designed by Natale Masuccio. The Baroque façade was added later. Beyond the monumental former Collegio dei Gesuiti (now a school), preceded by a portico, is the **Cathedral of San Lorenzo**, built by Giovanni Biagio Amico in 1743. On the fourth altar in the south aisle is a *Crucifixion* attributed to the local 17th-century artist Giacomo Lo Verde, a follower of Pietro Novelli. On the second north altar is a painting of *St George* by Andrea Carreca and on the fourth, a fine *Deposition*, showing Flemish influence.

In front of the cathedral Via Giglio leads to the **church of the Purgatorio** (*closed for repairs*) where the figures of the *Misteri*, statuary groups made of wood, cloth, *papier-mâché* and glue, are kept in between the Good Friday processions. The church has a fine tiled dome and elaborate façade by Giovanni Biagio Amico.

Nearby in Via San Francesco is a 17th-century **ex-prison house**, with four caryatids on its façade, and, further along, on the opposite side of the street, the church of the

Immacolatella, with a delightful apse by Giovanni Biagio Amico (1732). At the end of the street, the green-domed church of **San Francesco** (13th–17th centuries) can be seen, next to a beautiful doorway. Inside, on the left, is a curious 17th-century tombstone dedicated to the 'death of the nation of Armenia', with a bilingual inscription.

The Corso continues past (left) the 18th-century Palazzo Berardo Ferro, which has an inviting courtyard, and then Palazzo Alessandro Ferro (1775), decorated with a clock and busts in medallions. Beyond on the right is the little **Porta delle Botteghelle** (13th century); outside can be seen the defensive fortifications which protected the town from the sea.

The Torre di Ligny headland

The promontory ends at the **Torre di Ligny** (*map 1*), a fortress built in 1671 by the Spanish viceroy. It has been well restored to house the Museo del Mare e di Preistoria (*open 9–12.30 & 3.30–6.30, Aug also 10.30–midnight, Sun and holidays open mornings only; T: 0923 23600, may be closed for rearrangement*), with a particularly interesting section devoted to submarine archaeology, displaying Phoenician, Greek, Roman, Spanish and Egyptian anchors and amphorae, and a bronze helmet probably lost at sea during the First Punic War. Many of the objects on display were recovered by local fishermen. There is a spectacular panorama from the roof.

From beside the Torre di Ligny there is a view across the bay to the small island dominated by the **Castello della Colombaia** (*map 5*), once the main defence of the port, and the base for the Romans' siege operations in 241 BC. Diodorus Siculus tells of a castle built here by Hamilcar Barca in 260 BC. Under the Arabs the castle was restored and used as a lighthouse, and the Normans strengthened it. In 1320 Frederick III of Aragon added the beautiful octagonal tower, and in 1714 the lantern was added by Giovanni Biagio Amico. It was first used as a prison in 1821, for rebellious Sicilians who were claiming independence, and later for common criminals, until 1965 when it was abandoned; at the time of writing a local association was fighting to save it, and restoration work was planned to begin (*see www.colombaiatrapani.altervista.org*).

Santuario dell'Annunziata

Inland, in the modern part of town, at Via Conte Agostino Pepoli 179 is the Santuario dell'Annunziata (*c. 4km from the centre, beyond map 4; bus nos 1, 10 and 11; open 7–12 & 4–7, July–Aug late closing at 8; T: 0923 539184, www.madonnaditrapani.com*). A church on this site has belonged to the Carmelite Order since the 13th century, when they arrived here as refugees from Mt Carmel in the Holy Land. The present structure dates from the early 14th century, rebuilt in 1760. Little remains of the 14th-century church except the west front with a rose window which overlooks a garden. The bell-tower dates from 1650.

The unusual grey and white interior was redesigned in the 18th century by Giovanni Biagio Amico. Off the south aisle is the beautiful Cappella dei Pescatori (the fishermen's chapel), built in 1481, perhaps an adaptation of an earlier chapel. On the left of the presbytery is the Cappella dei Marinai (the sailors' chapel), another attractive chapel built in the 16th century in a mixture of styles. From the sanctuary, which has a lovely apse, two elegant 16th-century doorways lead into the Cappella della Madonna; here another arch, with sculptures by Antonino Gagini (1531–37) and a bronze gate of 1591 by Giuliano Musarra, gives access to the inner sanctuary containing a highly-venerated 14th-century statue of the Madonna and Child, known as the **Madonna di Trapani**, a very fine work by Nino Pisano or his workshop. Below the statue is a tiny silver model of Trapani by the 17th-century silversmith Vincenzo Bonaiuto, who also made the silver reliquary statue in the Chapel of Albert of Trapani (a 14th-century Carmelite, patron of the city), to the right of the Cappella della Madonna.

The Museo Regionale Pepoli

The Pepoli museum (*beyond map 4; entrance to the right of the Santuario church façade, open Mon–Sat 9–1, Sun and holidays 9–12, Wed, Fri and Sat also 3–7; T: 0923 553269*), housed in the former Carmelite convent, holds a municipal collection formed in 1827, a group of Neapolitan paintings which belonged to General Giovanni Battista Fardella, and a large fine and applied art collection donated by Count Agostino Pepoli in 1906. The exhibits are beautifully arranged and well labelled. The entrance is through the paved 16th–17th-century cloisters, with palm trees.

Two rooms on the ground floor contain architectural fragments and a wooden ceiling salvaged from a chapel, along with a sculpted 16th-century portal by Bartolomeo Berrettaro, a stoup of 1486 from the Santuario dell'Annunziata, and works by the Gagini, notably a figure of St James the Great (1522), by Antonello Gagini.

The first floor is devoted to the museum's collections of paintings and decorative arts, the archaeological collection and the Arab art section. Paintings range from Roberto di Oderisio's *Pietà* (c. 1380) and the early 15th-century Master of Trapani's polyptych, *Madonna and Child with Saints* (from the church of Sant'Antonio Abate), and *St Francis Receiving the Stigmata*, attributed to Titian, to a portrait of the politician Nunzio Nasi (c. 1902) by Giacomo Balla. Displays of wooden figurines by Giovanni Matera illustrate the *Massacre of the Innocents* in 16 tableaux.

The superb collection of decorative arts, the work of local craftsmen from the 17th–19th centuries, includes scenes of the *Adoration of the Magi* and *Nativity* by Andrea Tipa in wax, alabaster and coral; a late 17th-century salt cellar; magnificent 18th–19th-century Sicilian coral jewellery and a 17th-century chalice. Particularly important are the charming crib figures, the best by Giovanni Matera, and Nativity scenes. Elaborate 17th-century objects in red coral, a skill for which Trapani is particularly famous, include a *Crucifixion* and a candelabrum.

The archaeological collection contains finds from Erice, Selinunte and Mozia, and coins of the 5th century BC. Arab art displays textiles, majolica, lamps, glassware and funerary inscriptions (10th–12th centuries). At the top of the stairs, in the first corridor, are majolica-tiled floors, including one with a splendid scene of tuna fishing (*the Mattanza; see box on p. 168*). The small prints and drawings collection here includes works by the printmakers Stefano Della Bella and Jacques Callot. The flag of *Il Lombardo*, the ship sailed by Garibaldi and the 'Thousand', is owned by the museum.

View across the salt-pans at Trapani.

THE SALT-PANS OF TRAPANI

The *saline* or salt-pans of Trapani can be seen from the secondary road which runs from the port to Marsala. A number of windmills survive, turning Archimedes' screws in order to raise the seawater from one pan to the next in spring, and to grind the salt in summer. Much of the area is now a nature reserve run by the WWF (Riserva Naturale delle Saline di Trapani e Paceco; *T: 0923 867700, 327 5621529, www.salineditrapani.it*), and flamingoes, great white herons, avocets (symbol of the reserve) and black-winged stilts are frequently seen. At Nubia, on the coast c. 5km south of Trapani, is the **Museo del Sale** (*map p. 543, B2; open 10.30–5; Sun and holidays call first to make sure, T: 0923 867442 or 0923 867700*). Here an old wooden mill is now used to illustrate the ancient salt-extracting industry, started here by the Phoenicians and still working a number of pans between Trapani and Marsala. Mounds of salt, protected by tiles, are a common sight in the area, the salt being exported all over the world. The wind and sun here favour evaporation, while the seawater has a naturally high level of salinity. From February to March seawater is pumped by the windmills from a canal into the salt-pans. The water level is gradually decreased, encouraging the evaporation process and the water assumes a reddish colour as the mineral content becomes more concentrated. The harvest begins in July, before total evaporation, avoiding the deposit of harmful minerals; the salt is then raked from the pans into mounds to dry.

ERICE

Erice (*map p. 543, B1*) is a medieval walled town perched on top of Mt San Giuliano (751m), an isolated limestone spur high above the sea. It can be reached in 10mins by cableway from Trapani. The number of permanent residents is about 300, and many of the houses are occupied only in summer by people from Trapani or Palermo, who come here to escape the heat: the number of inhabitants in August rises to about 5,000. By far the most populous part of Erice is at the foot of the hill, close to Trapani. The locals call their town *'u Munti*, the mountain. It is often shrouded in a mist, known as *il velo di Venere* (the 'veil of Venus'), and it can be very chilly here, the steep cobbled streets deserted and slippery, even snowy in winter, which contributes to the feeling of isolation. The perfect triangular shape of the town makes it difficult to find one's bearings, despite the fact that it is so small. The view to the north of the pyramid-shaped Mt Cofano, one of the most beautiful promontories on the coast of Sicily, is exceptional. To the southwest there is another memorable view of Trapani and the Aegadian Islands and, on a clear day, Cape Bon in Tunisia can be seen, and looking east, even Mt Etna.

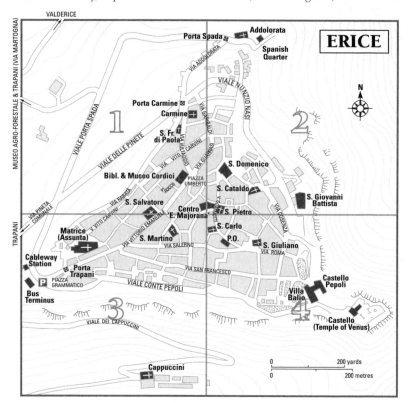

HISTORY OF ERICE

Eryx, an Elymian city said to have been founded by Aeneas and his surviving Trojans, was famous all over the Mediterranean for the magnificent temple of the goddess of fertility, known to the Romans as Venus Erycina. This splendid site, naturally defended and visible for miles around, was a noted landmark for navigators from Africa. An altar to the goddess was first set up here by the Sicans and the sanctuary was much frequented during the Elymian and Phoenician period. Every year, the Carthaginians (who venerated her as Astarte) released from here hundreds of white doves and one red one to represent the goddess, which arrived nine days later at the temple of Sicca Veneria at Carthage. This ceremony took place in mid-August (by a strange coincidence, the feast of the patron saint of Erice, Our Lady of Custonaci, is always held on 16th August). In 415 BC the inhabitants of nearby Segesta took the visiting Athenian ambassadors to see the rich treasury of the temple, which convinced Athens to take their side against Selinunte and Syracuse (they were pretending to be richer than they were, and thus capable of financing the expedition), a decision which led to the fatal attack on Syracuse in 413 BC and the consequent defeat of the Athenians. Captured by Pyrrhus in 278 BC, Erice was destroyed in 260 by Hamilcar Barca. The Roman consul Lucius Junius Pullus took the hill in 248 and was besieged by Hamilcar, who was himself blockaded by a Roman army, until the Carthaginians were defeated by the Romans, led by Catulus. The cult of Venus Erycina reached its maximum splendour under the Romans and the sanctuary was restored for the last time by Tiberius and Claudius. The Saracens called the mountain *Gebel Hamed*. Count Roger, who had seen St Julian in a dream while besieging it, changed its name to Monte San Giuliano, a name it kept until 1934. The city thrived in the 18th century (with a population of around 12,000) and there were many religious communities. The town is now known for its Ettore Majorana Cultural Centre, founded by the local physicist Antonino Zichichi in 1963.

EXPLORING ERICE

The grey stone houses of Erice (mostly dating from the 14th–17th centuries), hidden behind their high walls, as well as the beautiful cobbled streets, give the town an austere aspect. But behind the walls are many charming courtyards, some of which have little gardens. There are no fewer than 60 churches in the town, testifying to the once large population. The entrance to the town is by Porta Trapani, beyond which Via Vittorio Emanuele climbs steeply uphill. Just to the left is the **Matrice** (Assunta; *map 3; open 10–1 & 3.30–6*), which has a beautiful fortified Gothic exterior. The porch dates from 1426. The splendid detached campanile was built as an Aragonese look-out tower c. 1315 by Frederick III, several years before the foundation of the church. The interior

Annunciation by Antonello Gagini (1525) in the Biblioteca Comunale of Erice.

received its impressive neo-Gothic form, with an elaborate cream-coloured vault, in 1852. The apse is filled with a huge marble altarpiece (1513) by Giuliano Mancino. In the sanctuary, through a small round opening on the left wall, a fresco fragment of an angel can be seen, the only part of the 15th-century decoration of the church to have survived. In a chapel on the left, the 16th-century painting of the *Madonna of Custonaci* (the venerated patron of Erice) was replaced in 1892 by the present copy when the original was taken back to the sanctuary of Custonaci on the coast. The next chapel, with a beautiful dome, dates from 1568. In a chapel on the right-hand side is a marble *Madonna* (1469) by Domenico Gagini, with a finely-carved base. Outside, on the south wall, there are nine iron crosses, said to come from the Temple of Venus (*see p. 132*).

Via Vittorio Emanuele continues steeply uphill past several old shopfronts and characteristic courtyards. At a fork, the road continues left past the old ruined Gothic church of **San Salvatore** beside a lovely old narrow street which leads downhill (and has a distant view of the sea). To the right Via Bonaventura Provenzano ends at a house with a Baroque doorway and window near the church of **San Martino** (*map 3; open 3–6*), with another Baroque portal, and an interesting 15th-century statue of the *Madonna* in the interior. Just before reaching Piazza Umberto, beside a charming café in a 19th-century palace, a flight of steps leads down left to the monumental doorway with four columns of San Rocco (*closed*).

Piazza Umberto

The central Piazza Umberto (*map 1*) is the only large open space in the town. An elegant *palazzo* is now used by a bank, and a long 19th-century building houses the Town Hall and the **Biblioteca Comunale e Museo Civico Cordici** (*open Mon–Fri 8–2*), named after the local historian Antonino Cordici (1586–1666). The library was founded in 1867 with material from the suppressed convents of the city. It now has c. 20,000 volumes. In the entrance hall is a beautiful relief of the *Annunciation* by Antonello Gagini, one of his finest works (1525), and a number of inscriptions. Upstairs in the small museum are interesting local archaeological finds (including a small Attic head of Venus, 5th century BC), Church vestments, paintings, and a 17th-century wooden Crucifix. Close by is the tiny **opera house**, Teatro Gebel el Hamid.

Via Guarrasi leads north out of the piazza and immediately on the left, a stepped street (Via Argentieri) leads down across Via Carvini into Via Vultaggio, which continues to wind down past the 17th-century church of **San Francesco di Paola** (*open 10.30–12.30*) with a Classical façade. The beautiful interior was restored in 1954 by an American benefactor. It has white stucco decoration in very low relief on the walls and the barrel vault, a worn tiled floor in the sanctuary, fine woodwork, and popular votive statues.

Lower down on the right is the 14th-century Palazzo Militari with Gothic traces, next to the Gothic church of the Carmine (*closed*). **Porta Carmine** stands nearby, with a worn, headless statue of the Blessed Albert of Trapani, a patron of Erice, in a niche on its outer face.

The town walls

The magnificent walls, which stretch from Porta Spada (*map 2*) to Porta Trapani (*map 3*), protected the only side of the town which has no natural defences: on all the other sides the sheer rockface made Erice one of the most impregnable fortresses on the island. The walls are constructed on huge blocks of rough stone which probably date from the Elymian period (c. 1200 BC), above which the square blocks added by the Carthaginians can be seen. The masonry in the upper parts, with stones of smaller dimension, date from the 6th century BC. The defences were strengthened in the Roman era and in the Middle Ages, and six postern gates and 16 medieval towers survive. Inside the gate the stepped Via Addolorata leads down past a well-preserved stretch of the walls, with a distant view ahead of Mt Cofano, to the church of the **Addolorata** (or Sant'Orsola; *closed*), surrounded by a little garden. It has an interesting 15th–16th-century plan. The 18th-century *Misteri* sculptures are kept here, which are taken in procession through the streets of Erice on Good Friday.

In this remote and picturesque corner of the town is the Norman **Porta Spada** (*map 2*; where the Jewish cemetery was situated). Outside Porta Spada is the so-called Spanish Quarter (Quartiere Spagnolo), a desolate group of buildings on a spur, intended by the Spanish to be the barracks for their troops in the 17th century, and for some reason never finished.

From Porta Carmine (*map 1*), Via Rabatà leads back to Porta Trapani following the walls, where there are a number of postern gates. Tiny narrow alleyways, designed to provide shelter from the wind, lead up left to Via Carvini and Piazza Umberto.

In and around Piazza San Domenico

In Piazza San Domenico, the former church of San Domenico, with a Classical porch (*map 2*), has been restored as a lecture-hall for the Ettore Majorana Centre (*see below*). From the right side of the church, Via San Cataldo leads downhill (and right) past a neo-Gothic electricity tower to the bare façade of **San Cataldo** (*open for services only*) on the edge of the old town. It was founded before 1339 and rebuilt in 1740–86. It contains a stoup of 1474 by the workshop of Domenico Gagini.

Further downhill and to the right is the church of **San Giovanni Battista** (*deconsecrated; opened on request by the religious community here*) on the cliff edge, with a 15th-century dome whose shape recalls Arab architecture, and an ancient side doorway. It contains a statue of St John the Evangelist by Antonello Gagini, and of St John the Baptist by Antonino Gagini.

From Piazza San Domenico, Via Guarnotti leads up right to the church of **San Pietro** (*open for services only*) with an 18th-century portal. The beautiful white interior by Giovanni Biagio Amico (1745) has a worn tiled floor. Beside it is an arch over the road and on the right (at no. 26) a convent has been restored as the headquarters of the **Ettore Majorana International Centre for Scientific Culture**. Founded in 1963, this has become a famous centre of learning where courses and seminars are held for scientists from all over the world.

Via Guarnotti continues past the former convent and orphanage next to the bare façade of **San Carlo** (*map 4; open 10.30–12.30*). It has a pretty majolica floor and on a side altar there is a statue of *Our Lady of Succour* with a tiny relief of St Michael Archangel on the base. The nuns' choirs are protected with carved wooden screens. On the right is the Post Office and downhill on the left is a pleasant raised piazza with the statue of the Blessed Albert of Trapani in front of the church of **San Giuliano** (*deconsecrated and used by a religious community*), which has an elegant 18th-century campanile.

Villa Balio and the Castello di Venere

Villa Balio (*map 4*) are delightful public gardens with wonderful views, laid out in 1870 by Count Agostino Pepoli on the summit of the hill. There is a monumental entrance with a double staircase on Via San Francesco. Above is the **Castello Pepoli** (*still privately owned by the Pepoli; no admission*), a Norman castle reconstructed in 1875–85 by Count Pepoli, with a 15th-century tower restored in 1973. The marvellous panorama from the terrace on the left encompasses Mt Cofano, the coast, and San Giovanni Battista on the side of the hill. Below, among the trees, you can see the abandoned neo-Gothic **Torretta**, also built by Count Pepoli.

A ramp leads down from the gardens beside the castle to Viale Conte Pepoli, on the southern edge of the hill, which continues left, ending at the 17th-century steps up to the **Castello di Venere** (*open Jan–March Sat, Sun and holidays 10–4; April–May 10–6; June–14 July 10–7; 15 July–14 Sept 10–8; 15 Sept–Oct 10–7; Nov–Dec Sat, Sun and holidays 10–4. Other days on request; T: 366 6712832 at least 24hrs before; www.comune.erice. tp.it/minisitocastello*). Above the entrance to the castle is the coat of arms of Charles V and a Gothic window. In the disappointing interior, the ruined Norman walls surround

Count Agostino Pepoli's neo-Gothic Torretta, built in the late 19th century.

the sacred area which was once the site of the famous **Temple of Venus**, many fragments of which are embedded in the masonry of the castle. A few very worn Roman fluted column drums can be seen here and the so-called Pozzo di Venere, once thought to be a ceremonial pool but more probably a silo or a water cistern. The view is breathtaking, extending to Mount Etna, Enna, and Caltabellotta.

THE TEMPLE OF VENUS & RELIGIOUS DIPLOMACY

The Temple of Venus in Eryx was highly regarded by the Phoenicians (who worshipped the goddess as Astarte) and by the Greeks, who considered it to be one of the most important temples of Aphrodite in the Mediterranean. This status allowed the city to maintain a privileged position on the island while it was being contested by the Carthaginians and Greeks between the 6th and 3rd centuries BC. Thanks to a quirk of mythological fortune, the people of Eryx were also able to build an important relationship with the rising power of the Mediterranean, Rome, that was of even greater benefit to them in the long run. Aeneas, one of the key figures in Roman mythology, was the son of Venus and the story was told that he had visited Eryx and founded the temple on his way to the Italian peninsula. This myth led, in 215 BC, to a temple of Venus Erycina being dedicated on the Roman Capitol, and another being founded near the city about 30 years later, outside the Porta Collina. The Roman governors of Sicily greatly honoured the temple in Eryx and funnelled tax contributions from some of the other cities of Sicily into its coffers. Thanks to this mythological kinship link, the people of Eryx were also able to persuade the Roman emperor Tiberius to pay for the later restoration of the temple.

The cult of Venus Erycina was also bound up with sacred prostitution. As Strabo notes, 'Eryx has a temple of Aphrodite that is held in exceptional honour, and in early times was full of female temple-slaves, who had been dedicated in fulfilment of vows not only by the people of Sicily but also by many people from abroad.' (*Geography, 6.2.6*). Such temple slaves began their careers at the age of 12 or 13, were trained in the art of love-making and retired at 21, rich and much sought-after as wives. Visitors to temples where sacred prostitution was practised were expected to leave gifts for the girls in exchange for the act of love, during which it was believed that they assumed the guise of the goddess herself. The girls were fed on large quantities of milk and honey to make them pleasantly fat. They seldom conceived, perhaps because they were made to drink a concoction specially prepared by the priests.

Environs of Erice

On the hillside below the town is the interesting **San Matteo Forest Museum** (*open April–Oct 8–7, Aug 9–2, Nov–March 8–4; T: 0923 869532*). It is reached from the Raganzili road. About 3km below Erice a signposted turn leads in c. 500m to the gates of the estate, run by the Azienda Forestale. A rough road (c. 1km) continues to the museum in the lovely old Baglio di San Matteo, arranged in rooms around the courtyard. The exhibits include wine and olive-presses, farm carts, saddle and tack, agricultural implements and household objects. There is also a natural history section. The beautifully kept farm of c. 500 hectares may also be visited, where San Fratello horses and Pantelleria asses are raised. It occupies a spectacular site with fine views towards Capo San Vito, and the vegetation includes dwarf palm trees, cypresses, fruit trees and forest trees.

THE NORTH COAST OF THE PROVINCE

North along the coast from Trapani, at the foot of Mt San Giuliano, is **San Cusumano** (*map p. 543, B1*) where a salt-pan windmill (now a hotel) can be seen. Ships are alerted to the low-lying islands offshore here by a lighthouse. **Pizzolungo** is the spot where, according to Virgil, Aeneas came ashore, welcomed by King Acestes of Eryx, and where his father Anchises died, obliging Aeneas to bury him here (an event commemorated by a white column). The Tonnara di Bonagia at **Bonagia** is a picturesque tuna fishery which has been restored as a hotel. Beside the little fishing port are hundreds of rusting anchors and an impressive tall tower.

Just inland, **Custonaci** has a sanctuary church, a frequent pilgrimage destination, because of the venerated 16th-century panel-painting of the *Madonna of Custonaci*, particularly generous with miracles. The economy, once based on agriculture, is now supported by a number of stone-quarries where the beautiful red marble called *perlato di Custonaci* is extracted. On the outskirts, a road (signposted 'Grotte Mangiapane') leads past an old quarry to the enormous **Grotta di Scurati** (*map p. 543, B1*) at the foot of Mt Cofano. The cave contains a hamlet, now no longer inhabited. On either side of the paved street are little houses with courtyards, bread ovens and workshops, and high above, the vault of the cave serves as a second roof. The village comes to life at Christmas, in a very successful venture called *Presepe Vivente*, or 'Living Crib' (*see p. 181*), when local people demonstrate the various trades and crafts of the area in the old houses.

Surrounded by barren hills, **Castelluzzo** has a picturesque sloping main street with one-storey houses and palm trees, and outside the town are groves of almonds and olive trees on the plain which descends to the seashore. There is a fine view of the lovely headland of Mt Cofano, with Erice in the distance. **Mount Cofano** (659m), a perfect pyramid in shape, is now a nature reserve run by the Azienda Forestale; apart from its sheer beauty, it is interesting for the abundant spring wildflowers, several of which are endemic. On the main road stands the little 16th-century domed church called the **Cubola di Santa Crescenzia**, derived from Arab models.

San Vito Lo Capo

At the tip of the headland, San Vito Lo Capo (*map p. 543, B1*) is a seaside resort, with gorgeous beaches of pale velvety sand that are among the most beautiful in Italy, and are regularly awarded the European Union Blue Banners for quality. Laid out on a regular plan in the 18th–19th centuries, the houses are bright with geraniums and bougainvilleas. In Piazza Santuario, the heart of the town, the unusual church (*open 8–8, July–Sept closes at midnight*) is a square fortress first built by the Byzantines, and later fortified by Arabs, Normans and Spaniards in turn, incorporating the ancient 4th-century chapel dedicated to the patron saint Vitus, martyred under Diocletian. In 2003 the crypt was brought to light, with a 5th-century baptismal font. Part of the building is used as a museum (*open July–Sept only 6pm–8pm & 9pm–11.30pm; T: 0923 972327*) for the collection of ex-votos and other material donated by worshippers from all over the world, and the robes said to have been worn by the saint. From the roof there is a glorious view over the bay. On the eastern side of the lovely promontory of Mt Monaco is a disused tuna fishery overlooking the Gulf of Castellammare.

A deserted road (signposted 'Calampiso') continues high above the shore across bare hills through a North African landscape, with dwarf palm trees and giant carobs, where broom and wildflowers blossom in spring, to the secondary northern entrance to the Zingaro Nature Reserve (*see below*).

Castellammare del Golfo

Cradled by mountains, Castellammare del Golfo (*map p. 543, C1*) lies on the bay, a jumble of small houses in pink, cream, yellow and orange. The fishing fleet is still active here, and the town has not yet been entirely won over to tourism. The charm of the place has attracted many second-homeowners from Northern Italy, drawn by the different pace of life, to enjoy summer evenings watching the sun drop behind the mountain and the fishermen sitting on the quay preparing the *conzu*, the bait for the night's fishing, while tempting cooking aromas waft from open doorways.

The town was originally founded by the Elymians as the harbour for the city of Segesta. The 18th-century Chiesa Madre houses a life-size majolica statue of *Our Lady of Succour* in the act of threatening the enemies of the town with her distaff, balancing the Christ Child on her left arm. The statue has been attributed to the 16th-century Della Robbia workshop in Tuscany. The castle, built by the Saracens in the 9th century and then enlarged by the Normans and later again by the Swabians, is now the seat of the Museo Civico (*open Mon–Fri 9–1; summer also Sat and Sun*), dedicated to life in the area, displaying antique clothes, furniture, tools, pots and pans, and equipment for making wine and olive oil. The old tunnery warehouses on the seafront are very attractive; some of these, too, are being restored and turned into summer homes and hotels.

Scopello

A byroad follows the coast north of Castellammare for **Scopello** (*map p. 543, C1*). Paths lead down to Cala Bianca, Cala Rossa and Baia Guidaloca, beautiful bays on the rocky coast, where the sea is particularly clear. Baia Guidaloca is locally claimed to be the fabled spot where Nausicaa found the shipwrecked Odysseus, and led him back to her father's court. Scopello itself is a tiny picturesque village (although it is in the process of being developed with hotels to provide some 8,000 extra rooms). From the little piazza, with its large drinking-trough, an archway leads into the old paved courtyard of an 18th-century *baglio*, with a few trees surrounded by one-storey houses, a number of them now used as cafés or restaurants.

Just beyond the village is the **Tonnara di Scopello**, sometimes called Marfaraggio, an important tuna fishery from the 13th century up to the middle of the last century. It is easily visible on the sea below the road, beside fantastically-shaped rocks on which ruined defence towers are situated. The buildings have been beautifully preserved. A footpath leads down to the seafront where hundreds of anchors are piled up beside the picturesque old buildings. The sea is very clear in the small cove, where feral cats teach their kittens the art of survival. The life of the fishermen who used to live here was vividly described by Gavin Maxwell in *The Ten Pains of Death* (1959).

The Zingaro Nature Reserve

The coast road soon ends at the main southern entrance to the Riserva Naturale dello Zingaro (*map p. 543, C1; open Oct–May 9–4, June–Sept 7–7.30; T: 0924 35108, www. riservazingaro.it*), a beautiful nature reserve, the first to be instituted in Sicily (6th May 1981), with 7km of unspoilt coastline that can be explored on foot along marked paths. There are also several beaches where you can swim. Dwarf palms, Mediterranean maquis, ilex, carob, olive and cork oak flourish here amid wheatfields and meadows. No motorised transport of any kind is allowed inside the park; the keepers use mules to carry out their work. Traditional farming methods are also preserved: durum wheat is sown and reaped by hand, and threshed by mules, before being ground into flour at the old mill inside the reserve.

The **museum**, about 500m from the Scopello entrance, illustrates the life of the peasants who once lived in the area, and also traditional fishing methods. The **Grotta dell'Uzzo**, also in the reserve (about 5km from the Scopello entrance), was inhabited in the Palaeolithic era and is now home to six different species of bat. Among the birds, nesting species include Bonelli's eagle, peregrine falcon, and the Sicilian form of the rock partridge; among the mammals are fox, rabbit, porcupine and the garden dormouse. An important part of the reserve consists of the coastal waters, where no fishing is allowed. There is another entrance to the park on its northern border, approached by the road from San Vito Lo Capo (*see above*), but visitors are encouraged to use the Scopello access.

SEGESTA

The temple and theatre of Segesta (*map p. 543, C2*) are two of the most magnificently-sited Classical monuments in the world. From the old road, the view of the Doric temple, on a bare hillside in deserted country amid the rolling hills west of the Gaggera river, has been admired by travellers for centuries. The theatre is on a second, higher hill to the east. The surrounding countryside is beautiful, with extensive vineyards, tiny olive trees and old farmhouses or *bagli*, and it is peaceful, despite the proximity of the motorway.

HISTORY OF SEGESTA

Segesta, also originally known as *Egesta*, was the principal city of the Elymians, one of the pre-Greek populations of Sicily. Legendary survivors of the Trojan war, the Romans thought they had been led here by Aeneas. The city was rapidly Hellenised, and was continually at war with Selinunte from 580 BC, seeking an alliance with Athens in 426 BC. After the destruction of Selinunte in 409 BC, Segesta became a subject-ally of Carthage, and was saved by Himilco (397 BC) from the attacks of Dionysius of Syracuse. In 307 BC, however, Agathocles sacked the city, changed its name to Dikeopolis, and from the flat area behind the temple catapulted some 8,000 of the inhabitants into the ravine below, over the course of three days. The city resumed its old name under the protection of Carthage, but treacherously murdered the Carthaginian garrison during the First Punic War, after which it became one of the first cities in Sicily to announce allegiance to Rome. The city's fortunes declined during the Arab period, and by the late 13th century it was abandoned.

The site

Open 9–2hrs before sunset July–Aug closes 8; last tickets 1hr before closing; possible combined ticket with Selinunte; T: 0924 952356; shuttle-bus tickets (every 30mins) to the theatre can be purchased.

The ancient city which covered the slopes of Mt Barbaro is now being extensively excavated, but the location of the necropolis has not yet been identified. Sporadic excavations have in fact taken place since the end of the 18th century, when the temple was first restored. The theatre was brought to light in 1822. An important sanctuary at the foot of Mt Barbaro was discovered in 1950 and the entire area has been declared an archaeological park.

The temple

The temple is situated on a low hill (at 304m) on the edge of a deep ravine formed by the Pispisa torrent, across which is a hillside covered with pinewoods. One of the grandest extant monuments of Doric architecture, it is peripteral and hexastyle, with 36 columns (c. 9m high, 2m wide at base) on a stylobate 58m by 23m. The high entablature and the pediments are intact. Its apparently perfectly straight lines are in fact curvatures: the corner columns are slightly thicker than the others, and lean a little towards the centre. All the columns bulge very slightly in the middle (entasis); the stylobate and the entablature are convex by a matter of millimetres, all being carefully calculated to avoid the optical illusion which, if the lines were perfectly straight, would make them appear distorted from a distance. The temple was almost certainly an unfinished building: although traces of the foundations of a cella have been found, it does not appear ever to have been completed (although one theory argues that it may have

View of the Doric temple at Segesta, the first thing a traveller sees on entering the area. It has been a breathtaking sight for almost two and a half thousand years.

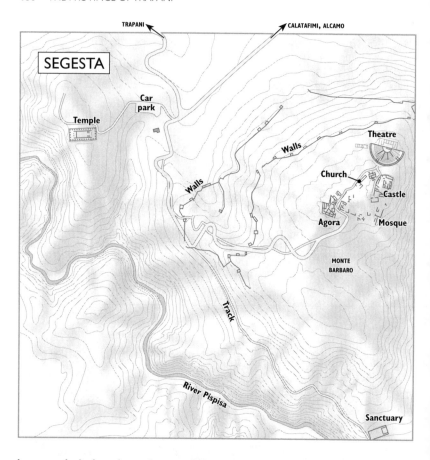

TRAPANI · CALATAFIMI, ALCAMO

SEGESTA

Car park

Temple

Walls

Walls

Theatre

Church

Castle

Agora

Mosque

MONTE BARBARO

Track

River Pispisa

Sanctuary

been wooden); the columns have not been provided with fluting; and the bosses used for shifting the blocks of stone have not been removed. It may have been constructed in a hurry, in order to impress the ambassadors from Athens whom the Segestans were anxious to win over to help protect them from Selinunte and Syracuse. It is possible that it is even the work of a great Athenian master and can tentatively be dated to 426–416 BC. Today the building is inhabited by a colony of jackdaws, their garrulous call adding to the mystery of the site.

The theatre

A road leads up to the theatre from the car park. At the foot of the hill, conspicuous excavations of part of the walls (and gate) of the ancient city can be seen. Yellow signs mark various excavations including an upper line of walls (2nd century BC) and a cave dwelling (re-used in Roman times; protected by a wooden roof). Near the top of the hill are two enclosures, the higher one with remains of medieval houses built over public buildings from the Hellenistic era and the lower one with a monumental Hellenistic edifice, reconstructed in the Roman period. A large expanse of fine paving from the agora has recently been uncovered, together with the bouleuterion. A path continues towards the theatre with a superb view of the temple below. On the right is an enclosure with a ruined church (12th–15th centuries). On the summit of the hill are the remains of a 12th–13th-century castle and, on the opposite side of the hill, a 12th-century mosque (destroyed by the owners of the castle in the 13th century).

The theatre occupies a spectacular position near the summit of Mt Barbaro (415m), facing the Gulf of Castellammare beyond Mt Inici (1064m), while higher mountain ranges rise to the east. It is well preserved and was built in the mid-3rd century BC or possibly earlier. With a diameter of 63m it could hold 3,200 spectators. The exterior of the cavea was supported by a high polygonal wall, which is particularly well preserved at the two sides. Beneath the cavea a grotto with late Bronze-Age finds was discovered in 1927 by the archaeologist Pirro Marconi. Classical drama productions are presented here in summer.

The sanctuary

In Contrada Mango at the foot of Mt Barbaro, to the east near the River Gaggera, is a large Archaic sanctuary (not fully excavated), of great importance, thought to date from the 7th century BC. The temenos measures 83m by 47m. A huge deposit of pottery sherds dumped from the town on the hill above has also come to light here.

Calatafimi Segesta

The nearest town to the ancient site is Calatafimi Segesta (*map p. 543, C2*), frequently visited by the writer Samuel Butler between 1893 and 1900. He identified in this corner of Sicily all the places described in Homer's *Odyssey*, and in *The Authoress of the Odyssey* he reveals his belief that the epic was actually written by a woman, Nausicaa. The old church of **San Giuseppe** (*open 9.30–12.30 & 4–7, closed Mon*) houses a collection of tools and equipment once used by the local farmers, and a fascinating *Altare di San Giuseppe*, a display of the decorative loaves baked for the feast of the saint (19th March).

Southwest of the town (signposted 'Pianto Romano', off the SS 113), an **obelisk** on top of a steep terraced hill commemorates Garibaldi's unexpected victory there on 15th May 1860 against the Bourbon troops, far superior in terms of numbers and the military preparation of their men. A cypress avenue leads to the monument, by Ernesto Basile (1892), on which Garibaldi's words on reaching the hill after his disembarkation from Marsala are inscribed: '*Qui si fa l'Italia o si muore*' ('Here we will create Italy or die'). There are beautiful panoramic views from the hilltop.

ALCAMO

At the eastern extremity of the province of Trapani is the agricultural town of Alcamo (*map p. 543, C2*), with numerous fine 18th-century churches. Founded at the end of the 10th century, it derives its name from the Arabic *manzil al-qamah*, perhaps meaning the 'farm of bitter cucumbers'. It was the birthplace of the 13th-century poet Cielo or Ciullo, short for Michele, one of the earliest exponents of the Sicilian School (*see box below*) and a forefather of Italian literature. The town has a strongly Arab flavour in its regular plan, with many attractive cobbled streets.

CIULLO D'ALCAMO & THE SICILIAN SCHOOL

The group of poets writing for the Palermitan court of the Holy Roman Emperor Frederick II, in the first half of the 13th century, were first identified as the 'Sicilian School' by Dante. He regarded his own work as an attempt to transcend their achievements, which included the adaptation of Provençal forms, largely lyrical celebrations of courtly love, into the local vernacular. One of their number, Jacopo da Lentini, is generally credited with inventing the sonnet, later perfected by Petrarch, with his *Io m'aggio posto in core* (I have a place in my heart...). Little is known about the life of Ciullo d'Alcamo, but his work *Contrasto Amoroso*, probably written c. 1230, was cited by Dante in *De Vulgari Eloquentia*. Ciullo's work contains bright and earthy parodies of the conventions of courtly love poetry. It begins *Rosa fresca aulentissima* ('Sweetest smelling fresh rose...') and tells of a young man's illicit seduction of a high-born lady, displaying such intimate acquaintance with life at court that some authorities have suggested that Ciullo was the *nom de plume* of a senior member of the nobility, close to the emperor himself. Other scholars maintain that Ciullo was never part of the Sicilian School, although his work provided inspiration for its members.

EXPLORING ALCAMO

On and around Corso VI Aprile

In Piazza Bagolino the terrace offers an ample panorama of the plain stretching towards the sea. Beyond the 16th-century Porta Palermo, Corso VI Aprile leads into the town. On the left is the church of **San Francesco d'Assisi**, founded in 1348 and rebuilt in 1716. It contains a beautiful marble altarpiece attributed to Giacomo Gagini (1568), statues of St Mark and St Mary Magdalene by Antonello Gagini and a 17th-century painting of the *Immaculate Virgin* by Giuseppe Carrera.

The Corso continues past the former church of **San Tommaso** (c. 1450), with a carved Gothic portal. Opposite, next to a convent, is the church of **Santi Cosma e Damiano** (*usually closed*), a domed, centrally-planned building of c. 1721 by Giuseppe Mariani. It contains two stucco statues by Giacomo Serpotta and two altarpieces by Willem Borremans; the interior is among the finest examples of Baroque architecture in Sicily.

The Corso crosses Via Rossotti, with a view left of the castle and right of San Salvatore. The **Castello dei Conti di Modica** (*open 9.30–12.30 & 4.30–7.30; T: 0924 22915*) was built c. 1350, on a rhomboid plan with four towers. For many years it was used as the local prison. Now it has been lovingly restored and is the seat of the Civic Historical Library and the Oenological Museum dedicated to the prize-winning Bianco d'Alcamo, one of Sicily's 23 DOC wines. Not far from the castle, tucked away in this part of town, is the **Torre De Ballis** (1495), one of the few surviving tower-houses in Sicily. It is now a private home with no public access.

The Corso continues past the former church of the Madonna del Soccorso (15th century), with a portal attributed to Bartolomeo Berrettaro, to the **Chiesa Madre**. Founded in 1332, it was rebuilt in 1669 by Angelo Italia, with a fine dome. In the interior are columns of red marble quarried on Mt Bonifato. The frescoes in the vault, cupola and apse are by Willem Borremans. In the second south chapel is a Crucifix by Antonello Gagini (1523); in the fourth a late 16th-century sarcophagus with portraits of two members of the De Ballis family; in the fifth there is a marble relief by Antonello Gagini. In the chapel to the right of the choir is a 17th-century painting of the *Last Supper*. In the adjoining chapel (right) are two marvellous Gothic arches and a beautiful fresco fragment of the *Pentecost* (1430). In the chapel to the left of the choir is a wooden statue of the Madonna (1721). On the altar of the north transept, the statue of St Peter is by Giacomo Gagini (1556). The inner door of the sacristy (beyond the wooden door in the north aisle) is decorated with carvings of fruit attributed to Bartolomeo Berrettaro. In the third north chapel there is a high relief of the *Transition of the Virgin* by Antonello Gagini.

Museo della Basilica Santa Maria Assunta

The long-abandoned oratory of the Holy Sacrament next to the Chiesa Madre, built in 1718, has been restored to house the Diocesan Museum (*entrance from Piazza IV Novembre 4; open 10–12.30 & 4.30–7.30, closed Mon; T: 0924 21578*), which has a rich array of paintings, vestments, codices and statues dating from the early 15th to the 19th centuries. Arranged in chronological order, the works were collected by the high priest Monsignor Vincenzo Regina during his period in office, from 1944–91. Among the highlights are the *Madonna of the Graces with Sts Vitus and Bartholomew* (1612) by Gaspare Vazano, the 'Zoppo di Gangi', with Palermo and its mountains in the background; a sensitive portrait of Baron Felice Pastore (1840) by Giuseppe Patania; and an equally revealing portrait of the high priest Benedetto Mangione (1793), by Giuseppe Renda. A rarity is the collection of *cerniglia*, discs of glass and gold enclosing small items of jewellery, precious stones or coral, dedicated as ex-votos to the miraculous Madonna of this church. Not to be missed on any account is the lovely statue in nut-brown alabaster of the *Madonna and Child*, by an unknown 16th-century artist, brought here from the church of the Rosario. The serene Madonna, enveloped in a heavy mantle picked out in gold and blue, is offering a pomegranate (symbol of humanity and also the Passion), to her Baby; gold-winged cherubim decorate the plinth.

Piazza Ciullo and environs

The Corso continues to the elegantly curved Piazza Ciullo, at the centre of town, which was the market place in the Middle Ages. On the corner is the **church of Sant'Oliva**, built by Giovanni Biagio Amico in 1724. It was restored in 1990 after a fire in 1987 destroyed the 18th-century frescoes and stuccoes in the vault of the nave. The interior has altars beautifully decorated with marble. In the fourth chapel of the south aisle is a statue of the titular saint by Antonello Gagini (1511). One of the four patron saints of Palermo, Oliva (9th century) was only 13 when she was kidnapped in Palermo and carried off to Tunis, where, somehow having avoided the sultan's harem, she lived in a cave healing the sick, performing miracles and converting many Muslims to Christianity. Arrested, she was tortured and beheaded. She remains respected by Muslims, and the great mosque of Tunis is dedicated to her. The high altarpiece is by Pietro Novelli and on the left wall is a 16th-century marble tabernacle. On the left side are 18th-century statues and a marble group of the *Annunciation* (1545) by Antonino and Giacomo Gagini.

Piazza Ciullo is dominated by the magnificent **Collegiate Church** (1684–1767) containing 18th-century stuccoes and altarpieces. On Sunday mornings a large proportion of the population—viticultors and their families, the women elegantly dressed, the men wearing black serge jackets and cloth caps—tends to congregate in front of this church.

Corso VI Aprile continues from Piazza Ciullo past 18th-century and Neoclassical palaces to the church of **Santi Paolo e Bartolomeo** (1689), with a splendid interior decorated by Vincenzo and Gabriele Messina and Antonino Grano. The oval *Madonna del Miele* (Our Lady of Honey), so-called because she is shown with a honeycomb symbolising her sweetness, dates from the late 14th or early 15th century.

In Via Amendola, the road leading out of the square to the north, opposite the church of Sant'Oliva, is the **church of the Rosario** (San Domenico), which contains a fresco attributed to Tommaso de Vigilia. Beyond the castle and the large Piazza della Repubblica is the church of **Santa Maria del Gesù** (1762). Beneath the portico is a portal attributed to Bartolomeo Berrettaro (1507). The church also contains a 16th-century altarpiece, the *Madonna and Saints with the Counts of Modica*, and a statue of the Madonna and Child attributed to Bartolomeo Berrettaro or Giuliano Mancino. The cloister of the adjoining convent is especially beautiful.

In Via Caruso is the church of **San Francesco di Paola**, rebuilt in 1699 by Giovanni Biagio Amico. The elegant interior has eight statues modelled in stucco by Giacomo Serpotta, commissioned in 1724, and an altarpiece of **St Benedict** by Pietro Novelli. The church is only open for services, but it is possible to ask for admission at the Benedictine convent next door.

Environs of Alcamo

On Mt Bonifato (825m), south of the town, in a pinewood, is the ruined **Norman castle** of the Ventimiglia, with the chapel of the Madonna dell'Alto (superb view). The medieval Fontanazza here is a huge reservoir or thermal edifice dating from the 14th century. Most of the mountain is a nature reserve (Riserva Bosco di Alcamo).

To the north, between the town and the sea, the spectacular castle on a spur known as **Calatubo** (*no access*) adequately protected Alcamo on that vulnerable side; probably Byzantine, the fortress was rebuilt and renamed by the Arabs in the 9th century. Close to the railway station is a spa, **Stabilimento Termale Gorga**, where water from hot springs flows into a pool prepared, according to Diodorus Siculus, by the local nymphs for Herakles 'to refresh his body'.

THE WEST COAST

The west coast of Sicily from Trapani to Mazara del Vallo is flat, with many salt marshes, which have given rise to one of the oldest salt-extracting industries in the world. Between Trapani and Marsala they are now protected, in part because of the interesting birdlife, and also as important sites of industrial archaeology. The coastal plain is dotted with white cube-shaped houses, palms and Norfolk Island pines. Beyond Marsala the plain is densely cultivated with olives, low vineyards, and gardens of tomatoes, melons and cantaloupes, stretching as far as colourful Mazara del Vallo, an important fishing port.

MOZIA

Four privately-owned islands lie close offshore in the beautiful shallow lagoon of **Lo Stagnone** (*map p. 543, B2*), which has an average depth of just over one metre, and is abundant in fish. Isola Longa is the largest, while the smallest is Isola Scola, site of an ancient academy where Cicero is said to have taught Oratory. The only island fully accessible to visitors is San Pantaleo, the site of ancient *Motya* (Mozia in Italian).

HISTORY OF MOZIA

Motya was founded in the mid-8th century BC by Phoenicians as a commercial base and industrial area (the name means 'mills'). By the mid-6th century BC the island was entirely surrounded by defensive walls, 2400m long and over 2m thick. It became an important Carthaginian station, controlling a large part of the western Mediterranean. In his determination to remove the Carthaginians from Sicily, Dionysius I of Syracuse brought a large army, formed partly of mercenaries, here in 398 BC. During the fierce battle which ensued, he used wooden towers that enabled his men to shoot over the walls and which served as mounts for catapults. When his fleet became trapped in the lagoon, Dionysius escaped by dragging his ships over an isthmus, 4km wide, using logs as rollers, to the open sea, where he finally defeated the enemy. By the following year the Carthaginians had moved their headquarters to Lilybaeum.

On the edge of the lagoon at **Ragattisi** (signposted from the coastal road), there are several jetties from which boats ferry visitors to the island (Signori Arini e Pugliese; *T: 347 7790218, 360 656053*). Near the main jetty is an old salt mill which is now a museum with a small hotel (Saline Ettore e Infersa; *open summer 9–8.30, winter 9.30–1.30 & 3–7.30; T: 0923 733003, www.salineettoreinfersa.com*). The various phases of obtaining salt from seawater are explained, and a film illustrates the method of production; canoes may be rented for exploring the lagoon, and of course you can buy some salt.

There are splendid views of the other islands from the water's edge, and on the far right the mountain of Erice is prominent beyond salt-pans, windmills and piles of salt. **San Pantaleo** itself is an oasis of luxuriant vegetation, a sanctuary for birds, with sweet-smelling plants, palm trees and pinewoods, and seven hectares of vineyards originally planted by Pip Whitaker, and now cared for by the Tasca d'Almerita company. Background music is provided by the cicadas. The ruins of Phoenician Motya (*open Nov–March 9–3, April–Oct 9.30–6.30*) are unenclosed.

Villa Whitaker and Zona E

The island was owned from 1888 by Joseph (Pip) Whitaker (1850–1936), a distinguished ornithologist and amateur archaeologist, and member of the famous family

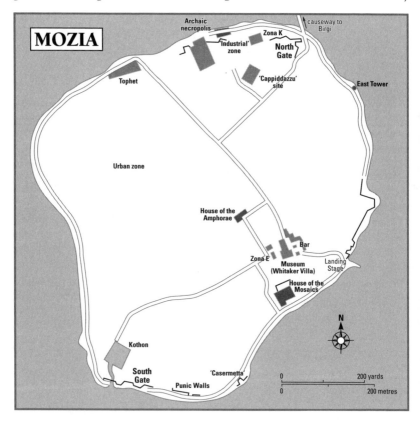

The 5th-century BC *Giovane di Mozia*. One theory suggests that the statue may represent Melqart (a Phoenician god identified by the Greeks as Herakles), the titular divinity of Tyre, who was probably wearing a lion's skin made of bronze (which would have partially covered the head) and a bronze band around the chest—the holes where this would have been fixed can still be seen. Other theories suggest that the statue may represent a charioteer, an athlete, or an unknown Carthaginian hero.

of Marsala wine merchants. The low vineyards here still produce an excellent wine. He began excavations around 1913. Since the death of his daughter Delia in 1971, the island has been the property of the Fondazione Whitaker (*Via Dante 167, Palermo; T: 091 6820522, www.fondazionewhitaker.it*).

The boat docks near a stretch of the fortifications of the Punic city, from which a path leads to the crenellated **Villa Whitaker** (*open Nov–March 10–12 & 1–2, April–Oct 10–12 & 3–5; T: 0923 712598*), founded as a museum in 1925. Some of the display cases brought at that time from Edinburgh and Belfast are still in use. The material comes from the excavations at Mozia, Lilybaeum and Birgi, carried out by Whitaker and (in the last few decades) by the Italian state. It includes Phoenician ceramics, the earliest dating from the 8th century BC, and Greek ware including proto-Corinthian and Corinthian vases, and Attic black- and red-figure vases. Other finds from the island include Phoenician glass, alabaster and jewellery.

Among the sculptural fragments is an extraordinarily vivid metope from the North Gate showing two lions attacking a bull, distinctly Mycenaean in style (late 7th or early 6th century BC), and a marble krater with bas-reliefs (Augustan period). The expressive statue of a young man in a finely-pleated linen tunic, *Il Giovane di Mozia*, was found by Vincenzo Tusa at Cappiddazzu on the northeast side of the island in 1979. In the stance of a victor, with hand on hip, the pose of the statue expresses great confidence in his youth, beauty and power. This remarkable work, made of white marble, is thought to be by a Greek master, perhaps Pheidias, and to date from c. 440 BC. The statue was found buried under a layer of rubble, face up in the road by the sanctuary. The face and the front are abraded, possibly from when the bronze accoutrements were torn from the statue during Dionysius' attack. The fact that it was not recovered and replaced in a temple, in spite of its enormous value, would be explained if it indeed represented a god (*see caption*). The shocked survivors of the battle may have thought their god profaned and buried it where it was found.

Nearby is a small building used until the 1970s for wine-making. During reconstruction work in 1995 remains of houses (called **Zona E**), dating from 7th–4th centuries BC, were found beneath the pavement: the excavations can now be viewed from a walkway.

The excavations

In front of the museum a path leads towards the lagoon to the **House of the Mosaics**, surrounded by a fence and rich vegetation, with bases of columns and pebble mosaics showing a panther attacking a bull and a griffin chasing a deer, among other designs (4th–3rd centuries BC).

A longer path (c. 400m) leads from the custodian's house across the southern part of the island to the waterfront at the southeast corner, beside the Kothon and the South Gate. The **Kothon** is a small basin (50m by 40m) within the walls, with a channel leading to the sea. It was long thought to have been a repair yard for boats, but recent digs (*www.lasapienzamozia.it*) have brought to light a large temple on the east side of the pool, with a portico facing the water. The pool (its four corners correspond to the cardinal points) was drained and cleaned, revealing that it was originally fed by a natural spring, which also provided water to a sacred well inside the temple—found to have been one of the oldest buildings on the island, going back to the mid-8th century BC, and rebuilt after Dionysius' attack. The channel connecting the pool to the sea was made later. The cult, which evidently required much water, and the divinity or divinities worshipped here are still mysterious, but inside the temple there were originally two upright stelae and an obelisk. Viewing the night sky at the winter equinox, the stones indicate the constellation of Orion, the Phoenician Baal, while at the spring equinox the portal of the temple, facing south-southwest, frames the same divinity, often together with the planet Venus, the Phoenician Astarte. Some scholars believe this temple was particularly sacred because it represented the spot where the inhabitants first disembarked, finding abundant fresh water and therefore the benevolence of the gods. A path leads back towards the villa along the edge of the south shore past an enclosure near a stand of pine trees. Excavations here have unearthed a building that was probably used for military purposes, known as the **Casermetta**.

The path continues along the water's edge below the villa, passing the jetty and the impressive fortifications (late 6th century BC), the best-preserved stretch on the island, along the eastern shore, reaching (after 400m) the **East Tower**, which preserves its flight of steps. Beyond some recent excavations (protected by a roof) is the imposing **North Gate**, with a triple line of defences. It defended a submerged causeway (meant to be invisible from land, but perfectly practicable for a horse and cart), which was built in the late 6th century BC to link the island to the mainland and a necropolis at Birgi. Several kilometres long, just wide enough for two carts to pass each other, it was in regular use until the 1950s.

A path leads inland through the North Gate to **Cappiddazzu**, the site of an important sanctuary, perhaps dedicated to Astarte or to Melqart, where Vincenzo Tusa found the statue of the *Giovane* in 1979. Above the level of the path is a building with mosaic remains. To the right is a field with low vines and two enclosed areas, the farthest of which, on the edge of the sea, is the **Archaic necropolis** with tombs dating from the 8th–6th centuries BC. Nearby a fence surrounds an 'industrial zone', known as **Zona K**, with interesting kilns, similar in design to some found in Syria and Palestine.

The largest enclosure is the **Tophet**, a Punic sacrificial burial-ground dedicated to the goddess Tanith and to her husband, the god Baal Hammon, where children, possibly the male first-born, were sacrificed; a cruel custom replaced after c. 475 BC by animal sacrifices, mostly cats and monkeys. Excavations here have produced cinerary urns, votive terracotta masks and stelae (some with human figures).

The West Gate (as yet unexplored) stood near a military fort, the largest building so far discovered on the island. From the Tophet a path, marked by low olive trees, leads back through a vineyard in the centre of the island towards the museum (c. 400m). It passes (right) an enclosure with remains of the **House of the Amphorae**, so called because a huge deposit of amphorae was found here.

MARSALA

Marsala (*map p. 543, B2*) is a pleasant town with a neat city centre and an attractive open seafront on Capo Boeo, the site of the Carthaginian city of *Lilybaeum*. The town gives its name to a famous dessert wine still produced here in large quantities from the vineyards along the coast.

MARSALA WINE

Similar to sherry and port, Marsala owes its worldwide fame to the British. In the late 18th century an English merchant tasted it and noted a striking similarity to the wines of southwestern Andalucia. By adding brandy to the base wine, he created a fortified liquor which he sold in England with enormous success. Production of top-quality Marsala began in 1880, when Paolo Pellegrino founded his winery and dedicated his life to the wine. The wine is stored in huge *bagli*, fortified farmhouses. The name derives from the Latin *balium* or *vallum*, being a group of buildings forming a square or a rectangle around a central courtyard, with one entrance, sometimes lavishly decorated, in the front wall. In the courtyard there is often a well-head above the rainwater cistern. On entering, the house immediately in front is that of the owner, usually with a private chapel to one side. Other buildings house the farm workers, the wine or olive presses and the stables.

Porta Garibaldi to the cathedral

The centre of town is entered from the port and southwest by the monumental **Porta Garibaldi** (*map 3–4*), formerly the Porta di Mare, reconstructed in 1685. On the left is the church of the Addolorata, with a fine circular domed 18th-century interior, and a venerated popular statue of the Madonna wearing a black cloak. Opposite, municipal offices occupy a restored 16th-century military building, behind which is the market square. Via Garibaldi continues to the central **Piazza della Repubblica** with the idiosyncratic Palazzo Comunale (Town Hall) which has original lamps on its upper storey. Opposite, on Via XI Maggio, is a wall and dome of the 17th-century church of **San Giuseppe**, with a lovely interior and a fine organ.

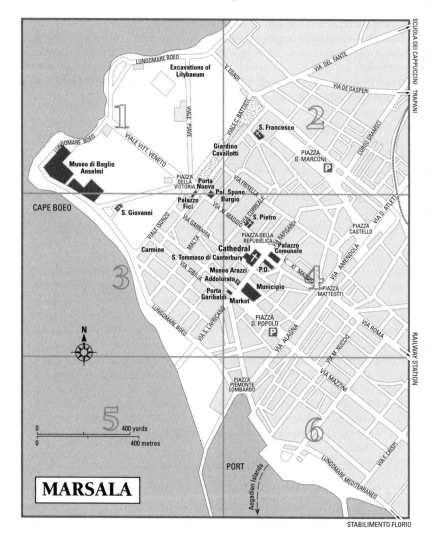

MARSALA

HISTORY OF MARSALA

Lilybaeum, founded by the Carthaginians in 396 BC, near the headland of Capo Boeo, the western extremity of Sicily, was peopled from Motya (*see p. 143*), and became their strongest bulwark in Sicily after the sack of that city by Dionysius. It succumbed to the Romans only after a siege of ten years (250–241 BC). During the Second Punic War, Scipio (later to become known as Africanus) set sail from Lilybaeum on his way to defeat Hannibal at the Battle of Zama near Carthage (202 BC). As the seat of the Roman governor of Sicily, the city reached the zenith of its importance. Cicero, made quaestor here around 75 BC, called it '*civitas splendidissima*'. In 47 BC Julius Caesar also pitched camp here on his way to Africa. A *municipium* during the Augustan age, it was later raised to the status of *colonia*. It kept its importance as an avenue of communication with Africa during the Saracen dominion under the name *Marsa Alì*, Harbour of Alì, but declined after 1574 when Don Juan of Austria (illegitimate son of Charles V) almost completely blocked its port to protect it from Barbary pirates. Garibaldi and the 'Thousand' landed here on 11th May 1860, being unobtrusively assisted by two British warships which had officially been assigned to protect the wine merchants. In 1943, Marsala was heavily damaged by Allied air attacks during preparations for Operation Husky.

The Marsala wine trade was founded by John Woodhouse in 1773, when he made the first shipment of local white wine to Liverpool, conserving it on its month-long journey by adding alcohol. In 1798, after the Battle of the Nile, Nelson placed a large order of Marsala for his fleet. In 1806 Benjamin Ingham and his nephew Pip Whitaker also took up trading in Marsala, with great success: by 1812 they were exporting the wine to North America. Production on an even grander scale was undertaken by Vincenzo Florio (d. 1868), an able businessman. In 1929 the establishments of Woodhouse, Ingham Whitaker and Florio were taken over by Cinzano and merged under the name of Florio. The house of Florio continues to flourish along with many other companies, including Pellegrino, Donnafugata and Montalto.

The **cathedral** (*map 4*) has a Baroque front completed in 1957. The first church on this site was built in 1176–82 and dedicated to St Thomas Becket, because the columns of various kinds of marble used in the building were recuperated from a shipwreck, and were intended for a church under construction in England, dedicated to this 'new' saint—Thomas was canonised in 1173. The renovated cathedral, begun in 1607 and completed in 1717, was ruined when the dome collapsed in 1893, and was partly re-built in the 20th century. The interior contains some important 17th-century paintings and sculptures. In the first south chapel there is an unusual statue of the *Assunta* and two reliefs on the side wall, all by Antonino Gagini. The delicately-carved tomb slab dates from 1556. In the second chapel there is a 15th-century statue of the Madonna, and a tomb with the effigy, attributed to Domenico Gagini, of Antonio Grignano (d. 1475) who fought with honour in the wars of King Alfonso. In the third chapel is an elaborate statue of the *Madonna dell'Itria* (derived from the Byzantine Hodegetria type, with the Virgin indicating Christ as 'the Way') and the tomb of Giulio Alazzaro with an amusing effigy, both by Antonino Gagini. The fifth chapel has a 15th-century Crucifix and an expressive, popular statue of the Virgin in mourning. In the south transept is a striking altarpiece of the *Presentation in the Temple* by Antonello or Mariano Riccio, and the tomb of Antonio Lombardo, who donated the tapestries to the cathedral (now in the Museo degli Arazzi; *see below*). In the chapel to the right of the sanctuary is an unusual statue of the Madonna (wielding a distaff), attributed to Giuliano Mancino, and a tomb with an effigy of Antonio Liotta (d. 1512), also attributed to Mancino. On either side of the sanctuary are two statues, one of St Vincent Ferrer attributed to Giacomo Gagini and one of St Thomas the Apostle by Antonello Gagini. In the apse is a 17th-century painting of the *Martyrdom of St Thomas* in the original frame. In the chapel to the left of the sanctuary is a beautiful gilded marble altarpiece of the *Passion* begun in 1518 by Bartolomeo Berrettaro and finished by Antonello Gagini (1532; four of the panels have been set into the walls). On the north side, in the sixth chapel is a charming polychrome wooden statue of *Our Lady of Carmel*, and in the second chapel is another wooden statue of the Madonna (1593), and two frescoed ex-votos with scenes of Marsala.

Behind the cathedral, at Via Giuseppe Garraffa 57, is the small **Museo degli Arazzi** (Tapestry Museum; *open 9.30–1 & 4.30–6, closed Sun, Mon and holidays; T: 0923 711327, 320 1860115*), displaying eight precious tapestries given to the duomo in 1589 by Antonio Lombardo, archbishop of Messina (1523–95), born in Marsala and buried in the cathedral. He became ambassador to Spain, and the very fine tapestries, depicting the capture of Jerusalem, were made in Brussels between 1530 and 1550 and are known to have come from the royal palace of Philip II in Madrid. They are displayed on three floors. Since their restoration they have to be kept in darkened rooms.

The museums of San Pietro and the Carmine

Via XI Maggio runs off Piazza della Repubblica. The 15th-century convent of **San Pietro** in Via Correale, with a massive pointed tower, is now used as the town library, cultural centre and Civic Museum (*map 4; open 9–1 & 4–8, closed Mon; T: 0923 718741*). It has sections on ancient history, the exploits of Giuseppe Garibaldi, and popular traditions.

Just off Via Malta (*map 3*), in Piazza Carmine, the former church and convent of the Carmine houses an interesting **contemporary art gallery** (*open 10–1 & 5–7, closed Mon, guided tours available; T: 0923 711631, www.pinacotecamarsala.it*), with paintings by Italian masters such as Alberto Sughi, Bruno Caruso, Corrado Cagli, Fausto Pirandello, Giacomo Baragli and the mythopoeic painter and sculptor Mirko. The former convent was founded in the late 14th century and has an 18th-century cloister.

Back on Via XI Maggio, just before Porta Nuova (on Piazza della Vittoria), is the façade (left) of **Palazzo Fici**, with a tall palm tree in its delightful Baroque courtyard. Opposite is the 19th–20th-century **Palazzo Spanò Burgio** (no. 15). Outside the gate is the entrance (right) to the **Giardino Cavallotti** (*map 1–2*), lovely public gardens with huge ficus trees, magnolias and ornamental Norfolk Island pines.

The excavations of Lilybaeum and Museo di Baglio Anselmi

Between Piazza della Vittoria and the seafront extends **Capo Boeo** (*map 1*), the site of ancient Lilybaeum and now an open area with lawns and trees. Some picturesque old *bagli* are still used as warehouses for wine; others have been converted into restaurants, and one of them houses the archaeological museum (Museo di Baglio Anselmi). The **excavations**, in the area known as the Insula Romana, are reached from the museum (*open 9.30–11.30 & 4.30–6, same ticket as Baglio Anselmi museum*). In a well-restored house are diagrams of the site, which includes a sumptuous Roman villa (surrounded by a fence and covered for protection) dating from the 3rd century AD, which was built over in the Arab period. Around the impluvium are four mosaics of wild beasts attacking each other (thought to represent circus animals), probably the work of African craftsmen. There are remains of baths and other rooms with mosaics, including a head of Medusa, the symbol of Trinacria and the Four Seasons. Nearby are more recent excavations including part of the walls, a necropolis and a Roman road. A hypogeum (*open Sat mornings 9–1; T: 0923 952535 to request visit*) with painted walls, where a certain Crispia Salvia was buried in the 2nd century AD, has also been discovered. The remains of a sanctuary dedicated to Isis are not yet open to the public.

The **Baglio Anselmi** itself is a former Marsala distillery and wine cellar, now restored as the regional archaeological museum (*open April–Oct 9–7.30, Nov–March 9–6, Sun always 9–1, last tickets 30mins before closing; T: 0923 953614, 0923 952535*), with a very interesting collection arranged in two huge vaulted warehouses. The display begins in the hall on the left with prehistoric material from the Marsala area, in particular from Mozia and also Phoenician articles from the Tophet (sacrificial burial area) of Mozia, along with some exquisite Hellenistic gold jewellery found in Marsala.

The finds from the Phoenician necropolis of Lilybaeum are displayed chronologically with diagrams and photographs, and include ceramics, funerary monuments, sculptures, terracottas and Tanagra figurines (graceful, elegantly dressed and coiffed female figures, so-called because their type was first found at Tanagra in Greece; they were placed exclusively in burials of women and girls). On the end wall are fragments of 3rd–2nd-century BC funerary monuments, stelae and aedicula with carved inscriptions or paintings from Motya and Lilybaeum. Also here are fragments from a large mausoleum in local stone covered with a fine layer of white and polychrome stucco (its hypothetical form has been reconstructed in a drawing). Finds from Roman Lilybaeum (3rd–4th centuries AD) follow, along with a model of the excavations on Capo Boeo, including fragments of wall-paintings, a hoard of coins, lamps and a fragment of a female statuette. A marble Aphrodite known as the *Aphrodite Callipige* ('of the firm buttocks'), recently discovered near the church of San Giovanni, has a room to herself; close by is a display of lamps found in a sanctuary of the Roman city. The displays conclude with photographs of Palaeo-Christian finds and a case of ceramics including Siculo-Norman ware. The last case illustrates the discovery of a Norman wreck in 1983, with a few finds from the boat.

The other hall on the right contains the Punic warship discovered by Honor Frost in 1971 off Isola Longa in the Stagnone lagoon. The well-preserved poop was recovered from the seabed and the rest of the hulk, 35m long, was carefully reconstructed in 1980. Manned by 68 oarsmen, it is thought to have been sunk on its maiden voyage during the First Punic War. The only warship of this period so far discovered, it is not known how the iron nails resisted the corrosion of the sea. The ship has been partly reconstructed around the original wood, which is conserved beneath a huge tent, which makes viewing awkward. Drawings illustrate the vessel's original appearance. Objects found on board are also displayed, including remains of ropes, a sailor's wooden button, a bone needle used for making nets, corks from amphorae, a brush, some ceramic fragments, and cannabis leaves and stalks—possibly an aid to the oarsmen during battle. The underwater finds include numerous amphorae, of which the contents, place of origin and date offer an interesting insight into trade in the ancient Mediterranean.

The little church of **San Giovanni** (*map 3; T: 0923 952535 to request visit, a few days in advance*) covers the so-called Grotto of the Sibyl, with a spring of water which later became an early Christian baptistery. There are still faint traces of ancient 5th-century AD frescoes.

THE SIBYL OF LILYBAEUM

Prophetesses or sibyls were popularly believed to be able to speak for the gods, and hence foretell the future. Apollo was especially generous in this respect, and is often referred to as 'the far-seeing one'. There were several places where these oracles could be consulted, such as Delphi or Cumae, but the Sibyl of Lilybaeum had a particularly good reputation for accuracy. The person requiring the information would enter the grotto where the priestess lived and put their question; she would then bathe his face and her own with water from the little pool. The pair would then take turns in sipping wine from a golden cup, after which the sibyl would enter a trance-like state and read the future in the dregs of wine remaining in the cup. The custom died out when Sicily became a province of Rome in the 3rd century BC.

The Florio winery (Stabilimento Florio)

On the road which continues along the seafront back towards town, lined with palms, is the former Baglio Woodhouse (the entrance is marked by two round towers in front of a jetty and next to a chapel built by the English). In the harbour only the base remains of the monument commemorating the landing of the Thousand, by Ettore Ximenes. It was destroyed in the Second World War. The road passes a number of old *bagli*, and, beside two tall palm trees, is the Stabilimento Florio (*Via Vincenzo Florio 1, beyond map 6; guided tours in English Sun–Fri 11 and 4.30, Sat 10.30; T: 0923 781111, www.cantineflorio.com*). The monumental buildings designed by Basile surround an inner courtyard planted with trees. Visitors are shown the historic cellars and invited to taste the wine (free of charge). In the small museum a letter is preserved from Nelson, Duke of Bronte, to John Woodhouse in 1800 with an order for Marsala for his fleet.

The Neoclassical villa built by Benjamin Ingham can be seen a little further along the waterfront.

MAZARA DEL VALLO

Mazara del Vallo (*map p. 543, B3*), at the mouth of the Mazaro, is the most important fishing town in Italy, with a large population of Tunisians who work on the farms and in the fishing fleet. It has a colourful waterfront and busy canal-port. The town, built in golden tufa, has a distinctly Arab flavour. Animated and attractive, with elegant shops and graceful squares, Mazara is one of the liveliest towns in western Sicily. The harbour lies at the mouth of the River Mazaro and is normally filled with the fishing fleet during the day, except on Saturdays. This is the more picturesque part of the city, together with the Tunisian district around Via Porta Palermo and Via Bagno. A short way upstream stands the little Norman-Byzantine church of San Nicolò Regale with a crenellated top. The Lungomazaro continues along the river to the bridge from which there is a splendid view of the boats.

HISTORY OF MAZARA DEL VALLO

Mazara, once a Phoenician trading-post, became an emporium of Selinunte and fell with it in 409 BC. It was held by the Carthaginians until 210 BC when it came under Roman rule. Here in AD 827 the Arabs, called in by the governor Euphemius to assist his pretensions to the imperial purple, gained their first foothold on the island. There followed the most important period in the town's history, when it became the capital of the Val di Mazara, one of the three administrative districts into which the Arabs divided Sicily. It was captured by Count Roger in 1075; and it was here in 1097 that the Sicilian parliament, one of the oldest in the world, was convened for the first time.

The cathedral and Diocesan Museum

The **cathedral** was founded in 1093 and rebuilt in 1690–94. Above the main door, which faces the sea, is a 16th-century sculpture of Count Roger on horseback. The interior contains a *Transfiguration* in the apse by Antonello Gagini (finished by his son Antonino, 1537). The statues of St Bartholomew and St Ignatius are by Ignazio Marabitti (1719–97). In the south aisle is a sculpted portal by Bartolomeo Berrettaro. In the vestibule of the chapter-house are two Roman sarcophagi. Off the north aisle is a chapel with a 13th-century painted Cross, and in the chapel of the Madonna del Soccorso is a Byzantine fresco (in a niche) of Christ Pantocrator.

Near the cathedral, at Via San Salvatore 14, is the **Museo Ornitologico** (*open week-days only 9–12 & 3–6.30*), a collection of 373 stuffed birds, some of them extremely rare, and a few mammals, prepared by a local taxidermist in 1924. Between the cathedral and the seafront is a **public garden** with huge trees, on the site of the Norman castle, one ru-ined wall of which faces the busy Piazza Mokarta at the end of the main Corso Umberto.

On the other side of the cathedral is the 18th-century **Piazza della Repubblica**, with a statue by Marabitti (1771) and the handsome Seminario Vescovile (1710) with a double portico. The **Diocesan Museum** (*open Tues–Sat 10–12.30, Wed, Fri and Sat also 4.30–6.30; T: 0923 909431; entrance from Via dell'Orologio to the south*) contains the tomb (1495) of Bishop Giovanni Montaperto, who ordered the construction of the cathedral in Agrigento, by Domenico Gagini, as well as paintings, vestments, and Church silver, including a processional Cross from Salemi dated 1386, by a Pisan artist, and another 15th-century Cross, along with numerous 18th-century reliquaries. Also on display is the carriage of another bishop, Antonio Salomone. The highlights of the museum are the tiny pink marble statue of *Christus Dolens* (an 18th-century ex-voto) and a stunning silver monstrance, glittering with diamonds, pearls, amethysts, emeralds, garnets and topaz; it was probably made using the jewellery of a noble lady on entering a convent.

Via San Giuseppe leads to the church of **Santa Caterina**, decorated in 1797 by Giuseppe Testa, with a statue of the saint by Antonello Gagini (1524).

Museo del Satiro Danzante and Museo Civico

On the west side of Piazza della Repubblica, Via XX Settembre leads to Piazza Plebi-scito, with the two 16th-century churches of the Carmine and Sant'Egidio, The church of Sant'Egidio now houses the **Museo del Satiro Danzante** (*open 9–6.30, holidays 9–1; T: 0923 933917*). In 1998 some local fishermen found a bronze statue of a satyr caught in their nets, while fishing in the Strait of Sicily. For a moment, while they were hauling up the catch, they thought it was a seaman who had fallen overboard and was clinging to the ropes, but an arm broke off and fell into the depths. A year earlier, the same crew had found a bronze leg. By returning to the same area a few weeks later they found a bronze elephant's foot, perhaps from the same statuary group; they are still trying to find the missing arms and the other leg. It has been suggested that the satyr could be Dionysus himself: he is shown with his body twisted in a dance of drunken ecstasy, his head thrown back, with wild hair and pointed ears. A little larger than life size, the statue is made of bronze about 7mm thick, the weight, including the stand, is about 140kg. Judging from other works of art on the same subject (statues, reliefs, cameos), the satyr would have been carrying an empty wine cup in his left hand and a long rattle in his right. A panther skin would have been thrown over his left arm with its legs and tail flailing, and this, plus his donkey tail behind him, would have increased the effect of his frenzied whirling. Research on the statue is still being carried out, but a tenta-tive date for it can be set between 404 and 280 BC. One authority has declared that the statue could even be the work of Praxiteles.

Close by is the church of Sant'Ignazio and the Collegio dei Gesuiti (1675–86), which now houses the municipal library and archives and the **Museo Civico** (*open 9–1, Tues* *and Thur also 3.30–5.30, closed Sat, Sun and holidays; T: 0923 949593, may be closed for rearrangement*), which has Roman finds from the area and two interesting sculpted elephants which once bore the columns outside the west porch of the Norman cathedral. Many drawings by the local sculptor Pietro Consagra are displayed here.

The little Norman church of the **Madonna dell'Alto**, erected in 1103 by Judith, daughter of Count Roger, to celebrate her father's victory over the Muslims, is on the outskirts of town 2km to the east.

SELINUNTE

One of the most impressive Classical sites in Sicily, because it was never subsequently re-developed, the extensive ruins (270ha) of the city of Selinunte (Selinous in Greek, Selinus in Latin) are in a superb position overlooking the sea (*map p. 543, C3*). On the coast nearby, the fishing village of Marinella has been developed as a small resort. The beautiful coast to the east, around the mouth of the River Belice (and as far as Porto Palo), with its sand dunes, is preserved as a nature reserve (Riserva Naturale Foce del Fiume Belice; *T: 0925 73875, www.focedelbelice.it*). The ancient town with its acropolis occupied a raised terrace between the River Selinon, or Modione, and the marshy depression now called Gorgo di Cottone or Galici, and possessed a harbour at the mouth of each valley. An important group of temples lay to the east of this site, and a necropolis to the north. The sandy soil is overgrown with wild celery, lentiscus, mandrake, acanthus and capers. The site has been enclosed, and is now the largest archaeological park in Europe.

The archaeological park of Selinunte

Open April–Oct 9–6, Nov–March 9–5, last tickets 1hr before closing; re-entry permitted with ticket on the same day; it is possible to buy a combined ticket with Segesta; T: 0924 46540, www.selinunte.net. A visit, best started early in the morning, takes at least three or four hours, to include the three quite widely separated areas.

The site was rediscovered in the 16th century by Tommaso Fazello, but systematic excavations were begun only in 1822–23 by the Englishmen William Harris and Samuel Angell, after a fruitless dig had been made in 1809–10 by Robert Fagan, British consul-general in Sicily. Harris and Angell found the famous metopes of temples C and E, but Harris died of malaria, contracted while excavating here, and Angell was killed by bandits on a successive visit.

The majority of the temples are distinguished by letters as their dedications are still under discussion. They are among the few temples in Sicily to have had sculptured metopes, and many of these works are now displayed in the archaeological museum in Palermo. All except temples B and G are peripteral and hexastyle. The measurements given in the following descriptions refer to the temple stylobates. Many architectural fragments bear remains of stucco, and throughout the site are underground cisterns, built to collect rainwater. Beside most of the temples are sacrificial altars.

HISTORY OF SELINUNTE

Selinunte was a colony of Megara Hyblaea, perhaps founded as early as 650 BC. It takes its name from the wild celery, *Apium graveolens* (Greek, *selinon*), which still grows here in abundance, and which appears on its coins. The colony's most prosperous period was the 5th century BC, when the great temples were built and the city was laid out on a rectangular plan. After the Battle of Himera in 480 BC, Selinunte took part with Syracuse in an alliance against Carthage, and in 409 BC the Carthaginians, summoned to the help of Segesta, the mortal enemy of Selinunte, sent an army of 100,000 under Hannibal, son of Gisco, which captured Selinunte before the allied troops of Akragas and Syracuse could arrive. The city, which fell in only nine days, was sacked and destroyed, and its inhabitants sold as slaves. A later settlement, led by Hermocrates, a Syracusan exile, was dispersed by Carthage in 250 BC, and the population resettled at Lilybaeum. It is thought, however, that the utter destruction of every building, scarcely a single column being left upright, could also have been due to earthquakes. In fact, around and under the columns of Temple C are the ruins of a Byzantine settlement, and a later, Arab village called *Rahal al-Asnaan*, or 'village of the columns', which must have been destroyed by an earthquake in the Middle Ages.

A bronze statue (Phoenician, 12th–11th centuries BC) of Reshef (kept in the Museo Archeologico in Palermo), found in the vicinity, perhaps suggests that the Phoenicians traded here before the foundation of Carthage.

The East Hill

The East Hill shows the ruins of three large temples. Behind the ticket office (bookshop and toilets) is a large modern dyke that isolates them from the village of Marinella.

Temple E: A Doric building of 490–480 BC, measuring 67.7m by 25.3m and probably dedicated to Hera. It had beautiful sculpted metopes, four of which were discovered in 1831 and are now in Palermo's archaeological museum. Toppled by an earthquake, its columns were re-erected in 1958.

Temple F: The oldest on this hill (c. 560–540 BC), possibly dedicated to Aphrodite, now almost completely ruined. It once had a double row of columns in front and 14 at the sides. Part of one column rises above others which are now only a few metres high.

Temple G: Perhaps dedicated to Zeus. Octastyle in form, it is the second largest (110m by 50m) Sicilian temple after the Olympieion at Agrigento. The columnar arrangement (8 by 17) is the same as that of the Parthenon. Laid out in the 6th century and left incomplete (with unfluted columns) in 409 BC when the city was destroyed by Hannibal. It is now an impressive pile of overgrown ruins, although a recently awarded

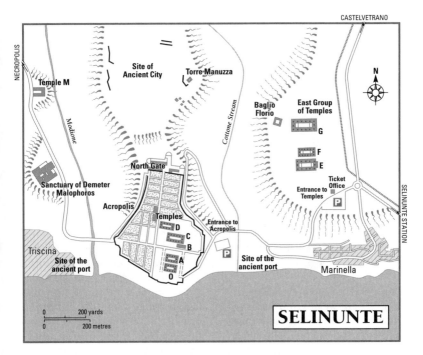

European Union grant to begin reconstructing it may soon change that. One column still stands, locally known as *'u fusu d'a vecchia* ('the old lady's distaff'). The columns, over 16m high with a base diameter of 3.4m, were built up of drums, each weighing c. 100 tons, from the quarries at Cusa. Blocks of stone destined for the site can still be seen there (*see p. 161*). The cella, preceded by a pronaos of four columns, had a central colonnaded way (open to the sky) leading to the shrine of the divinity. The fallen capitals give some idea of the colossal scale of the building and the crepidoma is in itself a marvel of monumental construction.

The Acropolis

From the first car park a road continues downhill across the Gorgo di Cottone (site of one of the ancient harbours) and up to the Acropolis, where there is a second car park (*see plan above*). From here a path continues up between the sea and massive double walls, in which five towers and four gates have been located, dating from c. 307–306 BC. On the clifftop is an old farmhouse, the Casa del Viandante, with a plan and explanation of the site, and a small antiquarium housing objects found here; small vases, pottery sherds, coins, and copies of the metopes now in the archaeological museum in Palermo. Some large fragments of the decorative stucco from Temple C are painted in bright colours.

Temples O and A: Only the stylobate of Temple O remains; the superstructure has disappeared. Next to it is the stylobate of Temple A with some fluted drums. The cella was one step higher than the pronaos and the adyton one higher still. Between the cella and pronaos two spiral staircases led to the roof. Fragmentary ruins of a monumental entrance exist to the east. Temples A and O, both built in 490–480 BC, and identical in form and dimension (40m by 16m; 36 columns), were the latest and probably the most perfect of the Selinuntine temples. In front of Temple O a sacred area has been excavated, thought to date from after the destruction of the city in 409 BC.

Temple C: The ruins of the Acropolis are crossed by two principal streets at right angles, with lesser streets running parallel in a grid pattern. To the north

are the remains of the great Temple C, on the highest point of the knoll, and the most conspicuous monument on the Acropolis. It measured 63.7m by 24m, and dates from the early 6th century BC, when it would have replaced a more simple megaron. Probably dedicated to Apollo, it was once adorned with metopes, found here in 1823 and now in the Palermo archaeological museum. In order to accommodate the sacrificial altar, the temenos was artificially extended some way eastwards, supported by monumental steps. The colossal columns (6 by 17), some of which were monolithic, are nearly 2m in diameter at the base, except for the corner-columns which are even thicker; they fell during an earthquake in the Middle Ages, burying a Byzantine village that had grown up in the 5th century (a Crucifix and a Christian bronze lamp were found here) and a later Arab village. The north colonnade, now the temple's most salient feature, was re-erected in 1925–27. Part of the sacrificial altar remains.

To the south of the temple is a megaron (17.6m by 5.5m), dating from 580–570 BC. In the east corner of the temenos a stoa has been excavated which was probably built at the same time as the acropolis walls (late 6th century).

Temple B: The small shrine known as Temple B takes the form of a prostyle aediculum with pronaos and cella; recent archaeological work has suggested that it was dedicated to Demeter. The path leads left, following the east–west thoroughfare of the city, passing in front of the pronaos

Ozymandian scene in Selinunte. The rubble of Temple G, toppled and never rebuilt.

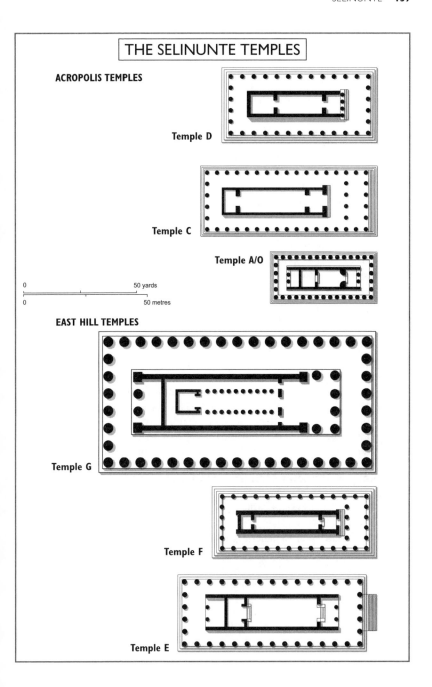

THE SELINUNTE TEMPLES

ACROPOLIS TEMPLES

Temple D

Temple C

Temple A/O

0   50 yards

0   50 metres

EAST HILL TEMPLES

Temple G

Temple F

Temple E

of Temple A. Near a solitary ancient ilex tree is a crude mosaic floor depicting an image of the Punic goddess Tanith.

Temple D: The wide main northern thoroughfare of the city (the North Gate can be seen at its end) leads away from the sea, past the stylobate of Temple D (570–554 BC), which stands beside the road: it carried 34 columns, measures 56m by 24m, and was the second temple to be built on the Acropolis, probably dedicated to Athena. Some of its blocks still have their bosses. Beyond, by a small pine tree, is a row of modest constructions thought to have been shops, each with two rooms, a court-yard, and stairs up to the living quarters on the first floor. Nearby are the founda-tions of the temple of the Small Metopes, named after the six small metopes found here, now in Palermo. It had a simple cella and adyton and measured 15.2m by 5.4m.

Just before the North Gate there is a good view east of the splendid, partially recon-structed Temple E on its hill. The **North Gate**, one of the main gates of the city, is well preserved. Beyond is a sophisticated defence system once thought to date from the time of Hermocrates, but probably constructed by Agathocles in 307–306 BC. The fortifica-tions include three semicircular towers, and a second line of walls c. 5m outside the earlier ones which were reinforced after their destruction by Hannibal in 409 BC using material from the acropolis, including capitals. The imposing remains are explained in a diagram at the site.

A sandy path continues through the low vegetation to the most recent area of excava-tions of the ancient city (*not yet open to the public*), near an old farmhouse, where the remains of a small industrial area have been found, dedicated to the manufacture of terracotta votive offerings. The city was orientated north–south and recent research has suggested it may originally have extended beyond the (later) perimeter wall to the north and into the valleys of the Cottone and Modione rivers. Another area of the city farther north, on the sand-covered hill of Manuzza, may have had a slightly different orienta-tion. Further north was a necropolis (probably on the site of a prehistoric burial-place).

Sanctuary of Demeter Malophoros and necropolis

Outside the North Gate, to the west, can be seen the excavations on the right bank of the Modione. These can most easily be reached by the rough road (c. 1km, used by the custodians) which branches off from the main crossroads near Temple C. Here the interesting **Sanctuary of Demeter Malophoros** (*open 9–1hr before sunset*), the 'Bearer of Fruits', consists of a sacred area enclosed by walls. It is now approached by a monu-mental entrance (late 5th century) and portico. In the centre is a huge sacrificial altar, and beyond, the temple (a megaron), thought to have been built c. 560 BC, with a Doric cornice. Nearby are the scant remains of two other sacred precincts, one of them dedi-cated to Zeus Meilichios with two altars, where numerous stelae carved with a male and female head were discovered. More than 5,000 terracotta figurines have been found in the vicinity, and an old farm building has been adapted as an antiquarium. Another temple is being excavated to the south.

Near a spring, some 200m north, a sacred edifice has recently been excavated and called **Temple M**. This may, in fact, be an altar or a monumental fountain of the 6th century BC. The **necropolis** proper extends for some kilometres to the west: several tombs and heaps of bones are still visible, behind the modern holiday village of Trisci-na, but at least another two burial-grounds have been located, besides this one.

THE CAVE DI CUSA

Off the road between Selinunte and Castelvetrano a country road (signposted) leads through extensive olive groves and vineyards to **Campobello di Mazara** (*map p. 543, C3*), a wine-producing centre. From Campobello a road (signposted) leads south to-wards Tre Fontane on the coast. At a crossroads by the Baglio Ingham, a right turn continues past a disused sewage plant to end at the **Cave di Cusa**, the ancient stone quarries used for building the temples of Selinunte (*open from 9 until 2hrs before sunset*). The early 19th-century Baglio Florio is now the Visitors' Centre (*open 9–1 & 3–6; T: 338 3627999, Sig. La Rosa*), where you will find detailed information about the quarries and the ancient city of Selinunte, how the columns were cut and transported, besides toilet facilities and a café.

The quarries have not been worked since the destruction of Selinunte in 409 BC and no excavations have ever been carried out here. Ancient olive trees grow among the peaceful ruins, and the beautiful site, inhabited by birds, is surrounded by olive and orange groves and vineyards. Only some 120m wide, the quarries extend for 2km, unenclosed, unannounced and often, especially in winter, utterly deserted and roman-tic. The various different processes of quarrying can be studied here, from the first incisions in the rock to the empty spaces left by the removal of the completed drums for columns. One block, still attached to the rock, seems to have been intended for a capital. Around each column carved out of the rock, a space of c. 50cm allowed room for the stonemason to work. Four drums stand close together, carved along the whole of their length and apparently waiting simply to be detached at their bases. The large cylindrical masses of stone (c. 3m by 2m) were probably intended for Temple G. It is thought that wooden frames were constructed around the columns and that they were transported to Selinunte, about 18km away, on wheels of solid wood strengthened by iron bands and pulled by oxen.

CASTELVETRANO & THE BELICE VALLEY

Castelvetrano (*map p. 543, C3*) is a farming community in the centre of a wine- and oil-producing area. The olive trees are very small, the fruits being gathered by hand for preserving or for making oil, thought to be the finest in Sicily; the local bread is par-ticularly good, too, and has been recommended by the Slow Food Foundation as wor-thy of protection. To the south, the view falls away across the cultivated plain towards the sea and the ruins of Selinunte. The simple architecture of many of the houses, with internal courtyards, is interesting, although the town was damaged in the Belice earth-quake of 1968. The body of the bandit Salvatore Giuliano was 'found' here in 1950.

EXPLORING CASTELVETRANO

The town centre

In the centre of town is the cramped and oddly-shaped Piazza Garibaldi, which is planted with trees. The **duomo** (usually entered by the side door in Piazza Umberto) is a 16th-century church with an unusual ornately decorated portal. The central roof beam has preserved its painted decoration. Two triumphal arches are bedecked with white stuccoes of cherubs, garlands and angels, by Antonino Ferraro and Gaspare Ser-potta (who also carved the four saints in the nave). In the presbytery there is gilded decoration by Antonino Ferraro and an *Assumption* (1619) by his son Orazio. The chapel to the right of the sanctuary has a 16th-century wooden Crucifix. The chapel to the left of the sanctuary has a marble Gaginesque statue, and, on the wall, a paint-ing attributed to Pietro Novelli. Off the north aisle, the Cappella della Maddalena has fine decoration, especially in the dome, by Tommaso Ferraro. The detached campanile dates from the 16th century.

On the corner of **Piazza Umberto** is an elaborate fountain with a statue of a nymph (1615) by the Neapolitan designer Orazio Nigrone. The church of the Purgatorio, now used as a lecture hall, has a decorative 18th-century façade. The Neoclassical Teatro Selinus of 1870 by Giuseppe Patricolo (*open 9–1 & 3–6.45, Aug mornings only; T: 0924 909610*) is also in the piazza. The little opera house, with 350 seats, looks like a mini-ature Doric temple, with four columns in front; in the entrance is a marble sculpture of *Children at Play* by Mario Rutelli.

From the top of Via Garibaldi, Via Fra' Pantaleo leads downhill southeast to **Piazza Regina Margherita**, where there is a little public garden and two churches. San Do-menico, which has a plain façade, contains a riot of 16th-century Baroque terracotta figures, coloured and stuccoed, by Antonino Ferraro, who included his self-portrait in the choir, and unusual funerary monuments, the richly-decorated tombs of the family of Don Carlos de Aragona, the first prince of Castelvetrano and later governor of Milan, who had commissioned Ferraro's meticulous work. On another side of the piazza is the 16th-century church of San Giovanni Battista, newly restored after the earthquake, with an elaborate façade and a green cupola. The interesting interior contains a remark-able statue of St John the Baptist by Antonello Gagini (1522) and three 17th-century paintings.

The Museo Civico

Via Garibaldi continues downhill southeastwards past Via Francesco La Croce, on the corner of which is the Biblioteca Comunale, which houses the Museo Civico (*open 9–1 & 3–6.30, Sun and holidays mornings only; T: 0924 909605*), displaying objects excavated at Selinunte. On the ground floor is an unusual little room, purposely designed to display the bronze statuette known as the *Efebo di Selinunte* (5th century BC), stolen

from the Town Hall (the mayor used it as a coat hanger) in 1962 and subsequently recovered in 1968. It was restored and displayed in the archaeological museum of Palermo for many years, before returning here. Found by a nine-year-old boy at Selinunte in 1882, it is thought to be a locally-produced work of c. 480–460 BC, made using the lost-wax method. The collection also includes the *Lamina plumbea*, a 5th-century BC transcription of a sacred law on a thin sheet of lead, coming from the archives of one of the Selinunte temples. It is the largest of its kind in existence and was recently returned from the Paul Getty Museum in Malibu, to whom it had been sold by clandestine diggers. Among the other finds from Selinunte are a red-figure krater with four satyrs (470–460 BC), Corinthian ware, terracottas, coins, and a two-headed stele from the sanctuary of Demeter Malophoros. The tawny alabaster *Madonna and Child* by Francesco Laurana and his workshop (c. 1460) comes from the ruined church of the Annunziata. The tourist office is on the first floor, over the museum.

Santissima Trinità di Delia

This lovely church (*map p. 543, C3*), about 3km west of the town, is reached by taking Via Pietro Colletta downhill from Piazza Umberto and continuing straight ahead (signposted 'Trinità di Delia'). After c. 1km, at a fork, the road (unsignposted) continues left past a gravel works and straight on (signposted 'Lago di Trinità'). It passes a small eucalyptus wood and then follows the white wall of the farm, which incorporates the church. The key is kept at the modern house on the right. The chapel, dating from the 11th–12th centuries, is a very fine building derived from Arab and Byzantine models. It was beautifully restored in 1880, and contains 19th-century family tombs. The crypt beneath is entered by an outside staircase. In the churchyard in a little wood is a romantic tombstone by Benedetto Civiletti, erected by the Saporito family. Beneath the hill is the beautiful reservoir of Lago della Trinità.

THE BELICE VALLEY

The Belice is one of Sicily's most important rivers. Once known as the *Hypsas*, it is formed by the union of the Belice Destro (the ancient *Crimissus*) from the mountains of Piana degli Albanesi, and the Belice Sinistro, or River Frattina, from Rocca Busambra. The two rivers meet near Poggioreale, forming the boundary between the provinces of Trapani and Agrigento. The Belice Valley, east of Castelvetrano, together with the parallel Mazaro, Modione and Carboj valleys, lie upon natural fault lines in the earth's crust, and earthquakes are therefore to be expected—but that of 15th January 1968, only 6.1 on the Richter scale, was exceptionally destructive. The inhabitants are still recovering from the impact. At least 370 people died and some 70,000 people were made homeless; reconstruction was long, slow, and fraught with scandal, and is still not complete.

Gibellina

The town of Gibellina (*map p. 543, C2*) was the worst affected in the earthquake. It stood below a ridge of sulphur-bearing hills and was abandoned completely after its destruction. The new town, relocated some 20km to the west, occupies a badly-chosen position that becomes unpleasantly hot in summer. Several of Italy's most prominent artists and sculptors provided the new town with works of art, some of which were clumsily made and are now already dilapidated. In 1994 the new church collapsed without warning. Little thought was given to town planning: the new houses have no balconies where people can put a pot of basil or a few geraniums, and the streets have no porticoes and only a few trees to provide protection from the relentless sun.

At the entrance to Gibellina is the **Porta** (1980), a five-pointed star designed by Pietro Consagra, who dedicated much of his artistic activity to the reconstruction of the town. In the central Viale Segesta is the **Museo Civico di Arte Contemporanea** (*open 9–1 & 4–7; closed Sun, Mon and holidays; T: 0924 67428*), which displays the models for the monuments of the new city, and paintings by Renato Guttuso, Fausto Pirandello, Mario Schifano and many others.

The ruins of the old town, **Rovine di Gibellina**, were covered with 13 hectares of white cement as a work of 'Land Art' by the Tuscan artist Alberto Burri; on the death of the artist in 1995 the work was still unfinished, and many years of neglect have led to the progressive decay of the cement. During the summer, open-air theatrical performances called *Orestiadi* are held here; for the first production, in 1983, the sculptor Arnaldo Pomodoro made items of scenery in wood and fibreglass, decorated with gold leaf. These have recently been restored and are shown in a special museum called the **Museo delle Trame Mediterranee** (*open 9–1 & 3–6, closed Mon; T: 0924 67844, www. orestiadi.it*), in the old wheat farm known as Baglio Di Stefano, c. 2km from Gibellina. It also houses a collection of local Elymian and Greek archaeological material, and there is an ethnographical section with costumes, jewellery from the Maghreb, and more than a hundred 14th-century majolica dishes from Spain. The gallery displays works donated to Gibellina by contemporary Italian artists such as Scialoja, Consagra, the Pomodoro brothers and Schifano.

Santa Ninfa, Poggioreale and Partanna

Even though the 1968 earthquake caused the collapse of a large majority of its houses, **Santa Ninfa** (*map p. 543, C2*) was rebuilt where it stood; it was a good choice. In Piazza Aldo Moro, near the public library, is the Museo Cordio (*open weekdays 9–1; www.museocordio.net*), dedicated to the genial local artist Nino Cordio and displaying a selection of his opus. His etchings are notable, as are his poignant little bronze statuettes. Near the town is a cave with splendid stalactites and 'cave pearls', and a necropolis of the Elymians, called Grotta di Santa Ninfa, protected as a nature reserve (*Visitor's Centre, Castello Rampinzeri, open Tues, Thur, Sat, Sun and holidays; T: 329 8620473/5, they will provide a guide, www.legambienteriserve.it*).

On the eastern border of the province is the old town of **Poggioreale**, also destroyed in the earthquake and later rebuilt. To the east of it, excavations in 1970 revealed part of an ancient city and a necropolis (with 7th- and 6th-century BC tombs). **Salaparuta** (*map p. 543, C3*), famous for its vineyards belonging to the Corvo family, was abandoned after the earthquake and a new town partially reconstructed.

Partanna (*map p. 543, C3*) is an agricultural centre which was also badly damaged. The Castello Grifeo (*open Oct–April 9.30–12.30 & 3.30–6.30, May–Sept 9.30–12.30 & 4.30–7.30, sometimes closes midnight in July–Aug; T: 0924 923970*), a Norman castle rebuilt in the 17th century, houses the Museo della Preistoria, displaying the prehistoric remains discovered nearby and elsewhere in the Belice Valley; including a remarkable collection of primitive vases in the style of Naro. In the courtyard is a damaged coat of arms sculpted by Francesco Laurana, who visited here in 1468. The Chiesa Madre has been partially reconstructed after being almost totally destroyed in the earthquake. It contains stuccoes by Vincenzo Messina, an organ by Paolo Amato, and a statue of the Madonna by the workshop of Francesco Laurana. Nearby in the Parco Archeologico di Contrada Stretta are numerous rock-hewn tombs, caves, and trenches for collecting water for irrigation, which have revealed the presence of a group of Beaker people who lived here c. 5,000 years ago. Objects discovered during the excavations are in the museum of Castello Grifeo (*see above*).

Salemi

North of Castelvetrano is Salemi (*map p. 543, C2*), probably the site of *Halicyae*, a town of the ancient Sicans or Elymians, and later an important Arab city. Even now the town's layout is clearly Arab in character. When Ferdinand of Aragon signed the famous edict on 31st March 1492 banishing Muslims and Jews from Sicily, Salemi was one of the few places to offer them refuge. The town was badly damaged in the 1968 earthquake, when the Chiesa Madre and the Capuchin Monastery were destroyed.

The steep and slippery Via Garibaldi leads up to the impressive golden 13th-century **castle** (*open 10–1 & 4–7, closed Mon*), with fine vaulted rooms and three towers, two square and one round, from which on 14th May 1860 Garibaldi raised the three-coloured banner, proclaiming Salemi to be capital of Italy, a privilege it maintained for only three days. The **church of the Collegio** (in Via D'Aguirre, near the summit of the hill), with its twisted Baroque columns either side of the entrance, became the new Chiesa Madre (among the various works of art, note the beautiful 18th-century organ) while the enormous Collegio itself, the Jesuit monastery, was restored to house the town's museums. The **Museo Civico** (*open 10–1 & 4–7, closed Mon; T: 0924 982376*) contains paintings and sculptures attributed to Domenico and Antonello Gagini and Francesco Laurana, brought here after the earthquake of 1968 from damaged churches, and an archaeological section, with material excavated at Mokarta and Monte Polizzo. The **Museo del Risorgimento** (*same opening times*) is dedicated to the Sicilian phase of the Unification of Italy, with memorabilia of Garibaldi's time in Sicily in 1860. A third museum, subject of much polemical discussion, is the **Museo della Mafia 'Leonardo Sciascia'** (*same opening times*). Some of its displays are so violent that they are not accessible to minors or sensitive people. The intention of the organisers was to shock, in order to underline the intolerably unpleasant character of the Mafia. A series of eight small cabins present progressively intensifying moments of horror. Other works of art on the subject, including sculptures and paintings, are displayed in the gallery. Further museums are planned for this complex.

Close to the Collegio is Largo 4 Novembre, with the Civic Library containing over 50,000 volumes, and the **Oratory of San Bartolomeo** (*open 10–1 & 4–7, closed Mon; T: 0924 982376*), which houses a display of the decorative loaves baked for the feasts of St Blaise and St Joseph (Feb 3 and March 19), for which Salemi is famous.

Continuing down the stairs at the end of Via D'Aguirre, you reach Piazza della Dittatura and the Town Hall. On the right is the charming **Rabato district**, and the church of Sant'Agostino (*open 10–1 & 4–7, closed Mon*), with a permanent exhibition of diocesan gold and silverware.

On the northern outskirts of the town is the early Christian basilica of **San Miceli**, with mosaic floors.

THE AEGADIAN ISLANDS

The Aegadian Islands, Favignana, Levanzo and Marettimo (*map p. 543*), lie 15–30km off the west coast of Sicily. They are connected by boat and hydrofoil services from Trapani or Marsala. The inhabitants, famed as skilled fishermen, are now turning to tourism to earn a living. The varied birdlife includes migratory species in spring and autumn and the islands now form a marine nature reserve, the largest of its kind in Italy. The waters around the islands are popular with divers, and those between Favignana and Marsala are also of great interest to marine archaeologists because of the many sea battles fought here. These islands were the ancient *Aegades* or *Aegates*, off which Lutatius Catulus routed the fleet of Hanno in 241 BC, one of the most resounding Roman victories over Carthage, thus putting an end to the First Punic War. In the mid-16th century the islands were given to the Genoese Camillo Pallavicini, from whom they were purchased in 1874 by the Florio, a family from Calabria, who settled in Palermo (*see p. 69*) and became important entrepreneurs on the west coast of Sicily.

FAVIGNANA

Favignana, 17km southwest of Trapani, is the largest island in the group and is mostly flat with a rather bare landscape, used mainly as pastureland. The best swimming is at the rocky bay of Cala Rossa, on the north coast; there are more crowded sandy beaches on the south coast between Grotta Pergiata and Punta Longa, where there is a tiny port and fishing village. In the eastern part of the island are numerous disused tufa quarries (the soft white tufa found here is an excellent building material). The small quarries are now mostly used as orchards, although one quarry still operates, supplying the local market, and some have been transformed into hotels. Near the cemetery, several wells with huge wooden water wheels of Arab origin survive, once used for irrigation. At Punta Marsala there is a view of Marsala and (on the left) the low, green island of Mozia. The prettiest part of the island is to the west beyond Mt Santa Caterina, where a Norman castle, once used as a prison and now abandoned, can be reached in about 1hr on foot.

The town

The little medieval town, where most of the inhabitants live and where all the shops are situated, was refounded in 1637 by the Pallavicini family. **Palazzo Florio**, a large Art Nouveau palace near the port, was built in 1876 for Ignazio Florio by Giuseppe Damiani Almeyda. It is now used as a police headquarters. Nearby is a smaller 19th-century palace, now the Town Hall, with a statue of Ignazio Florio in front of it. The little church of Sant'Antonio da Padova is close by. Via Vittorio Emanuele, the main street, leads to **Piazza Matrice**, where there is the main church with a green dome, near the tourist office. Numerous shops sell smoked tuna fish and *bottarga* (dried tuna roe).

The town has a peaceful, rather run-down atmosphere, with a number of the cube-like houses half-restored, half-built, or for sale. The passenger boats and hydrofoils dock at the picturesque harbour, filled with fishing vessels. Here the **Stabilimento Florio delle Tonnare di Favignana e delle Formiche** (*open summer 6pm–midnight; T: 0923 808444, 0923 808111*) is an enormous old tuna-canning facility built in 1859 by Giulio Drago for the Pallavicini, and beautifully restored. It used to be among the most important in the Mediterranean, processing 10,000 tuna a year. The bluefin tuna (*Thunnus thynnus*), renowned for its excellent quality, is no longer caught here, to give the fish (on the verge of extinction) the chance to recuperate. Before the cannery was built the fish were salted, hung up by the tail, then cut in pieces to be smoked, cooked or preserved in oil. Every piece of the fish was used: the skin was used as sandpaper; the tail and fins became brooms; some bones were used to make tools; and other parts either boiled to make glue or fishmeal. The industry thrived and in 1874 Drago ceded his contract to the Florio who ran this factory until 1937. By 1977 it had closed down owing to competition from Atlantic tuna fishing (yellowfin). The buildings, a splendid example of industrial archaeology, are now owned by the region of Sicily, and house a theatre and a concert hall; soon to come will be a restaurant, artisans' workshops, a marine-research centre, and the Archaeological Museum. This last will display an intriguing collection of objects found on the seabed. A few years ago some fishermen discovered the wreck of an Arab ship dated c. 1000, with its storage jars still intact. More recently, four young divers found sherds of pottery among the seaweed not far offshore, and also an enormous octopus, guarding a pewter wine bottle (which they retrieved with some difficulty). Still sealed and intact, it is believed to be the oldest bottle of wine in the world, dated to the 14th century.

LEVANZO

Levanzo (pron: Lévanzo), 15km from Trapani, has no natural springs, and virtually no cars. The ancient *Phorbantia* or Pliny's *Bucinna*, its austere, windbeaten landscape is set in a transparent sea of turquoise and cobalt blue. The island is particularly interesting for botanists: many of the plants are endemic. It is also famous for its caves, notably the Grotta del Genovese, which has the most interesting prehistoric wall-art in Italy, discovered by chance in 1950. The cave paintings, comparable with those at Lascaux in France or Altamira in Spain, date from the Neolithic period; the primitive paint is made of animal fat, ochre and charcoal; fish and people are represented. The stunning incised drawings of bison and deer date from the Upper Palaeolithic period, when the island was still joined to Sicily. A track leads across the island from the port to the cave, which can also be reached by boat. Visits (jeep or boat) must be booked in advance (*the excursion lasts 2hrs by jeep, 3hrs by boat; departures at 10.30 and 3; T: 0923 924032, 339 7418800, www.grottadelgenovese.it*).

LA MATTANZA

Tuna fishing has historically been an important part of life in these islands, as this scene from a red-figure krater shows (in the Mandralisca museum in Cefalù).

In the deep channel between Levanzo and Favignana, the traditional method of tuna fishing known as *la Mattanza* was practised in spring since prehistory. A series of net traps formed a corridor leading to a square pen called the *camera della morte* (death chamber), which was activated under the instructions of the head fisherman, called the *rais*. The wind called the *Favonio* which brings the fish here for spawning, starts to blow at the end of May or in early June; choosing the right moment for fishing was all important. The females, already fertilised by the males, escaped the trap because they swim deep down, about 20m below the surface, while the males are much closer to the surface. When there were around 100 fish in the pen, the area was encircled by boats, with that belonging to the *rais* in the centre, and the nets were slowly hauled in, accompanied by the ancient haunting chants of the fishermen, called *cialome*: 'aja mola, aja mola, aja mola e iamuninni ... Gesù Cristu cu' li Santi ... nianzò ... nianzò ...', to maintain the correct rhythm. It was very hard work; one fish caught in 1974 weighed 600kg. Tuna tend to dive when in danger, so that during this operation they often collided with one another and hit their heads: by the time the net reached the surface (the whole operation took about an hour) many of them were wounded and stunned. They were then harpooned and pulled into the boats. The sea ran red with blood; it was a horrid but fascinating spectacle which had changed little since the Bronze Age. The catch drastically declined in recent years, due in part to modern fishing techniques and to over-exploitation encouraged by the high prices offered by Far Eastern markets. Sicily once had many tuna fisheries: they have all closed now, because the bluefin tuna is in grave danger of extinction, and if the fishing is not stopped, in four or five years there will be no more left at all.

A capsized Roman cargo-ship was recently located close to Levanzo, with its cargo of garum amphorae still intact. In 2004 underwater archaeologists discovered some wrecks of military vessels dating back to 241 BC on the seabed just off the north coast of the island: several anchors, a bronze helmet, and an impressive bronze ram from a Roman ship have so far been brought to the surface.

GARUM

In Roman times, Levanzo was noted for the production of *garum*, a fish sauce much appreciated by connoisseurs. Garum was widely used in ancient times for preparing dishes of meat, fish or vegetables, as well as in fruit recipes and drinks. The flavour of the sauce varied according to the type of fish used in its manufacture, and gourmets could distinguish between different provenances. There were famous garum factories in Sardinia, Tunisia, Morocco, Lebanon, Spain and Sicily. The garum produced on Levanzo was one of the most highly prized. To make the sauce, small fish, or the intestines of big fish, or both, were placed in terracotta pots or stone vats, together with salt, sea water, and aromatic herbs. After a week in the sun, the mixture was stirred and again left to ferment. After 20 more days, the garum, or *liquamen*, was strained off into amphorae. The solids, called *allec*, left in the vats, were not thrown away, but sold in the markets, where the poor were only too glad to eat them with bread.

MARETTIMO

Marettimo (pron: Maréttimo), once known as *Hiera* or *Hieromesus* (sacred place), is the most isolated of the Aegadian Islands, 38km from Trapani, and immersed in a transparent deep blue sea. Only 16km square, wild, beautiful and mountainous, it is rich in natural springs and grottoes, and is the best preserved of the three islands, mainly because it was once a notorious pirate stronghold, which discouraged settlers. There are many birds, especially during the migratory passage, and the nesting species include Bonelli's eagle, peregrine falcon, kestrel, lesser kestrel, buzzard, black wheatear as well as many interesting sea birds, including the storm petrel, gannet, and Cory's shearwater. In the interior of the island there are even boars and mouflons. The island is cared for by the Azienda Forestale, and there are well-signposted tracks to the various points of interest. With a charming little Moorish-style village, there are no roads, no cars and no hotels. Samuel Butler suggested that this was the island described in the story of the Cyclops in Homer's *Odyssey*, the islets of Le Formiche being the rocks hurled by Polyphemus at Odysseus. A rewarding and spectacular hike leads to the ruins of the ancient castle called Castello Saraceno at Punta Troia. Some Roman ruins and a small Palaeo-Christian church can also be found. Boat trips around the island and its sea caves can be arranged at the harbour. At the end of the 19th century many islanders from Marettimo found their way to Monterey in California, where they established a successful canned-fish enterprise, immortalised by John Steinbeck in his *Cannery Row* (1945).

PANTELLERIA

Far away to the southwest, about 110km from the Sicilian mainland (and only 67km from Tunisia) lies Pantelleria (83km square, pop. 8,000), the largest of Sicily's offshore islands. The wild scenery includes volcanic phenomena such as hot springs (the last eruption was in 1891). The central conical peak rises to a height of 836m. Tiny capers, full of flavour, said to be the finest in the world, figs, and sweet raisin grapes called *zibibbo* are cultivated, and the island is especially famous for its wines, Moscato di Pantelleria and Moscato passito. In fact, most of the mountainsides are terraced, with tiny gardens descending to the sea, each with its dry-stone wall to protect the crops from the wind. The cube-shaped black stone cottages, with domed whitewashed roofs, called *dammusi*, are of Arab origin. The inhabitants of Pantelleria are farmers rather than fishermen, showing considerable patience and fortitude in caring for their crops in the difficult, windswept volcanic terrain. As well as the capers and grapes, they produce superb olive oil and citrus fruits, in spite of strong winds, little rain and no underground springs. Sufficient water is provided for cultivation thanks to the lava-stone walls built around the plants to protect them from the wind; humidity condenses during the night onto the cold stone, and then gradually seeps through the porous rock until it reaches the roots of the plants. This simple, ancient method is now being studied at an international level, in the hope answers may be provided for other areas in the world with similar problems.

Now protected as a nature reserve run by the Azienda Forestale, Pantelleria is also particularly attractive to lovers of the sea. There are no beaches, but swimming from the rocks is very pleasant, because the water is clean and clear. Dolphins are common, and the rare nun seal is once again occasionally being spotted, after many years of absence from Italian waters. Scuba diving is exceptionally good here. It is a good place for birdwatching too, especially during the migratory passage, when herons, cranes, flamingoes, geese and ducks can be seen. During the summer the hoopoe is resident, as is the cattle egret, the Tunisian chaffinch and the blue rock thrush. Among the mammals, the wildcat is still present. The Pantelleria ass is a kind of donkey native to the island, where it has been used since the 1st century BC. It is large (the size of a pony), sure-footed and very strong, with a smooth, shiny black pelt. It became extinct 20 years ago because islanders were no longer using them (the last one slipped into the sea and drowned). However, forestry technicians at the San Matteo stud farm at Erice have been able to recreate the animal by taking genes from donkeys throughout Italy which had the Pantelleria ass in their ancestry. It has taken them 17 years, but recently the first four Pantelleria asses were shipped to their island, where they will be used for tourism (trekking around the volcanoes). Of Pantelleria's 597 plant species, 13 are endemic.

HISTORY OF PANTELLERIA

The island was the legendary home of Calypso, the nymph who was able to distract Odysseus from his travels for seven years. Archaeological evidence has proved the island was inhabited in the Neolithic era, when the obsidian on the southern shores would have been particularly useful, and later it was home to a Phoenician settlement called *Hiranin*, meaning 'place of the birds'. The Greeks called it *Cossyra*, meaning 'small one', a name it maintained under the Romans, who took it in 217 BC. The Arabs gave it the name it still bears, *Bint er-rhia*, or 'daughter of the wind'. After conquest by Count Roger in 1123 it remained a Sicilian possession. During the Second World War it was used as a base for harrying Allied convoys. Reduced by heavy bombardment during May 1943, the island was captured from the sea on 11th June with 11,000 prisoners, Allied casualties being reported as 'one soldier bitten by a mule'. The island was once used as a place of exile for political prisoners. It is now popular with the rich and famous: Gerard Depardieu, Sting and Giorgio Armani, among others, own properties on the island.

EXPLORING PANTELLERIA

The port of Pantelleria was completely rebuilt after the Second World War; the little houses around the harbour go back to the 1950s, and are not renowned for their architectural elegance. The oldest building is the forbidding **Castello Barbacane** (*open Mon–Fri 9–1 & 7–11; Sat, Sun and holidays 9–1 & 7–midnight*), first built by the Arabs, when it was surrounded by water and entered by a drawbridge; successive dominations each altered the castle to adapt it to their particular needs; it was used as a prison until 1975, and now it is intended that the museum of Pantelleria will be situated within its walls; objects found during recent archaeological excavations, including the Roman sculptures (*see below*) will be displayed here.

At **Mursia** 58 prehistoric tombs known as *sesi* were discovered by Paolo Orsi in the 19th century. These large domed tumuli were built in blocks of lava in the 17th century BC, and were probably founded in order to exploit the deposits of obsidian, the volcanic glass used for making knives. Only 27 have survived, notably the Sese Grande, the others having either fallen into ruin or been engulfed by new buildings. Several of them still contained human remains, buried in the foetal position, with their personal possessions close by. Recent excavations revealed a square stone hut, in which a cloth bag with some items of bronze jewellery with glass beads was found, perhaps from Egypt or Syria.

More recent excavations at Cossyra have brought to light an exceptional series of three finely-carved Roman heads. Two of them, a portrait of Julius Caesar and another of Antonia the Younger, daughter of Mark Antony, sister-in-law to Tiberius and mother of Claudius, are of Paros marble, and were found in a cistern, where apparently they had been placed with care; the third (also found in a cistern) is a stunningly realistic portrait of Titus, son of Vespasian. The finds are evidence of the vitality of Cossyra in the 1st–2nd centuries AD, and will be displayed in the museum of Castello Barbacane. In another recent exceptional find, close to shore at Cala Tramontana on the east coast, 3,418 Carthaginian bronze coins, minted between 264 and 241 BC, were found scattered on the seabed. On one side the coins show Tanith crowned with wheat, and on the other a horse's head. With all probability the money was intended to pay the soldiers taking part in the First Punic War.

Among the villages of the island, **Scauri** is high on the edge of a cliff, with a spectacular view down to its little fishing-harbour. **Nicà** is a fishing-village, on a narrow inlet, while the inland village of **Rekhale**, close by, is still intact, with the typical stone cottages and tiny, luxuriant gardens. Spectacular views can be had at Saltalavecchia and the ancient landing-place of **Balata dei Turchi**, both on the south coast. The most famous viewpoint is at **Punta dell'Arco**, where there is good swimming and the rock formations look like the head and the trunk of an elephant extending into the sea. **Gadir** is another fishing-village, where the sea is easily accessible even for inexperienced swimmers.

The extinct volcanoes in the middle of the island, **Montagna Grande** (836m) and **Monte Gibele** (700m) offer rewarding treks through vineyards and pinewoods; the wobbly song-flight of the fan-tailed warbler can be observed, even in the middle of the day, and the Algerian form of the bluetit can also be spotted. The old volcanic cones are called *cuddie*. The beautiful inland crater-lake of **Bagno dell'Acqua** (Lago di Venere, or the lake of Venus) is about 6km from the port. It is fed by a hot-water spring and is 500m in diameter and 2m above sea-level.

PRACTICAL INFORMATION

GETTING AROUND

• **By air:** There are daily flights to Vincenzo Florio Airport at Birgi, equidistant from Trapani and Marsala (*www.aeroportotrapani.com; www.airgest.it*) from several mainland Italian airports. Buses connect the airport to Trapani, Marsala, Mazara del Vallo and Palermo. Flights to Pantelleria from Palermo and Trapani are run year-round by Meridiana (*www.meridiana.it*), and from June–Sept by Blu Express (*www.blu-express.com*) and Alitalia (*www.alitalia.it*) from Milan and Rome.

• **By sea:** *NB: When sailing to Pantelleria, always check beforehand that ferries are leaving: high seas are common.*

Siremar (*www.siremar.it*) runs ferries from Trapani to Pantelleria daily except Sat in winter (4–5 hrs) and to the Aegadian Islands (Favignana and Levanzo 4 daily, c. 50 mins; Marettimo twice weekly, 3 hrs) from Molo della Sanità. **Traghetti delle Isole** (*www.traghettidelleisole.it*) runs ferries from Trapani to Pantelleria every day in summer and daily except Sun during the rest of the year. Hydrofoils (more expensive) for the Aegadian Islands, run by **Siremar** (website above), leave from Molo Dogana, those run by **Ustica Lines** (*www.usticalines.it*) leave from the Banchina Dogana, Via Ammiraglio Staiti, several times a day in summer: services also for Pantelleria and Ustica. Ustica Lines also run hydrofoils from Mazara del Vallo to Pantelleria and Lampedusa.

Siremar ticket offices: In Trapani: Agenzia Sanges, Stazione Marittima, Molo Sanità. On Favignana: Compagnia delle Egadi, Molo San Leonardo. On Levanzo: Caterina Campo, Via Calvario 29. On Marettimo: Francesco Torrente, Piazza Umberto 2. On Pantelleria: Agenzia Rizzo, Via Borgo Italia 22.

Traghetti delle Isole ticket offices: In Trapani: Agenzia Egatour, Via Ammiraglio Staiti 13. On Pantelleria: Adriano Minardi, Via Borgo Italia 15.

Ustica Lines ticket offices: In Trapani: Banchina Dogana, Via Ammiraglio Staiti. In Marsala: Molo Porto Marsala, Piazza Piemonte Lombardo. In Mazara del Vallo: Agenzia MG Group, Lungomare Fata Morgana 20. On Favignana: Molo San Leonardo. On Levanzo: Molo Aliscafi. On Marettimo: Agenzia Polisano, Corso Umberto 15. On Pantelleria: Agenzia Minardi, Via Borgo Italia 15.

• **By train:** The central railway station in Trapani is in Piazza Umberto, with services to Palermo, Marsala (c. 40mins), Mazara del Vallo (c. 1hr) and Castelvetrano (c. 2–3hrs). Trains stop at Ragattisi, the nearest station for the boat to Mozia; jetties are about 1km walk from the station. Segesta is on the Palermo–Trapani line (infrequent services) but the station is a 20-min walk from the site (*www.trenitalia.it*).

• **By bus:** ATM (*www.atmtrapani.it*) runs services within Trapani, to the port and also to the cableway station for Erice. **AST** (*www. aziendasicilianatrasporti.it*) run to Trapani airport, also Alcamo, Erice, Castellammare, Marsala, Mazara del Vallo, Nubia Salt Museum, San Vito Lo Capo, Segesta and Selinunte. Lumia (*www.autolineelumia.it*) connects

Trapani to Agrigento and a wide variety of other destinations, and Marsala to Mazara del Vallo and Agrigento. **Salemi** (*www.autoservizi-salemi.it*) connects Marsala to Castelvetrano, Mazara del Vallo, Palermo, Salemi and Trapani airport. **Segesta** (*www.segesta.it*) runs intercity services from Piazza Malta in Trapani to/ from Palermo and Palermo Airport. There are buses from Castelvetrano to Selinunte (the stop is a 5-min walk from the entrance).

• **By cableway:** A cablecar (*funivia*) connects Trapani (*corner SP 31 Trapani–Erice and Via Capua, Casa Santa; www.funiviaerice.it) and Erice in just over 10mins, Tues–Fri 9.10–9pm, Sat and public holidays 9.30–midnight, Sun 9.40–9.30pm, closed Mon for maintenance*).

WHERE TO STAY

Alcamo (*map p. 543, C2*)

€€ **Centrale.** Restored *palazzo* where Goethe once stayed. Rooms are plainly and simply furnished. Good restaurant. Centrally situated. *Via Amendola 24, T: 0924 507845, www. hotelcentrale.sicilia.it.*

€€ **La Battigia.** On the beach at Alcamo Marina (completely deserted in winter), with 26 rooms, many with sea views. Pool, restaurant. *Lungomare La Battigia, T: 0924 597259, www. labattigia.it.*

€ **Terme Gorga.** Simple little hotel and spa between Alcamo and Segesta. Restaurant. Swimming pool filled with water from the nearby Caldo river. *Contrada Gorga, west of Alcamo and the A29, T: 0924 23842, www. termegorga.com.*

Calatafimi Segesta (*map p. 543, C2*)

€ **Mille Pini.** Well-organised small modern hotel in the pinewoods just out of town. Good value for money, with restaurant. Close to Segesta. *Belvedere Francesco Vivona 4, T: 0924 951260, www.hotelmillepini.com.*

Castellammare del Golfo (*map p. 543, C1*)

€€€ **Cetarium.** On the harbour, a beautifully restored tuna fishery; bright and comfortable rooms, excellent restaurant. Car park. *Via Zangara 45, T: 0924 533401, www.hotelcetarium.it.*

€€ **Al Madarig.** ■ Close to the castle and the old city, 38 rooms, good restaurant, car park. *Piazza Petrolo 7, T: 0924 33533, www. almadarig.com.*

€ **Cala Marina.** Attractive and practical little hotel, on the harbour, in a converted warehouse. No restaurant, car park. They can organise boat trips and diving. *Via Zangara 1, T: 0924 531841, www.hotelcalamarina.it.*

€ **Locanda Scirocco.** Unusual hotel with 12 rooms in two 18th-century *palazzi* in the old city centre. All rooms have air conditioning. Good breakfasts, no restaurant, but an excellent wine bar offering opportunites to taste local products. Airport/port shuttle on request, boat trips organised. *Corso Garibaldi 117, T: 0924 30010, www.locandascirocco.it.*

Castelvetrano (*map p. 543, C3*)

€ **Villa Mimosa.** ■ About halfway between Castelvetrano and Selinunte, in the countryside. Very attractive self-catering rooms, garden full of dogs and cats, pergola and veranda. The home of Jackie Sirimanne, a sommelier and expert on wine and olive oil, a charming and helpful person. Breakfast is provided, evening meals on some nights. *Contrada La Rocchetta, Castelvetrano, T: 0924 44583, 338 1387388, www.tenutamimosa.it.*

Custonaci (*map p. 543, B1*)

€€€ **Villa Zina.** New hotel with 89 rooms and suites, fitness centre, tennis, bowls, huge pool, good restaurant. *Baglio Messina, east of the centre. T: 0923 973937, www.villazina.it.*

€ **Cala Buguto.** Tiny hotel in an old house not far from the cave which encloses the hamlet of Scurati, with 9 rooms and a restaurant serving delicious food. *Via D1, Contrada Scurati, T: 0923 973953, www.hoteltrapanicalabuguto.it.*

€ **Il Cortile.** Delightful little hotel in a *baglio*

close to the sanctuary, with a small pool, car park, restaurant serving excellent local dishes (also vegetarian on request), pizza baked in a stone oven, and good local wine. The owner, signor Andrea Oddo, is founder-member of the Living Museum Association. *Via Scurati 67, T: 0923 1941540 and 0923 971750 (after 5.30pm at at weekends), www.hotelilcortile.it.*

Erice (*map p. 543, B1*)

€€ **Elimo.** Small and comfortable, on the main street, with a rooftop terrace, and lovely little courtyard garden; no restaurant. *Via Vittorio Emanuele 75, T: 0923 869377, www. hotelelimo.it. Map p. 126, 3.*

€€ **Moderno.** Fascinating old hotel with exceptionally good restaurant, part of the Buon Ricordo chain. *Via Vittorio Emanuele 67, T: 0923 869300, www.hotelmodernoerice.it. Map p. 126, 3.*

Guarrato (*map p. 543, B2*)

€€ **Vultaggio.** Hilltop farm south of Trapani, surrounded by citrus and olive groves, with pool and fitness centre. Good restaurant. Medieval castle nearby. Bowls and clay-pigeon shooting. *Via Quartana, Contrada Misiliscemi, east of Guarrato, T: 0923 864261, 347 6696059, www.misiliscemi.it.*

Marsala (*map p. 543, B2*)

€€€ **Stella d'Italia.** Built in 1873, Marsala's first hotel overlooks the cathedral. 35 delightful rooms, no restaurant. Part of the Best Western chain. *Via Rapisardi 7, T: 0923 761889, www.hotelstelladitalia.it. Map p. 148, 4.*

€€€ **New Hotel Palace.** Delightful 19th-century building, recently restored, lovely hall. 55 rooms and suites, garden, pool, car park, restaurant, excellent wine list. *Lungomare Mediterraneo 57, T: 0923 719492, www. newhotelpalace.com. Map p. 148, 6..*

€€ **Carmine.** A 17th-century monastery transformed into a modern, comfortable hotel, with 28 welcoming rooms, all different, and a garden. *Piazza Carmine, T: 0923*

711907, www.hotelcarmine.it. Map p. 148, 3.
€€ **La Finestra sul Sale.** Three comfortable rooms in an old salt mill, right in front
of the island of Mozia, north of Marsala on
the coast. Rooms have views of the salt pans.
*Saline Ettore e Infersa, Contrada Ettore Infersa,
T: 0923 733003, www.salineettoreinfersa.com.*
Mazara del Vallo (*map p. 543, B3*)
€€€ **Giardino di Costanza.** Situated among
palms, olive groves and orchards, this is the
only Kempinski hotel in Italy, and is also part
of the 'hotels of silence' chain. Spa centre
offers beauty treatments using the local salt.
It is some way from town, although they have
a private beach. *7km on Via Salemi, T: 0923
675000, www.kempinski-sicily.com.*
€€€ **Visir Resort.** Comfortable hotel a short
walk from the sandy beach of the Tonnarella,
with 27 luxurious rooms and suites, restaurant, cosy bar, huge pool and fitness centre.
*Via del Mare 211, Tonnarella, T: 0923 653738,
www.visirresort.com.*
€€ **Mahara.** Once the winery of the English
Hopps family, now an elegant hotel just out
of town, offering 81 comfortable rooms and
suites, good restaurant, garden, fitness centre.
Many special offers. *Lungomare San Vito 3, T:
0923 673800, www.maharahotel.it.*
€ **City Centre B&B.** Situated on the first
floor of the old railway station, 4 diminu-
tive rooms with private bath, TV and air
conditioning, ample parking space. *Piazza De
Gasperi 13, T: 0923 909769, 349 3779743, 340
2310013, www.bbcitycentre.it.*
€ **Foresteria Monastica.** It is possible to stay
at the Norman-built Benedictine convent of
San Michele. The nuns offer accommodation
for 40 people in double and triple rooms with
private bathroom, and dormitories separated
into monastic-like cells. Refectory. Central,
friendly, and very good value for money. *Via
Sant'Agostino, Piazza San Michele, T: 0923
906565, 347 7225069 (call 9.30–8, Sun and*

holidays 9.30–1), www.foresteriasanmichele.com.
San Vito Lo Capo (*map p. 543, B1*)
€€€ **Capo San Vito.** Right on the beach.
Garden, excellent restaurant for candlelit
dinners on the terrace, well-furnished rooms,
small fitness centre, car park. *Via San Vito 1,
T: 0923 972122 or 972284, www.caposanvito.it.*
€€ **Pocho.** Tiny inn 2km south of town, in
a spectacular position on a rocky point. 12
welcoming, nicely furnished rooms, pool and
good restaurant; car park. *Contrada Makari, T:
0923 972525, www.pocho.it.*
€–€€ **Baglio Cusenza.** Comfortable B&B
on the main street, 200m from the beach,
with two spacious rooms and a bed-sitter, all
with private bath, TV and air conditioning.
Prices slightly higher during the September
Cous Cous Fest. *Via Savoia 220 (corner of Via
Foritano), T: 0923 972427, 320 3757439, www.
bagliocusenza.it.*
Scopello (*map p. 543, C1*)
€ **Casale Corcella.** A panoramic B&B in an
old stone house in the country, with 5 comfortable rooms, 1km inland (west) of Scopello
and 2km from the Zingaro reserve. *Contrada
Scardina, T: 368 3654482 for info; to book see
www.casalecorcella.com.*
Selinunte/Marinella (*map p. 543, C3*)
€€€ **Admeto.** In a lovely position overlooking the fishing harbour and a short walk from
the temples, modern hotel with comfortable
rooms, good restaurant. *Via Palinuro 3, T:
0924 46796, www.hoteladmeto.it.*
€€ **Alceste.** Small, modern, family-run hotel
with Orazio's excellent restaurant; walking
distance from the archaeological park. *Via
Alceste 21, T: 0924 46184, www.hotelalceste.it.*
Trapani and environs (*map p. 543, B1*)
€€€ **Relais Antiche Saline.** Beautifully
restored *baglio* in the salt marshes at Nubia,
on the south side of the bay of Trapani. 18
lovely rooms, pool, good restaurant. *Via delle
Saline, T: 0923 868029, www.relaisantichesaline.*

com. Map p. 543, B2.

€€ **Ai Lumi.** Five minutes from the station, in the old quarter, lovely award-winning B&B in an 18th-century palazzo with courtyard, air conditioning, also restaurant and self-catering apartments, English, French and German spoken. Very good breakfasts. *Corso Vittorio Emanuele 71, T: 0923 540922, www.ailumi.it. Map p. 120, 6.*

€ **Duca di Castelmonte.** Comfortable old olive farm close to Trapani, with good home cooking. *Via Salvatore Motisi 3, Contrada Xitta, T: 0923 526139, www.ducadicastelmonte.it. Map p. 543, B2.*

€ **Maccotta.** In the old city, small guesthouse with 20 comfortable rooms and friendly owners, airport transfer on request, no restaurant. *Via degli Argentieri 4, T: 0923 28418, www.albergomaccotta.it. Map p. 120, 7.*

Zingaro Nature Reserve (*map p. 543, C1*)
€ From Oct–May you can stay in one of the refuges in the nature reserve; remember you have to carry everything with you, including food, water, and a sleeping-bag. *T: 0924 35108, www.riservazingaro.it. Click on 'Rifugi' and fill in the online form (Italian only) or go to their office at Via Segesta 197 in Castellammare.*

Aegadian Islands
Favignana

€€€ **Casa Favonio.** 19th-century villa with 5 carefully designed rooms, each with a terrace and a superb view over Marettimo. Open April–end Oct. *Contrada Seppi Torrente 3, T: 0923 921179, www.casafavonio.it.*

€€€ **Cave Bianche.** Modern design in a low-environmental-impact hotel in an old tufa quarry. Beautiful rooms with stone walls, wooden furniture made by local craftsmen. Pool, good breakfasts. *Strada Comunale Fanfalo, T: 0923 925451, www.cavebianchehotel.it.*

€€ **Aegusa.** Delightful little hotel, central, with 28 rooms in two old buildings. Very

welcoming, lots of rattan furniture, excellent restaurant on the patio. *Via Garibaldi 11 (at the port), T: 0923 922430, www.aegusahotel.it.*

€€ **Egadi.** The oldest hotel on Favignana. 11 cool and relaxing rooms. Book well in advance. Renowned restaurant. Closed in winter. *Via Colombo 17 (at the port), T: 0923 921232, www.albergoegadi.it.*

Levanzo

Holiday cottages are available at **Lisola Residence** (*lisola.eu*) and **La Plaza Residence** (*levanzoresidence.com*). For simple overnight stays there are two *pensioni*, both with restaurants: € **Pensione dei Fenici**, *Via Lungomare 18 (Via Calvario), T: 0923 924083, www.isoladilevanzo.it/ITA/ristorant_fenici/ristorante-fenici.htm* and € **Paradiso**, *Via Lungomare 133, T: 0923 924080, www.isoladilevanzo.it/ITA/albergo_paradiso/pensione-paradiso.htm. Closed mid-Dec to early March.*

Marettimo

Rooms can be rented in private houses: fishermen will meet you on the quay to propose this kind of accommodation. Islanders offering rooms or apartments and other services, such as boat excursions and fishing trips include **Rosa dei Venti**, *Via Punta San Simone 4, Contrada Crocilla, T: 0923 923249, www.isoladimarettimo.it* and **Simmar**, *Piazza Scalo Nuovo 1, T: 0923 923392, www.vacanze-marettimo.it.*
€ **Marettimo Residence** offers self-catering apartments in cottages for stays of one week or more, garden, very helpful hosts, *Via Telegrafo 3, Località Spatarello, T: 0923 923202, www.marettimoresidence.com.* € **La Perla** is a B&B overlooking the old harbour, simple comfortable rooms with private bath, panoramic rooftop terrace, English spoken. *Via Scalo Vecchio 13, T: 0923 923206, 333 2782602, 333 6512618, www.marettimolaperla.it.*

Pantelleria

NB: Hotels on Pantelleria usually take bookings on a weekly basis only.

€€€ **Santa Teresa Resort**. 18 rooms among the vineyards in the interior of the island. Three pools, golf, horse-riding. Open end April–end Sept. *Contrada Monastero Alto-Sibà, T: 0923 916389, www.santateresa.it.*

€€ **Relais Gli Euterpini**. On the southwest side, close to the sea, 8 *dammusi* surrounded by pine trees, good restaurant. Open June–Sept. *T: 0923 918070, www.euterpini.it.*

€€ **Zubebi Resort**. ■ Hilltop position overlooking the port for this Oriental-style resort, with beautifully restored and furnished *dammusi*, pool, fitness centre, open-air restaurant under the palms, car park. *Contrada Zubebi, T: 0923 913653, www.zubebi.com.*

€ **Le Case di Gloria**. Facing west, for glorious sunsets, close to the sea and to the village of Scauri, 9 *dammusi* each accommodating from 2–10 people, pool. *Contrada Penna, T: 328 2770934, 339 7551824, www.dammusidigloria.it.*

WHERE TO EAT

Bonagia (*map p. 543, B1*)
€€ **Sansica**. On the sea front, famous old restaurant renowned for pasta cooked in lobster broth and dishes based on tuna. *Lungomare Bonagia 45, T: 0923 573176.*

Castellammare del Golfo (*map p. 543, C1*)
€€€ **Ristorante del Golfo**. Fresh sardines in *agrodolce* (sweet-sour sauce), home-made *busiati* (macaroni) with new-born anchovies, *macco* (broad-bean potage). Leave room for the *cassatelle*, little pies filled with lemon-scented ricotta. Closed all day Tues in winter, open Tues evening in summer. *Via Segesta 153, T: 0924 30257.*

€€ **Al Burgo**. Well presented, imaginative food, prepared with marvellous fish or meat and local vegetables. Good wine list. Closed Mon lunchtime. *Via Malta 19, T: 0924 531882.*

Castelvetrano (*map p. 543, C3*)
€€ **Antiche Tradizioni**. Traditional simple

Sicilian dishes, good pasta and meat (the cook prepares her own special dessert with chopped almonds and chocolate), pleasant atmosphere, local wines. Closed Mon. *Via San Martino 11, T: 0924 907759.*

€ **Da Giovanni**. ■ Superb home-style cooking, using local vegetables, fish and meat. Closed Sun. *Via Milazzo 26, T: 0924 89053.*

Erice (*map p. 543, B1*)
€€ **Monte San Giuliano**. Refined restaurant offering carefully prepared seafood and marvellous *busiati*, home-made macaroni; finish your meal with an assortment of the local pastries. Good wine list. Closed Mon. *Vicolo San Rocco 7, T: 0923 869595. Map p. 126, 1.*

€€ **Osteria di Venere**. In the deconsecrated church of the Blessed Albert, a welcoming *trattoria* offering seafood, meat and vegetable dishes. Closed Wed. *Via Roma 6, T: 0923 869362. Map p. 126, 4.*

€€ **La Pentolaccia**. The best cous cous in Erice, fast service. Closed Tues. *Via Guarnotti 17, T: 0923 869099. Map p. 126, 2.*

€ **Caffè San Rocco**. Welcoming bar and restaurant, crowded with scientists from the nearby Majorana centre. Great atmosphere. Closed Wed. *Via Guarnotti 23, T: 0923 869337. Map p. 126, 2–4.*

Marsala (*map p. 543, B2*)
€€ **Le Isole del Gusto**. Just north of town, on the lagoon facing the island of Santa Maria, this is the best seafood restaurant in the area. Elegant locale and garden, delicious dishes prepared by chef Tommaso Bonnici, generous servings, good wines, and irresistible desserts. *Contrada Birgi Vecchi 390, T; 0923 966247.*

Mazara del Vallo (*map p. 543, B3*)
€€€ **Il Pescatore**. On the outskirts of Mazara, an elegant restaurant with a gourmet following, especially for the fish. Very good pasta dishes and cous cous, delicious desserts, good wine cellar, impeccable service. Closed Mon. *Via Castelvetrano 191, T: 0923 947580.*

€€€ **La Bettola.** Central position, very good local fare and wines. Take chef Pietro's advice and start with a dish of crudités from the sea: scampi, tuna, swordfish, shrimps, amberjack and sea-perch. Two special desserts, sponge cake with organic ricotta cream, toasted almonds and chocolate, or almond parfait. Closed Wed. *Via Maccagnone 32, T: 0923 946422.*

€€ **Alla Kasbah.** In the heart of the old city, offering Tunisian and Sicilian cuisine, cous cous prepared with fish, vegetables or meat. Closed Mon in winter. *Via Itria 10, T: 0923 906126.*

Santa Ninfa (*map p. 543, C2*)

€€ **Al Colle Verde.** Pina and Lucrezia will serve you all the best local dishes, including home-made pasta, *cinghiale* (boar), *lumache* (snails, when in season), and tripe. Good assortment of wines. Also has rooms. *Via Carducci 36, T: 0924 62377.*

San Vito Lo Capo (*map p. 543, B1*)

€€€ **Al Ritrovo.** In Castelluzzo, just south of town, the restaurant of a small hotel where chef Peppe prepares delicious seafood *antipasto* and memorable tuna in an almond crust. Closed winter. *Via Cristoforo Colombo 314, Castelluzzo, T: 0923 975656.*

€€€ **Syrah.** Refined restaurant on the main street, excellent pasta dishes and desserts. Booking necessary. *Via Savoia 5, T: 0923 972028.*

€€ **Casa del Cous Cous.** The delightful restaurant of Enzo Battaglia, son of a fisherman, who tackles whatever he does with passion. He offers the very best cous cous prepared with fish or meat and vegetables, accompanied by Sicilian wines and rounded off with a glass of Tunisian tea. Closed Tues and Nov. *Via Principe Tommaso 8, T: 0923 621488.*

€€ **Gnà Sara.** Cous cous, home-made pasta, fresh fish, served in a congenial little *trattoria*. Closed Mon. *Via Duca degli Abruzzi 8, T: 0923 972100.*

Selinunte (*map p. 543, C3*)

€ **Lido Zabbara da Jojò.** ■ Lunch here is a delightful experience; summer only, swimming facilities. *Via Pigafetta (on the beach under the Acropolis), T: 0924 46194.*

Trapani (*map p. 543, B1*)

€€€ **Taverna Paradiso.** Good cous cous, or try the spaghetti *con uova di cernia* (with grouper roe). Closed Sun. *Lungomare Dante Alighieri 22, T: 0923 22303. Map p. 120, 3.*

€€ **Cantina Siciliana.** Excellent *trattoria.* Try owner-chef Pino's *bruschette con uova di tonno* (croutons with tuna roe) as a starter, or some of his imaginative fish salads, perhaps followed by seafood cous cous, then *cassatelle di ricotta*, an irresistible dessert. Sicilian wines. Next door there is a well-stocked wine shop run by the same management. *Via Giudecca 36, T: 0923 28673. Map p. 120, 7.*

€ **Da Peppe.** The home-made pasta is delicious, as is the cous cous or the lobster soup. Closed Mon. *Via Spalti 50, T: 0923 28246. Map p. 120, 8.*

€ **Trattoria del Sale.** Out by the salt-pans at Nubia, open for lunch only, very tasty dishes prepared using 'on the spot' ingredients: fish from the salt pans, Nubia garlic, intensely flavoured tomatoes from the dunes. Closed Mon and Aug. *Via Chiusa Nubia, between Nubia and Paceco (5km from Trapani), T: 0923 867142, 338 3915967. Map p. 543, B2.*

Aegadian Islands
Favignana

€€ **Amici del Mare.** On the port, you can eat outside in a peaceful atmosphere, deliciously fresh seafood, good wine list. Closed Feb and Wed in winter. *Piazza Marina, T: 0923 922596, 347 8210574.*

Levanzo

€€ **Paradiso.** Simple little *trattoria*, marvellous food, prepared by chef Mimmo with the freshest fish and aromatic herbs from the island, and served on a shady veranda overlooking the harbour. Closed winter. *Via Lungomare 8, T: 0923 924080.*

Marettimo

€€ **Il Veliero.** ■ Meals served on the terrace; try Peppe's lobster soup in which he cooks spaghetti; the *pasta al pesto di Trapani*, made with raw tomato, is also good. Best to book the lobster soup and the table by the sea. *Via Umberto 22 (by the harbour), T: 0923 923274.*

€ **Il Pirata.** By the old harbour, serves appetising seafood risotto, lobster soup, and grilled fish. Also rooms to rent. *Via Scalo Vecchio 27, T: 0923 923027, 333 3030545.*

€ **Il Timone.** Signora Maria prepares homemade pasta and wonderful tuna dishes; the *antipasti* of seafood crudités and her delicate *cassata siciliana* for dessert are memorable. Closed Sat and Sun. *Via Mazzini 30, T: 0923 923142.*

Pantelleria

€€€ **Al Tramonto.** In a beautiful setting, try *ravioli amari* (filled with ricotta cheese and mint), spicy cous cous, *sciakisciuka*, a popular local dish made with vegetables, capers, and fresh sheep's milk cheese called *tumma*; good assortment of robust desserts. *Località Penna 12, Scauri Basso, T: 349 5372065.*

€€€ **Franco Castiglione.** Elegant restaurant serving excellent *antipasti*; the spaghetti with *ammogghiu*, the local tomato pesto, is exceptional; also good fish soup and a delicious dessert called *baci*, crispy pastry layered with sweet creamy ricotta. *Lungomare Borgo Italia 81, T: 0923 911448, 347 1560199.*

€€ **Il Cappero.** Among the best restaurants on Pantelleria, unfortunately no tables outside; delicious tuna dishes; pizza in the evenings; crowded on Sat. Closed winter. *Via Roma 31 (at the port), T: 0923 912601.*

€€ **Trattoria di Bugeber.** On a high point of the island, offers all the local specialities and

has a panoramic terrace. Closed Tues, also Sun evening in winter. *Contrada Bugeber, T: 0923 914009 or 912604.*

Alcamo The Bar 900 (*Corso VI Aprile 103*) opened in 1937 and is still the best coffee-house in town. Excellent DOC Bianco d'Alcamo wine is produced by Rapitalà (*Contrada Rapitalà, Camporeale, www.rapitalà.it*), on the gentle hills behind Alcamo.

Calatafimi Segesta The family-run Ceuso farm (*Contrada Vivignato, www.ceuso.it*) produces good red wines.

Campobello di Mazara This area produces excellent olive oil from the Nocellara del Belice variety. Azienda Agricola Latomie (*Via Umberto 34, www.latomie.com*) stock it, also gourmet sauces, blue and yellowfin tuna, and honey.

Castelvetrano Sapore Verde makes prize-winning olive oil (*Via Sirtori 10, www. saporeverde.it; they will ship abroad on request*). Olives are gathered by hand from the tiny trees of the Nocellara del Belice variety, and pressed the same day. There are several bakeries which make the local sourdough loaves: the bread is a characteristic coffee-brown colour, with a delicious flavour, and it keeps well. Try Rizzo (*Via Garibaldi 85, opposite the museum*) or Pierino Fratelli (*Via Garibaldi 169/171*). At the factory of Famiglia Bua (*Via Marinella, www.tappidisugherobua.com*) you can see the family at work making cork stoppers, as they have been doing for over a hundred years. The raw material is gathered exclusively in Sicilian forests and is seasoned for three years before the corks are made. Most Sicilian manufacturers use Bua corks.

Erice The pastries made here are unique in Sicily, and were once made by the nuns of the many convents. Go to **Pasticceria Grammatico** ■ (*Via Vittorio Emanuele 14, T: 0923*

869390) for Maria Grammatico's confectionery; she is one of the most accomplished pastry-cooks in Sicily. Ask for *brutti ma buoni* almond cookies, or *genovesi*, tiny shortcrust-pastry pies filled with confectioner's custard. The women of Erice also weave bright cotton rugs called *frazzate* and sell colourful pottery, try Signora Amico (*Via Guarrasi 5*) or Pina Parisi (*Via Vittorio Emanuele 76 and Via Conte Pepoli 55*).

Levanzo The *cannoli di ricotta* are excellent everywhere; they are freshly prepared every day with milk from the goats which roam the island. The Panetteria di Levanzo (*Via Pietre Varate 5, going towards lighthouse*) is the bakery and nerve centre of the village, where Signora Olimpia (who is also an artist) makes delicious currant biscuits.

Marsala There are several good places for buying DOC wines and if you call the wineries first they will show you around the cellars. Cantine Florio (*Via Vincenzo Florio 1, T: 0923 781111*) has a long tradition and their Marsala Vergine Baglio Florio is wonderful. Also Carlo Pellegrino (*Via del Fante 39, T: 0923 719911*): try the Soleras or the Fine Ruby. Enoteca La Ruota and Enoteca Luminario are close to each other on Lungomare Boeo, near the archaeological museum. Enoteca Fazio (*Via S. Bilardello 99, T: 0923 718125*) is a good example of how the younger generation is injecting new energy into long-established industries; their Marsala, Erice DOC wines and olive oil are winning recognition. Cantine Mothia is a small winery on the outskirts of Marsala (*Via Sappusi 12, www.cantine-mothia. com*), producing exceptionally good wines. Always crowded, Enzo e Nino (*Via XI Maggio 130; closed Wed in winter*), is the historic coffee-house of Marsala. Try the home-made ice cream, freshly prepared each day, or the little ricotta pies called *spagnolette*, or their famous chicken focaccia.

Mazara del Vallo There are only seven

Benedictine nuns remaining at the Monastero di San Michele Arcangelo on Piazza San Michele, baking delectable little sweets to the same secret recipes since 1600. Choose from an assortment of *croccanti* (crunchies), *cassatelle ai fichi* (with dried figs), *savoiardi* (delicate biscuits to dunk into hot chocolate), *pasta reale* (marzipan) and *muccunetti* (little pies of almond paste with a sweet pumpkin filling). Pasticceria Lamia (*Via Val di Mazara 44*) has a good reputation for local pastries. Ask for their *muccunate* and *mazaresi al pistacchio*. Pietro Rocca is another skilled confectioner, his specialities with ricotta are particularly inviting (*Via Marsala 29*). Mazara is also famed for its bread, which had to be skilfully made to provide an edible resource for the fishermen heading out to sea for a week at a time: try Forno Laudicina Tommaso (*Piazza Madonna del Paradiso 142*) or Panificio Roccaforte (*Corso Vittorio Veneto 149*).

Pantelleria Pantelleria wines are made using a high proportion of white Zibibbo grapes. Although they are usually considered to be dessert wines, they work as aperitifs when drunk chilled. DOCs to look out for are Moscato di Pantelleria, excellent with cheese; Moscato Passito di Pantelleria, made with grapes which have been allowed to shrivel in the sun before harvesting; Tanit, or Nikà, from the Case di Pietra cellars (*www.casedipietra.com*) in Contrada Nikà, and Ben Ryé, from the Donnafugata Rallo estate at Khamma (*T: 0923 915649, www. donnafugata.it, call for appointment*). Salvatore Murana at Mueggen (*open April–Nov; T: 0923 915231, www.salvatoremurana.com*) produces excellent quality wines.

Salemi The town is famed for its decorative loaves of bread, baked for the feasts of St Blaise (3 Feb) and St Joseph (19 March); they are also sold, and the proceeds go to charity. Prices are high, and can exceed 50 euros for one small, albeit very intricate, loaf. All the women of the town take part in the baking, which begins about ten days before the feasts. Award-winning DOP olive oil from the Cerasuola variety is produced by Società Agricola Alicos (*Via Cremona 21, www.alicos.it*); they prepare very nice gift boxes including honey, jam or gourmet sauces.

San Cusumano Buy local tuna products online, including canned bluefin (*tonno rosso*) and yellowfin (*pinna gialla*) and *bottarga* (tuna roe): www.ninocastiglione.it.

Trapani Platimiro Fiorenza (*Via Osorio 36, behind Villa Margherita*) is one of the few coral craftsmen remaining in Trapani. He makes exquisite jewellery, using silver and coral. Saverio D'Angelo (*Via Della Cuba 19*) is an old-fashioned shop specialising in antique coral jewellery. Ice cream here has a unique fluffy consistency and delightful flavours: try *croccantino* or *gelsomino*. Trapani is famous for 'jasmine'-flavoured *granita*: the aroma comes from the root of a wild parsnip called *scorsonera*, once used by herbalists as a cure for the plague and snakebite. The best address is Gino (*Piazza Generale Della Chiesa 4*).

FESTIVALS & EVENTS

Castelvetrano Easter Sun morning, the Aurora festival is celebrated with a traditional procession and an enactment of the meeting of the Madonna with her risen Son. Mid-May, *Corteo Storico di Santa Rita*, two days of celebrations for St Rita of Cascia, with parades in medieval costume, sword-dancers, jugglers, flag-tossers, medieval musicians and falconers.

Custonaci Christmas, the 'Living Crib' takes place in the cave of Scurati, involving 300 villagers who illustrate local crafts and trades. Very famous, it is a good idea to get your tickets online (*Info: T: 0923 973553, 0923 971029, www.presepeviventedicustonaci.it*).

Erice Good Friday, procession of the *Misteri*.

July–Aug, *Estate Ericina*, festival of music and art. Last Wed in Aug, Feast of Our Lady of Custonaci, the patron saint, with a magnificent procession organised by the women, who wear medieval dress. Christmas–New Year, *La Zampogna d'Oro*, international bagpipes and folk music competition.

Gibellina Aug–Sept, *Orestiadi* with plays, concerts and ballet, among the ruins of the old town (*Info T: 0924 67844, www.orestiadi.it*).

Marsala Maundy Thursday, procession representing the Via Crucis. The little girls dressed as Veronica are particularly impressive, as traditionally they must wear all the family jewels.

Mazara del Vallo Aug, *'U Fistinu di San Vitu*, celebrations for St Vitus, during which the fishermen pull a cart with his statue through the streets (*Info: T: 0923 941727*).

San Vito Lo Capo May, International Kite Festival, when kite-flyers from all over the world demonstrate their skills on San Vito's splendid beach (*Info: T: 0923 974300, www. festivalaquiloni.it*). 13–15 June, the patron St Vitus is celebrated, culminating with firework displays and a competition among the fishermen who try to walk along a slippery pole suspended over the water to get a flag at the far end. Sept, International Cous Cous Fest, with cooks from all around the Mediterranean competing for the coveted award (*Info: T: 0923 974300, www.couscousfest.it*).

Trapani Good Friday, procession of the *Misteri*, groups of life-size figures made in the 17th–18th centuries by local artists. Each group represents an episode in the Passion of Christ, and is carried by the representatives of the 20 corporations, or *mestieri*—hence the name. The procession starts at 3pm and continues all night long (*Info: www.processionemisteritp.it; www.francescogenovese.net*). July, *Luglio Musicale*, opera in the public gardens, Villa Margherita (*Info: www.lugliomusicale.it*).

THE PROVINCE OF AGRIGENTO

The province of Agrigento was once known for its sulphur mines, and the collapse of the industry brought much hardship. However, the district is now reaping benefits from tourism and from its export of high-quality agricultural produce: wine, oranges, wild strawberries, olive oil and vegetables. The area has also become an important international centre for the study of almond trees. The Pelagian islands (Lampedusa, Linosa and Lampione) form part of the province.

AGRIGENTO

Once one of the most prosperous of the ancient Greek cities on the island, Agrigento (*map p. 539, C3*) presents a remarkable series of Doric temples of the 5th century BC.

HISTORY OF AGRIGENTO

Agrigento, the *Akragas* of the Greeks and the *Agrigentum* of the Romans, claims Daedalus as its legendary founder, though it probably originated as a colony of Gela in 580 BC. An early ruler was the tyrant Phalaris (*see p. 192*). A century later the poet Pindar described Akragas as 'the fairest city of mortals', and some of its citizens were renowned for their wealth—a certain Gellias, during a storm, offered hospitality, fresh clothes and stabling to a group of 500 horsemen heading for Gela.

In 406 BC the Carthaginians captured the city after an eight-month siege. They burnt the city, and sold the inhabitants who had not escaped as slaves. Timoleon defeated the Carthaginians (340) and rebuilt the city, but it was taken by the Romans in 261 and again in 210, and remained in their possession until the fall of the Empire. It fell to the Arabs in AD 828, who improved the languishing economy by cultivating cotton, sugar-cane and mulberries for the silk industry: trade flourished so much that the old port at the mouth of the River Akragas (now the San Biagio) was abandoned in favour of the larger, deeper harbour at Porto Empedocle. The Normans arrived in 1087 and took the city after a pitiless siege of 116 days, depriving the inhabitants of any kind of food, to the point that they resorted to cannibalism. But after the surrender the city was rebuilt, and the bishopric was founded.

The present town occupies the acropolis of the Greek city. Long known as Girgenti, deriving from *Kerkent*, an Arabic corruption of the Roman *Agrigentum*, meaning 'People of the Fields', the name Girgenti was abandoned in 1927 on the orders of Mussolini.

THE VALLEY OF THE TEMPLES

The ancient city, encircled by a wall, occupied the angle between the rivers *Hypsas* and *Akragas* (now the rivers Sant'Anna and San Biagio), which meet near the coast to flow into the sea. The temples should, if possible, be seen at several different times of the day, especially in the early morning and at sunset; and at night when floodlit. In early spring, when the almond trees are in bloom, they are particularly beautiful. Butterflies are in the valley in abundance. The temples are a World Heritage Site.

Opening hours

The Valley of the Temples is open daily 8.30–7 (in summer also evenings Mon–Fri 7.30–9.30, Sat, Sun and holidays 7.30–11.30pm). Ticket office at the upper entrance by the Temple of Hera or at the lower entrance by Gate 5 (where there is also a bookshop, café and stalls selling local products). A combined ticket is available for the temples and museum. A separate ticket is required for the Kolymbetra Garden. T: 0922 621611.

Visiting the Valley of the Temples

The entrance areas and internal transit arrangements are currently in a state of flux. At the time of writing, there are three car parks: one just off the Strada Panoramica by the Temple of

Late 19th-century engraving of the Valley of the Temples, showing (with some degree of artistic licence) the Temple of Hera and Temple of Concord.

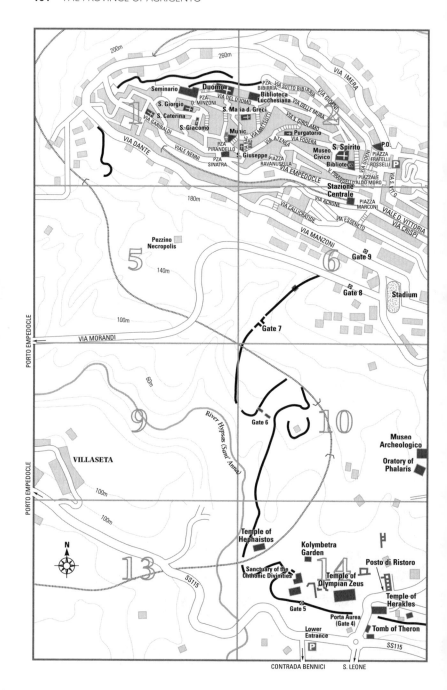

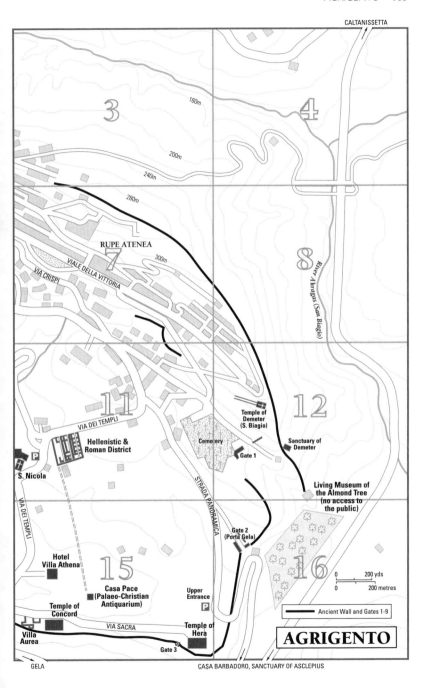

CALTANISSETTA

3

4

160m

200m

240m

280m

RUPE ATENEA

7

300m

VIALE DELLA VITTORIA

VIA CRISPI

8

River Akragas (San Biagio)

11

VIA DEI TEMPLI

Temple of
Demeter
(S. Biagio)

12

Cemetery

Sanctuary of
Demeter

Hellenistic &
Roman District

Gate 1

S. Nicola

Living Museum of
the Almond Tree
(no access to
the public)

VIA DEI TEMPLI

STRADA PANORAMICA

Gate 2
(Porta Gela)

16

Hotel
Villa Athena

15

0   200 yds

0   200 metres

Casa Pace
(Palaeo-Christian
Antiquarium)

Upper
Entrance

Temple of
Concord

Ancient Wall and Gates 1-9

VIA SACRA

Temple of
Hera

Villa
Aurea

AGRIGENTO

Gate 3

GELA

CASA BARBADORO, SANCTUARY OF ASCLEPIUS

Hera (map 15), one by the Museo Archeologico (map 11) and another by Gate 5 (map 14; drive west along the SS115 in the direction of Porto Empedocle and go straight across the roundabout just after the Tomb of Theron. The entrance to the car park is 200m further on, on the left). At the time of writing there was no public transport between the upper and lower car parks, but it is hoped that something will soon be inaugurated. In the meantime, the best way to visit the site is to arrive at the upper entrance by the Temple of Hera, progress down through the site past the Temples of Concord and Herakles, cross the road into the Temple of Zeus to see the rest of the site, then exit by Gate 5, where you can get a taxi or shuttle back to the upper entrance, or to another destination. Alternatively, walk back up through the site from Gate 5 to the Posto di Ristoro and then along Via dei Templi to the Archaeological Museum and the Hellenistic and Roman housing district, or hail a bus by the Posto di Ristoro to return to Agrigento town.

At least a whole day should be allotted to visiting the museum and the main ruins as the site covers a large area (ancient Akragas and its temples measured 4.5km by 3km). Those with less time should not miss the museum, the temples on the Via Sacra (it takes at least half an hour to walk from the Temple of Hera to the Temple of Herakles) and the Temple of Zeus. Several sites, such as the Casa Pace and the Pezzino Necropolis are only opened by prior request, and some sites, such as San Biagio and the Casa Barbadoro are only opened if there are sufficient site personnel to spare or if a prior request has been made. For information, T: 0922 621653.

Temple of Hera

The upper entrance leads directly to the much ruined but picturesque temple erroneously identified as being dedicated to Juno Lacinia (Hera to the Greeks), from a confusion with a temple dedicated to Hera on the Lacinian promontory at Crotone in Calabria. Since a landslide in 1976 threatened its stability, the entrance has been fenced off. The stylobate, on a massive artificial platform, measures 38m by 16.8m. Of its 34 columns (6 by 13), 6.4m high with a base-diameter of 1.3m, nine have fallen. It is slightly smaller and older (c.450 BC) than the nearby Temple of Concord, which it resembles in form. Traces of a fire (which probably occurred in 406) are still visible. The work of the Roman restorers was ruined by an earthquake. To the east is the sacrificial altar; to the west an ancient cistern.

Looking west there is a good view of the outer face of the wall of Akragas, in some places carved out of the natural rock, clinging to the brow of the hill. Nearby are the scant remains of Gate Three (one of the ancient city gates), and outside the city walls an ancient roadway used for transporting the stones for the temples: the deep wheel-ruts can still be seen.

The **Via Sacra** (*closed to cars, unless a request for disabled access has been made in advance*) traverses the ridge on which stand the temples of Hera, Concord and Herakles. Between the temples of Hera and Concord it leads through delightful countryside, with beautiful groves of almonds and ancient olive trees, and runs parallel to the ancient city walls, the inner face of which contains many Byzantine tomb recesses. On the right, about halfway between the two temples, is a café with free toilets and a bookshop (*open* *daily 8–7, in summer also 7.30–11pm*). There is a view on the right of the cemetery of Agrigento, to the right of which San Biagio can be seen beside a clump of trees. On the skyline, radio masts mark the Rupe Atenea.

The Casa Pace Palaeo-Christian Antiquarium

A little gate on the right of the Via Sacra, after the café and 100m or so before the Temple of Concord, gives access to the Casa Pace, an old building restored to house a Palaeo-Christian antiquarium (*only opened by prior request, entrance to the nearby catacombs can be requested at the same time; T: 0922 621653*). The two floors contain exhibits illustrating the Palaeo-Christian cemeteries excavated in Agrigento and the surrounding area, and the history of the three early Christian churches so far found in Agrigento: one outside the walls at the eastern edge of the temple ridge; one built inside the Temple of Concord; and one excavated beside the Hotel Villa Athena.

A path leads through olive groves from the Casa Pace up to a Palaeo-Christian necropolis with tombs cut into the surface of the rock, and the entrance to the extensive Fragapane catacombs with subterranean passages extending below the road (*only opened by prior request*), rejoining the Via Sacra by the Villa Aurea. In the field nearby are two tholos tombs thought to date from the 5th century BC.

Temple of Concord

The Temple of Concord at Agrigento is the second-best-preserved of all Greek temples after the Temple of Hephaistos in Athens, which it recalls in its majestic symmetry and rich colour. The name Concord occurs in a Latin inscription found here, but has no actual connection with the temple, which has not as yet been firmly attributed to any particular divinity (although there is a local tradition that the temple should be visited by a husband and wife on their wedding day to ensure a future free from marital strife).

The building, which probably dates from about 430 BC and was only slightly damaged by the Carthaginians, stands on a stylobate with four steps and is peripteral hexastyle in plan. Its 34 Doric columns are 6.8m high including the capitals, with a diameter of 1.4m at the base. Each column has 20 grooves. The intercolumniations of the façades become narrower towards the sides (to accommodate the corner metopes); this is one of the earliest instances in Sicily of this refinement in temple design. The roof was made of slabs of coloured marble, provided with lion-head water-spouts. The cella has a pronaos and an opisthodomos, both distyle in antis. From the east end of the cella two spiral staircases mount to the architrave. The complete entablature survives at both ends.

The excellent state of preservation of the temple is explained by the fact that it was converted into a church (moving the entrance to the west end, as is usual in Christian churches) dedicated to Sts Peter and Paul by San Gregorio delle Rape ('St Gregory of the Turnips'), bishop of Agrigento in the late 6th century. The building was restored as a temple in the 18th century, but the arches of the nave remain in the cella walls. The material of this and of the other temples is the local, easily-eroded sandstone, formerly protected by brightly-painted stucco (a brilliant white background with architectural details highlighted in strong hues, red, blue, green and yellow being the most favoured). This stucco has now almost completely disappeared and the stone has been burnt by the sun to a rich tawny gold.

The Villa Aurea

Beyond the Temple of Concord is the Villa Aurea, surrounded by a luxuriant garden that contains tombs and underground cisterns. Visible from the road, in the forecourt, is a memorial bust of Captain Alexander Hardcastle set up in 1984. This eccentric Englishman arrived as a tourist aged 49 in 1921, was captivated by Agrigento, repaired the villa and lived here with his brother Henry until his death in 1933. The captain provided substantial funds to restore and excavate the ancient city, supporting the work of the archaeologist Pirro Marconi. He also took an interest in the modern city, providing an aqueduct from there to the temple valley. In gratitude, the Italian government awarded him the important honorary title of Commendatore della Corona d'Italia and the Home Office allowed him to wear the insignia. The Wall Street Crash of 1929 caused his bank to fail, and he found himself bankrupt; unable to sell the villa, he lost his mind and was taken to the local lunatic asylum, where he died. The villa is now used for exhibitions and cultural activities, and is only open to the public when an event is in progress.

Temple of Herakles

On the left, towards the end of the Via Sacra, is a footbridge above a deep street of tombs carved into the rock which leads to the Temple of Herakles (Hercules in the Roman world), a heap of ruins showing traces of fire, with nine upright columns, eight of them re-erected in 1922–23 thanks to the generosity of Captain Alexander Hardcastle (*see above*). To the left of the bridge, on a small flat expanse of bedrock, are a few blocks from the altar of the temple.

This is probably the oldest visible temple of Akragas (built c. 500 BC). Peripteral hexastyle in plan, its 38 columns (6 by 15) were 9.9m high and 2m in diameter. It had a cella with pronaos and opisthodomos, both distyle in antis. Until a few years ago it was possible to walk around inside the temple, but a barrier has now been erected to prevent this. The cella was altered at some point after its construction (almost certainly between the Carthaginian destruction in 406 BC and the time of the Roman emperor Hadrian: it is not yet possible to be more precise), and three cult spaces were created at the rear. A damaged Roman statue of Asclepius was found in the southern chamber, and a beautiful marble statue of a warrior, perhaps from the pediment of the temple of Herakles, was found nearby. The attribution of this temple to Herakles is due to a reference in Cicero's *Verrine Orations* (II.4.43), and is not certain. If it is the temple referred to by Cicero, then in ancient times it was famed for its cult statue, which Verres (*see box opposite*) attempted to steal. It also contained a painting by Zeuxis, one of the most famous artists of the ancient world, of the infant Herakles strangling the serpents.

Returning to the Via Sacra, it is necessary to pass through a set of turnstiles and cross the main road by the Posto di Ristoro (*café, toilets, local bus tickets*), in order to enter the second part of the Valley of the Temples.

VERRES THE ART THIEF

In 73 BC the Roman politician Caius Verres was made praetor (governor) of Sicily. Cicero tells us that no sooner was he installed in the governor's palace than he began pillaging works of art to adorn it. At first, he requisitioned beautiful objects from private homes, but later he stole cult statues and paintings from the temples: a statue of Ceres from Catania, the gold and ivory doors of the Temple of Athena at Syracuse, together with paintings and the effigy of the goddess, whose face and hands are said to have been of gold. In Akragas, the magnificent bronze statue of Apollo, signed by Myron, was again stolen from the Temple of Asclepius (it had once before been carried away by the Carthaginians, in 406 BC, and returned by Scipio in 146). Verres sent a group of soldiers to steal the statue of Herakles from the temple at Akragas at dawn one day, but word of the raid got out and the soldiers were overpowered by furious citizens. Cicero, who had been called by the Sicilians in 71 BC to plead their cause in front of the senate, described the statue as the most beautiful work of art he had ever seen, and the effect of Verres on the island as more devastating than war. Cicero won his case, which launched his political career, but Verres was only nominally punished: he went into voluntary exile in Marseilles, where he died in 43 BC. The stolen artworks were never recovered.

Temple of Olympian Zeus

NB: The custodians of the archaeological park, whose offices are here, are very helpful and well-informed about the parts of the site that are currently accessible, but can only open them if a prior request has been made and authorised.

Immediately beyond the entrance are the vast, complex ruins of the altar and temple of Olympian Zeus (the Olympieion), thought to have been begun by Carthaginian prisoners taken at Himera in 480 BC, and left unfinished in 406. Temporarily transformed into a fortress in 255 BC, it was the last refuge for the inhabitants and the Roman garrison during a Carthaginian siege. Its destruction, partly due to earthquakes, was completed by quarrying in the 18th century, much of the stone going into the harbour mole of Porto Empedocle.

This huge Doric temple (110.1m by 52.7m, virtually a double square), is the largest Doric temple known, and is unique in form among Greek temples. The major architectural elements were built out of multiple individual blocks (each capital was composed of three blocks) and then covered in stucco. It is heptastyle and pseudoperipteral, i.e. the seven columns at each end and the 14 on each side were engaged in the walls, being rounded externally and presenting a square face towards the interior. In between the semi-columns, 16.7m high and 4m thick at the base, were 38 colossal telamones set on the outer wall; their exact arrangement is still under discussion, as is the location of the entrance/entrances. In the east pediment a Gigantomachia was represented, and in the west pediment the capture of Troy. The cella was divided into three aisles, separated by square pillars, and was almost certainly roofless.

Little remains in position except the stereobate, but this alone is sufficient to convey an impression of the immensity of the monument. Part of the north wall survives (note the outer face) and the foundations of the aisle pillars. To the east are the foundations of the huge altar. All over the stereobate are collapsed stones, amid which lies a copy (7.6m high) of one of the telamones and a partly-reconstructed original. The U-shaped incision visible on many stones is believed to have facilitated their being raised by ropes. Near the southeastern corner, below one of the colossal fallen capitals, is a small temple of Archaic date with a cella divided by piers, flanked by yet another partly-reconstructed telamon.

The lower agora and gymnasium

A path from the northeastern corner of the altar of the Temple of Zeus leads through an orange grove to the lower agora and the gymnasium. Both sites were poorly sign-posted at the time of writing, and the explanatory boards were faded or non-existent. The remains of the lower agora are poorly preserved and difficult to understand. The gymnasium, probably built in the Hellenistic period, consists of a long portico (a xystus or covered track) in which the row of seats now located in the inner courtyard of the archaeological museum (inscribed in the Augustan period with a dedication to Hermes and Herakles) were discovered. In the Roman Imperial period, perhaps in the 2nd century AD, a circular structure (nearly 22m in diameter) of unknown function, with column bases in its interior, flanked by two enormous rectangular rooms (12m by 37m), was built over the portico.

The area between the Temple of Zeus and Gate 5

To the west of the Temple of Zeus is a wide area of poorly-preserved remains from a densely-occupied section of the city. Three 5m-wide north–south roads (the eastern-most of which is practically buried under the fallen elements of the Temple of Zeus) divide two blocks of houses that were first constructed at the end of the 6th century BC, and rebuilt in the Hellenistic period after the Carthaginian destruction. Immediately to the west, between the housing blocks and Gate 5, are the traces of an L-shaped portico enclosing a complex sanctuary founded in the middle of the 6th century BC. The first phase consisted of a non-peripteral temple with pronaos, cella and adyton located right by the walls, surrounded by a paved square, and faced to the north by a rectangular building interpreted as a meeting room. In the second phase, between the 6th and 5th centuries BC, the area was renovated and enriched: a monumental altar and a sort of pro-pylon were built, a new pavement was laid in the square, and a sacred grove was planted. In the third and final phase, dating to the Hellenistic period, the buildings (which had been destroyed by the Carthaginians) were levelled, a new pavement was laid, a monumental altar was constructed, a sacred tholos and the L-shaped portico were built. The identity of the divinity worshipped in this sanctuary has not yet been ascertained.

The road that delineates the northern extent of this sacred area and the adjacent housing blocks runs in through Gate 5 and crosses the entire city to exit again at Gate

2. The carriageway from Gate 5 is obstructed by masonry which apparently fell in Greek times. It was probably a double gate defended by a large rectangular tower to the west and two smaller towers on either side of the entrance. The path leads down from here through a tunnel under the walls to the lower ticket booth and car park.

Sanctuary of the Chthonic Divinities

To the west of Gate 5 are various shrines that together formed the sanctuary of the Chthonic Divinities (the gods of the earth as opposed to the gods of Olympus). The shrines were entirely enclosed by a precinct wall, a portion of which is visible on the west side. The misnamed Temple of Castor and Pollux is here. The four columns bearing a portion of the architrave, which have been much used as the picturesque symbol of Classical Sicily, are a reconstruction of 1836 now known to incorporate elements from more than one building on this site. The traces of stucco and white plaster are original.

Superimposed ruins show the existence of shrines dedicated to the cult of the earth gods as early as the 7th century BC. The structures on the north side, notably the pairs of altars, one circular and one square, date from this period. To the south of these are the remains of two unfinished 6th-century temples; the third is that formerly misascribed to Castor and Pollux, which was probably similar in plan to the Temple of Concord. A fourth temple was built just to the south, in Hellenistic or Roman times. Many of the fallen column-drums belong to the last temple and the well-preserved altar east of the platform.

The Kolymbetra Garden

Beyond the house on the southern side of the terrace is a recently excavated area on the spur of the hill with a few poorly preserved structures, some of which were the bases for statues of the Chthonic divinities. This area was probably used for cultic songs and dances. From here two columns of the Temple of Hephaistos (*see p. 198*) can be seen, across a little valley verdant with orange trees. This is the Kolymbetra Garden (*open May–Oct 9–7, Nov–Jan 10–5, Feb–April 9–6, closed Mon, Jan and during the Almond Blossom Festival*). The garden was originally an artificial lake (a *kolymbethra*, or pool, in ancient Greek) dug by Theron's Carthaginian prisoners taken at Himera in 480 BC. It was intended for use as a reservoir and as a source of freshwater fish. Ancient sources describe it as a place of great beauty with swans, ducks and many other birds. After a relatively short time, probably little more than a century, the lake was drained and abandoned because the complex hydraulic system had not been maintained, and it became a fertile garden where the Arabs cultivated oranges. Abandoned for centuries, it has been restored by the FAI, the Italian conservation agency, who are caring for it. From the garden it is easy to cross the railway line to reach the remains of the Temple of Hephaistos.

THE ARCHAEOLOGICAL MUSEUM & UPPER AGORA

Museo Regionale Archeologico Pietro Griffo

On the main road (Via dei Templi), about 1km uphill from the Posto di Ristoro, is the exceptional archaeological museum (*open 9–7; Sun, Mon and holidays 9–1; sometimes open until midnight in Aug; T: 0922 401565*), spaciously arranged in a 1960s building. It is approached from the car park to the north through a garden and the 14th-century cloisters of the convent attached to the church of San Nicola. In the cloisters is a long stone bench carrying an inscription to Herakles and Hermes found in the gymnasium by the lower agora.

Room I: Beyond the ticket booth, between the bookshop and the entry barriers, are a couple of posters providing basic information about the history, topography and ancient sources for Akragas.

Room II: Early and late Bronze-Age material from sites near Agrigento, including a small Mycenaean amphora (probably found at Porto Empedocle) and painted vases. Also prehistoric objects found in Agrigento beneath the Classical area. Around the corner are objects from nearby Gela (6th–7th centuries BC), including Corinthian and Rhodian ware (note the head of a bull), as well as locally-made vases. A small dish shows the three-legged symbol of Sicily, the Trinacria or Triskeles, one of its earliest known depictions (7th century BC).

THE BULL OF PHALARIS

Phalaris, the 6th-century BC tyrant of Akragas is said to have had a hollow bronze bull built, into which he would force his victims and then light a fire underneath. As they roasted, their shrieks would issue from the creature's mouth, reverberating against the metal to sound like a bull in full bellow. Inevitably this instrument of torture has given rise to theory and speculation. Could there be a Cretan connection? Daedalus the inventor, who by curious coincidence emerges as the legendary founder of Akragas, was employed by King Minos and built a hollow cow for Minos' wife, Pasiphaë, to climb inside after she conceived a blind passion for a bull. The bull had his way with her, resulting in the birth of the Minotaur, half-man, half-bull, to whom children were sacrificed. But if Phalaris' bull was an instrument of ritual sacrifice, then was there also perhaps a Phoenician connection? The Phoenician sacrificial burial-ground dedicated to Baal at Mozia seems to yield traces of child sacrifice. Such connections are ill-explored and scholars give them short shrift. Perhaps the most interesting myth about the Akragas bull is that the first victim was the person who had made it, because his evil genius horrified Phalaris so much. And the last victim, it is said, was the tyrant himself.

Room III: Superb collection of vases, including a group of outstanding **Attic vases** from the mid-6th to the early 3rd centuries BC. Black- and red-figure kraters from the 4th–3rd centuries BC include a lekythos with Nike sacrificing (460–450 BC), and kraters depicting Dionysiac scenes (c. 440 BC); a stam-

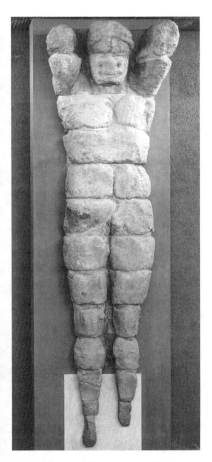

Reconstructed telamon from the Temple of Zeus. The reconstruction is conjectural. The discovery of a leg of one of the statues attached to a block of stone, for example, has shown that the feet must have been further apart than is indicated here.

nos (440–430 BC) shows a sacrifice to Apollo. At the end of the hall is a fine marble statue of a warrior (c. 480 BC), belonging to the Early Classical period, that may have adorned part of the pediment of the Temple of Herakles.

Room IV: Architectonic fragments including a remarkable variety of lion-head water-spouts from various buildings (including the Temple of Herakles and the Temple of Demeter).

Room V: Statuettes and heads in terracotta. Note the female votive statues, the mask of a black African of the 6th century BC, two cases of moulds, and a head of Athena with a helmet (c. 490 BC). The highlight is the 5th-century BC terracotta head of Persephone in case 51, showing her with a firm chin and a strong nose; the statuette was modelled by hand (you can still vaguely see the fingerprints of the craftsman) and not made using a mould. The cases on the north side of the room contain finds from the area near the Temple of Herakles, including architectonic fragments in terracotta.

Room VI: Devoted to **finds from the Temple of Zeus**. Here the remarkable telamon (7.6m high) is displayed, which was recomposed from fragments in the 19th century (a copy is on display in the temple itself); along the north wall are three colossal telamon heads illustrating three different types. The blocks of stone were originally covered with plaster. Plans and models suggest possible reconstructions of the temple, and the as-yet unresolved position of the telamones.

Room VII: Fragments of wall-paintings and mosaics from the Hellenistic and Roman housing district, and a fantastic cork model showing one possible reconstruction of the Temple of Zeus.

Rooms VIII and IX: The coin collection is displayed in a new gallery with well-written descriptive panels explaining the development of Agrigentine coinage. Four beautifully-lit display cases are equipped with movable magnifying glasses through which the fine details of the coins can be admired. The highlight is the **Agrigento Gold Hoard**, 52 Roman gold coins found near the bouleuterion (*see p. 196*) that were buried during the Second Punic War and never recovered, presumably because the owner had died in the war.

The north gallery of Room V: In the first part three statuettes are displayed: the 5th-century BC *Ephebe of Agrigento*, a marble statue of a young man, found in a cistern near the Temple of Demeter, is thought to represent an athlete from Agrigento victorious in various events at the Olympic Games. Also here are a fragment of a kneeling statue of Aphrodite (2nd–1st centuries BC) and a statuette of Apollo, or the river-god Akragas (c. 480 BC). The second part contains material found in the excavations for this museum.

Room X: A corridor, overlooking a garden with two Roman statues, contains inscriptions from Akragas, including the **Concordia inscription** found near the temple which now erroneously bears that name, and terracotta 'sulphur' tiles used to stamp bricks of sulphur with the name of their owner/producer. They are, naturally, inscribed in reverse.

Room XI: Finds from various necropoleis, notably that at Contrada Pezzino (*see p. 199*). The miniature vases were found in children's tombs. At the end of the room, the fine alabaster sarcophagus of a child, with poignant childhood scenes (ended by illness and death), a Hellenistic work of the 2nd century BC, was found near Agrigento.

Room XII: An introductory display of prehistoric material, and finds from Sciacca. The highlight is the burnt ter-

The *Ephebe of Agrigento* (5th century BC), a significant milestone in Greek sculpture, being suggestive of a body in motion.

racotta statuette from the Piano Vento necropolis that may represent a divinity.

Room XIII: Objects from the province of Agrigento, including finds from the Grotto dell'Acqua Fitusa and from Sant'Angelo Muxaro.

Room XIV: Material from Herakleia Minoa and Greek and Roman helmets; busts from Licata; also bronze cooking utensils.

Room XV: Contains a single magnificent **red-figure krater from Gela** (5th century BC) by the Niobid painter. In perfect condition, it displays an episode from the Trojan War: the battle with the Amazons on one side, and on the other Achilles falling in love with Penthesilea, Queen of the Amazons, as he strikes her to death. Photographs on the walls show other vases, now in the Gela museum.

Room XVI: Iron-age finds from Sant'Angelo Muxaro, dating from both before and during the period of Greek colonisation.

Room XVII: Finds from Caltanissetta (notably a fine red-figure krater of 450–440 BC showing horsemen).

The upper agora

The archaeological museum is located in a sector of the ancient city that was always of prime importance. In the Archaic and Classical period it was the location for a series of sanctuaries. In the rebuilt city of the 4th century BC it became the upper agora of Agrigento, and was furnished with important civic buildings such as the bouleuterion and ekklesiasterion, which remained in use until the late 2nd/early 1st century BC when, under Roman control, the area was remodelled in a process that is as yet not fully understood. The finds from the sanctuary over which the museum is built are displayed in the north gallery of Room V.

The area to the south of the museum

The area to the south of the museum is dominated by the so-called **Oratory of Phalaris**, a Roman prostyle tetrastyle podium temple with Ionic columns, a Doric architrave and an adjacent altar, built in the early 1st century BC. It was later transformed into a Gothic chapel, hence the windows in the cella. This podium temple was partly constructed over the Hellenistic ekklesiasterion (capable of accommodating 3,000 citizens for assemblies), which was levelled to create a terrace on which the temple was placed. The foundations on view held the tiered seats which would have risen up in the shape of a curved theatre. A path with a footbridge circles the temple and ekklesiasterion, crossing an area with remains of late Hellenistic houses, and mosaics from Imperial Roman buildings.

The early 13th-century **church of San Nicola** (*open 9–1hr before sunset*) has a curious façade made up of a Gothic doorway in strong relief between antae with a Doric cornice (the material probably came from a Roman edifice nearby). The architecture of the interior, reconstructed in 1322 and altered in 1426, is interesting. In the second south chapel there is a magnificent sarcophagus of white Parian marble, which with great delicacy and purity of style portrays four episodes in the story of Phaedra (Theseus' second wife) and Hippolytus (her step-son). Phaedra fell in love with Hippolytus, who ignored her desperate pleas and the love-letter she sent with her maid. She blamed her suffering on an attempted rape by him, and he died after his father Theseus cursed him. The sarcophagus could be a Greek work of c. 450 BC or a later Roman copy of the original, and was much admired by Goethe, who said that it was the best-preserved Classical relief carving he had seen. The front panel shows Hippolytus with his male companions and their horses and dogs, about to leave for the hunt, ignoring the maid who attempts to give him her mistress's letter. The right-hand end panel shows Phaedra in despair, while the unfinished scene on the left-hand panel shows Hippolytus falling from his chariot and trampled to death by his horses, terrified by Poseidon's bull emerging from the sea in fulfilment of the curse. The scenes are completed by a delicate frieze at the top and bottom. The rear panel is also unfinished, possibly because the sarcophagus was placed in the corner of a building. The church also contains a venerated wooden Crucifix, a statue of the *Madonna and Child* by the Gagini school, and an unusual stoup supported by a grey marble hand, bearing two dates (1529 and 1685). From the terrace there is a wonderful view of the Valley of the Temples.

The area to the north of the museum

A path leads from the north of the museum, near the exit to the car park, to a large viewing area overlooking an extensive and confusing area of excavations. At the time of writing there were no explanatory boards and the area was overgrown. Two interesting structures have been found here: a bouleuterion (to the east) that could hold 300 people, which was transformed into an odeon in the Imperial period; and a sanctuary built in the Augustan period and modified in the 2nd century AD comprising a podium temple and a triporticus that was probably dedicated to the goddess Isis. A second path leads north from the car park, alongside the excavation area just mentioned, to the Giacatello hypogeum (*only opened by prior request*). Another part of the enormous hydraulic system attributed to the architect Phaiax, it was perhaps originally intended to be a huge cistern, but in the Roman period it was transformed into a granary.

OTHER SITES OF THE ANCIENT CITY

The Hellenistic and Roman district

On the opposite side of the Via dei Templi, directly to the east of the archaeological museum, is the entrance to an enclosure (behind a green fence) with the conspicuous remains of the Hellenistic and Roman district of the city (*open 9–1hr before sunset, closed Sun and holidays*). Here an area of c. 120m square has been excavated, exposing four cardines running north and south, with their complex of buildings sloping downwards from east to west in a series of terraces, forming three insulae. The district was first developed at the end of the 6th century BC, but the scant traces from the Archaic and Classical inhabitation (which was presumably destroyed by the Carthaginians) were mostly covered over when the area was redeveloped from the end of the 2nd century BC onwards. The drainage system is elaborate, and traces of stairs show that buildings were of more than one storey. The houses take a variety of forms: some are built around a large peristyle courtyard in the typically Hellenistic tradition; others follow the typically Pompeian tradition and have an atrium in which there is a sunken tank to collect rainwater. Many of the rooms on view have well preserved floors (the best, which include the Casa della Gazzella and the Casa del Maestro Astrattista, are covered for protection) and some contain traces of a rich painted decoration. The size of the houses varied greatly, both between each other and over time (they expanded and contracted at the expense of their neighbours as the fortunes of the various households changed), but it is abundantly clear that this was one of the wealthiest housing districts in the city. Civic life in this district seems to have lasted until the 4th or 5th century AD.

San Biagio and the Sanctuary of Demeter

Drive north from the archaeological museum along Via dei Templi and turn right onto Via Demetra, following signs to the **cemetery**. Captain Alexander Hardcastle, who was responsible for excavating the ancient walls here, was buried in this cemetery beside a 'window' in the wall, cut purposely so he could enjoy the view over the Valley of the Temples for eternity. A gate on the left (signposted) is officially open at the same time as the temples but it is often locked due to lack of personnel (*best to call a day in advance on T: 0922 621653 to ensure that a custodian will be there*). Beyond it an unsurfaced road (c. 200m) leads (on foot) to the edge of the cliff.

On the hillside above is **San Biagio**. This Norman church was built on the cella of a small temple (peripteral hexastyle in plan, with a double cella distyle in antis), begun after the victory at Himera in 480 and probably dedicated to Demeter and Persephone (though the identification has recently been questioned). The pronaos and stylobate of the temple protrude beyond the apse of the church. To the north are two large round altars, one of which (the one to the west) was a bothros or sacred well, in which hundreds of votive statuettes were found. The temple was approached by the ancient track with deep wheel ruts, still clearly visible, mounting the side of the hill. On the rock face a marble plaque records Captain Hardcastle's excavations.

On the edge of the cliff the line of the ancient city walls can clearly be seen running from the Rupe Atenea, above San Biagio, to the Temple of Hera; beyond, the view extends along the temple ridge and to the sea. Just outside the walls and below the cliff edge is the entrance gate to the **rock sanctuary of Demeter**, reached by long, steep flights of steps (20th century) built into the rockface, which lead down through a delightful garden. Beside two natural caverns in the rock (in which numerous votive busts and statues dating from the 5th–4th centuries BC were found) is a tunnel which carries a terracotta aqueduct from a spring far inside the hill. In front is a complex series of cisterns on different levels and remains of what may have been a monumental fountain. The sanctuary was formerly thought to antedate the foundation of the city by some two centuries, but many scholars now believe it was constructed in the 5th century BC.

Another unsurfaced road (signposted) leads along the cemetery wall to (200m) an interesting wedge-shaped bastion built to guard this vulnerable spot where a valley interrupts the natural defence line. To the north is Gate One.

The Rupe Atenea (351m), a rocky hill, was part of the acropolis of Akragas. It is reached by a road which runs beyond the hospital, but as it is now military property, the ruins of a large ancient building found here are inaccessible.

Living Museum of the Almond Tree and Sanctuary of Asclepius

The Strada Panoramica leads south from Via dei Templi, passing near Porta Gela (Gate

2; *currently inaccessible*) and continues past the car park and ticket booth at the upper entrance to the Valley of the Temples, near the Temple of Hera. The road curves down to a roundabout that is crossed by the SS 115. The first exit to the right (the SS 115 heading west) runs beneath the temple ridge and walls, past a park of four hectares which has recently been designated to protect some 300 varieties of almond tree, of the 522 known to exist. This **Living Museum of the Almond Tree** (*no public access*) is run jointly by the province and the University of Palermo.

An unsurfaced road on the left (signposted) leads through an almond orchard to a farm beside the **Sanctuary of Asclepius** on the bank of the San Biagio, near a medicinal spring. The site is enclosed (*only opened by prior request*). There is a Doric temple in antis with a pronaos, cella and false opisthodomos. In spite of its much smaller size, it shows the advanced techniques of construction associated with the (contemporary) Parthenon. The stairway is preserved between the cella and pronaos. Asclepius was the god of medicine and the temple and its precincts would have been a clinic for the sick: rooms for this purpose have been discovered in porticoes to the north and west of the temple. Other structures include a pair of altars and a monumental fountain, and recent work has shown that the entire area between the buildings was planted with olive and oak trees, examples of which have recently been replanted. This is the temple mentioned by Polybius in his account of the siege of 262–261, when it was used as one of the Roman bases. It once contained a famous bronze statue of Apollo by Myron, signed by the artist in letters of silver on the right thigh, which was looted by Verres in 72 BC (*see box on p. 189*).

Casa Barbadoro

Further along the SS 115, accessed by an unsurfaced road on the right (poorly signposted) is a simple country cottage restored to house the Antiquarium Iconografico Casa Barbadoro (*9–1 in summer, closed Sun and holidays and throughout winter*), a beautiful collection of illustrations of the Valley of the Temples, consisting of drawings, watercolours, etchings and photographs made by earlier travellers.

Tomb of Theron

Continuing along the SS 115, the area to the north between the road and the temple ridge comprises an enormous Roman necropolis (1st century BC–5th century AD), the most noted element of which (just before the roundabout on the right) is a large mausoleum misnamed the Tomb of Theron, a two-storeyed edifice with a Doric entablature and Ionic corner columns that would probably have supported an obelisk. Local legend holds that this is the place where Theron buried his favourite horse, which had won several Olympic competitions.

Temple of Hephaistos

The SS 115 continues across the roundabout and passes (200m on the left) the car park and ticket office at Gate 5. A little further ahead (c.300m), just before a bridge at the bottom of a little valley, an unsurfaced road (not signposted) forks right. Follow it as far as the high railway viaduct. Here, steps (signposted) lead up past agaves and aloes to the

Temple of Hephaistos (the Roman Vulcan; the identification of the temple is actually not certain), beyond an orchard of contorted almond trees and beside an old farmhouse. The temple, hexastyle and peripteral, was built c. 430 BC and two columns remain upright. The cella was partly built over a small Archaic temple of the early 6th century. A marble stone beneath the stylobate on the south side records excavations here in 1928–29 by Alexander Hardcastle. From here the irregular line of walls leading up to Monte Camico and the old part of modern Agrigento is pierced by Gates 6, 7, 8 and 9.

The Pezzino Necropolis

The enormous Pezzino Necropolis (*map 5*) extends to the west of Gates 6 and 7. The visitable section is beneath the viaduct of Via Morandi (*only opened by prior request, but most parts can be seen from behind the fences*) and is accessed from Via Dante (turn right at the signpost for 'Il Rustichello', keep to the right, go through a tunnel, keep to the left and after a short while during which the track runs parallel to the main road—they are separated by a wire fence—it leads through the middle of the excavated part of the necropolis: the track is extremely rough, so proceed with caution or, better yet, walk from just before or just after the tunnel). Dating from the 6th–4th centuries BC, it was the largest necropolis at the time in Akragas, and probably one of the richest. Unfortunately, tomb robbers ransacked much of it before the archaeologists began work here. The uncovered area is only a tiny section of the entire necropolis, and the continuous undulations in the surrounding fields give some idea of its original extent. The tombs were separated by roads and there is evidence that they were grouped together on the basis of family ties.

EXPLORING AGRIGENTO TOWN

The oldest part of Agrigento town occupies the summit of Mt Camico (326m), the acropolis of the Greek city; modern suburbs extend along the ridge to the east below the Rupe Atenea, and the city is expanding down the hillsides to the north and south. Three connected squares effectively divide the centre; the area to the west contains the old city.

Santo Spirito and the Museo Civico

Via Atenea, the long main street of the old town (*map 2*), leads west from Piazzale Aldo Moro. Just out of the square to the right is **Palazzo Celauro**, where Goethe stayed while on his tour of the island. It is now a B&B (*see p. 222*). Via Porcello (right) and the stepped Salita Santo Spirito lead steeply up to the abbey church of the **Spirito Santo** (*if closed, T: 0922 20664*), founded c. 1290 for Cistercian nuns. The nuns still make delectable sweets which may be purchased here (*ring the doorbell of the door to the right when facing the entrance to the Museo Civico*). The church façade has a Gothic portal surmounted by a rose window; inside are lovely stuccoes (c. 1693–95) by Giacomo Serpotta and his school. The statue of the *Madonna Enthroned* is by the workshop of Domenico Gagini.

Part of the convent was restored in 1990 to house part of the **Museo Civico** (*map 2; open Mon–Sat 9–1, also 3–7 on Tues and Thur, closed Sun and holidays*), with a miscellany of poorly-labelled objects. It is approached through an over-restored cloister and up a modern flight of stairs. The two rooms on the top floor contain a local ethnographic collection of agricultural implements and domestic ware. On the first floor below, archaeological material and remains of frescoes of the Byzantine, Arabic and Norman periods are displayed. Steps lead down to the Stanza della Badessa in a tower with a Gothic vault and a painted 15th-century Crucifix. The beautiful dormitory has fine vaulting and an exhibition of international folk costumes, as well as a collection of butterflies, beetles and shells. On the ground floor a chapel with a Gothic vault has a crib, with charming domestic scenes, made by a local craftsman (1991). The chapter house (now used for weddings) is also shown. The paintings include works by Pietro Novelli, Luca Giordano and Fra' Felice da Sambuca.

Towards the duomo

The unfinished façade of Santa Rosalia stands beside the church of the **Purgatorio** or San Lorenzo (*map 2*), containing elegant statues of the *Virtues* by Serpotta. The lion to the left of the church sleeps above the locked entrance to a huge labyrinth of underground water-channels and reservoirs, built by the Greek architect Phaiax in the 5th century BC. Beyond the neo-Gothic Chamber of Commerce, Via Atenea widens at the undistinguished Piazza Nicola Gallo, once the centre of the old city. Beyond the church of San Giuseppe, at the top of the rise, the street descends to **Piazza Luigi Pirandello** (*map 1*; formerly Piazza del Municipio). On the right is the Baroque façade of San Domenico, while occupying the former convent (mid-17th century) are the Town Hall and the fine Teatro Pirandello opera house (*T: 0922 590360 or 0922 590220*) by Ernesto Basile, inaugurated on 24th April 1880.

To the right of San Giuseppe, Via Bac Bac leads to the stepped Via Saponara (signposted for Santa Maria dei Greci). From here it is a steep climb up the Salita Gubernatis and Salita Santa Maria dei Greci to (right; inconspicuous entrance) **Santa Maria dei Greci** (*usually open 8–12 & 3–dusk, closed afternoons on Sun and holidays*), preceded by a charming little courtyard with a palm tree. This small basilica was built with antique materials on the site of a Doric peripteral temple (6 by 13 columns) that may have been begun by Theron in the 5th century BC and was perhaps dedicated to either Athena or Zeus. The cella almost certainly had a pronaos and an opisthodomos, both distyle in antis. The interior preserves fragments of charming 14th-century frescoes, and the well-designed wood and glass floor provides views of the foundation blocks of the cella of the temple and also, near the church altar, a 15th-century Capuchin crypt used for mummification (the bodies were placed upright in the seats, and the fluids drained into the hole in the centre of the room). Ask for the under-floor lights to be turned on if this has not already been done. Several columns from the temple are visible inside the church, and in a passage below the north aisle (*entered from the churchyard; unlocked by the custodian on request*) are the stumps of six fluted columns on a c. 20m stretch of the stylobate.

The duomo

The duomo is approached by a magnificent old staircase (*map 1; closed for repairs at the time of writing: it stands partly on a layer of clayey rock which shifts periodically; cracks de-*

veloped in March 2011). Dedicated to the Norman St Gerland, first bishop of Agrigento, it is a mainly 14th-century building with an unfinished campanile (to the southwest) that shows in its Gothic windows a mixture of Arab-Norman and Catalan influences. The ancient blocks visible in the bell-tower were almost certainly brought here from the lower city and do not indicate the existence of a temple underneath. Inside, a single round arch divides the nave into two parts: at the entrance the tall polygonal piers support an open painted roof of 1518; in the sanctuary is a coffered ceiling of 1603 decorated with the two-headed royal eagle of the House of Aragon. At the end of the south aisle is the Chapel of St Gerland (who refounded the see after the Arab defeat), with a lovely 17th-century silver reliquary by Michele Ricca. Opposite, in the left aisle, is the tomb of the merchant Gaspare de Marino, by Andrea Mancino and Giovanni Gagini (1492), and other Baroque funerary monuments and fragments of 15th-century frescoes. A curious acoustic phenomenon (*il portavoce*) permits a person standing beneath the cornice of the apse to hear every word spoken even in a low voice near the main doorway, though this does not work in reverse.

The extensive façade of the Biblioteca Lucchesiana lines Via del Duomo. This fine building was founded by the bishop of Agrigento in 1765 as a public library. Its treasures number 40,000 volumes (including Arab MSS still housed in the original presses). Forming part of the building is the archbishop's palace, housing the **Museo Diocesano** or **MUDIA** (*open Oct–March 10.30–2.30, April–Sept 10.30–6.30, closed Sun; July–Aug also evenings 8–11 on Fri, Sat and Sun; T: 0922 490039*), with cathedral treasures from the 12th–19th centuries: paintings, frescoes, sculpture, Church silver and embroidery, including some rarities.

PORTO EMPEDOCLE (VIGATA) & KAOS

Porto Empedocle (*map p. 539, C2*) takes its name from the philosopher Empedocles (c. 495–430 BC), the most famous native of ancient Akragas. For Empedocles, cosmic history was a cyclical process of union and division under the alternating influences of Love and Strife and the four immutable Elements (the now canonical earth, air, fire and water). Little survives from his writings, but it is clear that his work influenced that of Aristotle and he is also said to have been a renowned doctor who composed in both prose and verse.

In 2003 the city, wishing to assert a new-found vocation for tourism (it boasts wide sandy beaches, good cuisine and delicious ice cream, but also a rather unpleasant cement factory, while a huge offshore re-gassification plant is planned), officially also assumed the name Vigata, in honour of locally-born Andrea Camilleri, the immensely popular writer who names it thus in his novels featuring the police inspector Salvo Montalbano. You will find a bronze statue of Montalbano mid-way along the main street, Via Roma, leaning casually against a lamp post. Close by, the glorious little 19th-century opera house, Teatro Empedocle, has just been restored.

The harbour is the point of departure for the remote Pelagian Islands: Lampedusa, Linosa and Lampione (*described below*). On the inner quay, built using stone from the temples of Agrigento between 1749 and 1763, is a massive tower built by Charles V, at the time of writing in the process of becoming a museum dedicated to the sea in all its aspects, the Museo Regionale del Mare. Close to the tower is a bronze monument to Empedocles by the American sculptor Greg Wyatt. Around the central statue of the philosopher are four smaller figures representing Earth, Water, Air and Fire.

Just outside Porto Empedocle is **Kaos**, birthplace of Luigi Pirandello (*see box below*) and now a delightful small museum (*open 9–1 & 2–7; T: 0922 511826*), with books, manuscripts, paintings and photographs. Under a wind-blown pine, the ashes of the dramatist and novelist were finally buried according to his wishes, beneath a 'rough rock in the countryside of Girgenti'.

Luigi Pirandello (1867–1936)

Pirandello was the son of a sulphur-dealer in Girgenti. He became famous as a playwright in 1921 with the first performance of *Sei personaggi in cerca d'autore* (*Six Characters in Search of an Author*), which caused a scandal in Rome. Quickly produced in Milan, Paris, London and Berlin, it was much admired by G.B. Shaw and was followed the next year by the equally successful *Henry IV*, dealing with themes of illusion, insanity and reality. From 1925, with the backing of Mussolini, Pirandello established and directed the Art Theatre. His short three-hander *The Man with a Flower in his Mouth* was the first-ever broadcast TV drama, being used by the BBC for test transmission in 1930. Four years later he was awarded the Nobel Prize for literature.

In his writings Pirandello conveys an idea of man suffering from solitude, disillusioned by his ideals. With a strong element of irony he suggests that his characters frequently reveal the necessity of 'wearing a mask', and this has been credited with inspiring the Theatre of the Absurd. Pirandello wrote some 40 plays, six novels, many novellas and hundreds of short stories, many of which are still in print. He was widely acclaimed in his lifetime: one of his most famous novels is *Il Fu Mattia Pascal* (*The Late Mattia Pascal*), published in 1904, but it is as a playwright and short-story writer that his genius fully emerged. For information on his literary park, see www.parcopirandello.it.

THE PELAGIAN ISLANDS

The Pelagian Islands (from the Greek *pelagos*, meaning sea) lie about 205km south-west of the Sicilian mainland and only 113km from Tunisia (*map p. 539*). Hauntingly beautiful, they lie tossed into a sea which varies in hue from pale green and lemon yellow through to turquoise and deep cobalt, a palette Matisse would have loved. There are three islands, Lampedusa, Linosa and Lampione, all quite individual and different in character. They fell to the Allies without resistance in June 1943; Lampedusa surrendered to an English airman who landed there by accident, having run out of fuel. All three islands now enjoy protected status as a nature reserve: Lampedusa's is run by Legambiente (*www.legambienteriserve.it*); with a small museum and library on the loggerhead turtles; Linosa's and Lampione's by the Azienda Forestale. The collective name of the reserve is Area Marina Protetta Isole Pelagie (*www.isole-pelagie.it*).

Lampedusa

Lampedusa is the largest of the three islands, some 20km square, with a population of about 6,000. On the African continental shelf, it is a flat limestone rock, similar to the Tunisian coast behind it, with crystal-clear waters and lovely sandy beaches, especially to the south, while the north coast forms a steep cliff. Until recently the island was crowded in July and August with holidaymakers from northern Italy, attracted by the clean sea and the memorable seafood, but its notoriety as the landing-place for boatloads of refugees and clandestine immigrants from Africa has had a negative effect on tourism. In the village square by the port is an obelisk by Arnaldo Pomodoro, dedicated to the immigrants, hundreds of whom drown on their way to Europe. Whale-watchers should come in March when the Rorqual, or fin whale, passes along the south coast of Lampedusa and mates off the east coast. After the American bombing of Tripoli and Benghazi in 1986, Libya fired scud missiles at the American transmitter base on Lampedusa (since closed), but the two missiles fell into the sea 2.5km from the island's shores.

The Isolotto dei Conigli, just offshore, is protected by Legambiente because of the loggerhead turtles (*Caretta caretta*), which still lay their eggs on the beach.

Linosa

Linosa, about 5km square in extent, 42km north of Lampedusa, is stunningly beautiful, formed of dark volcanoes, with cobalt-blue waters and tidy little houses painted in bright colours with contrasting borders around the doors and windows. This scheme was adopted to help fishermen recognise their own home when they were far out at sea. It is quite hilly, and the most fertile of the islands. The people are not all fishermen; most of them were in fact once cattle farmers, but they have been forced to stop this because there is no slaughter-house between here and Agrigento. They have also stopped extracting *pozzolana*, the stone formed by hardened volcanic ash (much in demand on the mainland for building), in order to preserve the landscape. The economy is now based on agriculture and tourism. The atmosphere is very peaceful on Linosa; just the place for a restful holiday. The small beaches are of black volcanic sand and there are lovely secluded rocky coves. Visitors are not permitted to bring cars, but they are not necessary as the island is so small. You can walk all the way round it in about 3hrs (strong shoes, water, sunhat, sunblock advised), or hire a motor-scooter or a bike. Sea daffodils cover the eastern slopes of Monte Nero in summer.

It has been suggested that Linosa is the lost Atlantis: offshore to the east there are great rectangular blocks of basalt on the seabed, and what appears to be a primitive divinity carved in stone, now covered with seaweed. The loggerhead turtle lays her eggs on one of the beaches (*no access*), and there is an important breeding colony of honey buzzards.

Lampione

Lampione, with an area of just 1.2km square, is uninhabited. Formed of white lime-stone like Lampedusa, with sheer cliffs, its deep waters are frequented by scuba divers in the summer. Practically inaccessible, it is home to an important colony of Cory's shearwaters.

SCIACCA

Sciacca (*map p. 539, B2*), thought to be the oldest spa in existence, has been known since Greek times, when it was perhaps the thermae of Selinunte. It took the name Sciacca after the Arab domination (9th–11th centuries AD): the town rises in front of a white lime-stone cliff that looks rather like an iceberg when seen from the sea, and the name probably derives from the Arabic *as-saqqah*, meaning ice. It has an important and picturesque fishing harbour, where every day about 5,000 tons of fish are disembarked, most of it for processing, and there is a renowned boat-building tradition. Along the tiny streets of the fishermen's district, both men and women sit in front of their doors to clean sardines and anchovies ready for salting. A local ceramics industry flourished here in the 16th and 17th centuries, and there are several artisans' workshops in the town. The colours and the patterns are quite different from those seen elsewhere in Sicily; often the bright floral designs or human figures stand out against a black or dark blue background.

Porta San Salvatore

The centre of Sciacca is still reached by most traffic through the fortified Porta San Salvatore (1581), a fine work in sandstone by local masons. Beside it in Piazza Carmine is the arresting façade of the **Carmine**, with a half-finished Neoclassical lower part and an asymmetrical 13th-century rose window. The dome, with green tiles, dates from 1807. The church contains a beautiful *Transition of the Virgin*, the last work of Vincenzo da Pavia, completed by another artist in 1572.

A short way up Via Geradi (left) is the **Steripinto**, a small fortified palace in the Catalan Gothic style. It has an interesting façade, with diamond-shaped stone facing, erected in 1501, and is now the symbol of Sciacca. Opposite the Carmine, on the other side of Via Incisa, is the north portal of the church of **Santa Margherita**, sculpted in 1468 by Francesco Laurana and his workshop. The church was deconsecrated many years ago and is now used for concerts and exhibitions. The coffered ceiling represents a starry sky. The polychrome stuccoes and marble reliefs (1623) by Orazio Ferraro, in the chapel of the titular saint, are impressive. Beyond is the Gothic portal of the former church of San Gerlando and the abandoned Ospedale di Santa Margherita. Opposite are the late-Gothic Palazzo Perollo-Arone and the 15th-century Torre di Pardo.

Corso Vittorio Emanuele continues into the central **Piazza Angelo Scandaliato**, shaded with trees. From here there is a view of the pastel-coloured old houses rising in terraces above the fishing harbour. The former Collegio dei Gesuiti (now the Town Hall), begun in 1613, has an elegant courtyard.

The Corso continues to the dilapidated Piazza Duomo where the duomo, called the Basilica and dedicated to Mary Magdalene, has statues by Antonino and Gian Domenico Gagini on its façade. It was rebuilt in 1656 and the vault fresco was completed in 1829. It has some good sculptures including a *Madonna* (1457), a marble altarpiece with reliefs by Antonino Gagini, and (on the high altar) the *Madonna del Soccorso* by Giuliano Mancino and Bartolomeo Berrettaro. In Piazza Don Minzoni next to the duomo, there is the **Scaglione Museum** (*closed for repairs*), the private collection of paintings, coins, ceramics and *objets d'art* of Francesco Scaglione, a local 19th-century nobleman.

The Corso continues to Piazza Friscia, in a pleasant part of town, which has shady 19th-century public gardens with tropical plants. Via Agatocle leads past the new theatre to the edge of the cliff. Here, the **Nuovo Stabilimento Termale** (*open June–Oct*), a pink spa building in Art Nouveau style (1928–38), offers mud baths and thermal swimming pools with a temperature of 32°C.

The upper town

From Piazza Friscia, Via Valverde leads up to the gardens in front of the church of **Santa Maria delle Giummarre** (or Valverde), built by Judith, the daughter of Count Roger. Its façade is tucked in between two crenellated Norman towers; the restored chapel in the left tower has an interesting interior. The elaborate 18th-century Rococo decoration in the main church, perhaps by Marabitti, is remarkable. The vault was frescoed by Mariano Rossi (1768). Also in the upper town is **San Nicolò La Latina**, a simple 12th-century church. Above is the **Castello Nuovo**, the ruined castle of the Spanish Luna family. Their feud with the Perollo clan in the 15th–16th centuries became notorious as *i casi di Sciacca* (the Sciacca business); it was resolved only after the population of the town had been reduced to almost half its size.

The outskirts of Sciacca

Above Sciacca (signposted) is **Monte Kronio** (or Monte San Calogero; 388m), which has caves (*closed Dec–March*) with steam vapours, known since Roman times and now a little spa. The **sanctuary church of San Calogero** (1530–1644) has a statue of the saint by Giacomo Gagini. St Calogero is said to have discovered the healing properties of the vapours and to have provided accommodation here for the sick; he possibly lived in the largest of the caves. There is a small museum, Antiquarium Kronio (*open 9–1; T: 0925 28989*), with a collection of vases and fragments found in the grottoes and dating from the Neolithic to the Copper Age.

On the Agrigento road (SS 115) east of Sciacca is the well-signposted 'enchanted castle', the **Castello Incantato** (*open summer 9.30–1 & 4.30–8, winter 9–1 & 4–6, closed Mon; T: 0925 993044, www.castelloincantato.net*), a park with olive and almond trees where thousands of heads were sculpted in wood and stone by a local farmer, Filippo Bentivegna (d. 1967). After being hit on the head during a robbery in the USA (where he had emigrated), Bentivegna returned home and carved heads wherever he could find space in his garden. A room is dedicated to his work at the Museum of Art Brut, Lausanne, originally Jean Dubuffet's collection of 'outsider' or pathological art.

ISOLA FERDINANDEA

Twenty-six nautical miles southwest of Sciacca, in early July 1831, a volcanic island appeared, rising through the water with fountains of black mud and clouds of ash. It was spotted by HM sloop *Rapid*, en route from Malta under the command of Captain Charles Henry Swinburne, who reported the phenomenon: 'It gradually increased in dimensions, magnificent eruptions of cinders with white vapours rising to the height of from 400 to 1,000 feet, accompanied by a noise like thunder.' By 17th July the island was 9m high, and on 11th August it was 25m with a circumference of nearly 2km. Another enterprising British captain, Commander Senhouse, passing close by the island with his ship at the beginning of August, surveyed the island, planted the Union Jack and claimed it as British territory, naming it Graham Island after the then First Lord of the Admiralty. Adventurous people started organising boat trips and picnics, one such being the novelist Sir Walter Scott in the year before his death. The claim, however, was contested by the Bourbon king Ferdinand II, who sent warships to the spot. On 17th August the island was named Isola Ferdinandea and annexed by the Kingdom of the Two Sicilies; but the victory was short-lived. By November the island was seen to be gradually sinking, and it disappeared completely on 8th December. Renamed the Graham Shoal, it remained some seven metres below the surface, until in 2002 it was announced that the capricious island was once more on the rise.

MENFI & THE WEST OF THE PROVINCE

Northwest of Sciacca is **Menfi** (*map p. 539, A1*), laid out on a regular plan in 1698 with the houses arranged around courtyards off the main streets, many of which were made uninhabitable by the Belice earthquake in 1968. The beautiful Torre Federiciana, however, has been completely restored—it is the only remaining fragment of a Swabian castle built here by Frederick II in 1238. A new town now rises on the higher ground above.

On the coast, beyond lots of condominiums and holiday villas, is the fishing village of **Porto Palo**. There are still some unspoilt stretches of coast here, adjoining the nature reserve at the mouth of the River Belice, in the province of Trapani (which extends to Marinella and Selinunte); the Menfi beaches have been awarded the European Union Blue Banner for quality.

Santa Margherita di Belice

North of Menfi is Santa Margherita di Belice (*map p. 539, B1*), where the country house described by Giuseppe Tomasi di Lampedusa in *The Leopard* is located. Named Don-nafugata in his masterpiece, Palazzo Filangeri di Cutò was badly damaged in the 1968 earthquake but has now been repaired by the civic administration and houses the

Museo del Gattopardo (*open 9.30–1 & 4–6.30, closed Wed and Sun afternoons; T: 0925 31150*), where you will find the manuscript and the first typescript of the novel, clothes worn in that historical period, a recording of the voice of Tomasi, and a room with wax models of the characters in the book.

The old Matrice, now repaired, is the **Museo della Memoria** (*open 9–2, Mon and Thur also 3.30–6.30, closed Sat, Sun and holidays; T: 0925 30216*) with a collection of photographs and paintings, a moving testimony of the Belice valley, before and after the 1968 earthquake. In the **new church** of the town the magnificent stained glass is the work of Americo Mazzotta from Florence. Santa Margherita is renowned for prickly pears and for *vastedda* sheep's milk cheese. From the public gardens there is a splendid view over the valley.

Giuseppe Tomasi di Lampedusa (1896–1957)
Giuseppe Tomasi di Lampedusa, whose family were princes of Lampedusa and dukes of Palma di Montechiaro, was known to his friends simply as Peppino Palma. He wrote his famous novel *Il Gattopardo* (*The Leopard*, translated into English in 1960) at the end of his life. It was published posthumously in 1958. The book recounts the life of his great-grandfather Giulio Tomasi (1815–85; renamed Don Fabrizio Corbera, Prince of Salina), who reacted with instinctive resignation to the turmoil produced by the landing of Garibaldi on the island in 1860. Set over three periods in the course of half a century, Don Fabrizio awaits the fall of his class and the ruin of his family, approving of the desire of his young nephew Tancredi Falconeri to marry the daughter of a *nouveau-riche* rogue, Calogero Sedara. Invited to join the Senate of the new Kingdom of Italy, the prince declines, proposing Sedara in his place. Disenchanted, he waits for death. The novel had enormous success, which was confirmed when it was made into a film by Luca Visconti in 1963, with Burt Lancaster and Claudia Cardinale. Tomasi di Lampedusa also wrote a collection of short stories, *I Racconti*, translated in 1962 as *Two Stories and a Memory*. In Palermo, Palma di Montechiaro and Santa Margherita, 'Literary Parks' (*T: 091 6160796, www.parcotomasi.it*) have been established in his honour.

Montevago (*map p. 539, B1*), close to Santa Margherita, was destroyed in the 1968 earthquake and rebuilt close to where it was before, leaving a poignant heap of ruins as a perpetual memory of old Montevago. This was the town with the highest number of victims. Many contemporary artists have donated works of art to Montevago, such as the stone sculpture by Giò Pomodoro of the *Deposed Sun*, and the bronze group by Lorenzo Cascio of the *Embrace*. There is a new spa centre, with a pool into which thermal mineral waters gush constantly at a temperature of 40°C; mud baths are also available.

Sambuca and Monte Adranone

Sambuca di Sicilia (*map p. 539, B1*) has an old centre with the best-preserved Islamic layout in Sicily (around Piazza Navarro, with cobbled streets). Known as Sambuca Zabut until 1921, this town escaped the 1968 earthquake unscathed. The economy is based on the production of wine (Planeta), on the shores of nearby Lake Arancio.

The main street of town, Corso Umberto, leads up to the old district. On the right is the little opera house with 250 seats, Teatro L'Idea (1850; *request visit at the Antiquarium, same opening times*); to the left Via Marconi leads to the church of the Concezione, with a 14th-century portal. Back on the Corso, on the left is the church of Santa Caterina, of which the convent is an **antiquarium** (*open 9–1 & 3.30–7.30; T: 0925 940239*) housing a rich and informative collection of finds from the archaeological area of Monte Adranone (*see below*). In Piazza Vittoria is the Neoclassical church of the Carmine (or Santuario della Madonna dell'Udienza), with 19th-century stuccoes and a much-revered statue of the Madonna attributed to Antonello Gagini. Corso Umberto continues up to Palazzo degli Archi, the Town Hall, from where Via Belvedere leads to Piazza Navarro. On the left is a little street leading to the **Arab quarter**, called Vicoli Saraceni, and the Renaissance-style Palazzo Panitteri (*request visit at the Antiquarium, same opening times*), with a curious collection of wax figures engaged in a political discussion. At the time of writing the building was being adapted for the planned archaeological museum, which will be second in importance in the province to that of Agrigento. The Chiesa del Collegio and that of the Cappuccini have works by Fra' Felice da Sambuca, who was born here.

The successful and well-known **Planeta winery** is near the village of Ulmo, on the shores of Lake Arancio near Sambuca. About 7km north of Sambuca, in Contrada Adragna, is the 1000m-high **Monte Adranone** (*open 9–1hr before sunset, closed Sun and holidays; T: 0925 946083*), on the provincial border with Palermo, site of the Sican city of *Adranon*, re-founded by Selinunte in the 6th century BC, and destroyed by Carthage in 408 BC. With the arrival of the Romans in 263 BC the site was abandoned. Excavations have brought to light traces of the walled city and the Iron-Age necropolis, with some impressive rock-hewn tombs including the so-called Tomba della Regina (Queen's Tomb), with a suitably imposing entrance. Other remains include the walls and the south gate, a sanctuary, and part of the acropolis to the northeast.

Caltabellotta

Northeast of Sciacca, **Caltabellotta** (*map p. 539, B1*) is a little town in a beautiful and commanding position, on a southeastern slope of its mountain, and visible from vast distances around. Some historians believe this to be ancient *Kamikos*, the Sican kingdom of Kokalos, who befriended Daedalus after he came to Sicily from Crete (*see box on p. 210*). The Arabs erected a fortress, which they called *Qal'at al-Ballut*, or Fortress of the Oak Tree. Here the peace treaty ending the war of the Sicilian Vespers (*see p. 69*) was signed in 1302. In 1194 the castle sheltered Sibyl of Acerra, widow of King Tancred, along with her two daughters and her infant son, who reigned for a few months as William III, shortly before they were imprisoned in Germany by the new king of Sicily, Henry VI. The little boy was never seen again; it is said that he was blinded and castrated, and ended his days in a monastery. The same castle inspired Wagner, who imagined it as the dwelling of Klingsor in his *Parsifal*.

The Norman Chiesa Madre has Gagini statues and an isolated square bell-tower to the left, probably once a watch-tower, while in the church of San Francesco there is a splendid panel-painting of the *Madonna*. The church of the Salvatore, below the rock-face, has a late Gothic portal. From here is the narrow path and steps to the fortress, worth the climb for the marvellous views over much of Sicily.

On the western outskirts of town is the old **monastery of San Pellegrino** (17th–18th centuries; now derelict). To the left of the church are two caves, one on top of the other, used by early Christians as churches. Many prehistoric rock-hewn tombs were used as dwellings through the centuries, noticeably near the church of Santa Maria della Pietà, which is itself also partly carved into the rock.

Burgio

Burgio (*map p. 539, B1*), across the valley of the River Verdura from Caltabellotta, is an agricultural town with a local ceramics industry founded in the 16th century, and the only remaining bell foundries of Sicily. The beautiful **carved stone portals** and doorways, of churches and palaces and also of the most humble private dwellings, are a characteristic of the town—there are over a hundred of them. Burgio has developed around the remains of a castle built by the Arabs on a spur, dominating the surroundings. In the **Chiesa Madre** (where you will find a beautifully restored 13th-century icon of the *Madonna and Child*), the third altar is dedicated to the *Madonna of Trapani*. Among frescoes, stuccoes and marble reliefs, there is a marble *Madonna* by Vincenzo Gagini, signed and dated 1566, and a 13th-century wooden Crucifix, much revered, and carried in procession every year to the sanctuary, 8km away, of Santa Maria di Rifesi, built in the 12th century by Ansaldo, steward of the royal household of Palermo.

The 17th-century **Convento dei Cappuccini** has been restored and opened to the public; during the works a painting by Zoppo di Gangi (Giuseppe Salerno) was discovered, complete with the original early 17th-century frame, considerably the worse for wear after being exposed to the elements for several years. A small museum, called La Dimora delle Anime (the Dwelling-place of Souls) or **Museo delle Mummie** (*open every day; T: 0925 65013 to request visit, they will provide a guide*) has been created to display a collection of 49 mummies, once carefully preserved by the monks, then allowed to decay after the convent was abandoned, and now restored and rearranged. Mummification was once a privilege restricted to members of the Church and wealthy citizens, and in Sicily the art of preserving bodies was almost exclusively confined to the Capuchins. Mummification was something that people planned and paid for while still in good health, even stipulating the clothes in which they should be dressed on their death. The best examples of preserved bodies can be seen at the Capuchin convent of Palermo (*see p. 65*), but there are plenty more elsewhere in Sicily, such as at Savoca near Taormina.

In Piazza Santa Maria, the important **Museo della Ceramica** (*10–1 & 3–6, closed Mon; T: 0925 64016, www.muceb.it*), dedicated to the production of local ceramics through the centuries, has been opened in the 16th-century former monastery of Santa Maria delle Grazie. The attractive pottery, business-like in function (floor and wall tiles, jugs, dishes and pharmacy vases) is decorated with medieval designs; particularly popular were profiles of moustachioed men wearing helmets, but suns and moons, replete with brilliantly coloured rays, are frequently found. The predominant colours are delicate yellow (the envy of rival craftsmen elsewhere in Sicily, who were never able to match it), green and cobalt blue, on a white background.

HERAKLEIA MINOA & THE COAST

The excavations of Herakleia Minoa (signposted 'Eraclea Minoa'; *map p. 539, B2*) are in a magnificent, isolated position at the mouth of the ancient *Halykos* (now the Platani). The road off the main coast road follows the lovely meandering river valley as it climbs the hill, passing vineyards. Beyond the turning for the seaside village, an unsurfaced road continues for the last 500m. Here part of the town defences can be seen.

Above the dirt road on the left are the foundations of a circular Greek tower and a section of well-preserved wall (ending in a square Roman tower). The continuation of the walls has been lost in landslides. A splendid view extends along the wooded shore, the pearly-coloured sand, and the white limestone cliffs to Capo Bianco, beyond the river.

HISTORY OF HERAKLEIA MINOA

The name Herakleia Minoa suggests that this was originally a Minoan colony; a legend that Minos pursued Daedalus from Crete (after the Athenian inventor had helped Theseus and Ariadne escape from Knossos) and founded a city here was reiterated by Diodorus Siculus, who records that Theron of Akragas found the bones of Minos close to this spot. The Cretan King is supposed to have been murdered in his bath with boiling oil poured through a pipe in the roof by the daughters of the Sican king Kokalos. A colony was founded here by the inhabitants of Selinunte in the 6th century BC, and the name Herakleia was probably added later in the century by Spartan emigrés. The town thrived during the 4th century BC when it was resettled by Timoleon, but it seems to have been abandoned at the end of the 1st century BC, perhaps because of malaria.

The excavations

The archaeological area of Herakleia Minoa (*open 9–1hr before sunset; the main entrance is beside the ruins of Hellenistic houses; T: 0922 846005*) includes a small **antiquarium**, which houses finds from the site and has informative plans of the area so far excavated. A path leads on through the beautifully-kept site, where the visible remains (excavations in progress) date mainly from the 4th century BC. The well-preserved **theatre** was built at the end of the 4th century. The soft sandstone is now protected by a Perspex cover. The site of the city is on the hillside in front of the theatre. Under cover is the so-called **Governor's House**: part of the wall decoration and mosaic floor survives.

Also here is a little **sacrificial altar** (under glass). Outside excavations have revealed three levels of destruction; the level of the Archaic city is at present being uncovered. The second line of the walls (built when the eastern part of the town was abandoned) is visible nearby. A path (or steps) leads up to the top of the hill above the theatre and a paved path leads over the hillside to the line of walls to the northeast, with square towers, built in the 4th century BC.

The coast towards Agrigento

The tidy little agricultural town of **Montallegro** (*map p. 539, C2*) was rebuilt in the 18th century below its abandoned predecessor on the hill, where a grotto has produced finds from the early Bronze to the Copper Age. The enticing-looking ruins are in fact practically inaccessible, due to a mud slide which has obliterated the path. Between the town and the sea is a small artificial lake, **Oasi Lago Gorgo di Montallegro**, much frequented by water-birds during migration; it is protected as a nature reserve run by the LIPU, the Italian association for the protection of birds, (*Info: T: 091 320506, 339 7645940, 0922 474541, www.lipu.it/oasi*). Besides cormorants and rare ducks, there are hosts of dragonflies and butterflies and, very rare for Sicily, the terrapin, now symbol of the reserve.

Further inland, **Cattolica Eraclea** was founded in 1610, close to the Platani. Originally called Cattolica (*Kata Halykos*, 'close to the Halykos'), it took the second name Eraclea in 1874, by order of Vittorio Emanuele II. The town, with its regular 17th-century street plan, is particularly attractive.

Siculiana, on a low hill between Eraclea Minoa and Agrigento, has a prominent domed church (1750–1813), and is very picturesque when seen from a distance. The castle on the top of the hill dates from 1350. A byroad leads down to the beach beside the Torre di Monterosso, where there is also a WWF nature reserve open to the public, protecting a spectacular stretch of coast with white cliffs, deep blue sea, and Mediterranean maquis.

Closer to Agrigento is the old city of **Realmonte**, with the only salt mine still functioning in Sicily, with tunnels extending for over 25km. On the outskirts, a Roman villa found while building the railway in 1907, the **Villa Romana di Durrueli** (*open 9–1; T: 349 8194223*), dating from the 1st century AD, has been excavated; the oldest yet discovered in Sicily and the only one built so close to the sea. Nearby at Punta Grande is the **Scala dei Turchi**, remarkable white rocks of limestone and sandy clay which have been eroded by the sea into fantastic shapes, used by Giuseppe Tornatore as a set for *Malena*.

THE PLATANI VALLEY

This part of Agrigento province consists of peaceful countryside studded with small, sun-baked towns, a landscape defined by the River Platani, the ancient *Halykos*, 84 km long, which often formed the boundary between the Greek and Carthaginian territories in Sicily. Sulphur was mined in the hills here up until the mid-19th century (*see box on p. 215*).

ARAGONA & ENVIRONS

Aragona (*map p. 539, C2*), c. 12km north of Agrigento, was founded in 1606. It has an interesting street plan: straight, regular streets demarcating blocks of houses, which reveal a host of tiny alleys and little courtyards, Arab-style. The tiny central square, Piazza Umberto, is dominated by the 17th-century Palazzo Feudale, now the Town Hall, and the Baroque façade of the church of the Purgatorio. Close by is the 17th-century Chiesa Madre, which houses a rare 18th-century crib with large wooden statues. Almonds and pistachios are cultivated in the surrounding fields.

Four kilometres southwest of the town are the **Vulcanelli di Macalube**, tiny conical volcanoes, only 0.5–1m high, filled with salty bubbling mud, now part of a Legambiente nature reserve (*Riserva Naturale Integrale Macalube di Aragona; T: 0922 699210, www.legambienteriserve.it*). They fascinated Guy de Maupassant when he visited the area in the late 19th century: 'If Satan has an abode, it is here, here in this monstrous sickness of nature, amid these pustules which in every respect resemble some loathsome suppuration of the soil, abscesses of the earth which from time to time burst noisily, spewing stones, mud and gas high into the air…'

Due east of Aragona, on the other side of the main highway, is the village of **Comitini** (*map p. 539, C2*), in a panoramic position on a hill. There are numerous sulphur mines around the town, and in the central Piazza Umberto the 16th-century Palazzo Bellacera houses a museum on the subject—Museo della Storia delle Zolfare (*open 8.30–1.30 & 3–8, closed Sun and holidays; T: 0922 600359*). In the same building is an antiquarium with a collection of objects found in the area, dating from prehistory to the Arab domination.

Around Raffadali

Raffadali (*map p. 539, C2*) has a Roman sarcophagus depicting the *Rape of Persephone* in bas-relief in the 16th-century Chiesa Madre. A prehistoric necropolis on the hill of Busone has yielded finds including a number of statuettes of a female divinity, each carved from a pebble (now in the archaeological museum of Agrigento). **Joppolo Giancaxio**, to the south of Raffadali, is a pretty village in a fine position with an 18th-century castle and church.

North of Raffadali, perched on a mountain-top, is **Sant'Angelo Muxaro**, in the heart of the Platani valley, surrounded by rugged farming country, another candidate for the site of the ancient *Kamikos* (*see p. 208*). Prehistoric tombs pepper the hillside. Those near the foot of the road which mounts to the village date from the 11th–9th centuries BC; the higher domed tombs were used in the 8th–5th centuries BC. These tombs have revealed interesting finds, some of which are in the archaeological museum of Agrigento (a gold dish, with a pattern of animals in relief, is in the British Museum). At the foot of the mountain is an interesting cave, Grotta dei Ciavoli, extending for over 1200m, with a flourishing population of bats; it is protected as a nature reserve (*Info: Legambiente, T: 0922 919669, www.legambienteriserve.it*).

Mini volcanoes of mud, the Vulcanelli di Macalube, which fascinated Maupassant.

THE NORTH OF THE PROVINCE

Casteltermini

Above the narrow Platani valley, with its odd-looking sulphurous hills, is Casteltermini (*map p. 539, C1*), once a sulphur-mining town. The Cozzo Disi mine, one of the largest in Europe, will soon be opened as a museum. An interesting festival known as the *Tataratà* takes place on the last Sunday in May. The name refers to the sound of the drums which accompany the colourful processions. The celebrations commemorate the miraculous discovery of an ancient Crucifix in the 17th century: a cow kept on kneeling down in a particular spot, in spite of the farmer's attempts to move her; out of curiosity, he dug a hole in the ground where she sat and revealed the Crucifix. The Cross, carbon-dated to the 1st century AD, is made of wood, about 3.5m high and just over 2m wide. It is thought to be the oldest in the world and is kept in a little church 3km from the village, where the processions go on the Friday and the Sunday of the last week in May. The participants wear magnificent costumes, and even the horses are richly arrayed. The last procession, on Sunday evening, is a frenetic dance of hordes of 'Moors', accompanied by the drums. It is said that the Muslims in this area were miraculously converted when the Cross was discovered.

This area has been densely inhabited since the Bronze Age, and material recovered from recent excavations in the vicinity is displayed in the **Museo Civico Di Pisa Guardì** (*Via Cacciatore 1, open Mon–Fri 9–1 & 3–7*). The contents include a hoard of bronze fragments; pottery painted with brown fishing-net designs, or bearing incised patterns; a 4th-century BC jug in the shape of a boot, all accompanied by explanatory panels. One room is dedicated to the work of a local sculptor, Michele Caltagirone (1854–1928), known as the Quarantino, who specialised in modelling rather *naïf* terracotta figurines. His scene of *Paradise*, with a host of angel trumpeters, is particularly interesting.

Cammarata

Cammarata (*map p. 539, C1*) is a little medieval town on the northeastern slopes of Mt Cammarata (1578m), the highest peak of the Sicani Mountains. The town is surmounted by the ruins of its 13th-century **castle**. Many of the streets are very steep, and some of them are formed of steps, which makes the religious processions particularly exciting to watch. There are several ancient churches housing precious works of art.

The surrounding **Sicani Mountains** and their extensive forests, which abound in indigenous flora and fauna, are protected as a nature reserve (Riserva Naturale di Monte Cammarata), run by the Azienda Forestale.

Santo Stefano Quisquina and Bivona

Santo Stefano Quisquina (*map p. 539, C1*) is a sleepy town in a panoramic position, where the Chiesa Madre has a lovely altarpiece of the *Resurrection of Lazarus* by the Carracci school. Four and half kilometres east of the town, a track leads from the Cammarata road for c. 2km to an oak wood, where at 986m the 17th-century **Santuario di Santa Rosalia** (*open July–Aug every day, Sept–June on Sat, Sun and holidays; T: 0922*

989805, www.quisquina.com) is situated. The convent, inhabited by a small congregation of monks until the 1950s, now houses two small museums, one dedicated to monastic life and the other to farming activities in the area. There is a grotto where St Rosalia is said to have lived before she went to Mt Pellegrino near Palermo.

Bivona, where renowned peaches are cultivated, also has a number of fine churches, though most of them are in bad repair. A few years ago the beautiful carved stone portals were saved, thanks to an initiative of the local schoolchildren.

SULPHUR MINING

The sulphur mines in central Sicily, which were worked throughout the 19th century, gave Italy a world monopoly of the mineral by 1890. It is used, among many things, in the manufacture of sulphuric acid, electrical insulators and match heads, and in the vulcanisation of rubber. Some 32,000 miners were employed by 1860, and of the 700 or so mines in operation, steam engines were used in only four, and horses in only ten; the formation of the seams of mineral allowed for nothing else. In most mines sulphur was extracted manually from an average depth of 60m, and many of the workers, known as *carusi*, were children under 14. Children were used because they were small enough to crawl through the tunnels; many of them only saw the light of day once a week. By the end of the century American sulphur was dominating the market, being much cheaper (a more economical method of refining, using steam, had been discovered, but the system was impossible to use in the Sicilian mines). The consequent decline of this part of the economy is one of the reasons for the mass emigration at the end of the 19th century, from Sicily to Australia, Venezuela, Canada and the USA. In 1934 legislation was introduced forbidding employers to use women or boys under 16 in the mines that still remained. The life of these people influenced many native writers, including Pirandello and Sciascia, as well as painters such as Guttuso. The last mines in the province of Agrigento were closed down in 1988, while those in the province of Caltanissetta were abandoned in the 1970s. You can see models of the mines in the Museum of Mineralogy in Caltanissetta (*see p. 230*). It may have been tough work, but the miners earned more than the peasants. The girls used to sing: '*cu surfuraru m'haju a fari zita, ca iddu lu sciallu mi lu fa di sita*', 'I must choose a sulphur-miner for a fiancé, because he will buy me a silken shawl.'

LICATA & THE EASTERN PROVINCE

A plain surrounds **Licata** (*map p. 539, D3*), a seaside town that was once a busy port, first for the shipping of wheat and later for Sicilian sulphur, but which became isolated after that industry collapsed, cut off as it is from world trade routes. Frederick of Hohenstaufen pronounced it *dilettissima* in 1234, and gave it the imperial eagle as a coat of arms. It occupies the site of *Phintias*, the Greek city founded by the eponymous tyrant from Gela, and is situated between the sea and a low hill, with the Bourbon Castel Sant'Angelo (*open Mon–Sat 9.30–1.30 & 4–7.30, Sun and holidays 9–1*) of 1640 on the top and the mouth of the River Salso to the east; the new section of town is on the far side of the river. Phintias was a prosperous town with a series of wells, water-cisterns and aqueducts; among these, the Pozzo della Grangela well can still be seen, a short distance from the Town Hall. On 10th July 1943, at 2am, the beaches of Licata were the scene of the Allied landings of Operation Husky, a turning-point in the Second World War.

In and around Piazza Progresso

In the central Piazza Progresso, where the main streets of the town converge, is the Art Nouveau-style Town Hall, **Palazzo del Municipio** (1935, Ernesto Basile), housing a small collection of antique reliefs, a gorgeous early 17th-century triptych, the *Madonna with Saints*; and the white marble *Madonna della Mazza* by Domenico Gagini (1470). The Art Nouveau opera house, Teatro Comunale Re Grillo (19th century) has recently been restored. Corso Roma leads north, passing (left) two palaces: Palazzo Canarelli, which is decorated with grotesque heads, and Palazzo Urso-Ciarcià. To the right is the church of **San Domenico**, which has two paintings by Filippo Paladini: one is the splendid *St Anthony Abbot and Stories of his Life*, a masterpiece of *trompe l'oeil*. The kindly saint, dressed in freshly-pressed robes, appears to be stepping out from his niche, which is surrounded by little 'theatre settings', each one with a different episode to narrate. The other painting shows the *Holy Trinity with Saints* (1611).

A little further along the street is the convent and church of the **Carmine**, designed by Giovanni Biagio Amico in 1748 on 13th-century foundations, which houses ten beautifully-modelled medallions with stories of the Old and New Testaments. The 16th-century cloister is interesting, with a double-lancet window and Gothic portal.

From Piazza Progresso, by taking Via Santa Maria uphill, you reach the old church of **Santa Maria La Vetere**, probably built in 580 by Benedictine monks together with their abbey. In the 16th century, it passed to Franciscan friars.

Corso Vittorio Emanuele and the Museo Archeologico

Going towards the sea, Corso Vittorio Emanuele passes the 16th-century church of **San Francesco**; its fine convent (now a school) was reconstructed in the 17th century and the marble façade added in 1750 by Giovanni Biagio Amico. It is also possible to see the peaceful cloister. In the single-nave interior are a handsome 18th-century organ, elaborately carved wooden choir-stalls, and some interesting old tombs.

Behind the church is the favourite meeting-place of the people of Licata, **Piazza Sant'Angelo**, surrounded by imposing 18th-century buildings. The 17th-century church of Sant'Angelo has an unfinished façade and elegant cupola attributed to Angelo Italia. Inside, the 17th-century silver urn contains the bones of St Angelo, the patron saint of Licata, who was martyred in 1220. The 16th-century Cistercian abbey (entrance from Via Dante) houses in its cloister the important **Museo Archeologico**

della Badia (*open 9.30–1.30 & 4–7.30, Sun and holidays 9–1; T: 0922 772602*), which contains local archaeological material from the prehistoric and Greek periods, including Hellenistic votive statuettes, ceramics and red-figure vases from a necropolis of the 5th century BC; also a beautiful 5th-century BC statue of a female divinity, probably Hera, in Greek marble; and a curious boat-shaped oil lamp. Notice in the first gallery the beautiful, slender, long-stemmed vases from the prehistoric sites of Monte Sole and Stagnone Pozzillo. Finds recovered from shipwrecks on the seabed, including two cannons, can be seen in the basement.

The Chiesa Madre

The Corso ends at the 15th-century Chiesa Madre, or Santa Maria La Nuova. The interior, a central nave and two aisles, has glowing 19th-century frescoes on the vault. The aisles are adorned with several canvases by the Capuchin Fra' Felice da Sambuca. On the main altar is a 17th-century Flemish panel-painting of the *Nativity of the Virgin*. An elaborately-decorated chapel in the south transept, with a magnificent coffered ceiling, has an unusual wooden Crucifix with a black Christ, which narrowly escaped destruction at the hands of the raiding Turks on the 11th July 1553: the notorious Anatolian corsair Dragut and a handful of pirates overpowered the garrison, crucified the chatelaine, and enslaved his two young sons and 600 citizens, but failed in their attempts to burn the Crucifix, which would not catch fire. The frustrated pirates tried to make away with some bronze church bells, but they were attacked by a swarm of bees, and the bells fell into an inaccessible crevasse.

INLAND FROM LICATA

Palma di Montechiaro and Campobello

On the edge of lonely countryside west of Licata, planted with almond trees, olives and vineyards, is **Palma di Montechiaro** (*map p. 539, D3*), founded in 1637 by the Prince of Lampedusa, ancestor of novelist Giuseppe Tomasi di Lampedusa (*see p. 207*). The town is surrounded by hundreds of half-constructed houses (now abandoned concrete shells), begun in the 1960s by emigrants, some of whom returned when the wine, table grapes, almonds, cherry tomatoes, and especially the cantaloupe melons of the area achieved fame on the international market. The conspicuous 17th-century Chiesa Madre, by the Jesuit architect Angelo Italia, is a fine building with twin bell-towers and 'stocky columns of red marble', as Tomasi di Lampedusa described them, approached by a long flight of steps. The 17th-century Palazzo Lampedusa, now owned by the town council, has been partially restored and is sometimes open in summer at weekends. The famous pastries known as *mandorlati del Gattopardo*, a favourite both with Tomasi di Lampedusa and Leonardo Sciascia, are still made by the Benedictine nuns in the Monastero del Santissimo Rosario, the cloistered convent where the Beata Corbera, the prince's sainted ancestor, received an enigmatic letter from the Devil.

Campobello di Licata (*map p. 539, D2–D3*) was founded in 1681. In the Parco delle Pietre Dipinte (Park of the Painted Stones), a series of 110 blocks of local stone have been polished and painted by a local artist, Silvio Benedetto, with scenes from the *Divine Comedy*, creating an unusual open-air museum. The surrounding area is excellent for wine production.

THE RIVER HIMERA

There are several Salso rivers in Sicily, so called because of their slightly salty waters. The one known as Imera (after the old city of *Himera*) enters the sea just east of Licata and is the second longest river on the island (112km). It springs from Bafurco in the Madonie Mountains, meets up with the River Gangi, and then joins the Imera Meridionale at Ponte Cinque Archi. It passes through the sulphur-rich interior, flowing north–south, neatly dividing Sicily into two parts. It once separated Sicans from Sicels. For the Arabs it defined the limits of the Val di Mazara, while for the Normans it was the dividing line between the diocese of Syracuse and that of Agrigento. It forms deep gorges as it winds its way towards the sea. Subject to frequent, abundant floods, the river was only provided with a bridge to replace the ferry in 1870. The Roman consul Attilius Regulus defeated a Carthaginian fleet off the mouth of the river in 256 BC, but in 249 BC another Roman fleet was almost completely destroyed during a tempest in the same spot.

Naro

Naro (*map p. 539, D2*), which bases its economy on the production of table grapes, stands on a hilltop, once defended by battlemented walls (1263), with one surviving gate of the original six, the **Porta d'Oro**, so-called because it led into the Jewish quarter, renowned for its goldsmiths. Naro has a dignified Baroque aspect, almost comparable to Noto, and an assortment of crumbling old churches with wildflowers bravely growing in the cracks, ranging from the ruined Norman duomo (reached by 210 steep steps from Via Dante) to early 17th-century churches. The robustly crenellated **Castello Chiaramontano** (*open 10–1 & 5–8, until 6.30 in winter, closed Mon; T: 0922 953021*) houses Vento di Donna, an interesting exhibit on women's clothes and accessories, and their evolution through the 19th and 20th centuries. On the first floor, in the Sala dei Baroni, are the remains of frescoes painted by the local artist Cecco di Naro. The castle is haunted by the ghost of Giselda, who on moonlit summer nights sometimes appears on the terrace, where she is comforted by her murdered lover, the minstrel Bertrano, who sings to her in the form of a nightingale.

In the main street, Corso Vittorio Emanuele, close to Piazza Garibaldi, is the 15th-century Palazzo Giacchetto-Malfitano, which houses the **Museo della Grafica** (*open 8–1 & 3–7.30, closed Mon, entrance from Via Piave 54; T: 0922 953021*), with a display of some 250 works by artists ranging from Goya to the Expressionism of Renato Guttuso. Some rooms are dedicated to 4,400 ancient books, incunabula and manuscripts from the library of Naro. The museum was opened in 2000 to show a number of works donated by the artist Bruno Caruso. Close by is the Baroque church of **San Francesco** (*open 9–12*), with a highly decorated, frothy façade. The single-nave interior was frescoed by Domenico Provenzano, and houses a life-size silver statue of the *Immaculate Virgin* and an altarpiece of the same subject by Vito d'Anna. In the sacristy you will find beautifully carved and decorated wooden cupboards.

Racalmuto

The little town of Racalmuto (*map p. 539, D2*), named from the Arabic *rahal-maut*, 'village in ruins', surrounded by barren, hilly countryside, is imbued with the spirit of Leonardo Sciascia, one of Italy's most important writers (*see box below*).

Leonardo Sciascia (1921–89)

Sciascia, one of the best-known Italian novelists of the last century, was born in remote Racalmuto, and lived there for most of his life. He is commemorated by a life-size bronze statue (1997) on the pavement in the main street near the Chiesa Madre, by a local artist (the cigarette, which never left his fingers when he was alive, is repeatedly replaced by a fan). His simple white marble tomb, surrounded by jasmine, is in the little cemetery nearby. His best novels, including *Il giorno della civetta* (*The Day of the Owl*, 1961), *A ciascuno il suo* (*To Each His Own*, 1966), *Il Consiglio d'Egitto* (*The Council of Egypt*) and *Todo modo* (*One Way or Another*; both 1974), written in a particularly simple and direct style, are detective mysteries with a distinctive Sicilian flavour. In a number of essays and articles he also wrote about the problems which afflict the island, and exposed political corruption and the insidious power of the Mafia long before these two evils of Italian society were widely recognised. Sciascia was very reserved and often pessimistic, but had a high standing in Italy in the 1970s as an intellectual figurehead. His 'Literary Park' (*www.regalpetra.it*) is in Racalmuto, as is the foundation housing his books and papers, in the specially re-designed, elegant old Electricity Board building (*Fondazione Sciascia, Viale della Vittoria 3, T: 0922 941993, www.fondazioneleonardosciascia.it*).

The quiet streets present a typically Arabian pattern, with blocks of houses facing onto narrow alleys, with stepped streets and the occasional tall palm tree. At the top of the hill is the main square, Piazza Umberto, with the 17th-century **Chiesa Madre**, or Annunziata. The interior is decorated with stuccoes, and there are five paintings by the local artist Pietro d'Asaro. Also facing onto the square are the 17th-century church of San Giuseppe, and the superb 13th-century **Castello Chiaramontano** (*open 9–1 & 4–8, closed Mon; T: 0922 948820*), with two large cylindrical towers. The ample galleries of the castle house permanent collections of works by local artists, and an exhibit of the works of Hungarian photographer Robert Capa, taken just after the Allied landings in Sicily in July 1943.

Steep steps lead up from the left of the Chiesa Madre to the former monastery of Santa Chiara, now the Town Hall; close by in Via Sciascia is the beautiful little 19th-century opera house (a miniature version of the one in Palermo), Teatro Regina Margherita. The stairs end at the sanctuary church of Santa Maria del Monte (1738), with a Gaginesque statue of the Virgin on the main altar; an important feast takes place here in July, attracting pilgrims from many nearby towns.

5km north of Racalmuto is a smaller Chiaramonte castle called the **Castelluccio** (720m). From the battlements, Mt Etna is visible on a clear day.

Canicattì and Favara

Canicattì (*map p. 539, D2*) is a market town of some importance and a railway junction. It is surrounded by vineyards, pergolas of a table grape called Italia. They can be marketed during the winter months thanks to the technique of covering the vines with thick plastic in August, when the grapes are just beginning to ripen. This blocks the ripening process indefinitely. When the farmer wants to sell his grapes, he takes off the plastic three or four days before picking. When covered with the plastic sheeting, the vineyards look like an endless silver sea. Peaches, nectarines and plums are also grown in this area.

In Piazza Cavour at **Favara** (*map p. 539, C2*; between Canicattì and Agrigento on the old SS 122), there is a castle of the Chiaramonte family (1275, enlarged in 1488; *open 9–1 & 3.30–7.30, Sun and holidays 9–1; T: 0922 438192*), now used by the council for meetings and exhibitions. The chapel, entered from the courtyard, has a superb Gothic portal. The town is dominated by the 18th-century church of the Rosario, with a beautiful blue-tiled dome and a delightful interior, overflowing with Baroque stucco decoration. It also preserves the original floor of majolica tiles and a coffered ceiling with paintings of saints. The pastry shops prepare famous Easter lambs made of marzipan filled with pistachio. They are so popular that they are now made throughout the year.

PRACTICAL INFORMATION

GETTING AROUND

• **By train:** From Agrigento there are services to and from Palermo, Syracuse, Catania and Caltanissetta. Cammarata, Casteltermini and Aragona are on the Agrigento–Palermo line but services are infrequent. In the eastern part of the province the nearest station for Racalmuto is Aragona (14km); Canicattì is a railway junction, from which Campobello

and Licata can be reached. Sciacca can be reached from Palermo (*www.trenitalia.it*). **Ferrovie Kaos** (*T: 329 9570774, www.ferroviekaos. it*), using trains, lines and stations no longer in regular service, run from Agrigento to Porto Empedocle in July–Aug, stopping at the temple of Hephaistos; also in summer the Akragas Express runs from Canicattì–Racalmuto–Grotte–Aragona–Agrigento–Porto Empedocle.

• **By bus:** In Agrigento small buses run by **TUA** (T: 0922 412024) cross the upper town along Via Atenea. Nos 1, 2 and 3 run from Piazza Marconi to the Valle dei Templi. Bus no. 1 continues to Kaos (Pirandello's house) and Porto Empedocle. Bus no. 2 to San Leone on the coast.

Inter-city buses: Tickets and information for all lines are available from **Omnia** (*Piazza Fratelli Rosselli, Agrigento; map 2, T: 0922 29136*). **ATA** (*www.atabusservice.it*) operates services linking Gela, Licata, Palma di Montechiaro and Palermo.

Autolinee Licata/Sal Autolinee (*www.autolineesal.it*) runs services for Porto Empedocle, Palma di Montechiaro and Racalmuto, and three buses a day connecting Porto Empedocle (and Agrigento) with Palermo Punta Raisi Airport (journey time slightly over 2hrs) and vice versa, in connection with ferries to Lampedusa.

Camilleri, Argento e Lattuca (*www.camilleriargentoelattuca.it*) connects Agrigento to Aragona, Raffadali and Palermo.

Cuffaro (*www.cuffaro.it*) has services for San Biagio Platani and Sciacca.

Lattuca (*www.autolineelattuca.it*) for Aragona, Comitini, Raffadali and Sant'Angelo Muxaro.

Lumia (*www.autolineelumia.it*) runs services from Agrigento for Burgio, Caltabellotta, Campobello di Mazara, Castelvetrano, Cattolica Eraclea (from where you can catch another bus to Eraclea Minoa, 15 mins' drive), Marsala, Mazara del Vallo, Menfi, Montallegro, Montevago, Palma di Montechiaro, Porto Empedocle, Realmonte, Ribera, Sambuca, Santa Margherita di Belice, Sciacca and Trapani. Trapani airport is linked to Menfi (80mins), Sciacca (1hr 40mins) and Agrigento and Porto Empedocle (approx. 3hrs). At the time of writing, services were due to begin to Palermo.

Panepinto (*www.panepintobus.it*) goes to Bivona, Cammarata, Casteltermini, Mussomeli, Palermo and San Giovanni Gemini.

SAIS Autolinee (*www.saisautolinee.it*) runs services for Caltagirone, Caltanissetta, Catania, Enna, Gangi, Gela, Messina, Palermo and Piazza Armerina.

SAIS Trasporti (*www.giamporcaro.it*) connects Agrigento with a variety of destinations all over the island, including Caltagirone, Caltanissetta, Canicattì, Castelvetrano, Catania and Catania Airport, Gela, Giardini Naxos, Marsala, Mazara del Vallo, Menfi, Messina, Palermo, Porto Empedocle and Sciacca.

Pelagian Islands

• **By air:** Direct flights to Lampedusa from Palermo, Catania and several mainland Italian cities are operated by Meridiana (*www.meridiana.it*), Alitalia (*www.alitalia.it*), Air One (*www.flyairone.it*), and Blu Express (*www.blu-express.com*).

• **By sea:** *For up-to-date information on shipping lines, timetables and tariffs, consult www.bookingitalia.it.*

Siremar (*www.siremar.it*) runs car ferries from Porto Empedocle to Linosa (6hrs) and Lampedusa (8hrs) every day; visitors are not allowed to bring cars to Lampedusa in July and August, and never to Linosa.

Ustica Lines (*www.usticalines.it*) run hydrofoils from Porto Empedocle twice daily from May–Oct except Tues, in winter Wed and Sat only, to Linosa (4hrs) continuing on to Lampedusa (5hrs). Ustica Lines also run hydrofoils from Mazara del Vallo to Lampedusa, stopping also at Pantelleria, three days a week from July–Sept.

Ferry and hydrofoil ticket offices: Lampedusa: Siremar, Lungomare Rizzo, T: 0922 636777; Ustica Lines, c/o Strazzera, Lungomare Rizzo, T: 0922 970003. **Linosa:** Siremar and Ustica Lines, c/o Cavallaro, Via Re Umberto 46, T: 0922 972062.

Inter-island transport: Hydrofoil connections run twice a day between Lampedusa and Linosa in summer, once a day the rest of the year, run by Ustica Lines.

WHERE TO STAY

Agrigento (*map p. 539, C2*)
€€€ **Villa Athena.** ■ Magical atmosphere, the first and the finest hotel in Agrigento, in a peerless location right in front of the Temple of Concord, with a garden, car park and pool. *Passeggiata Archeologica 33 (Via dei Templi), T: 0922 596288, www.hotelvillaathena.it. Map p. 185, 15.*

€€€ **Domus Aurea.** Enchanting house 7km south of the centre, built in 1781, with beautiful Mediterranean garden and hydromassage tub; the old-fashioned red-plush sitting room is adorable. 20 lovely rooms, car park, nice breakfast but no restaurant. Private beach. *Contrada Maddalusa 150, SS 640 km 4, T: 0922 511500, www.hoteldomusaurea.it.*

€€ **Colleverde Park.** Comfortable, straightforward hotel close to the town and within walking distance of the temples, with 50 rooms, beautiful garden, car park and very good restaurant. *Via dei Templi (just north of the Archaeological Museum), T: 0922 29555, www.colleverdehotel.it. Map p. 185, 11.*

€€ **Villa Goethe.** The villa belonging to Baron Celauro where Goethe stayed in 1787 is an elegant, central B&B with a shady hanging garden, lots of stairs, and 5 rooms, all with air conditioning, private bath and TV. *Via Celauro 7 (north of Via Atenea, before the fork with Pirandello), T: 0922 816240, www.villagoethe.it. Map p. 184, 2.*

€€ **Camera con Vista.** Six comfortable rooms, simply but adequately furnished, in this 60s-built relais with car park (but no restaurant). Views over the temples. *Via Porta Aurea 4, Contrada Bennici (near the hospital,* just west of Porta Aurea), *T: 0922 554605, www.cameraconvista.net. Beyond map p. 184, 14.*

€ **B&B Monastero Santo Spirito.** The Cistercian nuns offer accommodation for women and families only. Light, airy rooms with private bath, TV and air conditioning, some with self-catering facilities. Central position, good value for money, and the breakfasts prepared by the nuns are something to write home about. *Via Santo Spirito, T: 0922 20664, 328 7370299, www.monasterosantospiritoag.it. Map p. 184, 2.*

Aragona (*map p. 539, C2*)
€€ **Ciuci's Manor.** Country house in panoramic position close to Aragona with lake and pool; donkeys and the local *girgentana* goats are raised. 5 spacious rooms with *en suite* bath, good restaurant. *Aragona, T: 334 6748055, www.ciucismanor.com.*

Cammarata (*map p. 539, C1*)
€€ **Casalicchio.** The farm has belonged to the same family since 1816. Comfortable rooms or self-catering apartments, pool, lake, tennis, sauna, good restaurant, organic food, mostly of local production. *Contrada Casalicchio (just east of the SS 189, T: 0922 908144, 339 6555609, www.casalicchio.info.*

Comitini (*map p. 539, C2*)
€ **'U Cavallaggeri.** A charming small hotel in the main square, 5 rooms over their excellent restaurant. *Piazza Umberto 22, T: 0922 600062, www.ucavallaggeri.it.*

Licata (*map p. 539, D3*)
€ **Antica Dimora San Girolamo.** Delightful B&B in a medieval house of the fishermen's quarter; lovely breakfasts and very comfortable accommodation. *Piazza San Girolamo 20, T: 0922 875010, www.dimorasangirolamo.it.*

Menfi (*map p. 539, A1*)
€€€ **Foresteria di Planeta.** This renowned wine producer offers accommodation on a beautiful estate, with many hectares of well-groomed vineyards; 14 elegant, pastel-

coloured rooms with floor tiles from Burgio and Caltagirone, surrounded by a garden of aromatic herbs. Good restaurant serving the best local cuisine, where much attention is paid to the wine. Cookery courses organised. *Contrada Passo di Gurra (west of Menfi, south of the SS 115), T: 0925 1955460, www.planeta.it.*

€€€ **Baglio San Vincenzo.** ■ An old-fashioned farm immersed in delightful countryside, offering 12 comfortable rooms, restaurant and pool, within easy reach of Menfi town, Sciacca, Selinunte and Castelvetrano. The farm produces olive oil and the award-winning Lanzara red and white wines, and both white and pink *spumante. Contrada San Vincenzo (just east of Menfi, north of the SS 115), T: 0925 75065, www.bagliosanvincenzo. net.*

Montallegro *(map p. 539, C2)*

€€€ **Relais Briuccia.** ■ A welcoming little hotel in what was a country nobleman's town house (lots of stairs!), in a strategically situated village on the road between Agrigento and Sciacca. All 7 rooms have beautiful old tiled floors, comfortable beds, bathrooms with jacuzzi. The restaurant, Capitolo Primo, is famous throughout Sicily. *Via Trieste 1, T: 339 7592176, www.relaisbriuccia.it.*

Porto Palo *(map p. 539, A1)*

€ **Da Vittorio.** Ten simple rooms with private bath on the lovely unspoilt beach of Porto Palo (awarded the EU Blue Flag), very quiet, garden and car park. Incredible restaurant, one of the best in Sicily, if you like fish. Closed Nov–Feb. *Via Friuli-Venezia Giulia 9, T: 0925 78381, www.ristorantevittorio.it.*

San Biagio Platani *(map p. 539, C2)*

€€ **Serra Pernice.** Farm producing cheese and vegetables using only organic methods in a beautiful position in the Turvoli Valley (5km from San Biagio on the road to Alessandria della Rocca). Also organises excursions to various destinations. 7 comfortable rooms, all

with private bath, very good restaurant serving home-grown food to local recipes. *Contrada Capraria, T: 331 3834736, 345 3433187 (Enrico Caldara), www.serrapernice.it.*

Sant'Angelo Muxaro *(map p. 539, C2)*

€ Accommodation is available in restored village houses; breakfast is included. Italian courses available. Walking tours and other activities are arranged. A delightful experience. *Contact Val di Kam, Piazza Umberto 31, T: 0922 919670, 339 5305989, www.valdikam.it.*

Sciacca *(map p. 539, B2)*

€€€ **Verdura Golf & Spa Resort.** A Rocco Forte Collection hotel, services are excellent. 203 rooms and suites, each with private terrace and sea view. Two golf courses, infinity pool, fitness centre, good restaurants. *SS 115 km 131, T: 0925 998001, 0925 998180, www. verduraresort.com.*

€€ **Villa Palocla.** Lovely old country house surrounded by orange groves, a short way out of town to the northwest. Nine rooms, pool, winter garden, elegant restaurant with frescoed ceilings. *Contrada Raganella, T: 0925 902812, 340 5290146, www.villapalocla.it.*

€–€€ **Jacaranda.** In a modern villa surrounded by a garden in the eastern outskirts of town, a colourful B&B with 4 comfortable rooms. Good breakfasts, car park. *Via delle Sequoie 1, T: 392 8123231, www.casajacaranda.it.*

€ **Al Moro.** A 13th-century ex-watchtower in the town centre, transformed into a tiny German-run inn with 13 rooms, patio. Excellent breakfasts but no restaurant. Lots of stairs, both inside and out. *Via Liguori 44, T: 0925 86756, www.almoro.com.*

Pelagian Islands

NB: Accommodation on the islands is considerably more expensive than in similar establishments on the mainland. The hotels usually demand a minimum stay of three nights or a week; many close in winter.

Lampedusa

€€€ **Cala Madonna.** Elegant resort with 14 spacious rooms in stone *dammusi*, in a quiet position facing the sea. Garden, restaurant, boat for excursions. Closed winter. *Contrada Madonna 28, T: 0922 971626, www.calamadonnaclub.it.*

€€€ **Cupola Bianca.** Very chic Moresque structure, the 23 rooms are in *dammusi* (stone cottages); peaceful position with a lovely garden and palm trees; open-air dining, tennis. Closed winter. *Contrada Madonna, T: 0922 971274 or 975793, www.hotelcupolabianca.it.*

€€ **Martello.** Comfortable modern hotel (though one of the oldest on the island), run by the owners, 25 rooms, most with sea view, very good restaurant, good value for money. Open mid March–mid Nov. *Piazza Medusa 1, T: 0922 970025, www.hotelmartello.it.*

€€ **Paladini di Francia.** Comfortable modern hotel with 25 rooms, also two-room apartments sleeping four with cooking facilities, ideal for families. Breakfast room. Half-board can be arranged with the Hotel Martello (same management). *Via Alessandro Volta, T: 0922 970550, www.hotelpaladinidifrancia.it.*

Linosa

€€ **Posta.** In a good central position, occupying the old post office, B&B with 10 rooms, air conditioning, garden, dinghy for excursions. *T: 0922 972507, 320 6010556, 339 7410705, www.linosaresidencelaposta.it.*

€ **Linoikos.** Part of an arts centre (Sanlorè), 13 simple but comfortable rooms, decorated with flotsam, lovely terraces overlooking the sea, evening meals on request. No TVs in the rooms. *Open June–Sept. Via Alfieri, T: 0922 401810, www.linoikos.it.*

WHERE TO EAT

Agrigento (*map p. 539, C2*)

€€ **La Posata di Federico II.** Elegant restaurant (you eat on the veranda in summer), imaginative chef who makes good use of his very fresh ingredients, nice desserts, Sicilian wines. Closed Sun. *Piazza Cavour 19 (Viale della Vittoria), T: 0922 28289, 348 5481497. Map p. 185, 7.*

€€ **Spizzulio.** Owner Carmelo is chef, waiter and sommelier, but he is passionate about what he does. Understandably slow service, but the food is good, and accompanied by the perfect Sicilian wine for each dish. *Strada Panoramica 23 (just after the junction with Via dei Templi), T: 0922 20712. Map p. 185, 11.*

€€ **Ruga Reali.** For a subtle mix of country cooking and marine cuisine, local wines, simple relaxed atmosphere. Open evenings only, closed Mon. *Cortile Scribani 8 (Piazza Pirandello), T: 0922 20370. Map p. 184, 1.*

€ **Villa Kephos.** Attractive restaurant surrounded by almond groves and beautiful views, serving delicious thin-crust pizza, both for lunch or dinner. Closed Mon. *Valle dei Templi (close to Porta Aurea), T: 0922 556031 & 330 661895. Beyond map p. 184, 14.*

Licata (*map p. 539, D3*)

€€€ **La Madia.** ■ Renowned, Michelin-star chef Pino Cuttaia's restaurant for excellent fish, meat and vegetables, well prepared to original recipes and beautifully served, accompanied by his own home-made bread and served with Sicilian wines; central position—a meal here is certainly worth the trip to Licata. Closed Sun evening, all day Tues (all Tues and Sun lunch in Aug). *Corso Capriata 22, T: 0922 771443.*

Montallegro (*map p. 539, C2*)

€€€ **Capitolo Primo.** ■ This restaurant is so good it would be worth the journey to Sicily, but it is in a strategic position along the route from Agrigento to Sciacca, and offers comfortable accommodation (*see p. 223*). Damiano, a chef with flair, will tickle your palate and delight your eye at the same time, using tradition and local ingredients to the best advantage, in a way they have never been used before. His cellar is stocked with the best Sicilian wines. Closed Mon. *Via Trieste 1, T: 339 7592176.*

Porto Palo (*map p. 539, A1*)

€€ **Da Vittorio.** ■ Family-run restaurant of long standing, on the beach, renowned for the sumptuous fish soup and seafood salads; rooms also available (*see p. 223*). Vittorio hails from the mountain town of Bergamo, but he has a real flair for cooking seafood. House wines are excellent. Closed Sun and Mon evenings in winter. *Via Friuli-Venezia Giulia 9, T: 0925 78381.*

Racalmuto (*map p. 539, D2*)

€€ **Lo Zenzero.** ■ Close to the opera house, a historic restaurant run by the same family for many years; the home-made food prepared to traditional recipes is delicious. Local wines. Closed Mon. *Via Sciascia 18, T: 0922 941087.*

Ribera (*map p. 539, B2*)

€ **Agorà.** Good restaurant worth the journey to Ribera, vast menu includes local fish (fried baby cod or squid) and delicious desserts made using the famous wild strawberries. Excellent pizza in the evenings. Closed Mon. *Via Buoni Amici 15, T: 0925 62014.*

Sciacca (*map p. 539, B2*)

€€€ **Hostaria del Vicolo.** Local fresh fish is used to prepare some very special dishes: *spaghetti frutti di mare e finocchietto* (spaghetti with shellfish and wild fennel), *merluzzo ai fichi secchi* (cod with dried figs), or swordfish ravioli. Closed Mon. *Vicolo Samaritano 10, T: 0925 23071.*

€€€ **Disio.** Tiny restaurant in the centre for memorable seafood, but start with delicious *zuppa di porri*, leek soup with grated *caciocavallo* cheese. Closed Mon. *Via Vittorio Emanuele 107, T: 0925 86922.*

€€ **La Lampara.** Trattoria serving simple local dishes, very well prepared. Closed Mon. *Via Secondo Grande Caricatore 33 (Lungomare Cristoforo Colombo), T: 0925 85085.*

Pelagian Islands

NB: Eating out is expensive on the islands; a popular dish is siluri di Gheddafi (Gaddafi's missiles), a filling version of stuffed squid. Dishes are often spicy and cous cous is frequently on the menu. Most restaurants are closed in winter.

Lampedusa

€€€ **Gemelli.** For the best seafood crudités and sea-perch cous cous, also bouillabaisse and paella; irresistible desserts. Expensive. Closed winter. *Via Cala Pisana 2, T: 0922 970699.*

€€ **Mille e Una Notte.** Beautiful restaurant in a large cave, excellent cuisine. Closed winter. *Lungomare Luigi Rizzo 133, T: 0922 971555.*

€€ **Trattoria Pugliese.** A cosy and quiet *trattoria* next to the airport. The chef is from Puglia; this guarantees excellent pasta dishes. Open evenings only in summer. *Via Cala Francese 17, T: 0922 970531.*

€€ **Ciccio's,** No-frills *trattoria*, ideal for lunch or dinner; tasty snacks, seafood salad, sea-perch cous cous, nice atmosphere. Closed Thurs in winter. *Via Vittorio Emanuele 63, T: 339 7723493.*

Linosa

€€ **Errera.** Close to the sea, wonderful pasta or cous cous; refreshing fruit *granita* for dessert. *Via Scalo Vecchio 1, T: 0922 972041.*

€€ **Trattoria da Anna.** ■ Her lentil soup is famous, or try the *pasta con gli sgombri* (pasta with mackerel). *Via Veneto 1, Belvedere, T: 0922 972048.*

LOCAL SPECIALITIES

Agrigento At the convent of Santo Spirito in Via Santo Spirito, the nuns make *cous cous* *dolce* with pistachios and cocoa; the recipe hasn't changed for 500 years. Dalli Cardillo (*Piazza Pirandello 32*) bakes all kinds of local bread, including the special rolls for the feast of St Calogero. Sammartino 1961 (*Via Pirandello 24*) is a good place to buy olive oil, wines, liqueurs, the local pesto made with wild fennel, cheese, anchovies with chilli pepper, swordfish paté. The historic coffee house is Infurna (*Via Atenea 96*). Try their ice cream made with wild strawberries from Ribera.

Aragona Cacciatore (*Via Venezia 1*) is a historic pastry-shop, for excellent *cannoli di ricotta*.

Burgio The oldest surviving bell foundry is that of Luigi Cascio (Fonderia Mario Virgadamo in Piazza Roma). The typical pottery can be found at La Ceramica di Burgio (*Via Vittorio Emanuele 19*).

Campobello di Licata Fine wines are produced by the Azienda Agricola Milazzo, on the Terre della Baronia estate (*SS 123 km 12.7, T: 0922 878207, www.milazzovini.com*).

Favara Famous for its marzipan Easter lambs; they are so good that the pastry shops make them year-round. Pasticceria Vita (*Via dei Mille 98*) is an excellent address.

Lampedusa Cose Buone, a very up-market bakery at Via Cavour 8, has fresh bread and pastries. Visit Famularo in Via Francesco Crispi for all kinds of local fish, smoked or in olive oil, and sponges. Titti Sanguedolce, at Via Roma 98, has a vast array of sponges, and wooden model boats. Lampedusa's historic coffee house is the Bar Dell'Amicizia (*Via Vittorio Emanuele 60*), with a particularly congenial atmosphere.

Menfi The Settesoli estate (*SS 115 di Menfi, www.mandrarossa.it*), produces the prize-winning Mandrarossa wine.

Racalmuto Pasticceria Taibi (*Via Garibaldi 127*) for the delicious local pastries, *taralli*

racalmutesi, delicate lemon biscuits.

Raffadali Di Stefano (*Via Murano 23*) for home-made ice cream, freshly prepared every day, some unusual flavours, such as *pecorino* made with sheep's milk. Espresso coffee is good too; try it with pistachio cream. Closed Wed.

Ribera A small company preparing jams and marmalades using local fruit, especially the renowned wild strawberries, is Colle Vicario (*Via Gramsci, 18, www.collevicario.it*). Very elegant packaging. Try the wild strawberry with orange blossom and pink champagne.

Sambuca The special pastries of Sambuca are called *minni di virgini* (virgin's breasts), delicate pies filled with confectioner's custard, chocolate and candied pumpkin, first made by Suor Virginia in 1725 in honour of Marquis Pietro Beccadelli and his wife Marianna; you will find them (along with numerous other delectable sweets) at Pendola (*Via Baglio Grande 42*). The Planeta estate at Ulmo (*request visit at least 2 days before, T: 0925 1955460, www.planeta.it*) produces a marvellous white wine called Cometa, a perfect accompaniment to rich fish dishes.

Sciacca Bar Sant'Angelo (*Corso Vittorio Emanuele 66*) is an excellent choice for home-made ice cream and granita, this coffee-house hasn't changed at all since 1963, when it was chosen by Pietro Germi as a film-set for his *Seduced and Abandoned*. Another charming Art Nouveau locale is the Bar Scandaglia (*Piazza Scandagliato 5*), which opened in 1919. Pastries made according to the traditional recipes of the nuns of Sciacca (*cucchiteddi* and *ova marine*) can be found at Pasticceria La Favola (*Corso Vittorio Emanuele 234*). Coral is still worked in Sciacca, with excellent results, by Conti (*Piazza Matteotti 10, www.orodisciacca.it*), while a good address for the local pottery is Cascio (*Via Vittorio Emanuele 115*).

Agrigento First week in February: *Sagra del mandorlo in fiore*, an international folklore festival, held at the temples (*Info: www.mandorloinfiore.net*). First week in July: Feast of St Calogero with processions and fireworks; when the saint is carried along Via Atenea, he is pelted with decorative loaves of bread.

Cammarata First Sun in May: unusual and picturesque feast with procession of the Cross of St Anthony called *Crocifisso di Tuvagli*. Last Sun in May: procession of the Cross of the Angels, with a cavalcade. Last Sunday in August: procession of the Cross of the Rain. 19 Dec-6 Jan: Living Crib in the district of San Vito, when local people enact tableaux representing the birth of Christ and the Epiphany, and bring to life ancient crafts (*Info: www.presepeviventecammarata.it*).

Casteltermini Last week in May: *Tataratà* (*see p. 214; Info: www.tatarata.it*).

Lampedusa July, Lampedusainfestival, summer event presenting films, concerts, open-air theatre (*Info: www.lampedusainfestival.com*).

Licata 3–6 May: *Festa di Sant'Angelo*, including a traditional fair, parades of Sicilian carts, handicrafts, fireworks and music in honour of St Angel, a Carmelite monk from Jerusalem, martyred in the 13th century. In years of good harvest, the farmers take a mule laden with flowers into the church; in dry years the statue of the saint is taken out to sea on a boat and threatened with being thrown overboard, in the hope that he will send rain (this invariably works).

Palma di Montechiaro May: *Festa della Madonna del Castello*, a procession of barefoot devotees, accompanied by musicians and richly-bedecked mules, accompany the Madonna up through the steep little streets to the castle.

Racalmuto 2nd Sun in July: Colourful procession of riders on festooned horses goes up the stairway to Santa Maria del Monte.

San Biagio Platani Easter Sun: *Gli Archi di Pasqua* dates back to the early 17th century; special bread is baked and streets are decorated with flowery arches made of branches of palm leaves, fruit, bread and dates, to celebrate the meeting of the Madonna with her Risen Son (*Info: 0922 910605*).

Sciacca February: the figure of *Peppe Nappa*, the sharp-witted Sicilian peasant, is burnt at the end of the Carnival processions with allegorical floats, thought to be the oldest in Sicily (*Info: www.carnevaledisciacca.com*).

THE PROVINCE OF CALTANISSETTA

Caltanissetta, the province between Enna and Agrigento, is neatly divided into two parts by the river Imera Meridionale (the ancient *Himera*). The town of Gela, on the south coast, dominates the southern part, while Caltanissetta, the capital, presides over the northwest. Particularly favourable in position and constitution for human settlement, the entire area has been inhabited since the early Bronze Age. In the 16th century much of the land was divided up among the more powerful aristocratic families with a view to farming it more efficiently, and many new towns were founded. The economy, after the decline of the sulphur mines, is now based on the production of wheat, fruit and vegetables, especially artichokes, table grapes, peaches and plums, and there is also an oil refinery at Gela. The famous bitter liqueur Amaro Averna is still produced near the capital, according to a secret recipe owned by the Averna family for more than 150 years. Craggy castles and beautiful beaches of golden sand are some of the prime attractions of this little-known part of Sicily.

CALTANISSETTA

The capital of the province (*map p. 540, B2*) is a small but prosperous provincial town, built of golden-yellow sandstone. It has a charming, colourful old centre, inviting displays in the shop windows, and a bustling daily fish and vegetable market.

HISTORY OF CALTANISSETTA

For many years the name was thought to derive from the ancient Sican city of *Nissa*, with the Arabic prefix *kal'at* (castle); but it could also come from *kal'at en-nissaat*, or 'castle of the young women'. Excavations in 1989 on Mt San Giuliano (or Redentore) yielded 7th–6th-century BC finds. The site was then abandoned until the Roman period. Conquered by Count Roger in 1086, it was given as a feudal estate to his son Jourdain, passing subsequently into the hands of Corrado Lancia (1296) and the Moncada family (1406). The province was once the centre of the most important sulphur-mining area in the world, from the 18th century up until the early 20th century (the last mines were closed down in the 1970s).

Piazza Garibaldi and the duomo

In Piazza Garibaldi is an amusing **fountain** depicting two bronze sea-monsters squirting water at a triton and a hippogryph by the local sculptor Michele Tripisciano, whose works also adorn Corso Umberto, the Town Hall and the public gardens. Dominating the square is the honey-coloured façade of the **duomo**, dedicated to Santa Maria La Nova e San Michele (1570–1622), much damaged by bombing raids in 1943. In the luminous interior, decorated with white and gold stuccoes and bright frescoes, the vault painting (1720), a brilliant, swirling triumph of *trompe l'oeil*, is considered the Flemish artist Willem Borremans' masterpiece. In the second south chapel is a wooden statue (covered with silver) of the Immaculate Virgin (1760). In the chapel to the right of the sanctuary is a charming polychrome wooden statue of the Archangel Michael by Stefano Li Volsi (1625), flanked by marble statues of the Archangels Gabriel and Raphael by Vincenzo Vitaliano (1753). St Michael is particularly venerated in Caltanissetta, because he is thought to have saved the people from epidemics of the plague. The high altarpiece of the *Madonna with Saints* is by Borremans, and the richly painted, carved and gilded organ dates from the 17th century. In the north transept is a painting of *Our Lady of Carmel* by Filippo Paladini, and in the second north chapel is a Crucifix attributed to Fra' Umile da Petralia. One of the altars is taken up by an elaborate gilded urn, containing a very realistic *Dead Christ*, made by local sculptor Francesco Biangiardi in 1896.

The church of **San Sebastiano**, opposite, has an unusual façade (1891), painted bright red, and a blue campanile. It is said to have been founded in the 16th century in thanksgiving to St Michael and St Sebastian, after a devastating epidemic of plague.

Another side of the piazza is occupied by a former convent which now houses the **Town Hall** (with statues by Tripisciano) and the **opera house**, Teatro Regina Margherita.

Corso Umberto

Running alongside the Town Hall, Corso Umberto leads up to a **statue of Umberto I** (the second king of Italy, wearing a flamboyant hat) by Tripisciano, outside the former Jesuit collegiate church of **Sant'Agata** (1605), painted red, and preceded by an outside stairway. The Greek-cross interior is finely decorated with inlaid marble, especially the two side altars. The north altar (with a delightful frontal with birds) is surmounted by a relief of St Ignatius by Ignazio Marabitti. The high altarpiece, the *Martyrdom of St Agatha*, is by Agostino Scilla (1654). His work here is framed in black marble adorned with cherubs by Marabitti. The first north chapel has frescoes by Luigi Borremans, the son of Willem (including an *Assumption* in the vault, and a *Nativity* on a side wall).

Off the right side of Corso Umberto, on Salita Matteotti, is the grand Palazzo Moncada (1635–38), now the seat of the Pro Loco tourist office, and on the first floor, the **Museo Michele Tripisciano** (*open 9.30–1 & 5–8, closed Sun in summer, T: 0934 585890*), a remarkable collection of sculptures by this unsung local artist, who lived from 1860–1914. The palace was built by Countess Luisa Moncada, when in an attempt to gain independence for the island her grandson was chosen by the Sicilians to become their king. Unfortunately the plot was discovered and the revolutionaries were executed, while Don Luigi Guglielmo himself (the grandson) was exiled to Madrid. His palace was never completed.

San Domenico and the Castello di Pietrarossa

A street on the left side of the duomo leads downhill to the east to Via San Domenico, which continues to the church of **San Domenico**, with a sinuously curving Baroque façade fitting an awkward site, in the oldest district of the city. The stuccoes inside have been painted bright blue, while the nave is decorated in pastel shades. The fine canvas of the *Madonna of the Rosary* (1614) is by Filippo Paladini.

From here along Via Angeli the 14th-century church of **Santa Maria degli Angeli** (*closed at the time of writing*), the first Chiesa Madre, can be reached in ten minutes. Sadly ruined, the church's west door survives. Beyond, on a rocky outcrop, stand the scattered ruins and lonely tower of the Arab-built **Castello di Pietrarossa**, so-called because of the red stone from which it was constructed.

Two small museums

Near Villa Amedeo (the beautiful public gardens) at Viale Regina Margherita 51 (south-east of the duomo) is the seminary which houses the **Museo Diocesano** (*to request visit T: 0934 21165 or ask at Pro Loco; Palazzo Moncada, Salita Matteotti, T: 0934 585890*), with 17th- and 18th-century vestments and a fine collection of paintings, including two by Luigi Borremans, who was employed in Caltanissetta as a fresco painter; also a very expressive *Martyrdom of St Flavia* by Fra' Felice da Sambuca. In the western part of town, in a school at Viale della Regione 73, is the **Museo Mineralogico Paleontologico e della Zolfara** (*to request visit call T: 0934 591280, possible Mon–Fri 9–1*), an interesting collection of some 3,000 minerals, and scale models of many of the sulphur mines that once operated in the provinces of Caltanissetta and Agrigento.

Abbazia di Santo Spirito and the Museo Archeologico

The **Abbazia di Santo Spirito**, 3km north of Caltanissetta, is the oldest church in the province, founded by Count Roger and his wife Adelaide (probably between 1086 and 1093), and consecrated in 1153. It was attached to a fortified building, parts of which now form the sacristy. The church has a fine triple apse, recently restored. The charming small interior (*to request visit call priest 0934 566596, or ring at the door on the right marked Abbazia*) contains a large font, where people were baptised by immersion, below a painted Crucifix dating from the 15th century. On the walls are three detached 15th-century frescoes. The striking 17th-century fresco *of Christ in Benediction* was repainted in 1974. On the arch of the apse is the dedication stone (1153), and nearby is a little Roman cinerary urn (1st century AD), with rams' heads, birds and a festoon. A 17th-century sedan chair, with its original fittings, which was once used as a confessional, has been removed to the priest's house (*shown on request*).

Close by, at Via Santo Spirito 57, is the **Museo Archeologico** (*open 9–1 & 3.30–6.30; T: 0934 567062*), with a particularly interesting archaeological collection from pre- and post-Greek colonisation sites in the province, including objects from tombs at Gibil Gabib, Polizzello, Capodarso, Vassallaggi and Sabucina; some fine kraters (many with animal illustrations); black- and red-figure vases; and figurines found recently on Mt San Giuliano (on the northern outskirts of Caltanissetta) which represent the earliest portrayal of the human figure so far discovered in Sicily, after the Palaeolithic graffiti in the Addaura caves near Palermo. Dating from the early Bronze Age, they are thought to have been used in a prehistoric sanctuary. Finds from the Byzantine period include the splendid gold earrings from Monte Mimiani. One of the most important objects on display is a 6th-century BC bronze helmet found recently at Polizzello, the cheekpiece of which is decorated with the figure of an armed warrior. It is very similar to a helmet of Cretan manufacture now on display in Berlin.

ENVIRONS OF CALTANISSETTA

Sabucina and Ponte Capodarso

Off the Enna road, on the peak of Mt Sabucina, is the **site of Sabucina** (*to request visit call the Sovrintendenza, T: 0934 554965*). The approach road climbs up past several disused mines, and there is a view up to the right above an overgrown mine of the line of walls of Sabucina, just below the summit of the hill. After 2km the asphalt road ends beside recent excavations of a necropolis. An unsurfaced road continues downhill for another 500m to a gate by a modern house at the entrance to the site, in a splendid position with wide views. Mt Sabucina was first occupied in the Bronze Age. A thriving Iron-Age village was then settled by the Greeks in the 6th century BC. The city declined after the revolt of Ducetius in 451–450 BC. The long line of Greek fortifications with towers and gates were built directly onto the rock. Sacred edifices can also be seen here.

In the valley below Caltanissetta to the east, the River Salso is crossed by the **Ponte Capodarso** (*map p. 540, B2*), a graceful bridge built in 1553 by Venetian engineers. A legend says that once a year the devils hold a market on the bridge; anyone lucky enough to see it may purchase just one fruit, which next day will turn into solid gold. Nearby is the **archaeological area of Capodarso**, an ancient city which had disappeared by the beginning of the 3rd century BC. Part of the walls and necropolis survive. Finds from the site are kept in the Museo Archeologico in Caltanissetta, and the area is now part of a large nature reserve run by Italia Nostra, Monte Capodarso e Valle dell'Imera Meridionale (*Viale Conte Testasecca 44, Caltanissetta, T: 0934 541722, www. riservaimera.it, call to book visit*). There are many old mines, water-mills and caves in the reserve, some of which have thriving populations of various bat species.

Gibil Gabib

South of Caltanissetta is the site of an ancient settlement at Gibil Gabib (*map p. 540, B3; to request visit call Sovrintendenza T: 0934 554965*). The name derives from the Arabic *jebel habib* (pleasant hill), and it was discovered in the 19th century. A necropolis has yielded finds from three periods of occupation, in the 7th, 6th and 4th centuries BC.

SOUTHWEST FROM CALTANISSETTA

Some 20km southwest of Caltanissetta, close to the border with the province of Agrigento, are two little-visited towns. **Delia** (*map p. 540, B3*) was re-founded as a farming community in the early 17th century, on an older medieval settlement. The name derives from the Arabic *daliyah*, meaning vineyard. A regular street plan divides the town into rectangular blocks, which in turn present a typical Arabian network of tiny alleys, serving also as courtyards for the dwellings, often built of blocks of yellow sandstone.

There are many of the old fountains where the families used to collect their supply of water, and life is still lived largely in the open air, as in the past, in a very sociable manner. The southern part of the town is recognisably the old centre, gathered around the Palazzo del Principe and the 16th-century Chiesa Madre, dedicated to the Madonna of Loreto. The painting of *St Rosalia of Palermo* over the altar is by Pietro d'Asaro, the 'Monocolo di Racalmuto' (*see p. 506*). Turreted ruins of the **Castellazzo**, the old castle (11th century) of Delia, still stand, 1km from the town.

Close to Delia is **Sommatino** (*map p. 540, B3*), a bright little town founded in the 14th century as the feud of the Del Porto family, who populated it with farmers. Here too, the older quarter of the town is clearly recognisable in the eastern part.

NORTH & WEST OF CALTANISSETTA

North of Caltanissetta is **Santa Caterina Villarmosa** (*map p. 540, B2*), founded in 1572 by Giulio Grimaldi, baron of Risigallo. The centre of this quiet agricultural town is Piazza Garibaldi, with the 18th-century Chiesa Madre. Many of the women are expert at embroidery and lace-making; you will see them sitting in front of their doorways in the early afternoon, hard at work.

About 2km northeast of the town, on the slopes going down to the Vaccarizzo stream, an area of particularly interesting geology is protected as a nature reserve run by the provincial administration, the **Riserva Geologica di Contrada Scaleri** (*Provincia di Caltanissetta, Via Regina Margherita 28, Caltanissetta, T: 0934 534413 and 0934 534111*). Slabs of limestone have collapsed through the centuries, eroded by the streams of water; resulting in formations that are unique in Sicily.

Resuttano (*map p. 540, B2*) stands above the Imera in the northernmost pocket of the province. An Arab farming village, it was re-founded in 1625 by the Di Napoli family, to whom it belonged until feudalism came to an end here in 1812. The ruins of the Castello di Resuttano are c. 5km east of the town, on the left bank of the river. The castle, which is incorporated into a 19th-century farmhouse, can be reached by a little road which branches off to the left from the country road to Alimena. It was probably built by the Arabs (*rahsul et-tan* meaning fortified house, hence the name of the town), and was important during the Middle Ages because of its position on the river, controlling the southern part of the Madonie Mountains. In 1337, the last year of his reign, Frederick II of Aragon, while travelling from Palermo to Enna and Catania, stayed the night here and is supposed to have written the will that sparked off a notorious feud between the Ventimiglia and Chiaramonte families.

Marianopoli and its archaeological sites

Along the old Palermo road, which skirts the southern foot of Mt Chibbò (951m), is **Marianopoli** (*map p. 540, A2–B2*), founded in 1726 by Baron Della Scala, who brought a group of immigrants from Montenegro here to farm the land. The town centre is built on a chequerboard street plan around Piazza Garibaldi. On the west side is the 18th-century church of San Prospero (or Santa Maria Addolorata); the body of the saint, patron of the town, is enclosed in the main altar. At the town hall (Piazza Garibaldi 1) is the Museo Archeologico (*open 9–1 & 3–7, T: 0934 674357*), on two floors, with a collection of finds from the nearby archaeological sites of Monte Castellazzo (Neolithic, early Bronze Age, Iron Age, Greek), Balate and Valle Oscura (Vallelunga culture, early Bronze Age), and from the 6th-century BC necropolis of Valle Oscura.

East of Marianopoli is the rocky summit of **Monte Castellazzo**, where excavations (*signposted*) have brought to light a prehistoric necropolis with rock-hewn tombs, signs of burial in large pots, and Greek tombs. On top of the crest are the remains of a city with walls (6th–3rd centuries BC), probably the ancient *Mytistraton*, which put up fierce resistance to the Romans in the First Punic War.

Continuing south along the road, after c. 7km is a private road (right), leading to an ancient settlement on **Monte Balate**; parts of the walls and the acropolis have been explored, the material is at the museum in Marianopoli. Still further south is the valley signposted **Valle Oscura**, where the inhabitants of an early Bronze Age village buried their dead in cracks in the rock; the same 'tombs' were used again by the Hellenised population in the 6th century BC. If you decide to visit these three sites, of difficult access, please inform the museum beforehand (so they know where you are in case of accidents), but they are not fenced; trekking boots and considerable agility are required.

Southeast of Mt Mimiani and Marianopoli, c. 8km from the town, is a nature reserve run by Legambiente, **Lago Sfondato** (*map p. 540, B2; for information and to book visit, Legambiente, 14/a Via Rosso di San Secondo, Caltanissetta, T: 0934 564038, www.legambienteriserve.it*), created to protect a small lake and the surrounding area.

Villalba and Vallelunga Pratameno

These villages (*map p. 540, A2*) are in an isolated northern pocket of the province, in a particularly spectacular part of the interior of Sicily. **Villalba** was a Roman colony in the 3rd century BC and later a Muslim village. **Vallelunga** is an important agricultural centre.

MUSSOMELI & ITS ENVIRONS

Mussomeli (*map p. 540, A2*) presents itself to the visitor as a cascade of ochre houses on the southern slopes of Mt San Vito, dominating a fertile and well-watered territory. The valley was formed by the River Platani (the ancient *Halykos*), 84km long, which enters the sea near Capo Bianco. It was founded by Manfredi III Chiaramonte in the late 14th century with the name Manfreda, near a Muslim farming community. Very soon the name Manfreda was forgotten in favour of the Arabic toponym *Menzil el-emir*, the mansion of the emir. On the north side of the central Piazza Umberto is the palace of Barone Mistretta; close by, preceded by a stairway, is the 16th-century church of San Francesco. The west side of the square gives onto the old district of Terravecchia, with quiet little streets surrounding the Chiesa Madre, which was founded by Manfredi III Chiaramonte and dedicated to St Louis of Toulouse. In the church of the Madonna dei Miracoli is a splendid vault fresco (1792) by Domenico Provenzano, showing heretics being flung

Perched on its crag near Mussomeli, the 14th-century Castello Manfredonico.

into Hell. In the crypt is a stone with an old painting of the Madonna, found near the spot where a cripple suddenly and miraculously regained the use of his legs.

By taking the road for Villalba, after c. 2km you reach the magnificent, gravity-defying **Castello Manfredonico** (*open summer 9–12 & 3–6, closed Mon; winter Sat and Sun 9.30–12*), a good example of medieval military architecture, and one of the most beautiful castles in Sicily; it seems to have grown out of the rock it was built upon. Manfredi III Chiaramonte built it on top of an older fortification. It is said to be haunted by the ghosts of three sisters, walled up in a small triangular room by their brother for their own safety when he went away to fight in a war. Leaving plenty of food and water, he was forced to stay away longer than expected, returning to find the corpses of his unfortunate sisters and the half-eaten soles of their shoes.

Acquaviva Platani is c. 8km west of Mussomeli (*map p. 540, A2*). The name is a reference to the abundant springs in the area (*acquaviva* = 'living water'). Of ancient origin and with panoramic views, facing north and west over the upper Platani valley towards Mt Cammarata, the town was re-founded in 1635 by Francesco Spadafora as an agricultural centre. Many years of depression and mass emigration are now giving way to new hopes for the future, thanks to the production of high-quality olive oil and wines.

SUTERA & CAMPOFRANCO

Standing in a spectacular position on the chalky white slopes of the steep Mt Paolino, **Sutera** (*map p. 540, A2*) dominates the wide, hilly interior of the island. Its ancient castle (now completely destroyed) was once of fundamental importance for the defence of this strategic point. Probably founded by the Byzantines, the town was developed by the Muslims. The typically Arab district of Rabato is the oldest part of town, with its tiny alleys and courtyards, while the Chiesa Madre, dedicated to the Assumption, stands on the site of the mosque. In 1366 the village was assigned to Giovanni Chiaramonte, Count of Caccamo, son of Manfredi III, the founder of Mussomeli. After a period of stability, development ground to a halt in the 16th century, because many inhabitants left the town to live in the nearby settlements of Acquaviva, Campofranco and Casteltermini, where it was easier to farm the land.

Entering Sutera from the north, Via del Popolo leads to Piazza Umberto, with the Town Hall, the 15th-century church of Sant'Agata, and the monastery of Santa Maria delle Grazie. Continuing along Via Sant'Agata, you reach Piazza San Giovanni, with the church of San Giovanni; inside there are some very good stuccoes of the Serpotta school. From here, Via del Carmine leads from the Rabatello district to Rabato. From the square (Piazza Carmine), Via San Paolino leads up on the left by the church of the Carmine to the top of the hill via many flights of steps, where there is an old convent and the sanctuary church of San Paolino, built in the 14th century for Giovanni Chiaramonte in place of the old castle, with far-reaching views. Back in the village, Via del Carmine continues up to the ancient Chiesa Madre (1370).

Campofranco

Close to Sutera is Campofranco (*map p. 540 A2*), a friendly village founded in 1573 by Baron Giovanni del Campo, which prospered during the sulphur-mining period in the 19th century. The **Chiesa Madre**, dedicated to St John the Baptist, was completed in 1575, but considerably modified in later centuries. Inside is a dramatic 17th-century canvas of the *Beheading of St John the Baptist*, perhaps by Pietro d'Asaro or one of the Flemish painters active in Palermo at the time. In the central Piazza Vittorio Veneto is a magnificent bronze fountain, the **Fontana della Rinascita**, 5m in diameter and with abundant jets of water, the work of architect Vittorio Ziino and sculptor Giovanni Rosone. It was a gift from the Sicilian Regional Government in 1955 because 99 percent of the population had turned out to vote in the elections.

The statue of the patron St Calogero is kept (together with numerous other works of art) in the church of **San Francesco d'Assisi**, and is carried around the town twice a year, on the shoulders of 20 stalwarts, an honour passed down from father to son.

Frequently seen in the countryside in this area are little stone 'igloos' in the fields, some in good condition, some not. Called *cubuli*, they were used by the peasants as emergency dwellings, for storing equipment, or to protect sick animals. Try to look inside one, you will be amazed at the intelligent use of space. Smaller ones were built to cover wells.

MILENA

South of Campofranco is the salty little River Gallo d'Oro, the 'Golden Cockerel', a tributary of the Platani. On the other side of the valley is Milena (*map p. 540, A3*), a farming community formed of the central village and many hamlets, called *robbe*, distributed on the hills around: San Martino, Vittorio Veneto, Cavour, Piave, Crispi, Roma, Monte Grappa, Cesare Battisti, Masaniello, San Miceli, Mazzini, Garibaldi and Balilla, are just some of the tiny villages, most of which are now abandoned. The area shows signs of human settlement going back to the Copper Age and even the Neolithic, and Milena itself was certainly an important Arab centre. For many centuries known as Milocca, it was donated to the monastery of San Martino delle Scale near Monreale, which held it until 1866. The monks granted the peasants perpetual lease of the land, which along with the abundant water allowed the inhabitants to enjoy relative prosperity. In the hamlet of Masaniello is a beautiful little two-storey cottage, now the **Casa-Museo della Civiltà Contadina** (*open daily July, Aug, Sept 9–12 & 3–6; closed Sun afternoon*), a collection of objects and equipment used by the farmers.

In Milena town centre, on Piazza Europa, is the **Antiquarium Comunale Arturo Petix** (*open Mon–Fri 9.30–1*), exhibiting archaeological finds from the area, including a terracotta mould for cooling liquid sulphur stamped as the property of the emperor Commodus. The slopes of Mt Conca, running down to the Gallo d'Oro stream, with many caves, are now protected as a **nature reserve** run by the CAI, Club Alpino Italiano (*for information, T: 0934 933254, 339 4652106*). The river is fringed by tamarisks, a haze of pale pink in spring, and is home to many small birds: Cetti's and fan-tailed warblers and the penduline tit, as well as kingfishers, little ringed plovers, black-winged stilts, kestrels and buzzards. Two caves here are of great speleological interest.

WEST FROM CALTANISSETTA

San Cataldo (*map p. 540, B2*) is a farming community, 5km west of Caltanissetta, founded in 1607 by Baron Nicolò Galletti, who named it after St Cathald, an Irish disciple of St Patrick who became the first bishop of Taranto. During the 19th century the economy prospered thanks to the sulphur mines. Time stands still on the quieter back streets, where you will occasionally see women embroidering or making lace, sitting in front of their homes, working away at their threads with deft fingers.

On the road to Serradifcalco, after c. 5km, a path on the right leads to the archaeological site at **Vassallaggi** (*map p. 540, B3*), five small rocky hills, where excavations have brought to light the remains of a settlement which was perhaps the Sicel town of *Motyon*, scene of a great battle in 451 BC between Ducetius and his Sicels and the Greeks of Agrigento and Syracuse. So far some streets have been located, a sanctuary and a necropolis. The finds are in the Museo Archeologico in Caltanissetta.

Serradifalco (*map p. 540, A3*) is a neat and tidy town in a strategic position controlling the major roads, and with abundant sources of water. It was once an important sulphur-mining centre. Not far from the town is Lago Soprano, a small, beautiful natural lake, set like a gemstone in the arid highlands; it is fed by underground springs and is protected as a nature reserve (*to book a visit, procedure as for Lago Sfondato, see p. 233*).

Across the valley of the Gallo d'Oro, **Montedoro** (*map p. 540, A3*) stands on a small plateau on the slopes of Mt Croce. Founded in 1635 for agricultural purposes by Don

Diego Tagliavia Cortes, prince of Castelvetrano, the town flourished in the 19th century thanks to its sulphur and potassium-salt mines. One of these has been opened as a museum, the Museo della Zolfara (*to request visit call the town hall, T: 0934 934404*). Clear skies and low light interference make this a good place for astronomy; there is an observatory (*to request visit, see www.speculapanormitana.it*), and a planetarium is close to completion.

At Montedoro and in the farming village of **Bompensiere** (*map p. 540, A3*), several housefronts are decorated with murals illustrating the history of the communities.

GELA & THE SOUTH

Gela (*map p. 540, C4*) is an important port and the fifth largest town in Sicily. Renowned for its splendour in the past, it was the last abode of the dramatic poet Aeschylus. Now it is frankly unattractive, thanks to uncontrolled building activity and the presence of an oil refinery and related industries. Among the town's many fine qualities are the exceptional courtesy of the inhabitants; the archaeological museum; and the unique Greek fortifications at Capo Soprano. Recent excavations at Bosco Littorio, site of the ancient emporium and harbour, have brought to light warehouses buried in the sand, untouched since the 5th century BC.

HISTORY OF GELA

The modern city, known until 1927 as Terranova, was founded by Frederick II in 1230 on the site of *Gela*, a colony of Rhodians and Cretans established in 688 BC. Gela soon rose to importance, founding its own colony at *Akragas* (Agrigento) in 580 and contributing to the Hellenisation of the interior of the island. Under Hippocrates (498–491 BC) the city reached its greatest prosperity, but Gelon, his successor, transferred the seat of government and half the population to Syracuse in 485. Aeschylus, the great 5th-century BC playwright, died in Gela in 456, supposedly because an eagle flying above him dropped a tortoise on his bald head, mistaking it for a stone. The Carthaginians destroyed the town in 405, but Timoleon refounded it in the 330s. The new city was larger than the earlier one and was given a new set of walls. In 282 BC, Phintias, tyrant of Akragas, transferred the inhabitants to his new city (now Licata) and Gela disappeared from history.

Museo Archeologico Regionale

At the east end of the town, at Corso Vittorio Emanuele 1, is the archaeological museum (*open 9–6, T: 0933 912626*), with one of the richest archaeological collections in Sicily. This includes some of the painted vases for which Gela is best known, the three famous terracotta altars found in the emporium area of the city, and a superb coin collection.

Section I: Dedicated to the acropolis area (east of the modern city), inhabited from prehistoric times to the 5th century BC.

Section II: Later material from the acropolis (4th–3rd centuries BC), when it was an artisans' district. There is also material salvaged from an Archaic Greek ship found off the coast of Gela in 1988.

Section III: Devoted to Capo Soprano, where a residential area and public edifices were erected in the late 4th century BC; this is followed by a pottery exhibit, including some pots with dedicatory inscriptions on their bases.

Section IV: More than 50 amphorae (7th–4th centuries BC) attest to the importance of Gela's commerce with other centres in the Mediterranean.

Section V: Finds from sanctuaries outside Gela, most of them dedicated to Demeter and Persephone.

Section VI: Prehistoric to Hellenistic finds from the surrounding territory.

Section VII: Roman and medieval material found during the restoration of the Castelluccio, together with Roman finds from Philosophiana (*see p. 242*).

In front of the coin room are three **terracotta altars**, with relief images, found in the emporium of the ancient city. Dating from the end of the 6th/early 5th centuries BC, the two larger ones are unique for their size, artistic quality, subject matter and state of conservation. That on the left represents the Gorgon Medusa, running with her babies in her arms, Pegasus the winged horse and the warrior Chrysaor, tightening her snake belt as she goes. The smaller central altar shows a slender lioness attacking a bull in the top part, and underneath the goddess of dawn, Eos, making away with the huntsman Cephalus, husband of Procris, who in revenge seduced King Minos of Crete. The altar on the right shows three goddesses, probably Hera, Demeter (smoothing her braids) and

Archaic heads of Maenads in painted terracotta, in the archaeological museum of Gela.

Aphrodite. The exceptional **numismatic collection** has over 2,000 pieces found in and around Gela, including a magnificent hoard of some 600 silver coins minted in Akragas, Gela, Syracuse, Messina and Athens, between 515 and 485 BC, one of the most important such collections in existence. Discovered in Gela in 1956, the coins were stolen in 1973, but most have been recovered. **Section VIII:** Important 19th-century Navarra collection of **ancient Sicilian vases** (with a fine group of Attic black-and-red figure vases, and Corinthian ware from the 8th–6th centuries BC). Also here is the smaller Nocera collection and two cases of finds from the necropolis, including an Attic lekythos showing Aeneas and Anchises on a white ground (460–450 BC) and an exquisite Attic red-figure lekythos by the Nikon painter.

Molino a Vento Acropolis

Outside the museum is the entrance to the Molino a Vento Acropolis (*open 9–6, closed Sun afternoon; same ticket as museum*), overlooking the oil refinery. This was part of Timoleon's city, on a terraced grid plan with shops and houses (c. 339–310 BC), above the ruins of a small sacred enclosure. In the garden on the site of the acropolis of the earliest city stands a single (re-erected) column of a temple probably dedicated to Athena (6th century BC) and the foundations of a second earlier temple also dedicated to Athena. This area had been abandoned by 282 BC.

The Archaic emporium at Bosco Littorio

A little to the south of the Acropolis, in the Bosco Littorio area, is the Archaic emporium of the early Greek colony (6th – 5th centuries BC). This was the commercial part of the settlement, consisting of various adjoining rooms facing onto open courtyards, in which goods from the nearby port of Gela were unloaded, stored and redistributed. The site is archaeologically important because of the excellently preserved mud brick walls of the rooms, which are preserved up to the level of the roof beams. Mud brick is notoriously fragile, and in this case it survived only because it was covered over by sand dunes. The three terracotta altars now on display in the museum were discovered in front of these rooms. The site was abandoned at the beginning of the 5th century due to a natural disaster (perhaps an earthquake or seaquake) and was never reoccupied (*to visit, ask at the Museo Archeologico Regionale, T: 0933 912626*).

Capo Soprano

The most pleasant way of reaching Capo Soprano and the Greek fortifications (over 3km from the museum) is along the seafront. First excavated in 1948, the remarkable Greek fortifications (*open 9–6, closed Sun afternoon, same ticket as museum*) have been excellently preserved after centuries beneath the sand: they extend for several hundred metres and reach a height of nearly 13m. The construction is unique for Sicily, because they were built partly of blocks of stone and partly of mud brick. The walls were begun by Timoleon in 333 BC and completed under Agathocles. Their height was regularly increased to keep ahead of the encroaching sand, a danger now removed by the planting of trees.

A path (right) leads past excavations of battlements to a circular medieval kiln (*under cover*). From here there is a view of the coast. The path follows walls (*partly under cover*) and foundations of the brick angle towers to the West Gate, and then descends to the most complete stretch of walls: the lower course is built of sandstone, while the top consists of mud bricks. A small postern gate in the walls can be seen here (filled in with mud bricks soon after it was built), near a well-preserved drain. Steps lead up past a little house which contains photographs of the site.

About 500m from the fortifications (signposted 'Bagni Greci'), now engulfed by modern apartment blocks, are remains of Greek baths (4th century BC), including hip baths with seats. Though protected by a roof, they are always open.

The coast east and west of Gela

Behind the sand dunes, along the coast east of Gela, is a shallow coastal lake, the largest of its kind in Sicily: the **Biviere di Gela** (*map p. 540, C4; info: LIPU, T: 0933 926051, 345 6612743, 345 5755044, www.riservabiviere.it*). Now protected as a nature reserve, it is particularly interesting during bird migration periods in early spring and late summer. Short-toed eagle, spoonbill, pratincole, garganey, ferruginous duck, little bittern, Audouin's and slender-billed gulls, Terek and buff-breasted sandpipers, red-necked grebe, black-tailed godwit, slender-billed curlew, purple heron, glossy ibis (symbol of the reserve), even the mute swan (very unusual for Sicily) nest or have been seen here, while the black-winged stilt nests in the marshy area nearby; another nester is the collared turtle dove, until recently only found locally on Pantelleria and Linosa (but it has now started nesting even in downtown Gela). Birds which winter here include the jack snipe, short-eared owl, marsh harrier, hoopoe and bluethroat; in September and October orange monarch butterflies from Africa are commonly seen.

On the coast west of Gela is **Falconara** (*map p. 540, B4*), with its well-preserved, spectacular 14th-century castle on the sea, now a beautiful hotel. There is an inviting sandy beach. Beyond are vegetable and melon fields, protected from the wind by cane fences, and often covered with plastic sheeting, which gives the countryside a strange, watery aspect, like a billowing sea.

NORTH & EAST OF GELA

Butera

Butera (*map p. 540, B4*), perched on a flat rock in a strategic position, with fine views towards the sea, is dominated by the bell-tower of the church of San Rocco. As *Butirah* it was one of the largest cities in Arab Sicily, later becoming a Lombard centre under the Normans (for the followers of Roger's Lombard wife Adelaide). William I destroyed the town in 1161 when he suspected its baron of taking part in a plot against his person. Later rebuilt, it became the seat of the Santapau family, Catalans who became the first feudal lords on the island to receive the title of prince, from Philip II of Spain in 1563.

In Piazza Duomo (approached from the north) is the plain, elegant 17th-century **Chiesa Madre**, dedicated to St Thomas the Apostle. The a Latin-cross interior, surmounted by a dome and decorated with stuccoes, houses an exquisite 13th-century enamelled copper Crucifix from Limoges and a collection of paintings, including a fine canvas by Filippo Paladini of *St Mary of the Angels* (1606). From here the main street, Via Principe di Piemonte, winds its way through to Piazza Dante, with a spectacular view over the hills to the Madonie Mountains and Mount Etna. Here is the interesting 15th-century triangular **Town Hall**, surmounted by a clock tower, and the 18th-century church of **San Giuseppe**, a simple façade with a large window, and an unusual 16th-century painted wooden Crucifix.

Via Aldo Moro leads to Piazza della Vittoria, where the romantic and imposing 11th-century **castle** (*same opening times as tourist office, they will provide guide*) was once thought to be impregnable. The keep is still in good condition; it now houses a collection of archaeological material found in the area. From the castle, Viale Diaz leads to the eastern crest of the hill, overlooking the plain, and the 18th-century sanctuary church of **San Rocco**, dedicated to the patron saint of Butera. The single-nave interior is richly decorated with stucco and 18th- and 19th-century canvases by local artists, representing episodes from the life of the saint, who is frequently invoked against the plague and often shown in art pointing to an abscess on his thigh. The historical St Roch was a French nobleman of the 14th century who contracted the plague in Piacenza while on pilgrimage to Rome. Retiring to the forest to die, he made a miraculous recovery thanks to the devotion of a prince's dog which brought him food from its master's table. Once cured, he tried to return the dog, but the prince told him to keep it, saying '*my dog knows his master*'. The saint and his dog are always represented together.

Important excavations of a **Bronze-Age settlement** (perhaps the Sican town of *Omphake*) have been carried out near Butera; the finds are in the Gela museum. Southwest of Butera is an artificial reservoir (*signposted from the railway station*), Lago Comunelli, used as a resting-place by many species of migratory bird in spring and autumn.

Mazzarino

Mazzarino (*map p. 540, B3–C3*) was the ancient Sicel city of *Maktorion*, which in the 14th century became the seat of the Branciforte family from Piacenza, renowned for their culture, learning and magnificence. In 1507 King Ferdinand II of Aragon invested Niccolò Branciforte with the title of Count of Mazzarino. His descendant, Prince Carlo Maria Carafa Branciforte (1651–95), embellished and enlarged the town, and built an enormous residence, a miniature royal palace, with its own theatre and printing-shop. Parts of the building survive, though much neglected. Convents and monasteries were built around the palace by all the major religious orders, and there were 25 churches.

The attractive main street, Corso Vittorio Emanuele, runs west to east for c. 1km, passing numerous aristocratic palaces in decay. At the west end is the 16th-century church and convent of **Santa Maria del Gesù**, containing the funerary monument of Prince Carlo Maria Carafa Branciforte. In the middle of the Corso is the Carmelite complex. The church of **Santa Maria del Carmelo** houses notable works of art, including a Branciforte funerary monument and paintings by Filippo Paladini. Another Branciforte funerary monument, by the Gagini school, is in the courtyard of the Town Hall, once the cloister of the monastery. Via Concezione runs north from the Corso to the church of **San Francesco**, or the Immacolata; on the main altar is a splendid canvas by Filippo Paladini of the *Immaculate Virgin and St Francis*, signed and dated 1606. Paladini died in Mazzarino in 1615. From here there is a view over the valley.

In Piazza Crispi, on the south side of the Corso, in front of Palazzo Branciforte, is the wide Baroque façade of the **Chiesa Madre** (Angelo Italia), dedicated to the Madonna of the Snow; inside are some paintings of the Paladini school. Close by to the east is Piazza Colajanni. In the Dominican church here is a masterpiece by Filippo Paladini, signed and dated 1608, the *Madonna of the Rosary*. Pink, white, mauve and dark green are the dominant colours; from the top corners, cherubs toss down pink roses, and in the bottom left-hand corner is the astonished-looking donor, a certain Pasquale Rondello.

At the eastern extremity of the Corso is the 18th-century church of **Santa Maria del Mazzaro**; the 15th-century triptych on the main altar, showing the *Madonna with Sts Agatha and Lucy*, has been damaged by two fires, and poorly restored.

Environs of Mazzarino

Mazzarino is dominated by the ruins of its pre-13th-century **castle**, north of the town, on an isolated hill, with a round tower; it is known as *'u Cannuni*, the cannon; not far away are the ruins of yet another, called *Grassuliato*. These fortresses, and ancient *Maktorion* itself, on Mt Bubbonia, were built to defend the vast plain of Gela and the valleys leading out of it towards the interior of the island.

About 12km east of Mazzarino are the remains of a Byzantine village called **Philosophiana** (signposted *Statio Philosophiana—Itinerarium Antonini; map p. 540, C3*), probably representing a resting-point on the Roman road from Catania to Agrigento. A small bath-house has been excavated, and a Palaeo-Christian basilica.

At **Riesi** (*map p. 540, B3*), a small town to the west of Mazzarino, where sulphur miners and farm workers have always led a hard existence, a kind of trade union uniting them all became strong enough for the community to declare itself a Socialist Republic in 1893. Although short-lived, the episode remains a source of local pride.

NORTHEAST OF GELA

On the Caltagirone road is the 13th-century **Castelluccio** (*map p. 540, C4*), a castle said to be haunted by the ghost of a mysterious lady who sometimes entices travellers inside; when this happens they are never seen again. The likelihood of this happening at the time of writing is small, as the castle is officially closed for lack of custodians (*if it should re-open, ticket available at the archaeological museum of Gela*). Otherwise it can be admired from the outside. It occupies a prominent site on the surrounding plain, now cultivated with artichokes. On the approach road there is a war memorial, appropriately sited beside two pill-box defences, commemorating the battle of 1943, which followed the landings of the American assault forces on the beaches in the Gulf of Gela.

There is a **prehistoric necropolis on Monte Disueri** or Dessueri (*no signs, but exactly 7.4km along the SS 190 to Mazzarino from the junction with the SS 117bis to Gela; on the* *left-hand side; map p. 540, C3–C4*) with more than 2,000 rock-cut tombs, found by accident during forestry work in the 1970s. It is the most important ancient necropolis in Sicily after Pantalica (*see p. 361*), and dates from the 11th–9th centuries BC. The paths have all but disappeared and there are no explanatory information boards; trekking boots are advisable for exploring. In spring the mountain is covered with wildflowers.

Niscemi (*map p. 540, C4*) stands on a plateau in a panoramic position facing west over the plain. Like others in the area, the town bases its economy on artichokes, of which it grows 12 percent of the entire world production. It was completely rebuilt, following a regular street plan, after the 1693 earthquake. To the east of the rectangular central square, Piazza Vittorio Emanuele, is the 18th-century Chiesa Madre (Santa Maria dell'Itria), with a lovely portal, while opposite is the interesting, octagonal church of the Addolorata (18th century, Rosario Gagliardi). Another side of the square is occupied by the elegant Neoclassical town hall. The highest part of Niscemi is a panoramic terrace called the Belvedere, offering wonderful views and cool breezes on summer evenings.

East of the town is a residual forest of cork, kermes and holm oaks, with tree heath, now protected as a nature reserve, the **Sughereta di Niscemi**, run by the Azienda Forestale, and occupying one third of Niscemi's territory (*Azienda Forestale Niscemi, T: 0933 954308, www.ceaniscemi.it*). The reserve boasts a small nesting colony of bee-eaters; until recently these handsome, colourful birds were only spotted here during their migratory flights; other nesting species include the greater spotted woodpecker and the hoopoe.

PRACTICAL INFORMATION

GETTING AROUND

• **By train:** The station at **Caltanissetta** is in Piazza Roma. Services via Canicattì to Agrigento, Gela, Ragusa and Syracuse. The station of **Caltanissetta Xirbi**, 7km north (bus connection with the town), is on another line connecting Palermo, Enna and Catania. **Gela** is on the Syracuse, Ragusa, Canicattì, Agrigento line.

• **By bus:** Yellow city buses leave from Gela station to Capo Soprano and the archaeological museum; info and tickets from the booth opposite the station. City buses in Caltanissetta leave from Piazza Roma (SCAT, *www.scattrasporti.com*). There are frequent inter-regional services (usually faster than the

trains) from the bus station in Caltanissetta, in Via Rochester (*www.orariautobus.it*). **ASTRA** (*T: 0934 588554*) runs services from Caltanissetta to Gela, San Cataldo, Enna, Piazza Armerina, and other towns in the province. **Etna Trasporti** (*www.etnatrasporti. it*) goes to Gela, Butera and Niscemi as well as to Catania and other destinations outside the province. **SAIS Autolinee** (*ticket office Via Colajanni 20/22, www.saisautolinee.it*) for Enna, with connections for Piazza Armerina, Santa Caterina Villarmosa, Caltagirone, Gangi, Palermo, Catania and Messina. **SAIS Trasporti** (*Via Colajanni 20/22, www.saistrasporti.it*) has services for Agrigento, Palermo and Catania airport. Destinations within the province include Acquaviva Platani, Bompensiere,

Campofranco, Delia, Marianopoli, Mazzarino, Milena, Montedoro, Mussomeli, Resuttano, Serradifalco, Sommatino, Sutera. **SARP Trasporti** (*T: 0934 597831*) connects Caltanissetta to Mazzarino, Riesi and Sommatino.

WHERE TO STAY

Butera (*map p. 540, B4*)
€ **Portico dei Normanni.** Panoramic old palace in the town centre with 5 comfortable rooms, all with air conditioning. Bar-restaurant-pizzeria, same ownership, on ground floor. *Via Mazzini 3, T: 0934 346146, 328 2747195, www.ilporticodeinormanni.it.*

Caltanissetta (*map p. 540, B2*)
€€€ **San Michele.** Large modern hotel just outside town, with garden, pool, restaurant, 136 rooms and suites. *Via Fasci Siciliani, T: 0934 553750, www.hotelsanmichelesicilia.it.*
€€ **Hotel Giulia.** Charming small hotel, 18 rooms, friendly service, central and comfortable, car park. No restaurant, but it is next door to L'Archetto, a good restaurant and pizzeria. *Corso Umberto 85, T: 0934 542927 www.hotelgiulia.it.*
€ **Piazza Garibaldi.** Central B&B offering 3 spacious rooms with fanciful murals, air conditioning, terraces, helpful owners, English spoken. *Piazza Garibaldi 11, T: 0934 680510, 340 3795803, www.piazzagaribaldi11.it.*

Falconara (*map p. 540, B4*)
€€€ **Castello di Falconara.** Crenellated Norman castle in a quiet position on a crag above a lovely beach. The whole castle can also be rented for up to 2 weeks (9 rooms, sleeps 16). Also B&B accommodation in 7 large rooms on the first floor. *Contrada Falconara, SS 115 km 245, T: 091 329082, www.castellodifalconara.it.* On the beach 200m from the castle and run by the same owners, is the €€€ **Falconara Resort**, with 65 rooms in a modern building, fitness centre, tennis, restaurant, pool. On

the down side, the beach is small and it can be noisy due to road traffic. *Closed Oct–April. Contrada Faino, SS 115 km 243, T: 0934 349012, www.hotelfalconararesort.com.*

Gela (*map p. 540, C4*)
€ **Villa Keratea.** Comfortable villa surrounded by carob trees 7km north of Gela. 12 rooms and a good restaurant. *Contrada Settefarine, SP81 Gela, T: 0933 1937062, 347 8004063, www.villakeratea.it.*
€ **Sole.** Simple, friendly hotel, all 22 rooms have sea views and air conditioning; car park, restaurant. Close to the Archaeological Museum. *Via Mare 32, T: 0933 925292, www. hotelsolecl.com.*

Mazzarino (*map p. 540, C3*)
€ **Hotel Alessi.** Comfortable modern hotel, family-run, central, with restaurant. *Via Caltanissetta 20, T: 0934 381549, www.alessipalacehotel.com.*

Montedoro (*map p. 540, A3*)
€ You can stay in one of the little houses in the centre, self-catering or B&B; excellent value for money. *For information call Pietro Petix of the Cupolette Rosse restaurant, T: 349 8654614, www.vacanzepetix.it.*

WHERE TO EAT

Caltanissetta (*map p. 540, B2*)
€€ **Vicolo Duomo.** Local dishes in an old building in a tiny alley where snow was once stored. Menu includes *farsumagru*, an appetising festive dish made of cheap cuts of meat, cheese, breadcrumbs, hard-boiled eggs, mortadella and salami. *Closed all day Sun and midday Mon. Piazza Garibaldi 3, entrance from Vicolo Neviera 1, T: 0934 582331.*

Gela (*map p. 540, C4*)
€€ **Casanova.** Restaurant and wine bar, with a good list of Sicilian wines. Also simple dishes. Exceptional fish crudités, especially the octopus. *Closed Mon in winter and Sun in*

summer. Via Venezia 89, T: 0933 918580.
Montedoro (*map p. 540, A3*)
€ **Cupolette Rosse.** Country food from the
Sicilian interior; try home-made pasta with
wild fennel dressing, or wild boar (*cinghiale*),
also cooked with local wild fennel. The restaurant also acts as the information centre for
Montedoro. *Via Sacramento, T: 349 8654614
(Pietro Petix).*
Mussomeli (*map p. 540, A2*)
€ **Il Giullare.** Snack bar and pastry shop,
offering good light lunches, *'mbriulata* (*see
below*) and home-made ice cream. *Via Barcellona 50, T: 328 7794790.*
Niscemi (*map p. 540, C4*)
€€ **Cibus.** Original dishes making good use
of the famous local artichokes when in season. The *antipasti* are not to be missed; simple
desserts. *Closed Sun evening. Via Mazzini 3, T:
0933 953277, 329 6045024.*
Sutera (*map p. 540, A2*)
€€ **Civiletto.** Elegant restaurant in a 12th-
century convent, marvellous local dishes,
good wine list. *Via San Giuseppe 7, T: 0934
954874, 333 9189601.*

LOCAL SPECIALITIES

Caltanissetta Torronificio Geraci, a nougat
factory opened in 1870 (*Via Canonico Pulci
10/14, www.geraci1870.it*), offers sweets in elegant packages or tins; closed Sun afternoon.
Gran Café Romano is a historic coffee-house,
renowned for ice cream and nougat (*Corso
Umberto 163*). Calogero Garzia (*Via Calabria
2*) is a traditional bakery with a stone oven for
sourdough bread.
Delia For the *cuddrireddra* biscuits, try Pasticceria del Corso (*Corso Umberto 183*). They are
found only in Delia and look like little golden
knots of twisted dough. It is said they were
invented to cheer up the noble ladies who
took refuge here during the Sicilian Vespers

(*see p. 69*). You can also order them online
from Alaimo & Strazzeri (*Viale La Verde 85/87,
T: 0922 826825, www.lacuddrireddra.com*).
Mussomeli *'Mbriulata* is a tasty and filling
winter snack, found in bakeries and *trattorie*;
flaky pastry encloses cheese, olives, potatoes
and minced pork.

FESTIVALS & EVENTS

Butera 15 Aug: *'U Sirpintazzu*, pantomime in
which a man dressed as a snake is appeased
with sweets and a goose, reference to a serpent which threatened the community many
centuries ago (*Info: www.sanrocco-butera.it*).
Caltanissetta Holy Week: Procession of *I
Misteri*, depicting the Passion of Christ. End
Sept: Feast of St Michael Archangel, the
patron saint; huge processions of barefoot
faithful, a traditional fair, and fireworks.
Campofranco 17 Jan: Feast of St Anthony
with a procession and fireworks. 11 Jan and
last weekend in July: feast of the patron St
Calogero, also dedicated to bread—*Sagra dei
Pupi di Pane*—almost life-size 'bread men'.
Delia Good Friday: *La Scinnenza*, Easter procession involving almost all the inhabitants.
Gela 18–19 March: Feast of St Joseph, many
families spend weeks preparing the lavish
altari di San Giuseppe, feasts for three poor
people chosen to represent the Holy Family;
one 'family' for each altar.
Mussomeli 1–2 September, *Corteo Storico*,
pageant in medieval costume.
Niscemi early April: *Sagra del Carciofo Violetto*,
celebrating the artichoke harvest, with plenty
of opportunities to sample the vegetable prepared in dozens of different ways, even with
chocolate (*Info: www.sagracarciofoniscemi.it*).
Sutera Christmas–6 Jan, Living Crib in
the tiny streets of the Rabato quarter (*Info:
Kamicos, Via Chiesa 2, T: 0934 954289, www.
kamicos.it*).

THE PROVINCE OF ENNA

Enna is the capital of the only landlocked province in Sicily. Its huge castle, dominating practically the whole island, was for centuries an almost impregnable stronghold. Although small, this province boasts some of Sicily's greatest treasures, such as Piazza Armerina with its Roman villa; Aidone with an array of unique antiquities in its lovely museum; Villarosa with three interesting museums (one in a train, one in a baron's villa, and the third a complete country hamlet); and Pergusa, a mysterious lake connected in myth to Persephone and Hades. The province is important for the production of cereals and provides a large proportion of the durum wheat used by the Italian pasta industry; the wheat fields of the dramatically hilly landscape provide a palette of ever-changing colours.

ENNA

Enna, at 931m (*map p. 537, B2*), is the highest provincial capital in Italy, often called the Belvedere of Sicily because of its position on the top of a precipitous hill. Enna Alta is the old city on the mountaintop, gradually being abandoned because of the harsh climate (even in August the nights are chilly). The new districts on the southern slopes and on the plateau of Pergusa are known as Enna Bassa.

HISTORY OF ENNA

The city occupies the site of *Henna,* a Sicel stronghold subjected to Greek influences, perhaps from Gela, as early as the 7th century BC. In one version, the legendary rape of Persephone occurred here, and it became a major centre of the cult of her mother Demeter (Ceres to the Romans), to whom Gelon of Syracuse erected a temple in 480 BC. Enna fell by treachery to Dionysius of Syracuse in 397 and the Romans conquered it in 258 during the First Punic War. In 214, during the course of the Second Punic War, the Roman consul feared a rebellion here in support of Syracuse and ordered a large part of the population to be executed before sacking the city. In 135 the First Servile War broke out here under the slave Eunus (*see box on p. 250*), and the town was taken in 132 by the Roman army after two years' siege. The Saracens took it in 859 AD and named it *Kasr Janni* (from the Roman name *Castrum Ennae*); and it was not captured by the Normans until 1087. From then on the town was known as Castrogiovanni until 1927, when on the decision of Mussolini it became the capital of a new province, in spite of the fact that Piazza Armerina had a larger population and was easier to reach.

EXPLORING ENNA

Enna Alta (the upper city)

The centre of town is Piazza Vittorio Emanuele (*map 1*). On the north side is the church of San Francesco, with its fine 16th-century tower. On the left is Piazza Crispi, which offers a marvellous view across the valley to Calascibetta and, on a clear day, to Etna. The bronze statue on the fountain in the middle is a copy of Bernini's celebrated *Rape of Persephone* (now in the Galleria Borghese in Rome). West of the square is Piazza Cataldo, with the church of San Cataldo, rebuilt in the 18th century on a preceding construction. The font (1473) is the work of Domenico Gagini. The vast 16th-century marble polyptych of the *Annunciation, Nativity and Madonna and Child with Sts Cathald and Blaise*, is by an unknown sculptor. St Cathald, to whom the church is dedicated, was a 6th-century Irish missionary who preached widely in southern Italy and Sicily.

Via Roma

The main street of the town, Via Roma (*map 1*), leads uphill traversing a series of squares. In Piazza Umberto is the Neoclassical Municipio (Town Hall), which incorporates the opera house, Teatro Garibaldi. The Baroque façade of San Benedetto (or San

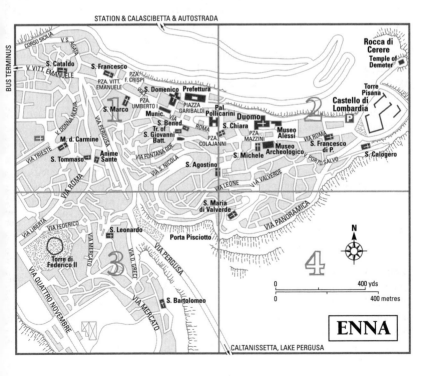

Giuseppe) decorates Piazza Coppola, off which is the 15th-century bell-tower of San Giovanni Battista with Gothic arches, crowned by a Moorish-style cupola.

On the north side of Via Roma the tall tower of the Rationalist-style Prefettura (1939) rises from Piazza Garibaldi; the building, visible from a long way around the town, was the result of Mussolini proclaiming Enna a provincial capital. Santa Chiara, in Piazza Colajanni, is a war memorial and burial chapel. Two majolica pictures (1852) decorate the tiled floor, one celebrating the advent of steam navigation, and the other the triumph of Christianity over Islam. The bronze statue in the piazza outside commemorates Napoleone Colajanni (1847–1921) a statesman and social reformer born in Enna. It is the work of Ettore Ximenes.

The sturdy Palazzo Pollicarini stands on the north side of the square. With its impregnable-looking stone walls and tiny windows, it retains one or two Catalan Gothic features. Via Roma continues up towards the duomo past several narrow side streets on the left which lead to the edge of the hill, with views over the valley to Calascibetta.

The duomo

The duomo (*map 2*), founded in 1307 by Eleonora, wife of Frederick II of Aragon, and damaged by fire in 1446, was slowly restored in the 16th century. The façade, with a 17th-century bell-tower, covers its Gothic predecessor. The transepts and polygonal apses survive in their original form (they can be seen from the courtyard of the Alessi Museum; *see below*). The Catalan Gothic south door was walled up in 1447, when Pope Nicholas V, after passing though it, declared it holy and only for the use of popes.

The interior has dark grey basalt columns with splendid bases, carved with grotesques, and Corinthian capitals (1550–60), the work of various artists including Gian Domenico Gagini, grandson of Domenico, who carved the symbols of the Evangelists on the first two at the west end. The nave ceiling is by Scipione di Guido, who also carved the walnut choir-stalls. On either side of the west door are 16th-century statues of the Angel Gabriel and Virgin Annunciate. The two stoups in the nave date from the 16th century, and at the east end of the nave are richly-carved 16th-century organ lofts. The altarpieces on the south side (c. 1722) are by the Flemish artist Willem Borremans (the painting of *Sts Lucille and Hyacinth* on the second altar is particularly good). In the presbytery are five paintings (1613) of New Testament scenes by Filippo Paladini, which clearly show the artist's late phase, when he had rejected his earlier Mannerism in favour of *Caravaggismo*. The chapel to the right of the sanctuary has 18th-century marble decoration and a painting of the *Visitation* also attributed to Paladini. There are more works by Borremans in the north transept and on the fourth north altar.

The city museums

The **Museo Civico Alessi** (*map 2; temporarily closed*) is named after Canon Giuseppe Alessi (1774–1837), a native of Enna, who left his remarkable collection to his brother intending that he should donate it to the Church. Instead, the Church was forced to buy it in 1860, and the museum was first opened to the public in 1862. The main highlights are on the first floor, where the cathedral treasury is exhibited. There are splendid 16th- and 17th-century works, including four reliquaries (1573) by Scipione di Blasi, a precious gold crown encrusted with jewels and enamels, made for the statue of the *Madonna of the Visitation* by Leonardo Montalbano in 1653; and a beautiful 16th-century jewel in the form of a pelican (symbol of Christ's sacrifice). Alessi's important numismatic collection is displayed here. The Greek, Roman and Byzantine coins are arranged topographically and include many in bronze used in everyday transactions. A charming archaeological collection (with some of Alessi's original labels) is also on view. It includes missiles (*glandes*) used in the Servile War, bronzes and pottery. In the last room the Egyptian ushabti figurines (664–525 BC), which also formed part of the Alessi collection and were presumably found in Sicily, are of great interest.

Across Piazza Mazzini the attractive 15th-century Palazzo Varisano, where Garibaldi made the speech in August 1863 that ended with the famous phrase '*o Roma o morte*' (Rome or death), houses the **Museo Archeologico Varisano** (*map 2; open Mon–Fri 9–1, also open 1st and 3rd weekends of the month, same times; T: 0935 5076323*). The collection is housed on the first floor (no lift); at the top of the stairs is the marble head of a lady with an elaborate coiffure, found at Piazza Armerina. In a series of small galleries with frescoed ceilings are finds from Calascibetta and Capodarso; the prehistoric rock-tombs of Realmese; Enna (Greek, Roman, and medieval ceramics, including an Attic red-figure krater); Cozzo Matrice (where the necropolis was in use from the Bronze Age up to the 5th century BC); prehistoric material from Lake Pergusa and elsewhere, and an interesting display on fake terracotta figurines and vases from Centuripe.

At Via Roma 533 is the latest of Enna's museums, the **Museo Musical Art 3M** (*map 2; open daily 10.30–1 & 4–6, or on request; T: 338 5023361, 339 2002463, 339 1079940*), which offers the opportunity to view the works of Sicily's greatest painters on a high-definition screen, while listening to specially-composed music designed to complement the subject, the historical period, and the character of the artists, who range from Antonello da Messina to Renato Guttuso. It is also possible to follow on-screen the religious processions of Enna.

Castello di Lombardia

The 13th-century **Castello di Lombardia** (*map 2; open 9–1 & 4–6*), or Cittadella, was adapted as a residence by Frederick II of Aragon. One of the best-preserved medieval castles on the island, six of its 20 towers remain. Outside is a First World War memorial by Ernesto Basile (1927), and a bronze statue of the rebel slave Eunus.

Steps lead up to the castle entrance. The first courtyard forms a permanent open-air theatre used in summer. Beyond the second court, planted with trees, the third has remains of a church, and (beneath a roof) tombs carved in the rock. Here is the entrance to the Torre Pisana, which can be climbed by a modern flight of stairs. The view from the top encompasses Etna, Centuripe on its hill and Lake Pozzillo. In the other direction, Lake Pergusa and Calascibetta can be seen. At the edge of the hill, beyond the castle, are the unenclosed remains of the **Rocca Cerere**, where old hewn stones mark the site of the **Temple of Demeter** (Ceres). Steps lead up to the summit with a view of Etna straight ahead.

EUNUS & THE FIRST SERVILE WAR

Eunus, originally from Syria, and a slave in Enna, organised a rebellion in 135 BC which led to the First Servile War. Sicilian slaves were notoriously badly treated. The best near-contemporary accounts we have are by Diodorus Siculus (c.90–20 BC) and Florus, quoting Livy. They say that Eunus claimed to be acting in the name of the Syrian goddess Atargatis, the equivalent of Demeter (Ceres). He is said to have convinced his followers that the goddess spoke through him by breathing out fumes from a sulphur-filled nut secreted in his mouth, a trick that he had previously used to entertain his master and guests at dinner parties. Having persuaded his confederates to murder their Roman owners but to respect the farms, he crowned himself king (Antiochus I), and even minted coins. His forces put the majority of the citizens of Enna to the sword, sparing only the metalworkers. Joined by the ex-herdsman Cleon from Agrigento, they put together an army said to number some 200,000 men, and took Taormina before laying siege to Messina. The revolt was only eventually suppressed by the Roman consul Publius Rupilius in 132 BC, who laid siege to Taormina and starved the rebel slaves before buying the loyalty of the garrison commander who let in the Roman troops. The slaves (15,000 of them) were thrown off the cliffs of Taormina (some sources say crucified). Cleon committed suicide. Pursued by Rupilius, Eunus fled from Enna. His men turned on each other in desperation and he died in prison at Morgantina, after atrocious torture.

Enna Bassa (the lower town)

Enna Bassa is reached by following the branch of Via Roma which takes a sharp turn to the south below Piazza Vittorio Emanuele (*map 1*). On the right are the churches of San Tommaso, with a 15th-century tower and a marble altarpiece by Giuliano Mancino (1515), and the Carmine (behind San Tommaso), with another 15th-century campanile and a curious stair-tower. On the left, near the southwest end of Via Roma, rises the octagonal Torre di Federico II (*map 3; open 9–1 & 4–6*), thought to have been built by Frederick II of Hohenstaufen in the 13th century. This tower, 24m high, is surrounded by a public garden, all that remains of Frederick's former hunting reserve.

CALASCIBETTA & ENVIRONS

Calascibetta (*map p. 537, B2*) is perched on a flat-topped hill opposite Enna. It is particularly picturesque when seen from a distance (and provides one of the most delightful views from Enna). The narrow main street leads up to the main square, with its Fascist-era monuments and the **Chiesa Madre**, built between 1310–40 for Peter II of Aragon, who replaced the castle with this church; the façade, surmounted by the bells, was rebuilt after the 1693 earthquake. The spacious interior, with a central nave and two side aisles, is divided by ten magnificent columns of a local hard red stone called *di cutu*; three of them are monolithic. The bases are cube-shaped, with faces and animals carved on the corners. The fourth base in the north aisle shows Peter of Aragon, his queen, his son, and the anonymous sculptor.

A one-way street leads back down to Piazza Umberto, where the signposted road to Enna leads downhill past the church and convent of the **Cappuccini**, on the edge of the hill. In the church is a splendid large altarpiece of the *Epiphany* by Filippo Paladini, in an enormous original wooden frame.

Realmese and Contrada Canalotto

No fewer than ten archaeological areas have been located around Calascibetta, a region which has been inhabited continuously since prehistoric times. One of the easiest to visit is the **Realmese necropolis** (*unenclosed; map p. 537, B2*), c. 3km northwest of Calascibetta, well signposted; the road suddenly finishes on the brink of an old quarry, and paths lead down into the valley, where some 300 rock-hewn tombs (9th–4th centuries BC) have been found (stout boots needed in winter). A short distance away (500m) in **Contrada Canalotto**, is a Byzantine village, its houses and church carved into the soft sandstone rock. In summer the mountainside is covered with deep purple thyme (*satra*) and yellow mullein; there are many shrikes in this area.

Villarosa

Villarosa (*map p. 537, A2*), in the sulphur-rich hills west of Enna, was founded in 1762 by Placido Notarbartolo, who asked the painter Rosa Ciotti to design the town for him; the result is an octagonal central square onto which four main streets converge. Villarosa became quite prosperous in the 19th century, thanks to the sulphur mines. An intriguing museum devoted to the subject is housed in a train parked in a siding in the railway station: the **Museo di Arte Mineraria e Civiltà Contadina** (*open 9.30–12 & 4.30–8, closed Mon; T: 0935 31126 or 338 4809721, www.trenomuseovillarosa.com*). One carriage is dedicated to the history of steam trains in Sicily, the others to mining activities and farming methods. On the road connecting the station to the town is the local baron's home, Villa Lucrezia, where another small museum has been opened: the **Museo della Memoria** (*T: 0935 567095 or 338 4809721 to request visit*), with a collection of 19th-century clothes and furniture, and at 9km from the station of Villarosa is the intact hamlet of **Villapriolo** (*to request guide, T: 0935 30166 or 329 0929972*), where until recently farmers and sulphur workers lived. You can visit their homes and their shops, such as the bakery and the cobbler's, and see the beautiful drinking-trough for animals, carved of deep red *di cutu* stone, the water-mills for grinding the wheat, and the washerwomen's sinks.

LAKE PERGUSA

Pergusa, 9km south of Enna (*map p. 537, B2*), is one of the few natural lakes in Sicily. It is said to occupy the chasm from which Hades emerged to carry Persephone down to the underworld, as mentioned by Milton in *Paradise Lost*:

Not that fair field
Of Enna, where Proserpin gath'ring flow'rs
Herself a fairer Flow'r by gloomy Dis
Was gather'd, which cost Ceres all that pain
To seek her through the world...

Paradise Lost, Book IV

Today the lake has no visible inlet or outlet and is apparently disappearing, perhaps because building activity nearby has damaged its underground sources. The vegetation on its shores, as well as the birdlife, have suffered greatly since the 1950s, when a motor-racing track was built around it. Paradoxically, the lake is also a nature reserve.

DEMETER & PERSEPHONE

Bust of Persephone from Morgantina, with characteristic *polos* headdress.

The goddess Demeter, patroness of the sowing of seed and the harvesting of corn, was already ancient when Homer wrote about her in his *Iliad*: 'Blonde Demeter separates fruit and chaff in the rushing of the winds'. Demeter's daughter by Zeus is Persephone or Kore; they were known as Ceres and Proserpine to the Romans. There is the legend, placed either in Eleusis in Greece or by Lake Pergusa near Enna in Sicily, that Persephone and her companions were gathering flowers in a meadow when the earth opened and Hades, the god of the underworld, charged out in his chariot and seized Persephone. The Sicilian version says that he re-entered the earth with his captive at the Fonte Ciane near Syracuse: there are records that there were drowning sacrifices at that site in ancient times, which may be linked to the myth. Demeter, after lighting a pine tree in the crater of Etna to use as a torch, wandered the earth desolate, eventually finding her daughter, but Persephone had eaten six seeds of a pomegranate Hades had offered her, and had married her kidnapper. Zeus decided that Persephone should spend six months of the year with her husband (who was also Zeus' brother) and six with her mother. While she is underground, Demeter is in despair and nothing can germinate or grow, her tears are the rainfall, but when she returns everything is blissfully fragrant and colourful with flowers. This myth, of the cycle of death and rebirth, is an ancient one with echoes in many different cultures. As Sicily was an oasis of fertility compared with the home cities of the Greek colonists, it is not surprising that the legends surrounding Demeter should become so well rooted here.   C.F.

On a hill above the lake are the excavations (*not open to the public*) of the necropolis, city and walls of **Cozzo Matrice**, a Bronze-Age settlement. About 10km southwest of the lake, in Località Gerace, a Roman villa with polychrome mosaics was discovered in 1994, but the excavations have since been covered over.

A short way southeast of Pergusa is the neat and tidy farming town of **Valguarnera Caropepe** (*map p. 537, B2*; the second part of the name, meaning 'expensive pepper', is now usually dropped). It was founded by the Valguarnera family in 1628 and prospered thanks to its sulphur mines. In the countryside east of Valguarnera are the isolated ruins of the medieval **castle of Gresti** (*map p. 537, B2–B3*), on an enormous rock split in two—a very rough track for the last part of the way, but incredibly beautiful at sunset.

PIAZZA ARMERINA

The town of Piazza Armerina (*map p. 537, B3*) has a medieval character, with dark cobbled streets and interesting Baroque monuments. The inhabitants are of Lombard origin; many of them have blue eyes and blond hair, and they have their own dialect.

HISTORY OF PIAZZA ARMERINA

The original Sicel settlement was probably near Casale, where a luxurious Roman villa would later be built. It is a well-watered, fertile area, which was conquered by the Arabs in 861 and named *Iblatasah*. The name may derive from *palatia*, a reference to the imperial villa, whose ruins were visible for many centuries after its abandonment. In 1091 Count Roger gave it to his Lombard troops, who had taken it after a ferocious battle; the Lombards called their new home *Platia* or *Plutia*. The town grew, entirely covering the ruins of the Roman villa. Less than a century later, in 1161, William I (the Bad) discovered that Ruggero Sclavo of Plutia was one of the ringleaders in a plot against him; he sent Muslim troops to destroy the city and scatter the inhabitants (barely a hundred survived). When his son William II (the Good) came to power in 1163, the Lombards begged him to allow reconstruction; he replied that he could not disobey his father's edict, but they could build a new town 3km away, on Monte Mira (now the Monte quarter); it was called Piazza Armoria, now Piazza Armerina. The abandoned ruins of Plutia became a farming hamlet called Casale. After the Sicilian Vespers (*see p. 69*), Piazza Armerina was vocal in demanding independence for the island, and at a meeting of the Sicilian Parliament convened here in December 1295, Frederick II of Aragon was declared king. The townspeople stoutly resisted the attempts of Robert of Anjou to reclaim the island for his family. In recognition of this loyalty, King Frederick granted the town many privileges, which are listed in a manuscript, *Il Libro dei Privilegi*, still in the civic library.

Exploring Piazza Armerina: upper town

The town is divided into four districts: Monte (on the highest point of Monte Mira, where the new town was built in 1163); Castellina (the district around the church of San Francesco d'Assisi, so called because of a small castle which once protected it); Canali (once the Jewish Ghetto; the church of Santa Lucia was the synagogue); and Casalotto (a separate village, which was incorporated into the city only in the 16th century). Though it was once far more important and more populous than Enna (which was named capital of the province by Mussolini), it was little known to travellers before the discovery of the Roman villa nearby at Casale (*see opposite*).

A number of streets converge on the central **Piazza Garibaldi**, a favourite meeting-place, with tall palm trees. Here is the 18th-century Palazzo di Città (Town Hall) next to the church of the Fundrò (or San Rocco), with a carved sandstone doorway. Between them Via Cavour leads up past the former seat of the electricity board, restored as the law courts. Further uphill is the former convent of San Francesco, with an elaborate Gagini balcony high up on the corner. The road continues past the 17th-century Palazzo del Vescovado to **Piazza del Duomo**, at the top of the hill, with a marvellous panorama from its terrace over the district of Monte, and a statue of Baron Marco Trigona, who was responsible for financing the rebuilding of the duomo in 1627. The brick façade of the duomo was added in 1719 and the copper-covered dome in 1768. The lovely bell-tower (c. 1490) survives from an earlier church. The fine façade (also brick) of the large 18th-century Palazzo Trigona is also in the square.

The entrance to the **duomo** is by one of the side doors. The interior is decorated in white and blue, and is unusually light and spacious. On the high altar is a copy of a venerated Byzantine panel-painting, the *Madonna of the Victories*; the original is preserved behind it in a 17th-century silver tabernacle. The painting was given by Pope Alexander II to Count Roger in 1063, after the battle of Cerami, and entrusted to the group of Lombards who took the city from the Muslims. Three of the 17th-century paintings in the sanctuary are by the Zoppo di Gangi (Gaspare Vazano). Above the door of the chapel to the left of the sanctuary is the *Martyrdom of St Agatha*, 1600, by Jacopo Ligozzi. Hanging in the nave is a Cross, painted on wood, attributed to a Provençal artist (1485). The altarpiece of the *Coronation of the Virgin* (1612) in the north transept is by Filippo Paladini. The organ is by Donato del Piano (1760). The font is surrounded by a Gaginesque frame in mottled beige marble, decorated with monsters' heads, which survives from the earlier church. Admire the magnificent carved walnut cupboards (1612) in the sacristy. The Trigona coat of arms of the spread eagle, star and triangle, is prominent throughout. An equestrian statuette of Count Roger and a late 14th-century reliquary by Paolo d'Aversa are also among the duomo's treasures, which may one day be exhibited in the former Bishop's Palace, the **Diocesan Museum**, at present used for temporary exhibitions (*Piazza Duomo 1, open 9–1 & 3.7.30; T: 0935 680214*).

The lower town

From Piazza del Duomo the picturesque Via Monte leads downhill through an attractive part of town, while Via Floresta leads down past the rear façade of Palazzo Trigona, with its Renaissance loggia, and ends in Piazza Castello. Here is the 14th-century castle, overgrown with ivy, and four small 17th-century palaces. From here Via Vittorio Emanuele continues down past the Jesuit Collegio on the right, now housing the **Biblioteca Comunale** (*open Mon–Fri 8–2, Tues and Thur also 3–6; T: 0935 686177*). This is one of the most important libraries in Sicily, with a small museum of antiquities including some swords, First-World-War shotguns, statuettes of terracotta and bronze, and the *Libro dei Privilegi*, a list of concessions granted by the kings of Sicily from 1300 to 1760.

To the east of the centre, in Piazza Umberto, is **San Giovanni dei Rodi**, the plain 13th-century chapel of the Knights of St John, with lancet windows. Nearby are the eccentric façades of Santo Stefano and the opera house, Teatro Garibaldi (1905; *T: 0935 684136*). Downhill are the lovely public gardens, Villa Garibaldi, near the 16th-century church of San Pietro. On the rise to the south, the church of the Carmine (*open Sun and holidays 10–1; info Domus Artis, T: 392 2068111*) preserves a campanile and cloister of the 14th–15th centuries.

VILLA ROMANA DEL CASALE

The celebrated Roman villa (*map p. 537, B3; open 9–6.30; T: 0935 680036, www.villaromanadelcasale.it*) lies 5.5km southwest of Piazza Armerina in the contrada of Casale. The road from Piazza Armerina (signposted) leads under a high road viaduct and then along a pretty valley. The complex, which has some of the most extensive and most beautiful Roman mosaics known, is a World Heritage Site and receives thousands of visitors a day. It is currently undergoing a long restoration which will include illumination, so in future it will be possible to see the mosaics also by night.

HISTORY OF THE VILLA

There is still no certainty as to the original owner of the villa. One theory is that it was the retreat of a Roman emperor, possibly Diocletian's co-emperor Maximian, but it is more likely to have been owned by someone of slightly lesser stature, who was nevertheless an important aristocrat. It lay in a wooded and secluded site at the foot of Monte Mangone (where the plundered tombs of the villa's necropolis have been found); the nearest Roman settlement was *Philosophiana* (Soffiana), 5km to the south, a station on the route to *Agrigentum*.

In richness and scope, the villa is comparable to Hadrian's Villa at Tivoli or Diocletian's Palace at Split, but while enough remains of the walls to give an idea of the elevation (and many of them are still covered with painted decoration, both inside and out), it is the extent of the polychrome floor mosaics (4103 square metres, with an average of 36,000 tesserae per square metre, a total of 120 million tesserae in the whole villa), mostly of the Roman-African school, that makes the building unique. The owner was a person of great wealth; the variety and quality of the marble and the coloured tesserae are unparalleled elsewhere; some of the rare marble was certainly reused from earlier buildings, because the quarries it came from were already exhausted at the time the villa was built. Several groups of craftsmen must have been working on the floors at the same time, in order to complete the assignment within a reasonable time. The signs on some of the cupids' foreheads, 'x', 'v' or a small diamond, were perhaps the 'signatures' of the craftsmen, and sometimes appear on North African floors of the same period. It is possible that some of the floors were pre-fabricated in North Africa and brought here in sections; the geometric designs would have been particularly suitable for this. The mansion is a single-storey building, made of rubble-and-mortar concrete faced with irregular brown stones, in some places painted to imitate marble.

Built between the 2nd and 4th centuries AD on the ruins of a 1st-century building, the villa, which consists of four distinct though connected parts on different levels, was perhaps inhabited for about 150 years. In Byzantine times the frigidarium, where lamps with Christian motifs have been found, was used as a church, before being partly destroyed by a flood, when much of the villa was covered with a thick layer of mud. Some rooms were reused by the Arabs or the Normans, who set up a furnace there, but after the destruction wreaked on the town by William the Bad in 1161 (*see p. 253*), the villa was completely abandoned. The buried ruins remained unexplored until 1761, when they became a source of columns for churches, and it was not until 1881 that anything but spasmodic excavations took place. In 1929, Paolo Orsi brought the triclinium to light. Work continued in 1935–39, and finally, in three campaigns from 1950–54, the main structure of the building was exposed, under the direction of Vinicio Gentili. The slaves' quarters and the outbuildings are only now being explored, and exciting discoveries are being made: the servants had their own bath-house, for example. Apart from the floors themselves, any archaeological evidence (such as coins or pottery) discovered during the early excavations remains unpublished.

NB: *At the time of writing, the mosaic and marble floors and the surviving murals have all been painstakingly restored and the transparent roof was being removed and replaced with copper-covered wooden roofing. The missing walls have been substituted with lightweight opaque panels, and the windows with copper mesh. A definitive route for the visit had not yet been established, and the description below is linked to the numbered plan opposite and does not reflect the way in which the building may be presented to the public in future.*

1: The original **main entrance** to the villa recalls in its massive form the Roman triumphal arch. It had two fountains on each face, probably fed from a reservoir.

2: The **atrium** is an ample polygonal courtyard with a portico of marble columns; the capitals are identical to those at Diocletian's villa near Split.

VILLA ROMANA DEL CASALE

PUBLIC & RECEPTION ROOMS

1 Main entrance
2 Atrium
3 Tablinum
4 Peristyle
5 Aediculum
6 Small latrine
7 Circus Room
8 Vestibule
9 Room of the Four Seasons
10 Room with cupids fishing
11 Room of the Small Hunt
12 Corridor of the Great Hunt
13 Room of the Ten Girls
14 Music Room
15 Xystus
16 Mosaics of fishing
17 Mosaics of grape harvesting
18 Triclinium

PRIVATE APARTMENTS & BASILICA

19 Small latrine
20 Atrium
21 Room with Arion mosaic
22 South vestibule
23 Bedchamber
24 North vestibule
25 Bedchamber
26 Basilica
27 Bedchamber
28 Anteroom
29 Bedchamber

BATHS (THERMAE)

30 Frigidarium
31 Room with massage mosaics
32 Tepidarium
33 Caldaria
34 Aediculum
35 Vestibule
36 Great Latrine

3: The villa proper was entered through the **tablinum** or reception-hall. On the mosaic floor, members of the household can be seen receiving their guests, with olive branches and torches; they are wearing garlands of flowers on their heads to indicate their joy.

4: The tablinum opens onto the **peristyle**, a quadriporticus of ten columns by eight, interrupted on the east side by an arch, and forming a garden with a pool and fountain in the centre. By studying the pollen, specialists have found that the garden was originally planted with sweetly-perfumed flowers and herbs such as roses, sage, carnations, marjoram, lavender and rosemary, and that climbing roses covered the latrines.

From the raised walkway the peristyle floor can be seen, consisting of square panels with geometric borders, in which animal heads are framed in laurel wreaths, with birds native to Sicily in the corners, and a recurrent ivy-leaf motif.

5: Opposite the entrance is an **aediculum**, the shrine of the household deity.

6: On the left below the walkway is the **small latrine**, the floor decorated with pictures of animals, including an ocelot. Just beyond, it is possible to look down into the **Circus Room (7)**, an exercise-room intended for use before entering the baths, and so-called from the scenes depicted on the floor of the chariot races at the Circus Maximus in Rome; the viewpoint of the onlooker is from the emperor's box.

8: The passageway leads by a **vestibule** (this was formerly another entrance to the baths). Its mosaic, showing the lady of the house with a girl and boy (wearing a yellow tunic, he squints, a characteristic of Maxentius, son of Maximian), and two slave-girls carrying bathing necessities and clean clothing, is doubly interesting because it reveals their style of dress, and because it probably represents the owners in a family scene.

9–11: The majority of the rooms (probably for use by guests) on the north side of the peristyle have geometric mosaics, several of them damaged by Arab or Norman structural alterations. One floor shows young people dancing very vivaciously. There is a room with the **Four Seasons (9)** and another with **cupids fishing (10)**. Of most interest is one called the **Room of the Small Hunt** (*Piccola Caccia*; **11**), where a number of hunting scenes are depicted in great detail. On five 'levels', we see different techniques for catching and killing birds and animals, using dogs, falcons, nets, lime-sticks and double-pointed lances. Some of the dogs (upper left-hand corner) are *cirnechi*, originally imported by the Phoenicians from Cyrene in Libya, and still bred at Adrano on Mt Etna (*see p. 398*). A dangerous accident during a boar-hunt is vividly portrayed in the bottom right-hand corner, while in the centre, under a red awning, a sacrifice to Artemis/Diana is being held, and slaves are emptying baskets in preparation for the picnic, while others raise their glasses to the company. Some of the characters in the scene would appear to be portraits of the owner of the house and his guests. As this room could not be closed by a door, it is thought that it was a sitting-room or small dining-room.

Detail from the Corridor of the Great Hunt showing an overseer and bodyguard.

12: The long **Corridor of the Great Hunt** (*Grande Caccia*), 65.93m long, runs the width of the building to isolate the private apartments, and is closed at either end by an exedra. This is certainly the focal point of the whole building. The corridor is paved throughout with a superb series of scenes of the capture of animals (*venationes*), one of the finest Roman mosaics known. Close to the centre is a dignified figure protected by two 'bodyguards' holding shields, who appears to be the overseer. It has been

noted that perhaps two different groups of craftsmen were working together. The left-hand part of the design is more detailed, and more colours are used, at least 25 types of stone, while for the right-hand area only 15 colours appear, in simpler compositions. In the apses are personifications of two regions, flanked by wild beasts, representing perhaps the two poles of the Roman world, Africa (north, much consumed, with a leopard and a lion) and India (south, with a tiger, tusks of ivory and an elephant, and a

phoenix beside her; she embraces a san-
dalwood tree with her right arm. The red
streamers hanging on the branch over
her are *formidines*, markers used during
Roman tiger-hunts to indicate the 'passage' along which the animal should be
driven by the beaters). The landscape between contains a fish-filled sea on which
large galleys sail, transporting exotic animals, and cleverly devised to show them

being loaded and then disembarked at
their destination. Some authorities identify Egypt in these scenes, and the port of
Alexandria, while the arrival could be at
Ostia. The scenes are remarkable for the
number and detail of the species of wild
animal (African elephants along the corridor, and an Indian elephant and tiger
in the south apse) and for the accuracy
with which they are depicted in action

MOSAICS

The richly-tessellated floor mosaics which were such a feature of Roman villa life
throughout the Empire originally developed from Greek models of the Hellenistic
period (323–27 BC) when for the first time ordinary homes adopted some
comfort and luxury. In Sicily the first mosaics of the 3rd century BC are crude:
chips of stone placed in pavements of crushed tile and mortar. One example
is the floor of Temple A at Selinunte (*see p. 158*), where the decorative motifs
appear to have been copied from local Carthaginian examples. By the end of the
3rd century there is more local experimentation, as in the House of Ganymede
at Morgantina (*see p. 267*), where a mixture of styles include patterned floors
and figures (notably Ganymede) with shaped tesserae now in several colours.
However, home-grown experiments are eclipsed in the later Hellenistic period
by wider Mediterranean influences as Sicily adopted styles and motifs from the
Aegean, notably Delos, and then transmitted them on to Italy. Then, in the early
centuries AD, Italian styles in black and white fed back into Sicily and by the 2nd
century AD there seems to have been an influx of mosaicists from the prosperous
workshops of North Africa. The great period of Sicilian mosaics was the 4th
century AD, above all here at the opulent villa at Piazza Armerina where a wealthy
family with connections to official life in Rome flaunted their status with an
amazing array of themes and subjects. It is assumed that the mosaic teams were
from North Africa and there is some evidence, from the villa on the River Tellaro
(*see p. 354*), for instance, that they settled in Sicily in order to exploit the island's
prosperity. As so often in Sicily, the island becomes part of a wider Mediterranean
culture, sustained in this case by the underlying stability of the Empire.   C.F.

13: At the southeast corner of the peristyle the walkway passes above the **Room
of the Ten Girls**, whose mosaic shows
young women in bikinis, competing and

performing gymnastic exercises, and
receiving prizes: the most famous floor
in the villa, yet of inferior artistic quality
compared with the others. In one corner

is part of an earlier geometric pavement, covered over to accommodate this one.

14: Adjacent is the **Music Room**, with a damaged mosaic representing the Orphic myth; again the animals are carefully depicted. There was a statue of Apollo here, and a fountain to cool the air.

15–17: The **xystus (15)** is a large elliptical court, formerly with fountains along the centre. The west end is closed by a wide exedra and the east by the great dining hall or triclinium. Six small rooms lead off the xystus, their floors decorated with playful **mosaics of fishing (16)** and **grape-harvesting (17)**. Amorini are shown on ladders picking grapes, which in Roman Sicily and southern Italy were trained to grow up trees.

18: The triconchos or **triclinium**, the ceremonial banqueting-hall, is 12m square with deep apses on three sides (hence the name). The theme of the superb central pavement is the *Labours of Hercules*, the violent episodes being combined into a single turbulent composition. Ten of the Labours can be distinguished, those missing being the man-eating Stymphalian Birds and the Girdle of Hippolyta, the Amazon Queen. In the apses you find the *Glorification of Hercules* (North), *Conquered Giants* (East) and a particularly beautiful depiction of *Lycurgus and Ambrosia* (South).

19: Close to the line of the aqueduct is a **small latrine**, beside the original entrance to the private apartments. Here Pompeian-style frescoes on the wall imitate marble. The narrow doorway, in complete contrast to the sumptuous spa-ciousness of the villa, was for the slaves, and the widening at the top was to allow the passage of whatever they were carrying on their heads.

20–21: The original approach, for the householder and his guests, was through the semi-circular **atrium** (with a mosaic of cupids fishing), divided by a tetrastyle portico into a nymphaeum and an ambulatory. On either side of this atrium a vestibule leads into a bedchamber, while the centre opens into a room with marble-covered walls **(21)**; the overcrowded, *horror-vacui* mosaic shows the poet Arion riding on a dolphin, surrounded by naiads and marine creatures—sea-lions and sea-horses among them—and is the best-known representation of this myth. The inventor of dithyrambic poetry, and the toast of the court of King Periander of Corinth, Arion was rescued by a dolphin after being thrown into the sea by the mariners (who stole his prize money) on his way back to Greece after winning a musical contest in Sicily.

22–23: The **south vestibule (22)**, decorated with nursery scenes, leads into a **bedchamber (23)** in which the mosaic shows scenes of drama; the musical instruments and the indication by Greek letters of musical modes are of unusual interest.

24–25: Off the **north vestibule (24)**, with its scene showing the contest between Eros and Pan (the bearded man wearing a purple toga and the boy opposite him could be the owner and his son), is a **bedchamber (25)** with scenes of children hunting, those in the centre already amusingly routed by their quarry.

26: The **basilica** was the administrative centre of the villa, where guests and clients were received. It is an imposing hall, 100 Roman feet long (c. 30m), richly decorated with columns of red Egyptian granite at the entrance and a porphyry disc in front of the place where the throne would have stood. Porphyry was almost exclusively used in imperial commissions, which lends support to the theory that Maximian was the owner of this villa. Above the throne stood a statue of Hercules (its head is now at the town hall of Piazza Armerina). The apse and floors are clad in *opus sectile*, made of marble from 40 different quarries in the Mediterranean area. An enormous copper-covered semi-dome of wooden laminate has been raised over the apse, and a massive coffered ceiling covers the rest of the room, the source of some controversy because not all scholars agree that the basilica would have had a dome, and if it did, perhaps not one of this size.

27–28: The northern group of private apartments consists of a **bedchamber (27)** with a mosaic depicting a variety of fruit, and an **ante-room (28)** with a large mosaic of *Odysseus and Polyphemus*, showing Odysseus offering wine to the unsuspecting three-eyed Cyclops.

29: The adjoining **bedchamber** has well-preserved, colourful frescoes on the walls, and a famous erotic scene in the 12-sided centre floor panel.

30–33: The thermae. The **frigidarium (30)** is in the form of an octagon with radiating apses of which two served as vestibules and two, larger than the rest, as plunge-baths. It was formerly covered with a dome. The mosaics show slaves helping people to dress or undress, and in the centre, marine myths (some of these show signs of having been clumsily repaired at a later date). Those in the adjoining room **(31)**, show the massage of bathers by slaves, a function consistent with its position between the cold baths and the **tepidarium (32)** and **caldaria (33)**, which lie beyond.

34: The **aediculum** designed for a statue of Venus was the original entrance to the baths.

35: The **vestibule** was the entrance to the long narthex (or Circus Room). In both these a partial loss of floor has exposed the hypocaust beneath.

36: Near the atrium are the remains of the **great latrine**, the marble seats of which are lost; the water-channel for washing and the niches for sponges can be seen.

Southwest of the villa the remains of a 12th-century village have been found, perhaps the Lombard *Plutia* (*see p. 253*).

NORTH & WEST OF PIAZZA ARMERINA

To the north of Piazza Armerina is the Norman **church of Sant'Andrea** (*map p. 537, B3; open Sun and holidays only, 10–1; Info: Domus Artis, T: 392 2068111*). Dating from 1096, the austere interior contains 12th–15th-century frescoes, including one of the *Cruci-*

fixion of St Andrew, making this church particularly important for the history of Sicilian medieval art. The abbey was one of the oldest religious communities in the area. The prior was elected by the local Aleramici counts and the nomination approved by the King of Sicily. After final ratification by the pope, the appointed prior had a permanent seat in the Sicilian Parliament and was one of the most powerful men in the kingdom.

West of the town, reached from the road to Casale, a rough track climbs the **Piano Marino** (or Armerino; so called because from there you can sometimes see the sea) to the church of Santa Maria di Platea, where the Byzantine *Madonna of the Victories* was found in 1348, during an epidemic of plague which miraculously stopped. Apparently the precious little painting, carefully packed in a cypress-wood box, had been hidden in 1161 to protect it from the Saracens. Nearby are the ruins of a castle, traditionally thought to have been founded by Count Roger. The views are delightful.

At **Montagna di Marzo**, northwest of Piazza Armerina, there was a Sicel settlement, possibly the 8th-century BC *Herbessos*, where recent excavations have revealed an extensive sanctuary of Demeter and Persephone, in use from the 6th–3rd centuries BC. Votive statuettes and coins have been found.

Due west of Piazza Armerina is **Barrafranca** (*map p. 537, A3*), a farming community of ancient origin. Some historians believe that this could be *Hybla Heraia*, an important Sicel town which has not yet been located with certainty. Still further west is **Pietraperzia**, a town of medieval character, especially in the old district at the foot of the photogenic Castello Barresio (*closed; sometimes open in summer for guided tours*), which was built by the Normans in 1088 on top of an existing (probably Arab) structure. The façade of the 16th-century Chiesa Madre (Santa Maria) in Piazza Vittorio Emanuele is incomplete, but inside there are some Gagini statues, the lovely marble sarcophagi of the local Barresi princes, and over the main altar is a masterpiece by Filippo Paladini, the *Madonna with Saints*. In the same square is the little opera house, where a 14th-century Catalan Gothic portal has been placed on display. Found abandoned and in very bad condition, it was restored and experts believe it comes from the castle.

MORGANTINA & AIDONE

The extensive remains of the ancient city of Morgantina (*map p. 537, B3*) lie on a high ridge surrounded by open, wooded countryside. With its superb views, the usually deserted and very peaceful site is one of the most memorable places on the island. The huge archaeological area (c. 20ha) occupies the long ridge of Serra Orlando to the west, once a Greek and Sicel city loyal to Hieron II of Syracuse, separated by a deep valley from the conical Cittadella hill to the east, where the original Sicel settlement had stood several centuries earlier.

Open 8.30–1hr before sunset, last tickets one hour before closing; T: 0935 87955, combined ticket with the archaeological museum of Aidone. NB: if you intend to continue to the Citadella, bring water and a sunhat.

Morgantina was first excavated in 1955 for Princeton University by the Swedish archaeologist Erik Sjoqvist; he was under the impression that the city was *Erbessa*, until coins and a wooden die carved with the initials MGT suggested that he had found Morgantina. The main excavations consist of the area of the agora, laid out in the 3rd century BC, and the residential areas on the two low hills to the east and west of it. Later excavations were carried out by Virginia University, under the direction of Malcolm Bell III.

HISTORY OF MORGANTINA

Here, in the centre of a rich agricultural plain near the source of the River Gornalunga, a group of Sicels called Morgetians (from the name of their leader Morges) founded a town c. 850 BC on the Cittadella hill, the site of an Early Bronze-Age settlement. They probably came from the Aeolian Islands, judging by their similar pottery. Morgantina would have been an important point on the route through to Agira and southern Sicily from the north coast. Groups of Greek settlers, from both Gela and Katane (Catania), fought over the site in the 6th century BC and rebuilt the city, which however was not abandoned by the Sicels, who continued living there, side by side with the newcomers. In 459 BC Ducetius, leader of the Sicels, seeing Sicels and Greeks living peacefully together as inimical to his dream of expelling the Greeks from Sicily, sacked the city. The Cittadella was abandoned and a new city was built on Serra Orlando, which probably reached its zenith under the protection of Hieron II of Syracuse (307–215 BC; he came to power in 276 BC). Almost all of Sicily was under Roman rule when he died, but his young successor chose to side with the Carthaginians, causing the inevitable destruction of Morgantina in 211 BC. By the time of Augustus, Morgantina was a mere shadow of its former self, and was gradually completely abandoned.

Residential area: West Hill

A path leads west from the ticket office to the recently excavated **Hellenistic bathhouse**, which is currently being studied and prepared for publication and at the time of writing does not have an explanatory signboard. Dating from the period of Hieron II, it is a fascinating example of an early bathing establishment and is visibly different from the later, Roman, versions that can be seen in so many other cities in Sicily.

Returning to the ticket office, a path leads east to the main part of the site, entered from the West Hill. This was a residential district at the intersection of two streets, Plateia B and Stenopos West 4, where a number of houses have been excavated. To the right, on Plateia B, is the **House of the Tuscan Capitals**, completely rebuilt in the 2nd century BC. Part of the house has been reconstructed to protect the walls and floors.

Across the street, near a large olive tree, is the **House of the Wine-press** (or Pappalardo House, after the engineer who first discovered it in 1884). Built in the 3rd century BC, the most prosperous period for Morgantina, and paved with early mosaics,

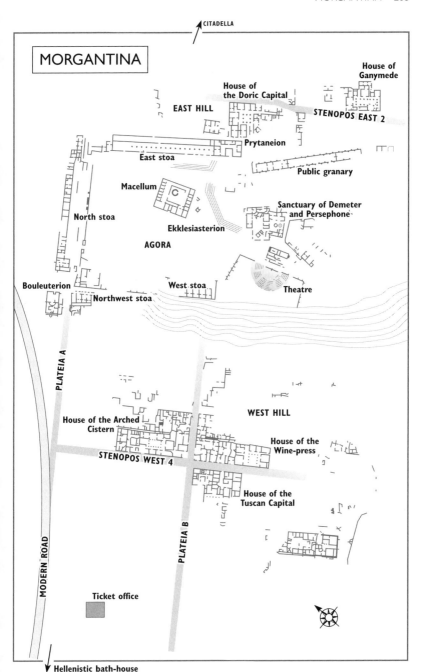

MORGANTINA

CITADELLA

House of Ganymede

House of the Doric Capital

EAST HILL

STENOPOS EAST 2

Prytaneion

East stoa

Public granary

Macellum

North stoa

Sanctuary of Demeter and Persephone

Ekklesiasterion

AGORA

Bouleuterion

West stoa

Northwest stoa

Theatre

PLATEIA A

House of the Arched Cistern

WEST HILL

House of the Wine-press

STENOPOS WEST 4

House of the Tuscan Capital

PLATEIA B

MODERN ROAD

Ticket office

Hellenistic bath-house

the house measures c. 500m square, and had a peristyle with twelve columns. It would have been one of the more luxurious homes in the city. In 1966, in one of the houses in this district, a pot containing 44 gold coins was found, probably buried hastily during the attack of 211 BC.

Returning to the intersection and heading northwest along Stenopos West 4, you will see the largest house in Morgantina (partly covered), the **House of the Arched Cistern**, built around two courtyards, with a cistern beneath a low arch and several mosaics. On the north side of the hill (near the approach road to the site) new excavations of another house are in progress. The views from the West Hill over the agora, one of the largest public spaces in ancient Sicily, are incomparable.

The agora

Stenopos West 4 leads down hill to join Plateia A, which brings you into the public heart of the city, with the **bouleuterion** on your left. This was the meeting-place of the city council, with a courtyard, a portico, and originally four semicircular rows of seats that could hold up to 80 councillors. The remains of a paved street can be seen here. The **northwest and west stoa** were arcades of shops built into the hillside. Beyond a long **terracotta water-conduit** (with holes at regular intervals provided with little lids to allow cleaning), you arrive at the **theatre**, still with appreciably good acoustics, with room for an audience of over 1,000 in 14 rows of seating. Note the dedicatory inscription (in Greek) on the 9th row of the 3rd section (counting from right to left).

In the centre of the agora is a monumental **ekklesiasterion**, a three-sided flight of steps unique in the Greek world, 55m wide, which descends to the lower agora. It separated the upper agora, dedicated to commerce and political meetings, from the lower, where religious functions took place. Beside the steps is a **Sanctuary of Demeter and Persephone**, with two round altars (under cover), and the pottery kilns used for manufacturing the votive offerings.

In the centre of the upper agora is the large rectangular **macellum**, a covered market with 14 shops arranged around an open yard in the middle of which was a large circular building with thick walls designed to store fresh food, and a stepped altar, which was built in 125 BC. Beyond it to the north is the **north stoa**, 90m long, with the remains of shops and offices and possibly a schoolroom. A number of lava millstones, used for grinding wheat, have been placed here—most of them were found in the residential quarters.

The long **east stoa** (87m) consisted of a narrow portico. A monumental fountain (under cover) with two basins has been excavated at its north end and at its extreme south end is a large building paved in brick, the **prytaneion**, or office of the magistrates, which could also be used as a reception-centre for visiting dignitaries. The three large holes you can see carved in a stone are enigmatic. They may have accommodated amphorae used for wine or water, or they may have been part of a cashier's till, with another (now lost) block placed over the holes in such a way that money could be deposited in the holes by people standing outside and scooped out by the cashier inside, who would then deposit it in a strongbox placed in the large hole in the floor.

Interlocking terracotta water pipe at Morgantina. The individual sections had circular lids which could be lifted off to allow cleaning. A few of these still survive.

Beyond the prytaneion is the huge **public granary**, a storehouse for wheat, with a small pottery kiln (under cover) which was added later, and at the other end (by the fence) a larger kiln with elaborate ovens for tiles, bricks and storage vessels.

Residential area: East Hill

From the prytaneion a stepped street zigzags up the East Hill. Just below the summit is the elegant **House of the Doric Capital**, so called because one was found incorporated into a wall. It has the word EYEXEI, meaning 'welcome' in Greek, inlaid into one of its floors, to the right of the entrance. A hip-bath found in the house is now in the Aidone museum.

Leaving the house on Stenopos East 2, and walking c. 50m along the summit, you reach the **House of Ganymede**, built c. 260 BC, and destroyed in 211 BC, with two columns and mosaic fragments in two little huts (seen through glass doors). The Ganymede mosaic is particularly interesting as one of the earliest known made with cut-stone tesserae, which also incorporates natural pebbles. There is a fine view of the agora and, on a clear day, of Etna to the east. From here you can also see the original site of the settlement, the Cittadella (*see below*).

The Cittadella

To the east of the site can be seen the conical Cittadella hill (reached from here by a rough road, about 30 mins' strenuous walk), which was separately fortified. On the summit is a long narrow temple of the 4th century BC. Here a hut village of the Morgetians (850–750 BC) was excavated, and rock-hewn tombs of Sicel type on the slopes have yielded considerable finds of pottery. Parts of the walls (7km in circumference) of Serra Orlando, and the west gate, can be seen near the approach road to the site.

AIDONE

The little red-stone town of Aidone stands in a panoramic position in the Heraean Mountains, close to lovely woods of pines, oaks and eucalyptus, where the fallow deer has been re-introduced; part of the forest is protected as a nature reserve, the *Riserva Naturale Russomanno*, run by the Azienda Forestale. In the heart of the reserve is a photogenic group of large, mysterious stones, called the Pietre Incantate—the 'enchanted stones'. Legend says they are a petrified band of dancers.

Aidone was founded by Count Roger for the families of the Lombard troops from Monferrato, who accompanied his third wife Adelaide, mother of Roger II. In 1282 the town took a leading role in the famous uprising against the Angevins, the Sicilian Vespers (*see p. 69*). The Chiesa Madre is dedicated to St Lawrence, the patron saint of Aidone; the old sacristy has been transformed into a small museum of church treasures, including a 16th-century silver reliquary containing the arm of the saint. Inside the church is a magnificent 18th-century organ, recently restored and in regular use.

Museo Archeologico

In the upper part of the town, a long steep walk from the centre, in Piazza Torres Truppia, is a restored 17th-century Capuchin convent, now the Archaeological Museum (*open 9–7, late closing sometimes in summer; combined ticket with Morgantina; T: 0935 87307, www.deadimorgantina.it*), with a well-displayed collection of finds, including the silver treasure, the acroliths and the statue of the Goddess of Morgantina (*Dea di Morgantina*), recently returned from the museums which acquired them from illegal sellers, after 30 years of international bickering. The entrance is through a charming little church with painted wooden statues.

THE REPATRIATION OF ANTIQUITIES

The acroliths, the *Dea di Morgantina* and the Treasure of Eupolemos were each discovered at Morgantina in the second half of the 20th century by clandestine diggers, who sold them on through a well-established antiquities smuggling chain. They eventually found their way to the United States, where they were put on display in various museums. Long recognised for what they were, various requests were made for their return, but it was only in 2005 that the Italian state began successful international legal proceedings for the return of these and other stolen treasures, and only in the last couple of years that they were finally returned to Italy and put back on display where they belong.

The earliest exhibits include huge storage-jars or pithoi from Morgantina and prehistoric, Bronze-Age and Iron-Age finds from the Cittadella and Contrada San Francesco, including material from huts inhabited by the Morgetic colony.

Three pieces from the Hellenistic silver and gilt hoard found in the House of Eupolemos at Morgantina. From left to right: bowl with elaborately embossed base; medallion showing Scylla hurling a rock; female figure with child and cornucopia, the lid of a pyxis.

The treasures of the museum are on the ground floor. The Sala degli Acroliti displays the famous **marble acroliths**: three feet, three hands and two heads, beautifully arranged by Marella Ferrera, with the help of some twists of tulle, to represent two seated goddesses. While the hands and the faces are perfect, the feet are worn, consumed by the caresses of generations of worshippers (notice the misshapen toe on Persephone's surviving foot, she appears to have a bunion). The features are typical of the 6th century BC, with Archaic smiles and almond-shaped eyes; scholars date them to c. 530 BC. The statues themselves would have been made of wood, covered by mantles of linen or wool, with the visible extremities made of marble. Hair, diadems, earrings and other ornaments might have been made of precious metals, and the goddesses would have been wearing veils. The position of the fingers suggests that they would have been holding an object. The left-hand figure is slightly larger than the other; after much debate, they are believed to be both female and to represent Demeter and her daughter Persephone.

The **Treasure of Eupolemos** is a group of 16 beautiful objects in gilded silver dating to the 3rd century BC and probably made in Syracuse. They may have been intended for use during temple rites: one of them is clearly inscribed with the words 'sacred to the gods'. Some also bear the embossed name of Eupolemos, who might have been the high priest at the temple. The treasure consists of two large oval situlae; three cups with flowers and leaves in relief at the bottom; a small bowl with a fish-net pattern (resembling a modern football); a jug; a two-handled cup; an offering-dish with sunray relief; a miniature cylindrical altar; a ladle; two pyxides with lids decorated with figures in relief, one representing a cupid with a torch, and the other a female figure with a cornucopia and a child on her lap (an allegory of Peace or Justice); a wonderful medallion (probably from a missing cup) showing Scylla in the act of throwing a large stone, and two slender horns, perhaps belonging to a leather priest's mask.

One of a series of terracotta bath tubs found in excavations at Morgantina This one was found in the House of Ganymede.

The magnificent **Dea di Morgantina** (c. 410 BC) has a room to herself (and a brand-new gallery is planned for her). Found broken into 83 fragments, it is thought that the statue was toppled from her pedestal and smashed during the 211 BC attack on Morgantina, or during an earthquake. The statue is pseudo-acrolithic: carved from local limestone with head, feet and arms of Parian marble, 2m 20cm tall, weighing 600kg, and thought by some to be the work of a follower of Pheidias. Tests show that her drapery was originally painted red (faded to pink on the fragments) and blue. Scholars continue to argue about which goddess she represents: Aphrodite, Demeter or Persephone.

Other exhibits in the museum include examples of the architecture of Morgantina and a remarkable collection of **objects found in the thermae**, which, more than anything else, give an idea of the high standard of living of the inhabitants. Other objects illustrate life in Morgantina during its moment of greatest splendour, in Archaic times: Corinthian and Attic ceramics, antefixes with gorgons' heads (6th century BC), a large red-figure krater by the Euthymides painter, an Attic Corinthian krater with birds, and lekythoi. There is also a fine collection of ceramics from the agora zone of Serra Orlando (including a plate with three fish), and from the houses excavated on the west and east hills (including statues). There are displays of household objects, cooking utensils, agricultural implements, toys and masks. Hellenistic and Roman finds from Serra Orlando include fine large **busts of Persephone** (3rd century BC) from the three sanctuaries of Demeter and Persephone so far found there, and grave goods found in tombs in the necropoleis.

NORTHEAST OF ENNA

The River Salso, so-called because of its slightly salty water, springs from Mt Bauda in the Madonie Mountains and flows east, forming the lovely Lake Pozzillo (Sicily's largest), before joining the Simeto. The countryside along its course is particularly spectacular, and there are numerous interesting old towns.

LEONFORTE

Leonforte ('Strong Lion'; *map p. 537, B2*) is a delightful little town founded in 1610 by the local overlord Nicolò Placido Branciforte. Seeing the potential of such a well-watered area, he founded a city, naming it after the lion on his family coat of arms. Today the town bases its economy on the production of lentils, broad beans, and highly-prized late-ripening peaches.

Via Porta Palermo leads to the main street, Corso Umberto or Cassaro, just before which, below the road to the left, is the **Chiesa Madre** (17th–18th centuries), with a striking façade in a mixture of styles. It contains numerous interesting wooden statues.

A very short steep road, Via Garibaldi, can be followed on foot downhill past the church of Santo Stefano to the church of the Carmelo, beside the magnificent **Granfonte** (built in 1651 by Nicolò Branciforte) an abundant fountain of 24 jets. The water is collected in a stream which follows a picturesque lane downhill. Beside it is the gate of an overgrown botanical garden, with palms and orange trees.

Just beyond the Chiesa Madre is **Piazza Branciforte**, with the impressive façade of the 17th-century Palazzo Baronale and, at the end, a stable-block for 100 horses built in 1641 (the prince of the time was a famous horse-breeder). The well-proportioned Corso leads gently up through a pretty circular piazza. Beyond, a side street (left) leads to the convent and church of the **Cappuccini**. It contains an enormous canvas of the *Calling of St Matthew* by Pietro Novelli, very reminiscent of Caravaggio. On either side are niches with Gaginesque statues. A finely-carved arch (1647) precedes the Branciforte funerary chapel, with the sumptuous black marble sarcophagus (1634) of Caterina di Branciforte, supported by four lions.

Fifteen kilometres to the west of Leonforte is **Mt Altesina** (1193m), thought by the Arabs to be exactly in the centre of the island; it is said that on this spot they decided the division of Sicily into three administrative districts, the Val Demone, Val di Noto and Val di Mazara. Set in a nature reserve run by the Azienda Forestale, it is a pleasant trek through the woods to the top, where the remains of a Sicel village are to be found, and panoramic views.

ASSORO

To the east of Leonforte is Assoro (*map p. 537, B2*), a town founded by the Sicels. Ally of Syracuse until 260 BC, it changed sides, became a Roman stronghold, and was even prosperous enough to mint coins. In 72 BC the notorious Roman governor Verres (*see p. 189*) was forced by the indignant inhabitants to abandon his attempt to steal the statue of Crisa, the town's patron god, from the temple. Assoro was taken by the Arabs in 939, who fortified it, and by the Normans in 1061; during the Middle Ages, Assoro was particularly fortunate, eventually becoming the fiefdom of the Valguarnera family.

The old centre, once surrounded by walls, is medieval in character. The main street, Via Crisa, leads up to Piazza Marconi (Piazza Matrice) and the 12th-century **Chiesa Madre** (San Leone), a national monument, with a square bell-tower. It is entered by a Catalan Gothic doorway and has an unusual interior with five aisles and three apses, twisted columns and a carved and painted wooden ceiling. The gilded stucco decoration dates from the early 18th century. In the raised and vaulted presbytery is a fine marble altarpiece of the Gagini school (1515) with statues and reliefs, and two early 16th-century Valguarnera funerary monuments on the side walls. Over the nave hangs a Crucifix (late 15th-century), painted on both sides. The high altar has three Gothic statues. To the left of the presbytery is a double chapel, the first with Gothic vaulting and bosses, and the second with Baroque decoration. Here is a carved processional Crucifix attributed to Gian Domenico Gagini, and two 17th-century sarcophagi. In the nave are some particularly interesting 16th-century polychrome gilded wooden statues. The porch of the church is connected by a Gothic arch to Palazzo Valguarnera, which has a balcony supported by grotesque heads. The Baroque portal of an oratory is also in the square.

On the top of Monte Stella is the **Castello Valguarnera**, separated from the town by a steep slope, now protected as an urban park. It is only accessible from the west. Some of the stones used for building the walls show Greek inscriptions—probably an example of recycling building material in the past. Most of the visible ruins go back to the 14th century, when the Valguarnera family took over Assoro.

AGIRA

The little town of Agira (*map p. 537, B2*) is perched on a conical hill. The ancient *Agyrion* was a Sicel settlement, important for its position between Sicel territory and that of the Sicans. It was colonised with Greeks in 339 BC by Timoleon of Corinth (the parent-city of Syracuse), who came to Sicily to oust the tyrant Dionysius II. Games were regularly organised in honour of Herakles, who had a strong cult following. Traces have been found here of Roman houses with mosaic pavements, a temple on what must have been the acropolis, and necropoleis of the 4th–3rd centuries BC. Diodorus Siculus, the historian (c. 90–20 BC), was born in Agira: in his description of Timoleon's city he declares the theatre to be the most beautiful in Sicily after that of Syracuse. The town was the scene of the miracles of the apocryphal St Philip of Syria, who is said by the local people to have imprisoned the devil in a nearby cave, where he can be heard wailing on stormy nights. Pope Leo II (682–83), who instituted the kiss of peace during High Mass, was probably born here.

The magic moment to be in Agira is just before dawn, when the town is still enveloped in the shadows of night, and the rising sun gradually outlines the profile of Mt Etna with a pink glow.

Exploring Agira

The highway SS 121 becomes Via Vittorio Emanuele, leading to Largo Mercato, with the church of **San Filippo** (12th and 14th centuries). The interior has a central nave and two aisles; on the main altar is a Crucifix by Fra' Umile da Petralia. The walnut choir-stalls, carved with scenes of the life of St Philip, are the work of Nicola Bagnasco (1818–22). In the left aisle are two paintings by Olivio Sozzi and three panels of a 15th-century polyptych. There is a crypt with two statues of St Philip, and a relief of the Gagini school.

Piazza Garibaldi is in the centre, with the large church of **Sant'Antonio da Padova** (1549); inside there is a 16th-century polychrome wooden statue of St Sylvester, a beautiful painting on marble by Willem Borremans, with a precious silver frame, and a 16th-century Flemish-School canvas of the *Deposition*. Via Diodorea continues steeply up to Piazza Immacolata and the 13th-century church of **Santa Margherita**, the largest in the town, with 13 sumptuous altars and several paintings by Olivio Sozzi. By taking the street to the right of the church, passing under an arch, and going through Largo Raccommandata, you reach Piazza Roma, with the Norman church of the **Santissimo Salvatore**; it has a beautiful bell-tower. Inside the church is a fine Aragonese portal from the oratory of Santa Croce (once the Jewish synagogue), a 15th-century panel painting of St Philip of Agira, and a 13th-century bishop's mitre of red silk embroidered with coral and pearls.

By returning to Largo Raccommandata and taking via Sant'Antonio Abate, you reach the top of the hill, and the romantic ruins of the castle. Just below it is the church of **Santa Maria Maggiore** (11th century), with an unusual interior: two asymmetric naves divided by three arches on columns, with decorated capitals; immediately in the right-hand nave, a 16th-century wooden Crucifix by Pietro Ruzzolone, and a 16th-century polychrome marble statue of the *Madonna*. In the chapel at the end of the left nave is a 15th-century wooden Crucifix, painted on both sides. A short distance away is the 16th-century church of **Sant'Antonio Abate**, with a modern façade. Inside there are some remarkable works of art: a painted wooden Crucifix by Pietro Ruzzolone, 14 small 17th-century canvases of the Venetian School, and a dramatic *St Andrew* by Polidoro da Caravaggio.

Environs of Agira

On the road to Regalbuto, just outside Agira (left; signposted) is a **Canadian Military Cemetery** (490 graves), beautifully kept in a clump of pine trees on a small hill; Canadian forces were engaged in heavy fighting here in 1943. Close to Agira is the beautiful, wooded **Lake Pozzillo**, the largest artificial lake in Sicily, measuring 6km by 1.6km, usually with cattle and sheep grazing around it. It was created in the 1950s by means of a dam on the River Salso, in order to provide water for irrigating the orange groves of the Plain of Catania.

South of Agira is a beautiful, remote valley in the central Heraean Mountains known as **Piano della Corte**, where a stream, flowing to join the River Dittaino, has created strange formations in the rock. It is protected as a nature reserve. The vegetation is typical Mediterranean maquis, together with poplars, willows and tamarisks; there are rabbits, foxes, porcupines and hedgehogs, while the birds include the woodchat shrike, barn owl, buzzard, and the Sicilian sub-species of the long-tailed tit.

Regalbuto

The ancient *Ameselon*, destroyed by Hieron II of Syracuse in 270 BC, has been identified near Regalbuto (*map p. 537, C2*) on Monte San Giorgio. It was later re-founded as an Arab village, *Rahal-butah*, at the site of the modern town. The people historically feuded with the inhabitants of nearby Centuripe, who completely destroyed their town in 1261. Fortunately, the appeals of the townsfolk to King Manfred were crowned with success, and Regalbuto was rebuilt the following year at his expense. The curving medieval streets, with narrow side streets and courtyards, are particularly attractive. Via Ingrassia leads north to the vast Piazza Re, with the **Chiesa Madre** dedicated to St Basil. The church has a sumptuous curving Baroque façade, and a tall campanile crowned by a spire. Inside is a towering altar, 10m high, with a wooden statue of St Vitus (Giuseppe Picano, 1790). The little town has some fine 18th-century buildings and a public garden, from whence, beyond hills flushed with ochre and crimson on the left, there is a splendid view ahead of Etna. The plain is filled with lustrous green citrus groves, many of them protected from the wind by 'walls' of olive trees, and Centuripe can be seen on its hill to the right.

CENTURIPE & ENVIRONS

Centuripe (*map p. 537, C2*) is lonely and remote, a cascade of coloured houses surrounded by harsh countryside; hills dappled with light, an occasional prickly pear, a few almond trees. The city has grown out in five directions on the top of its ridge, like a starfish. Founded by the Sicels and known by the Greeks as *Kentoripa*, it occupies a superb commanding position facing Etna, at a height of 719m; when Garibaldi saw it in 1862 he aptly named it '*il balcone della Sicilia*'. With the advent of Greek colonisation, the city maintained good relations with the newcomers, but later she discovered that her true sympathies lay with Rome, an alliance that brought prosperity, wealth, power and the gratitude of Augustus, who rebuilt the town after the destruction wreaked by Sextus Pompey during the Civil War in the 1st century BC. In the early Middle Ages decadence set in, although it remained an important strategic stronghold. The people made the mistake of rebelling against Frederick II of Hohenstaufen in 1232, who got his revenge by forcibly removing the entire population to Palermo after razing Centuripe and its castle to the ground (an incorrect, but widely reported, reading of the sources has led to the idea that he sent them instead to the southeast coast, to found the city of Augusta). Some people trickled back, however, and started rebuilding; but it was a forlorn effort. Crushed once more in 1268 by Charles I of Anjou, it was not until 1548 that it was re-founded by Francesco Moncada. Its capture by the Allies in 1943 caused the Germans to abandon Sicily.

Exploring Centuripe

The town centre is the piazza near the 18th century pink and white **Chiesa Madre**, with an attractive symmetrical façade with a clock in the middle and bell-tower above. On the edge of the cliff an avenue of pines leads to the remains of a monument on a knoll, of Roman (2nd century AD) origin, which resembles a mausoleum. Locally it is known as **Il Corradino** in allusion to a certain Corrado Capece, a Swabian who probably fortified this monument while supporting Conradin of Swabia against the Angevins. He surrendered under false promises, and was tortured and executed at

Catania. There are impressive views from this point. Another 2nd-century AD Roman funerary monument, originally similar to this one and known locally as *La Dogana*, is to be found on the northern limits of the town, not far from an enigmatic Roman Imperial monument known as *La Panneria*.

The archaeological and anthropological museums

In Via Giulio Cesare is the regional archaeological museum (*open 9–7; T: 0935 73079, ticket includes visit to the Anthropological Museum, www.museocenturipe.it*), housing a display of some 3,000 objects discovered in the area, including a few of the famous **Centuripe vases**. Unfortunately, a large part of the collection was stolen while the museum was being built. The vases are unique in Sicily for their shape and decoration. The terracotta itself is a particularly rich hazelnut colour, and the ceramicists decorated the pieces further by picking out details in relief before firing, and adding brightly-coloured painted motifs afterwards. They date to the 3rd and 2nd centuries BC. More recently, in the 19th century, and especially after the Second World War, its particular beauty gave rise to a rash of illegal, clandestine excavations for the black market, supported by unscrupulous collectors. Several local craftsmen also proved to be adept at faking old vases, some of which apparently still hold pride of place in important museums of the world. Today, however, the craftsmen are limiting their activities to making souvenirs for tourists.

The museum is organised on three floors. The ground floor presents the local prehistoric sites side by side with a marvellous bust of Hadrian and a rich collection of Imperial sculpture found in the Sede degli Augustali (*see overleaf*). On the first floor there are displays about the various aspects of life in the Hellenistic city, and an interesting section about the forging of the Centuripe vases, and objects found in clandestine excavations. The second floor has material from the necropoleis, including an interesting reconstruction of a typical tomb, spanning the period from the first Sicel inhabitants in the 8th century BC to Roman cinerary urns.

The museum is conveniently situated in the archaeological area and the remains are all within walking distance. The local people are extremely friendly, proud of their town, and more than willing to show visitors around. In the valley (Vallone Difesa), east of the town, excavations beneath and near the church of the Crocifisso

Example of a Centuripe-type vase of painted terracotta, in the form of a kylix with a distinctive conical lid.

have revealed an important 2nd-century AD edifice, known as the **Sede degli Augustali**. To the northwest in Vallone dei Bagni, is a large Roman thermal edifice with five niches. Close by in Via Genova, in what used to be the slaughterhouse, is the **Anthropological Museum** (*open 9–1.30 & 3–7; T: 0935 919093*), a well-arranged collection of tools, furniture, and equipment used until quite recently by farmers, artisans and labourers.

On the road to Adrano, near the Ponte del Maccarone, a large **aqueduct** (31 arches) constructed in 1761–66 by the Prince of Biscari can be seen.

Catenanuova

South of Centuripe and close to the motorway is the prosperous farming community of Catenanuova (*map p. 537, C2*), overlooking the River Dittaino, and founded in the 18th century in a strategic spot on the Palermo–Catania road. Goethe stayed here during his travels in Sicily in 1787, and appreciated the legendary hospitality of the people. In 1714, when the Duke of Savoy (proclaimed King Vittorio Amedeo II of Sicily the year before, although forced by the Great Powers to drop the title in exchange for Sardinia) and Queen Anna were passing through Catenanuova, a local baron ordered his farmworkers to pour all that day's milk into a nearby stream, thus creating for their majesties a river of milk. The royal pair were suitably impressed, and the baron was made captain of the Royal Guard.

NICOSIA & THE NORTH

Founded by the Byzantines with the name meaning 'victorious', **Nicosia** (*map p. 537, B1*) became a place of some importance in the Middle Ages, and was given by Count Roger to his Lombard troops, hence the noticeable local dialect. The beautiful stonebuilt medieval city was damaged by a landslide in 1757, by an earthquake in 1968, and by a flood in 1972. It is known locally as the town with two cathedrals and two Christs, because for a time the churches of Santa Maria Maggiore (Byzantine rite) and San Nicola (Latin rite) took turns in being the cathedral, and therefore two processions for Good Friday were organised, with two Crucifixes—and considerable rivalry between the two groups, sometimes resulting in bloodshed.

EXPLORING NICOSIA

The cathedral (San Nicola)

The cathedral of San Nicola di Bari has an elegant 15th-century portico with six slender marble columns. The Arab-Norman bell-tower is one of the most important in Sicily: 40m high, it consists of three sections, in three different architectural styles. The base of the tower once formed part of a defensive structure, devised by the Arabs to protect the castle. The decorative 14th-century main door is in extremely poor repair; the entrance is through the north door.

Dormition of the Virgin. Detail of the marble high altarpiece in Santa Maria Maggiore, Nicosia, the work of Antonello Gagini (1512).

In the Latin-cross interior, a new vault was erected in the early 19th century, unfortunately covering the 15th-century trussed and painted wooden ceiling, among the most important in Sicily. The paintings, in panels representing saints, angels and mysterious personages, alternating with borders of fruits, flowers and geometric designs, have been newly restored, and it is possible to see them close-up from a viewing platform (*a virtual reconstruction of the panels can be seen at the Centro Civico in Palazzo Nicosia, opposite the Town Hall*). Over the second south altar is a *Martyrdom of St Placidus* by Giacinto Platania. The 16th-century pulpit is attributed to Gian Domenico Gagini. In the right transept is a Gaginesque statue of the *Madonna of Victory*. Suspended over the crossing, in the octagonal vault, surrounded by 17th-century paintings, is an unusually large statue of St Nicholas by Giovanni Battista Li Volsi. In the chapel to the right of the high altar is a venerated wooden Crucifix by Fra' Umile da Petralia, called *Padre della Provvidenza*, one of the two carried in procession through the town on Good Friday. In the presbytery the intricately-carved walnut choir-stalls (c. 1622; with a relief showing the old town of Nicosia) are by Giovanni Battista Li Volsi and his son Stefano, while the altarpiece is a *Resurrection* by Giuseppe Velasquez. In the chapel to the left of the high altar is delightful polychrome marble decoration. On the left side is a font by Antonello Gagini and, in the base of the bell-tower, the funerary monument of Alessandro Testa by Ignazio Marabitti. In the chapter-house (*opened by the sacristan on request*) are some more fine paintings, including the *Madonna with Sts John and Rosalia* by Pietro Novelli, the *Martyrdom of St Sebastian* by Salvator Rosa, and the *Martyrdom of St Bartholomew* by Jusepe de Ribera, 'Lo Spagnoletto'.

Santa Maria Maggiore and the rest of town

Further uphill is the imposing **Santa Maria Maggiore**, with a handsome Baroque portal, once belonging to an aristocratic palace and donated by the family when the church (founded by Count Roger, c.1062) was being rebuilt after the 1757 landslide. The campanile collapsed in 1968, and the bells were re-hung on a low iron bracket beside the façade. The interior, a central nave and two aisles separated by pilasters, contains a huge painted marble high altarpiece by Antonello Gagini (1512; *see illustration on previous page*), over 10m high, carved with scenes from the life of the Virgin. A statue in the left transept of the *Madonna* is thought to be by Francesco Laurana. There is a view from the terrace of the modern buildings of the town, and the church of San Salvatore perched on a rock. Via Carlo V and Via del Castello lead up behind Santa Maria Maggiore to the ruins of the **Norman castle**. The views from here are splendid.

From Piazza Garibaldi, Via Fratelli Testa, a narrow alley with lots of steps, leads up to a rocky outcrop at the top of the hill, and the 13th-century church of San Salvatore, rebuilt in the 17th century, with an attractive portico and bell-tower. On the outside wall of the tower are the ***Calendari delle Rondinelle***, carved stones giving the arrival and departure dates of the house-martins, from 1737–98 and from 1837–45. In the opposite direction, it leads down past the closed churches of San Calogero (with a fine ceiling and works by Filippo Randazzo) and Sant'Antonio Abate, ending at Via Li Volsi with (left) the church of the Carmine which contains statues of the Angel Gabriel and Virgin Annunciate attributed to Antonello Gagini. At the top of Via Li Volsi, which is lined with trees, the Baroque façade of Palazzo Speciale can be seen, now propped up with concrete pillars.

In the 14th-century church of **San Michele** (just east of Nicosia) is a 16th-century font and two wooden statues by Giovanni Battista Li Volsi; the marble statue of St Michael Archangel is a youthful work by Antonello Gagini.

The landscape is particularly beautiful east of Nicosia, with frequent glimpses of Etna in the distance. In the rugged countryside at the foot of the Nebrodi mountains the fields are dotted with *pagliari*, conical huts of straw and mud, used by the shepherds as temporary refuges.

SPERLINGA

Sperlinga (*map p. 537, B1*) is the only Sicilian town which took no part in the Vespers: on an arch inside the castle are inscribed the words *Quod Siculis placuit, sola Sperlinga negavit* ('What pleased the Sicilians, was shunned only by Sperlinga'). By offering refuge to the Angevins, Sperlinga earned herself a reputation for betrayal which is still remembered today. The approach road offers beautiful views over the valley. The village is a delightful little place at the foot of the conspicuous castle rock; part of the town and all of the castle are carved into the stone. The people base their economy on raising cattle and sheep. The road enters the town past the 17th-century church of Sant'Anna and on the right you will see some cave dwellings, inhabited until recently and now protected by the local administration as an urban park.

Further along the main road, a road (signposted right) leads up past the large 17th-century Chiesa Madre to a car park just below the entrance to the **castle** (*open 9–1 & 4–7; T: 0935 643265*), which probably goes back to the days of the Sicels; recent archaeological surveys have found a small prehistoric sanctuary with a Mycenaean-type domed roof, and a chamber with twelve niches, illuminated by the sun passing through a hole in a similar domed roof. Two grottoes are used as local ethnographical museums with agricultural implements. Steps lead up across a small bridge (on the site of the drawbridge) through the double entrance. Stables, carved out of the rock in the Middle Ages, were later used as prisons. In one room are old photographs of Sperlinga, some taken during Operation Husky in 1943 by the great photographer Robert Capa. From a terrace a flight of high steps hewn out of the rock leads up to the battlements from which there are wonderful panoramic views.

Between Sperlinga and Gangi is an old fortified farmhouse near a **chapel dedicated to St Venera**, long the scene of country fairs in her honour; traces have now been discovered of an ancient processional route sacred to the goddess Cybele, leading to a spur with altars carved into the rock, illegible inscriptions, and many tombs, one of which has the form of a perfect tholos.

TROINA & ENVIRONS

Troina (*map p. 537, C1*), on a steep ridge, is the highest town in Sicily (1121m). Its early capture by the Normans in 1061 is recalled by Norman work (1078–80) in the Chiesa Madre which has a 16th-century campanile, and a Byzantine panel-painting of the *Madonna*. Count Roger and his young bride Adelaide allegedly spent a very cold winter in the castle in 1061, with little food, sharing one blanket between them, while they were besieged by Greeks and Arabs who had improvised an alliance. Count Roger also instituted the first of his Basilian monasteries here, and in 1082 made it the first diocese of the island, entrusting it to a bishop of his own choice. Nothing much remains of the castle, which must have been imposing; the Normans maintained the Royal Treasury here for many years, even after taking Palermo. Parts of the Greek walls remain, and the Belvedere has a superb view.

In a breathtaking position among the mountains, south of Troina, is **Gagliano Castelferrato** (*map p. 537, B2*), a picturesque village dominated by a huge rock which incorporates the castle. The numerous tombs carved into the rock show that the mountain has been inhabited continuously since the early Bronze Age. Though the castle resisted the Arab onslaughts, the town acquired importance under their domination, and later under the Normans. The Chiesa Madre (1304), by the castle ruins, has a plain façade and a spire covered with brightly coloured majolica tiles, and is dedicated to the Irish saint Cathald, who preached widely in Sicily. Inside is an old organ and a lovely 16th-century carved wooden choir. In the southern part of the village is the church of Santa Maria di Gesù, which contains an impressive wooden Crucifix by Fra' Umile da Petralia.

West of Troina, **Cerami** (*map p. 537, B1*) is a little medieval town on a crest, built on top of a series of earlier settlements; it was the scene in July 1063 of a decisive victory of Count Roger's Lombard troops over the Muslims. Four camels taken from the enemy were presented to Pope Alexander II. The name derives from the Greek *Keramion*, meaning terracotta. The church of the Carmine houses a Crucifix by Fra' Umile da Petralia, while over the main altar in the abbey-church of San Benedetto is a charming, newly-restored 17th-century painting on slate of the *Madonna and Child*, known to the local people as the *Madonna della Lavina* because it was found in a torrent (*lavina*), and said to be miraculous. It has recently been attributed to Pietro Antonio Novelli, the father of 'Il Monrealese'.

To the north of Cerami, **Lake Ancipa** or Sartori, at a height of 949m and full of fish, was formed in 1952 when the River Troina was dammed for hydro-electric works; the dam itself is 120m high. There is a nature reserve run by the Azienda Forestale, where the two peaks of the Nebrodi chain, Monte Sambuchetti (1559m) and Monte Campanito (1514m), are protected for their flourishing beech forest, the southernmost in Europe. Other trees include chestnuts, varieties of oak (including the cork oak), holly and maple; the wildlife includes the endemic form of the marsh tit, the wildcat and pine marten.

PRACTICAL INFORMATION

• **By train:** Enna railway station (*T: 0935 501228*) is in the valley, 5km from the town centre, on the Palermo–Catania line. On the same line are Villarosa, Leonforte (Stazione di Pirato) and Centuripe (nearest station Catenanuova at 15km; *www.trenitalia.it*).
• **By bus:** The bus station (*T: 0935 500902, opens 11am*) in **Enna** is in Viale Diaz. **Troina** has a shuttle-bus leaving every 20mins, connecting Piazza Conte Ruggero and Loggiato Sant'Agostino.

Etna Trasporti /INTERBUS/Segesta (*www.interbus.it*) run services for most towns in Sicily, including Catania airport, Aidone, Piazza Armerina and Valguarnera.
Fratelli Romano Autolinee (*T: 0935 73114*) run a few buses to Centuripe and Catania.
ISEA Autolinee (*www.iseaviaggi.it*) for Catania, Nicosia and Troina.
SAIS Autolinee (*www.saisautolinee.it*) runs the bus service in Enna itself, also inter-city coaches for many places in Sicily, including Catania airport (75mins from Enna). Destinations within the province include Aidone,

Barrafranca, Calascibetta, Enna, Piazza Armerina, Pietraperzia, Sperlinga and Valguarnera.

WHERE TO STAY

Aidone (*map p. 537, B3*)
€ **Morgantina**. Friendly and welcoming if
somewhat Spartan modern building in the
centre of Aidone with 27 rooms (some with
views of the mountains), restaurant, and a car
park. *Via Adelasia 42 (Piazza Cordova), T: 0935
88088, www.hotelmorgantina.it.*

Assoro (*map p. 537, B2*)
€ **Casa Museo Elio Romano**. 5 comfortable
rooms in the fascinating country house of
a local artist and anthropologist. Car park,
airport/station shuttle on request. *Contrada
Morra, SP Acquanuova–Morra km 5.2, T: 338
1137595, 328 8737060, francesco.1509@
hotmail.it.*

Centuripe (*map p. 537, C2*)
€€ *Kento Park*. Hillside position between
Centuripe and Mt Etna, elegant little hotel
with 10 rooms and suites, large wooded
garden, pool, car park, panoramic restaurant,
shuttle-bus for Centuripe. *Contrada Ta-
gliacasse, T: 0935 74205, www.kentoparkhotel.it.*

Enna (*map p. 537, B2*)
€ **Grande Albergo Sicilia**. Popular, central
hotel with car park and 60 comfortable
rooms, many with views. No restaurant.
*Piazza Colajanni 7, T: 0935 500850, www.
hotelsiciliaenna.it. Map p. 247, 1.*

Leonforte (*map p. 537, B2*)
€€€ **Villa Gussio**. Elegant 17th-century
country house full of frescoes and Baroque
stucco reliefs, approached by a magnificent
stone stairway, with 49 rooms, library, pools,
tennis and golf, fitness centre, excellent restaurant making much use of local ingredients,
such as the late-ripening peaches or the broad
beans, when in season. *Contrada Rossi (Stazione Pirato; just south of Leonforte on the SS121,*

km 94.75), T: 0935 903268, www.villagussio.it.
Nicosia (*map p. 537, B1*)
€ **Umberto I**. A welcoming B&B in the heart
of town; 3 comfortable rooms. *Corso Umberto
34, T: 0935 361135, 347 1535382.*
Piazza Armerina (*map p. 537, B3*)
€€€ **Villa Trigona**. ■ A short way from
town to the south, the homely and friendly
country seat of the princes of Piazza Armerina, 15 pleasant rooms with antique furnishings, good food. *Contrada Bauccio, T: 0935
681896, 333 3999601, www.villatrigona.it.*
€€ **La Casa sulla Collina d'Oro**. Small
relais in a panoramic position overlooking the
old town, 6 comfortable rooms with private
bathrooms, car park, shuttle service to/from
Catania airport or station on request. *Via
Mattarella, T: 0935 89680, 333 4668829, www.
lacasasullacollinadoro.it.*
€ **Del Centro**. B&B in the central square,
5 large rooms on two floors, lovely Sicilian
breakfasts in the bar down below. *Piazza
Garibaldi, T: 0935 681900, 328 4553530, 339
7054250, www.bandbdelcentro.com.*
€ **La Volpe e L'Uva**. Welcoming B&B in the
heart of town, 3 comfortable rooms, excellent
breakfasts. *Via Santa Veneranda 35, T: 0935
680752, 328 4455062, 329 1661188, www.
volpeuva.it.*
€ **Gangi**. Comfortable little hotel (the oldest
in town) in a medieval palace near the public
gardens, 19 small, spotless rooms, nice breakfasts, no restaurant. *Via Generale Ciancio 68,
T: 0935 682737, www.hotelgangi.it.*
€ **Mosaici da Battiato**. ■ Country inn within walking distance of the Roman villa, car
park, 23 quiet rooms, very good restaurant
serving robust local cuisine; excellent grilled
mutton (*castrato*). *Contrada Casale Paratore 11,
T: 0935 685453, www.hotelmosaici.com.*
Pietraperzia (*map p. 537, A3*)
€ **Marconi**. Central, modern building with
23 rooms, breakfast but no restaurant. On

request you can sleep in their Neolithic cave. *Via Kennedy 5, T: 0934 461983, www.hotelmarconi.sicilia.it.*

Regalbuto (*map p. 537, C2*)

€ **Castel Miralago.** Country hotel overlooking Lake Pozzillo, 26 rooms all with panoramic views, good restaurant much favoured for wedding banquets. Good value for money. *Località Pettoruta (just west of town), SS 121 km 60, T: 0935 72810, www.hotelcastelmiralago.it.*

Villarosa (*map p. 537, A2*)

€€ **San Giovannello.** 4km north of Villarosa and close to the sulphur mine, the farm offers 6 comfortable rooms and an apartment, all with TV and air conditioning. The farm produces organic durum and timilia wheat and, in alternate years, vegetables and pulses; also saffron (you can buy the products and the saffron bulbs). *Contrada San Giovannello, T: 0935 31260, 328 8677270, www.sangiovannello.it.*

WHERE TO EAT

Aidone (*map p. 537, B3*)

€€ **La Vecchia Aidone.** In an ancient *palazzo* with a small garden, restaurant serving simple, delicious local dishes, very well presented; open fireplace makes it cosy in winter. Closed Mon. *Via Cordova 88, T: 0935 87863.*

Enna (*map p. 537, B2*)

€€ **Bottiglieria Belvedere.** Wine bar and restaurant, good assortment of cheeses, ham and salami, absolutely delicious risotto and pasta dishes; the menu changes every day. Closed Sun. *Via Vulturo 26, T: 0935 23396. Map p. 247, 1.*

Leonforte (*map p. 537, B2*)

€ **La Piramide.** Homely atmosphere, simple food in generous portions; excellent grilled meat, vegetables, also pizza. Local wines. Closed Mon. *Via Pirandello 26, T: 0935 902121.*

Morgantina (*map p. 537, B3*)

€ **Eyexei.** ■ The name means 'welcome' in Greek (inspired by the floor mosaic in the House of the Doric Capital), and this country restaurant close to the ruins offers a welcome break after hours of exploring. Local dishes, home-made food, presented with their own wines. *T: 0935 87074.*

Piazza Armerina (*map p. 537, B3*)

€€€ **Al Fogher.** In an old railway building at the crossroads on the 117b just before reaching the town from the north. Chef Angelo Treno presents an imaginative blend of tradition and new ideas. Closed Sun evening and Mon. *Contrada Bellia, T: 0935 684123, 339 1579005.*

€ **Da Gianna.** Very simple family-run *trattoria*, excellent *antipasti*, good fresh fish from Licata, also meat and vegetable dishes; generous helpings. Closed Mon. *Commenda dei Cavalieri di Malta (yellow awning), T: 347 3064581.*

€ There are places to eat behind the car park at the **ruins of the Villa del Casale.** Simple food and good wine at very reasonable prices.

LOCAL SPECIALITIES

Centuripe At Ken Art Ceramica (*Via Lazio 67, www.kenart.it*) you will find perfect replicas of antique pottery. For very special confectionery, unique to Centuripe, go to Pasticceria Centrale (*Piazza Sciacca 11*).

Enna The historic coffee-house is Caffé Italia (*Via Mastro Chiaramonte 12*), for superb coffee, breakfast pastries and *granita*. Campisi (*Piazza Umberto 22*) is a bakery where they still make *ciabattina*, miners' bread which lasts a week, and simple local biscuits.

Piazza Armerina Pasticceria Diana (*Piazza Generale Cascino 34*) is famous for the typical local nougat, thin chewy toffee squares with nuts, cherries and candied citron, covered with white or plain chocolate.

Sperlinga A special cake is made here called *tortone*, with durum-wheat flour, olive oil, cinnamon and sugar. Try it at Bar Li Calzi (*Piazza Marconi 1*).

FESTIVALS & EVENTS

Agira Christmas Eve: A Living Crib, the only one in Italy to take place on Christmas Night, a play and procession involving hundreds of locals, starting in the old town and finishing under the castle (*Info: www. presepeviventeagira.it*).

Aidone Palm Sunday: *I Santuni*, procession of 12 giant figures representing the Apostles, each carrying his symbol.

Cerami 27–28 August: Procession for St Sebastian, including a cavalcade of riders in Roman costume.

Enna Holy Week: the religious ceremonies culminate with a Procession of the Confraternities on Good Friday; probably the eeriest of the Easter celebrations in Sicily, because it takes place in total silence. Starting in the afternoon, 2,000 hooded representatives of the 15 corporations solemnly escort the symbols of the Passion through the town, from the church of San Leonardo to the duomo, then to the Addolorata. They wear a wooden number around their necks which is passed down from father to son.

First week of June until 2 July: Festivities for the *Madonna della Visitazione*, which almost certainly go back to the ancient rites for Demeter and Persephone. The celebrations begin a month before, finishing with

124 barefoot bearers carrying the statue of the Madonna in procession, on a magnificent float called the *nave d'oro*, the golden ship, made by Scipione di Guido in 1590.

Gagliano Castelferrato 29–31 August: Feast of the patron St Cathald, with a procession of farmers riding horses, donkeys and mules carrying branches of laurel to the church for blessing on the first day; the urn with the relics is carried through the town on the second; and finally the statue of the saint.

Leonforte Oct: celebrations for the unique late-ripening peaches, *Sagra delle Pesche*, with many gastronomical opportunities (*Info: www. sagradellepesche.it*).

Piazza Armerina 19 March: San Giuseppe, with the traditional banquets and ornamental loaves. July, Jazz in Piazza, a four-day festival with jam sessions and concerts, involving musicians from all over Italy (*Info: www.piazzajazz.it*). 12–14 August: *Palio dei Normanni*, medieval jousting to celebrate Count Roger's victory over the Saracens. 15 August: Our Lady of the Victories procession: the banner given to Count Roger returns to the cathedral.

Pietraperzia Good Friday: *'U Signuri di li Fasci*, procession through the streets of the Crucifix on top of a tall standard, to which the faithful tie strips of linen 36m long as ex-voto. 15 August: an hour after midnight, Mass is held in a cave for the *Madonna della Cava*, followed by an open-air feast.

Troina 2 January: Feast of St Sylvester, during which the crowd is pelted with hazelnuts. This much-loved saint is also celebrated in May, June and Sept.

THE PROVINCE OF RAGUSA

Ragusa, smallest of the Sicilian provinces, is also one of the wealthiest. Off-shore oil wells provide a sizeable proportion of the national requirement. The hill towns of the area, devastated by earthquake in the late 17th century, were rebuilt with opulent Sicilian Baroque-style churches and palaces, a concerted architectural accomplishment that represents, in its quality and consistency, a vivid final flowering of the style in Italy. Some of them, such as Ragusa, Modica and Scicli, are now UNESCO World Heritage Sites, and apart from their beauty, they enjoy a good reputation for their cuisine and hospitality. The landscape is a limestone plateau, deeply scored by waterways, which have formed canyons and gorges luxuriant with vegetation in their depths. The uplands provide smooth green pastures, a chequerboard of tidy dry-stone walls, dotted with the intense green, almost black, of the shady carob trees, the shimmering foliage of ancient olives, and the contorted almonds which surround old stone farmhouses. The limestone rises to form the Monti Iblei (Hyblaean Mountains), named after a great king of the Sicels, Hyblon.

RAGUSA SUPERIORE & RAGUSA IBLA

In the southern part of the Hyblaean mountain range, the town of Ragusa Superiore (*map p. 538, C2*) is an elegant provincial capital laid out after the earthquake of 1693, on a spot chosen by a group of survivors as being more suitable for their new city—the others stayed where they were, and rebuilt Ragusa Ibla. Ragusa Superiore occupies a ridge that runs from west to east between two deep gorges, and has expanded across the river gorge to the south, where three breathtaking bridges now connect it to the modern town. On another hill just below it to the east is Ragusa Ibla, an old town of finely carved golden stone, one of the best preserved in Sicily. An intricate maze of stepped streets, it is connected to the upper town by a steep winding road. The two centres have many exceptionally fine Baroque palaces and churches.

EXPLORING RAGUSA SUPERIORE

The cathedral

The monumental, creamy-gold **cathedral of San Giovanni Battista** (*map 2*), built after 1694 by Mario Spada of Ragusa and Rosario Boscarino of Modica, has a wide façade with a pretty campanile and spire. It dominates Piazza San Giovanni, at the centre of the well-kept upper town. The Latin-cross interior, suffused with light from the cupola, houses richly decorated chapels and many works of art: paintings, including a canvas of *St Philip Neri* by Sebastiano Conca, gilded stuccoes; marble and wooden statues; and a monumental organ. Fronting the cathedral is a terrace and small garden.

HISTORY OF RAGUSA

Ragusa Ibla occupies the site of the Sicel *Hybla Heraea*; the Romans called it *Heresium*, and the Byzantines *Reusia*; during their rule it was repeatedly attacked by Vandals, Goths and Visigoths. The Arabs refounded it as *Rakkusa*, an important centre for trade and agriculture. The county of Ragusa, created in 1091 by Count Roger for his son Godfrey, was united in 1296 by Manfredi Chiaramonte with that of Modica. The Chiaramontes were succeeded by the Cabrera family, most of whom were disliked by the people of Ragusa, resulting in a rebellion in 1448. Because of this the seat of government was transferred to Modica, which became one of the most important towns in Sicily until 1926. After the Val di Noto earthquake of 1693, which killed 60,000 people, 5,000 of whom were the inhabitants of Ragusa, the wealthy aristocracy, who were devoted to St George, decided to rebuild the town where it was (Ibla), while the equally wealthy middle class, who were devoted to St Joseph, decided they wanted a modern city with a rational street plan, and chose a new site to the west (Ragusa Superiore). The two groups, with the encouragement of the clergy, competed in building a large number of beautiful churches (in 1644 there were 41 churches for a population of 15,000), but considerable controversy arose over which of the two could legitimately house the cathedral. Rivalry continued for centuries, and because of the friction, the upper and lower towns became separate communities from 1695 to 1703, and from 1865 to 1926, when they were united again as a new provincial capital.

The area is known for its asphalt mines. The limestone impregnated with bitumen hardens quickly in contact with the air, providing an attractive black stone which can be easily worked, while the bitumen itself has been used for paving the streets of many Italian and European cities. Oil was found here in 1953, and there used to be oil wells scattered about the upper town. Drilling now takes place offshore, and the oil is piped from Marina di Ragusa to Augusta. Numerous small farms in the area provide durum wheat, olives, fruit, vegetables, and also milk from the local breed of cattle, Modicana, used for making excellent cheese, especially the famous *caciocavallo*. Close to the sea, where the Arabs cultivated sugar cane, are market gardens, protected by plastic frames in winter, hence in production year-round.

Around the cathedral

Next to the cathedral is the **Diocesan Museum** (*open 9–12.30 & 4–6; T: 0932 621658*), with a precious collection of works of art from the churches, many dating back to before the earthquake. Just beyond the east end of the cathedral is the elegant 18th-century Casa Canonica. Across Corso Italia is the imposing façade of the collegiate church of Santa Maria Addolorata (1801), next to its convent.

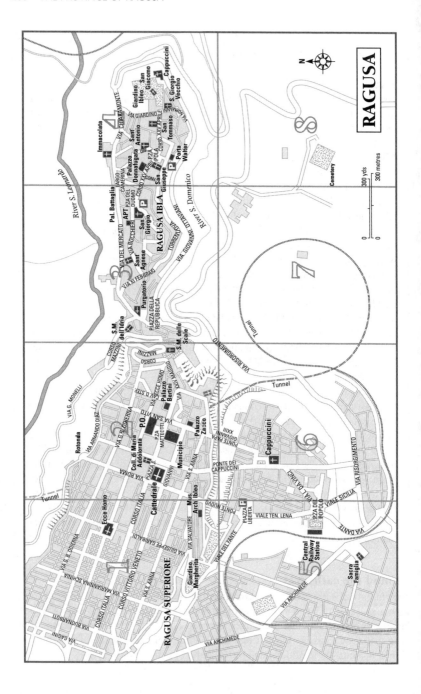

RAGUSA

N

300 yds
300 metres

River S. Leonardo

Cemetery

RAGUSA IBLA

Cappuccini
Giardino Ibleo· San Giacomo
S. Giorgio Vecchio
Immacolata
VIA GIARDINO
VIA CHIARAMONTE
Sant' Antonio
San Tommaso
CORSO XXV APRILE
Palazzo Donnafugata
PZA POLA
San Giuseppe
Porta Walter
LARGO CAMERINA
Pal. Battaglia
APT
PZA DEL DUOMO
CORSO XXV APRILE
VIA DEL MERCATO
VIA BOCCHIERI
San Giorgio
TORRENUOVA
VIA GIOVANNI DI QUIVOVA
River S. Domenico
Sant' Agnese
VIA XI FEBBRAIO
Purgatorio
PIAZZA DELLA REPUBBLICA
S.M. delle Scale
S.M. dell'Idria
Tunnel

7

Tunnel

CORSO MAZZINI
VIA G. MONELLI
CORSO MAZZINI
VIA ARMANDO DIAZ
VIA RISORGIMENTO
VIA ECCE HOMO
VIA DI STEF
VIA XX SETTEMBRE
Palazzo Bertini
Rotonda
P.O.
VIA B. CADERNA
Coll. di Maria Addolorata
VIA SAN VITO
PZA S. MATTEOTTI
Palazzo Zacco
VIA S. ANNA
VIA ROMA
Municipio
PZA S. GIOVANNI
Ecce Homo
Cattedrale
Mus. Archeologico Ibleo
PONTE DEI CAPPUCCINI
PONTE PAPA GIOVANNI XXIII
Cappuccini
PONTE NUOVO
VIA SALVATORE
VIA DEL FANTE
VIALE DUOMO
PIAZZA LIBERTA
VIALE TEN. LENA
PZA DEL POPOLO
VIALE SICILIA
VIA DANTE
VIA DA TINCI
VIA RISORGIMENTO

RAGUSA SUPERIORE
Giardino Margherita
CORSO ITALIA
VIA C. B. CADERNA
CORSO GIUSEPPE GARIBALDI
CORSO VITTORIO VENETO
VIA S. ANNA
VIA MARIANNINA SCHININA
VIA BUONARROTI
VIA GAGINI
Central Railway Station
Sacra Famiglia
VIALE ARCHIMEDE
VIA ARCHIMEDE

Corso Italia, the handsome long main street, lined with trees, descends steeply to the edge of the hill above Ibla. Uphill, above the cathedral, it crosses Via Roma, which to the north ends in a belvedere, **La Rotonda** (*map 2*), with a view of Ibla and the San Leonardo canyon. Going south on Via Roma takes you towards **Ponte Nuovo** (*map 1–5; 1937*), which crosses the little Santa Domenica stream high above the public gardens of Villa Margherita. From the bridge, there is a good view (left) of Ponte dei Cappuccini (1835) and Ponte Papa Giovanni XXIII (1964) beyond. Across the bridge is **Piazza Libertà** (*map 5*), with Fascist-era buildings, and the modern town.

Museo Archeologico Ibleo

Just before the Ponte Nuovo bridge, in a building beneath the road viaduct which also houses the Hotel Mediterraneo, is the Museo Archeologico Ibleo (*map 1; open 9–1.30, 4.30–7.30. T: 0932 622963*). The collection displays finds from the province, dating from prehistory to Roman times. In the **prehistoric section**, the Bronze-Age civilisation of Castelluccio is particularly well represented. Pride of place in the museum is given to a unique sculpture known as the ***Warrior of Castiglione***, discovered by a farmer in 1999 while ploughing his field north of Ragusa. Made to fit over a door, this carved stone probably stood over the entrance to a warrior's tomb. Castiglione would have been a Sicel centre when this warrior died at the end of the 7th century BC. The relief, carved from a single block of local limestone, shows the warrior on horseback with his shield in front, at one side a bull and at the other a sphinx, probably symbolising his nobility (horse), strength (bull) and wisdom (sphinx). The carving bears an inscription with the name of the warrior, 'Pyrrinos son of Pyttikas', and is even signed by the sculptor, Skyllos, very unusually for the times.

Another section displays **finds from Kamarina** from the Archaic to the Classical period, while yet another is dedicated to the inland indigenous centres inhabited by the Sicels; in case 15 is a rare **Ionic vase** with an inscription in the Sicel language. Further on, a **potter's workshop** from the ancient site at Scornavacche near Chiaramonte Gulfi (its ancient name is as yet unknown) has been reconstructed, and the terracotta figurines are particularly interesting. The **Roman section** includes finds from Kaukana, and early Christian mosaics from Santa Croce Camerina.

Towards Ragusa Ibla

Corso Italia descends steeply from Piazza San Giovanni to **Piazza Matteotti**, passing on the right at no. 90 the 18th-century Palazzo Lupis, with ornamented balconies and corbels. Here is the Municipio (Town Hall; 1880; enlarged 1929) opposite the monumental Post Office (1930), with colossal statues on the top. In the centre of the square is a large fountain with bronze dolphins. Corso Italia next crosses Via San Vito in which, on the right, is the fine Baroque **Palazzo Zacco**, with the magnificent family coat of arms on the corner of the building and elaborate balcony corbels.

Further down Corso Italia is the late 18th-century **Palazzo Bertini** (no. 35), famous for its three grotesque gargoyles known as i *Tre Potenti*. They are usually interpreted as representing Poverty, Aristocracy and Wealth. The Corso ends at Via XXIV Maggio, with two palaces at the corner, which narrows and becomes steeper as it begins the descent to Ragusa Ibla (called *iusu* by the local people, meaning 'down'), now seen in its magnificent position on a separate spur. At the foot of an elegant Baroque palace, a small tabernacle recalls a cholera epidemic here in 1838; in front, wide steps descend to an appealing group of houses with courtyards, overlooking the valley. The road continues downhill, passing the pretty **Via Pezza** (left), which runs along the hillside, and **Via Ecce Homo** which climbs uphill to the left. Via XXIV Maggio ends at the balcony beside the bell-tower of **Santa Maria delle Scale** (*map 2*), where there is a superb bird's-eye view of Ragusa Ibla, with its beautiful expanse of tiled roofs, in various shades of terracotta, grey and gold. The large building on the top of the hill is an old military barracks occupying the site of the castle of the Chiaramonte family. Many fragments of the 15th-century structure of the church (*open for Mass only, 7.30, holidays also 11*) survived the 1693 earthquake. Outside, beneath the campanile, is part of a Gothic doorway and the remains of an outside pulpit. Inside is an elaborate Gothic arch decorated with sculptures and (over a side altar) a relief of the *Dormition of the Virgin* in coloured terracotta, by the Gagini school (1538).

RAGUSA IBLA

Crumbling away on its hilltop, with a maze of mysterious, inviting little stepped streets, Ragusa Ibla lends itself to exploration on foot. UNESCO recognition, a new university, and use as a location for the extremely popular Police Inspector Montalbano TV series, have saved it from depopulation, which was becoming a problem in recent years; many old houses are being restored, and there are several delightful small hotels. Ibla can be reached from Ragusa Superiore by the zig-zag Corso Mazzini (*map 2*), or on foot by various flights of steps. By the road is a relief of the *Flight into Egypt* (15th–16th century), probably once part of a votive tabernacle. Also on the way is the delightful **Palazzo Nicastro** (or Vecchia Cancelleria), erected in 1760 and once the seat of government, with tall pilasters, a decorative doorway, and windows with large balconies.

To the left is the bell-tower and little dome decorated with blue majolica tiles of the church of **Santa Maria dell'Idria** or San Giuliano (*map 3*), built in 1626 for the Knights of Malta, and rebuilt after the devastating earthquake: the cross of the Order can be seen over the doorway. The interior is sumptuously decorated. The Salita Commendatore continues down, passing (left) the 18th-century **Palazzo Cosentini** (*used for temporary art exhibitions*), with splendid Baroque pilasters, capitals, and more fantastic balconies, the corbels illustrating scenes from daily life, such as a group of travelling minstrels. These are thought to be the finest Baroque corbels in Ibla, and have recently been cleaned and restored. In one corner St Francis of Paola can be seen travelling over to Sicily on his cloak. In 1464 the saint had been refused passage by the boatmen and used his cloak and staff to sail safely across the Straits of Messina with his companions. Franz Liszt composed a piece inspired by the miracle. The main façade is on Corso Mazzini, which now continues right to Piazza della Repubblica at the foot of the hill of Ragusa Ibla.

To the left of the 17th-century church of the **Purgatorio** (*map 3*; the bell-tower was built on top of the old walls of the pre-earthquake city), Via del Mercato leads up around the left side of the hill with a view of the massive Baroque Palazzo Sortino Trono above the road. Further on it continues left past the old market building and has splendid views over the unspoilt San Leonardo valley. Via XI Febbraio, peaceful and well paved, forks right off Via del Mercato for the centre of Ibla. On a bend there is a view (left) of the hillside traced with characteristic dry-stone walls. Via Sant'Agnese continues left, and then steps lead up to the wide Via Tenente Di Stefano near the church of Sant'Agnese. It continues uphill and soon narrows with a good view ahead of the cathedral's dome. On the left are the six delightful balconies of **Palazzo La Rocca**. It has an interesting double staircase in black asphalt stone, and a little garden with citrus trees.

Duomo di San Giorgio

FAÇADE OF THE DUOMO DI SAN GIORGIO.

Via Di Stefano continues round the side of the cathedral into the charmingly asymmetrical Piazza del Duomo, which slopes up to the magnificent three-tiered golden façade of the Duomo di San Giorgio (*map 3*), designed by Rosario Gagliardi and built 1744–75, standing above a flight of steps enclosed by a beautifully crafted 19th-century balustrade, the work of Angelo Paradiso of Acireale, a much sought-after artisan. The Neoclassical **dome**, 43m high (hidden by the façade but visible from the road behind or from the extreme left side of the piazza), was constructed in 1820 by Carmelo Cutraro, a local craftsman, who modelled his design on that of the Pantheon in Paris.

The **interior** (*entered by one of the side doors*), with a central nave and two aisles, is lit by the impressive dome which rises above its high drum with windows between the coupled columns. The stained glass dates from 1926. In the south aisle, above the side door (and behind glass), is an equestrian statue of St George; on the third altar is *The Immaculate Virgin* by Vito d'Anna (c. 1729–69), and on the fourth altar, *Rest on the Flight into Egypt* (1864) by Dario Guerci. In the north transept is *St George and the Dragon*, also by Dario

Guerci. In the sacristy is a lovely stone tabernacle with the equestrian statue of St George between Sts Hippolytus and Mercurius, with ruined reliefs below; and Rosario Gagliardi's original plans for the cathedral. By the west door is a stone statue of St George by the Gagini school. The organ in the nave is by the Serassi brothers of Bergamo.

The **museum** of the cathedral (*open Sat and Sun 10.30–12.30 & 3–7; T: 0932 654113*) contains interesting works of art, vestments and church silver.

Along Corso XXV Aprile

Palazzo Arezzi forms an attractive corner of the Piazza Duomo, with a wide arch passing over a side street. At the lower end of the piazza is a charming little fountain and the handsome Palazzo Veninata (early 20th century). The Neoclassical **Circolo di Conversazione** (c. 1850), at Via Alloro 5 (*open 9–1 & 3–9*), which preserves an interesting interior, houses an exclusive private members' club. The carved sphinxes over the doorways symbolise wisdom and supposedly refer to the intelligent conversations being held within. Next to it is **Palazzo Donnafugata** (*admission only with special permission*) with its delightful little wooden balcony, from which it was possible to watch the passers-by in the road below without being seen. The palace contains a private art collection formed in the mid-19th century by Corrado Arezzo de Spuches (*see p. 308*) and a little theatre built in the late 19th century (150 seats) where public performances are sometimes held.

The wide Corso XXV Aprile continues to **Piazza Pola** (*map 4*), with the splendid tall Baroque façade of the church of **San Giuseppe** (1590, re-designed in the second half of the 18th century by the Carmelite monk Alberto Maria). In the oval domed interior there are still the raised galleries used by the nuns. The beautiful floor is made with black asphalt, mined locally, while the unusual altars along the sides are made of shiny painted glass. In the centre of the dome is a painting of the *Glory of St Benedict* by Sebastiano Lo Monaco (1793). Above the high altar, in an elaborate frame, is the *Holy Family* by Matteo Battaglia. The side altarpieces include a *Holy Trinity* by Giuseppe Cristadoro.

Corso XXV Aprile continues to wind downhill past the closed church of the Maddalena and the high wall of the church of **San Tommaso**, which has a photogenic belltower. In the oval interior is an unusual font in black asphalt (1545), and a masterpiece by Vito d'Anna—*Our Lady of Carmel*.

Giardino Ibleo public gardens

Just beyond San Tommaso, beside the church of St Vincent Ferrer, is the entrance to the **Giardino Ibleo** (*map 4; open 8–8*) or Villa Comunale, a delightful public garden laid out in 1858, with a splendid palm avenue, goldfish pool, flower beds, and wide views over the Irminio Valley. It contains three small churches. Beyond the colourful campanile of St Vincent Ferrer is the church of San Giacomo, founded in the 14th century and rebuilt in the 18th century, with a façade of 1902. At the bottom of the garden is the 17th-century church of the Cappuccini (*closed*), with a simple interior, and a very fine altarpiece, a triptych by Pietro Novelli of the *Madonna with Angels and Saints* that is widely considered to be his finest masterpiece. It is still in its original, minutely-carved frame. The attached convent is currently undergoing restoration. There are good views from here, and, beyond the war memorial, the church of San Giorgio can be seen on the skyline, with the large church of the Immacolata on the right.

In an orchard below the balustrade some late antique hypogea (once thought to be ancient Sicel tombs) have been carved into the rock. Outside the entrance to the gardens, in Via Normanni, is the 15th-century Gothic side portal of the church of **San Giorgio Vecchio** (*map 4*), with a relief of St George. The church, which was very large, was completely destroyed in the earthquake of 1693, but this portal has become the symbol of the town of Ibla.

North of Piazza Pola

From Piazza Pola, with a view of the top of the façade of San Giorgio and its dome, Via Orfanotrofio leads past the church of **Sant'Antonio** (*map 4*) with remains of a Gothic portal next to a little Baroque side doorway. Just beyond is the 18th-century Palazzo di Quattro with a balcony along the whole length of its façade.

A road descends on the left past Santa Teresa to reach the **Immacolata**, with a fine campanile. It contains interesting works in asphalt stone. Its Gothic portal stands in Piazza Chiaramonte, in a little garden of orange trees. The narrow Via Chiaramonte leads up past the campanile to the rear side of **Palazzo Battaglia** (no. 40; *map 3*), a very original building, with two completely different façades. You can see the main façade beyond the arch on the left, on Via Orfanotrofio, leading to the church of the **Annunziata**. This church houses the oldest bell in the city, dated 1501.

Porta Walter

A road leads out of Piazza del Duomo, under the arch of Palazzo Arezzi, to (left) the Salita Ventimiglia (steps) which lead down to the simple façade and the rich portal of the church of the **Gesù** (*closed for restoration at the time of writing*). The interior has stuccoes and frescoes by Matteo Battaglia (1750). Behind the church is the **Porta Walter** (1644; *map 4*), the only one of Ibla's five ancient gates to have survived the earthquake and subsequent developments. It is a Romanesque arch, about 5m high and 3m wide, with a very faded Latin inscription recording the visit of the Viceroy Alfonso Enriquez. Along the road outside it are some old houses carved into the rock.

MODICA

Modica (*map p. 538, C3*) is an unusual town divided into two parts, Modica Bassa and Modica Alta, with decorative palm trees and elegant Baroque buildings. The lower town (Modica Bassa) occupies a valley at the confluence of two rivers, which were channelled and covered over in 1902 after a disastrous flood. On the steep spur between them the upper town rises in terraces above the dramatic church of San Giorgio. There is a sharp contrast between the ample main streets, built over the rivers, and the tiny alleys and courtyards of the six ancient city districts, each still with its own distinctive character: Francavilla, behind the castle, a populous district reminiscent of an Arab kasbah; Cartellone, once the Jewish Ghetto, between Corso Umberto and Via Vittorio Veneto; Corpo di Terra, the district around St Peter's, with handsome houses and gardens; Malvaxia, a very poor district, also called Vignazza, on the Gigante hill opposite Porta d'Anselmo; Casale, the 'modern' district, with steep cobbled streets, behind Piazza Matteotti; and Porta d'Anselmo, a poor district under the castle, where until recently many people still lived in cave-houses.

HISTORY OF MODICA

The site of Modica was first occupied by the Sicels, then by the Greeks and the Romans, becoming an important centre in Byzantine times. Under the Normans it became a county, one of the most powerful fiefs of the Middle Ages, and passed from the Chiaramonte in 1392 to the Spanish Cabrera family. It controlled Ragusa, Comiso, Chiaramonte Gulfi, Scicli, Spaccaforno (now Ispica), Pozzallo, Vittoria, Monterosso and Giarratana, and reached its maximum splendour in the 16th century; at the end of the 17th century Modica was the fourth largest town in Sicily. It owed its prosperity to its custom of renting out the land to the peasants on a long-term basis, which was to prove extremely profitable, both for the landowners, who were assured of a regular income, and for the farm-workers themselves, who found they could make improvements and invest for the future. Like many towns in this corner of Sicily it had to be rebuilt after the earthquake of 1693. There has always been considerable rivalry between the two churches of San Giorgio and San Pietro, both of which aspired to the role of Chiesa Madre. After the earthquake, the king expressly forbade the people to rebuild both churches, in the hope they would build only one, dedicated to both saints, but in the course of time the ban was forgotten—and so, fortunately, was the rivalry. After 1704 Modica came through Spanish connections to the seventh Duke of Berwick and Alba. For many centuries Modica was known as the 'Venice of Sicily', both for its rivers, then in use as waterways, and for the intellectual fervour of its inhabitants.

EXPLORING MODICA

Corso Umberto

The main street of Modica Bassa is **Corso Umberto**, unusually wide because it occupies the bed of a river, covered over in 1902. Lined with handsome 18th- and 19th-century palaces, it provides a splendid view of the monumental church of San Giorgio (*see p. 295*), halfway up the hillside between the lower and upper town. On the extreme right, on top of a bare rockface, the round tower surmounted by a clock is all that remains of the **castle** of the counts of Modica. Secret tunnels (*not accessible*) run from the castle to the river and to the church of Santa Maria di Betlemme.

Detail of four of the Apostles (*Santoni*) on the steps of the church of San Pietro. From bottom to top they are St Jude, St Bartholomew, St Matthew and St Andrew.

San Pietro

A monumental flight of steps, decorated with statues of the Apostles, leads up from the Corso to the elegant façade of the church of San Pietro (*open Mon–Sat 9–1 & 3.30–7.30, closed Sun and holidays; T: 0932 941074*), rebuilt after the earthquake of 1693, and provided with a balcony. The vast interior presents a central nave and two aisles, separated by 14 columns with Corinthian capitals. In the south aisle is a large chapel, with a splendid **Madonna of Trapani** by the Gagini school, while a little further along on the same aisle is a sculpted group by Benedetto Civiletti of *St Peter and the Paralysed Man* (1893). To the right of the church is the inconspicuous entrance to a grotto used for many years as a storeroom. Three layers of frescoes were discovered here in 1989, the earliest of which may date from the 11th century. They decorated the ancient church of **San Nicolò Inferiore** (*open Tues–Sun 10–1 & 4–7; pm may be closed; T: 0932 752891 (Etnos)*); the baptismal font carved into the rock is very unusual.

Teatro Garibaldi and Via Marchesa Tedeschi

By turning right along Corso Umberto after coming down the steps in front of San Pietro, you will see the Neoclassical façade of the opera house, **Teatro Garibaldi** (*open Tues–Sun 9–1 & 4–8; T: 334 8277958; for guided tours call Cooperativa Sant'Antonio Abate T: 0932 774778 or 333 6531261*), with a lovely interior, recently restored and embellished inside with paintings by Piero Guccione.

In the centre of town, at the former confluence of the two rivers, the Corso forms a fork with the broad **Via Marchesa Tedeschi**, also on the site of a riverbed. Here is the Town Hall, ex-convent of the church of San Domenico (*crypt open 9–1 & 4–8, closed Sun afternoon*) which contains a 16th-century painting of the *Madonna of the Rosary*. At no. 1 Via San Domenico is a small museum dedicated to local poet Salvatore Quasimodo (*request visit at the Casa-Museo, see below*). On the other side of the Corso, in Via De Leva, is a fine Arab-Norman doorway in a little garden, probably once part of a 13th-century palace. Also in Via Marchesa Tedeschi is the simple façade of a national monument, the church of **Santa Maria di Betlemme** (*open Mon-Sat 9–1 & 3.30–7.30, closed Sun and holidays; T: 0932 941470*) which incorporates four preceding churches, including a beautiful 15th-century chapel called the Cappella Palatina. At the entrance is a stone with an inscription, indicating the level reached by the flood waters in 1902.

On the other side of the Town Hall, Corso Umberto continues past **Piazza Matteotti** with its decorative palm trees. Here is the fine rose window and Gothic portal of the 13th-century church of the **Carmine** (*open Mon–Sat 9–5, closed Sun and holidays; T: 0932 945696*), which contains a superb marble group of the *Annunciation* by Antonio Gagini. On the other side is the Art Nouveau ex-Cinema Moderno, now a lecture hall.

Museums of the Palazzo dei Mercedari

Corso Umberto ends at Viale Medaglie d'Oro above which, in Via Mercè, is the majestic, but unfinished, sanctuary church of **Santa Maria delle Grazie** next to its huge former convent, the Palazzo dei Mercedari, restored as the seat of the civic museums. On the ground floor the **Museo Archeologico Belgiorno** (*open Tues–Sun 10–1 & 4–7; T: 0932 752897 (Etnos)*) has an archaeological collection arranged in chronological order from the Neolithic onwards, with finds from Cava d'Ispica and Modica; pride of place is given to the *Ercole di Cafeo* (the 'Herakles Alexikakos', 3rd century BC), a bronze statuette found locally in 1966. The hero's lion-skin cloak is marvellously portrayed; so well, in fact, that many scholars believe that the author could be Lysippus, or one of his school. On the top floor, in the lovely vaulted rooms of the old convent, is the **Museo Ibleo delle Arti e delle Tradizioni Popolari S.A. Guastella** (*entrance from Via Mercè, open Tues–Sun 10–1 & 4–7, closed for restoration at the time of writing*). This fascinating ethnological collection of artisans' tools and utensils is displayed in reconstructed workshops. Local artisans give demonstrations of their skills; a typical farmhouse has also been reconstructed and there is a fine collection of Sicilian carts.

MODICA ALTA

Roads and steps continue steeply uphill to the highest point of Modica Alta. The main street, **Corso Regina Margherita**, is lined with handsome 18th- and 19th-century palaces. At the highest point of the hill another monumental flight of steps leads up to its most important church, **San Giovanni Battista**, which occupies the site of a preceding church and Benedictine monastery, one of the six founded in Sicily in the 6th century by St Gregory. The top of the bell-tower represents the highest point in Modica

(449m), from where it is possible to spot Malta on a clear day. The Baroque façade was erected in 1839. In another part of the upper town, Piazza del Gesù at the end of Via Don Bosco, which can be reached by taking the alley to the right of San Giovanni, is the elaborate doorway (1478) of the recently restored church of **Santa Maria di Gesù**.

MODICA CHOCOLATE

During the 16th century, cocoa beans imported from Mexico by the Cabrera family were made into chocolate by the confectioners of Modica, using the ancient Aztec method of slowly grinding the beans between two stones (to avoid overheating) and then adding maize. Elsewhere in Europe the method of manufacture evolved to industrialise the product, improve the flavour and lower the cost. In Modica, however, the method is still basically the same, the only difference being that sugar instead of maize is added towards the end of the grinding, giving a grainy consistency to the finished product. Natural flavourings are also added, such as cinnamon, vanilla, orange essence or chilli. See www.cioccolatodimodica.it.

San Giorgio

The imposing **church of San Giorgio** (*open 8–1 & 3.30–7.30; T: 0932 941279*), built from the 11th century–1848, is mostly the work of local stonemasons, directed later by the architect Paolo Labisi, and dedicated to the patron saint of Modica Alta. It is reached from Corso Garibaldi, which runs parallel to Corso Umberto. Some 250 steps (completed in 1834) ascend to the pale honey-coloured church. It has five original doorways and a very tall, central bell-tower. In the interior, with double side aisles and a central nave, the apse is filled with a large polyptych with episodes from the gospels and the life of St George, attributed to Bernardino Niger (1573). The silver high altar was made in 1705. In the south aisle is a 16th-century painting of the *Nativity* and (on the second altar) an *Assumption* (1610) by Filippo Paladini, comparable in quality with his canvases in the cathedral at Enna. In the chapel to the right of the presbytery is a much-venerated equestrian statue of St George, while in that to the left of the presbytery is a statue of the *Madonna of the Snow* (1511) by Giuliano Mancino and Bartolomeo Berrettaro. There is a meridian on the floor of the transept, traced by the mathematician Armando Perini in 1895. The fine Serassi organ dates from 1886–88. Among the treasures of the church is a silver ark with the relics of St George, made in Venice in the 14th century. On completion in 1848, the happy parishioners placed a plaque over the main doorway with the words Mater Ecclesia (Chiesa Madre), to put an end once and for all to the rivalry with San Pietro.

Left of San Giorgio is the 18th-century **Palazzo Polara**, which houses the civic art gallery and from which there is a fine view of the lower town and the hillside beyond. Uphill behind San Giorgio, on Corso Francesco Crispi, is the Baroque **Palazzo Tomasi-Rossi**, with attractive carved balconies—the caryatids are said to be portraits of the owner.

The Nobel Prize-winning poet Salvatore Quasimodo (1901–68) was born at Via Posterla 84, just under the castle clock. It is possible to visit his house at no. 5, **Casa-Museo Salvatore Quasimodo** (*open Tues–Sun 10–1 & 4–7; T: 0932 752897 (Etnos), www.quasimodo.it*). Together with Eugenio Montale, Quasimodo is considered to be one of the most important of Italy's 'hermetic' poets. He worked for many years in northern Italy as a surveyor, where his intense homesickness for Sicily inspired many of his most beautiful poems, which are written in a characteristic lyrical style.

THE SICILIAN BAROQUE

Characterised by a strong sense of movement and a theatrical handling of space, the Baroque was the dominant European style of architecture during the 17th and early 18th centuries. It achieved distinctive and concerted expression in southeastern Sicily after the earthquake of 11th January 1693, which killed more than 60,000 people. Within half a century, more than 100 towns and villages, including some 600 churches, were rebuilt in this triumphant and exaggerated style, an exceptional legacy thanks to the experience and traditions of the native craftsmen, the flair of the architects and the beautiful colour of the hard, local limestone. Formerly dubbed 'Sicilian Rococo', the style is now recognised as late Baroque, an idiosyncratic continuation of the mid-17th-century Italian style perfected in Rome by Bernini and Borromini. Streets and squares are arranged as theatre settings for the population to act out their lives. Carefully detailed carvings on balcony corbels and around windows attest to the skill of the stonemasons and sculptors. Faces can be portraits of members of the family, or enigmatic monsters. Garlands of flowers and leaves, birds and animals, dragons, hippogryphs, cherubs and harpies, jostle for space, each with their own significance. The churches have imposing façades, playing daring games with convex and concave curves, light and shade, the lines drawing our gaze up from the opulent stairways to the highest pinnacles; the dazzling interiors are decorated with gold and silver, inlaid marble, paintings, stuccoes and statues; the people of southeast Sicily certainly did their best for the saints whom they hoped would ward off further catastrophes.

SOUTHEAST OF RAGUSA

The attractive countryside southeast of Ragusa and Modica is well cultivated, with low dry-stone walls between fields of pastureland and crops, and small farmhouses built of the local grey stone. Scicli is a bustling Baroque market town. Ispica is built on chalk, which has been tunnelled over the centuries for tombs and dwellings. Cava d'Ispica is visited for its rock-cut churches and catacombs. There are fine beaches at Pozzallo.

SCICLI

Described by Elio Vittorini, author of the lyrical anti-Fascist novel *Conversations in Sicily* (1941), as 'the most beautiful town in the world', Scicli (*map p. 538, C3*) has occupied the floor of its valley, surrounded by rocky cliffs, since the 14th century. The landscape around the site of the old medieval town on the hillside, dominated by the old Chiesa Madre of San Matteo (and abandoned after the 1693 earthquake) is a good place for some gentle trekking, especially in spring. There are many caves, once used as homes. There are plans to transform this area, known as Chiafura, into an open-air museum; it already provides the setting for theatre performances during the summer.

Prosperous under the Saracens (when it was known as Sikli), legend has it that Scicli was taken by the Normans after a tremendous battle, in which the Madonna herself took part. It is one of the region's charming Baroque towns, rebuilt after the 1693 earthquake and prosperous again today thanks to its production of flowers and vegetables, especially 'date' tomatoes (to find out more about this famous product, see www.datterino.com).

Piazza Italia

In Piazza Italia, planted with trees and surrounded by Neoclassical buildings, and a favourite meeting-place for the people of Scicli, is the richly ornate façade of the 18th-century **duomo**, dedicated to St Ignatius and to St William of Noto, who is the patron saint of the town. The interior, a central nave with two aisles, is bright with gilded stuccoes and frescoes by local artists. Here also you will find the brilliantly coloured *papier mâché* statue of the **Madonna delle Milizie** which is carried in procession in May (*see p. 316*).

Opposite is the Baroque **Palazzo Fava**, with a large entrance, flanked by elaborate columns on plinths, surmounted by Corinthian capitals crowned with cherubs. On top of the arch is a mysterious face, with acanthus leaves for hair. The balconies are splendid, especially those looking out over Via San Bartolomeo, with corbels shaped into galloping horses, winged dragons, and mythical creatures ridden by cherubs. The area which opens out in front of the **church of San Bartolomeo**, in front of a rockface, was created in 1824 when the river was covered. The pastel-coloured façade, crowned with a cupola, was built at the beginning of the 19th century by Salvatore Alì; the single-nave interior was decorated with stuccoes by the Gianforma, father and son. There is a monumental crib with 29 almost life-size statues by Pietro Padula (1773–75). It comes from Naples, and the figures (some of them dating back to 1573; there were originally 65) are carved in lime wood.

Via Nazionale and Via Penna

Via Nazionale leads uphill and on the right, at the end of a short street, is the corner of **Palazzo Beneventano** (*pictured overleaf*). The most famous building in Scicli, described by art historian Anthony Blunt as 'Sicily's most beautiful Baroque palace', it was designed not by an architect but by local master-builders. It has elaborate balconies supported by fantastic creatures, as well as the unusual addition of a richly decorated zig-zag design running up one corner: on the top are two Moors and at the bottom is St Joseph.

Off the other side of Via Nazionale is the decorative central street, **Via Mormino Penna**. The relatively sombre Town Hall (1906) stands next to the elegant church of San Giovanni, with a fine façade. Via Penna winds on past the oval church of San Michele, past **Palazzo Spadaro** (*open Mon, Wed, Fri 9–1; Tues, Thur 9–1 & 3.30–6.30; T: 0932 839611*), with its splendid wrought-iron balconies and elegant carved stone window frames, and the stupendous façade of the **church of Santa Teresa**, now used as a meeting hall.

Via Nazionale continues to **Piazza Busacca**, planted with trees and flowers. In the centre is a 19th-century statue (by Benedetto Civiletti) of the rich local merchant and philanthropist Pietro Di Lorenzo Busacca (d. 1567). Here is the church of the **Carmine** (1751–69), beside its convent (1386) with a decorative balcony. Palazzo Busacca (1882), surmounted by a clock between two

The stylised heads of two Moors function as gargoyles on Palazzo Beneventano.

mermaids, is now used as council offices. Inside, the rooms are still decorated with wonderful frescoes and stuccoes, and 18th-century paintings. Beyond, to the right, is the elegant church of **Santa Maria della Consolazione**, once dedicated to St Thomas; with a wooden statue (1560) of Christ at the Column.

The church of Santa Maria la Nova

East of Via Nazionale, surrounded by a rocky crag in an interesting part of the old town, is the large church of Santa Maria la Nova (15th century). The Neoclassical façade dates from 1816. In the interior, decorated with stuccoes, there is a high altarpiece of the *Birth of the Virgin* by Sebastiano Conca, The presbytery was designed by the Neoclassical architect Giuseppe Venanzio Marvuglia. Among the paintings is a particularly beautiful *Immaculate Virgin* by Vito d'Anna; there is also a Gaginesque marble statue of the Madonna. On the second left-hand altar is a highly venerated statue of the *Madonna della Pietà*, made of cypress wood and thought to be Byzantine.

From Scicli to the sea

On leaving Scicli and going towards the coast, after c. 1.5 km you will see the sanctuary church of the **Madonna delle Milizie** (*map p. 538, B3*). Local legend states that it was an ancient temple of Bacchus transformed into a church by Count Roger after his victory over the Arabs in 1091, in which battle the Madonna came to his aid (the church exhibits a stone which purports to be imprinted with the hoofmarks of the Madonna's warhorse). There is no certain evidence for an ancient temple, but the Normans may well have won an important victory here. The bell-tower dates from late medieval period (it is not Byzantine, as is sometimes claimed).

Southwest of Scicli is the town's natural harbour, the charming, simple little fishing village of **Donnalucata** (*map p. 538, B3*), often used as a film set. The name refers to the appearance of the Madonna one night in 1091 'bathed in light'. To the east, near **Cava d'Aliga**, is a sandy bay, perfect for swimming.

ISPICA

The small town of Ispica (*map p. 538, C3*) was rebuilt on its present site after the earthquake of 1693 destroyed the former town on the valley floor. It has fine 18th–19th-century buildings. Known in the Middle Ages as Spaccaforno, derived from *Ispicae Fundus*, it re-adopted its old name in 1935. The chalk eminence on which it stands is pierced with tombs and cave dwellings. These can best be seen in the **Parco della Forza** at the south end of the Cava d'Ispica (*described overleaf but best approached from the town itself*).

The town centre

In the new town centre, Piazza Regina Margherita is dominated by the elegant lines of the **Chiesa Madre** (*T: 0932 959274*), dedicated to St Bartholomew.

Nearby is the church of **Santa Maria Maggiore**, an attractive building by Vincenzo Sinatra of Noto, with a daring semi-elliptical loggia around it inspired by the colonnaded porticoes in front of St Peter's in Rome. The startling interior is decorated with 18th-century frescoes painted by Olivio Sozzi during the last two years of his life. He included in his scheme a self-portrait as one of the elderly Apostles admiring the Ascension, in the central apse. The large (40m square) fresco on the vault, with scenes from the Old and New Testaments, is considered his masterpiece, while the whole group of 26 frescoes is one of the most important in Sicily. Over the main altar is a luminous canvas of the *Madonna* by Vito d'Anna, while to the right of the altar is a panel painting of the *Madonna of the Rosary*, dated 1567, by an unknown follower of Polidoro da Caravaggio or Vincenzo da Pavia. The most venerated chapel is that dedicated to Christ at the Column, in the left transept, with a very ancient Crucifix, thought to be miraculous, and brought from the preceding church after the 1693 earthquake, which it survived. The brightly-painted soldiers of wood and *papier mâché* were added in 1729 by Francesco Guarino, a sculptor from Noto. Near the main door is the Casa della Cera, a room containing many of the wax figurines which it is customary to offer as an ex-voto to Christ at the Column; there is also a glass case containing the body of Olivio Sozzi.

Palazzo Bruno di Belmonte, an Art Nouveau building (the finest in the province) by Ernesto Basile (1906), has been restored as the Town Hall. The most imposing building in the town is the 1704 church of the **Annunziata** (*T: 0932 951912*), with its theatrical façade; it is filled with stuccoes carried out in the mid-18th century by

Giuseppe Gianforma. In the sacristy is a painting erroneously attributed to Caravaggio, *St Andrew of Avellino*; notice the cleverly-depicted hands, and the expressive face. Mounted on one of the side walls is the head of a bull, supposedly the cause of a miraculous event in the 18th century: a child wearing a red cloak was attacked and carried off on the horns of this bull, which suddenly stopped and knelt down in front of the church, allowing the little boy to escape unscathed.

A little road leads 8km to the south of Ispica, to its inviting beach of golden sand at **Santa Maria di Focallo** (*map p. 538, C3*), awarded the European Union Blue Banner.

Cava d'Ispica and Parco della Forza

The **Cava d'Ispica** (*map p. 538, C3; open April–Oct 9–7, Sun and holidays 9–1.30, Nov–March 9–1.30, T: 0932 771667*) lies 11km east of Modica (*signposted*). It is a deep gorge 13km long which follows a river (now usually dry) with luxuriant vegetation—many rare terrestrial orchids in early spring. It is also good for birdwatchers, who might see sparrow hawks, buzzards, kestrels, jays, and colonies of ravens. The sides of the canyon are honeycombed with prehistoric tombs, early Christian rock-hewn churches, and medieval cave-dwellings: the presence of man can be traced from the earliest times to the most recent, although the valley was greatly damaged in the earthquake of 1693.

Just below the entrance are extensive Christian catacombs known as **Larderia** (4th–5th centuries AD). They extend for some 36m inside the rock, and contain 464 tombs. Across the main road is the little church of **San Nicola** (*unlocked on request*), which contains very damaged traces of (?)early Norman frescoes. A path near here leads along the dry riverbed to **Baravitalla**, with prehistoric tombs dating from the Castelluccio period (1800 BC), and one with a design of pilasters on its façade.

From the entrance a gravel road (c. 400m) leads past numerous caves, including some on more than one storey, ruined by the earthquake. Outside the enclosure an overgrown path runs along the valley passing numerous **rock tombs and dwellings**, including the so-called **Castello** on four floors.

At the far end is the **Parco della Forza** (best approached from Ispica; *open daily 9–6.45, mornings only in winter; T: 0932 951133*). It has lush vegetation, water-cisterns, tombs and churches, all carved out of the rock, and a remarkable tunnel known as the Centoscale (hundred stairs), 60m long, formerly used by those carrying water from the river to the town. The museum displays a notable collection of finds from the site, including amphorae, fragments of pottery and Bronze-Age tools.

Further along the valley is the area known as **Ispicae Fundus**, with more interesting caves and churches, and part of the old main street, which was paved with limestone.

POZZALLO

Pozzallo (*map p. 538, C3*) is a busy port with a prominent square tower, Torre Cabrera, built by the Cabreras to protect it from pirate raids in the 15th century, reconstructed after 1693, and now a national monument. It is located in Via delle Sirene. The port was used in the Middle Ages as the loading point for shipping the enormous quantities of wheat grown in the county to various destinations. Giorgio La Pira, the *sindaco santo* (saintly mayor), who for many years was mayor of Florence, was born in Pozzallo. A great politician, he played an important role in the drawing up of the Italian Constitution after the Second World War; but it was his intense efforts to secure conciliation among different religions, and his strong ideas about guaranteeing dignity to the poor, that won him the reputation of saintliness (the Vatican is evaluating his case). The harbour is increasingly used both for trade and tourism. The lovely beaches, awarded the EU Blue Banner, are hidden behind tree-covered dunes where cane fences control the sand.

WEST OF RAGUSA

The small towns of Vittoria, Comiso, and Santa Croce Camerina have fine Baroque and Art Nouveau buildings and the surrounding countryside is beautiful. Traditional ways of life have been preserved here, involving the production of wine, olive oil, vegetables and limestone for paving.

VITTORIA

Vittoria (*map p. 538, B2*) is a prosperous agricultural town and centre of the wine trade, especially for the famous Cerasuolo di Vittoria, the only Sicilian wine in the DOCG category. It was built for, and named after, Vittoria Colonna, wife of Luigi III Enriquez, Count of Modica and daughter of the viceroy Marcantonio Colonna, in 1607. Constructed according to a grid plan on a large plain overlooking the Ippari, a small river bordered by pine forests, it escaped the 1693 earthquake with little damage, but a tragic death-toll: the Chiesa Madre collapsed, killing 40 children at a prayer service.

The opera house and the Chiesa Madre

In the main square, Piazza del Popolo, the elegant Neoclassical **Vittoria Colonna Opera House** (1877; *T: 0932 861517*), particularly admired by the critic Bernard Berenson, stands next to the church of the Madonna delle Grazie, with an attractive Baroque façade of 1754, complete with a clock. The simple interior has polychrome marble altars along the sides, with 18th-century wooden statues and canvases.

From here, the central Via Cavour, with its Art Nouveau buildings and enticing shop windows, leads to the rectangular, shady Piazza Ricca, and the **Chiesa Madre**, San Giovanni Battista, dedicated to the patron saint of Vittoria, with an unusual Moorish façade and dome (18th–19th centuries). The four bells in the tower are dedicated to St John the Baptist, Our Lady of Carmel, St Rosalia and St Victoria, all of whom were thought to be suitable patron saints for the town when it was founded; the four names were placed in an urn, and drawn out by a blindfolded child. John the Baptist came out three times running. The Latin-cross interior, divided into a central nave and two side aisles by Corinthian columns, is richly decorated with gilded stucco, marble inlay, statues, and 17th–19th-century paintings. The marble floor in front of the main altar was completed with an interesting ex-voto in the 19th century, two vases of grapes: the one on the right, dated 1798, is a withered vine, that on the left, dated 1801, is flourishing; a reference to a terrible blight which destroyed the local vineyards, and their miraculous recovery only three years later, thanks to the intercession of the saint. The wooden statue of St John the Baptist over the main altar is by an unknown sculptor who has depicted him as black, and wearing camel skins. To the right of the main altar, under the large canvas of the *Beheading of St John the Baptist* (1600, ?Mario Minniti), is an urn with the remains of Vittoria Colonna, brought here from Spain in 1991. The magnificent organ (1748) is by Donato Del Piano.

The museums

The **Museo di Arte Sacra Monsignor Federico La China** (*open 9–1; closed Sun and holidays*) at Via Cavour 51, contains a collection of material from the Chiesa Madre (stone carvings, sculptures and fragments of altars), together with fine examples of 18th-century Sicilian gold and silver work.

Among the Art Nouveau palaces in the town, perhaps the finest is **Palazzo Traina**, on Via Rosario Cancellieri, in the Venetian-Gothic style, a good example of the skill of the local stonemasons. The **Museo Civico Virgilio Lavore** (*open Mon–Fri 9–12, Sat on request, T: 0932 864038*) is at Piazza Enriquez 15, in the oldest building in town, once the castle of Countess Vittoria. It has an interesting exhibit on the 19th-century equipment used for obtaining sound effects for the opera house, as well as a picture gallery with a section devoted to modern art, a collection of Sicilian carts, archaeological finds, and some stuffed birds.

In Via Garibaldi, the former prisoner-of-war camp where some 20,000 Austro-Hungarian soldiers were imprisoned in 1916 (the largest of such camps in Sicily), is the EMAIA trade fair centre and the interesting **Museo Storico Italo-Ungherese** (*open Mon–Fri 8–1.30; T: 0932 865994*). The museum was prepared with the help of the Budapest Museum of Military History. In the local cemetery is a chapel dedicated to the Hungarian soldiers who died here.

The Villa Comunale and the nature reserve

The **Villa Comunale**, public gardens, once the garden of the Capuchin monastery, offers a beautiful view over the Ippari valley. Along the River Ippari, between Vittoria and the sea, is a pinewood protected as a nature reserve, **Riserva Naturale Pino d'Aleppo**. The trees are the last remaining examples of a variety of Aleppo pine, endemic to Sicily. Other species have benefited from the protective measures too, including typical Mediterranean trees and flowers, mammals such as the hare and the garden dormouse, the tortoise, and a wide variety of birdlife.

About 8km northwest of Vittoria is **Acate** (*map p. 538, B2*), so-called because of the agate which was once abundantly found along the banks of the River Dirillo. It is surrounded by olive groves and vineyards, some of which produce excellent Chardonnay.

In the central Piazza Libertà is the impressive 15th-century Castello dei Principi di Biscari, flanked by the church of San Vincenzo, opposite the Chiesa Madre, rebuilt in 1859.

COMISO

On the slopes of the Hyblaean Mountains, the pretty Baroque town of Comiso (*map p. 538, B2*) is unmistakable for its skyline of church domes. Nearby, at Cozzo di Apollo, are the ruins of a currently unidentified Greek settlement. Under the Byzantines the settlement here was called *Jhomiso*, or 'fountain of water'. It became a fief of various aristocratic families until 1453, when it passed to the Naselli, who held it until 1812; Comiso flourished under their intelligent, far-seeing administration. Many inhabitants died during the 1624 plague epidemic, and the 1693 earthquake destroyed much of the town. Today the handsome paving on the streets of the old centre is made from the local stone, which has the appearance of marble. Comiso has a strong economy, based partly on the quarrying of that stone and also on the year-round production of vegetable crops and carobs. There is an old Fascist-era airport which has been transformed for civil use, but is not yet open because of bureaucratic tangles.

Santissima Annunziata and the Chiesa Madre

Three palm trees stand outside the church of the **Santissima Annunziata**, with a spectacular stairway in front and a beautiful blue dome above. It was rebuilt in 1772–93 on the ruins of the Byzantine church of St Nicholas. The plans, which can be seen in the sacristy, were drawn up by Rosario Gagliardi. The luminous interior has stucco decoration in blue, grey and white. It contains a wooden 15th-century statue of St Nicholas on the first right-hand altar, and an impressive Crucifix attributed to Fra' Umile da Petralia in the right transept. On the second north altar is a panel-painting of the *Transition of the Virgin* (1605) by local artist Narciso Cidonio. The font (1913) is a fine piece in marble and bronze by Mario Rutelli. In the apse is a painting of the *Nativity and Resurrection of Christ* by native artist Salvatore Fiume.

Via Papa Giovanni XXIII leads downhill in front of the church, and Via degli Studi leads right to the central **Piazza Fonte Diana**, with its amusing fountain (1937). The waters of this spring were said to refuse to mix with wine when poured by unchaste hands; in Roman days they supplied a bath-house, with a mosaic of Neptune, the remains of which are visible beneath the Town Hall. Nearby, in Piazza delle Erbe, which was the old market-place, rises the imposing **Chiesa Madre**, Santa Maria delle Stelle, also with a dome. The fine 18th-century façade is attributed to Rosario Gagliardi. The interior has a wooden ceiling painted in the 17th century with scenes of the Old Testament, attributed to Antonio Alberti 'Barbalunga', and interesting altars with the statues protected by curtains.

Local museums and the Fondazione Bufalino

Piazza delle Erbe has a fountain, onto which faces the handsome market building, with a raised portico, built in 1867. It has been restored as the seat of the civic library and museums, entered from the delightful courtyard, also with a fountain. The collection of paintings includes 19th-century portraits. The library is now officially known as the **Fondazione Bufalino** (*open Mon and Wed 9–2, Tues, Thur, Fri 9–2 & 4–7; T: 0932 962617, www.fondazionebufalino.it*), because it houses the private collection of more than 10,000 books once belonging to the local writer Gesualdo Bufalino (1920–96), born in Comiso. He achieved recognition relatively late in life, at the age of 61, with his novel *Diceria dell'Untore* (1981), published in English seven years later as *The Plague Sower*. Semi-autobiographical, it is set during and immediately after the Second World War, and chronicles the disturbing reflections upon life, death, and the Christian faith of the sole survivor of a Sicilian TB clinic. Writing in a highly literary, allusive style which critics quickly described as 'Baroque', Bufalino shared with other contemporary Italian authors a playful distrust of his own narrative. The museum also has newspaper articles written by or about Bufalino, photographs and other memorabilia. The same building houses the **Museo Civico di Storia Naturale** (*entrance from Piazza delle Erbe 13, open 9.30–1 & 4–7.30, closed Wed, Fri and Sun afternoon and all day Mon; T: 0932 722521*), with a collection dedicated to fossils of whales, dolphins and turtles and an interesting exhibit on rare creatures found after being washed up on the beaches of Sicily and Calabria. The sections dedicated to Palaeontology and Zoology are housed nearby, on the first floor of the former Art School, at Via degli Studi 9. Opposite the library is the **church of Gesù** (San Filippo Neri), with a magnificent wooden ceiling into which paintings by Olivio Sozzi have been inserted, with stories of the life of St Philip Neri.

Monuments of the Naselli family

From Via Giovanni XXIII, Via degli Studi leads shortly (right) to the lovely church of **San Francesco**, or the Immacolata (*if locked, ring at the convent*), founded in the early 14th century. The present church was built in 1478, and the very interesting Cappella Naselli (1517–55) was added at the east end by Gaspare Poidomani, using an imaginative pastiche of architectural styles. Arab-Norman squinches support the dome, and classical details are incorporated in the decoration. It contains the marble funerary monument of Gaspare Naselli, Count of Comiso, attributed to Antonello Gagini. At the west end is a 15th-century wooden choir-loft. It is also worth asking to see the beautiful 15th-century cloister.

At the entrance to the town, and from a similar period, is the **Castello Feudale** (*closed*). Once owned by the Naselli family, it has been much altered over the years, but traces of an octagonal tower, probably once a Byzantine baptistery, and the square 15th-century keep, can still be seen. In 1841 a Neoclassical opera house, **Teatro Naselli** (*T: 0932 963933*) or Teatro Diana, which brought fame to the town and is still in use, was built on the east side of the castle.

SANTA CROCE CAMERINA

A direct descendant of the ancient settlements of *Kamarina* and *Kaukana*, Santa Croce Camerina (*map p. 538, B3*) is a little town which never fulfilled its true potential, thanks

Marble effigy of Gaspare Naselli, Count of Comiso (16th century), attributed to Antonello Gagini.

to pirate attacks, malaria, cholera, and other setbacks. After the 1693 earthquake, many refugees from badly-hit centres came to live here, giving the town new energy. Today the economy is based on cattle-rearing and the cultivation of flowers (especially roses, tulips and gladioli) for export. Many of the buildings in the centre are in the Art Nouveau style.

In the central Piazza degli Studi is the **Museo Civico** (*open Mon–Fri 9–1, Sat, Sun open by prior request*) with interesting collections of objects from nearby archaeological sites, and tools and equipment used by farmers and craftsmen until the 20th century. On the coast south of the town, several ruined watchtowers against pirate attacks can be seen, now surrounded by a seemingly endless rash of holiday bungalows.

The sandy headland of **Punta Secca** on Capo Scalambri has a series of coves, one of which was the site of a Byzantine settlement, *Kaukana* (*T: 0932 826004 or 0932 916142 to request visit*), a large harbour-town mentioned by Procopius, where the fleet of Belisarius put in on the way to Africa, and where Roger II departed for the conquest of Malta. The remains are protected as an archaeological park, with three distinct groups of ruins corresponding to the different districts of the town. Unfortunately the site, although screened with trees, has been surrounded by unattractive holiday bungalows.

Marina di Ragusa

Southeast of Santa Croce, Marina di Ragusa (*map p. 538, B3*) is a crowded resort, with an elegant marine promenade flanked by palm trees and a yachting harbour, which grew up in the 1950s on the site of an old Arab port. A fast *superstrada* connects it to Ragusa. Oil is drilled offshore and piped from here to Augusta. The beach (awarded the EU Blue Banner) is sandy, once continuing into extensive sand dunes, many of which are now covered with holiday homes or market gardens. The well-preserved reedy dunes around the mouth of the River Irminio near Playa Grande are protected as a nature reserve (**Riserva Macchia Foresta dell'Irminio**; *T: 0932 675525-6, entrance c. 2km from Marina di Ragusa on the road to Donnalucata*), where black-winged stilts and avocets nest, and historic remains include a Sicel bee-farm and a Greek forge; there is even a small colony of coypu, originating from a pair accidentally freed here a few years ago.

KAMARINA

Situated on the coast is the archaeological park and museum of Kamarina (*map p. 538, B3*), an important Greek city.

HISTORY OF KAMARINA

Kamarina was a colony founded c. 598 BC by Syracusans and perhaps Corinthians, which suffered alternate sacking and repopulation by Syracuse, Gela and Carthage, because the inhabitants were of a particularly rebellious nature and tended to take sides with the Sicels. They first rose up against Syracuse only 45 years after their founding, in 552 BC, and suffered destruction in 533 and 484. After being sacked by the Romans in 258 BC, the inhabitants were sold as slaves. There are signs of occupation in the Republican and Imperial eras and also of a late Arab-Norman settlement.

Kamarina was a nymph, daughter of the god Oceanus, who lived in a nearby lake and in the River Hypparis (now Ippari). She can be seen on the 5th-century BC coins minted in the city (some are kept in the coin department of the archaeological museum in Syracuse), riding on a swan and holding her dress out of the water, while fish jump around her. This was a good place to build a city, with a large flat area protected by mountains and rivers, and in a strong strategic position on the south coast of the island. Archaeologists have discovered traces of prehistoric settlements here, and some scholars believe the Phoenicians established a trading-post on this spot; the cult of Herakles, corresponding to the Phoenician Melqart, had a strong following in Kamarina. The site was first located by the historian Tommaso Fazello in the 16th century. Sporadic digs took place in the 18th and 19th centuries, followed by scientific excavations under the direction of Paolo Orsi from 1896–1910. The recent and extensive excavations began in 1971.

The archaeological museum and the excavations

The road passes several enclosures with **excavations** (*if closed, they are sometimes unlocked on request at the museum*) before reaching the **Museo Archeologico** (*open 9–2 & 3–7; T: 0932 826004, last tickets 30mins before closing*). The museum is housed in a restored 19th-century farmhouse built above the remains of the Sanctuary of Athena. A room displays underwater finds made offshore where nine shipwrecks have so far been identified. These include a Greek bronze helmet (4th century BC), and objects from Punic and medieval boats. In 1991 a hoard of 1,272 bronze coins was found from the treasure-chest of a Roman cargo ship which sank offshore in AD 275. The headland by the city is surrounded by treacherously sharp rocks: an entire Roman fleet foundered here in 255 BC.

One of the most interesting exhibits shows a rare set of 3rd–2nd-century BC square lead weights, found under the sea in front of the acropolis in 1993, allowing experts to calculate the measuring system used by the inhabitants of this area. Outside in the courtyard, beneath a porch, are sandstone sarcophagi and a circular stone tomb. Beyond, part of the temple's sanctuary wall can be seen. Another building contains a plan of the site and explanatory diagrams, and Bronze-Age finds from the area. Material from the 6th century BC includes a beautiful Corinthian black-figure vase with a hunting scene.

In another building the foundations of the temple, dating from the early 5th century BC, have been exposed (it was re-used as a church in the Byzantine era). A room on two floors has a splendid display of amphorae (mostly Corinthian and Carthaginian), around one thousand of which were found in the oldest necropolis of Kamarina, known as Rifriscolaro. The various excavated areas overlooking the sea include fragments of the walls, part of the street layout and houses with three or four rooms opening on to a courtyard (built after 405 BC) and part of the agora. The necropoleis have yielded a great number of tombs, revealing different methods of burial and cremation, varying through the years: it was customary for a time, for example, to provide the corpses with pillows made of seaweed. Studies of skeletons show that the inhabitants were stocky and robust, with good teeth, but some had serious back problems. Traces of the canal-port have been found at the mouth of the River Ippari.

On the coast not far from Santa Croce Camerina is **Scoglitti** (*map p. 538, B3*), the beach resort of Vittoria. It overlooks the Gulf of Gela, a long shallow bay whose beaches provided the chief landing-place for the American assault forces on 10th July 1943, during Operation Husky.

Castello di Donnafugata

A quiet byroad (signposted Santa Croce Camerina) leads southwest from Ragusa through lovely countryside with numerous farms to the Castello di Donnafugata (*map p. 538, B3; open 9–1, Tues, Thur, Sun also 2.45–5.30, closed Mon; T: 0932 619333*). On the site of a 17th-century building, the present castle was constructed by Baron Corrado Arezzo de Spuches in the 19th century. It is a large country villa, built in an eclectic style, with a Venetian-Gothic loggia. In 1893 the owner was able to have the Syracuse–Licata railway line diverted, to bring his guests and himself right up to the entrance by train. Its delightful setting survives, with its farm and a large park. The exotic gardens contain a stone maze entered over a miniature drawbridge guarded by a stone soldier, a coffee house, a little Neoclassical temple above a grotto and an amusing little chapel with a *papier mâché* friar inside, which pops up to frighten people. The asphalt-stone monument to Corrado Arezzo de Spuches (2005) is the work of the Anglo-French artist Peter Briggs. In recent years the castle has been used in the Police Inspector Montalbano series and many of the 122 rooms of the castle have been restored. The most interesting are the **Salone degli Specchi**, displaying some paintings of the Neapolitan school, and the **Salone della Musica**, containing three pianos and with frescoes on the walls, and also the tiny **theatre**. In the oldest part of the building, a small chamber is indicated as the prison of Blanche of Navarre, widow of King Martin of Sicily. She was captured (in ?1410) after being chased across Sicily by Count Bernardo Cabrera, who was aiming to improve his claim to the throne by forcing her into marriage. This claim should be taken with a generous pinch of salt, as nearly every castle in Sicily has a room indicated as her prison, several of which (as with this example) were constructed long after her lifetime.

Baron Corrado Arezzo de Spuches (1824–95)
Baron Corrado Arezzo de Spuches was several times mayor of Ragusa, member of the Sicilian parliament in 1848, and later senator of the Kingdom of Italy, besides editing a ferociously satirical magazine and being a farmer. Nicknamed *Terremoto* (earthquake), he married Concettina Trifiletti and had one daughter, Vincenzina, who at the age of 16 married a prince and had two daughters, before the prince absconded with another woman. Vincenzina died of a broken heart, followed soon after by her mother. De Spuches became the legal guardian of his granddaughters. The youngest, Maria, abandoned him to marry a commoner and live in Messina (where she died in the 1908 earthquake), and the other, Clementina, fell in love with a Frenchman and was carried off by him on board his ship. A gardener saw them going and raised the alarm. Another ship was sent to intercept the lovers, who were taken back to the castle. They were allowed to wed, in Malta to avoid scandal, and it was a happy marriage, but Clementina was never forgiven by her grandfather, who cut her out of his will. On his death she brought a court case against distant relatives and succeeded in gaining possession of the castle. Her daughter was the last of the de Spuches line.

CHIARAMONTE GULFI & THE NORTH

Chiaramonte Gulfi (*map p. 538, B2–C2*) was founded by Manfredi Chiaramonte for the survivors of *Gulfi*, an Arab town destroyed in 1299 by the Angevins, who killed most of the inhabitants, including women and children, in a massacre still remembered for its ferocity. Called the 'Balcony of the Hyblaean Mountains' and the 'City of Museums', of which it has eight, it is also famous for its olive oil, as well as excellent bread, pasta and cured hams. The remains of an ancient Greek settlement have been found at the foot of the hill, at Scornavacche.

Churches of Chiaramonte

In the central Piazza Duomo is the Gothic-style **Chiesa Madre** dedicated to Santa Maria la Nova (begun in the 17th century; finished in the 19th century), and nearby is the 18th-century church of **San Filippo**, which houses a beautiful chapel dedicated to St Philip of Argirò, the masterpiece of Nicolò da Mineo. The stonework is very ornate; just over the doorway is a highly unusual naked mermaid, and up above, two winged sphinxes. Nicolò da Mineo, who lived until he was 83, is buried by the altar.

In the highest part of town is the Gothic **Arco dell'Annunziata**, the northwestern doorway to the castle, and the only one to survive the 1693 earthquake. Through the archway is a lovely view of the simple church of San Giovanni, with Doric columns on either side of the portal.

Chiaramonte museums

There are eight museums in Chiaramonte, some of which have been set up in the historic Baroque Palazzo Montesano (in Via Montesano). The others are close by in the town centre (*all museums open 24 June–31 Aug Mon–Thur 8.30–1.30, Fri 8.30–12.30, Sat 10–1 & 6–9; Sun and holidays, afternoons only from 6.30–10; 1 Sept–23 June Mon–Thur 8.30–1.30, Fri 8.30–12.30, Sat, Sun and holidays 9.30–1 & 3–6; T: 0932 711239, tourist office*).

Museo di Arte Sacra (Piazza Duomo) is considered to be one of the finest collections of its kind in Italy. Among the rare and precious objects from the churches of the town there is a crib of 40 terracotta figures about 30cm high, dressed in the traditional 19th-century costumes of the people of Modica. The **Collezione di Cimeli Storici Militari F. Gulino** (ex-Casa del Fascio, Piazza Duomo) contains about 1,000 interesting mementoes, most of them relating to the two World Wars.

Pinacoteca Giovanni De Vita (Corso Umberto) houses about 60 paintings by this local Impressionist artist, donated by his family when he died.

Museo di Liberty, at Palazzo Montesano, illustrates with photographs, paintings and furniture the fervid period between 1895 and 1913 when the Liberty style (Art Nouveau) was fashionable in Sicily. The **Museo dell'Olio d'Oliva** (Olive-Oil Museum; also Palazzo Montesano) gives information about the town's most precious product, with a complete collection of presses and tools used through the ages. Things have not changed very much; even now the excellence of this oil is due to the fact that the olives are gathered by hand and processed the same day, using only stone presses. The **Collezione Ornitologica Fratelli Azzara** in Palazzo Montesano shows about 500 stuffed birds of Sicily and Italy (some now extinct), prepared by the Azzara brothers, expert taxidermists. Also in Palazzo Montesano is the **Collezione di Strumenti Musicali Etnici**, a beautiful arrangement in seven rooms of more than 600 rare musical instruments from all over the world.

Museo del Ricamo e dello Sfilato Siciliano (Via Lauria, one of the tiny alleys off the stairway to the church of San Giovanni) has a display of beautiful embroidery and lace made by local women. Its success has led to the creation of the first Town School for Embroidery in Sicily, where more than 60 experts teach whoever wants to learn, so that this precious skill is not lost. Many of the traditional designs can be traced back to the pottery of the Middle Ages or even further back to prehistoric art, showing fishing-nets, honeycombs, flowers, leaves, ears of wheat and birds.

Around Chiaramonte

A short walk (c. 2km east) from Chiaramonte Gulfi, in the pinewoods on the slopes of Mt Arcibessi, is the **sanctuary church of the Madonna delle Grazie**, built in 1576 by the local population as thanksgiving for being spared a terrible epidemic of the plague. The people chose this spot because a spring of water had miraculously appeared. The views towards Mt Etna from here are spectacular.

GIARRATANA & MONTEROSSO ALMO

Giarratana (*map p. 538, C2*) is the smallest town in the province, basing its economy on the production of wheat, almonds and vegetables, especially large flat onions, to which a feast is dedicated every August (*see p. 316*). Rebuilt after the earthquake of 1693, it is dominated by three Baroque churches: **San Bartolomeo** has a fine façade, perhaps the work of an apprentice of Gagliardi; **Sant'Antonio Abate**, on the top of the hill, contains gold stuccoes and a beautiful 18th-century floor of asphalt stone and bright ceramic tiles; and the **Chiesa Madre**, similar in appearance to the cathedral of Noto. Inside the church of St Bartholomew, the patron saint, is a glass urn containing the mummified body of St Hilary, a Roman virgin and martyr; her body was sent here as a gift by Pope Alexander VII in 1664. The highest part of the town, around the ruins of the castle built in 1703, and centred on via Galilei, is the **Museo a Cielo Aperto** (*open Mon–Fri 9–1, Sat and Sun by prior arrangement, closed Nov–Jan; T: 0932 976012*), an open-air museum showing what the local houses once looked like inside and how the tradesmen and craftsmen carried on their occupations. In 1988 the remains of an Imperial Roman villa dating from the 3rd–4th centuries AD were discovered close by, at **Orto Mosaico** (*not normally open to the public, but you can try calling the Town Hall, T: 0932 976012 or 0932 622150*), with fine mosaics, which have been re-buried to protect them. At 10km from the town is a dam on the River Irminio, which forms the beautiful artificial **lake of Santa Rosalia**.

Monterosso Almo

North of Giarratana is Monterosso Almo (*map p. 538, C2*) at 691m the highest town in Ragusa province. Monterosso is renowned in Sicily for cherries and ricotta, both remarkably good. The inhabitants are currently under study by an international group of scientists, for their exceptionally long lives and the low incidence of cancer. Because of its quaint atmosphere, it is often used as a film set.

In the large central Piazza San Giovanni is the **church of San Giovanni Battista** (attributed to Vincenzo Sinatra), preceded by an immense stairway. Inside there is a precious glass chandelier from Murano. Over the main altar is a 15th-century wooden statue of St John the Baptist, shown only on the first Tues of each month. Via Roma leads down to the golden-brown and red neo-Gothic church of the **Assunzione**, sometimes called the Matrice, this is the oldest parish in the diocese of Ragusa, and the building suffered little damage during the 1693 earthquake. By the side entrance is an 11th-century holy-water stoup on a 5th-century Palaeo-Christian column.

Opposite the Matrice, surmounted by an attractive triple belfry, is the church of **Sant'Antonio Abate** (17th century), or Sanctuary of Our Lady of Sorrows, the patroness of Monterosso Almo. This part of town was the centre before the earthquake.

In the **public gardens** is a small astronomical observatory with a telescope available to the public; the clear skies and low light interference guarantee good visibility.

PRACTICAL INFORMATION

GETTING AROUND

• **By rail:** Ragusa is on the Caltanissetta–Gela–Ragusa–Modica–Noto–Syracuse line (*www.trenitalia.it*). From April–Oct the **Treno Barocco** runs every alternate Sun from Ragusa to Syracuse and back, and the other alternate Sun from Syracuse to Ragusa, stopping in the Baroque cities with time for guided tours of Modica, Scicli and Noto (*Info and booking: Tourist Office Modica call centre T: 0932 759634, www.treno-barocco.blogspot.com*). Also from April–Oct, every Sat, the **Treno di Montalbano** operates from Syracuse to Scicli and return, with guided tours of the TV-series locations, and a typical 'Salvo Montalbano' lunch in a *trattoria* used during the filming (*Info as for the Treno Barocco above*).
• **By bus:** AST (*www.aziendasicilianatrasporti. it*) connects Ragusa to Ragusa Ibla, also to Acate, Marina di Ragusa, Punta Secca, Scoglitti, Santa Croce Camerina and Kamarina.
Etna Trasporti/Interbus (*www.interbus.it*) goes to towns all over the island, including Catania airport, Messina and Syracuse. Places in Ragusa province include Acate, Giarratana, Marina di Ragusa, Monterosso Almo and Santa Croce Camerina.
Giamporcaro (*T: 0932 981632, 0932 869612*)

runs services to Comiso, Marina di Ragusa, Santa Croce Camerina, Scoglitti and Vittoria.
SAIS Autolinee (*www.saisautolinee.it*), goes to Acate, Comiso, Marina di Ragusa, Santa Croce Camerina and Vittoria. Also Catania airport.
SAL (*www.autolineesal.it*) connects Ragusa to Agrigento, Gela and Licata.
Simili (*www.viaggisimili.com*) has services for Caltagirone, Comiso and Modica.
Tumino (*www.tuminobus.it*) runs from Ragusa railway station to Marina di Ragusa, Punta Secca, Santa Croce Camerina, and in summer to Kamarina.

WHERE TO STAY

Cava d'Ispica (*map p. 538, C3*)
€€ **Villa Teresa**. 4km from Cava d'Ispica, a convivial and hospitable little country hotel, with restaurant, garden and pool. *Via Crocevia Cava d'Ispica 2, Contrada Bugilfezza, T: 0932 771690, 334 1579156, www.villateresaweb.it.*
Chiaramonte Gulfi (*map p. 538, B2–C2*)
€€ **Antica Stazione**. The old railway station on the dismantled Ragusa–Vizzini–Syracuse line, which passed through Pantalica (the passengers had to get off and walk when the gradient was too steep) is now a comfortable hotel, with 18 rooms, a good restaurant,

garden and car park. *Contrada Santissimo (southeast of Chiaramonte), T: 0932 928083, 334 9386264, www.anticastazione.com.*

€ **Villa Nobile**. Pretty little hotel, efficient, with 22 basic rooms but splendid views, car park, friendly service, no restaurant but close to town centre. *Corso Umberto 168, T: 0932 928537, www.albergovillanobile.com.*

Comiso (*map p. 538, B2*)

€ **Cordial**. Simple but spotless, with restaurant and pizzeria, just out of town. *SS115 km 1 per Vittoria, T: 0932 967866 or 967867, www.cordialhotel.com.*

€ **Balcone di Sicilia**. Perched high in the hills, a stone-built farmhouse with breathtaking panoramic views towards Mount Etna and the sea. Delicious breakfasts, children more than welcome. English spoken. *Contrada Margitello, SS115, km 313, T: 320 7750545, 320 0141674, www.balconedisicilia.it.*

Ispica (*map p. 538, C3*)

€ **Corte Statella**. Aristocratic B&B in town centre, with 4 palatial rooms, all with air conditioning, TV and en suite bathrooms, small fitness centre, garden and terrace. English and German spoken. *Corso Umberto 141, T: 0932 793380, 333 6460555, 338 2634068.*

Marina di Ragusa (*map p. 538, B3*)

€€€ **La Moresca**. Designer boutique hotel, 15 rooms with character, patio with lemon trees. *Via Dandolo 63, T: 0932 239495, www.lamorescahotel.it.*

Modica (*map p. 538, C3*)

€€€ **Palazzo Failla**. Old town house in the centre of Modica Alta with 10 rooms individually decorated in a 'baroque' style, marvellous breakfasts and an excellent restaurant. *Via Blandini 5, T: 0932 941059, www.palazzofailla.it.*

€€ **FerroHotel**. Near the railway station which inspired the décor of this self-styled 'concept hotel', very comfortable, modern design, 21 rooms with up-to-date bathrooms, restaurant, car park, bikes available. *Via Stazi-*

one, T: 0932 941043, www.ferrohotel.it.

€€ **Grana Barocco**. Built in 1600, tiny eco-friendly hotel in very central position, 7 rooms and suites, all different, fitness centre and restaurant in caves under the building, good breakfasts. *Corso Umberto 133, T: 0932 754704, www.granabarocco.it.*

€€ **L'Orangerie**. Superior B&B accommodation in the heart of town, with 7 beautiful rooms and a good restaurant at Vico Napolitano 14, the Fattoria delle Torri (*T: 0932 751286, closed Mon*). *Vico de Naro 5, T: 347 0674698, www.lorangerie.it.*

€€ **Cambiocavallo Resort**. In the countryside 5km south of town, 8 bright, modern and elegant rooms., pool. *Contrada Zimmardo, SP Modica–Pozzallo km 5, T: 0932 779118, 334 7091959, www.cambiocavallo.it.*

Pozzallo (*map p. 538, C3*)

€ **Villa Ada**. Charming, elegant little hotel in a centrally-located 1920s building, with a restaurant and car park, close to the beach, quiet rooms. *Corso Vittorio Veneto 3, T: 0932 954022, www.hotelvillaada.it.*

€ **Mare Nostrum**. Simple, comfortable B&B in the centre of Pozzallo, 7 rooms named after Sicilian writers, very good breakfasts. *Via Giunta 12/14, T: 0932 958769, www.villasara.it.*

Ragusa Ibla (*map p. 538, C2*)

€€€ **San Giorgio Palace**. Group of old houses clinging to the hillside, remarkably well recuperated, lovely modern interiors. 13 rooms and suites, very good panoramic restaurant. From the road a tunnel and lift take you straight up to the front desk and to the old streets of Ibla. *Via Torrenuova 50, T: 0932 686983, www.sangiorgiopalacehotel.it. Map p. 286, 3.*

€€ **Le Chicche**. B&B behind the cathedral, with 5 rooms offering spectacular views over the rooftops, all with TV and air conditioning. *Via Salita Specula 7, T: 0932 239180, 330 849862, www.bblechicche.com. Map p. 286, 3.*

€ You can stay in one of the little houses of Ibla, which functions as *paese-albergo*, by contacting Associazione Zuleima, *Piazza della Repubblica 3, T: 0932 061656, 338 7862198, www.zuleima.org.*

Ragusa Superiore (*map p. 538, C2*)

€€€ **Antica Badia Relais**. In a beautifully restored 18th-century building; the 12 rooms and suites are all different, some with the original floors of Caltagirone tiles. Small spa, very good restaurant, have breakfast or dinner on the rooftop in an unbelievable setting. *Corso Italia 115, T: 0932 247995, www. anticabadia.com. Map p. 286, 1.*

€€€ **De Stefano Palace**. 15 elegant rooms and suites, all different, in an 18th-century palace with frescoed ceilings, no restaurant. *Via Cavaliere De Stefano 15, T: 0932 682872, www.destefanopalacehotel.com. Map p. 286, 2.*

€€€ **Villa Carlotta**. Just outside the new town to the west, an old farm has been transformed into a comfortable, modern hotel surrounded by a garden, with a pool and a car park. 26 beautiful rooms and suites, good restaurant. *Via Gandhi 3, T: 0932 604140, www. villacarlottahotel.com. Beyond map p. 286, 1.*

€ **Rafael**. Small family-run hotel, with 28 straightforward, clean rooms in a fairly central renovated 19th-century building. *Corso Italia 40, T: 0932 654080. Map p. 286, 2.*

Ragusa environs

€€€ **Eremo della Giubiliana**. A restored villa with authentic antique furniture, once a convent and then a fortified farmhouse. Private airstrip. Excursions (on request) by private plane or private boat to Lampedusa, Aeolian Islands, Etna. Very good restaurant, excellent wine list. *8km south of Ragusa, on the SP25 Ragusa–Marina di Ragusa, Contrada Giubiliana, T: 0932 669119, www.eremodellag-iubiliana.com.*

Santa Croce Camerina/Punta Secca (*map p. 538, B3*)

€ **La Casa di Montalbano**. The house on the beach used as the setting for Inspector Montalbano's home, now a comfortable B&B with 4 double rooms. Min 2 nights. *Via Aldo Moro 44, T: 0932 915376 (9am–6pm) and 393 9621306 (weekends and holidays), www. lacasadimontalbano.com.*

€ **Kaukana Inn**. On a lovely stretch of beach south of Santa Croce, a bright little hotel just right for families, 16 rooms, good restaurant, pizzeria and tennis. *Località Punta Secca, T: 0932 915273, www.kaukanainn.it.*

Scicli (*map p. 538, C3*)

€€€ **Palazzo Hedone**. Beautiful hotel created by French designers after restoring a group of crumbling Baroque palaces and voted by the Sunday Times as among the '100 Best Hotels of the World'; the 10 rooms are all different, and the restaurant is very good too. *Via Loreto 51, T: 0932 841187, www.palaz-zohedone.it.*

€€ **Novecento**. Elegant hotel in a tiny aristocratic palace in the heart of the Baroque town consisting of 6 (small) rooms and a suite, good restaurant. Unforgettable breakfasts on the flowery patio. *Via Duprè 11, T: 0932 843817, www.hotel900.it.*

€ **Conte Ruggero**. 5 lovely renovated rooms (all with air conditioning, en suite bathrooms & TV), in an 18th-century palazzo overlooking the town's main square; English spoken. *Piazza Italia 24, T: 0932 931840, 335 8218269, www.conteruggero.it.*

€ **Torre Camarella**. Six km from Scicli towards the sea, a friendly family home in the countryside with 3 clean, simple rooms with en suite bathrooms; excellent home-grown food, fresh milk and ricotta from the farm. *Contrada Mosca, SP 64 2km, T: 339 5277855, www.torrecamarella.it.*

Scoglitti (*map p. 538, B3*)

€€ **Al Gabbiano**. Welcoming little hotel used as a location for the Police Inspector

Montalbano series, with quiet rooms and a good restaurant serving local dishes accompanied by the excellent local wines, right on the beach; perfect for families with young children. *Via Messina 52, T: 0932 980179, www.hotelsulmare.it.*

Vittoria (*map p. 538, B2*)
€€€ **Locanda Cos.** ■ This beautiful farm 10km north of Vittoria town offers 6 luxurious suites and two double rooms, good restaurant and pool. Cos are the only vintners in Sicily to use huge terracotta amphorae to ferment their award-winning wines, Nero d'Avola and Cerasuolo di Vittoria DOCG. *SP Chiaramonte–Acate, km 14.5, T: 0932 876145, 392 7691544 (Giuseppe de Caro), www.cosvittoria.it.*

WHERE TO EAT

Chiaramonte Gulfi (*map p. 538, B2–C2*)
€€ **Majore.** An institution. Excellent local dishes, using the best ingredients Sicily can offer; pork is a speciality. Closed Mon. *Via Martiri Ungheresi 12, T: 0932 928019.*

Comiso (*map p. 538, B2*)
€ **Antica Comiso** They are justly proud of their seafood antipasti in this little trattoria; try the crudités of the day. Closed Tues, in summer also Sat and Sun lunchtime. *Via Di Vita 5, T: 0932 066631.*

Donnafugata (*map p. 538, B3*)
€ **Al Castello.** Simple family-run *trattoria* offering Hyblaean Mountain cuisine, next to the castle. Closed Mon. *T: 0932 619260, 333 2143959.*

Donnalucata (*map p. 538, B3*)
€€€ **Al Molo.** On the sea front, a friendly trattoria often featured in the Police Inspector Montalbano series, where chef Claudio prepares imaginative fish dishes; for dessert try the local version of blancmange with toasted almonds—*biancomangiare alle mandorle ab-*

brustolite. Open every day in summer, closes Mon in winter. *Via Perello 90, T: 0932 937710.*

Ispica (*map p. 538, C3*)
€€ **Greenway.** Spectacular restaurant in the grottoes of the archaeological park, offering tasty, typical local dishes. Open summer only. *Parco della Forza, T: 0932 951355.*

€ **Hotel Ispica.** Exceptionally good restaurant in a modest hotel—the cook is gifted. Closed Fri in winter. *Contrada Garzalla (railway station), T: 0932 951652.*

Marina di Ragusa (*map p. 538, B3*)
€€€ **Lido Azzurro da Serafino.** Long-standing reputation for fish dishes, Michelin star. Closed Mon and Tues lunchtime in winter. *Lungomare Andrea Doria, T: 0932 239522.*

Modica (*map p. 538, C3*)
€€€ **La Gazza Ladra.** This famous restaurant is the domain of brilliant young Michelin-star chef Accursio Craparo, who prepares exciting, original dishes with an eye for colour and flavour. Closed Sun evening, all day Mon. *Via Blandini 5, T: 0932 941059 (Hotel Palazzo Failla).*

€€ **Taverna Nicastro.** An old-fashioned, award-winning trattoria serving exceptionally good pasta and meat dishes, tasty arancini (fried rice balls), lentil or chickpea soups in winter, friendly and relaxed. Open evenings only, booking advisable, closed Sun and Mon. *Via Sant'Antonino 30 (Modica Alta), T: 0932 945884.*

€€ **Hosteria San Benedetto.** Restaurant serving generous portions, Sicilian dishes, also wine-beer-coffee-snack bar. Closed Tues. *Via Nativo 30 (Modica Alta), T: 0932 754804.*

€ **L'Arco.** Good home-made pasta or ravioli, simple desserts such as lemon or cinnamon jelly, Sicilian style. All accompanied by wine from their own vineyard. Closed Mon (July and Aug open every day). *Piazza Corrado Rizzone 11, T: 0932 942727.*

Pozzallo (*map p. 538, C3*)

€€ **Ippocampo**. Local fish, cooked to perfection and served in beautiful surroundings, with a sea view. Closed Wed. *Contrada Tegolaio (eastern outskirts), T: 0932 953658, 334 9691343.*

€€ **Il Delfino**. Central and on the seafront, absolutely delicious fish dishes, good value for money. Closed Mon. *Piazza delle Sirene 4, T: 0932 954732.*

Ragusa Ibla *(map p. 538, C2)*

€€€ **Ristorante Duomo**. One of Sicily's best restaurants, presided over by famous 2-Michelin-star chef Ciccio Sultano; excellent wine cellar; ideal for a special dinner, very imaginative and appetising fare. Expensive. Closed all day Mon and Sun evening in winter, all day Sun and Mon lunchtime in summer, Aug open every day. *Via Bocchieri 31, T: 0932 651265. Map p. 286, 3.*

€€ **La Locandina**. Charming restaurant in the heart of Ibla, attentive service, inventive cuisine, excellent pizza. Closed Thur in winter. *Via Orfanotrofio 39, T: 0932 220231. Map p. 286, 4.*

€ **'U Saracino**. A favourite with the locals. Excellent ricotta ravioli with pork ragout, delicious soups in winter; inexpensive set menu. Closed Wed. *Via del Convento 9, T: 0932 246976. Map p. 286, 4.*

Ragusa Superiore *(map p. 538, C2)*

€€€ **Caravanserraglio**. Refined restaurant offering excellent seafood, including bluefin tuna when in season and garfish, also lamb, rabbit and duck. Interesting desserts, extensive wine-list. Closed Mon and Sat lunchtime. *Via Nenni 78, T: 0932 654342. Beyond map p. 286, 5.*

Scicli *(map p. 538, C3)*

€€ **Pomodoro**. Chef Giuseppe favours tradition with a twist, making the most of fresh local ingredients. Try his *tortino di melanzane con pomodoro e crema di ricotta* (aubergine tart with tomato and ricotta cream). Closed Tues.

Corso Garibaldi 46, T: 0932 931444.

€€ **Satra**. ■ A tiny restaurant where you can appreciate the particular local cuisine, enhanced by the use of locally-grown herbs, adding just the right fillip to every dish. Local wines. *Via Duca degli Abruzzi 1, T: 342 0616781 (Enrico) or 348 6726875 (Rita).*

Scoglitti *(map p. 538, B3)*

€€€ **Sakalleo**. In the centre of the village. Fresh fish and good wine; the antipasti are very special; renowned for cous cous and fish soup. Closed Mon lunchtime in winter. *Piazza Cavour 12, T: 0932 871688.*

LOCAL SPECIALITIES

Chiaramonte Gulfi For olive oil made with Tonda iblea olives, Pianogrillo was voted 'Best of Sicily' in 2011. Some of the trees in their groves are 700 years old. *(Contrada Pianogrillo, near the archaeological area of Akrillae; T: 338 8193102, www.pianogrillo.it for online purchases.)*

Modica Antica Dolceria Bonaiuto, founded 1880 *(Corso Umberto 259, www.pianogrillo.it)*, sells delicious, unusual local sweets including *'mpanatigghi* (light pastry filled with minced beef, chocolate and spices), *cedrata* (honey and citron rind), *cobaita* (honey and sesame seeds), and Modica chocolate. Another good address is Casa Don Puglisi *(Vico De Naro 4, www.laboratoriodonpuglisi.it, closed Sun and Wed afternoon)*; it is a foundation which takes in girls in a difficult situation (mostly unmarried mothers refused by their families, thieves and repentant prostitutes), looks after them, gives them a place to live, and trains them as confectioners, so they will easily be able to find employment once they are back on their feet. Rizza *(Corso Umberto 128)* is the place to go for olive oil, fresh roasted coffee, herbs, pepper and Modica chocolate, including *cioccolato al peperoncino* (chilli-flavoured chocolate). Casa del Formaggio *(Via Marchesa*

Tedeschi 3) has all the local cheeses, hams and salami, Modica chocolate, carob products and liqueurs. Ottavia Failla makes unusual and decorative handbags using luxurious materials (*Hotel Palazzo Failla, www.ottaviafailla.it*).

Monterosso Almo At Terranova, in Piazza San Giovanni, you will find the exquisite ricotta ice cream, served in the little wicker *cavagne* where the cheese is prepared.

Pozzallo Gelateria Fede (*Corso Vittorio Veneto 29*) for exquisite sorbet and *granita*—chocolate *granita* was invented here.

Ragusa Ibla Gelati DiVini has an excellent reputation for ice cream, including novel flavours such as olive, beetroot, red wine; made using only local ingredients (*Piazza Duomo 20*).

Ragusa Superiore Casa del Formaggio Sant'Anna (*Corso Italia 387; closed Wed afternoon*) for local cheeses, including the superb *caciocavallo ragusano*. Maddalena (*Via Lombardia 86*) for sourdough bread, baked in a stone oven. Forno San Paolo (*Via Giusti 121*) is another traditional baker. Di Pasquale (*Via Vittorio Veneto 104; closed Mon*) is one of the finest confectioners in Italy, and has won many prizes. Try *testa di turco* (Turk's head), a creamy confection, or *cannoli di ricotta*.

Scicli–Sampieri Aromatic herbs grow well in this corner of Sicily, with constant sunshine and sea breezes. Visit the Herb Garden to see, touch and smell hundreds of varieties. You can order online (*Gli Aromi, Contrada Santa Rosalia, T: 342 0616781 (Enrico), www.gliaromi.it*).

FESTIVALS & EVENTS

Acate Good Friday, *Scinnenza*, a procession of the statue of Christ, accompanied by girls dressed in white, representing Veronica. Third Sun after Easter, Feast of St Vincent.

Chiaramonte Gulfi Feb, *Carnevale della*

Contea, including a feast of the local sausages.

Comiso 3 Feb, Feast of St Blaise, with fireworks and distribution of blessed loaves. First week of June, *L'Isola dei Mestieri*, a fair dedicated to Sicilian handicrafts.

Giarratana 14 Aug, *Sagra della Cipolla*, festival of the large, flat, very tasty onions. 21–22 Aug, *Fiera di San Bartolomeo*, traditional cattle-market followed by a festival on 24 August to celebrate St Bartholomew.

Modica Easter Sun, *La Maronna Vasa-Vasa* (the 'Kiss-Kiss Madonna'), the culmination of Easter week with the meeting of the Madonna and her Son, the two statues exchanging joyful kisses. Sun on or after 23 April, Feast of St George, patron saint of Modica Alta. End of June, Feast of St Peter, patron saint of Modica Bassa, with a fair.

Pozzallo Second Sun in Aug, *Sagra del Pesce*, fish are cooked and served in Piazza Rimembranza, using a pan 4m wide.

Ragusa Ibla Last Sun in May, Feast of St George, procession and fireworks. Oct, Ibla Buskers, street musicians from all over the world (*Info: www.iblabuskers.it*).

Ragusa Superiore 29 Aug, Feast of St John, the patron saint, with colourful celebrations and fireworks.

Santa Croce Camerina 18–19 March, celebrations for St Joseph, including the *tavolate*, lavish banquets for the poor.

Scicli Mid-March, *Cavalcata di San Giuseppe*, bonfires on street corners light the Flight into Egypt. Palm Sun, procession culminating in woven palm leaves offered to the Madonna. Easter Sun, *Festa dell'Omu Vivu*, a dramatic procession of young people carrying the statue of the Risen Christ, shouting '*Gioia! Gioia!*' (Joy! Joy!). Last Sun of June, *Madonna delle Milizie* in commemoration of the famous battle between the Normans and Saracens.

Vittoria 18 March, *Tavolata di San Giuseppe*, when banquets for the poor are prepared.

THE PROVINCE OF SYRACUSE

The province of Syracuse is famed above all for its many delightful Baroque cities, all of which were rebuilt in this style after the devastating earthquake of 1693: Syracuse itself, Noto, Palazzolo Acreide, Sortino, Buccheri and Buscemi are the most noted. Syracuse itself is home to many fascinating remains from its ancient Greek past. Other highlights include the quiet fishing villages such as Marzamemi, peaceful country towns like Avola or Floridia, the Sicel necropolis of Pantalica, and spectacular gorges at Cassibile and Ispica. The wine produced in the province is famed for its quality, and fruit and vegetables are grown in abundance: strawberries from Noto or Rosolini, carrots from Ispica, and Pachino cherry tomatoes, cantaloupes and melons are known throughout Europe.

SYRACUSE

Syracuse (*Siracusa* in Italian; *map p. 538, D2*) is the successor of the magnificent *Surakousai*, which rivalled Athens as the largest and most powerful city of the Greek world. The beautiful island of Ortigia (literally 'the island of the quail', after its shape) has many monuments of great interest. Though it suffered from depopulation a few years ago, it is now once again the heart of the city, with good restaurants and a lively atmosphere in the evenings. The principal ruins of the Greek city, including the famous theatre, are close by on the mainland, as is the archaeological museum. Cicero noted that Syracuse knew no day without sun, and it does indeed enjoy a mild marine climate throughout the year. It is a World Heritage Site, and one of the more popular destinations in Sicily.

Clay altar of the 6th century BC showing a lion attacking a bull. Found at Centuripe in Enna province and now on display in the archaeological museum in Syracuse.

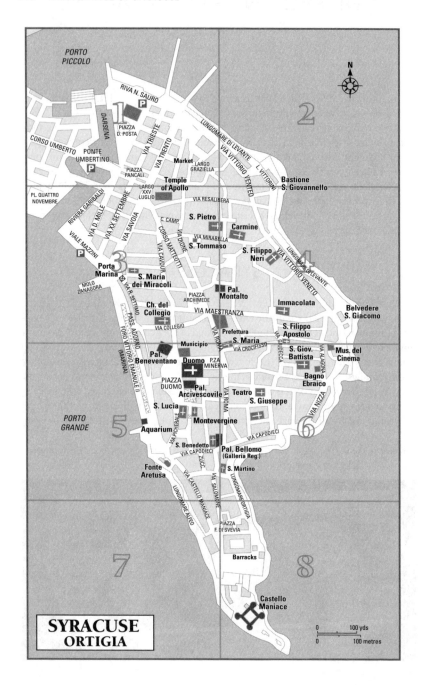

PORTO
PICCOLO

N

RIVA N. SAURO

DARSENA

P

PIAZZA
D. POSTA

CORSO UMBERTO

PONTE
UMBERTINO

P

PIAZZA
PANCALI

VIA THESTE

VIA TRENTO

LUNGOMARE DI LEVANTE

VIA VITTORIO VENETO

L. VITTORINI

Market

LARGO
GRAZIELLA

Temple
of Apollo

LARGO
XXV
LUGLIO

Bastione
S. Giovannello

PL. QUATTRO
NOVEMBRE

RIVIERA GARIBALDI

VIA D. MILLE

VIA XX SETTEMBRE

VIA SAVOIA

VIA RESALIBERA

C. CAMP.

S. Pietro

Carmine

VIA MIRABELLA

S. Tommaso

S. Filippo
Neri

LUNGOMARE DI LEVANTE

VIA VITTORIO VENETO

CORSO MATTEOTTI

VIA DIONE

VIA CAVOUR

Porta
Marina

MOLO
ZANAGORA

VIALE MAZZINI

P

VIA R. SETTIMO

PASS. ADORNO

FORO VITTORIO EMANUELE II

(MARINA)

S. Maria
dei Miracoli

Ch. del
Collegio

VIA COLLEGIO

PIAZZA
ARCHIMEDE

Pal.
Montalto

VIA MAESTRANZA

Immacolata

Belvedere
S. Giacomo

Prefettura

Municipio

Pal.
Beneventano

Duomo

PIAZZA
DUOMO

PIAZZA
MINERVA

P.ZA
MINERVA

Pal.
Arcivescovile

S. Lucia

S. Maria

VIA CROCIFISSO

VIA ROMA

VIA GIUDECCA

S. Filippo
Apostolo

S. Giov.
Battista

VIA ALAGONA

Mus. del
Cinema

Bagno
Ebraico

Teatro

S. Giuseppe

VIA NIZZA

PORTO
GRANDE

Aquarium

VIA PICHERALE

Montevergine

S. Benedetto

VIA CAPODIECI

ZUCC.

VIA CAPODIECI

Pal. Bellomo
(Galleria Reg.)

S. Martino

Fonte
Aretusa

VIA CASTELLO MANIACE

VIA SALOMONE

LUNGOMARE ORTIGIA

LUNGOMARE ALFEO

PIAZZA
F. DI SVEVIA

Barracks

Castello
Maniace

SYRACUSE
ORTIGIA

0   100 yds
0   100 metres

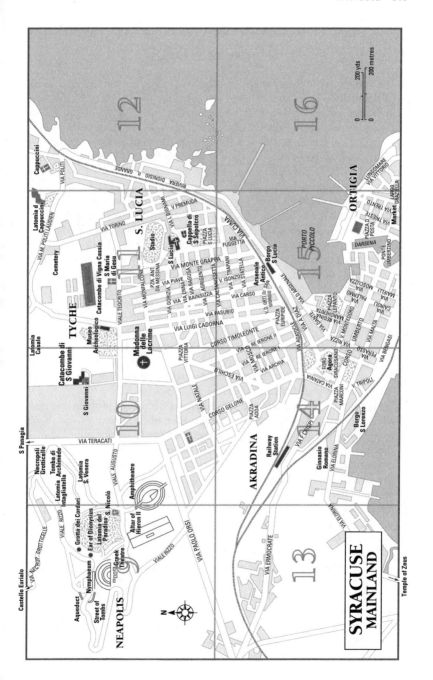

HISTORY OF SYRACUSE

The ancient city of Syracuse was founded on Ortigia, an island so close to the mainland that it would later be joined to it by a causeway. The island had a famous freshwater spring, Arethusa (today's Fonte Aretusa; *map 5*), and it helped provide shelter for two superb harbours (the Great Harbour to the south and west (now Porto Grande; *map 5*), and the Small Harbour to the north, now the Porto Piccolo used by fishing-boats; *map 1*). The city was founded in 733 BC by Corinthian settlers led by Archias, and links with Corinth remained close. The city grew fast, and its accumulated wealth was channelled into the creation of sub-colonies, such as *Akrai, Kasmenai, Heloros* and *Kamarina*. Much of the new settlement on the mainland, the districts of Akradina, Tyche and Neapolis, were on the slopes of the Epipolai plateau, which was to provide an outer defence line for the city.

Landed aristocrats were the first rulers of Syracuse, and when challenged by an emerging democratic movement, they called on a 'tyrant' from the outside, Gelon, ruler of the city of Gela, who forcibly settled much of Gela's population in Syracuse and made it his capital in 485. In 480 he defeated the Carthaginians at Himera, with the aid of his father-in-law, Theron of Akragas (Agrigento). The temple of Athena, built to celebrate this victory, is now the cathedral. Gelon was succeeded by his brother Hieron I (478–c.467), who married Gelon's beautiful widow Damarete and defeated an Etruscan fleet off Italy (474). He won a chariot race at the Olympics, and patronised the arts, welcoming the poets Aeschylus, Pindar, Simonides and Bacchylides to his court. Much of the expansion of the city dates from this period of cultural fervour.

Following Hieron's death, the city became a democracy, with an assembly, administrative council and elected generals. Even when Dionysius I was chosen as 'general with full powers' in 405, he preserved the democratic institutions. By this time Syracuse had fought off the great Athenian invasion fleet of 415–413, commanded by Nikias. The Athenians had tried to close off the city with a double row of walls and blockade it, but eventually, thanks to an eclipse of the moon, an omen that was misinterpreted by Nikias, their fleet was trapped inside the Great Harbour and annihilated. Dionysius I made sure that the city was made invulnerable against siege by obliging the whole population, himself included, to build a 30km wall around the city which would also enclose springs, pastures and gardens, starting from the heights of Epipolai. Although none of the four wars Dionysius fought against Carthage drove the Carthaginians from the island, under his rule Syracuse became a major power in Sicily and southern Italy.

It all collapsed under Dionysius' son, Dionysius II, who, in spite of personal tutoring by the philosopher Plato, was dissolute and arrogant. Syracuse was forced to ask her mother city for help to restore order. The Corinthian Timoleon did have some success in confronting the Carthaginians and setting up an oligarchic government, of some 600 leading citizens, modelled on that in Corinth, but Timoleon's constitution was overthrown after his death by Agathocles, who established his own tyranny in 316. Agathocles was an opportunistic adventurer who led campaigns to Africa and southern Italy and proclaimed himself king. However, he brought no long-term stability to Syracuse which lapsed once again into anarchy after his assassination in 289. In fact, Syracuse's security was compromised by a group of his mercenaries, the Mamertines. The city had to call on the ambitious ruler of Epirus, Pyrrhus, who was already supporting Greek cities in southern Italy against the Romans, for help against both the Mamertines and a resurgent Carthage. It was from this weak position that Syracuse enjoyed an unexpected revival. When the Mamertines called for help from Rome, a new king of Syracuse, Hieron II, realised the advantages of allying with, rather than resisting Rome, and for the next 60 years he exploited his favoured position to bring about an Indian summer of prosperity. Once again trading links extended across the Mediterranean. One of the largest theatres of the Greek world, surmounted by a huge stoa, and a massive altar to Zeus, were among the grand building projects of his day. Such grandeur masked the city's reliance on Rome, though, and when, after Hieron's death in 215, his successor unwisely moved towards the Carthaginians who, under their general Hannibal, were threatening Rome from inside Italy, Rome's retaliation was inevitable. Even the genius of Archimedes (*see box on p. 330*) could not save Syracuse in 211/212, after two years of siege.

The Romans made Syracuse a provincial capital under a praetor (a magistrate elected annually in Rome) and adopted Hieron's system of a grain tax to feed Rome and her armies. Some praetors, notably the notorious Verres (praetor 73–71), used their rule to despoil the city, but evidence of Roman building—an amphitheatre, a triumphal arch and a new forum—attest to a steady prosperity. The city remained a stopping-point for any voyager coming to Italy from the East (in AD 59 the apostle Paul spent three days here on his way to Rome), and it had some status as a tourist attraction. Catacombs show the growth of Christianity (they date from a century before Constantine's Edict of Toleration of 313 and then expand rapidly after it).

After the Roman period, Syracuse's power declined rapidly, although the Byzantine emperor Constans II resided there from 662 until his assassination in 668. Syracuse was badly damaged by the Saracens in 878, but freed from Arab rule for a time by General George Maniakes (1038–40), sent by Basil II of Byzantium. The importance which Syracuse regained between 1361 and 1536 by holding the quasi-independent seat of the Camera Reginale or Queen's Chamber, a kind of miniature Parliament, did not last. In 1837, having rebelled unsuccessfully against the Bourbons, it was punished by losing its role as provincial capital. After the Italian conquest of Libya the port expanded again but during the Second World War it was a target first for the Allied air forces and, after its capture on 10th July 1943, for German aircraft.

ORTIGIA

The island of Ortigia, just under 1km square, is joined to the mainland by three bridges. It forms the charming old town of Syracuse and is best explored on foot. It is certainly the most pleasant place to stay in the city.

Entering Ortigia

From Ponte Umbertino (*map 1*), the main bridge connecting the island to the mainland, numerous colourful little fishing-boats and excursion boats can be seen. On the left, the monumental former Post Office by Francesco Fichera (1934) was being turned into a hotel at the time of writing. Soon reached from the foot of the bridge, through an avenue (with a taxi rank) of shady ficus trees, is Piazza Pancali. On the right, in Via XX Settembre, are the remains of the Porta Urbica, a gateway in the old Greek fortifications.

To the left, a daily market for fresh fish, fruit and vegetables is held every morning except Sunday in the streets surrounding the old covered market place, a fine turn-of-the-century building. Nearby to the northeast is the fishermen's district, a small area of interesting narrow streets, once the old Arab quarter, centred on Largo della Graziella.

The Temple of Apollo

The temple of Apollo (*map 3*), surrounded by lawns and papyrus plants, is the earliest peripteral Doric temple in Sicily, built of local limestone in the late 7th century BC and attributed to the architects Kleomenes and Epicleos. Some scholars have identified it with the Artemision recorded by Cicero, but the dedication to Apollo cut in the steps of

Greek inscription on the steps of the Temple of Apollo, east side. The 'ΚΛΕΟ' of the name Kleomenes, the architect, is clearly visible.

the stereobate (still visible on the eastern side) seems conclusive. Transformed through the centuries, first into a Christian church, then an Arab mosque, and lastly into a Spanish prison, it was freed in 1938 from overlying structures, and two monolithic columns and part of the cella walls remain intact. Fragments of its polychrome terracotta cornice are preserved in the archaeological museum (*see p. 336*).

From Porta Marina to the Chiesa del Collegio

Via Savoia leads to the waterfront overlooking the Porto Grande, near the elaborate Chamber of Commerce building. Here is **Porta Marina** (*map 3*), a plain 15th-century gateway to the Great Harbour with an aedicule in the Spanish Gothic style. The long promenade by the water's edge, planted with splendid *Ficus benjamin* trees, called Foro Vittorio Emanuele II, is known locally as the Marina. There is a lovely view across the harbour to the wooded shore on the Maddalena headland, the ancient *Plemmyrion*.

Within the gate to the left is the attractive little church of **Santa Maria dei Miracoli**, in the street of the same name, with a fine doorway resting on little lions, with a sculptured lunette, and a worn tabernacle in the Catalan Gothic style. Straight on from the gate, Via Ruggero Settimo emerges on a terrace above the trees of the Marina, and Via del Collegio leads away from the sea skirting the high walls of the imposing Counter-Reformation **Chiesa del Collegio**, with its Corinthian pilasters and overhanging cornice (1635–87). The interior (now a temporary exhibition venue) contains altars from the former Jesuit college in Palermo, moved here in 1927–31.

Piazza Duomo

NB: The duomo itself is described overleaf.

The most beautiful square in the city is Piazza Duomo (*map 5*), where there are some fine Baroque buildings: to the left of the duomo itself, the **Municipio** (Town Hall) occupies the former Seminary (begun in 1628 by Giovanni Vermexio; notice his signature lizard on the extreme left-hand side of the cornice). Under the building lie the remains of an Ionic temple (*open 10–1.30, closed Sun and holidays; a new entrance in Via Minerva was under construction at the time of writing*) that was probably dedicated to Artemis (the Roman Minerva) and almost certainly never completed.

Adjoining the duomo is the **Palazzo Arcivescovile** (Archbishop's Palace; c. 1750, Louis-Alexandre Dumontier), part of which now houses the prestigious Biblioteca Alagoniana, with precious old manuscripts and incunabula. It has a shady hanging garden with oranges, lemons and palm trees. Archbishop Alagona, who founded the library in 1780, loved books so much that he excommunicated anyone caught stealing them. A doorway opening onto the square under the garden allows access to the subterranean passages called **Ipogeo** (*open 10–1, closed Sun and Mon*), some carved out in the Byzantine era, which house an exhibition on their use as an air-raid shelter during the Anglo-American bombing in 1943. The self-guided route through impressive dry and dripping caverns emerges at sea level on Foro Vittorio Emanuele II.

On the other side of the square, opposite the Town Hall, is **Palazzo Beneventano del Bosco**, a very fine building by the local master-builder Luciano Alì (1778–88),

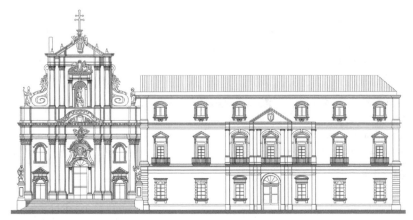

FAÇADE OF THE SYRACUSE DUOMO & ADJOINING ARCHBISHOP'S PALACE

enclosing a particularly attractive courtyard. Next to it is the curved, pink façade of Palazzo Gaetani e Arezzo.

At the south end of the square, with a balcony on the corner, is Palazzo Impellizzeri and the church of **Santa Lucia alla Badia**, which has a fine Bavarian-Baroque façade of 1695 by Luciano Caracciolo, who provided it with a balcony so the cloistered nuns could watch the festivities for St Lucy (*see p. 333*). Displayed over the high altar is a marvellous **painting by Caravaggio** of the *Burial of St Lucy*, carried out in 1608 after his adventurous escape from Malta, while he was the guest of his admirer Mario Min-niti, and completed in less than two months. Notice the despair of Lucy's mother, who believes herself responsible for her daughter's death, and the impatience of the uncouth grave-diggers (the one on the left is perhaps a self-portrait of the artist), waiting for the priest to finish his prayer so they can go home to their dinner. Also displayed here are two medieval Crucifixes, one of them T-shaped (15th century), the other of the 13th century. All three of these artworks come from the church of Santa Lucia on the mainland (*see p. 333*) but have been exhibited here indefinitely.

Just out of the piazza is the church of **Montevergine** (*closed*) with a façade by Andrea Vermexio; the convent next door is the gallery of modern art, **Galleria Civica d'Arte Contemporanea Montevergini** (*open 9–12 & 4–8; T: 0931 24902*), housing temporary exhibitions by local artists.

The duomo

Dominating the square with its authoritative presence is the duomo (*map 5; open 8–8; T: 0931 65328*), or Santa Maria del Piliero or delle Colonne. In the 7th century Bishop Zosimus repaired the Byzantine church built from the ruins of Gelon's Doric Temple of Athena and declared it the cathedral of the city. The present façade is a powerful Sicilian-Baroque composition erected in 1728–54 and designed by Andrea Palma; on the summit is a double-armed Cross, symbolising the presence of the archbishop. The marble statues of Sts Peter and Paul flanking the steps are the earliest known works of Ignazio Marabitti; he also sculpted the other statues (1754) on the façade: *Bishop Marcian* (*see p. 339*), the *Madonna* and *St Lucy*. The façade gives no hint that this building was once a Doric temple, but turn into Via Minerva and you will see twelve columns, with their architrave and triglyphs, punctuating the medieval north wall of the church. Their cornice was replaced by Muslim crenellation when the church was used as a mosque. Excavations beneath the duomo carried out by Paolo Orsi from 1912–17 revealed details of an Archaic temple, demolished to make way for the later temple, and, at a lower level, pre-Greek huts of the 8th century BC; more recently, while re-paving, an ancient Sicel necropolis of rock-cut tombs was discovered under Piazza Duomo.

HISTORY OF THE TEMPLE OF ATHENA (DUOMO)

In 480 BC the victorious Gelon returned home from Himera with thousands of prisoners of war to be used as slaves. In celebration of his victory, the finest craftsmen among them were selected to build a new temple to Athena on the summit of the island of Ortigia. Work probably continued for about ten years, although some scholars suggest that it took only two years to complete. Doric and peripteral, with 14 columns on the long sides and six on the short, the temple had doors inlaid with ivory and gold. Inside, the statue of Athena, larger than life-size, was made of Paros marble, with face, hands, feet and weapons of gold. Paintings by Zeuxis lined the walls of the cella. The magnificence of the building and these works of art were famous throughout the Mediterranean. The golden shield in the tympanum, which reflected the rays of the sun, was a landmark for sailors. All these treasures were later stolen by the praetor Verres (*see p. 189*).

Under Byzantium the temple was converted into a church: arches were cut in the wall of the cella, the entrance was moved to the west, and the space between the columns filled by a wall. Under the Arabs it became the Great Mosque. The Normans raised the height of the roof and added clerestory windows and the side chapels. The Spanish added the ceiling (of chestnut wood from Mt Etna) in 1518. Damaged by several earthquakes, it was rebuilt after 1693 when the Norman façade fell.

Interior of the duomo

Stripped of Baroque decoration between 1909 and 1927, the nave arcades were reduced to the plain massive piers formed by the eight arches opened by the Byzantine Christians in the side walls of the cella, which is the original 480 BC construction. The stained-glass windows are modern. On the internal entrance wall, two columns from the opisthodomos of the cella are preserved, and 19 columns of the peristyle are incorporated in the aisles, those on the left side being engaged. In fact, 24 columns of the temple survive, of the original 36. Along both sides of the nave, more or less where

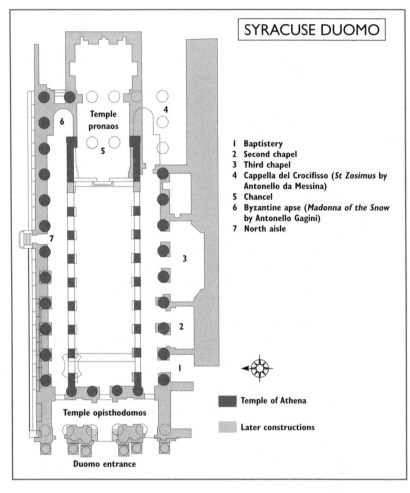

SYRACUSE DUOMO

Temple pronaos

Temple opisthodomos

Duomo entrance

1 Baptistery
2 Second chapel
3 Third chapel
4 Cappella del Crocifisso (*St Zosimus* by
  Antonello da Messina)
5 Chancel
6 Byzantine apse (*Madonna of the Snow*
  by Antonello Gagini)
7 North aisle

Temple of Athena

Later constructions

the roof of the temple would have been, is an inscription in Latin describing this as the oldest Christian community in Europe: *Ecclesia Syracusana prima Divi Petri filia et prima post Antiochenam Christo dicata*: 'The church of Syracuse is the first daughter of divine Peter and the first to be dedicated to Christ after Antioch'.

South side: The first chapel (**1**) is for baptisms. The **font** is a Hellenistic marble krater with a Greek inscription, standing on seven miniature bronze lions (13th century). It was found in the catacombs of San Giovanni (*see p. 339*), where it had been used as a burial urn. On the wall are fragments of mosaics which survive from the earlier Byzantine church.

In the second chapel **(2)**, with wrought-iron gates by Pietro Spagnuolo (1605), is kept a silver statue of St Lucy by Pietro Rizzo (1599), shown only on certain festivals and carried in procession in May and on 13th Dec. The two marble medallions are attributed to Ignazio Marabitti. The third chapel **(3)**, also with magnificent wrought-iron gates (1811), was designed in 1650–53, probably by Giovanni Vermexio. The vault frescoes are by the natural scientist and artist Agostino Scilla (1657). The altar frontal bears a beautiful relief of the *Last Supper* by Filippo Della Valle (1762). Above is a ciborium by Luigi Vanvitelli (1752).

On the left wall of the **Cappella del Crocifisso (4)** is a panel-painting of St Zosimus, attributed to Antonello da Messina; notice the innovative three-quarters positioning of the bishop, his expressive face, the varying textures of his sumptuous robes. Opposite is a damaged early 16th-century panel-painting of St Marcian. In the sanctuary is a Byzantine Crucifix and 13 panels from a polyptych by the school of Antonello (or early work by Antonello himself?).

Chancel: The bronze candelabra in the chancel **(5)** date from 1513, while the splendid main altar is the work of Giovanni Vermexio (1659), incorporating a monolith originating from the temple of Athena. The altarpiece, by Agostino Scilla (1653), is the *Nativity of the Virgin*. The two paintings over the choir, of *St Paul Preaching to the Christians of Syracuse* and *St Peter Sending Marcian to be Bishop of Syracuse*, were carried out by Silvio Galimberti in 1950.

North side: In the Byzantine apse **(6)** is a *Madonna of the Snow* by Antonello Gagini (1512). The end of the pronaos wall of the temple with its column can be seen here. The noticeable irregularity of the pillars on this side is due to earthquakes.

Along the wall of the north aisle **(7)**, between the temple columns, are three arresting statues in white Carrara marble: *St Lucy* by Antonello Gagini, *Madonna and Child* by Domenico Gagini, and *St Catherine of Alexandria* by the Gagini school.

Fonte Aretusa to Castello Maniace

From Piazza Duomo, Via Picherale passes the Hotel des Etrangers, which incorporates part of the medieval Casa Migliaccio, and leads down to a wide terrace on the waterfront surrounding the **Fonte Aretusa** (*map 5*), one of the most famous fresh-water sources of the Greek world. The spring of the nymph Arethusa was celebrated by Pindar and Ovid: when Arethusa was bathing in the River Alpheus near Olympia, the river god fell in love with her. In order to escape from Alpheus, Arethusa plunged into the Ionian sea and reappeared here. Transformed by the goddess Artemis into a spring, she was pursued here by Alpheus, who mingled his river water with that of the spring: it was believed that the river in the Peloponnese was connected, via the sea, to the fountain of Arethusa. A freshwater spring, called the Occhio della Zillica and said to be Alpheus, still occasionally wells up in the harbour. The spring of Arethusa diminished after the erection of the Spanish fortifications. Nelson took on supplies here before the Battle of the Nile in 1798, and noted in a letter that 'surely, watering at the fountain of

Arethusa, we must have victory'. The fountain now flows into a pond (built in 1843), planted with papyrus, abounding in fish and inhabited by white ducks, under a venerable old Morton Bay fig tree.

By the spring is the **Aquarium** (*open 10–4.30, until 10 in summer; T: 333 1674461*), with some of the types of fish to be found in the Ionian Sea. The attractive seafront here with its shady *Ficus benjamin* trees, is the favourite spot for the local *passeggiata*.

The end of the promontory, beyond Piazza Federico di Svevia, is occupied by the 13th-century **Castello Maniace** (*map 8; open 9–1.30, last tickets 30mins before closing, closed Mon; T: 0931 464420*), built c. 1232 by Frederick II of Hohenstaufen but named after the Byzantine general George Maniakes, supposed (in error) to be its founder. The 51m square keep, with cylindrical corner towers, has probably lost a third of its original height. On either side of the imposing Swabian doorway are two consoles, formerly bearing splendid 4th-century BC bronze rams, thought to be the work of Lysippus. One of these is now in the Salinas archaeological museum of Palermo. Overlooking the harbour are the remains of a large three-light window. Beneath the castle is the so-called Bagno della Regina, an underground chamber once probably a reservoir.

Via Salomone and Via San Martino return past (right) the church of **San Martino** (*map 6*), founded in the 6th century, with a doorway of 1338. The interior, dating from Byzantine times, contains a fine triptych by a local 15th-century master. At the opposite end of the street stands the church of **San Benedetto** (*map 5*), with a huge canvas of the *Ecstasy of St Benedict* by Mario Minniti.

Palazzo Bellomo and the Regional Gallery of Art

Palazzo Bellomo is the seat of the Galleria Regionale (*map 5–6; open 9–7, Sun and holidays 9–1, last tickets 30mins before closing, closed Mon; T: 0931 69511*). The building combines elements of its Swabian construction (c. 1234) with alterations of the 15th century. The splendid collection, recently rearranged, includes some great masterpieces. The galleries are not numbered; the description below follows the sequence, with the works displayed in loose historical order.

Ground floor

Entrance is through the two courtyards. In the first are stone inscriptions, including some from the Jewish cemetery. In the second courtyard are aristocratic coats of arms carved in stone, and a large window affording a view of the 18th-century state carriages of the city. In the small rooms opening onto this courtyard are elements of medieval art: sculptures, polyptychs, and some lustre-ware bowls from Valencia. Steps lead up to the principal galleries (*lift available*).

First floor

In the first room is a large wooden relief map of the city of Syracuse, made in the 18th century. High up on the wall is a painted wooden beam from the cathedral. To the left is **Gallery 1**, displaying the *Madonna Annunciate* by Antonello da Messina, painted for the church of the Annunziata of Palazzolo Acreide in 1474, and discovered by chance in the church in 1897. Painted on wood and much decayed, apart from the figures of the Virgin and the Angel, the fragments of colour were transferred onto canvas during a long and difficult restoration. Close by are other contemporary works of art: an illuminated book of hours, and a lustre bowl, both made in Syracuse. In the other part of the room, in front of the huge fireplace, is the *Madonna of the Goldfinch* by Domenico Gagini, and the marble tombstone of Giovanni Savastida, who died in 1472, showing his effigy on one side and a *Pietà* on the other, probably the work of Francesco Laurana. **Gallery 2** has a collection of crib figurines in wax and cloth, and Sicilian ceramic bowls and jugs in the centre. **Gallery 3** shows 17th-century paintings, mostly anonymous, and a model in wood and ivory of the city of Syracuse. Beautiful coloured marble intarsia work dominates **Gallery 4**, together with a stunning *Immaculate Virgin with Saints* by Willem Borremans. The showcases display church silverware and embroidered vestments, and a large model ship in silver, a reliquary of St Ursula. In **Gallery 5** are paintings by Giuseppe and Giovanni Reati, a *Martyrdom of St Lucy* and other paintings by Mario Minniti, and some interesting little figurines and reliquaries, examples of the skills of the local craftsmen. Large statue-reliquaries are to be seen in **Gallery 6**, and a sketchbook belonging to Filippo Paladini. Stone carvings and more paintings are in **Gallery 7**. In the middle of the room there is a marvellous collection of old Byzantine icons, panel-paintings of saints, and a series of pictures portraying episodes from the Old Testament, from the Creation to the Expulsion of Adam and Eve from the Garden of Eden.

Via Roma and Piazza Archimede

Via Roma, with delightful overhanging balconies, is the backbone of Ortigia. On the corner of Via Crocifisso (*map 6*) is the church of **Santa Maria della Concezione** (1651), which has a lovely interior with a tiled floor. On the vault is a late 18th-century fresco by Sebastiano Lo Monaco, while the altarpieces on the left side and on the first right altar are by Onofrio Gabrieli (1616–1706), depicting the *Madonna of the Letter*, patroness of Messina, Gabrieli's home town; the *Martyrdom of St Lucy* and the *Massacre of the Innocents*.

Piazza Archimede (*map 3*) was laid out between 1872 and 1878 in the centre of Ortigia, but some of its palaces and courtyards preserve medieval elements. In the centre is the cement Fountain of Diana by Giulio Moschetti (1906). Off the square, reached by Via Montalto, is the façade of **Palazzo Montalto** in the Gothic-Chiaramonte style of 1397; it has been propped up with concrete bastions. From the car park behind, the shell of the building is visible, with a fine loggia.

The handsome little Baroque Palazzo Pupillo, standing at no. 11 on the square houses the **Arkimedeion** (*open 9.30–7.30, last tickets 30mins before closing, café and well-stocked bookshop; T: 392 9928351, www.arkimedeion.it*), a science museum dedicated to the city's most illustrious citizen. On two floors, a series of fascinating interactive displays and models perfectly illustrate the intellectual fervour of Archimedes, and the way in which his theories provide the basis for modern science and technology. Particularly effective are the Stomachion, the 14-piece composition puzzle, the Sphere contained by the Cylinder, and the Burning Mirrors. Explanatory panels in Italian, English and Spanish.

Archimedes (?287–212 BC)

The mathematical genius Archimedes may have been a close friend or relative of King Hieron II of Syracuse; certainly it was Hieron who sponsored his journey to the great library of Alexandria, where he was able to discuss his theories with his peers. Among the discoveries attributed to Archimedes are the cogged wheel (hence the winch); the spiral tube for lifting water; the relationship between the circumference and the diameter of a circle; the lever; the displacement of liquid method for ascertaining the composition of metals (which he famously discovered in the bath); and the calculation of the volume of a sphere contained inside a cylinder. In 240 BC he designed a luxurious cruise ship for Hieron, called the *Syrakosia*, described by an engineer, Moschyon, who took part in the construction. The great ship was a catamaran, built of timber from Mt Etna, rope from Iberia, ivory and rosewood from Africa, and weighed 4,000 tons. Intended to demonstrate the power of Syracuse in the Mediterranean, the ship was in fact impractical, being too large for most ports. Hieron made the generous gesture of sending it to Egypt loaded with wheat, as a gift to Ptolemy IV Philopator during a famine. When Marcus Claudius Marcellus captured Syracuse in 211/212 BC, he ordered his men to take Archimedes alive but, distracted by his calculations, Archimedes refused to give his name, and was killed by an impatient legionary.

Via Maestranza and the Giudecca

The elegant Via Maestranza (*map 3–4*), once seat of the wealthy city corporations, leads east from Piazza Archimedes towards the sea, past several Baroque palaces and the church of **San Francesco** (or Immacolata), with an attractive little convex façade. It has a fine late 18th-century interior, with twelve small paintings of the Apostles in the apse. Two Gothic portals have been exposed. Via Giudecca, to the right, recalls the Jewish district of the city. By following it south, after 150m you find on the right the tiny church of **San Filippo Apostolo**, once a synagogue. Opposite the church a little street leads to Piazza del Precursore, with the 12th-century church of **San Giovanni Battista**, usually known as San Giovannello (*to request visit of both churches call Kairos; T: 0931 64694*). This was one of the four basilicas built in the city by the English bishop Richard Palmer in 1184, and later rebuilt under Swabian rule. Also in this district, at Piazza San Giuseppe 33, is the interesting puppet museum, **Museo dei Pupi** (*open Sept, Oct, Dec and March, April, May 11–1 & 4–6; June, July, Aug 10.30–1 & 4–6.30; closed Sun and Jan, Feb, Nov; T: 0931 465540, 347 3810826, www.pupari.com*), offering the opportunity to view the typical marionettes of Syracuse, together with the stage settings and the posters.

Back on Via Maestranza, the last turning on the right is Via Alagona, where at no. 41 you will find Palazzo Cordaci, which houses the **Museo del Cinema** (*open Wed 9–12.30; T: 0931 65024, 339 4258654*). Besides a vast library of books about cinema

Detail of the nymph Arethusa on the Fountain of Diana in Piazza Archimede.

and theatre, there is a collection of more than 2,600 films, and posters going back to the early days of cinema. Close by, at no. 52, is the **Bagno Ebraico**, an intact Jewish mikveh, a spring for ritual ablutions, which came to light during restoration work in an ancient palace (*guided tours at 11, 12, 1, 3.30, 4, 5, 6, 7; T: 0931 22255*).

Via Vittorio Veneto

Via Vittorio Veneto, once the *Mastrarua*, the main street in Spanish times, is lined with 17th–18th-century Spanish-style palaces, and emerges on the sea by the church of **San Filippo Neri** (*map 4*), which bears the lizard symbol, signature of the architect Vermexio, beside the left-hand mascheron. Next door is the fine restored Palazzo Interlandi. Via Mirabella (with Palazzo Bongiovanni on the corner) leads away from the seafront past the church of the **Carmine**, which preserves part of its 14th-century structure.

AKRADINA & TYCHE

The area on the mainland opposite Ortigia corresponds to the ancient district of *Akradina*, northeast of which is *Tyche*, where the Regional Archaeological Museum is situated. Akradina centres on the **Foro Siracusano** (*map 14*), a large and busy square with a Fascist-era war memorial (1936) and fine trees. Here are some remains of the ancient **agora**; recent excavations have revealed other parts of the agora near Corso Umberto and Corso Gelone, where dwellings of the late 8th century BC have also come to light, the earliest of the Greek period so far found in Syracuse.

Ginnasio Romano

From Piazza Marconi, Via Crispi forks right to the railway station. Via Elorina (left) leads to the so-called Ginnasio Romano (*map 14; open 9–1; may be closed Sun and holidays*), a complex ruin surrounded by lawns and palm trees, with a portico on three sides, an altar, a temple and a small theatre. The portico on the north side and part of the high temple podium remain. The theatre's orchestra is now under water, but a few of the lower steps of the cavea are visible. The buildings, all of Imperial date, probably formed part of a serapeum, a Roman sanctuary dedicated to the Egyptian god Serapis.

Arsenale Antico

From the Foro Siracusano, Via Diaz leads towards Borgo Santa Lucia (*map 15*). On the left are two excavated sites: the first (straddled by a modern condominium) includes a small **bath house** of Roman origin, possibly the Baths of Daphne in which Emperor Constans II was assassinated in 668; the second, just beyond, behind railings, marks the **Arsenale Antico**, where the foundations of the mechanism used by the Greeks to drag their ships into dry dock can be seen.

In a simple house at no. 11 in Via Orti di San Giorgio, a little plaster image of the Virgin is supposed to have wept in 1953 (plaque in Piazza Euripide; the sanctuary of the Madonna delle Lacrime is described on p. 338).

Church of Santa Lucia

The church of Santa Lucia (*map 11*) is fronted by a large shady square. The façade, which recently collapsed without warning, has been faithfully reconstructed. the church was begun in 1629 to a plan by Giovanni Vermexio and completed in the 18th century (perhaps by Rosario Gagliardi), on the spot where St Lucy (?281–304), patron saint of Syracuse (*see box below*), was buried. The portal, the apses and the base of the campanile are Norman work and the rose window is of the 14th century. Outside can be seen the chapel of the Santo Sepolcro, which has a pretty exterior. Inside the church, in the sacristy, is a copy of Caravaggio's *Kiss of Judas* (the original is in Dublin). The church's other Caravaggio, together with two medieval Crucifixes, has been transferred to the church of Santa Lucia alla Badia in Ortigia (*see p. 324*).

ST LUCY OF SYRACUSE

According to Vatican files, Lucy of Syracuse would have been about 24 years old when she was martyred in 304, during the persecution of Diocletian. She had accompanied her wealthy, ailing mother to Catania to pray at the tomb of St Agatha. Having obtained a miraculous recovery, the two women returned to Syracuse, where they proceeded to donate all their possessions to the poor, as testimony of the miracle. Lucy was denounced by her betrothed for practising Christianity, and imprisoned. As punishment for her refusal to make sacrifices to the gods, the consul Pascasius sentenced her to be taken to the brothel, stripped, and raped. The soldiers, however, could not move her; she seemed rooted to the ground. Not even a team of oxen was sufficient. By now the people of the city were rejoicing and calling out her name. Pascasius told the soldiers to pile logs of wood around her to burn her, but even with the help of generous quantities of oil, the pyre would not catch. She was finally killed by a soldier who thrust his dagger into her neck. Portrayals of Lucy show the saint with her eyes in a dish or cup, about which the Vatican says nothing, but she is constantly invoked by people with eye problems, and also by the Swedish, to whom light is so important. Swedish girls traditionally take part in her procession in Syracuse on 13th December, once thought to be the shortest day in the year, harbinger of spring. The name Lucy derives from the Latin word *lux*, 'light', and the goddess Artemis, bringer of light, was once an important divinity in Syracuse.

A tunnel from the church leads past the entrance to the **catacombs of St Lucy** (*open 9–12.30; T: 0931 64694 to request visit*). These are the oldest in Sicily and the most extensive in existence after those in Rome, but only a small part are currently visitable. Caverns in the limestone existed here before the Christian era; there are Christian remains of the 2nd century and fragmentary Byzantine paintings. The tunnel emerges in Santo Sepolcro, the domed octagonal chapel by Giovanni Vermexio, partly below ground. This was the burial-place of St Lucy (the empty tomb remains behind the altar) and from here her body was taken to Constantinople in 1038; it was later seized as booty by the Venetians and taken to Venice, where it can still be seen, in the church of San Geremia. The 17th-century statue of the saint is by Tedeschi.

The Museo Archeologico Regionale Paolo Orsi

The Archaeological Museum (*map 11; open Tues–Sat 9–7, Sun and holidays 9–2, last tickets an hour before closing; T: 0931 464022*), dedicated to the great archaeologist Paolo Orsi, superintendent for antiquities from 1895–1934, has one of the most interesting archaeological collections in Italy, especially representative of the eastern half of Sicily. The material from excavations made by Paolo Orsi is outstanding. The collections are displayed in an unusual, low-level functional building in the shape of a broken triangle designed by Franco Minissi in 1967 and opened to the public in 1988.

The approach is through the garden, with splendid trees and some antique remains, which was once used as a Protestant cemetery. Among the 19th-century British and American tombstones (reached by the upper path which encircles the garden) is that of the Classicist German poet and scholar August von Platen (1796–1835).

Beyond the entrance hall the centre of the building has a display illustrating the history of the museum and the organisation of the exhibits, which are in three sections on the ground floor, starting from the bookshop and moving clockwise: (A) Geology, Palaeontology and Prehistory; (B) Greek colonies in eastern Sicily; (C) sub-colonies and Hellenised centres. On the upper floor (D) presents Hellenistic and Roman statuary, (E) Syracuse in the early Middle Ages, while (F), still on the drawing-board, will illustrate the territory of Syracuse during the Hellenistic period. In the basement is the Medagliere, the numismatic collection.

Section A (Ground floor): Geology, Palaeontology and Prehistory

Prehistory: An enlightening display illustrates the geology and the palaeontology of Sicily, with models of the famous dwarf elephants, the skulls of which, casually found in the past, gave rise to the legend of the Cyclops.

Neolithic Period: Represented by the Stentinello culture, characterised by fortified villages and the use of impressed pottery.

Early Bronze Age: Display relating to the site of Castelluccio (between Noto Antica and Palazzolo Acreide), with objects recovered by Paolo Orsi, including brown painted pottery and carved

stone doors from rock-cut tombs, each presenting spirals, yin-yang signs and male-female motifs, presumably symbolising death, rebirth and eternity.

Middle Bronze Age: Material from Thapsos on the Magnisi peninsula, a metropolis of the Mycenaean world, with inhabitants from various parts of the Mediterranean. The necropolis was excavated by Paolo Orsi, but the inhabited area (1500–900 BC) has only recently been examined. Finds include imported pottery (from Mycenae, Cyprus and Malta) and some splendid large storage jars, made using the 'coil of clay' method (some had been recycled as tombs). There are also some fascinating lebetes, water-bowls with a pedestal underneath and strangely-modelled upright backs, with what could be eyes and ears, or nipples and upheld arms, perhaps recalling a divinity who protected water. They had handles behind, so they could be carried from one place to another, perhaps for important rites. People of this culture used long-stemmed dishes for serving food, indicating that they were probably reclining on the floor while eating. **Late Bronze Age:** An absorbing display is dedicated to Pantalica, the most important Late Bronze-Age site in Sicily, which was naturally defended by its position,

and inhabited by the Sicels, who are thought to have migrated here from the Italian peninsula c. 1700 BC; their culture remained virtually unchanged until the arrival of the Greeks. There are many of the handsome, characteristic red vases, made this time by using a potter's wheel, and some of them (the heart-shaped jugs for carrying water) are reminiscent of Mycenaean ware, with shiny glaze.

Nearby are some of the numerous bronze artefacts found at Pantalica. Interesting reconstructed tombs, illustrating different burial methods, and a fine hoard of bronze fragments from Mendolito near Adrano, complete this part of the museum.

Section B (Ground floor): Greek colonies in Eastern Sicily

Greek colonisation: This period began in the mid-8th century BC, when settlers from Naxos, Corinth and Chalcis arrived on the island. Among the finds is a superb kouros (late 6th century BC) from Leontinoi, the head of which is in the Civic Museum of Catania. Ample space is dedicated to **Megara Hyblaea**, founded in 728 BC by Lamis of Megara and his people—late-comers successful enough to found Selinunte in their turn, exactly 100 years later. The objects displayed include imported Greek ware and local products, a fusion of the two cultures.

The most interesting sculptures include a marble statue of a young man (c. 560–550 BC), thought to be a funerary monument, with an inscription on the leg naming him as the physician Sambrotidas, son of Mandrocles, and a headless statue made from painted local limestone of a seated mother goddess suckling twins (550 BC). When found

in the 1950s it was smashed into more than 900 pieces by workers building the oil refineries for fear of having their employment stopped; the head was never found, probably pulverised when the statue was thrown over a cliff.

Syracuse: Finds from Ortigia are arranged topographically, giving an idea of the continuous habitation of the island: Arab pottery shards along with Roman glass and Greek vases, and a very life-like 5th-century BC marble fragment of a male figure. Akradina is represented by material from excavations in Piazza della Vittoria (the intended car park for the sanctuary of the Madonna delle Lacrime), where a sanctuary of Demeter and Persephone of the 5th–4th centuries BC was found, with hundreds of votive statuettes and an exceptional polychrome terracotta bust of Artemis. The necropoleis of the city have revealed much of interest. The artefacts are arranged here in chronological order and displayed as they were found in the tombs. They include an exquisite proto-Corinthian lion-shaped perfume vase (725–700 BC; Case 190) and a fine bronze 8th-century BC geometric-style statuette of a horse, now the symbol of the museum (Case 188). Artefacts imported from all over the known world, mostly of exceptionally high artistic value, demonstrate the wealth, influence and power of Syracuse.

Models of the temples of Apollo and Athena and terracotta fragments from them are exhibited. The frieze of seven lion-faced gargoyles comes from the Temple of Athena. The stunning polychrome marble relief of the running Gorgon with Pegasus, the earliest-known representation (7th century BC) of the unfortunate lady, was part of the older temple on the same site, replaced by Gelon's magnificent new building in 478 BC.

Section C (Ground floor): Sub-colonies and Hellenised centres

Heloros, **Akrai** and **Kasmenai**: These sites are represented by a high-relief in limestone (570–560 BC) of Persephone holding a dove, and weapons left as ex-votos. **Kamarina**: Finds include a large terracotta horse and rider (6th century BC), perhaps one of the Dioscuri, used as part of the roof decoration of a temple. **Grammichele**: A fine marble torso by a Greek artist (c. 500 BC) and a terracotta goddess enthroned (late 6th century BC). **Francavilla di Sicilia**: A remarkable series of pinakes, little terracotta pictures in relief (470–460 BC), which previously had only been found at the sanctuary of Persephone at Locri, in Calabria. **Centuripe**: A beautiful little clay miniature altar bears a relief from the 6th century BC showing a lion attacking a bull.

Adrano: The bronze statuette known as the *Ephebus of Mendolito* dates from c. 460 BC. **Gela** and **Agrigento**: The last section on the ground floor is devoted to Paolo Orsi's work here, with architectural terracottas, cinerary urns and sarcophagi. The vases from Gela include a krater signed by Polygnotus (440 BC); part of a cup signed by Chachyrylion (520–510 BC); a lekythos with a Nike, signed by Douris (470–460 BC), and a bronze dish with relief of horses (7th century BC). Also, a fragment by the Painter of Panaitos, and fine bronze kraters. The finds from Agrigento include three rare wooden statuettes of Archaic type dating from the late 7th century BC, found by a sacred spring at Palma di Montechiaro (Case 309).

Section D (Upper floor): Hellenistic and Roman Statuary

A colossal head of Zeus found in the Syracuse amphitheatre, a delicate statuette of Asclepius, a marvellous figure in marble of an Old Fisherman (a Roman copy of a Greek original), and several other fine works are to be admired in this gallery, but the highlight is the

remarkable headless statue of **Venus Anadyomene**, 'emerging from the water', an Imperial Roman copy of a 2nd-century BC Hellenistic original. Found in Syracuse in 1804 by the aristocrat and amateur archaeologist Saverio Landolina, she was greatly admired by Guy de

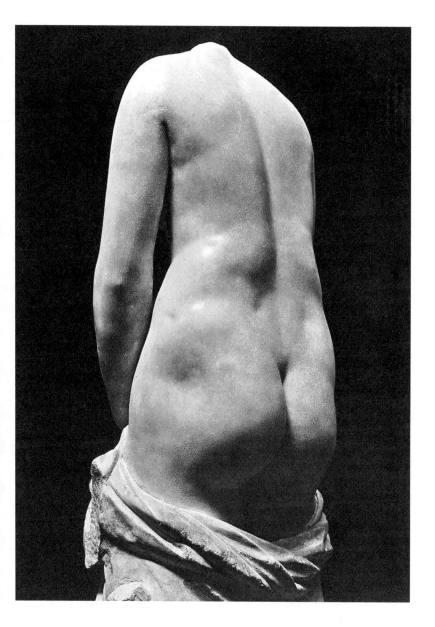

The celebrated *Venus Anadyomene* (Venus emerging from the water) seen from behind. The work is a Roman-era copy of a Hellenistic original.

Maupassant, who came purposely to see her in 1885 and left a vivid description of his emotions when he saw her: 'It is not woman poeticised, idealised, divine or majestic like the Venus de Milo; it is woman as she is, as she is loved, desired and should be embraced.'

Section E (Upper floor): Late Antique Syracuse

This section is devoted to a somewhat shadowy period in the history of the city. The highlight is the Sarcophagus of Adelphia, a white marble coffin carved in high relief with episodes from the Bible, including the *Nativity*, the *Flight into Egypt* and the *Massacre of the Innocents*, surrounding the central medallion with the magistrate Valerius and his wife Adelphia. Notice also the beautifully-crafted liturgical receptacles in bronze—goblets, small platters, lamps and a bell—recovered from the seabed off the Plemmyrion headland where the ship that was transporting them from Constantinople to Syracuse sank during a storm. The display is called *Il Relitto del Plemmyrion*. There were plans to transfer the wedding-ring of Emperor Constans II from the archaeological museum in Palermo for the inauguration of the section.

Medagliere (Basement)

The exceptional numismatic collection (*open Tues–Sat 9.30–1.30, Wed 9.30–5.30, closed Sun and Mon*) includes coins from the Greek cities of Sicily and southern Italy, together with examples of Roman, Byzantine and Islamic coins, and the first coins minted by the Normans, followed by Swabian, Aragonese and Spanish examples. There are also interesting examples of the art of Sicilian goldsmiths through the ages, from Prehistory to modern times, with lovely seal-rings from Sant'Angelo Muxaro, Byzantine earrings from Pantalica, and necklaces.

Museo del Papiro

Next door to the archaeological museum, at Viale Teocrito 66 is the Papyrus Museum (*open Tues–Sun 9–2; T: 0931 22100, 0931 61616, www.museodelpapiro.it*) with displays illustrating the manufacture through the centuries of paper and other articles (even boats) from the papyrus plant, here in Syracuse, but also in Egypt, Ethiopia, Sudan and Chad.

Madonna delle Lacrime

The vast tepee-shaped sanctuary of the Madonna delle Lacrime, or Our Lady of Tears (*map 10; open 7–1 & 3–8, until 9 on Sun and holidays; T: 0931 21446*) was begun in 1970 to enshrine a small mass-produced plaster image of the Madonna. The figure is supposed to have wept for four days in 1953 in a nearby house. The building where the miraculous image is preserved (by Michel Andrault and Pierre Parat), incorporates a late Roman tomb in the crypt, where there are also numerous ex-votos. The huge conical spire (98m high including the statue) towers incongruously above the city.

Adjoining it to the south, in Piazza della Vittoria, extensive excavations begun in 1973 during the construction of the sanctuary have revealed a group of Hellenistic and Roman houses, a sanctuary of Demeter and Persephone (late 5th or early 4th century BC), and a monumental 5th-century BC fountain. Five thousand terracotta votive statuettes were found here, some of which are now exhibited in the archaeological museum.

Church and Catacombs of San Giovanni

Off Viale Teocrito, just to the northwest of the Museo Archeologico, Via San Giovanni leads right. Here, amidst modern buildings, are the ruined church and catacombs of San Giovanni (*map 10; open 10–12.30 & 2.30–4, until 6 in summer, guided tours only, every 30mins; T: 0931 64694, www.kairos-web.com*). The façade is preceded by three arches constructed of medieval fragments. To the right is the main entrance and ticket office, beyond which are the entrances (right) to the catacombs and (left) to the ruined church and crypt. The catacombs are the remains of an early Christian burial ground, probably in use from the 3rd century to the end of the 6th, which had been built into an ancient quarry from the Greek era. The quarry was the supposed scene of the martyrdom of Marcian, first bishop of Syracuse, sometime in the 1st century. His grave, according to tradition, was also here, and a crypt was constructed around it. Above that crypt a basilica was erected at the end of the 6th or beginning of the 7th century.

The catacombs

The catacombs preserve examples of various types of burial, including loculi, arcosolia and tombs cut into the rock floor. From the decumanus maximus, or principal gallery, adapted from a disused Greek aqueduct, smaller passages lead to five domed circular chapels, one with rock-cut tombs, possibly those of seven nuns, members of one of the first religious houses established after the persecutions in Syracuse. One of the rock-niches contains a sarcophagus bearing a Greek inscription.

The church and crypt

On the left of the main entrance, a garden now occupies the ruins of the roofless **church**. The original basilica, once the cathedral of the city, was probably destroyed by the Arabs in 878. The Normans reconstructed it in 1200 and some of the visible remains date from that period. In the early 17th century it was remodelled on a smaller scale and with a different orientation. The earthquake of 1693 finally reduced it to the ruins from which it has never subsequently risen. A fine Gothic cusped rose window survives, as well as the 7th-century apse.

The **crypt** is in the form of a Greek cross, with three apses. The faded frescoes date from the Norman reconstruction. The fine Byzantine capitals, with symbols of the Evangelists, are thought to have been reused from the first basilica. In one apse are traces of 4th- and 5th-century frescoes from a hypogeum. The column against which the saint was allegedly flogged to death, and his tomb, surrounded by some of the earliest catacombs, can be seen. An altar is said to mark the site of St Paul's preaching in Syracuse: he probably spoke to the Christians of the city in the latomies.

To the east of the archaeological museum is the **Vigna Cassia** (*map 11; T: 0931 64696 to request visit*), a particularly attractive latomy with 3rd-century catacombs.

Latomia dei Cappuccini

Close to the former Capuchin convent, this latomy (*map 11; open 9.30–1, closed Sat, Sun and holidays*) is one of the most extensive of the twelve ancient quarries that surrounded the city. It is now overgrown by plants and trees. Adjacent is Villa Politi, the hotel where Winston Churchill stayed on his painting holidays in Syracuse. From Piazza dei Cappuccini, in front of the 17th-century church, is a fine view of Ortigia.

Neapolis: the Archaeological Park

Map 9–10. Entrance on Viale Augusto. Open summer 9–1hr before sunset, last tickets 1hr before closing; winter 9–3 (9–1 Sun and holidays in winter). NB: Call first to be sure of closing time. A visit can take at least 2hrs; a single ticket gives access to the Latomia del Paradiso, the Greek theatre and the Roman amphitheatre; combined tickets with the archaeological museum are available; T: 0931 65068. Just inside the entrance to the park is the little Norman church of **San Nicolò**. The funeral service of Jourdain de Hauteville, illegitimate but favourite son of Count Roger, was held here in 1092. The church has been restored but is kept locked. Below it, part of an aisled *piscina* can be seen, a reservoir used for flushing the amphitheatre, to which it is connected by a channel.

The Roman amphitheatre

The first entrance on the left leads to the Roman amphitheatre, approached past stone sarcophagi from necropoleis in Syracuse and Megara Hyblaea. An imposing Roman building probably of the 1st century AD, partly hollowed out of the hillside, in external dimensions (140m by 119m) the amphitheatre is only a little inferior in size to the one in Verona. Beneath the high parapet encircling the arena runs a corridor with entrances for the gladiators and wild beasts; the marble blocks on the parapet have inscriptions (3rd century AD) recording the ownership of the seats. In the centre is a rectangular depression, probably for the machinery used in the spectacles. The original entrance was at the south end, outside which a large area has been exposed, including an enclosure thought to have been for the animals, and a large fountain. Excavations have revealed an earlier roadway and the base of an Augustan arch here.

The altar of Hieron II

From the amphitheatre the path continues to the huge Ara di Ierone, hewn out of the rock; the monument can only be viewed from above. The altar, built between 241 and 217 BC, was used for public sacrifices to Zeus, when as many as 450 bulls could be killed in one day. It was 198m long and 22.8m wide (the largest altar known), and was destroyed by the Spaniards in 1526 in order to use the stone for harbour fortifications. The altar was presumably about 15m high, and elaborately decorated; the sacred area in front of it contained a rectangular pool for ablutions, and was delimited by a colonnade, more or less where the cypress trees stand today.

The Greek theatre

The Greek theatre is the most celebrated of all the ruins of Syracuse, and the largest Greek theatre in Sicily (138m in diameter). Archaeological evidence confirms the existence on this spot of a wooden theatre as early as the 6th century BC, and it was here that Epicharmus (c. 540–450 BC) worked as a comic poet. In c. 478 BC Gelon excavated a small stone theatre, engaging the architect Damokopos of Athens. It was inaugurated by Aeschylus in 476 BC with the first production of *Women of Aetna*; his *Persian Women* was performed shortly afterwards. The theatre was enlarged in the 4th century BC, under Timoleon, by excavating deeper into the hillside; it was again enlarged under Hieron II (c. 230 BC) by extending the cavea upwards, using blocks of stone. It could thus hold an audience of 15,000; some scholars think even more.

Under the Romans the **scena** was altered several times, eventually to make it suitable for gladiator battles. The foundations of the scena remain, but successive alterations make it difficult to identify their function. The Romans probably also cut the trapezoidal lines around the **orchestra**, when creating a *kolymbethra*, an ornamental fish pool, but it was abandoned in the 1st century AD in favour of the elegant new amphitheatre.

The existing **cavea**, with 42 rows of seats in nine wedges, is almost entirely hewn out of the rock. This is now believed to represent Hieron II's auditorium of 59 rows, less the upward extension, the stone of which has been removed. The extent of Timoleon's theatre before Hieron's excavations is marked by the drainage trench at the sixth row, above the larger gangway. Around the gangway runs a very worn frieze bearing, in large Greek characters, the names of Hieron (II), Philistis (his queen), Nereis (his

Detail of one of the side walls of the Street of Tombs. The niches cut in the wall in the Hellenistic period have all been long since despoiled of their votive tablets.

daughter-in-law, wife of Gelon II), and Zeus Olympius, which served to distinguish the blocks of seats. The little house which dominates the cavea is a medieval watch-tower against pirates.

Steps at the far end of the theatre, or a path near the entrance (which passes behind the medieval watch-tower) lead up to the rock wall behind the theatre. Here there are recesses for votive tablets and a **nymphaeum or grotto** in which the Galermi aqueduct ends in a gushing waterfall after traversing Epipolai bringing water from the River Bottigliera near Pantalica, 33km away. At the left-hand end of the wall the **Street of Tombs** (Via dei Sepolcri) begins, rising in a curve 146m long. The wheel-ruts in the limestone were made by carts in the 16th century serving the mills which used to occupy the cavea of the theatre. The Byzantine tombs and Hellenistic niches in its rock walls were all rifled long ago. Its upper end (*no admission*) crosses the rock-hewn Galermi aqueduct.

Immediately to the west of the theatre a sanctuary of Apollo Temenites has been discovered. A smaller and probably older theatre lies to the southwest, the Teatro Lineare, with seats arranged in straight lines.

Latomia del Paradiso and the Ear of Dionysius

A path leads down through a garden of lemons, oleanders and pomegranates to the **Latomia del Paradiso**, the largest and most famous of the twelve ancient quarries and since then one of the great sights of the city. The size of the latomies testifies to the colossal amount of building stone used for the Greek city, and for Dionysius' famous fortifications. Following the northern limit of Akradina from here to the Cappuccini near the sea, the quarries also served as a defensive barrier. They were sometimes used as concentration camps: according to Thucydides some 7,000 Athenians were incarcerated in one of them in 413 BC. By taking the steps down after the barrier, and following the path, you will see a tall isolated column of rock, the only surviving support for the roof of the enormous cave which the stone-cutters had formed, both to reach the fine-quality limestone deep under the surface, and to shelter themselves from the sun and the rain. The great blocks of stone fell when the vault collapsed during the 1193 earthquake. The path continues to the **Ear of Dionysius** (*Orecchio di Dionisio*), a sinuous artificial cavern, 65m long, 5–11m wide, and 23m high, in section like a rough Gothic arch. Its name was given to it by Caravaggio in 1608. Because of the strange acoustic properties of the cavern, it has given rise to the legend that Dionysius used the place as a prison and, from a small hole in the roof at the far end, heard the whispers of his captives. Before Caravaggio, local people called the cave the 'grotto of the noises'. It amplifies every sound and has an interesting echo, which only repeats each sound once. Now it is filled with the strange echoes of noises made by the pigeons which nest here. Once your eyes become accustomed to the dark you can walk to the far wall. The entire surface bears the marks of the slaves' chisels, and you can see the regular size of the blocks they were cutting—exactly one square cubit.

The entrance to the cavern known as the Ear of Dionysius, famous for its peculiar acoustic properties. Its walls are covered with the chisel marks made by slave quarrymen.

To the right of the Ear of Dionysius is the **Grotta dei Cordari**, named after the rope-makers who worked here for centuries. The vault of this picturesque cavern is supported by huge pillars, and the walls are covered with maidenhair ferns and coloured lichens. Access, unfortunately, is prohibited because of its perilous state.

A short way to the north of the church of San Nicolò is the beautiful, verdant **Latomia di Santa Venera** (*very regrettably closed*), the walls honeycombed with niches for votive tablets. At the far end is the **Necropoli Grotticelle**, a group of Hellenistic and Byzantine tombs, one of which, with a triangle over the entrance, is arbitrarily known as the Tomb of Archimedes. The 20th-century excavations here can be seen from the fence along the main road, Via Teracati.

ENVIRONS OF SYRACUSE

Dionysius the Elder (c. 432–367 BC)

Dionysius was one of the most remarkable rulers of his day. He exploited tensions in his native Syracuse after the failure of a campaign against the Carthaginians in order to seize control of the city and declare himself 'general with full powers' in 405 BC. He was clearly a charismatic speaker; several accounts tell of the theatres emptying as the citizens rushed to greet his arrival in a city. Dionysius was flamboyant in his personal life (one story tells of him consummating two marriages on the same night) but equally open to Greek culture. He loved making a display, flaunting the wealth of his city at the Olympic Games of 384. He supported Sparta against Athens but then was wooed back by the Athenians and even won first prize for a play at the city's drama festival. It is said that he was so excited by the news that he drank himself to death.

Ultimately, however, his position rested on a large force of mercenaries drawn from all over Sicily and Italy which sustained him in power even against popular uprisings. While his central mission to rid Sicily of the Carthaginians was never achieved, he came to control much of the island and extended his rule to the Greek cities of the mainland. An important innovator in siege warfare at a time when Greek armies usually gave up as soon as they met city walls, his capture of the Carthaginian stronghold of Motya (Mozia) in 397 was a major achievement. It is sometimes argued that if Dionysius had defeated the Carthaginians he might have conquered much of Italy and stayed the growing power of Rome. The fortifications around Syracuse which he completed between 402 and 397, culminating in the Castello Eurialo, are his most visible legacy.

Castello Eurialo

At the western limit of the ancient city, on the open, barren plateau of Epipolai, is the Castello Eurialo (*beyond map 9; open winter 9–3, summer 9–7, last tickets 1hr before clos-*

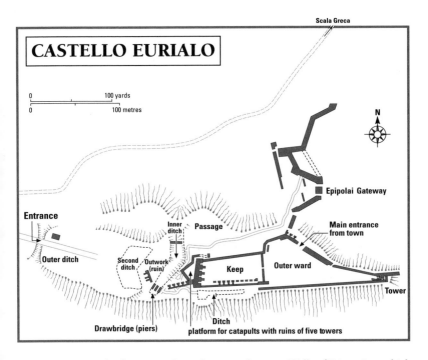

ing; T: 0931 711773). The approach road crosses the great Walls of Dionysius, which defended the Epipolai ridge. Begun in 402 BC by Dionysius the Elder (*see box opposite*), they were finished by 397 and were 30km long. Just before the main road to Belvedere crosses the walls, a path (50m) leads right to the **Latomia del Filosofo** (or Bufalaro). Philoxenus of Cythera was supposedly confined here for expressing too candid an opinion of the verses of Dionysius. The quarry supplied stone for the walls and the castle. The main road winds up towards the town of Belvedere; just after the signpost for the town, a narrow road (signposted) leads right for Castello Eurialo.

Three ditches precede the west front: the **outer ditch** is near the custodian's house. Between the second and the third are the ruins of an **outwork**, the walls of which have partly collapsed into the second ditch. On the left, steps lead down into the **inner ditch**, the principal defence of the fortress, which gave access to a labyrinth of casemates and passages. On the right the three piers of the **drawbridge** are prominent. There are eleven entrances from this main ditch to the gallery parallel with it; from here three passages lead east; the longest, on the north (174m long), connects with the Epipolai Gateway (*see below*). Prominent in this part of the castle are the **ruins of five towers**, originally 15m high, and surmounted by catapults invented by Dionysius.

The dark corridor to the south leads to a ditch outside the south wall of the castle. At the end, steps (which were concealed from the enemy) lead up to the outer ward of the castle proper, which consisted of a **keep** with the irregularly-shaped **outer ward** on the east. The barracks and cisterns were located in these parts of the castle. On the northeast side of the outer ward was the **main entrance from the town**; on the southeast rose a **tower** connected with the south wall of Dionysius. From here there is a good view of the **Epipolai Gateway** below, a 'pincer' type defence work on the spur of the north wall of Dionysius, which can be seen, broken at intervals by towers and posterns, stretching towards the sea. It was united to the keep by a complicated system of underground works, notable for their ingenious provisions for shelter and defence. An arch leads back towards the entrance into the keep. There are plans to re-open the antiquarium of the site, with its interesting collection of maps, plans and artefacts found during the excavations, but at time of writing no firm date had been given.

The Temple of Zeus

The temple of Zeus or Olympieion (*beyond map 13; open 9–1, closed Sun and holidays*) is on the right bank of the Ciane. On the approach the two remaining columns of the temple can be seen among trees on the skyline of a low hill, the *Polichne*, a point of great strategic importance, invariably occupied by the besiegers of Syracuse. About 1km after the bridge over the Ciane, at the top of the rise, a road (right; signposted) leads in less than 1km (keep right) to the temple in a cypress grove. Built in the 6th century, just after the Temple of Apollo on Ortigia, it was the second Doric temple in Sicily, hexastyle and peripteral with 42 monolithic columns, two of which remain standing on part of the stylobate. There is a superb view from here of the island of Ortigia.

Fonte Ciane

The Fonte Ciane, source of the river and now a nature reserve run by the provincial administration (*map p. 538, D2; Riserva Naturale Orientata Fiume Ciane e Saline di Siracusa*), is reached by a turning off the Canicattini Bagni road SP 14. After crossing the Anapo, a byroad (left; signposted) leads for 3km through a fertile valley with orange and lemon groves and magnificent old olive trees. Beyond a tributary of the Ciane, a road (signposted) continues left to end in a grove of eucalyptus and cypress trees beside the romantic spring (the ancient *Cyane*), overgrown with reeds and thick clumps of papyrus. This plant grows only here and along the River Fiumefreddo in Sicily, and in no other part of Europe. The name of the spring (in Greek, blue) describes the azure colour of its waters, but a myth relates how the nymph Cyane, who tried to prevent Hades from carrying off Persephone (*see p. 252*), was changed into a spring and condemned to weep forever. Wooden decking allows you to walk out over the water to examine the papyrus plants from close quarters. The water is inhabited by numerous waterfowl and noisy frogs. Both springs, the Testa della Pisma and the smaller Pismotta, have pools with papyrus.

Plemmyrion and the coast to the south

The ancient district of Plemmyrion, now known as the **peninsula of the Maddalena** (*map p. 538, D2*), was on the headland opposite Ortigia on Syracuse's Great Harbour. The headquarters of Nikias were established here after his defeat on Epipolai by Gylippus, in the famous battle between Athens and Syracuse in 415–413 BC. Although now disfigured by concrete villas and holiday apartment blocks, the coast is still intact and is protected as a marine nature reserve (*T: 0931 449310, www.plemmirio.it*), one of six such reserves around the coast of Sicily. You can book a guide for an immersion to do some seawatching, or you can birdwatch along the 7km of protected coastline—the many interesting birds include kingfishers, here adapted to fishing in the sea.

Neolithic settlements have been found further south on the offshore **islet of Ognina**, where Neolithic and Early Bronze Age pottery finds suggest that it may have been a Maltese trading outpost. There is a little port here and sea-bathing at Capo Sparano, just to the north.

The bay to the south, Fontane Bianche, is the crowded bathing resort of Syracuse. Nearby is **Cassibile**, where a huge Bronze-Age necropolis and hut village yielded extremely interesting finds, now in the archaeological museum in Syracuse. In an olive grove near the bridge over the river, close to the road, on the afternoon of 3rd September 1943, Generals Bedell Smith and Castellano signed the military terms of surrender of the Italian army to the Allies. Several pill-boxes survive along the road and on the bed of the river. At the mouth of the Cassibile, the ancient *Kakyparis*, the Athenian general Demosthenes, covering the rear of Nikias' forces during the retreat from Syracuse, was cut off and forced to surrender. The countryside here is particularly lovely, with old olive trees, carobs, almonds and citrus groves.

NOTO

Noto (*map p. 538, C2–D2*) is perhaps the most fascinating of the 18th-century Baroque cities of Sicily. It was built after the earthquake of 1693 when the former town (now known as Noto Antica) on Monte Alveria was abandoned. An excellent example of 18th-century town planning, the local limestone has been burnt gold by the sun. The inhabitants call their city *il giardino di pietra*, the garden of stone. The surrounding vineyards produce an exquisite dessert wine, Moscato di Noto, also rich gold in colour. Made from white Muscat grapes, the wine comes in three varieties: *naturale*, *spumante* and *liquoroso*.

HISTORY OF NOTO

This was ancient *Neas*, founded in 448 BC by Ducetius; a city which enjoyed several privileges under the Romans, who called it *Netum*, and was chosen by the Arabs in 903 to be the capital of the Val di Noto, one of the three administrative areas of the island. The economy flourished, thanks to the introduction of citrus, mulberry trees for the silk industry, almonds, rice, sugar-cane and cotton; there were wool mills and tanneries. Trade was encouraged and there was a flourishing Jewish community. (*contd overleaf*)

These happy conditions continued through the successive dominations of Sicily, until 1492, when the Jews were expelled, and 1693, when the great earthquake struck, followed by epidemics of cholera. The town on the Alveria was so severely damaged that a new site about 14km away was chosen by the Spanish government, against the wishes of the Church and the majority of the inhabitants, making reconstruction slow. Only in 1702 was the old town abandoned for the rational new city, planned and built by some of the greatest engineers, architects and master-builders of the time.

In 1817 Syracuse was preferred by the Bourbons as provincial capital (briefly returned to Noto from 1837–65), and the economy languished. A further blow was the governmental decision in 1866 to expropriate the monasteries and convents; Noto, seat of a bishopric, had always had a very strong religious community, which had a considerable influence on the life of the city. People started to abandon Noto, in favour of new districts to the south. Because of neglect, buildings started to crumble; in 1986 many of the most beautiful were propped up with scaffolding and closed. A serious earthquake in 1990 did further damage, and in 1996 the dome of the cathedral collapsed. A World Heritage Site, the town is still partly undergoing restoration.

EXPLORING NOTO

NB: It is possible to a buy a combined ticket for the monuments and museums of Noto.
At the east end of the main street of Noto is the bronze statue of the patron San Corrado Confalonieri (*see box on p. 352*) by Mario Ferretti (1955), near the luxuriant public gardens (Giardino Pubblico), where the thick evergreen *Ficus benjamin* trees form an impenetrable roof over the road. To the south is the Neoclassical church of Ecce Homo or **Pantheon** (*map 4; open for Mass Sun morning 8, 10.30*), now a sanctuary dedicated to local soldiers who died in the Second World War.

Porta Reale, surmounted by the three symbols of the people of Noto, a tower for strength, dog for loyalty, and pelican for self-sacrifice, was erected for the visit of Ferdinand II of Bourbon in 1838. It leads into Corso Vittorio Emanuele, along which the town rises to the right and falls away to the left. By skilful use of open spaces and monumental flights of steps, this straight and level street, 1km long, has been given a lively skyline and provides successive glimpses of the countryside. The main streets are paved with blocks of stone, while the side streets are cobbled. On the right, a grandiose flight of steps leads up to **San Francesco all'Immacolata** (*map 4*; 1704–48), by Vincenzo Sinatra, with a decorative façade and an interior of lavish white stucco by Giuseppe Gianforma; there are two canvases here by Olivio Sozzi: over the first left-hand altar, *The Ecstasy of St Francis*, and opposite, *St Anthony Preaching to the Fish*. The convent of San Salvatore (now a high school) faces Via Zanardelli with a fine long 18th-century façade and attractive tower (possibly designed by Rosario Gagliardi).

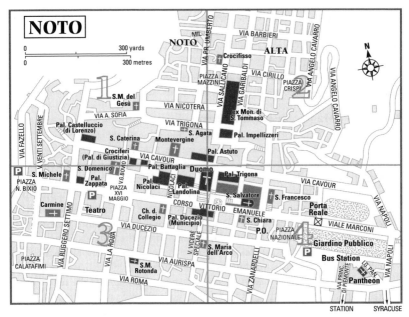

Opposite San Salvatore is the church of **Santa Chiara** (*map 4; open for Mass 8.30*), with an oval interior by Gagliardi (1730–48), and a *Madonna* by Antonello Gagini, from Noto Antica. The convent now houses the civic museums (*open 9.30–1.30 & 3–7 in winter, 3.30–8 in summer, but times are variable so call in advance; T 0931 836462*), including the **Galleria di Arte Moderna**, a collection of sculptures and drawings by the local artist Giuseppe Pirrone (1898–1978), responsible for the impressive bronze doors of the duomo. Also, many poignant remains from the old pre-earthquake city, and the **Museo della Carta**, an interesting museum dedicated to paper, its manufacture and its various uses as a vehicle for culture and knowledge.

Around the duomo

At the heart of the town, the immense façade of the **duomo** (*map 3*), rising above a dramatic stairway, looks down on Piazza Municipio with its symmetrical horseshoe hedges of ficus. The Cattedrale San Nicola (18th century, Rosario Gagliardi and Vincenzo Sinatra) has been newly repaired after part of the dome, which was rebuilt in the 19th century, collapsed in 1996. Beside the cathedral is the Neoclassical Bishop's Palace, and **Palazzo Sant'Alfano Landolina**, once the residence of this privileged local family, the only one to have a palace on the main street, and the only one allowed to offer hospitality to visiting kings and queens. Beyond the Bishop's Palace is the **basilica of San Salvatore**. The façade was designed by Andrea Giganti of Trapani and probably built by Antonio Mazza (1791). The polychrome interior, with a vault painting by Antonio Mazza, contains 18th-century paintings by Giuseppe Velasquez.

On the south side of the piazza, facing the cathedral, is the Town Hall, **Palazzo Ducezio** (*the Sala degli Specchi, Hall of Mirrors, is open 9–1.30 & 3–7*), a splendid building of 1746 by Vincenzo Sinatra. The upper floor was added in 1951. To the right is the **Chiesa del Collegio** (*open 10–1 & 3.30–7*), with a curved façade probably by Gagliardi (1730; restored by Vincenzo Sinatra in 1776). It has a luminous interior, with frescoes on the vault. It is possible to climb up the bell-tower, for a view over the rooftops.

Piazza XVI Maggio and Via Ducezio

The long façade of the former Collegio dei Gesuiti (now a school) stretches as far as Piazza San Domenico (or Piazza XVI Maggio; *map 3*), with the opera house, **Teatro Vittorio Emanuele** (*open 9–1.30 & 3–7*), a perfectly preserved building of 1861 with a beautiful interior and 330 seats. In front of the building, in a little garden, is a 17th-century Baroque fountain from Noto Antica with a statue of Hercules, thought to be Roman. In the pavilion behind is the Tourist Information Bureau. Above to the left is the soaring, glorious golden façade of **San Domenico** (*1737–56; closed for restoration*) by Gagliardi, perhaps his most successful building in the town. In Via Bovio above is the former convent of the **Casa dei Crociferi** by Paolo Labisi (1750), finished by Vincenzo Sinatra. It has been restored for use as the law courts.

From Piazza XVI Maggio, Corso Vittorio Emanuele continues to the rather severe **Palazzo Zappata**. To the left Via Ruggero Settimo leads past an aristocratic palace to the pretty Via Ducezio, which runs parallel to the Corso to the south. It is closed at the west end by the fine concave Baroque façade (with Rococo details) of **Santa Maria del Carmine** (or Carmelo), a late work by Gagliardi with a charming elliptical interior. At the east end of the street, on Via Viceré Speciale, is the church of **Santa Maria dell'Arco** (1730; *map 3–4*), also by Gagliardi, with an elegant portal and a decorative stucco interior with two stoups from Noto Antica; the organ is dated 1778 and the wooden Crucifix over the altar is 14th century. Nearby is an attractive Art Nouveau house. Via Aurispa, parallel to Via Ducezio on the south, is another pretty street with simpler buildings and the church of **Santa Maria Rotonda**, which has a Baroque façade.

Via Nicolaci and Via Cavour

From Santa Maria dell'Arco, Via Viceré Speciale leads up to the splendid rear façade of the Town Hall. To the left is **Palazzo Rau della Ferla**, which has a handsome front and a courtyard covered with jasmine. Part of the palace houses the Costanzo pastry shop. At the end the impressive wall of the Collegio dei Gesuiti can be seen, which a road now follows uphill back to the Corso, straight across which Via Corrado Nicolaci continues uphill towards the church of Montevergine. Via Nicolaci is overlooked by the delightful Baroque balconies of **Palazzo Nicolaci Villadorata** (*map 3; open 9–1.30 & 4–8*), built between 1737 and 1765, once the residence of Don Giacomo Nicolaci, a patron of the arts. He donated part of his collection of books to the important City Library, housed here, consisting of 80,000 volumes, incunabula, rare editions and manuscripts.

The façade of the church of **Montevergine** is attributed to Vincenzo Sinatra. Deconsecrated, it has a magnificent 18th-century floor of majolica tiles from Caltagirone, and paintings by Costantino Carasi. The church is on the handsome Via Cavour, an 18th-century street with views of the countryside at either end. It leads west past **Palazzo Battaglia** (1735), on the corner of Via Rocco Pirri, in which a charming little market-place, with a loggia supported on iron pillars surrounding a fountain, has been restored and used for open-air concerts in the summer. Via Cavour continues west past the former Oratorio di San Filippo Neri (1750) and the church of Santa Caterina (right; attached to the oratory, on Via Fratelli Ragusa). Beyond, near the end of Via Cavour, is the large Neoclassical **Palazzo di Lorenzo (Castelluccio)**, built for the Knights of Malta. At the other end of Via Cavour, to the east of Montevergine, is the beautiful **Palazzo Astuto** (late 18th century; Vincenzo Sinatra or Paolo Labisi; *map 1–2*). Further on, on the right, is **Palazzo Trigona** (1781), part of it renovated as an exhibition room and auditorium.

Noto Alta

The upper part of the town is known as Noto Alta. This simpler district was laid out facing north and south, on a different plan and orientation from the lower monumental area, with its four long, straight, parallel streets running east–west. There is a view of the battlemented former Convento di Sant'Antonio di Padova on the top of the hill. The **Palazzo Impellizzeri San Giacomo** (1752; *map 2*) has a balcony along the whole length of the first floor. Part of the palace is now used to house the city archives (*open Mon–Thur 8.30–1.30 & 3.30–6.30, Fri and Sat mornings only*), often used for exhibitions. In one room there is a splendid 18th-century crystal chandelier. The corner and bell-tower of the former Ospedale Trigona are visible here. Via Trigona leads past the former convent to the deconsecrated church of **Sant'Agata** (*map 1*), attributed to Gagliardi and completed by Paolo Labisi. It contains stuccoes by Labisi and paintings by Costantino Carasi. Opposite is the **Santissima Annunziata e Badia**, another church dating from 1720. Just beyond, approached by a double stairway, is **Santa Maria del Gesù**, next to its convent.

Via Trigona leads back to the impressive former **Monastero di San Tommaso** (1720; *map 2*), with an attractive façade and double stairway. It is now used as a prison, which extends as far as Piazza Mazzini. On the summit of the hill, at the centre of Noto Alta, is the enormous church of the **Crocifisso** (1715, Gagliardi; *map 2*), which contains a number of works of art from Noto Antica, including (in the right transept) a beautiful statue of the *Madonna della Neve* (Our Lady of the Snows) signed by Francesco Laurana (1471) and two Romanesque lions. The Cappella Landolina contains paintings by the school of Costantino Carasi. On the high altar is an 18th-century reliquary designed by Gagliardi, which contains part of a venerated Crucifix from Noto Antica. A relic of the Holy Thorn also belongs to the church (only shown on Good Friday).

ENVIRONS OF NOTO

San Corrado di Fuori

The most beautiful road from Noto to Noto Antica (12km, signposted for Palazzolo Acreide) leads uphill from the public gardens, crossing Noto Alta and passing through the village of San Corrado di Fuori (*map p. 538, D2*), with attractive early 20th-century houses. Outside the town to the west is the Valle dei Miracoli, a verdant paradise and home to the hermitage of San Corrado Confalonieri, who lived here in the 14th century; the monks are now so numerous that they can no longer offer accommodation to visitors. The 18th-century sanctuary contains a painting of the saint by Sebastiano Conca.

San Corrado Confalonieri (1284–1351)

Corrado Confalonieri was born an aristocrat in Piacenza in 1284. While out hunting a white deer, he set fire to the forest to flush out the animal, but the ensuing blaze did a great deal of damage to the nearby crops and villages. A vagabond was blamed, who confessed after atrocious torture. On the point of the man's execution by hanging, Corrado saved his life by admitting his responsibility. All Corrado's possessions were confiscated to make good the damage, but he saw in this episode a sign that he should change his way of life. He told his young wife to enter a nunnery, while he himself joined the Franciscans. After a few years he came down to Sicily, where he lived as a hermit in the hills between Noto and Avola, gaining a reputation for wisdom and sanctity. It is said that he could conjure loaves of bread from the air, whenever he was hungry. On his death, on 19th February 1351, his body was hotly contested by the two towns, so it was placed on an ox-cart with no driver, allowing Corrado to choose the place of his burial. He ended up in Noto, and is portrayed with a flame on his right hand and a white deer by his side.

Noto Antica

The road north from San Corrado continues across a beautiful upland plain with old olive trees. It then descends to cross a bridge decorated with four obelisks. The byroad (left) for Noto Antica is lined with early 20th-century Stations of the Cross on the approach to the large sanctuary of **Santa Maria della Scala** (*open 9.30–12.30 & 3–6 in winter, 4–7 in summer*), next to a seminary with an elegant façade (1708) surmounted by three statues and a balcony. The road now descends to cross another bridge over a ravine before reaching **Noto Antica** (*map p. 538, C2*), abandoned since the earthquake of 1693 and now utterly deserted. The scant ruins, reduced to rubble and overgrown, are very romantic and provide inspiration for artists, photographers and writers. The settlement here long antedates its legendary foundation by the Sicel chief Ducetius in 448 BC, and was the only Sicilian town to resist the depredations of Verres (*see box on p. 189*). For its later history, see pp. 347–48.

The entrance is through the monumental Porta della Montagna, with remains of the high walls on either side. A rough road leads up past a round tower and along the ridge of the hill. The conspicuous wall on the left (the highest one to survive) belonged to the Chiesa Madre. After 1km, beside a little monument, the right fork continues (and the road deteriorates) to end beside the Eremo della Madonna, a small deserted chapel, with a good view of the surrounding countryside.

Some distance to the west is the remote prehistoric village of **Castelluccio** (c. 18th–14th centuries BC), which has given its name to the most important Early Bronze Age culture of southeast Sicily. The rock tombs had carved portal-slabs (now in the archaeological museum at Syracuse).

Cava Grande del Cassibile and Avola Antica

The Cava Grande (*map p. 538, D2; open Oct–March 8–4, April–Sept 8–8*), formed through the centuries by the River Cassibile, where centuries-old plane trees and colourful oleanders grow, is a nature reserve (*Riserva Naturale Orientata Cavagrande del Cassibile*) run by the Azienda Forestale. A spectacular gorge nearly 10km long, it reaches a depth of 300m and is the deepest canyon in Europe, containing a series of rock pools, waterfalls, and ancient cave-homes. The river was the first in Sicily to be exploited to produce hydroelectric energy, in 1910. Thousands of tombs (11th–9th centuries BC) have been identified here (finds in the archaeological museum of Syracuse). The easiest approach to the gorge is through **Villa Vela**, a little village with some Art Nouveau villas on the road between Noto and Palazzolo Acreide. The gorge can be entered from there, or from the Belvedere (where you will find a restaurant and an Azienda Forestale information kiosk) at the end of the very winding road to **Avola Antica**, the site of the pre-earthquake town c. 6km inland. The deserted and desolate streets can also be explored here, overgrown with vegetation, the buildings destroyed, as at Noto Antica, in 1693. The path down into the gorge (about 40mins) from the Belvedere is steep and overgrown with vegetation, but it is the most impressive approach and brings you right to the lakes (*NB: Visiting the Cava Grande is strenuous and can be dangerous; mobile phones do not function; trekking-boots advisable*). Birds that may be heard or spotted include dippers, ravens, kingfishers, Cetti's warblers, blue rock thrushes, spotless starlings, shrikes, nightingales and owls; but the Cava Grande is particularly important for the resident populations of different bat species.

Avola

Avola (*map p. 538, D2*) is a prosperous agricultural town and an important centre for almond cultivation. It has expanded in a disorderly way around its centre, which retains the hexagonal plan to which it was designed after 1693 by Angelo Italia. The central square is Piazza Umberto, where the **Chiesa Madre**, dedicated to St Nicholas and St Sebastian, is situated. The interior, a central nave and two side aisles, houses two splendid canvases, the *Madonna of the Rosary* by Sebastiano Conca and the *Marriage of the Virgin* by Olivio Sozzi. In the choir is an 18th-century organ by Donato Del Piano, while the Chapel of the Sacrament is richly decorated with stuccoes in Rococo style. Near the church is one of Sicily's most famous cafés, the **Caffè Finocchiaro**. Four smaller squares open off the outer edge of the hexagon, one of which, Piazza Vittorio Veneto, has an early 20th-century fountain with three lions stooping to drink, by Gaetano Vinci. The 18th-century churches include Sant'Antonio Abate in Piazza Regina Elena, which houses a wooden statue of Christ at the Column from Avola Antica, and, in Via Manzoni, the Santissima Annunziata (with a façade by Giuseppe Alessi). There are a number of **Art Nouveau buildings**, evidence of the flourishing economy here in the early 20th century. The 16th-century church of the **Cappuccini**, outside the hexagonal centre, in Piazza Francesco Crispi, has a lovely 17th-century altarpiece, a painting by an unknown artist of *The Invention of the Cross*.

THE GULF OF NOTO

Noto Marina (or Lido di Noto; *map p. 538, D3*) is a little seaside resort with some of the best beaches on the east coast of the island. The beautiful landscape has huge old olive, carob, almond and citrus trees. The River Asinaro, which reaches the sea near Calabernardo, a fishing village and popular spot for swimming, is the ancient *Assinaros*, where the Athenian general Nikias' forces, trying to reach Heloros, were overtaken while drinking at the river and killed after the great battle between Syracuse and Athens in 413 BC.

Ancient *Heloros*

Near the mouth of the Tellaro river, on a low hill in peaceful countryside, are the remains of *Heloros* (Eloro; *map p. 538, D3, open 9–1, closed Mon*), the first sub-colony to be founded by Syracuse, probably at the beginning of the 7th century BC. The excavations are in a lonely, deserted position by the sea and there is a good view inland of the Pizzuta column (*see below*), with Noto seen beyond green rolling hills. The view along the unspoilt coastline extends to the southern tip of the island.

The road passes the foundations of a **temple dedicated to Asclepius**. To the right of the road, in a large fenced enclosure sloping down to the canal, is the **Sanctuary of Demeter**, consisting of a larger temple and a monumental stoa. A theatre has been partially excavated nearby. To the left, beyond the custodian's house, is another enclosure of recent excavations. An ancient road continues to the **walls and north gate**. Outside the walls, another later (Hellenistic) **temple of Demeter and Persephone** has been found.

The **Pizzuta** or Torre di Vendicari (*open 9–3*), a column over 10m high, can be reached by returning to the approach road beyond the railway bridge. This is now known to be a funerary memorial of the 3rd century BC; the archaeologist Paolo Orsi found the burial-chamber underneath it, with three stone funerary couches complete with skeletons.

Villa del Tellaro

From the main road (SS 115), just by the bridge across the river, a road leads inland towards a farmhouse (conspicuous to the right of the road) in the locality of Caddeddi, less than 1km from the main road. Beneath the farmhouse in 1972 a wealthy Roman villa of the mid-4th century AD, known as the Villa del Tellaro (*open 9–7; T: 0931 573883, 331 5771472*) was discovered. The villa was destroyed by fire in the mid-5th century, then in the 17th century the farmhouse was built right in the middle of the site, creating difficulties for the archaeologists. The mosaic floors were detached, and after restoration, replaced *in situ*. The farmhouse has become a visitors' centre.

Vivid polychrome mosaics with a decoration of medallions surrounded by garlands of laurel can be seen in the 20m by 20m peristyle courtyard and the portico. The portico and the rooms on the north side of the courtyard are the best preserved. In the first (east) room is a fragmentary scene representing the *Ransom of Hector*, with the corpse of Hector in the centre on one of the dishes of a large set of scales, balanced by his weight in gold on the other dish; to the left stand Odysseus, Achilles and Diomedes, and to the right are the Trojans and Priam. The floor of the room to the west of this, the Room of the Kraters, has a rich decoration of festoons of leaves and flowers sprouting from kraters in the corners, which divide the floor into four areas; the central scene is sadly lost. Next comes the large (6.4m by 6.2m) Room of the Hunt, a scene with episodes of a day's hunting, framed by an elegant series of swastikas and wildfowl. At the top (badly damaged), animals are being directed into a cage, whose door is held open by a crouching man. In the centre an allegorical figure, perhaps representing Africa, watches over the proceedings. At the bottom of the scene, a banquet is taking place in the woods; the six protagonists, sheltered by an awning and reclining on a long bolster around the *stibadium* or barbecue, are having their hands washed by a slave, while another pours wine.

Although reminiscent of the mosaics at Piazza Armerina, these are different in style and use of materials and exceptional for the skilful use of space, fluidity of motifs and sense of colour. They were probably the work of prestigious North African ateliers.

The Vendicari nature reserve

The eight-kilometre stretch of coast south of the mouth of the River Tellaro is the **Oasi Faunistica di Vendicari** (*map p. 538, D3*), run by the Azienda Forestale. This beautiful wetland, of the greatest interest for its wildlife, has been protected since 1984 after opposition led by the Ente Fauna Siciliana succeeded in halting the construction of a vast tourist village. More than 250 different species of birds have been recorded, some nesting (including black-winged stilts), some migratory (many ducks, herons, cormorants and flamingoes).

From the main road, beyond the railway, a track closed to cars continues for c. 1km through lemon groves to the entrance (*open 9–dusk, further information and guides are available at the entrance*). At the south end is the 18th-century farmhouse of San Lorenzo Lo Vecchio, with remains of a Hellenistic temple transformed into a Byzantine church. On the edge of the shore are ruins of a Norman tower and an old tuna fishery.

The landscape from here to the southern tip of the island is less striking. In the shallow bay by the charming fishing village of **Marzamemi** (*map p. 538, D3*; the name derives from the Arabic *Marsa el-hamaam*, Bay of the Pigeons), a wonderful place for diving, excavations begun in 1959 have brought to light 14 ancient shipwrecks (four Greek, five Roman and five Byzantine), as well as more modern wrecks, such as the *Chillingham*, a British cargo ship that sank in the 19th century; a Hurricane fighter plane which came down in 1943; and a submarine, the *Sebastiano Veniero*, which sank in 1925 after colliding with a merchant ship. On the waterfront is the sturdy Palazzo Nicolaci, next to an old tuna-fishing establishment, one of the sources of wealth for the Nicolaci princes of Noto, and close to the shore is a tiny island almost entirely occupied by a pink house, once the home of writer Vitaliano Brancati (1907–54).

Pachino and Portopalo

Pachino (*map p. 538, D3*) is not particularly attractive as a town, but is world-famous for its wine production. In recent years Pachino has also acquired fame for cantaloupe melons, and especially for its deliciously tasty cherry tomatoes, with which the town has now become synonymous, especially in Italy.

Beyond almond and olive trees and an inland lagoon is the fishing-port and tiny municipality of **Portopalo di Capo Passero**. An imposing early 17th-century fortress stands on the eastern end of the island of Capo Passero, the ancient *Pachynus*, the southeast horn of Sicily. A few years ago it was restored at great expense and transformed into a Museum of the Sea, which was mysteriously never opened. Overshadowing the fortress is the bronze statue of the *Madonna Guardian of the Sea of Sicily* (1959, Mario Ferretti), 5m tall on a pedestal of 20m. A Roman necropolis has been excavated on the island, which until recently was joined to the mainland by an isthmus, and is of interest to naturalists for its exceptional endemic vegetation, and for the migratory passage of birds.

The southernmost point of Sicily is the little Isolotto delle Correnti, with a lighthouse. West of Pachino, on the border with the province of Ragusa, several marshy areas now form a nature reserve for the protection of migrating birds, known as the Pantani Cuba e Longarini.

Rosolini

Rosolini (*map p. 538, C3*) is a town of very ancient origin, re-founded in 1713 by the aristocrat Francesco Moncada. In the spacious central Piazza Garibaldi is the elegant Town Hall, surmounted by a clock, and the sturdy Chiesa Madre, which dominates all the buildings around it. Begun in 1720 on the orders of Moncada, it was only finished in the late 19th century, thanks to the town's carters, who transported the blocks of stone from the quarry to the site, free of charge—it was a question of pride. A rock-hewn Palaeo-Christian basilica lies beneath the Castello del Principe (1668) amid extensive catacombs (now used as a garage).

PALAZZOLO ACREIDE

Successor to the Greek city of *Akrai*, of which the impressive remains can be seen on the western outskirts, Palazzolo Acreide (*map p. 538, C2*) is a charming town with a good climate. Akrai was a sub-colony founded by Syracuse in 663 BC, in a strategic point for dominating southeast Sicily and the route to the interior. After periods of independence, a treaty between Rome and Hieron II assigned Akrai to Syracuse in 263 BC. Its period of greatest splendour followed, and its main monuments, including the theatre, were built at this time. Hieron built himself a magnificent summer residence here, hence the name Palazzolo. Under Byzantium it had a conspicuous and vocal Christian community, which probably caused its destruction in the 9th century by the Arabs, who were otherwise fairly easy-going in Sicily as far as other faiths were concerned.

Count Roger assigned the town to his son Godfrey and from 1374 it was governed for two centuries by the Alagona family. Its finest buildings were erected after the earthquake in 1693, in Baroque style, for which the town is a UNESCO World Heritage Site.

EXPLORING PALAZZOLO ACREIDE

The lower town

The **Chiesa Madre** (San Niccolò, 13th century, 18th-century façade by Vincenzo Sinatra) is in the central Piazza Moro. Inside there are two late 19th-century carved thrones used for transporting the 16th-century statue of St Nicholas in procession. The charming sacristy with its painted vault dates from 1778 and retains its original furniture. Opposite is the extremely elegant church of **San Paolo** (18th century, Vincenzo Sinatra), with statues on the façade and the bell-tower on the top. The interior is richly decorated with stucco.

From San Paolo a road leads down to Piazza Umberto and the red 18th-century **Palazzo Zocco**, with a decorative long balcony supported by grotesque heads, all different. Via Annunziata leads downhill from the piazza towards the edge of the town and one of its oldest churches, the unfinished **Annunziata**, with a lovely 18th-century portal decorated with four twisted columns and vines and festoons of fruit. In the dazzling, luminous interior, covered with stuccoes, is a fine high altar in marble. The *Annunciation* by Antonello da Messina that is now in the Palazzo Bellomo Regional Gallery in Syracuse, was commissioned for this church in 1474.

From Piazza Moro, Via Garibaldi leads uphill past **Palazzo Caruso** (or Judica-Cafici) at no. 127, with monsters' heads beneath its Baroque balconies, the longest in the world. Further uphill, after a flight of steps, is Palazzo Ferla (no. 115) with four graceful balconies. Close by, at Via Gaetano Italia 36, is the Art Nouveau **Palazzo Cappellani**, which will one day house the rich collection formed by the local historian Baron Gabriele Judica, who in 1809 was the first to excavate the monuments of Akrai.

The upper town

The centre of the busier upper town is **Piazza del Popolo**. Here is the 18th-century church of San Sebastiano, which is approached by a flight of steps and has a splendid façade and portal by Paolo Labisi. In the interior are a painting of *St Margaret of Cortona* by Vito d'Anna (fourth north altar) and a pre-earthquake statue of St Sebastian. The handsome Town Hall, with the municipal clock on the top, dates from 1808. In Corso Vittorio Emanuele the 19th-century Palazzo Judica has an imaginative façade and vases on the roof.

Just off the piazza, at Via Macchiavelli 19, entered through a courtyard, is the **Casa-Museo Antonino Uccello** (*open 9–1 & 2.30–7; ring the bell; T: 0931 881499, www. casamuseo.it*), a delightful local ethnographical museum created by schoolteacher and anthropologist Antonino Uccello (1922–79) and displayed in his 17th-century home. The material from the provinces of Syracuse and Ragusa includes farming utensils and tools, household objects, puppets and terracotta statuettes; recently some of the rooms lived in by the aristocratic family who owned the rest of the building have been included in the museum itinerary.

An old 17th-century convent later transformed into an aristocratic dwelling, Palazzo Vaccaro at Via Maestranza 5, now houses the **Museo dei Viaggiatori in Sicilia** (*open 9–1 & 3–7, closed Mon; T: 0931 883880, www.museoviaggiatori.it*), a fascinating museum dedicated to travellers in Sicily through the last few centuries.

At the top of the road, Via Acre continues uphill to Piano Acre and the church of the **Immacolata**. Its convex façade is difficult to see as the church is now entered through the courtyard at the east end (*ring at the central door, at the house of the custodian of a school*). It contains a very fine statue of the Madonna by Francesco Laurana.

The ruins of *Akrai*

Beyond the Immacolata a road continues westwards up to the entrance to the remains of ancient Greek *Akrai* (*map p. 538, C2; open summer 9–8; winter Mon–Sat 9–4.30, Sun and public holidays 9–1; T: 0931 876602*). It is a well-kept site, with signposted pathways offering splendid views of the site and surrounding area.

The path from the ticket booth at the entrance leads past a long stretch of the **de-cumanus** (on the right), the main street, constructed in basalt and later altered by the Romans. A gap in the dry-stone wall to the left takes you to the small **theatre** (seating for 600), built in the late 3rd century BC, which is well preserved and now used regularly in spring for Greek drama presented by school students. The scena was altered in Roman times, and in AD 600 a mill with round silos was built over the ruins. Nearby is a small round altar for sacrifices. To the right of the theatre (when facing it) is the **bou-leuterion**, a tiny council-chamber which is connected to the theatre by a passageway, now closed for safety reasons. To the left of the theatre various paths lead to two stone quarries with traces of a heroic cult and of later Christian occupation. The path furthest from the theatre leads to the abandoned site antiquarium (functioning toilets), across from which niches can be seen in the quarry face (they were formerly closed with com-memorative plaques carved with reliefs and inscriptions) and an interesting **funerary bas-relief** of c. 200 BC, showing a complicated scene in which a warrior is making sacrifice and two adults recline on a couch. Further on from the relief are extensive Byz-antine catacombs (*currently locked*), some of which were adapted by the Arabs as dwell-ings. The larger family chapels are decorated with unusual lattice-work transennae.

The path closest to the theatre leads into a quarry in which a smaller network of **Byzantine catacombs** can be visited, although care should be taken as the rock is slippery underfoot and a flashlight is needed. The middle path curves up to the high-est point of the site, from which the views are magnificent. A fenced-off area contains the foundations of a peristyle **temple of Aphrodite** (6th century BC) and its associated sanctuary. From here, another path drops down towards the entrance, passing on the left a second sanctuary (probably dedicated to Persephone), of 3rd-century date. It contained a circular temple covered by a cupola with a circular opening in the centre, supported on girders of terracotta (no longer *in situ*, but preserved); the holes for them are visible in the walls, and the pavement survives.

Worn relief of Cybele, one of the Santoni near the ruins of Akrai.

Leaving Akrai, the road from the theatre goes down the hill to the Ragusa road, off which a paved byroad (left) ends beside a gate. Here, on a cliffside, you can see the **Santoni** (*to request visit, T: 0931 876602 a few days beforehand; visit not possible on Sun*), a series of twelve very worn but interesting reliefs of Cybele, carved in a rockface, probably in the 3rd century BC. Her role as the mother-goddess is sometimes conflated with that of Demeter, because in some of the carvings she is seen together with Persephone. Most of the carvings show the goddess enthroned, with two lions at her feet. The path once led to a sacred spring and a small sanctuary (*no access*).

ENVIRONS OF PALAZZOLO ACREIDE

East of Palazzolo Acreide, on the fast road to Syracuse, is **Canicattini Bagni** (*map p. 538, C2*), now surrounded by new buildings. Founded in 1678, it contains interesting early 20th-century houses decorated in the local stone in Art Nouveau style, and a beautiful 18th-century bridge, known as Ponte di Sant'Alfano, over the Cava Cardinale stream. Canicattini has a beautiful museum at Via Marconi 2, the Museo del Tessuto e dell'Emigrante (*T: 0931 945322 to request visit, www.galleriadelricamo.com*), dedicated to mainly locally-made textiles and embroidery, very well displayed, and with some very rare pieces. An evocative gallery explains the reasons behind emigration, which has so much affected Sicily over the last 150 years: from 1880–1910 alone nearly one and a half million emigrants, 50 percent of the population, left the island. Poignant testimonies include their house-keys, which they left behind, knowing they would never return.

Near Canicattini is the **Grotta Perciata**, the largest cave so far discovered in Sicily, where prehistoric artefacts have been found.

Buscemi

Across the Anapo valley north of Palazzolo Acreide is the attractive little town of Buscemi (*map p. 538, C2*), rebuilt after 1693. The main road runs uphill past its four impressive churches. Sant'Antonio di Padova has an 18th-century façade which incorporates ten splendid large columns on its curving front (with three bells hung across the top). Higher up is San Sebastiano, preceded by a stairway, and then the elliptical 19th-century church of San Giacomo, high up on a terrace. At the top of the town is the 18th-century Chiesa Madre, which houses a wooden statue of *Our Lady of Sorrows* by Filippo Quattrocchi (1732). A number of artisans' workshops and houses in the town can be visited, along with a water-mill in Palazzolo Acreide, making up a museum of 19th-century life in the Hyblaean Mountains: I Luoghi del Lavoro Contadino (*ticket office: Via Libertà 10, next to the church of San Giacomo, open Mon–Sat 8.30–1.30, closed holidays; T: 0931 878528, 0931 452932, www.museobuscemi.org*).

Buccheri

On the barren Piana di Buccheri, with views to Mt Lauro (986m), the highest point of the Hyblaean Mountains, and of Etna to the north, pinewoods have recently been planted. **Buccheri** (*map p. 538, C2*) was destroyed in the 1693 earthquake and rebuilt in Baroque style. Corso Vittorio Emanuele passes the 18th-century church of Santa Maria Maddalena, which contains a statue of Mary Magdalene by Antonello Gagini (1508). From Piazza Toselli a steep flight of steps rises to the towering façade of the church of Sant'Antonio Abate: the rich interior, a nave and two aisles, is decorated with stuccoes by Giuseppe Gianforma (1760) and houses two signed and dated (1728) paintings by Willem Borremans: *Sts Vitus, Modestus and Crescenza* in the right aisle, and *Ecstasy of St Anthony Abbot* over the main altar.

To the south of Buccheri, on the road to Giarratana, a few kilometres south of Mt Lauro and right on the border between the provinces of Syracuse and Ragusa, is a vast archaeological site that is almost certainly **ancient *Kasmenai***, the second colony founded by Syracuse. The views from here are stunning, but the site has been closed for some time due to lack of staff.

THE ANAPO VALLEY

The plateau above the Anapo valley to the south is beautiful open countryside, with attractive farmhouses and low dry-stone walls. Dark carob trees provide welcome shade, and the olive groves are renowned for the high quality of their oil. Shepherds pasture their flocks and small herds of cattle wander around apparently untended; the sound of their bells lingers after their passage. Byzantine tombs and caves in the area show evidence of Neolithic and Bronze-Age occupation.

Near the village of **Cassaro**, famous for excellent olive oil from the Tonda iblea variety, and a very picturesque place, is the **Valle dell'Anapo** (*open 8–1hr before sunset*). A beautiful deep limestone gorge, and a protected area since 1988, it is run by the Azienda Forestale. A map of the paths in the area is available at the entrance. No private cars are allowed (there is a small car park) and there are a large number of other restrictions: in particular, no animals can be taken in. The route follows the course of the disused narrow-gauge railway track (and its tunnels), which runs along the floor of the valley, once the Syracuse–Vizzini line. The interesting vegetation here includes ilexes, pines, figs, olives, citrus trees and poplars, and the only buildings to be seen are those once used by the railway company. Horses are bred here and picnic places are provided with tables. In the centre of the valley there is a good view of the tombs of the necropolis of Pantalica (*see below*), high up at the top of the rockface. There is another entrance to the valley from the Sortino road, at which maps of the area can also be obtained.

On the Ferla road is the site of the destroyed town of Cassaro, which was moved after the earthquake of 1693 up to the top of the cliff face (seen above the road). Orange trees, prickly pear and pomegranates have been allowed to grow wild on the approach to **Ferla** itself (*map p. 538, C2*). A small stone-built town, it is traversed by one long main street climbing steeply uphill past four Baroque churches with imposing facades, lined with interesting early 20th-century houses, and makes the best approach to Pantalica.

Pantalica

A lonely road leads from Ferla for 12km along a ridge through beautiful remote pastureland and pinewoods to the extraordinary prehistoric necropolis of Pantalica (*map p. 538, C2*), in deserted countryside, now a UNESCO World Heritage site and a nature and archaeological reserve run by the Azienda Forestale (*Riserva Naturale Orientata Pantalica, Valle dell'Anapo e Torrente Cavagrande, www.parks.it/riserva.pantalica*). All around rock tombs carved in the cliffs (*see plan*) can be seen. The Azienda Forestale has set up a visitors' centre just off the road into Pantalica, about 5km before the end of the asphalt road, equipped with toilets, a picnic area and a large carpark. The wardens can provide you with a map, and they also show a 30-min film about Pantalica on request. They currently have 50 mountain bikes (ten of which are electric) that they provide for free (a valid ID document must be produced, and a simple form completed). It has been rumoured for years that access to Pantalica will be regulated and an entrance fee charged, but this has yet to happen. For those who wish, it is possible to drive beyond the visitor's centre and park closer to the tombs or the Anaktoron.

Visiting the site

The deep limestone gorges of the Anapo and Cava Grande rivers almost encircle the plateau of Pantalica. It seems as though the inhabitants of nearby coastal settlements such as Thapsos moved to this naturally defended site in the 13th century BC. The cliffs of the vast necropolis, one of the largest and most important in Europe, are honeycombed with some 1,000 tombs of varying shapes and sizes. The settlement was abandoned after the arrival of the Greeks. Some of the tombs were later converted into cave-dwellings at the time of the fall of the Western Roman Empire, and subsequently inhabited by Christians.

THE PANTALICA NECROPOLIS

A necropolis is literally 'a city of the dead' where bodies are buried away from the centre of habitation. Existing caves are sometimes used, or soft rock can be tunnelled to make tomb-chambers. Necropoleis are of immense importance to archaeologists as they usually contain well-preserved objects which can be dated and used to hypothesise the status of those buried. The chambers may be in a local style or influenced by neighbouring cultures, while the way a chamber is used—to contain one or many burials, or a sequence of burials—can illustrate how kinship groups work and are sustained over time. About a hundred burials have been recovered from the thousand tombs cut into the limestone rocks of Pantalica and there is some sign in the early ones (13th century BC onwards) of Mycenaean influence in the way that the tombs have been cut, with corridors embellished with masonry leading to the grave entrance, while some of the pottery is either directly imported from Mycenaean Greece or copied from Mycenaean models. Although the size and importance of graves vary, women are given some status and one of the wealthier tombs of c. 1200 contained a female body with an array of golden goods. A common feature is a basin placed on a large pedestal, evidence of some kind of feasting rite at the time of burial, with the basin left after the sealing of the tomb. In the Late Bronze Age (1200–900 BC) a few larger tombs connected by corridors suggest a stratified society at Pantalica based on strong kinship groups. Clearly the local Sicel community was an effective and self-supporting one with some limited contact in earlier times with the Mycenaeans. However, with the coming of Greek settlement in the 8th century, the community was dispersed and burials at Pantalica cease. The objects discovered in the official archaeological excavations are displayed in the archaeological museum in Syracuse.

An easy footpath (signposted 'Villaggio Bizantino') at the beginning of the road leads to **San Micidiario**, a tiny Byzantine oratory carved in the rock (with traces of frescoes), and the **South Necropolis**. Off the road, further on, a track leads up to the top of the hill and the so-called **Anaktoron**, or Palace of the Prince, a megalithic building dating from the Late Bronze Age, only the foundations of which survive (35m by 11m); it was the only stone construction in the settlement. Nearby are short sections of wall and a defensive ditch, the only remains of the settlement, recently identified with the legendary *Hybla*, whose king, Hyblon, allowed the Megarese colonists to found Megara Hyblaea.

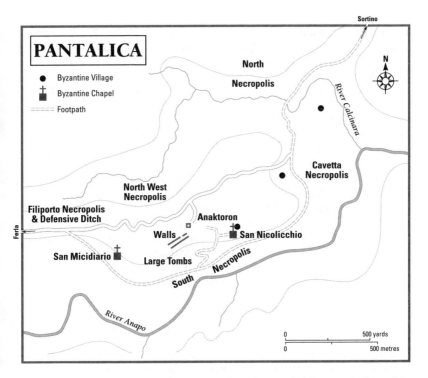

PANTALICA

● Byzantine Village

✝ Byzantine Chapel

===== Footpath

Sortino

North Necropolis

N

River Calcinara

Cavetta Necropolis

North West Necropolis

Filiporto Necropolis & Defensive Ditch

Anaktoron

Ferla

Walls

San Nicolicchio

San Micidiario

Large Tombs

South Necropolis

River Anapo

0 ———— 500 yards

0 ———— 500 metres

The Anapo Valley can be seen far below, with a white track following the line of the old railway. Further on, downhill, near the end of the road, a signpost indicates the **Cavetta Necropolis** (9th–7th centuries BC) and another Byzantine village.

A path leads towards the **North Necropolis**, beyond the stream in the valley. The road ends abruptly here and the road from Sortino, which will now never be completed, can be seen across the valley. There is a view of Sortino in the distance. In the early months of the year, flocks of ravens can sometimes be seen here, performing a mysterious mating flight, almost like a joyous dance, during which they fly upside down and link feet for a moment.

Sortino

Reached from Solarino, on the main road between Ferla and Syracuse, Sortino (*map p. 538, C1*) is well known for the production of honey and oranges, and for its traditional puppet theatre. The town developed at the foot of an Arab watch-tower (a *shortin*), but it was destroyed in the 1693 earthquake and rebuilt close by. It contains some elegant 18th-century churches and palaces and, in the old Franciscan convent at Piazza San Francesco 9, the **Museo dei Pupi** (*temporarily closed, www.opradeipupi.it*), a collection of puppets, posters and scenery accumulated by the Puglisi family, illustrious *pupari*. At Via Gioberti 5 is a museum dedicated to the production of honey, the **Museo dell'Apicoltura** a **Casa d'o Fascitraru** (*to request visit, T: 333 9003816, 0931 952992, 3398420366, www. museoapicoltura.beepworld.it*), which explains all the secrets of this fascinating craft.

Floridia

Floridia (*map p. 538, D2*) was a Sicel stronghold (in 1909 Paolo Orsi found a Mycenaean vase in a necropolis here, indicating Bronze-Age trading activities), re-founded in 1628 and rebuilt after 1693. The Madonna delle Grazie, now in disrepair, was built by the Spaniards to celebrate their victory over the Austrians in 1720. A supposedly miraculous image of the Madonna, painted on sandstone, was stolen from this church in 1970 and never recovered.

About 3km from Floridia is the **Cava di Spampinato**, one of the deepest gorges in the area. The road leaving the town from the south, signposted Canicattini Bagni, immediately crosses the gorge and goes to the right. At the first crossroad, where the road curves left, take the byroad right (it becomes a track after 800m) to reach the entrance to this beautiful and little-known gorge. There are many caves here, and tombs carved into the rock. It was through this gorge that the defeated Athenian army tried to retreat inland in 413 BC, but they were blocked by defending Syracusan forces and marched instead to the Assinaros, where they were defeated.

THAPSOS & THE GULF OF AUGUSTA

Capo Santa Panagia, the headland north of Syracuse, has been identified with **ancient Trogilus**. Fossils are found in the limestone caves and in the overlying clays are remains of Neolithic habitation.

The flat peninsula of Magnisi, a little further north along the coast, was the **ancient Thapsos** (*map p. 538, D1*), under whose northern shore the Athenian fleet anchored before the siege of Syracuse. It is almost an island (2km long and 700m wide), connected to the mainland by a sandy isthmus 2.5km long and little more than 100m wide at one point. The fleet of Marcellus also moored near here during the Roman siege of Syracuse. Finds from the settlement and its vast necropolis have given the name to a Bronze-Age culture and interesting domed rock-tombs line the shore west of the lighthouse. The excavations at Thapsos show three periods of occupation: c. 1500–1400 BC, characterised by round huts; c. 1300–1200 BC, where the square houses are of the Mycenaean type (a bronze bar with figures of a dog and fox, unique in prehistoric Sicily, and thought to be of Aegean origin, was found here); and a final period c. 1100–900 BC, with finds of remarkable large terracotta vases (now in the archaeological museum in Syracuse).

The Magnisi peninsula and the coast alongside are protected as a nature reserve run by the LIPU, the Italian association for the protection of birds (Riserva Saline di Priolo e Penisola Magnisi; *T: 0931 735026, www.lipu.it/oasi*). The coastal wetland, once exploited as salt-pans, is an ideal resting-place for migrating birds; about 215 different species have been spotted, including some rarities: marsh harrier, glossy ibis, avocet, black-winged stilt, greater sand plover (the only sighting for Italy), shoveler, ferruginous duck, and Caspian tern.

MEGARA HYBLAEA

Near the port of Priolo, a fast road signposted 'Zona Industriale' and 'Catania Via Litorale' (the old SS 115 coast road) branches off towards the sea. Yellow signposts indicate the way to the excavations of the ancient city of Megara Hyblaea (*map p. 538, D1*).

HISTORY OF MEGARA HYBLAEA

The city was founded by Lamis of Megara in 728 BC. Having delayed their departure because of his illness, his settlers found no land available for them in the area, beaten to it by the Corinthians of Syracuse and the Chalcidian sub-colony of Leontinoi. After uncomfortable sojourns at Leontinoi and then at Thapsos, where Lamis died, King Hyblon of the Sicels magnanimously donated a small but choice stretch of land still under his control, at the mouth of the River Cantera; the grateful people remembered this when choosing a name for their new home, Megara Hyblaea.

A century later, wanting to found a sub-colony of their own, they again found no room and were forced all the way to southwestern Sicily in order to found Selinunte. Megara Hyblaea was destroyed by Gelon in 483. A second city was founded here by Timoleon in 340, which in its turn was obliterated by the Romans in 214, after which the site was abandoned. Excavations were begun by the French School in Rome in 1949. In spite of the industries all around, the site is enchanting in spring, when wild chrysanthemums (*fiori di maggio*) carpet the surrounding countryside with gold.

The excavations

The lonely, overgrown excavations (*open winter 9–4, summer 9–7, last tickets 1hr before closing; T: 0931 512364*) are approached by a byroad which runs alongside a citrus grove behind a line of cypresses. The road continues right (signposted 'Scavi') and here in a group of pines is a stretch of Archaic walls (6th century BC) with four semicircular towers (a fifth has been destroyed). The walls can be followed on foot for some 250m as far as the west portal. A number of tombs have been placed near the walls, salvaged from excavations of the two necropoleis which are now covered by industrial plants. The third necropolis was located in the vicinity of these walls. Further on, below ground level, is an oblong construction with seven bases for columns. Excavated in 1880, it is of uncertain significance. Just before the little bridge over the railway is a car park; cars can continue over the narrow bridge along a rough road past some abandoned farmhouses. The road passes over the second line of **Hellenistic walls** built around the Hellenistic town (they follow a line of cypresses). To the left of the road here the Hellenistic **North Gate** has been identified near the remains of Archaic walls. The road ends at the custodian's house in a little garden. The farmhouse here will be used as an antiquarium to house the finds, including a tomb with a decorative

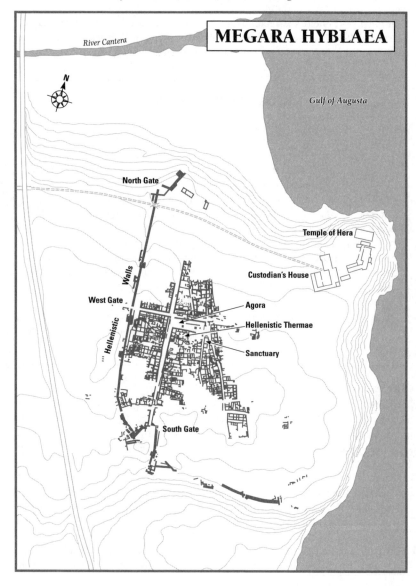

frieze, although the most important Archaic sculptures excavated here are now in the archaeological museum in Syracuse.

A path leads across a field to the main area of excavations: the complicated remains include buildings from both the Archaic and Hellenistic periods (the red iron posts indicate the Archaic areas, and the green posts the Hellenistic buildings). At the intersection of the two main roads is the **agora**, near which are a sanctuary, interesting **Hellenistic thermae** with intact floors, and a poorly-preserved small **Doric temple** of the 4th century (protected by a roof). The main east–west road leads from the agora to the narrow Hellenistic **West Gate** (with two square towers) along the line of cypresses. Near the gate, on a lower level to the south, are ovens and houses of the Archaic period. The main north–south road ends at the Hellenistic **South Gate**, a 'pincer'-type defence work.

AUGUSTA

The shores of the Gulf of Augusta (*map p. 538, D1*), once lined by the ancient cities of Syracuse, Thapsos and Megara Hyblaea, are now a jungle of industrial facilities, and oil tankers anchor offshore. The industrial zone extends from here to Priolo Gargallo and Augusta, and has the largest concentration of chemical plants in Europe. After the Second World War, the industrialisation of the area seemed the answer to many peasants' prayers, and the population of Syracuse rocketed from 44,000 to 135,000, the newcomers attracted by the possibility of employment and the hope of avoiding emigration. The industries are now going through a difficult period, however, and many workers have been laid off. After years of pollution problems and criticism from many quarters, what was once thought of as the solution to the economic woes of southeastern Sicily is revealing its shortcomings.

Augusta itself is the most important oil and military port in Italy. It stands on a rocky islet connected to the mainland by a long bridge. To east and west are two capacious harbours, the Porto Xifonio, and the Porto Megarese with two old forts.

HISTORY OF AUGUSTA

Augusta was founded by Frederick II in 1232 as a refuge for the inhabitants of Montalbano, which he himself had destroyed. In 1269 it was sacked by Philip and Guy de Montfort. It was taken by the French in 1676 after Admiral Duquesne defeated a Dutch fleet commanded by De Ruyter in the bay. De Ruyter was mortally wounded in the action and died a few days later at Syracuse, where he still lies.

Augusta was completely destroyed by the earthquake of 1693, and the modern town suffered severe damage from air raids in the Second World War. Another earthquake hit the town and the provinces of Syracuse, Catania and Ragusa on 13th December 1990 (St Lucy's Day; hence the name by which it is commonly remembered, *Terremoto di Santa Lucia*), leaving 13,000 people homeless.

The town and environs

The main road enters the town through the old Spanish bastions (1681): on the left is the battered, but still imposing, **Castello Svevo**, built by Frederick of Hohenstaufen in 1232–42 and surrounded by a double circle of walls. Until recently it was used as a prison, and is now the police headquarters. Further ahead on the left are the public gardens. From here Via Principe Umberto leads south through the city. It crosses Via Garibaldi, with some fine churches and convents. Via Umberto continues to Piazza Duomo, with the severely damaged Chiesa Madre (Santa Maria Assunta, 1644). The north side of the square is taken up by the Municipio (1699), with a long balcony and the Swabian eagle under the cornice. The sundial was erected to record a total eclipse of the sun in 1870. On the first floor is the opera house (1730).

On the coast to the north is the ruined **castle of Brucoli**, erected by Giovanni Bastida in 1468, near a beautiful little fjord used by fishing-boats, often used as a location for the Police Inspector Montalbano films. *Trotilon*, one of the oldest Greek settlements in Sicily, probably stood on the bay of Brucoli, which now has a large holiday village.

Melilli

Clearly visible on the hill to the right as you approach Syracuse from Augusta, is Melilli (*map p. 538, D1*), destroyed and rebuilt after the 1693 earthquake, famous in the past for its production of wild thyme honey, highly prized by both Greeks and Romans. This town has suffered a lot from the proximity of the industrial area, which has also affected the health of the population.

In the centre is the **Chiesa Madre**, dedicated to St Nicholas, with a beautiful wooden ceiling into which paintings by Olivio Sozzi have been set, representing the Triumph of Faith. In the lower part of the town, to the east, is the church of **San Sebastiano** (1751, Louis-Alexandre Dumontier), approached by a large square with a portico where country fairs used to be held. The church is decorated inside with a remarkable series of frescoes by Olivio Sozzi, carried out between 1759 and 1763. The priest will show you on request the tiny statue of St Sebastian, reported to be miraculous, and usually only shown on his feast days.

Tombs along the nearby rivers Mulinello and Marcellino (the ancient *Mylas*) have both revealed extremely interesting archaeological remains (now in the archaeological museum of Syracuse), proving that trade with the Greeks existed before the mid-8th century BC colonisation. Melilli also has some really beautiful **caves** to explore, in the district of Villasmundo (signposted from Villasmundo village, c. 12km north of Melilli on the Carlentini road); they are now protected as a nature reserve run by the University of Catania (Riserva Naturale Integrale Complesso Speleologico Villasmundo-Sant'Alfio; *T: 095 7215769, www.cutganambiente.it*). The caves extend for a total of nearly 3km (the longest in Sicily), with a series of narrow tunnels on different levels, with magnificent stalactites and stalagmites, underground streams and a small lake. The bat colonies are extremely interesting; several different kinds of snake and unusual reptiles can be found outside the caves; birds include buzzards, kestrels, blue rock thrushes and tawny owls.

LENTINI & ENVIRONS

The medieval town of Lentini (*map p. 538, C1*), a busy agricultural centre, was destroyed in the earthquake of 1693, and the modern town was again badly shaken in 1990. The Chiesa Madre, dedicated to the patron saint Alphius, was built over a 3rd-century Christian hypogeum, said to be the saint's grave, and also preserves a 9th-century icon of the Madonna covered with silver. The churches of San Luca and Santa Trinità have interesting 16th-century paintings.

The small **Museo Archeologico** (*open Tues–Sat 9–6, Sun 9–1.30, last tickets 30mins before closing, closed Mon; T: 095 7832962*) is located at Via del Museo 1. It houses a small collection of local finds dating from the Bronze Age to the 2nd century BC, including three fine kalyx kraters and a reconstruction of the South Gate of ancient Leontinoi (*see below*).

Ancient *Leontinoi*

The ancient Greek city of *Leontinoi* (*map p. 538, C1; T: Museo Civico, 095 7832962, to request visit*) was founded by the Chalcidians of Naxos in 730–728 BC, on the site of an earlier Sicel settlement, on two hills, the Metapiccola and the San Mauro, probably in order to control the fertile plain of Catania. In the 6th century BC Panaetius set himself up as tyrant of Leontinoi, the first such ruler in Sicily. In the early 5th century BC it was taken by Hippocrates of Gela, and soon afterwards succumbed to the Syracusans. In 427 BC the city sent the orator Gorgias (480–c. 380) to invoke the assistance of Athens against her tyrants. Hieronymos, the last native tyrant of Syracuse, grandson of Hieron II and barely 14 years old, was assassinated at Leontinoi in 215 BC, a month or so after coming to power, during which time he had declared allegiance to Hannibal and the Carthaginians. The Roman general Marcus Marcellus captured Leontinoi in the same year.

The excavations are neglected and overgrown. A path leads down from the entrance to the elaborate South Gate. Across the valley steps lead up to a path which follows the walls to the top of the hill, from which there is a fine view of the site and the surrounding hills. The area of the prehistoric settlement, with a necropolis (6th–4th century BC) and hut village, is not at present open to the public, but most parts of interest can be viewed with ease over the low enclosure fence.

Lago di Lentini

Northwest of Lentini is a large artificial lake, the Biviere or Lago di Lentini (*no admission, you have to view through the fence*), a vast wetland thought to have been created by the Templars in the Middle Ages, which was drained in the 1950s, with disastrous effects on the climate, so it was filled again in the late '90s. Potentially, this is the most important area in Sicily for waders and water-birds, both as a resting-place during migration, and as a nesting site; but the level of the water in the lake varies constantly, as water is siphoned off for agriculture and for nearby industries, and this damages plant life, and sometimes nests. However, there is an important colony of white storks, which seem to be doing well. Princess Borghese, who lives in a villa close to the lake, will show you her beautiful gardens if you book beforehand (*T: 095 7831449, 348 3513110, biviere@sicilyonline.it*); besides being a good gardener, she is a competent botanist, and will provide lunch, brunch, cocktails or afternoon tea, on request.

Francofonte

Southwest of Lentini is the hill town of Francofonte (*map p. 538, C1*), whose Town Hall occupies the 18th-century Palazzo Palagonia adjoining the medieval castle. The town was damaged in the 1990 earthquake. Local orange groves produce the *tarocco di Francofonte*, voted the finest orange in the world by an international jury. Quite large, it peels easily and the flesh is tinged with red. The flavour is reminiscent of strawberries. Opera lovers will remember that in *Cavalleria Rusticana*, Francofonte is the place where Alfio the carter came to get his wine.

PRACTICAL INFORMATION

• **By rail:** Trains run from Syracuse north to Lentini, Melilli and Augusta on the Syracuse–Catania line, and southwest to Noto on the Syracuse–Gela line. For details, www.trenitalia.it. From April–Oct the **Treno Barocco** runs every alternate Sun from Syracuse to Ragusa and back, and the other alternate Sun from Ragusa to Syracuse, stopping in the Baroque cities with time for guided tours of Modica, Scicli and Noto (*Info and booking: T: 0932 759634, www.treno-barocco.blogspot.com*). Also from April–Oct, every Sat, the **Treno di Montalbano** operates from Syracuse to Scicli (return by coach), with guided tours of the TV-series locations, and a typical 'Salvo Montalbano' lunch in a *trattoria* used during the filming (*Info: as above, or Go Green Sicily, T: 329 1738801, www.gogreensicily.blogspot.com*).
• **By bus:** AST (*www.aziendasicilianatrasporti.it*) runs bus services within Syracuse. The main terminus is in Corso Umberto I, near the train station. Shuttle buses run to Ortigia and around the city, and from the main car park at

Molo Sant'Antonio to Ortigia and back.
AST also runs inter-city services from the main terminus in Corso Umberto I to Augusta, Avola, Buccheri, Buscemi, Canicattini, Cassaro, Cassibile, Ferla, Floridia, Francofonte, Lentini, Melilli, Noto, Palazzolo Acreide, Rosolini, Sortino, and many places outside the province including Catania, Modica and Ragusa.
SAIS/Interbus (*www.interbus.it*) operates services from Corso Umberto I to Avola, Noto and Portopalo di Capo Passero. Outside the province it serves Acireale, Catania (and airport), Messina, Pachino, Palermo, Piazza Armerina, Ragusa, Taormina and Trapani.

Augusta (*map p. 538, D1*)
€€€ **Palazzo Zuppello**. Augusta's only hotel, smart and modern, in an old city-centre *palazzo*. 20 comfortable rooms and suites (no lift), good restaurant, professional service. *Via Epicarmo 74/76, T: 0931 995633, www.palazzozuppellohotel.it.*

Brucoli (*map p. 538, D1*)

€€€ **Commenda di San Calogero**. ▇ In serene countryside on the edge of the plateau formed by the Hyblaean Mountains, a short way northwest of the tiny harbour of Brucoli, this country house offers 12 comfortable rooms all furnished with antiques, good restaurant for guests only, luxuriant Mediterranean garden full of birds, saltwater pool, evocative Turkish bath and spa. *Contrada San Calogero, T: 095 998417, 335 1961181, www. commendadisancalogero.com.*

Lentini (*map p. 538, C1*)

€€ **Casa dello Scirocco**. Charming rooms in an old farmhouse, or in an ancient cave, entirely carved out by hand thousands of years ago, buried by the family because it was used by a 17th-century baron for his clandestine love affairs, and only brought to light in 1987. Pool. *Contrada Piscitello, Carlentini, T: 339 4907743, www.casadelloscirocco.it.*

Noto (*map p. 538, C2–D2*)

€€€ **Flora**. Simple hotel overlooking the public gardens, close to the bus stop, 11 rooms all with air conditioning, TV and Wifi access, no restaurant (but they own one a short distance away), friendly proprietor. *Largo Pantheon, T: 0931 573052, www.hotel-floranoto.com. Map p. 349, 4.*

€€€ **Seven Rooms Villadorata**. 7 rooms of the prince's palace have been transformed into an elegant and exclusive guesthouse. *Via Nicolaci 18, T: 338 5095643, www.7roomsvilladorata.it. Map p. 349, 3.*

€ **Masseria degli Ulivi**. 18 comfortable rooms in a beautiful old farmhouse set in a centuries-old olive grove north of town, good restaurant run by an enthusiastic young chef. Pool. *Contrada Porcari, SS 287 Noto–Palazzolo Acreide, T: 0931 813019, www.masseriadegliulivi.com.*

Noto Lido (*map p. 538, D3*)

€€€ **La Corte del Sole**. Country hotel, once an olive mill, overlooking the Vendicari nature riserve; 24 beautiful rooms, good restaurant. *Località Eloro-Pizzuta, Contrada Bucachemi, T: 0931 820210, www.lacortedelsole.it.*

Pachino (*map p. 538, D3*)

€€ **Camporeale**. Country house with pleasant rooms, all different. Nice breakfasts; car park. *Contrada Camporeale, northeast of town on the way to Marzamemi, T: 0931 846543, 339 6061872, www.camporealerooms.it.*

Palazzolo Acreide (*map p. 538, C2*)

€€€ **Colle Acre**. A small wine farm just outside the town producing DOC wines from grapes grown in the Val di Noto and the territory of Eloro. 15 comfortable rooms, car park, restaurant serving marvellous food. *Via Giuseppe Campailla (northeast outskirts), T: 0931 040001 or 040002, www.hotelcolleacre.it.*

€€€ **Feudo Bauly**. Restored hamlet in an isolated position 5km to the southeast of Palazzolo, once belonging to amateur archaeologist Baron Judica, 25 beautiful rooms each with little sitting-room. Pool, fitness centre (expert massage) and wonderful restaurant (Feudo Bauly is run by the renowned Corsino confectioners), which on the down side is often used for wedding receptions. Mountain bikes and horse-riding in the nearby forest available. *Contrada Bauly, T: 0931 882088 or 881568, www.feudobauly.com.*

€ **Villa Claudia**. In a panoramic position on the SS124 just outside town, a country house with 8 welcoming rooms, some in the villa and some in the old farm buildings. Pool. No restaurant. *Contrada Bibbinello, T: 0931 464187, 339 3695280, www.albergovillaclaudia.com.*

Portopalo di Capo Passero (*map p. 538, D3*)

€€ **La Rosa dei Venti**. Isolated and panoramic, inland to the west. Ten rooms, rather Spartan atmosphere, splendid view over the sea. Car park, no restaurant. *Contrada Corridore Campana, T: 0931 844343 or 581608,* *www.hotellarosadeiventi.it.*

Syracuse (*map p. 538, D2*)

€€€ **Livingston.** ◾ Small hotel on the seafront of Ortigia, with a tiny beach just below. 17 beautiful rooms, luxurious bathrooms, good rooftop restaurant, fitness centre with indoor pool and whirlpool in a cave. *Via Nizza 17, T: 0931 463460, www.livingstonhotel.it. Map p. 318, 6.*

€€€ **Musciara Resort.** A tuna-fishery transformed into a small hotel with a delightful quiet, relaxing atmosphere, 11 lovely rooms and suites, all with views across the water to Ortigia, private sandy beach. Breakfast is provided, other meals on request. Expensive, but worth it. *Riviera Dionisio il Grande 42, T: 0931 463613, www.siracusaresort.it. Map p. 319, 12.*

€€€ **Roma.** Delightful pink hotel built in 1880, right next to the cathedral, with restaurant and private beach. *Via Roma 66, T: 0931 465626, www.hotelromasiracusa.it. Map p. 318, 5.*

€€€ **Des Etrangers.** Beautiful 19th-century hotel, comfortable, overlooking the historic old harbour, very professional staff. 76 rooms and suites, two restaurants, beauty and fitness centre, sauna, indoor pool. *Passeggio Adorno 10/12, T: 0931 319100, www.amthotels.it/desetrangers. Map p. 318, 3.*

€€€ **Villa Politi.** A short distance from the centre, on the Latomia dei Cappuccini, and once favoured by Winston Churchill for his painting expeditions, a charming old hotel built in 1862 as the retreat of a wealthy artist. 100 comfortable rooms and suites, car park, beautiful restaurant, huge pool. *Via Politi Laudien 2, T: 0931 412121, www.villapoliti.com. Map p. 319, 11.*

€€ **Gutkowski.** ◾ On the north side of Ortigia, a small hotel of 25 rooms for travellers of taste; no restaurant but nice breakfasts, cosy fireplace in winter. *Lungomare Vittorini 26, T: 0931 465861, www.guthotel.it. Map p. 318, 2.*

€ **Villa Mater Dei.** Nuns at this large monastery just southeast of town offer 14 rooms with private bath, air conditioning, good restaurant and large park. Very good value for money. *Via delle Carmelitane, Contrada Sinerchia, SP 77, T: 0931 744044, www.villamaterdei.it.*

WHERE TO EAT

Augusta (*map p. 538, D1*)

€€ **Osteria della Mattonella.** The oldest inn in Augusta, the menu offers traditional fare, including (in season) snails, salt cod, thick vegetable soups: in summer you eat outside. Sicilian and Italian wines. Closed Tues and Aug. *Via Garibaldi 88, T: 0931 1966271.*

Avola (*map p. 538, D2*)

€ **Cavagrande.** This little restaurant is the ideal lunch stop while exploring the area; simple, appetising dishes, also pizza in the evenings. They have a couple of rooms if you want to stay overnight. Closed Mon. *Piazzale Laghetti di Cava Grande, T: 0931 811220, 347 3502342.*

Buccheri (*map p. 538, C2*)

€€ **'U Locale.** ◾ Award-winning *trattoria* serving good country food; *macco* (broad-bean potage), *cinghiale* (boar), spaghetti with mint and lemon, pig's trotters, tripe; *cannoli di ricotta* for dessert. Closed Tues. *Via Dusmet 14, T: 0931 873923.*

Francofonte (*map p. 538, C1*)

€ **Antica Hostaria Le Streghe.** Delightful trattoria/pizzeria in the stables of the Cruyllas castle, near Piazza Garibaldi. Vast array of vegetable *antipasti*, excellent pasta, simple desserts, Sicilian wines. Closed Mon. *Via Verdi 5, T: 095 7843493.*

Lentini (*map p. 538, C1*)

€ **'A Maidda.** Owner-chef Salvo Bordonaro really cares about Sicilian food and wine; his restaurant (worth a detour) is recommended by the Slow Food Foundation, and has a lovely shady garden. Very unusual, inventive dishes. Closed Wed, and Sun lunchtime unless you book. *Via Alfieri 2 (corner of Via Alaimo), T: 095 941537, 339 7760134.*

Marzamemi (*map p. 538, D3*)

€€ **La Cialoma**. Chef Lina Campisi has a way with fish. Start with smoked tuna and swordfish; you eat outside in the square. *Piazza Regina Margherita, T: 0931 841772.*

Noto (*map p. 538, C2–D2*)

€€€ **Meliora**. Nice little restaurant tucked away in the back streets, where the owner will present each dish and suggest the right wine. Very good *antipasti*, selection of fish or meat, good wine list, delicious desserts. Closed Tues. *Vico Milazzo 9, T: 0931 892161. Map p. 349, 1.*

€€ **Trattoria del Crocifisso**. Very good vegetable antipasti and selection of local cheeses, tasty home-made spaghetti with sardines and toasted breadcrumbs, but the star dish is *coniglio alla stimpirata*, rabbit cooked the Sicilian way. Closed Wed. *Via Principe Umberto 46 (behind the duomo), T: 0931 571151. Map p. 349, 3.*

€ **Trattoria del Carmine**. With a superb view of the church of the Carmine, this simple restaurant serves pizza in the evenings, and sandwiches during the day, if you prefer these to a plate of pasta. Closed Mon. *Via Ducezio 1, T: 0931 838705. Map p. 349, 3.*

Noto Lido (*map p. 538, D3*)

€€ **Baglieri**. Both restaurant and pizzeria, offering excellent, imaginative cuisine, well prepared and presented; the fish is perfect, so are the desserts. Closed winter. *Viale Lido di Noto, Contrada Falconara, T: 0931 812571.*

Palazzolo Acreide (*map p. 538, C2*)

€€ **Andrea**. ■ Interesting dishes using ingredients from the local mountains: meat, cheese, ham, mushrooms and truffles. Very good desserts, excellent wine list. Closed

Tues. *Corso Vittorio Emanuele 4, T: 0931 881488, 338 8519092.*

Portopalo di Capo Passero (*map p. 538, D3*)

€€ **La Giara alla Tavernetta del Porto**. On the dockside, this delightful restaurant serves only fish. Try the *brezza marina* (sea breeze), spaghetti with 8 different kinds of fish; a meal in itself, or the appetising *fritto misto di paranza*, mixed fried fish. Closed Mon. *Porto, T: 0931 843217.*

Rosolini (*map p. 538, C3*)

€€€ **Locanda del Borgo**. Ancient building with frescoed ceilings in the oldest district of Rosolini, the Locanda offers carefully prepared and creative cuisine; mostly fish dishes, good wine list. Closed Sun evening and all day Mon. *Via Controscieri 11, T: 0931 850514.*

Syracuse (*map p. 538, D2*)

€€€ **La Foglia**. Very unusual restaurant, principally vegetarian; the experience is rather like eating in someone's front parlour, hospitable owners but nothing matches—all odd crockery, tablecloths and cutlery. Superb grilled vegetables and famous soups; it should not be missed. *Via Capodieci 29, T: 0931 66233. Map p. 318, 6.*

€€€–€€ **Zafferano**. Award-winning chef (he does TV programmes for RAI) offers modern Sicilian food. Just out of town close to the Temple of Zeus. *Via Elorina 154, T: 0931 69057. Beyond map p. 319, 13.*

€€ **Apollonion Osteria**. Great fish, just off Corso Matteotti. Closed Mon. *Via Carmelo Campisi 18, T: 0931 483362. Map p. 318, 3.*

€€ **La Rambla**. Old-fashioned restaurant serving exceptionally good *antipasto* and seafood risotto. *Via dei Mille 8, T: 0931 66638. Map p. 318, 3.*

€€ **Taberna Sveva**. Popular restaurant on the square in front of the castle. One of the nicest places to eat in town. *Piazza Federico di Svevia, T: 0931 24663. Map p. 318, 8.*

€–€€€ **Piano B**. Excellent pizza restaurant,

innovative approach. Evenings only. *Via Cairoli 18, T: 0931 66851. Map p. 319, 15.*

LOCAL SPECIALITIES

Avola The historic, award-winning Caffè Finocchiaro (*Piazza Umberto, closed Tues*) is renowned throughout Italy for ice cream, *granita* and the unique almond nougat covered with chocolate. Visit Sebastiano Munafò (*Via Monte Grappa 13*) for the famous local Pizzuta d'Avola almonds.

Floridia The picturesque Bar Centrale (*Piazza Umberto 17*) is the oldest café in town, with a very good reputation. Try the *crèpe al gelato*, ice cream in a pancake, or the irresistible *gelato al torrone*. A good savoury snack is the *strudel salato*.

Ispica Curto (*SS115 Ispica–Rosolini km 358, T: 0932 950161, www.curto.it*) produces Eloro Fontanelle, from very old Nero d'Avola vines which each yield only 500g of grapes; before bottling, the wine is aged for 8 months in oak.

Marzamemi Campisi (*Via Marzamemi 12, www.specialitadelmediterraneo.it*) is a charming old-fashioned shop stocking locally-prepared canned, bottled or smoked tuna, swordfish, mackerel, sardines and anchovies; also vegetables from Pachino, olives, artichokes, sun-dried tomatoes. If you are looking for the local DOC wines, Feudo Ramaddini (*Contrada Lettiera, T: 0931 1847100, www.feudoramaddini.com*) produces Al Hamen, a delectable Moscato Passito di Noto that has won many awards.

Noto Market day is Mon morning. There is a country fair on the first and third Tues of every month, and a flea market (public gardens) every third Sun of the month. Corrado Costanzo (*Via Silvio Spaventa 7–9*) is a famous old-fashioned confectioner's; of more recent foundation is Mandolfiore (*Via Ducezio 2*), which also sells very good cakes, biscuits

and ice cream; try tangerine sorbet or *dessert di carruba* made only with carobs; *cubbaita* nougat (sesame seeds and honey) is available all year round. The Caffè Sicilia (*Corso Vittorio Emanuele 125*) is famous for its unusual home-made jams and ice cream. Tenuta dei Fossi (*Contrada San Lorenzo, www.tenutadeifossi.it*) produces DOC Moscato di Noto.

Pachino For some DOC Moscato di Noto or Eloro Pachino, try Cantine Rudinì at Contrada Camporeale (*T: 0931 595333*).

Palazzolo Acreide Cose a Caso (*Via Antonino Uccello 11, T: 0931 883684, open afternoons only*) has beautiful bedspreads, tablecloths, curtains and cushions inspired by local Baroque and Art Nouveau motifs. Corsino (*Via Nazionale 2/Piazza Pretura, www.corsino.it*) opened in 1889 and is famous for excellent sweets, especially the nougat (*torrone*), but the fried rice balls (*arancini*) and other savoury snacks are superb too. For traditional *pignuccata* and *giuggiulena* made with local thyme honey, try Caprice (*Via Iudica 1*).

Syracuse A market of fresh fish, fruit and vegetables (daily except Sun) is held in the morning in Ortigia on the streets near the Temple of Apollo. A farmers' market is held on Sat afternoon in front of the old Post Office building of Ortigia. There are many places in Syracuse where craftsmen make paper by hand, using papyrus which grows naturally in the River Ciane (*see p. 346*). L'Angolo del Papiro (*Via Giuseppe Agnello 11*) sells papyrus writing-paper and envelopes. Fish House (*Via Cavour 29/31*) has ceramics inspired by the sea. Reoro (*Via Landolina 17*) is where Massimo Sinatra creates stunning jewellery in gold and precious stones, including the rare amber from the River Simeto. Another gifted goldsmith is Massimo Izzo (*Piazza Archimede 25, www.massimoizzo.com*), who draws his inspiration from the sea, preferring coral, diamonds and aquamarines.

Zappalà (*Via Po 11*) creates unique pieces using gold, coral, pearls and turquoise. Bazar delle Cose Vecchie (*Via Camera Reginale 7*) sells curios, antique jewellery and puppets.

Bianca (*Via Roma 43*) is the finest baker in Syracuse. Marciante (*Via Landolina 9*) makes excellent pastries and marzipan; they were suppliers of *cassata di ricotta* to the late British Queen Mother, who was very partial to it. An assortment of cakes and other local products are available from Le Antiche Siracuse (*Via Maestranza 2; they also rent apartments; www. leantichesiracuse.it*). Caffè Centrale (*Piazza Archimede 22*) is a good place to take a break from sightseeing.

For Moscato di Siracusa DOC wine, the Fausta Mansio farm (*Via Nausicaa 10, T: 0931 744508, www.faustamansio.it*), produces this delicious 'condensed sunlight' using organic methods; you can shop online.

FESTIVALS & EVENTS

Avola Feb, Carnival, famous for the processions of sumptuous allegorical floats.

Francofonte March, *Sagra del Tarocco*, festival of the famous blood oranges. Tasting opportunities, guided tours, concerts.

Marzamemi July, *Festival del Cinema di Frontiera*, open-air screenings of films dealing with adventure, explorations and heroism—the 'frontier' can be geographical, intellectual or cultural.

Melilli 20 Jan and 3–11 May, Feast of St Sebastian, with a procession, a fair and fireworks; many thousands of pilgrims arrive from all over the world.

Noto 19 Feb, last Sun in Aug, and 1st Sun in Sept: festivities in honour of St Conrad. Easter: the Procession of the Holy Thorn takes place on Good Friday, along the Corso, and other religious ceremonies during the week. 3rd Sun in May, the *Infiorata*, when Via

Nicolaci is carpeted with fresh flowers.

Noto Antica 4th Sun in May, *Festa dell'Alveria*, the inhabitants of Noto go for a stroll through the streets of the earthquake-destroyed town, accompanied by expert guides. Nostalgic and fun at the same time.

Pachino May, *Inverdurata*, to celebrate the rich variety of local produce, the roads of central Pachino from Via Roma to Piazza Vittorio Emanuele are decorated with fruit and vegetables, forming intricate designs. Free sampling (*Info: Municipio, T: 0931 592611*).

Palazzolo Acreide Jan, the great feast for St Sebastian, *Festa di San Sebastiano*, attracts thousands of enthusiastic worshippers (*Info: www.sansebastiano.org*). Feb, Carnival is unusual in this town because the allegorical floats are miniature. Live music every night in Piazza del Popolo (*Info: www.comune.palazzoloacreide. sr.it*). Aug, the dramatic, moving celebrations for St Paul are concluded by a firework display (*Info: www.sanpaolopalazzolo.org*).

Solarino 7 Nov, procession of tractors and other farm machinery to the church of Madonna delle Lacrime at Via Matteotti 97 for a solemn Thanksgiving. On the way people give them fruit, flowers, cakes, bread, meat etc, which are later distributed among the poor.

Sortino 1st weekend in Oct, Puppet Festival and a celebration of the area's famous thyme and orange-blossom honey.

Syracuse 1st and 2nd Sun in May, *Santa Lucia delle Quaglie*, commemorating a miracle of the saint which took place here in 1642, procession and fireworks. May–June, *Rappresentazioni Classiche*, the Greek plays presented yearly in the Greek theatre (*Info: INDA, Corso Matteotti 29, T: 0931 487248, www.indafondazione.org*). 8 Dec, *Immacolata*, a procession for the Madonna. 13 Dec, *Santa Lucia*, procession from the cathedral to the church of Santa Lucia.

THE PROVINCE OF CATANIA

The city of Catania is one of the liveliest and most interesting on the island, though it is seldom visited by tourists, who bypass it on their way from Syracuse to Taormina, unaware of what they are missing. The province includes Mount Etna, one of the world's most active volcanoes (and the largest in Europe), as well as interesting old cities such as Acireale, Randazzo, Mineo, Adrano, Militello and Caltagirone, famous for its ceramics. There are many historic castles such as Calatabiano and Aci Castello. The Simeto, Sicily's most important river, which springs in the Nebrodi Mountains, flows through this province for most of its 88km.

CATANIA

Catania (*map p. 541, C2*) is a stimulating city, the second largest on the island after Palermo. It has been destroyed nine times in the course of its history, variously by earthquakes, bombardments, and lava flows, yet has been rebuilt each time on exactly the same spot. Noisy and untidy, it is also generous and fun; a city of enormous cultural fervour; of many theatres and occasions to listen to music. The city enjoys a love–hate relationship with the volcano at whose foot it stands; the people never call Etna by its name, preferring instead to refer to it simply as *'a muntagna*, 'the mountain'. The harmonious appearance of the centre, a World Heritage Site, with long straight streets

Detail of a triton from the 19th-century Amenano Fountain in the Villa Pacini garden.

of imposing Baroque churches and palaces, dates from the reconstruction which followed the earthquake of 1693. The colour scheme of the city-centre buildings is black and dark grey, relieved with white limestone details around the doors and windows. The dark colour is provided by the lava sand used in the plaster on the exterior walls. The effect is rarely sombre; Catania is one of the sunniest cities in Europe and can well afford to use the glittering black *'azzolu* on the house fronts. The result is extremely elegant. Blocks of basalt have also been used for paving the streets.

Large quantities of fruit, vegetables, wheat, wine and raw materials of many kinds are brought to Catania to be sorted, graded, packed and shipped. The most prosperous city on the island, Catania was known in the 1960s as the 'Milan of the South'.

HISTORY OF CATANIA

The founders of Catania, from Chalcis on Euboea, seem to have chosen a previously uninhabited location for their new colony in 729 BC, which, as *Katane*, soon rose to importance. Hieron I of Syracuse took the city in 476 and exiled the inhabitants to Leontinoi, re-founding Katane as *Aetna*, with celebrations for which Aeschylus wrote his *Women of Aetna*; the exiles returned and drove out his Doric colonists in 461. In 415 it was the base of the Athenian operations against Syracuse, but it fell to Dionysius in 403, when the citizens were sold as slaves. After the defeat of the Syracusan fleet by Mago the Carthaginian it was occupied by Himilco. Catania opened its gates to Timoleon in 339 and to Pyrrhus in 278, and was one of the first Sicilian towns to surrender to the Romans (263). Its period of greatest prosperity began during the time of Augustus who rewarded it for taking his part against Sextus Pompey, and it flourished under the Antonine emperors, when the theatre and amphitheatre were rebuilt and a number of other major civic works completed.

In early Christian days Catania was the scene of the martyrdom of St Agatha (238–51; *see box on p. 390*). In the Middle Ages it was wrecked by an earthquake (1169), sacked by Henry VI (1194), and again by Frederick II (1232), who built the castle to guard the harbour and keep his subjects in check. His beloved wife Constance died here (she is buried in Palermo).

The 17th century saw the calamities of 1669 and 1693, the former the most terrible eruption of Etna in history, the latter a violent earthquake. The lava flows which reached the town in 1669 can still be seen from the ring road. In 1943 Catania was bombarded from the air and from the sea, receiving more bomb attacks than Naples.

EXPLORING CATANIA

Piazza Duomo

The old centre of Catania is the well-proportioned Piazza Duomo (*map 11*). In the

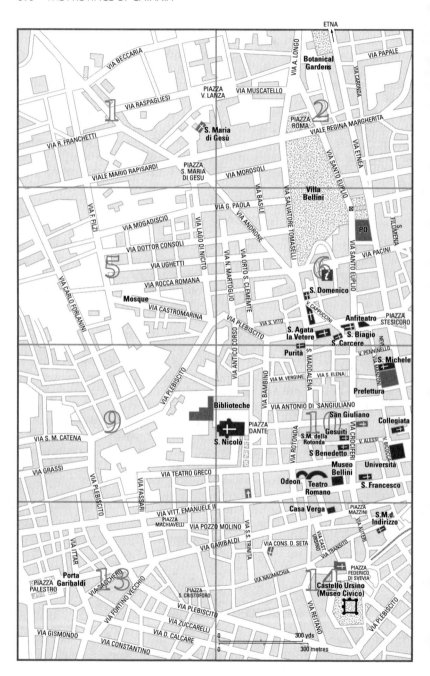

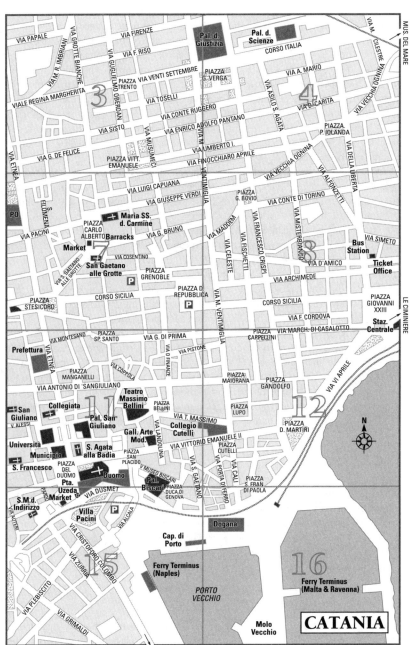

VIA PAPALE

VIA FIRENZE

Pal. d. Giustizia

Pal. d. Scienze

CORSO ITALIA

VIA M. CELESTRE

VIA M. DEL MARE

MUS. DEL MARE

VIA F. RISO

VIA GROTTE BIANCHE

VIA M. R. IMBRIANI

VIA GUGLIELMO OBERDAN

VIA VENTI SETTEMBRE

PIAZZA TRENTO

PIAZZA G. VERGA

VIA A. MARIO

VIA VECCHIO PANNINO

VIALE REGINA MARGHERITA

VIA TOSELLI

3

VIA ASILO S. AGATA

VIA D. CARITA

4

VIA DELLA LIBERTA

VIA CONTE RUGGERO

VIA SISTO

VIA ENRICO ADOLFO PANTANO

VIA M. VENTIMIGLIA

PIAZZA P. IOLANDA

VIA ETNEA

VIA G. DE FELICE

VIA MUSUMECI

VIA UMBERTO I.

PIAZZA VITT. EMANUELE

VIA FINOCCHIARO APRILE

VIA VECCHIA OGNINA

VIA ALFONZETTI

VIA LUIGI CAPUANA

PIAZZA G. BOVIO

PO

VIA GIUSEPPE VERDI

VIA CONTE DI TORINO

VIA FILOMENA

VIA PACINI

Maria SS. d. Carmine

PIAZZA CARLO ALBERTO

Barracks

VIA G. BRUNO

VIA MADDEM

VIA FRANCESCO CRISPI

VIA MISTERBIANCO

VIA SIMETO

Bus Station

Market

7

VIA COSENTINO

VIA CELESTE

VIA FISCHETTI

8

Ticket Office

VIA S. GAETANO ALLE GROTTE

San Gaetano alle Grotte

PIAZZA GRENOBLE

VIA D'AMICO

LE CIMINIERE

P

VIA ARCHIMEDE

PIAZZA STESICORO

CORSO SICILIA

PIAZZA D REPUBBLICA

CORSO SICILIA

PIAZZA GIOVANNI XXIII

P

VIA F. CORDOVA

Staz. Centrale

VIA MONTESANO

PIAZZA SP. SANTO

VIA G. DI PRIMA

VIA M. VENTIMIGLIA

PIAZZA CAPPELLINI

VIA MARCH. DI CASALOTTO

Prefettura

VIA ETNEA

VIA COPPOLA

VIA PISTONE

VIA D FINANZE

PIAZZA MAIORANA

VIA VI APRILE

PIAZZA MANGANELLI

VIA ANTONIO DI 'SANGIULIANO

Teatro Massimo Bellini

PIAZZA BELLINI

PIAZZA GANDOLFO

San Giuliano

Collegiata

11

PIAZZA LUPO

12

V. ALESSI

Pal. San Giuliano

VIA T. MASSIMO

PIAZZA D. MARTIRI

Università

Gall. Arte Mod.

Collegio Cutelli

VIA LANDOLINA

VIA VITTORIO EMANUELE II

Municipio

S. Agata alla Badia

PIAZZA SAN PLACIDO

PIAZZA CUTELLI

VIA S. GAETANO

VIA PORTA DI FERRO

PIAZZA S. FRAN DI PAOLA

S. Francesco

PIAZZA DEL DUOMO

V. MUSEO BISCARI

Duomo

Pta.

Pal. Biscari

PIAZZA DUCA DI GENOVA

VIA S. CALI

S.M.d. Indirizzo

Uzeda Market

VIA DUSMET

VIA AUTERI

Villa Pacini

P

VIA ALCALA

Dogana

VIA CRISTOFORO COLOMBO

Cap. di Porto

16

VIA ZURRIA

15

Ferry Terminus (Naples)

Ferry Terminus (Malta & Ravenna)

VIA PLEBISCITO

PORTO VECCHIO

N

VIA GRIMALDI

Molo Vecchio

CATANIA

AIRPORT, SYRACUSE

middle of the piazza stands a fountain supporting an antique lava-stone elephant, the symbol of Catania. On the elephant's back perches an Egyptian obelisk (perhaps once a turning-post in the Roman circus or, alternatively, part of a sanctuary of Isis and Serapis), erected here in 1736 by Giovanni Battista Vaccarini, who was responsible for much of the look of the square. The fountain is modelled on the monument by Bernini in Piazza Minerva in Rome. The Catanese refer to the elephant as *Liotru*, after Heliodorus, a Byzantine necromancer who is supposed to have used it as a 'Jumbo Jet' to fly between Catania and Constantinople in the 6th century AD. The square is surrounded by 18th-century buildings, many by Vaccarini, and dominated by the superb duomo on the east side.

To the right of the cathedral is the sumptuous **Diocesan Museum** (*open Mon-Fri 9–2, Sat 8–1, closed Sun; T: 095 281635; combined ticket with Terme Achilliane; www.museodiocesicatania.it*), which displays the cathedral treasure, fine art works and objects relating to the cult of St Agatha. From the terrace there is an interesting view over the old city centre and you can walk along a short stretch of the city walls. The museum staff also lead guided tours of the nearby **Terme Achilliane** (*same hours as Diocesan Museum*), the entrance to which is just outside the museum, in the courtyard of the duomo (*the museum guide will take you there*). This complex was used as an air-raid shelter in 1943, and has since then been closed for flooding and other problems; it is well worth the visit. Jean Houel succeeded in descending into the subterranean tunnels in the 18th century; he thought he had found a temple of Bacchus.

The Municipio (Town Hall), begun in 1695, was finished by Vaccarini in 1741. Two state carriages are on view in the entrance passage. The south side of Piazza Duomo is closed by the fine Porta Uzeda (1696), which leads to the little public garden called **Villa Pacini**, often busy with pensioners playing cards and talking, and beyond to the harbour. The streets behind the striking 19th-century white marble Amenano Fountain (an underground river which emerges at this point) are lined with a colourful daily food market, *'a Pescheria*, where fish, meat, cheese and vegetables are sold.

The duomo

Dedicated to St Agatha, the duomo (*map 11; open 7.30–12 & 4.30–7; T: 095 320044*) was founded by Count Roger in 1094. Consecrated on 15th May, the following day it was declared to be the cathedral, taking the place of the old Sant'Agata la Vetere, which had acted as such for 800 years. It was rebuilt after the earthquakes of 1169 and 1693. The granite columns on the lower storey of the Baroque façade (Vaccarini, 1736–58) come from the Roman theatre. The cupola, by Battaglia, dates from 1804. The north door, with three statuettes, is attributed to Gian Domenico Mazzola (1577). The structure of the mighty 11th-century black lava-stone apses can be seen from Via Vittorio Emanuele 159.

Interior of the duomo

The spacious simplicity of the interior, with its wide nave and two aisles separated by sturdy pilasters, is relieved by the side altars with their elegant 18th-century gilded wooden picture-frames, forming a remarkable collection. During restoration work in the 1950s, the foundations of the Norman basilica were revealed beneath the nave. On the right, against the second pier, is the **tomb of the composer Vincenzo Bellini** (1801–35) by Giovanni Battista Tassara (1876). The second and third altarpieces are by Borremans.

Under the last altar in the south aisle is the **uncorrupted body of the Blessed Giuseppe Benedetto Dusmet** (1816–94). Much revered by the local people even to-day, he was a sympathetic cardinal and archbishop of the city during difficult times. His motto was 'As long as we have a crust of bread, we'll share it with a poor person'. When he died he was already considered a saint by his flock, for his devotion to the poor and especially during epidemics of cholera, when he always refused to leave the city, preferring to stay with the people, helping as best he could. His face is covered with a silver mask, but you can see his portrait on the pilaster on the left.

The fine antique columns in the transepts and three apses (of late Imperial and Byzantine date) formed part of Count Roger's construction. In the south transept, a doorway by Giovanni Battista Mazzola (1545) leads into the Cappella della Madonna, which preserves a Roman sarcophagus with the figures (very worn) finely carved in the round, thought to come from Asia Minor. It contains the remains of Frederick II (d. 1337), Louis (d. 1355), Frederick III (d. 1377) and other illustrious members of the House of Aragon. Opposite is the beautiful **tomb of Queen Constance of Aragon** (d. 1363), wife of Frederick III, with contemporary scenes of Catania. The sculptured fragment above the door dates from the 15th century.

The chapel to the right of the high altar is the **Cappella di Sant'Agata**, seen through a magnificent wrought-iron gate which prompted wry comments since it was erected only after the body of the saint had been stolen. The chapel contains a marble altarpiece (*Coronation of the Saint*); the tomb (right) of the Viceroy Fernández d'Acuña (d. 1494), a kneeling figure attended by a page, by Antonello Freri of Messina; and (left) the treasury protected by seven doors, with the relics of St Agatha, including her reliquary bust by Giovanni di Bartolo (1376). These are displayed only for the saint's feast days (3rd Feb, 17th Aug, and, in procession, on 4th and 5th Feb). The walnut stalls in the choir, finely sculpted by Scipione di Guido (1588), represent the life and martyrdom of St Agatha and the miraculous events concerning her corpse.

In the north transept, the Norman Cappella del Crocifisso is approached through an arch designed by Gian Domenico Mazzola (1563). In the sacristy is a fresco painted in 1675 showing the destruction of Catania by the lava flow from Etna in 1669, by Giacinto Platania, an eye-witness of the disaster. The painting has proved of great interest to volcanologists.

San Francesco and the Museo Bellini

From Piazza del Duomo the handsome, long, straight Via Vittorio Emanuele, lined by a number of Baroque churches, leads west. In Piazza San Francesco (*map 11*), a large votive deposit of 6th-century BC pottery came to light in 1959, indicating the presence of an important sanctuary here, plausibly attributed to Demeter. Dominating the little square, which in the Middle Ages was the vegetable market, is the monument (1935) to the cardinal and archbishop Giovanni Benedetto Dusmet (*see previous page*), who died in 1894. The medallions at the foot of the monument represent some of his acts of charity. The majestic church of **San Francesco** (*open daily 8.30–12 & 4–7.30; T: 095 317687*) houses two of the *candelore*, the impressive candlesticks representing the city corporations used during the processions for St Agatha (*see p. 390*), and it is possible to take a close look at them and appreciate the strength of the bearers. Each one weighs about a ton, and is borne by eight stalwarts chosen from the corporation represented.

Facing the scenographic façade of San Francesco is Palazzo Gravina, which contains a small apartment that houses the **Museo Bellini** (*map 10; open Mon–Sat 9–1; T: 095 7150535*). This delightful little museum commemorates the great composer Vincenzo Bellini, who was born here and lived here for 16 years. Known as the 'Swan of Catania', he died of a mysterious illness in Paris, and was buried in the cemetery of Père Lachaise, before being returned to Catania in 1876, where a state funeral and a tomb in the duomo awaited him. The rooms have retained their character and are crowded with mementoes, including his harpsichord (in the alcove where he is thought to have been born), several pianos and his death mask. The music library (*open to students*) preserves the original scores of *Adelson e Salvini, Capuleti e Montecchi*, and *I Puritani*, besides fragments of all the remaining operas. On the opposite side of the same palace is the **Museo Emilio Greco** (*open Mon–Sat 9–1; T: 095 317654*), dedicated to the graphic works of the sculptor Emilio Greco, who was born in Catania.

San Benedetto and San Giuliano

From Piazza San Francesco, beyond the arch of San Benedetto (1704) begins Via Crociferi, the most representative 18th-century street in Catania, lined with Baroque churches, convents and palaces, many of them approached by flights of steps. Excavations here have revealed remains of Roman houses. On the left, the church of **San Benedetto** (*map 10; open Thur 7–12, 3.30–6, Sun and holidays 10–12; T: 7150499*) has an elegant façade and vestibule of 1762. The pastel-coloured interior (*entrance from Via San Benedetto*) has an elaborate nuns' choir, a frescoed barrel vault by Giovanni Tuccari (1725) and a beautiful floor. Across Via Alessi (its steps to the right are a popular gathering-place in the evenings), San Francesco Borgia or **Gesuiti** (*open Tues–Sat 9–1; T: 095 310762*) is now an exhibition venue. On the north side is a statue of St Ignatius by Marabitti and a wooden reliquary Cross (1760), with skulls dimly visible behind glass. Both the church and the large Jesuit college next door (with four courtyards) are the work of Angelo Italia (1754). Across the street, on the right, **San Giuliano** (*T: 095 7159360 to request visit*) was begun in 1739 and continued by Vaccarini, who was responsible for the façade. In the fine elliptical interior is a 14th-century painted Crucifix. At no. 14 is the **Herborarium Museum**, a delightful place for browsing among medicinal herbs and spices.

San Nicolò l'Arena

Via Antonio di Sangiuliano, a handsome street lined with oleanders, with views of the sea, leads uphill to the church of **San Nicolò l'Arena** (*map 10; open Mon–Sat 9–1; T: 095*

7159912). It faces a little crescent of houses designed by Stefano Ittar. This is the largest church in Sicily (105m long, transepts 42m wide), begun in 1687 by Giovanni Battista Contini and rebuilt in 1735 by Francesco Battaglia, probably to the design of Antonino Amato. The dome was designed by Stefano Ittar. The striking façade, with its gigantic columns, was left incomplete in 1796.

The simplicity of the interior emphasises its good proportions. The complex meridian line on the floor of the transept dates from 1841. The 18th-century choir-stalls were intricately carved by craftsmen from Naples. The huge organ (5 keyboards, 72 registers, 2,916 pipes), almost as big as a house, was intended to be played by three organists at once, and the monks also intended it to be the largest in Europe. Its builder, Donato Del Piano (d. 1775), lies buried beneath. The organ was recently the subject of an 18-year restoration project, longer than the 12 years it took Donato to build it. Goethe alluded to its wonderful sound when he heard it in 1787, and it was played by Vincenzo Bellini when he was still a child—being so small, he got his friends to move the pedals for him while he was at one of the keyboards. The chapels at the east end have been made into war memorials. The roof is accessible and there is a breathtaking view.

To the left of the church façade (surrounded by railings), are some remains of a **Roman bath complex**, well below ground level. The building in front is the remarkable **convent** (*guided tours Mon–Fri 9–5, Sat and Sun 9–1; T: 095 7102743*), the largest in Europe after that of Mafra in Portugal. When the traveller Patrick Brydone saw it in 1770 he thought it was a royal palace, only to discover it 'was nothing else than a convent of fat Benedictine monks, who wanted to assure themselves a paradise in this world, if not in the other'. It is now used by the university faculties of letters and philosophy. It was almost entirely rebuilt after 1693 to the design of Antonino Amato and his son Andrea; the rich detail of its Baroque ornamentation combines well with its simplicity of line. The first court is overlooked by the splendid façade with delightful windows and balconies, completed in the early 18th century and decorated with an exuberant display of grotesque masks, cupids, fruits and flowers in an opulent Baroque style. Excavations here have revealed prehistoric traces as well as Greek and Roman remains, including a lava-stone road. In one of the cloisters there is a beautiful enclosed garden with trees and a majolica neo-Gothic tabernacle. Another cloister has a graceful arcaded portico. The monumental Neoclassical staircase (1794) at the entrance was designed by Antonio Battaglia. The impressive long corridors have fine vaults.

To the right of the church façade, an iron gate leads into another courtyard past the department of Archaeology. An iron staircase leads to the **Biblioteche Civica ed Ursino Recupero** (*open Mon–Fri 9–1, Sat 9–12; T: 095 316883*), including the monastic archive and library, with thousands of ancient manuscripts held in their original 18th-century bookcases. The majolica floor dates to 1700 (the tiles are from Vietri).

Santa Maria della Rotonda

Via Gesuiti, with herring-bone paving in large blocks of basalt (typical of the side streets of the city), descends from San Nicolò and Piazza Dante towards Via Crociferi past modest houses. Via Rotonda branches off to the right. Remains of a **Roman bath**

complex are visible here, partly under the primitive domed church of Santa Maria della Rotonda (*map 10; open 9–1.30 & 2.30–7.30, Sun 9–1; T 095 7150508*), which has recently been reopened after a long period of restoration. From the 16th century onwards it was considered to be the oldest church in Catania, founded in 44 AD (this is the gist of the Latin inscription at the base of the dome), and it was only in the 18th century that it was finally identified as a bath complex of the Imperial period that had been turned into a church in the Middle Ages. The baths were used from the 1st–6th centuries AD, and its rooms were richly decorated. When it fell out of use, the area was reused as a cemetery. This complex is one of the main sites of the newly-founded archaeological zone, the offices of which are in the Teatro Romano.

Teatro Romano

At Via Vittorio Emanuele 266 is the inconspicuous entrance to the recently renovated **Teatro Romano** (*map 10; open Tues–Sat 9–1.30 & 2.30–7.30, Sun 9–1; T: 095 7150508*). This Roman theatre is thought to have been built on the site of the theatre where Alcibiades harangued the people of Catania to win them to the cause of Athens in 415 BC, in the first phase of the war against Syracuse, but the earliest architectural phase dates only to the 3rd century BC. The building is of basalt, practically all of the marble facing having disappeared. The underground passageways which gave access to the cavea, which has nine wedges of seats in two main tiers, are very well preserved and are partly lined with architectural pieces recovered in the various excavations. The diameter was 98m, the depth of the orchestra 22m, and the capacity was c. 7,000. The orchestra is sometimes flooded since the underground River Amenano tends to come to the surface here at certain times of the year.

From the top of the cavea a path leads west round to the small **Odeon**, a semicircular building used for rehearsals and for competitions, and which could accommodate 1,500 spectators. The stage building is covered over by a modern building that has not yet been demolished. The Androne house and Liberti house museums at the eastern end of the theatre provide fantastic views over the archaeological area and the surrounding buildings. Liberti house has been restored as an example of the many houses that covered the theatre before the archaeological work began, and contains a small archaeological collection. The Androne house contains an exhibition and conference space and a series of wall panels explaining the excavations of the area. The way out passes through a small antiquarium, with some of the marble decorative elements from the theatre. Note the marble dolphin that was probably one arm of a seat of honour.

Casa Verga

On the second floor of Via Sant'Anna 8, Casa Verga (*map 14; open Tues–Sat 9–1.30 & 2.30–7.30; T: 095 7150598*) is the spartan apartment of the parents of the writer Giovanni Verga, who lived and died here. Some of the original furnishings have been preserved in his study, library and bedroom. The library is open to students and contains photocopies of the manuscripts of his most famous works (stored at the University for safe-keeping).

Giovanni Verga (1840–1922)
One of Sicily's best-known writers, Giovanni Verga is famous for his naturalistic style, which gives a dramatic picture of the tragic social conditions of everyday Sicilian life using a simple and direct language. His first great success was *Storia di una Capinera* ('Story of a Black-cap', published in 1871), which was adapted for the screen by Franco Zeffirelli as *Sparrow* in 1993. His masterpieces include *Vita dei campi* (a collection of short stories, including *Cavalleria Rusticana*), *I Malavoglia* ('The House by the Medlar Tree'), and *Mastro-don Gesualdo*. Both these last were first translated by D.H. Lawrence, who was much influenced by Verga. By 1884 he was acclaimed as the greatest living Italian writer. He made contact with Emile Zola and remained a life-long friend of the writer Luigi Capuana, also born in the province of Catania. Both writers were fiercely proud of their Sicilian roots, which in Verga's case meant the town of Vizzini, and both made frequent use of the local idiom. Although his fame diminished towards the end of his life, his eightieth birthday was publicly celebrated in Catania with Luigi Pirandello as orator, and he was nominated senator in the same year. His influence on Italian novelists remained strong long after the Second World War.

Around Castello Ursino

At the far west end of the busy Via Garibaldi stands the Baroque Porta Ferdinandea (1768), or Porta Garibaldi. In Via San Giovanni is the church of **Santa Maria dell'Aiuto**, with an imposing Baroque façade designed by Antonino Battaglia, in golden limestone with antique columns. It preserves a full-size replica of the Holy House of Loreto, in the Marche, which was visited by the prelate Lauria in 1730. Impressed by the legend of the house of Jesus of Nazareth carried to Loreto by angels, he ordered that it be reproduced as closely as possible in Catania, using the finest materials, by the sculptor Michele Orlando.

Further west along Via Garibaldi is the imposing facade of the old tobacco factory (left), which at the time of writing was being turned into the Archaeological Museum of Catania. The entrance is in Piazza San Cristoforo (*map 13*).

Piazza Mazzini (*map 14*) is charmingly arcaded with 32 columns from a Roman building which stood close to the Odeon, probably on the ancient forum. South of the piazza, Via Auteri, in a dilapidated district of the city, leads south to Piazza Federico di Svevia, where low houses surround the **Castello Ursino** (*map 14; open Mon–Sat 9–1 & 3–7; T: 095 345830*), built by Richard of Lentini for Frederick II of Hohenstaufen. It was partly destroyed by the lava of 1669, which completely surrounded it. The castle was restored after 1837 to house the **Museo Civico**. Material from the monastery of San Nicolò was augmented by archaeological treasures collected by the Prince of Biscari in the 18th century. Extensive repairs have recently been completed, and a permanent display installed. Temporary exhibitions are also held here. The ground floor is devoted to a collection of ancient vases and sculpture and the upper floor displays a collection of paintings. New archaeological excavations around the castle have revealed long sections of the Norman fortifications.

Near the submerged railway line just outside the square is the simple little church of **Santa Maria dell'Indirizzo**. Behind it, in the courtyard of a school are the remains of Late Roman baths called **Terme dell'Indirizzo** and a tiny domed Greek-cross building in black lava stone. This archaeological site has recently been studied and restored during the establishment of the archaeological zone of Catania, and will hopefully soon open to the public with the same hours as the Roman theatre (*open Tues–Sat 9–1.30 & 2.30–7.30, Sun 9–1*).

Sant'Agata alla Badia and Palazzo Biscari

Via Vittorio Emanuele leads east out of Piazza Duomo between the north side of the cathedral and the majestic little church of **Sant'Agata alla Badia** (*map 11; open 8–1*), its dome harmoniously setting off that of the cathedral, when viewed from Piazza Duomo. It is a work by Vaccarini (1735–67), though the Rococo interior was completed after his death, but notice the side altars in precious yellow marble from Castronovo (a stone he used also for the royal palace of Caserta), with their glossy stucco statues, and the magnificent floor with an intricate design in white and grey marble. Beyond, in a little square on the right, is the church of **San Placido** (*usually closed*) with a façade of 1769, attributed to Stefano Ittar, and a pretty interior. The vast convent behind the church, which includes the 15th-century terrace belonging to Palazzo Platamone, is now used by the town council as a cultural centre. Opposite the church is the workshop of a chandler, skilled in making the enormous wax candles for the feast of St Agatha.

Via Museo Biscari is named after the **Palazzo Biscari** (*T: 095 321818 to request a visit*), the most impressive private palace in Catania, said to have 600 rooms; it was an obligatory stop for travellers on the Grand Tour. The best view of the magnificent exterior, by Antonino Amato, is from Via Dusmet. Here, in the 18th century, Ignazio Paternò Castello, Prince of Biscari, catalogued *objets d'art* for his famous collection, part of which is preserved in the Museo Civico (*see p. 385*). Concerts are occasionally held in the lovely Rococo Salone della Musica, and part of the building, entered from no. 16, houses **Museum & Fashion** (*open Tues–Sun 10–7; T: 095 2503188*), created by designer Marella Ferrera, who was born in Catania; it displays some of her 'nostalgic mementoes', items from her most famous collections, temporary exhibitions, and her atelier.

Teatro Massimo Bellini and Via Vittorio Emanuele

The splendid opera house, **Teatro Massimo Bellini** (*map 11; open for visits Mon, Wed, Fri 9.30–11.30; T: 095 7306110*), by Carlo Sada, was inaugurated on 31st May 1890 with the première of Bellini's *Norma*. During the construction of the building, the architect had been heavily criticised by local opera lovers and city administrators who thought it would be ugly, to the point that he was forced to buy his own ticket for the opening night, but when the audience heard the marvellous acoustic effects there was an ovation. Sada stood up, bowed, and left the theatre. In fact the tenor Beniamino Gigli pronounced this theatre to have the finest acoustics he had ever encountered, wherever he had sung in the world. The narrow streets in this area, once a run-down part of the city, are now full of life; many pubs and open-air cafés open in the evening, giving rise to the so-called '*movida*' of Catania: live music for all tastes, jazz, pop or classical, especially in the summer.

Via Vittorio Emanuele leads east towards the sea, passing on the right Via Bonajuto, where the **Cappella Bonajuto** (*open Tues–Sat 10.30–1, to book visit T: 095 321338 or ask at Via Vittorio Emanuele 97*) is a Byzantine chapel built between the 6th and the 9th centuries. The elegant Palazzo Valle at no. 122, designed by Vaccarini and until recently on the verge of collapse, was purchased, recuperated *in extremis*, and returned to the city by a benefactor (who created the Puglisi Cosentino Foundation for the purpose) as a stylish showcase for exhibitions of modern art: the **Galleria d'Arte Moderna** (*open Tues–Sun 10–1 & 4–7, late closing Sat 9.30 pm*). At the end of the street, **Piazza dei Martiri** has a statue depicting St Agatha trampling the Plague, on top of a column removed from the ancient theatre; the monument was erected by the city senate in 1743 when an plague epidemic miraculously spared Catania. Here a wide terrace, '*u Passiaturi*, popular in the 19th century for afternoon strolls, and often mentioned by Verga in his novels, overlooks the harbour and leads to the **railway station**. In front of the station is a large, dramatic fountain in cement representing the kidnapping of Persephone by Hades, made by Giulio Moschetti in 1904.

Via Etnea to Piazza Stesicoro

On the north side of Piazza Duomo is the handsome **Via Etnea**, nearly 3km long, the main street of the city. It is lined with elegant shops (especially for clothes) and cafés, and its wide lava-stone pavements are always crowded. It rises to a splendid view of the peak of Mt Etna in the distance.

Beyond the Town Hall (Municipio) is the distinguished **Piazza Università** (*map 11*), laid out by Vaccarini. The University, on the left, known as Siculorum Gymnasium, was founded in 1434 by Alfonso V of Aragon (the Magnanimous) as the first in Sicily, and rebuilt after the earthquake of 1693; the gorgeous courtyard was begun by Andrea Amato and finished in 1752 by Vaccarini; the shady portico with its loggia was designed to allow students to walk in the open air while repeating their lessons, and it could also protect them from the rain if necessary.

Just beyond is the **Collegiata**, a royal chapel of c. 1768 by Stefano Ittar, with a dazzling Baroque interior, much in request for fashionable weddings; the vaults were frescoed on the theme of the Glorification of the Virgin by Giuseppe Sciuti. The canvases are by the little-known local artist Francesco Gramignani (1770), while the splendid painting over the first south altar represents St Apollonia, by Olivio Sozzi. The main altarpiece is a copy made after the 1693 earthquake of a Russian icon, destroyed in the disaster. Still further north, at no. 85, is the imposing church of **San Michele Arcangelo ai Minoriti** (*open 8.30–12 & 4.30–8; T: 095 316974*), which dominates this part of Via Etnea, as the influential monastic community which commissioned Francesco Battaglia to build it for them in 1771 fully intended it to do. The circular interior is striking for its huge dome. In the third north chapel is a beautiful Crucifix by Agostino

Penna, and opposite, a fine *Annunciation* by Willem Borremans, painted in 1720. The monumental organ with its intricate gold-leaf trimmed ornamentation is the work of the famous Serassi brothers of Bergamo.

San Biagio, the amphitheatre and Via Manzoni

Piazza Stesicoro (*map 6 and 7*) is the heart of modern Catania, with a monument to Vincenzo Bellini by Giulio Monteverde (1882). The figures at the feet of the composer, who sits relaxed in an armchair with pigeons all over him, represent the protagonists of his four most famous operas, *Norma, Il Pirata, I Puritani*, and *Sonnambula*. Dominating the square from the west is the 18th-century church of **San Biagio** (*open Mon–Sat 9–12 & 3–7, Sun 9–1; T: 095 7159360*), said to stand on the spot where St Agatha's Roman torturers tried to burn her in a furnace, and more usually known to the local people as Sant'Agata alla Carcarella, 'St Agatha on the Hot Coals'; the mouth of the furnace can be seen in the interior on the right. In the centre of the square are the scant ruins of the **Roman amphitheatre** (*open Tues–Sat 9–1.30 & 2.30–7, Sun 9–1; T: 095 7472268*) in black lava stone, thought to date from the 2nd century AD. The external circumference was 389m, and the arena was one of the largest after the Colosseum in Rome. There were 56 entrance arches and 32 rows of seats, and it could hold 16,000 spectators. The visible remains include a corridor, part of the exterior wall, and fragments of the cavea supported on vaults. The rest of the structure still partly exists beneath the surrounding buildings, with labyrinthine tunnels which have given rise through the centuries to legends of citizens mysteriously vanishing. Its destruction had already begun under Theodoric when it was used as a quarry; Totila made use of the stone in building the city walls in 530, and Count Roger stole its decorative elements to embellish his cathedral in 1091. In 1693 the area was used as a dump for the rubble of the earthquake.

Via Manzoni, which leads out of the south side of the square parallel to Via Etnea, is interesting for its numerous well-stocked haberdashery shops and old-fashioned clothes shops for children; once it was the site of the *niviere*, pits where snow from Mt Etna was stored, covered with thick layers of straw or sawdust to keep it fresh for use in the summer. A little way along on the right is the tiny Via dell'Anfiteatro, at the end of which is a small section of the first and second *ordine* of the amphitheatre.

Santo Carcere and Sant'Agata La Vetere

The **church of the Santo Carcere** (*map 6; open Thur and Sat 4–7, Sun and holidays 9.30–12*) is flanked by a strong defence wall. Incorporated into the Baroque façade is a beautiful doorway, with grotesque animal heads, which dates from 1236 and was formerly in the façade of the duomo. In the interior is St Agatha's prison, with a Roman barrel vault, which is shown by the custodian on request; the magnificent altarpiece representing her martyrdom is by Bernardino Niger (1588).

Sicilian Baroque churches are often described as 'scenographic', which is to say, they resemble an elaborate stage set, in which holy mysteries would be acted out whenever Mass was celebrated. The one illustrated left is Catania's Collegiata.

Via Cappuccini leads uphill to Via Maddalena, where the church of **Sant'Agata la Vetere**, probably built only a few years after the martyrdom of the saint in the 3rd century, stands opposite the church of the Purità (or Visitazione), with a curving façade by Battaglia (1775) next to its handsome convent. Sant'Agata la Vetere was once Catania's cathedral; inside is the Roman marble sarcophagus that was the first tomb of the martyr. The lid is a substitute, the original was used for many centuries as the altar in the duomo.

A little to the north is the church of **San Domenico** (*open before 9.30 & 5–6.30; ring at the convent next door*). It contains a beautiful *Madonna* by Antonello Gagini (1526) and a painting of St Vincent Ferrer by Olivio Sozzi (1757). The most interesting piece, held by the monks, is the central fragment of a canvas representing the head of the Virgin (c.1518) by Cesare da Sesto Calende, a pupil of Leonardo da Vinci; on the right side of the nave is a *Madonna del Rosario*, attributed to Innocenzo da Imola (c.1530).

ST AGATHA OF CATANIA

The Feast of St Agatha (Sant' Agata) is one of the most lavish in the Roman Catholic world, being exceeded only by Corpus Domini at Cuzco in Peru and the Easter procession at Seville in Spain. It galvanises the whole population of the city during the first week of February, and again on 17th August. An early Christian martyr, Agatha was only thirteen years old when she was arrested for her religious beliefs. In spite of blandishments and then threats, she would not recant her faith. On 4th February 251 she underwent terrible tortures including the mutilation of her breasts. Miraculously recovering during the night after seeing a vision of St Peter, she also survived being burned the next day in the amphitheatre in front of the populace, on the orders of Quintian, Roman governor of Catania. The flames would not touch her, and a sudden earthquake caused the Romans to flee the town leaving Agatha unscathed. She asked to be taken to her prison cell, where she died. Her body, still intact, was carried off to Constantinople by the Byzantine general George Maniakes as a gift for Emperor Basil II in 1040, but on 17th August 1126 she was brought back to Catania by two soldiers of the Imperial Guard, who had cut her body into pieces in order to smuggle her back home.

St Agatha is the patron saint both of women who have undergone mastectomy, and also of firemen. The processions in her honour are impressive and richly Baroque, sometimes continuing for 24 hours. The huge, 20-ton float, carrying caskets containing parts of her body and the 14th-century reliquary, glittering with jewels, which holds her torso and head, is dragged through the streets by thousands of *divoti* wearing traditional white robes and black caps, preceded by the *candelore*, enormous highly-decorated candlesticks representing the corporations of the city. The celebrations are concluded with spectacular fireworks. The event is regularly attended by crowds of some 300,000 and has been declared a UNESCO World Heritage Tradition.

North of Piazza Stesicoro

Via San Gaetano alle Grotte, with its daily market, leads to the little church of **San Gaetano alle Grotte** (*map 7*), which dates from 1700. The former church, built into a volcanic cavern beneath in 1262, is now usually closed but is sometimes open for Mass. The cave itself probably represents the oldest Christian place of worship in the city, and perhaps the first burial place of St Agatha.

The main **market** for produce and textiles, known as *'a Fera d'o Luni*, the Monday Fair, occupies Piazza Carlo Alberto. The piazza is overlooked by the church of the Carmine and a handsome palace occupied by the Lucchesi-Palli barracks, in the courtyard of which is a fine 2nd-century AD Roman tomb traditionally and erroneously held to be that of the poet Stesichorus of Himera (died c. 540 BC).

The charming **Villa Bellini** (*map 6; open daily 6am–10pm*) is a fine public garden laid out c. 1870. It contains large boulevards, two hills, fountains and busts of famous citizens (all without noses, thanks to local vandals) and a monument to Giovanni Pacini (1796–1867), another local composer. At the north end of the garden a gate leads out to Viale Regina Margherita, part of the modern east–west artery of the city, c. 5km long.

Further north is the important **Botanical Garden** of the University (*map 2; open Mon–Fri 9.30–1.30 & 3.30–5.30, Sat and Sun 10–1.30; T: 095 430901 or 430902; www. dipbot.unict.it*), founded in 1858. The main gate is on Via Etnea, but the usual entrance is on Via Longo. It is particularly famous for its cactus plants and trees from all over the world, but the Orto Siculo contains rare plants from Sicily, growing in specially-prepared beds reproducing as closely as possible their natural habitat. Via Etnea ends at Parco Gioeni, on a lava flow, an attractive and unusual public park.

About 500m west of the Botanical Garden, surrounded by tall, modern apartment blocks, is the church of **Santa Maria di Gesù** (*map 1*; 1442 and built in 1465). On its north side is the pretty exterior of the Cappella Paternò which survived the earthquake of 1693. It is entered from the north aisle of the church through a doorway by Antonello Gagini (1519) with a *Pietà* in the lunette above. Inside is an altarpiece of the *Madonna with Sts Agatha and Catherine* by Angelo de Chirico (signed 1525). Above the main altar of the church is a Crucifix by Fra' Umile da Petralia (early 17th century), and in the second north chapel, a *Madonna with Two Angels in Adoration* by Antonello Gagini (1498). The church originally owned a celebrated polyptych by Antonello de Saliba (1497), now held in Castello Ursino.

Piazza Verga and Corso Italia

Piazza Giovanni Verga (*map 4*) is a large square dominated by the Palazzo di Giustizia (1952). It is the focus of post-war Catania. The fountain in the centre by local sculptor Carmelo Mendola (1975) is a monument to Giovanni Verga and represents the moment of tragedy in his masterpiece *The House by the Medlar Tree*, when the Malavoglia family lose their fishing-boat, symbolically named *Provvidenza*.

Further east, at Corso Italia 55, the **Palazzo delle Scienze** (*open Tues and Thur mornings; T: 095 7195767 to request visit*), of 1942, houses the geological and volcanological collections of the university. The Corso terminates at the sea in Piazza Europa, with a watch-tower on top of a mound of lava and, under the trees, a marble statue of a young girl by Francesco Messina. Viale Ruggero di Lauria leads from here along the waterfront to Ognina and the **Museo del Mare** (Museum of the Sea; *Piazza Ognina 15; open Mon–Sat 9–1*). Many of Catania's fishermen live in this part of town and the museum is a way of honouring the fishing community. Mementoes of fishing from the past, anchors and boats are on display, and traditional fishing methods are explained.

Le Ciminiere cultural centre

Beyond the railway station, Viale Africa runs parallel to the waterfront to Le Ciminiere (*open Tues–Sun 9.30–12.30, Tues and Thur also 3–5; last tickets one hour before closing*) with its tall chimneys, which was built in the 19th century as a sulphur refinery. It has been restored as a cultural centre with exhibition halls and space for theatrical performances and concerts, and houses the Puppet Theatre and several museums. The museum of the 1943 Allied landing in Sicily, **Museo Storico Sbarco in Sicilia 1943** (*T: 095 4011929*) is a collection of uniforms, weapons, memorabilia, photographs and films documenting the invasion codenamed Operation Husky. The **Museo del Cinema** (*T: 095 4011928*) offers an interesting excursion into the world of films made in Sicily, including virtual interviews with actors and directors, some film sets, and a luxurious little theatre furnished with antique Frau armchairs from which to view excerpts. The **Mostra Radio d'Epoca** (*T: 095 4013058*) is a large collection of beautiful old radio sets, the passion of local enthusiast Francesco Romeo, together with an interesting description of the pioneer work of Marconi, while the **Mostra Collezione 'La Gumina'** (*T: 095 4013072*) is an exhibition of precious old maps and atlases of Sicily. The **Museo del Giocattolo** (*T: 095 0947899, 095 539073 to book afternoon visits*), has a fascinating collection of toys: old dolls and teddy bears, tea sets and dolls' prams, card games and puppets. One room provides space for temporary exhibits and impromptu creativity, with a little puppet theatre.

RISERVA NATURALE OASI DEL SIMETO

The Simeto nature reserve (*map p. 541, C3; when arriving from Catania on the SS 114, you will see the entrance and car park on the left just before reaching the old bridge over the Simeto, Ponte Primosole*) sits at the mouth of the River Simeto, a few kilometres south of Catania. Although numerous holiday villas were built here illegally from the 1960s onwards, it was first protected in 1975 and became a nature reserve in 1984, thanks mainly to the strenuous efforts of Wendy Hennessy Mazza, a British local resident and birdwatcher, a representative of the Lega Italiana Protezione Uccelli (LIPU), the Italian society for the protection of birds. In 1989, 54 of the numerous houses erected within the area without building permission were demolished, but hundreds still remain. The marshes and brackish lakes offer protection to numerous birds, both nesting and migratory, including rare ducks, great white heron, flamingo, black-winged stilt, godwit, cattle egret, glossy ibis, avocet and spoonbill. The purple gallinule has been successfully reintroduced. Amber can sometimes be found on the shore here, the fossilised resin of almond trees which grew inland about 60 million years ago. The colour is rich chestnut brown, giving green or blue reflections in artificial light; sometimes there are insects or fragments of leaves trapped inside.

On the right bank of the Simeto, close to the bridge, where you can see a low hill, stood the ancient Sicel town of *Symaethus*, whose necropolis survives on the Turrazza estate. The River Simeto, 88km long, is the most important river in Sicily; it springs from Serra del Re in the Nebrodi Mountains, and picks up some important tributaries on its way to the sea—the Salso, Troina, Dittaino and Gornalunga. In the course of time it has formed the immense alluvial Plain of Catania. The mouth was a marshy delta, drained in the 1930s under Mussolini, to create farmland and eliminate malaria, but the disease continued to be a problem for the local farmers until 1943, when Allied troops eradicated it with DDT.

MOUNT ETNA

Mount Etna, to the northwest of Catania, is the highest volcano in Europe (c. 3350m) and one of the largest and most active in the world. Its regional park protects 59,000 hectares of unique geology, flora and fauna, villages and farms, and traditional methods of forestry, bee-keeping, wine manufacture, stonework and carpentry. The ascent of Etna is easy and is an experience which should not be missed, not only for the volcanic phenomena but also for the superb views. The extent of a visit is always subject to current volcanic activity, and visibility is determined by cloud conditions (which tend to build up in the course of the day) and the direction of the smoke from the main craters. There are splendid views of the lava fields on the approach roads to Rifugio Sapienza and Piano Provenzana, the two starting-points for the ascent. Higher up it is often possible to see smoking and gaseous fissures, and explosions from the main craters, of which there are four—it is not permitted to approach these. There may be a strong smell of sulphur, and here and there the mountainside is covered by yellow sulphurous patches. The view, beyond the mountain's hundreds of subsidiary cones and craters, can extend across the whole of Sicily, the Aeolian Islands and Calabria. The spectacle is unique owing to the enormous difference in height between Etna and the surrounding hills.

Etna statistics

Etna's circular cone is 45km in diameter at the base. From a distance it appears almost perfectly regular in shape and the great width of its base detracts from its height. But the terminal cone, with its four open summit craters, rises from a truncated cone 2801m high, on the sides of which are about 300 side craters. The smaller craters are often arranged along a regular line of fracture, and are thus called 'button formations'.

On the northeast side is the Valle del Bove, an immense caldera 19km in circumference, bounded on three sides by sheer walls of tufa and lava, in places 900m high; it formed about 20,000 years ago, when the crater known as Trifoglietto subsided. During recent eruptions the lava has been flowing into this huge natural reservoir, thus sparing the towns on the southeast slopes.

HISTORY OF MOUNT ETNA

Etna, called *Aetna* in ancient times and Mongibello (from *monte* and *jebel*, Italian and Arabic for mountain) by the Sicilians (often simply *'a muntagna*), probably originated from a submarine eruption which took place in the gulf which is now occupied by the Plain of Catania. In ancient Greece the volcano was held to be the forge of Hephaistos or of the Cyclopes, or the mountain from beneath which the Titan Enceladus, imprisoned by Zeus, forever struggled to free himself. Empedocles (*see p. 201*), the philosopher, scientist and statesman from Agrigento who lived in the 5th century BC, was said to have thrown himself into the crater to obtain complete knowledge. Among early eruptions, that of 475 BC was described by Pindar and Aeschylus, while that of 396 BC, whose lava reached the sea, is said to have prevented the Carthaginian general Himilco from marching on Syracuse. Hadrian climbed Etna to see the sunrise and the conical shape of the mountain reflected on the island. The eruption of 122 BC covered the city of Catania and the surrounding countryside under a thick layer of sand, disastrous enough for the senate in Rome to exempt the inhabitants from tax for ten years. In 1169, 1329 and 1381 the lava again reached the sea, twice near Acireale, the third time at Catania. The largest eruption ever recorded took place in 1669 when an open cleft extended from the summit to Nicolosi and part of Catania was overwhelmed. The resulting crater, which appears double, is called Monti Rossi.

Since 1800 there have been over 130 eruptions, that of 1928 being the most destructive, obliterating the town of Mascali. In 1908 a huge pit of lava opened in the Valle del Bove. The eruption of 1947 threatened Passopisciaro, and that of 1950–51 menaced Rinazzo and Fornazzo before the lava halted. The 1971 eruption destroyed the observatory and the second stage of the cableway on the summit, as well as vineyards and some houses near Fornazzo. In 1978–79 four new cones erupted and the lava flowed into the Valle del Bove; the town of Fornazzo was again threatened. Nine British tourists were killed by an explosion on the rim of the main crater in 1979. In the spring of 1983 activity started up on the opposite side of the mountain above Nicolosi and Belpasso, forming the southeast crater, which has since been the most active of the summit cones. In 1984 an earthquake damaged the town of Fleri. In 1991–92 eruptions took place over four months, threatening Zafferana Etnea. The eruption of summer 2001 started just below the Montagnola at 2800m, on 18th July, but within a few days 18 temporary craters had opened up all over the top of the volcano, providing spectacular firework displays at night. The lava was successfully prevented from doing too much damage by the use of bulldozers to create enormous dykes to contain and direct the flow. 2002 saw another eruption, which took the same path as that of the previous year, and an earthquake at Santa Venerina; since then there have been several explosive and eruptive phases, indicating perhaps that the volcano is increasing its activity.

Vegetation and wildlife

The soil at the foot of Etna is extraordinarily fertile because the volcanic ash is rich in nutrients. In the cultivated zone (*pedemontana*), oranges, lemons and tangerines are grown behind low black basalt dry-stone walls. The higher slopes of the mountain were forested up until the 19th century, but now they are planted with groves of olives, apples, pears, pistachios, hazelnuts and vineyards. The apparently delicate, willowy, pale green endemic Etna broom, *Genista aetnensis*, flourishes on many of the lava flows; it is one of the most important 'pioneer plants' which help to break up the rock and turn it into soil, a process which takes about 400 years. At 1300m forest trees grow, especially oaks, chestnuts, pines and beeches. This is the southernmost point in Europe where the beech tree can be found, and this is also where it reaches its highest altitude, growing up to 2250m. It is also the extreme southern limit for the silver birch, which is found in its endemic form, *Betula aetnensis*. From 2000–3000m the black lava is colonised by tough little plants, most of them found only on this volcano, such as the Etna holy thorn (*Astragalus aetnensis*), or the Etna violet (*Viola aetnensis*), creating a wonderful carpet of flowers in the spring and early summer. Botanists should not miss the 'Nuova Gussonea' Alpine Garden (*T: 095 7332111, 095 317097, 347 0033932 to request visit*), run by the University of Catania. It is in Contrada Carpinteri, not far from the Grande Albergo, and can be reached from the Nicolosi–Rifugio Sapienza road.

Since the creation of the park, the golden eagle has returned after an absence of more than a hundred years, and nests regularly; Etna is the only place in Sicily where the long-eared owl can be found. Wolves and boars no longer roam the forests, and there are no squirrels or badgers, but to compensate there are plenty of foxes and rabbits, hares, porcupines, wildcats, hedgehogs, the garden and the edible dormouse, many species of bats, five snakes (of which only the viper is venomous), the tortoise and two kinds of toad. There are plans to reduce access to the area of maximum protection (*Zona A*) to allow nature to take over again, and to reintroduce some long-absent species, such as the roe deer and the griffon vulture.

Pot-holers or spelaeologists will find the numerous lava tubes on Mount Etna fascinating, but exploration should not be attempted without expert help. Those interested should call the CUTGANA group at the University of Catania (*T: 095 7615769, www. cutgana.it*), for these or other caves in Sicily.

The heat of the rocks and the hot vapours from the terminal cones cause the snow to melt partly even in winter, but in certain depressions with a northern aspect the snow was kept fresh for refrigeration purposes throughout the summer by being covered with a layer of volcanic ash, and it was transported on mule-back down to the towns as necessary.

EXPLORING MOUNT ETNA

The summit can be visited from either the southern or the northern side of the mountain. There are organised excursions from Rifugio Sapienza on the southern slopes (Etna Sud) and from Piano Provenzana on the northern slopes (Etna Nord).

Both can be reached easily by car or bus. The upper part of the volcano can also be explored on foot from both these points, and there are some spectacular walks which are signposted on the lower slopes of the mountain. Near the top there is almost always a very strong wind and the temperature can be many degrees below freezing: a warm jacket, sturdy shoes and a close-fitting hat are in order (boots and jackets can be hired at the cableway station near Rifugio Sapienza). The four summit craters are strictly off limits.

The southern approach: Etna Sud

The Strada dell'Etna was opened in 1934 by Vittorio Emanuele III. It is well signposted beyond **Nicolosi** (*map p. 541, C2*), which is one of the best centres for visiting Etna. At Via Cesare Battisti 28 is the **Museo Vulcanologico Etneo** (*open 9.30–12.30, Tues and Thur also 3.30–5.30; closed Mon; T: 095 7914589*), an informative display about Etna and its phenomena, together with a collection of various types of lava and minerals. To the west of Nicolosi are the twin hills of the Monti Rossi (949m), which represent one of the most important subsidiary groups of craters (over 3km round), formed in 1669 by the biggest eruption ever recorded.

Beyond Nicolosi the road climbs through lava fields and some woods, crossing lava flows from 1886 and 1910; the names of the craters on either side of the road are indicated. Walks off this road are also signposted. The main road continues to the Casa Cantoniera at 1910m and ends at the 2001 lava stream beside the **Rifugio Sapienza**. Here there are souvenir shops, an information bureau, a first-aid point, cafés, restaurants and honey vendors. In the desert of hardened volcanic lava nearby, several extinct craters can be explored easily on foot, and the 400-metre-wide 2001 lava flow is impressive, superimposed with the lava from 2002.

A cableway ascends from here up the slopes of the **Montagnola** (2507m), a crater of 1763, through a desert of lapilli with splendid views of the sea and port of Catania. It takes about 15mins to reach the site of the Piccolo Rifugio, destroyed during the 2001 eruption. Although at present you are not allowed any nearer to the main crater, from this distance you can usually see (and hear) volcanic activity. A road has been cut through the 2001 and 2002 lava streams, making it possible to reach the **Silvestri Craters**, formed during the eruption of 1892, and continue down the thickly-wooded eastern slopes of the mountain and across the 1992 lava to Zafferana Etnea.

Getting to the summit

Organised excursions to the summit leave from the Rifugio Sapienza and take about 2hrs. Tickets can be bought at the cableway station near the refuge. The cableway itself was severely damaged during the eruptions of July 2001 and November 2002, but has since been repaired. If weather conditions are adverse, 4WD vehicles are used to reach a height of about 2800m, where the guides take people on foot to the more interesting areas. From the Rifugio Sapienza guides also take people walking to the 2001 crater close by (NB: It is absolutely forbidden to approach the rim of the summit craters). Before undertaking the climb independently, advice should be obtained about weather conditions at the SITAS offices at the cableway station, or at Nicolosi, where guides are available to accompany walkers. The easiest and most usual approach from Sapienza follows the track used by the 4WD vans. About 4hrs should be allowed for the return trip on foot from the refuge. The most spectacular time for the ascent is before dawn.

The northern approach: Etna Nord

Linguaglossa (*map p. 541, C1*) is the best centre for excursions on the northern slopes of Etna. The peaceful little town has a number of late 19th- and early 20th-century houses. The doorways and windows of the 18th-century church are decorated with lava stone, and elaborate 19th-century lamps ornament the façade.

The mountain road, known as the Mareneve, which climbs towards the summit of Etna, begins here. It leads up through the **Pineta Ragabo**, ancient pinewoods of great interest to naturalists, to the ski fields of **Piano Provenzana** (1800m), the main ski resort on Etna, with a refuge, and five ski-lifts (1800m and 2300m) completely destroyed by the earthquakes and lava during the 2002 eruption, and under repair at time of writing. From here excursions by 4WD vans are organised, arriving just below the summit. It is also possible to walk up the cone from here in c. 3hrs (the easiest way is to follow the track used by the excursion vans).

Another mountain road descends from Piano Provenzana following the eastern slope of the mountain passing beneath the Rifugio Citelli at 1741m, to Fornazzo.

THE SOUTHERN FOOTHILLS OF ETNA

ADRANO

Adrano (*map p. 541, B2*) was the ancient *Hadranon*, founded by Dionysius I close to the site of a Sicel temple dedicated to the god Hadranon, said to have been guarded by hundreds of dogs called *cirnechi* (from Cyrenaica), originally purchased from Phoenician merchants, and still raised in the area today. Of medium size, with upright ears, a long, thin straight tail, ginger in colour and with a pinkish nose, they are extremely intelligent and highly prized.

Overlooking the public gardens, **Giardino della Vittoria** (with superb trees), is the enormous former monastery of Santa Lucia, now a school, flanked by the towering façade (1775) of its church, which has a pretty oval interior. The imposing black lava-stone **castle** (*open Tues–Sat 9–1 & 4–7, Sun 9–1; T: 095 7692660*) was built in 1070 by Count Roger on the site of Greek and Roman fortifications. The interior houses an interesting local museum. The archaeological section includes prehistoric material from Stentinello and Castelluccio (ground and first floors). On the second floor the later finds from Mendolito include a hanging askos and a 6th-century BC bronze figurine, *Il Banchettante*. In a little Norman chapel, with an apse fresco, is a collection of coins from ancient Adrano. On the third floor are paintings, many of them in very poor condition.

Next to the castle is the **Chiesa Madre**, of Norman origin. The interior incorporates

16 basalt columns, possibly from the ancient temple of Hadranon. High up above the west door is a fine polyptych by the 16th-century Messina school in its original frame. The painted 15th-century Crucifix was damaged by restoration work in 1924. In the transepts are four panels (two saints and the *Annunciation*) by Girolamo Alibrandi. In the pretty sacristy is a fine painting of the *Last Supper* by Pier Paolo Vasta.

The opera house, **Teatro Bellini**, built in 1845 to replace an earlier theatre of 1742, has been restored and is now in regular use; its Art Nouveau façade was added in the early 20th century.

Off a byroad below the town (signposted 'Strada per il Ponte dei Saraceni'), a poorly-surfaced road between low lava-stone walls leads (in c. 1.5km) past citrus plantations and lovely old farmhouses to the Simeto river, spanned by the impressive 14th-century **Ponte dei Saraceni**, an extremely well-preserved bridge. It has four asymmetric arches decorated with black lava-stone and the path over the top is still passable. In this beautiful peaceful spot there is a view of Etna and a waterfall on the rocky bed of the Simeto. Nearby (not signposted) are a few remains of the walls and south gate of the ancient Sicel town of *Mendolito*.

EAST FROM ADRANO

Southeast of Adrano is **Biancavilla** (*map p. 541, B2*), where excellent oranges and clementines are grown; beside the extensive citrus plantations are olive groves and hedges of prickly pear. At **Paternò**, another important centre for orange-growing, the town sprawls at the base of an 11th-century castle (*open 9.20–12.40 & 4.15–7.30, Sat 9.20–12.40; closed Sun and Mon*). The austere tower built of volcanic rock commands the wide Simeto valley. It was restored in 1900, with a fine hall and frescoed chapel. From the terrace there is a good view. Frederick II of Aragon died near Paternò while journeying to Enna. The churches of San Francesco and Santa Maria della Valle di Giosafat retain Gothic elements.

From Paternò the road continues to the town of **Motta Sant'Anastasia**, perched on an extremely interesting rock formation, a 'neck' of lava (visible close-up from Via Montalto and Via Vittorio Veneto), with a fine 12th-century Norman castle (*open 9.15–12.40; closed Sat and Sun*) which preserves its crenellations. The unusual name of **Misterbianco**, a town now swallowed up by Catania, with an industrial area and several hypermarkets, comes from a Benedictine monastery, the *monastero bianco*, which was destroyed along with the town, in the eruption of 1669.

A secondary road from Paternò leads up the volcano to **Belpasso**. Once known as Malpasso, it was covered by lava in 1669 and rebuilt with the name Fenicia Moncada; destroyed once again by the 1693 earthquake, it was again rebuilt, this time with the more optimistic name, which it still holds. The bell in the tower of the Chiesa Madre, forged in 1815, is among the largest in Italy. The Art Nouveau opera house is dedicated to the popular local playwright Nino Martoglio.

The road continues to Nicolosi, Pedara, and **Trecastagni** (*map p. 541, C2*), where the Chiesa Madre is perhaps the purest Renaissance building in Sicily, thought to be the work of Antonello Gagini. The Chiesa del Bianco has an elegant 15th-century campanile. The town is renowned for the production of wine, especially Etna Rosso.

Zafferana Etnea is the main town on the east side of Etna. Its name derives from the saffron which once formed the base of the economy, but today Zafferana is one of the most important honey-producing areas of Italy, renowned for its *miele di zagara* or citrus-blossom honey. The area was damaged by an earthquake in 1984, and in 1992 a lava flow reached the outskirts of the town (this can now be visited, at the end of a signposted road, where a statue was set up as a thanksgiving to the Madonna). Climbs towards the Valle del Bove can be made from here.

THE NORTHERN FOOTHILLS OF ETNA

RANDAZZO

Above the Alcantara valley, Randazzo (*map p. 541, B1*) is a lava-built town of great antiquity, which has never in recorded history suffered volcanic destruction. Its medieval history resolves itself into a rivalry between the three churches of Santa Maria, San Nicolò and San Martino, each of which served as the cathedral for alternate periods of three years. The parishioners of each church (of Greek, Latin and Lombard origin) spoke different dialects until the 16th century. The town was damaged during Allied bombing in August 1943, when the Germans made it the strong point of their last resistance on the island.

Exploring Randazzo

The present **cathedral**, Santa Maria, is a 13th-century church with fine black lava-stone apses and a three-storeyed south portal (approached by two flights of steps) in the Catalan Gothic style of the 15th century. The dome is attributed to Venanzio Marvuglia. The black and white tower was restored in 1863. The terrace, with another fine doorway, and the sacristy with 16th-century portico, looks out over the Alcantara Valley. The interior (1594) has fine black columns and capitals, one of which serves as an altar. Over the south door is a small painting with a view of the town attributed to Girolamo Alibrandi (15th century); over the north door is a fragment of a fresco of the *Madonna and Child* (13th century). The church contains six paintings by Giuseppe Velasquez (on the first north altar, the fourth and fifth altars in the north and south aisles, and on the south wall of the sanctuary). The Crucifix in the chapel to the right of the sanctuary is by Fra' Umile da Petralia. The second left-hand and second right-hand altarpieces are by Onofrio Gabrieli. The third south altarpiece is by Jan van Houbraken. Outside, the south side shows beautiful windows of the original structure and a magnificent Catalan Gothic doorway with a tiny marble relief of the Madonna over it, probably from Pisa.

Via Umberto leads past the southern flank of Santa Maria past a little **natural history museum** (*open 10–1 & 4–7, summer until 10*), with an ornithological section and a collection of shells, to Piazza Municipio where the Town Hall occupies a 14th-century convent reconstructed in 1610. The lovely cloister has columns of lava stone.

From here the narrow, pretty Via degli Archi leads beneath four arches to the church of **San Nicolò**, which dates mainly from the 16th–17th centuries (damaged in 1943). The apse, however, is original (13th century). In the north transept is a seated statue of St Nicholas (with two small reliefs below) by Antonello Gagini, signed and dated 1523. In the south transept is a 16th-century painted Crucifix and four delicately carved bas-reliefs of the Passion by Giacomo Gagini. Outside, there is an 18th-century copy replacing the original, destroyed in 1943, of a curious antique statue of a man, thought to symbolise the union of the three parishes (*see above*). Called Old Randazzo or *Piracmone* by the local people, the eagle represents the regality of the Latins, the snake the wisdom of the Greeks, and the lion the strength of the Lombards. Nearby is Palazzo Clarentano (1509) where a medieval arch tunnels beneath houses back towards the Corso.

Via Umberto continues to the district of San Martino, with evidence of shell fire from the Second World War. At no. 197 is the information bureau (*open 9–1 & 3–7.30, Sun 9–1*). The damaged church of **San Martino** still has its fine 14th-century campanile. On the top is a charming old-fashioned iron weather-vane, in the form of a cherub. The façade has 15th-century reliefs of saints and martyrs. In the interior are black lava-stone columns and in the south transept a statue of the *Madonna and Child* by the Gagini school (which retains part of its polychrome decoration). In the north aisle is a triptych by a local painter influenced by Antonello da Messina. Here also is a *papier mâché* Crucifix, recently restored, the work of Giovannello Matinati, signed and dated 1540. It is known as the Crucifix of the Water, because when Matinati was transporting it from Messina, where he lived, to an unknown destination, he was waylaid by a deluge and took refuge in the church to protect his artwork. Every time he tried to leave, it started raining again. In the end he left the Crucifix in the church where it apparently belonged. The marble font was made in 1447.

In front of the church is the 13th-century **castle**, which was rebuilt in 1645 and used as a prison up until 1973. It has now been restored as the **Vagliasindi Museum** (*open 10–1& 3.30–7.30, closed Mon; T: 095 921861*). The collection includes some fine vases from a neighbouring Greek necropolis (5th–2nd centuries BC), including a 5th-century red-figure oinochoe, as well as coins and jewellery. A collection of puppets is also displayed here. There is a lovely view of the church of San Martino from the uppermost tower. Just beyond in the walls is the Porta San Martino (1753).

BRONTE

Bronte (*map p. 541, B1*) is an important centre for the cultivation of pistachios (90 percent of the pistachios produced in Italy are grown here). The trees are small and grey, with long contorted branches which almost reach the ground. The fruit is harvested every two years at the end of August and beginning of September. Pistachios are used in local cuisine for pasta dishes, sweets and ice creams, and exported to northern Italy for flavouring mortadella sausage.

Castello Maniace (Castello Nelson)

In a little wooded valley to the north of Bronte, on the Saraceno, a tributary of the Simeto, is the Castello Maniace or Castello Nelson (*open 9–1 & 3–5, closed Mon; T: 095 690018*). A convent was founded here in 1173 by Margaret of Navarre, mother of William II, on the spot where the Byzantine general George Maniakes defeated the Saracens in 1040, with the help of the Russian Varangian Guard and Norman mercenaries, among whom may have been the Scandinavian hero Harold Hardrada.

The house and estate were presented to Admiral Horatio Nelson in 1799 by Ferdinand IV (later King Ferdinand I of the Two Sicilies). Nelson was given the Duchy of Bronte in gratitude for his help the year before when the king had fled from Naples on Nelson's flagship during the Napoleonic invasion. Patrick Brunty from Ulster was a country parson in Yorkshire who was a great admirer of Nelson. In celebration of his hero's success he changed his name to Brontë and went on to father the Brontë sisters. Nelson himself apparently never managed to visit Maniace, but the title and estate passed, by the marriage of Nelson's niece, to the family of Viscount Bridport who sold the property in 1981 to the Bronte town council.

In the courtyard is a stone cross memorial to Nelson. The 13th-century chapel, with the original portal, has a Byzantine *Madonna and Child*, two charming primitive reliefs of the *Annunciation*, and two 15th-century paintings. In the barn, there are walkways above excavations of the former abbey church. The house retains its appearance from the days when it was the residence of Alexander Hood, who lived here from 1873 until just before the Second World War: it has majolica tiled floors and English wallpaper.

The dilapidated gardens, also designed by Hood (with palm trees, planted in 1912, magnolias, cypresses and box hedges), can also be visited. The Scottish writer William Sharp, who was once considered a father of the Celtic Renaissance and published under the pseudonym Fiona Macleod, died here in 1905 aged 55. He is buried beneath an Iona cross in the cemetery (*shown on request*).

Between Bronte and Randazzo the landscape is barren, with numerous volcanic deposits. The countryside, studded with little farmhouses built of black lava stone, is used for grazing and the cultivation of vineyards. There is a large lava stream of 1832 near **Maletto**, whose sandstone cliff called Pizzo Filicia (1140m) is the highest sedimentary rock on Etna (views). The vineyards in this region produce excellent red and white wines (Etna Rosso and Etna Bianco); the vines are grown close to the ground (known as the *alberello* method) for climatic reasons.

EAST OF RANDAZZO

East of Randazzo is the town of **Passopisciaro** (*map p. 541, C1*). Beyond it, near a massive lava flow (1981), oaks and chestnuts are now being replaced by vineyards and olive trees. Some of the prettiest scenery in the foothills of Etna can be seen here, with numerous handsome old russet-coloured houses (many of them now abandoned), excellent views of the volcano and, to the north, the wooded mountains beyond the Alcantara.

Francavilla di Sicilia, with its ruined Norman castle, stands in a dominant position overlooking the road. Above the cemetery on the outskirts is the well-signposted Convento dei Cappuccini (17th century), where the church has a beautiful 15th-century *Madonna and Child* attributed to the school of Antonello da Messina and the 17th-century funerary monument of the Ruffo family, among other works. A Greek sanctuary was excavated in the town in 1979–84 and the votive statues found here are now displayed in the archaeological museum in Syracuse. Among the objects discovered are *pinakes*, pictures made of terracotta relating to the cult of Persephone. It is believed that some of the survivors of Dionysius' destruction of Naxos in 403 BC took refuge here.

Castiglione di Sicilia is a quiet little town, in a stunning position perched on a crag. Founded by the survivors of the destruction of Naxos, wreaked by Dionysius of Syracuse, it was once a stronghold of Roger of Lauria, inveterate opponent of Frederick II of Aragon. Frederick II of Hohenstaufen loved the town, conceding it the privilege of minting its own coins, and called it *animosa* for the courage of the population. Its many churches are all closed most of the time, a great pity because they contain remarkable works of art. However, the Chiesa Madre (San Pietro), whose magnificent apse of 1105 is visible from outside, opens for Mass (*8 every day, also 10 on Sun*). Inside is an interesting meridian line traced by Temistocle Zona in 1882. Below it is the church of Sant'Antonio (*key at wine shop in front*), with an ingenious façade and campanile, in a charming little piazza. Inside, it preserves delightful marble inlay work (1700) and four octagonal paintings by Giovanni Tuccari. In the sanctuary is an elaborate wooden confessional supporting a pulpit and a simple painted organ loft.

The **Rocca del Leone** or Castel Leone (Castle of the Lion), which gives its name to the town, is worth the climb. Extremely interesting and of great antiquity, it is said to have been constructed in 750 BC by a Greek commander called Leon, even before the creation of the first colony at Naxos. The old stones are haunted by jackdaws and the views are peerless, over the rooftops to Mt Etna, the Alcantara valley and the Peloritan Mountains. Castiglione is magical, especially on certain winter mornings when the air is crisp and clear, Etna is covered with snow, and the scent of woodsmoke lingers in the air; or on hot summer evenings, when the sky is like a bowl of deep blue Murano glass, and swifts screech and whirl untiringly among the steeples.

Below the town, off the Randazzo road (well signposted for the '**Cuba Bizantina**'), is another abandoned Byzantine-Arab building surrounded by vineyards, usually called the church of Santa Domenica. It is approached along a narrow country road beyond a railway line. Built of lava stone, probably in the late 8th century, it has an interesting plan and although very ruined the vault survives.

There are pinewoods and hazelnut groves near **Linguaglossa**, an important centre for excursions on Etna. **Piedimonte Etneo** is a village surrounded by fine citrus groves, with views of Taormina and Castelmola.

To the south is **Sant'Alfio** (*map p. 541, C2*), near which is a famous giant chestnut tree known as the Castagno dei Cento Cavalli (*T: 095 968017*), because its branches were reputed to be able to shelter 100 horses with their riders. It has a circumference of over 60m and is over 2,000 years old. The area was once a forest of chestnuts, nowadays

largely coppiced for the timber of the saplings. The fruit from the orchards in the district is sold on the streets in the autumn, together with chestnuts and wild mushrooms.

ACIREALE

Famous for exquisite almond confectionery, the sound of church bells, and the stubbornness of its people, Acireale (*map p. 541, C2*) is a beautiful and atmospheric little city, perched between Etna and the sea on a cliff of lava, verdant with lemon trees and Mediterranean maquis, called the Timpa, now a nature reserve. The maze of tiny jasmine-scented streets in the centre is often used as a film set. The surroundings are rich in mineral springs, which have been exploited since Roman times for health cures. Ten towns and villages in this area derive their name from the Acis, a mythical river said to flow underground, which came into being on the death of Acis, the shepherd beloved by Galatea and killed by the Cyclops Polyphemus. Acireale derives the second part of its name from the decree of 1642, whereby Philip IV of Spain declared it a royal city. It is particularly interesting for its Baroque buildings, erected after the earthquake of 1693.

Exploring Acireale

The main Via Vittorio Emanuele leads up to Piazza Vigo. Here the church of **San Sebastiano** has a 17th-century façade in Spanish-Baroque style with numerous statues and a delightful frieze of cherubs with garlands, considered by some to be the loveliest in Sicily. The balustrade and statues are by Giovanni Battista Marino (1754). Entered by the side door, the Museo Basilica San Sebastiano (*open 9–1, closed Mon*) houses (partly in the old crypt) a collection of paintings, wooden statues, and embroidered silk priests' robes.

On the other side of Piazza Vigo, with two charming little kiosks, is the large Neoclassical **Palazzo Pennisi di Floristella**, belonging to the foremost aristocratic family of the city, which now offers accommodation (*see p. 417*). Beyond, the main streets of town meet at the elegant Piazza Duomo. Here is the 17th-century Town Hall, with splendid balconies supported by grotesque figures, and the basilica of **Santi Pietro e Paolo**, with an asymmetric early 18th-century façade and just one bell-tower, instead of the two which were originally planned. The 17th-century **cattedrale** (Acireale has been a diocese since 1844) has a neo-Gothic façade, added in the late 19th century by Giovanni Battista Basile, and an interesting early 19th-century meridian line in the transept. It is dedicated both to the Madonna and the patron St Venera, a Roman martyr. At the east end are 18th-century frescoes by Pier Paolo Vasta, although the best place to admire the work of this much-loved local artist is at the church of **Santa Maria del Suffragio** in Via Romeo, where a dazzling series of frescoes carried out in 1750 can be seen. There are more of his frescoes at the church of **San Camillo** in Via Galatea, called the 'church of the women' by the local people, because the theme chosen by Vasta for the paintings was women of the Old Testament, such as Bathsheba, Judith, Abigail and Rebecca.

Detail of the façade of San Sebastiano in Acireale, with the figure of St Christopher.

Opposite the cathedral, Via Cavour leads to the church of **San Domenico**, which is both graceful and dramatic, close to the large 17th-century Palazzo Musmeci, with an unusual curving façade and pretty windows. At Via Marchese di San Giuliano 15 is the **Accademia Zelantea** (*open Tues–Fri 10–1 & 3.30–6.30; T: 095 7634516, www.zelantea. it*) a handsome building of 1915. The Academy was founded in 1671 and the library in 1716. It now possesses a fine collection of artworks, a selection being displayed here, and some 150,000 volumes, one of the most important collections of its kind on the island. Note in particular the Roman marble statue bust found at Capomulini in the 17th century and thought to be of Julius Caesar.

The outskirts of Acireale

A surprising and lovely walk follows Via Romeo from the cathedral down to the perilous main road, which can be crossed by means of a footbridge, then down the many steps of the picturesque Strada delle Chiazzette through the Timpa nature reserve (run by the Azienda Forestale) to **Santa Maria la Scala**, a tiny fishing village. There are many springs of sweet water down here at sea-level: the fishermen's wives were washerwomen, using the steps to carry their baskets of laundry up and down.

The sulphur baths of **Santa Venera** are at the south end of town in a park overlooking the Timpa; water and volcanic mud are used for treating various ailments. The spa building is of 1873, and was visited by Wagner. Just south of Acireale, in the district of Reitana, a **Roman spa** has been brought to light, and at Capomulini the remains of a **Roman podium temple** can just be made out behind a locked gate.

The coast south of Acireale

South of Acireale is **Acitrezza** (*map p. 541, C2*), a fishing village described by Giovanni Verga in his masterpiece, *I Malavoglia* (*The House by the Medlar Tree*). In the sea in front of the tiny harbour, with its boats in various stages of construction or repair, are seven lava-stone rocks called the **Faraglioni del Ciclope**, now protected as a marine nature reserve run by the University of Catania (*T: 095 7117322*). According to legend, the rocks are those thrown by the Cyclops Polyphemus at Odysseus, who had just blinded him. They are the result of an ancient lateral eruption of Mt Etna, and represent the fragmentary rim of a crater. On one of the rocks, Isola Lachea, is a small house used by the University of Catania, which runs the reserve. The rocks have surprisingly varied fauna (as does the sea around them), including a tiny population of an endemic lizard, found only here, *Lacerta situla faraglionensis*, recognisable by its red throat.

Aci Castello is a large village on the coast close to Catania, with a small quay with colourful fishing boats beneath the castle (*open summer 9–1 & 4–8, winter 9–1 & 3–5; T: 095 272600*) on a splendid basalt rock which rises sharply out of the sea, with interesting formations of 'pillow lava'. The town was covered with lava in the eruption of 1169. It was rebuilt (1297) by Roger of Lauria, the rebel admiral of Frederick II of Aragon. Frederick succeeded in capturing it by building a wooden siege-tower of equal height alongside. A long flight of steps built in the lava leads up to the entrance to the small museum, with mineralogical, palaeontological and archaeological material, including underwater finds. According to Giovanni Verga, the castle is haunted by the ghost of an unfortunate lady, Donna Violante. From the terrace there is a fine view of the Faraglioni del Ciclope in front of Acitrezza. Further south, on a cove, is Ognina, now a suburb of Catania. The bay, originally much bigger, was half-filled with lava in the 14th century.

THE LEMON RIVIERA

To the north of Acireale the beautiful, fertile coastline is known as the Riviera dei Limoni: lemon groves are planted along the coast all the way to Taormina. The main road runs through **Giarre** (*map p. 541, C2*), where ceramics and Sicilian folk art are sold. The town has unexpectedly grand eclectic buildings and the huge church of Sant'Isidoro Agricola (1794), the patron saint, with an impressive dome and two bell-towers. The ancient *Callipolis*, Giarre was a suburb of Mascali until 1815; the name derives from *giare*, the terracotta storage jars where the tenth part of the entire agricultural production of Mascali was stored, before being sent to the bishop of Catania, by ancient right also the baron of Mascali. This meant enormous quantities of wine, olive oil and wheat.

Separated from Giarre by the railway line, on the sea, with an elegant yachting harbour and another imposing church, is **Riposto**, eternal rival of Giarre. The harbour was once used for shipping the baron of Mascali's wine to Catania; the local craftsmen are still able boat-builders. **Mascali** itself was completely rebuilt after being covered by the lava stream during the November 1928 eruption of Etna.

Fiumefreddo (*map p. 541, C1*) takes its name (cold river) from the short river (only 1800m long) close by, with abundant, but icy-cold, waters, which enters the sea at Marina di Cottone, a lovely beach awarded the EU Blue Banner for quality. The area is a nature reserve run by the province, protected since 1984, because of the papyrus which grows along its course. This is one of only two rivers in Europe where the plant can be found growing spontaneously; the other is the River Ciane near Syracuse.

Calatabiano

North of Fiumefreddo the dramatic ruins of the castle of Calatabiano come into view (*map p. 541, C1*), on a hilltop dominating the Alcantara valley, close to the mouth of the river. The **Castello Cruyllas** (*open winter 9–5.30, Sat–Sun 9–8, summer 9am–10pm every day; closed Mon; T: 095 640450, www.castellocruyllas.com, bookshop and restaurant on site*) has been rendered easily accessible by the installation of a lift on the mountainside, which makes it easily recognisable. Because of its Arabic name (Calatabiano translates as 'Castle of Bian'), it was previously thought that the castle dates back to the Arab domination, but recent archaeological surveys have revealed that the fortification was first built by the Greeks in the 4th century BC, and rebuilt or repaired as necessary through the centuries, providing—together with the castles of Taormina and Castelmola—a perfect defensive system to protect the vulnerable Alcantara valley, a highway towards the interior of the island. A settlement grew up at the foot of the castle, but it was destroyed during the 1693 earthquake, and the survivors moved to the present position lower down the hillside. The 360° panorama from the battlements is superb, encompassing Etna and the coast as far as Syracuse, Taormina and the Peloritan Mountains, the Straits of Messina and the coast of Calabria.

Just below the castle on the south side, you can see the winding path leading up from the village (c. 30mins' walk), and the two pretty churches of the **Carmelo** (the lower one) and **San Filippo** or the Crocifisso (1484; *closed except for the feast*), with its resident colony of jackdaws in the belfry. Inside is the statue of the patron St Philip, weighing over two tons, which is raced down the mountainside and through the town and back again for his feast in May (*see p. 424*).

Parco Fluviale dell'Alcantara

From Giardini Naxos, a road signposted Francavilla leads inland along the Catania-Messina provincial boundary, the Alcantara valley (*el-qantara*, meaning barrage-bridge in Arabic), which is verdant with lemon groves. The river, 50km long, springs from Mt Soro in the Nebrodi Mountains. Just before reaching the turning for Motta Camastra (c. 15km from Giardini Naxos), a sign on the left indicates **Gole dell'Alcantara** (Alcantara Gorge; *Via Nazionale 5, Motta Camastra, T: 0942 985010*). Beside the car park is a lift which descends into the unexpectedly deep gorge of basalt prisms. It was originally formed when a lava flow from nearby Mt Moio (a side crater) was eroded by the cold waters of the river, forming a narrow passage through the still hot basalt (waders can be hired; there is a restaurant and coffee bar by the lift, and a shop selling organic produce from the nearby farm. The whole river valley is now protected as a regional park (Parco Fluviale dell'Alcantara; *www.parcoalcantara.it*). Along the river the vegetation is luxuriant, including willow, beech, oleander, birch, elm and prickly pear. Mammals include the pine marten, porcupine, and wildcat; among the birds to be spotted are the golden eagle, red kite, dipper, blue rock thrush, kingfisher, bittern, and glossy ibis.

CALTAGIRONE

The old town of Caltagirone (*map p. 541, A3*), with dark, weathered buildings, is built on three hills, to which it owes its irregular plan and narrow streets, and its medieval name *Regina dei Monti*, or Queen of the Mountains. Traces of one or more Bronze- and Iron-Age settlements have been found in the area. During the Greek colonisation, the town came under the influence of Gela. The present name is of Arabic origin (*kal'at*, castle and *gerun*, caves). The town was conquered by Genoa in 1030 and destroyed by the 1693 earthquake. The old centre of Caltagirone, with its Baroque architecture, is a World Heritage Site. It has always been renowned for ceramic ware thanks to a rich vein of high-quality clay in the area. The Arabs opened many potteries here, introducing new techniques, colours and designs, and today there are numerous artisans' workshops, and a prestigious School of Ceramics. The use of majolica tiles and terracotta finials is a characteristic of the local architecture.

Detail of the Scala Santa Maria del Monte in Caltagirone, with its majolica risers.

Piazza Umberto and Piazza del Municipio

In the central Piazza Umberto a bank occupies the Neoclassical Monte delle Prestanze, erected by Natale Bonaiuto in 1783. The **duomo**, dedicated to St Julian, was completely transformed in 1920. In the south aisle are altarpieces by the Vaccaro, a 19th-century family of local painters, and in the south transept an unusual carved Crucifix attributed to Giovannello Matinati (1500). Beyond is the **Corte Capitaniale**, a delightful one-storey building decorated in the 16th–17th centuries by Antonuzzo and Gian Domenico Gagini. In **Piazza del Municipio** is the Neoclassical façade of the former opera house, which serves as an entrance to the Galleria Luigi Sturzo, a monumental building inaugurated in 1959. The Town Hall has a fine façade of 1895.

From Piazza del Municipio, Via Principe Amedeo returns to Piazza Umberto past (left) the **Chiesa del Collegio**, with a lovely façade decorated with statues, visible below the road. Built at the end of the 16th century, it contains a painting of the *Annunciation* by Antonio Catalano, and a *Pietà* by Filippo Paladini.

Adjacent to Piazza del Municipio rises the impressive long flight of 142 steps known as the **Scala Santa Maria del Monte**. It has colourful majolica risers, predominantly yellow, green and blue, on a white ground. They were designed and completed in 1606, and altered in the 19th century. It is a climb (past numerous little ceramic workshops) up to **Santa Maria del Monte**, once the Chiesa Madre. The Baroque façade is by Francesco Battaglia and Natale Bonaiuto. The campanile, by Venanzio Marvuglia, is one of the very few bell-towers which can be climbed in Sicily. A little spiral staircase, which gets narrower and lower as it reaches the top, leads to the bell-chamber, from which there is a fine view. In the church is displayed a statue of the Madonna attributed to the workshop of Domenico Gagini. Further up the hill is the attractive former church of San Nicola, in a maze of medieval streets.

Via Luigi Sturzo

From near the foot of the steps, Via Luigi Sturzo leads past the church of Santa Maria degli Angeli with a 19th-century façade, behind which the façade of Santa Chiara can be seen, by Rosario Gagliardi (1743–48), which contains majolica decorations. Further uphill is Palazzo della Magnolia (no. 76), an elaborate Art Nouveau house.

Just beyond, the 19th-century façade of San Domenico faces that of **San Salvatore**, by Natale Bonaiuto (1794). It has a pretty white and gold octagonal interior with a Gaginesque *Madonna*. A modern chapel contains the tomb of Luigi Sturzo. The politician and priest Luigi Sturzo (1871–1959) is a much-honoured native of the town. He advocated local autonomy and improved social conditions here while he was mayor. A founder of the national Partito Popolare in 1919, he remained secretary of the party until 1923. This was the first Catholic political party, a forerunner of the Christian Democrat Party which came into being in 1942, and was to remain at the centre of Italian political life for much of the 20th century.

Via Sturzo continues uphill past the former Ospedale delle Donne, an attractive building, now the **Galleria di Arte Moderna e Contemporanea** (*entrance from Viale Regina Elena 10; open 9.30–1.30, Sun 9.30–12.30; Tues, Fri, Sat and Sun also 4–7; closed*

Wed; T: 0933 21083), an interesting collection of contemporary art, mostly by local artists. The road ends at **San Giorgio**, rebuilt in 1699, which contains a beautiful altarpiece of the *Mystery of the Trinity*, attributed to Rogier van der Weyden. From the terrace (left) there is a fine view of the countryside.

San Giacomo

From Piazza del Municipio, the handsome Corso Vittorio Emanuele passes several fine palaces, and the Art Nouveau post office (still in use) on the way to the basilica of San Giacomo, rebuilt in 1708; at the side a pretty flight of steps ascends through the base of the campanile. In the interior, above the west door, the marble coat of arms of the city is by Gian Domenico Gagini. In the left aisle is a blue and brown portal (formerly belonging to the baptistery), and a blue and gold arch in the Cappella del Sacramento by Antonuzzo Gagini. In the left transept is the charming little Portale delle Reliquie, also by Antonuzzo, with bronze doors by Agostino Sarzana. In the chapel to the left of the sanctuary (behind glass doors) is a silver urn (*illuminated on request*), the masterpiece of Nibilio Gagini (signed 1604). In the sanctuary is a processional statue of St James by Vincenzo Archifel (1518), protected by a bronze canopy of 1964 (the saint's original gilded throne is kept in the Museo Civico). This and the urn are carried through the streets of the town in a procession on 25th July.

The Museo Civico and Via Roma

To the south of Piazza Umberto, at Via Roma 10, is the **Museo Civico** (*open 9.30–1, Tue, Fri, Sat and Sun also 4–7; closed Mon; T: 0933 31590*), housed in a massive former prison (Carcere Borbonico), built in 1782 by Natale Bonaiuto with an interior courtyard and double columns. On the stairs are architectural fragments and on the landing, four 19th-century terracotta vases by Bongiovanni Vaccaro. Beyond a room with modern local ceramics, another room contains the gilded Throne of St James (16th century, by Scipione di Guido; the statue is kept in the church of San Giacomo), a bishop's 19th-century sedan chair, and a Christmas crib. There is a room dedicated to the works (paintings and ceramics) by the local artists Giuseppe, Francesco and Mario Vaccaro. There are also some 16th–17th-century paintings (including *Christ in the Garden* by Epifano Rossi), and two terracotta cherubs by Bongiovanni Vaccaro. On the top floor are modern works. Beside the museum is the fine façade, also by Bonaiuto, of Sant'Agata (*closed*).

Via Roma continues south from Piazza Umberto to **Ponte San Francesco**, an 18th-century viaduct, which has pretty majolica decoration and a good view of Palazzo Sant'Elia below the bridge. The road continues past the piazza in front of the simple church of **San Francesco d'Assisi**, founded in 1226 but rebuilt after 1693. It contains paintings by Francesco and Giuseppe Vaccaro and a Gothic sacristy. Behind the church (reached by Via Sant'Antonio and Via Mure Antiche) is San Pietro, with a 19th-century neo-Gothic majolica façade.

The street continues past the Tondo Vecchio, an exedra built by Francesco Battaglia in 1766. Beside the church of San Francesco di Paola, a road leads up past the **Teatro Politeama Ingrassia**, with interesting Art Nouveau details, to the entrance gate of the delightful **public gardens**, laid out in 1846 by Giovanni Battista Basile. The exotic trees include palms, cedars, ficus and huge pines. There is a long balustrade on Via Roma decorated with pretty ceramics from the workshop of Enrico Vella, and throughout the gardens are copies of terracotta vases and figures by Giuseppe Vaccaro and Giacomo Bongiovanni. There is also a 17th-century fountain by Camillo Camilliani and a decorative bandstand. The palace of Benedetto Ventimiglia, also on Via Roma, is preceded by a colourful ceramic terrace.

Museo della Ceramica

The Museo della Ceramica (*open 9–6.30; T: 0933 58418, 0933 58423*) is situated in the gardens, entered through the elaborate Teatrino (1792) by Natale Bonaiuto. From the top of the steps there is a good view beyond a war memorial and some palm trees to the hills (with the town on the left). The museum contains a fine collection of Sicilian ceramics from the prehistoric era to the 19th century. In the corridor to the right are 17th- and 19th-century ceramics from Caltagirone. Beyond a room with 18th- and 19th-century works, the archaeological material is displayed, including Hellenistic and Roman terracotta heads and figurines. Prehistoric pottery from San Mauro and Castelluccio is also exhibited. In Case 26 is a krater depicting a potter at his wheel protected by Athena (5th century BC). Case 27 contains the Russo Perez Collection, including 5th-century BC red- and black-figure vases. In the courtyard, bases used in various potteries from the 11th–13th centuries are exhibited. In the large room on the left are Arab-Norman stuccoes from San Giuliano, 10th–12th-century Arab–Norman pottery, and medieval works.

On a lower level is a large hall with 17th–19th-century ceramics from Palermo, Trapani, Caltagirone and Sciacca, including blue enamelled vases and pharmacy jars. The fine collection of terracotta figures includes works by Giuseppe Bongiovanni (1809–89) and Giacomo Vaccaro (1847–1931). The hall is also used for exhibitions.

Via Santa Maria di Gesù leads south from the public gardens to (10mins) the church of **Santa Maria di Gesù** (1422), with a charming *Madonna* by Antonello Gagini, while on the opposite side of the city, at Viale Principessa Maria José 7/9, is the photography museum, **Museo della Fotografia Storica e Contemporanea** (*open 9–1, Tues and Thur also 3–5.30; closed Sun and Mon; T: 0933 54567*), with a collection of cameras and photographic equipment and a selection of interesting photographs, all beautifully displayed.

ENVIRONS OF CALTAGIRONE

North of Caltagirone is the clean and tidy **Mirabella Imbaccari** (*map p. 541, A3*), famous for its lace and embroidery. You can see the work at the Mostra del Ricamo e del Tombolo (*open 9–1 & 3.30–7.30; closed Mon*), in the central Via Alcide De Gasperi.

Grammichele, 15km east of Caltagirone, was founded by Carlo Maria Carafa Branciforte, prince of Butera, to house the people of Occhiolà, destroyed in 1693. The ruins of the old town, c. 2km away to the northwest, are now a very interesting archaeological park (*open 9–5, until dusk in summer*). The new town was built to a concentric hexagonal plan, around the spacious central six-sided Piazza Carafa, with an array of honey-coloured palaces between the six roads. Here the weather-worn, unfinished Chiesa Madre, begun in 1723 by Andrea Amato and dedicated to St Michael Archangel, who protects against earthquakes, stands next to the elegant red and gold Palazzo Comunale (Carlo Sada, 1896). The Museo Civico (*open 9–1 & 4–6*) has a well-arranged, small collection of finds from excavations in the district, begun in 1891 by Paolo Orsi, who identified a pre-Greek settlement at Terravecchia. Exhibits include prehistoric bronzes and Bronze-Age ceramics, vases found in tombs (6th century BC), terracotta votive statuettes and 15th–16th-century majolica from Occhiolà. In front of the Town Hall is the Art Deco Teatro Intelisano (1940s), the balconies supported by ledges reproducing the faces of great personalities of the past, including Rossini and Leonardo da Vinci.

THE SOUTH OF THE PROVINCE

Vizzini

Vizzini (*map p. 541, B4*) nestles among the Hyblaean Mountains. On the summit of two hills, it occupies the site of ancient *Bidis*, recorded by Cicero. In the central Piazza Umberto is a stairway decorated with majolica tiles like the one in Caltagirone, leading up to the church of Sant'Agata (14th and 18th centuries). In the square is **Palazzo Verga** (*open 8.30–1, closed Sun*), an unfinished 18th-century palace which used to be owned by Giovanni Verga's family: the great writer was born in Vizzini and most of his works are set here or in the vicinity, such as *Cavalleria Rusticana*, *La Lupa* (*The She-wolf*), and *Mastro-don Gesualdo* (*see p. 385*). Close by, in the 18th-century Palazzo Costa, at Via Vespucci 5, is the **Museo Immaginario Verghiano** (*open 9–1 & 3.30–7.30, closed Mon*), dedicated to the writer, with a collection of his photographs (he was a keen amateur photographer), interesting pictures of the Sicilian locations used for the films based on his books, and various memorabilia.

From Piazza Umberto, Via San Gregorio Magno winds its way up to the **Chiesa Madre**, dedicated to St Gregory the Great, who is the patron saint of Vizzini. His statue stands on a column by the side entrance into the church, which still shows some surviving pre-earthquake fragments, such as the splendid 15th-century Catalan Gothic portal on the right side. The interior is decorated with Baroque stuccoes; in the south aisle are two paintings by Filippo Paladini: the *Martyrdom of St Lawrence* (second altar), and the *Madonna of Mercy* (fourth altar).

Vizzini is a prosperous farming community, renowned for its excellent sheep's milk cheese, ricotta, olive oil, prickly pears and durum wheat, and in the past leather was tanned along the little River Dirillo, just outside the town. Now the workshops and the vats, many carved out of the rock, and the homes of the workers, all long since abandoned, are being repaired and transformed into a cultural centre called 'a Cunziria (the Tannery); accommodation is available (*see p. 420*). The mountains around Vizzini are ancient spent volcanoes, now rich pastures or wheat fields, where flocks of ravens still fly.

Licodia Eubea

Situated on a crest overlooking the River Dirillo to the south, Licodia Eubea (*map p. 541, B4*) was probably founded in the 7th century BC as a sub-colony of *Leontinoi* (Lentini). In the Middle Ages it had a formidable castle, of which few traces remain to-day—it was destroyed by the 1693 earthquake. In the 15th century the town and castle became the property of the Catalan Santapau family. In recent years there has been considerable archaeological research in the area; the finds are displayed in the Museo Civico Antonino Di Vita (*open 9–1; if closed ask at Town Hall*) in Corso Umberto, where besides the objects of Greek origin, there are interesting traces of the Sicel settlement which preceded their arrival.

Militello in Val di Catania

Thanks to the munificence of its prince, Don Francesco Branciforte, Militello in Val di Catania (*map p. 541, B3*) is a splendid little town with remarkable Baroque buildings, designated a UNESCO World Heritage Site. Don Francesco and his wife Donna Johanna of Austria, in the early 17th century, wanted their town to be the cultural centre of this part of Sicily, and poured money into public works, sponsoring religious communities and inviting artists, architects and writers of fame to their court. The 22 lovely churches here contain paintings by Vito d'Anna, Olivio Sozzi, Pietro Ruzzolone and others.

The main square, Piazza Municipio, houses the great abbey and church of **San Benedetto**, now the Town Hall, modelled on the Benedictine Monastery of St Nicholas in Catania. Inside the church, the 18th-century carved walnut choir-stalls are of particular interest.

In Via Umberto, in the crypt of the Chiesa Madre di San Nicola, is the **Museo di San Nicola** (*open 9–1 & 5–8, Tues closed; also guided tours of the town on request*) with 17th- and 18th-century works, including vestments, Church silver, sculpture and paintings. In the treasury of the church of **Santa Maria della Stella** (*T: 095 655329 for opening times*) there is an altarpiece in enamelled terracotta by Andrea Della Robbia (1487) with the *Nativity*, *Annunciation to the Shepherds*, and (in the predella) a *Pietà* and the *Twelve Apostles*. Another altarpiece, the *Retablo di San Pietro*, is thought to be the work of a follower of Antonello da Messina. For centuries these two churches, both said to have been founded before the 9th-century Arab invasion, one of Greek rite (San Nicola) and the other of Latin tradition (Santa Maria), were rivals for the title of Chiesa Madre and for the role of patron saint; the question was resolved only in 1966, when the pope was forced to intervene. Now St Mary is the patron saint, and the San Nicola is the Chiesa Madre.

Another interesting museum has been opened in the ex-prison of Militello, near the Branciforte Castle at Via Porta della Terra 21, the **Museo Civico Sebastiano Guzzone** (*open 9–1 & 3–7*), housing a collection of paintings, archaeological finds, medieval books, and the city archives. The half-ruined **Santa Maria la Vetere**, to the south of the historic centre, has a porch supported by lions and a magnificent doorway of 1506.

Not far from Militello is **Scordia** (*map p. 541, B3*), famous for its blood oranges. In the apse of the church of Sant'Antonio di Padova is an exceptional 18th-century floor of coloured tiles from Caltagirone, now rather fragmentary, showing a pelican shedding its own blood to feed its young, a symbol of Christ's sacrifice to redeem mankind.

Mineo

A small town on an ancient settlement founded by Ducetius, king of the Sicels, in the 5th century BC, Mineo (*map p. 541, B3*) was later occupied by the Greeks and Romans. High-quality olive oil, wheat and oranges are produced here, and edible snails are raised. The church of Sant'Agrippina, patron saint of the town, and that of the Collegio both have fine 18th-century stuccoes. Behind the church of San Pietro (which houses an organ by Donato Del Piano), at Piazza Buglio 40, is the house where the writer Luigi Capuana (1835–1915) lived, now a museum: the **Biblioteca Museo Luigi Capuana** (*open Tues–Thur 9–1, Sat and Sun 10–1 & 6-8; closed Mon and Fri; T: 0933 983056*). A close friend of Giovanni Verga, Capuana wrote various works both in Italian and Sicilian, including tales for children. The museum holds his books, manuscripts and photographs, and the library of the Capuchin monastery, with 16th- and 17th-century volumes. On the outskirts of the town, at Viale della Rimembranza 8, is the **Museo Civico Corrado Tamburino Merlini** (*open winter Tues–Sun 9–1, Sat and Sun 10–1 & 4–6; summer Tues–Sun 9–1 & 5.30–8.30, Sat and Sun 10–1 & 5.30–8.30; closed Mon; T: 0933 989059*) with a wide variety of finds (from Paleolithic flint tools to Greek and Latin inscriptions) from archaeological sites in the area. The medieval **castle** on the summit of one of the two hills of Mineo is now a romantically crumbling ruin. Near the town are two caves called **Grotte di Caratabia**, where some Sicel graffiti of the 5th century BC has been found, representing a hunting scene with horses, hunters and their servants, and deer. The caves, probably tombs of important personages, will eventually be opened to the public.

Palagonia

Palagonia (*map p. 541, B3*) stands on the edge of the fertile Plain of Catania, known to the Greeks as the Laestrygonian Fields, the home of the cannibal Laestrygones. Its vast groves are watered by the Simeto and its tributaries, the Dittaino and the Gornalunga. Today the district is well known for its oranges and tangerines. Outside the town is the 7th-century Byzantine church of Santa Febronia, with abundant traces of frescoes inside. The little basilica of San Giovanni, surrounded by orange groves, is now believed to be a Cistercian structure. The old Sicel town *Palike* is close to Palagonia, at a sacred lake with two small geysers emitting gases (no longer visible since being exploited for industrial purposes), said to be the Palikes, twin gods who guaranteed justice; the spot became a sanctuary for runaway slaves. The archaeological site, excavated since the mid-1990s, has recently been opened to the public (*opening hours were not fixed at the time of writing*). The earliest traces of human activity date back to the Palaeo-Mesolithic period, but it is only in the 6th century BC that the site indisputably became the principal religious sanctuary of the area. The most impressive structure is the hestiaterion, a ritual dining facility that dates to the 5th century BC and was perhaps built by Ducetius. The four larger rooms would have held seven couches for reclined dining, and the three smaller rooms were probably used as service areas.

RAMACCA & RADDUSA

Ramacca (*map p. 541, B3*) is an elegant little country town founded by Prince Ottavio Gravina in the early 18th century, often called 'City of Jesus' because its street layout resembles a Crucifix. It is famous for its delectable violet artichokes. The Museo Civico Archeologico (*open Mon–Sat 9–1 & 4–7, closed Sun; T. 095 7930110*) at Via Marconi 2 displays archaeological material from settlements in the vicinity, including some noteworthy grave goods (in particular a pair of attic black-figure skyphoi) from 6th–5th-century BC necropoleis. The museum staff are willing to give guided tours of the local archaeological sites if asked a day or two in advance.

Raddusa (*map p. 541, A2–A3*) has an interesting Tea Museum at Via Garibaldi 45 (*T: 095 662193, 339 2053677 (Salvo Pellegrino) to request visit, www.lacasadelte.it*), well worth a detour, where you can visit the tea plantation and sample some of the 600 different kinds of tea that form Dr Pellegrino's collection, including varieties belonging to Berber, Bedouin, Chinese, Japanese, Ethiopian, Iranian, English, French, Singalese and Burmese traditions, prepared with appropriate ceremony. He has discovered that tea was first cultivated in Sicily by the Arabs, from c. 950, for an emir who was fond of the beverage. There is also a surprisingly interesting museum dedicated to wheat, Raddusa's most famous product, at Via Tenente Sollima 41 (Museo del Grano; *open 9–1, closed Sun and Mon; T: 095 667003*).

PRACTICAL INFORMATION

GETTING AROUND

• **By air:** Catania airport at Fontanarossa (*www.aeroporto.catania.it*) has flights connecting the major Italian cities and many European destinations. All major car-hire companies have booths at the airport. Taxis are available, reaching Catania centre in c. 30mins. ALIBUS no. 457 runs every 20mins from 5am–midnight, connecting the airport to various points in Catania, including the railway station and the port. Other bus companies offer services to a selection of destinations around the island.

• **By train: Catania** station is at Piazza Papa Giovanni XXIII (*map 8*), for all services on the line to Palermo via Enna and on the coastal line between Syracuse and Messina (*www.trenitalia.com*). All trains stop at Acireale and Taormina, which are on the main line.

Caltagirone (station in Piazza della Repubblica) is on the Catania–Caltanissetta line, it has services to Catania in c. 2hrs. Several towns around Caltagirone are served by the railway, but sometimes (Vizzini, Mineo, Licodia, Militello) the stations are a long way from the towns.

The **Circumetnea**, opened in 1898, provides a classic rail trip, but you need to take two trains to circumnavigate Etna. Circumetnea Borgo station (*www.circumetnea.it*) is at the top of Via Caronda (*beyond map 2*), for the line which runs around the foot of Etna. Trains go to Randazzo (in c. 2hrs), continuing less frequently to Riposto (in c. 1hr); from there the direct return (poor connections) may be made by the mainline train on the Messina–Syracuse line.

• **By bus:** In Catania an efficient network of yellow city buses is run by **AMT** (*www.amt. ct.it*). **KATANE LIVE** (*www.katanelive.it*) runs sightseeing tours using yellow open-top buses with a multi-lingual audio-guide departing hourly 9–7 from the duomo.

Inter-city services:

AST (*www.aziendasicilianatrasporti.it*) runs services from Piazza Giovanni XXIII outside the station (*map 8*) to many places in and outside Catania province, including Acireale, Avola, Caltagirone, Ispica, Lentini, Modica, Nicolosi, Noto, Palazzolo Acreide, Piazza Armerina, Syracuse, Scicli, Vizzini and Zafferana Etnea. AST also runs a daily bus (in c. 2hrs) to the Rifugio Sapienza on Mt Etna, departing early morning. An extra service runs in July and Aug, leaving Piazza Giovanni XXIII in the later morning for Nicolosi, where a connecting bus continues to the Rifugio Sapienza. A bus returns to Catania in the afternoon.

Buda (*www.autolineebuda.it*) runs infrequent services from Piazza Giovanni XXIII to Giarre, Fiumefreddo and Calatabiano.

Etna Trasporti–Interbus (*www.etnatrasporti. it, www.interbus.it*) from Via Archimede (*map 8*) to a wide variety of destinations, including Acireale, Aidone, Avola, Gela, Giardini Naxos, Licata, Noto, Piazza Armerina, Ragusa, Santa Croce Camerina, Syracuse, and Taormina.

FCE (*www.circumetnea.it*) leaves from the entrance to the port of Catania, for Adrano, Biancavilla, Bronte, Castiglione di Sicilia, Fiumefreddo, Giarre, Linguaglossa, Maletto, Mascali, Randazzo, Riposto and Santa Maria di Licodia.

Giamporcaro (*www.saistrasporti.it*) links Catania Piazza Giovanni XXIII to Vittoria and Comiso.

Giuntabus (*www.giuntabus.it*) connects Catania airport to Milazzo port (for the Aeolian Islands) from April–Sept.

ISEA (*www.iseaviaggi.it*) leaves from Catania (Piazza Repubblica; *map 7*) to Capizzi, Cerami, Cesarò, Nicosia, San Fratello, San Teodoro, Sant'Agata Militello and Troina.

Molica (*www.orariautobus.it*) connects Catania airport to Porto Rosa, Gioiosa Marea and Capo d'Orlando from 15 June–15 Sept.

Romano (*www.romanobus.it*) leaves from Catania (Via VI Aprile near the railway station) to Centuripe, Catenanuova and Enna.

SAIS Autolinee (*www.saisautolinee.it*) from Piazza Giovanni XXIII run coaches about every hour via the motorway to Palermo (2hrs 40mins) and Messina (1hr 30mins); less frequently via the motorway to Enna (1hr 30mins), Caltanissetta and Gela. Most also stop at the airport.

SAIS Trasporti (*www.saistrasporti.it*) has services to Agrigento, Caltanissetta and Canicattì.

SARP Trasporti (*www.saistrasporti.it*) connects Catania to Sommatino, Riesi, Barrafranca and Pietraperzia.

• **By sea**: Boats from Catania serve the Italian mainland and Greece. For the Sicilian islands, boats leave from Trapani, Palermo, Cefalù, Porto Empedocle and Milazzo (see the relevant chapters).

WHERE TO STAY

Acireale (*map p. 541, C2*)

€€€ **Santa Caterina**. Breathtaking position on the cliffside for this charming hotel, 23 comfortable rooms, good restaurant, car park, pool and garden. *Via Santa Caterina 42/b, T: 095 7633735, www.santacaterinahotel.com.*

€€ **Palazzo Pennisi di Floristella**. Smart B&B in a princely palace offering two large rooms with private bath and a delightful little penthouse apartment. Roof garden where breakfast is served in summer, using products from the family farm. *Piazza Lionardo Vigo 16, T: 095 7633079, www.en.palazzopennisidifloristella.it.*

€ **Palazzo Leonardi**. B&B in a 19th-century house with garden, car park, 5 clean rooms, hospitable owners. *Corso Savoia 241, T: 095 891501, www.palazzoleonardi.it.*

Calatabiano (*map p. 541, C1*)

€€€ **Castello San Marco**. Close to the sea under the mountain of Calatabiano, a romantic castle built by an eccentric millionaire and now a comfortable hotel, 30 rooms all leading into the beautiful gardens. Pool and restaurant. *Via San Marco 40, T: 095 641181, www.castellosanmarco.it.*

Caltagirone (*map p. 541, A3*)

€€€ **Villa Tasca**. Stylish accommodation in this splendid old aristocratic villa 3km north of town. 10 rooms. Pool, gardens, sauna, cycling track, horse-riding. *Contrada Fontana Pietra, SP 37 km 11, T: 0933 22760, 334 1210205, www.villatasca.it.*

€€ **Vecchia Masseria**. Old country house in the heart of the woods west of town, in a convenient position for touring Caltagirone, Piazza Armerina, Niscemi, Butera and Gela, with 20 luxurious rooms and suites. Forms part of the Charme & Relax chain. Helicopter tours, boat trips and horse-riding are organised. Good food (you can purchase their products, including wine). *Contrada Cutuminello, SS 117bis, T: 333 8735573, 333 1826582, www.vecchiamasseria.com.*

€€ **La Pilozza Infiorata**. The beautiful Art Nouveau family home of the Vaccaro sculptors, in the centre of town, is now a welcoming B&B, with 5 rooms and lots of books, *Via Santissimo Salvatore 97, T: 0933 22162, 328 7029543, www.lapilozzainfiorata.com.*

€ **Tre Metri Sopra il Cielo**. Comfortable B&B in a marvellous position on the town's central stairway (Scalinata SS. Maria del Monte); 2 double rooms with bathroom, good breakfasts. *Via Bongiovanni 72, T: 0933 1935106, 339 2133228, www.bbtremetrisoprailcielo.it.*

Castiglione di Sicilia (*map p. 541, C1*)

€€ **Federico II**. In a 14th-century building right in the town centre, a charming hotel run by the owners with 9 rooms, garden, good restaurant serving Sicilian dishes accompanied by wines from Etna. *Via Baracca 2, T: 0942 980368, www.hotelfedericosecondo.com.*

Catania (*map p. 541, C2*)

€€€ **Una Hotel Palace**. Prestigious 19th-century hotel with 94 luxurious rooms, fitness centre with sauna and Turkish bath, roof garden, good restaurant, garage, courteous staff. *Via Etnea 218, T: 095 2505111, www.unahotels.it. Map p. 378, 6.*

€€€ **Liberty Hotel**. Beautifully restored in Art Nouveau style, the bathrooms are beautiful; some of the 18 rooms and suites have frescoed ceilings. No restaurant. Car park. *Via San Vito 40, T: 095 311651, www.libertyhotel.it. Map p. 378, 6.*

€€€ **Katane Palace**. Elegant 19th-century building, central, with 135 rooms, a good restaurant and garage parking. Cookery courses organised. *Via Finocchiaro Aprile 110, T: 095 7470702, www.katanepalace.it. Map p. 379, 4.*

€€€ **Il Principe**. This hotel, in the Baroque heart of Catania, has 12 very comfortable rooms and suites, some with jacuzzi, and a fitness centre with Turkish bath. It can be a bit noisy; the stairs of Via Alessi are a popular meeting-place for young people on weekend evenings. *Via Alessi 20/26, T: 095 2500345, www.ilprincipehotel.com. Map p. 379, 11.*

€€ **Novecento**. Art Nouveau elegance, just behind the Opera House. 18 comfortable rooms, no restaurant. *Via Ventimiglia 37, T: 095 310488, www.hotelnovecentocatania.it. Map p. 379, 12.*

€ **Bed and Breakfast Stesicoro**. In an aristocratic palace overlooking the Roman amphitheatre, entered from the little alley where snow for the city was once stored. All rooms with private bath, evening meals and airport shuttle on request. Good value for money. *Via Neve 7, T: 095 311178, 393 9193342, www. bbstesicoro.it. Map p. 378, 6.*

Giarre (*map p. 541, C2*)

€€ **Etna**. Historic villa with garden, pool, and panoramic views of Etna, 18 well-equipped and comfortable rooms, no restaurant. Car park. Shuttle service to/from Catania Airport on request. *Via Continella 10, T: 095 934070, www.etnahotel.it.*

Mascalucia (*map p. 541, C2*)

€€ **Borgopetra**. Conveniently situated in a small town at the foot of the volcano, a comfortable, historic and very beautiful B&B offering rooms and self-catering accommodation for long or short stays, helpful and informative owners. *Via Teatro 9, T: 095 7277184, 333 8284930, www.borgopetra.it.*

Paternò (*map p. 541, B2*)

€ **Il Casale dell'Etna**. Surrounded by groves producing oranges, lemons, tangerines and pistachios, old farmhouse offering comfortable rooms, good food and spectacular views of the volcano. *SP 56 Paternò-Belpasso, T: 095 7977996, 347 9123695, www.ilcasaledelletna.it.*

Ramacca (*map p. 541, B3*)

€€€ **Contea di Wagner**. Named after its most famous guest (Wagner's eldest daughter married Count Gravina, owner of the farm, and while staying here it is said that he found inspiration for his *Parsifal*), this old-fashioned country house offers comfortable accommodation in 35 rooms, delicious food. Well-placed for Catania airport. *SS 288 km 12, Contrada Mendolo, T: 095 653134, 329 9134283, www.conteadiwagner.com.*

€ **Paradiso della Zagara**. Good-value, basic albergo, family-run, 10 simple but comfortable rooms, good restaurant (closed Fri) spe-

cialising in local dishes, including artichokes when in season. *Piazza Sottotenente Di Fazio 8, T: 095 653279, www.paradisodellazagara.it.*

Randazzo (*map p. 541, B1*)

€€ **Scrivano**. Comfortable modern hotel in town centre, no frills, family-run, 30 rooms, good restaurant. *Via Bonaventura 2, T: 095 921126, www.hotelscrivano.com. http://www. hotelscrivano.it*

€€ **Nebrodi Monte Colla**. An out-of-the-way country house where horses are raised, very peaceful, within the boundaries of the Nebrodi Mountains Park at 1426 m, reached by a rough track (transfer to/from Randazzo on request), good food. *Frazione Monte Colla, T: 338 2376569, www.hotelnebrodi.it.*

€ **Parco Statella**. Gorgeous 18th-century villa surrounded by a park just east of Randazzo. The 10 comfortable rooms furnished with delightful antiques were once the farm buildings. Very kind owners. *Via Montelaguardia 2/S, Località Montelaguardia, T: 095 924036, 347 4097281, www.parcostatella.com.*

Riposto (*map p. 541, C2*)

€€€ **Donna Carmela**. Old winery producing award-winning Etna Rosso and also ornamental plants, beautifully restored farmhouse with 18 comfortable rooms, all different and subtly colourful, pool surrounded by centuries-old olive trees, restaurant. *Contrada Grotte 5, Carruba di Riposto (between Riposto and Acireale), T: 095 809383, www.donnacarmela.com.*

San Giovanni La Punta (*map p. 541, C2*)

€€ **Paradiso dell'Etna**. Pretty 1920s-style hotel, with 34 elegant rooms and suites, garden, and excellent restaurant. *Via Viagrande 37, T: 095 7512409, www.paradisoetna.it.*

San Michele di Ganzaria (*map p. 541, A3*)

€€ **Baglio Gigliotto**. A very beautiful large farm, with olive groves and vineyards, cereals and prickly pears, conveniently situated for Morgantina and Piazza Armerina. The farm buildings comprise the original 14th-century farmhouse and an ancient monastery. 14 comfortable rooms furnished with antiques, restaurant serves good home-made food using local organic products. *SS 117bis km 60, Contrada Gigliotto, T: 0933 97089, 0933 979092, www.gigliotto.com.*

€ **Pomara**. ◼ An efficient, family-run hotel in an excellent position for touring central Sicily, with car park and pool, 40 welcoming rooms. The restaurant serves marvellous local dishes, Sicilians come here from miles around, just for the food. *Via Vittorio Veneto 84, T: 0933 976976, www.hotelpomara.com.*

Vizzini (*map p. 541, B4*)

€ 'A **Badia**. In the highest point of Vizzini, accommodation in a wing of the Benedictine convent of Santa Maria de' Greci, built by St Gregory the Great on land belonging to his mother, St Sylvia. In the little church an ancient triptych of the *Madonna with Saints* has been found, dated 385. 17 comfortable rooms with private bathroom, restaurant serving traditional local food, pizzeria, shop selling local products and handicrafts. *Via Etrusca 17, T: 0933 966323, www.abadia.it.*

€ 'A **Cunziria**. Some of the workers' cottages of this old tannery have been transformed into clean and comfortable accommodation for a peaceful holiday. Plenty of activities are organised. *Contrada Masera, T: 0933 965507, www.acunziria.com.*

Acireale (*map p. 541, C2*)

€ Al Ficodindia. ◼ Excellent pizza, *antipasto* and pasta, in a beautiful setting. *Piazza San Domenico 1, T: 095 7637024.*

Acitrezza (*map p. 541, C2*)

€€ **Da Federico** (*Piazza Verga/Via Provinciale 115, T: 095 276364. Closed Mon*) and €€ **Verga da Gaetano** (*Piazza Verga/Via Provin-*

ciale 119, T: 095 276342. Closed Thur). These two restaurants are both renowned for long, leisurely fish dinners, up-market clientèle. Crowded at weekends, booking necessary.

Bronte-Maniace (*map p. 541, B1*)

€ **Don Ciccio**. A delightfully simple restaurant near Castello Maniace, serving country food and local wine (*T: 095 7722916*). Another good restaurant not far from the castle is € **Fiorentino** (*closed Sun evening and all day Mon; T: 095 691800*).

Caltagirone (*map p. 541, A3*)

€€ **Il Locandiere**. Tiny family-run *trattoria* serving only seafood (strange for an inland city!), to very high standards. Try the fish cous cous or the *ravioli di ricotta con bottarga* (tuna roe). Good wine list, obliging service. Closed Mon. *Via Sturzo 55, T: 0933 58292.*

€ **La Piazzetta**, Besides pasta, meat, or pizza, wonderful vegetarian dishes. Closed Thur. *Via Vespri 20/a, T: 0933 24178.*

Castiglione di Sicilia (*map p. 541, C1*)

€ **La Dispensa dell'Etna**. Simple local dishes, beautifully cooked, accompanied by all the best local wines (which they also sell). *Piazza Sant'Antonio 2/3, T: 0942 984258.*

Catania (*map p 541, C2*)

€€€ **Il Sale Art Café**. Dishes presented to please both the eye and the palate, made using the freshest exclusively Sicilian ingredients accompanied by local wines, very congenial and elegant locale, currently the most fashionable in the city. Evenings only. Booking essential, especially at weekends. *Via Santa Filomena 10, T: 095 316888. Map p. 378, 6.*

€€€ **Ambasciata del Mare**. Try *pasta con cime di rapa e bottarga* (tuna roe with turnip greens), or pumpkin flowers with shrimps, this restaurant offers combinations of fish and seasonal vegetables from the market just outside the door. Closed Mon. *Piazza Duomo 6, T: 095 341003. Map p. 379, 11.*

€€ **Osteria Antica Marina**. Tiny restaurant tucked away inside the fish market. Booking is essential. *Alici marinati* (raw anchovy salad) or *spaghetti coi ricci* (spaghetti with sea urchins) are both very tasty dishes. Closed Wed. *Via Pardo 29, T: 095 348197. Map p. 379, 15.*

€ **'U Fucularu**. Tiny family-run *trattoria*, serving exclusively home-made food, excellent grilled meats and vegetables, local wines. In summer, open every day evenings only. In winter open also midday Sun, but may close Mon or Wed, so call first. *Piazza Ogninella 6 (between the Collegiata and Teatro Bellini), T: 331 3735273. Map p. 379, 11.*

€ **Prestipino**. ■ In front of the duomo, close to the elephant fountain, the ideal spot for light lunch, snacks or ice cream while indulging in some people-watching. *Piazza Duomo 9, T: 095 320840. Map p. 379, 11.*

Militello (*map p. 541, B3*)

€ **'U Trappitu**. Delicious recipes typical of the interior of Sicily, served in a transformed oil press. Closed Mon. *Via Principe Branciforte 125, T: 095 811447.*

Nicolosi (*map p. 541, C2*)

€ **Antico Orto dei Limoni**. Old wine press, wonderful atmosphere, delicious food, closed Tues. *Via Grotte 4, T: 095 910808.*

€ **Café Esagonal**. ■ At the Rifugio Sapienza, right in front of the cableway station. Nunzio and Dominique serve delicious coffee, hot chocolate and salads, snacks or pasta, and all the latest information on the volcano's activity. Gift shop too. *T: 095 7807868.*

Randazzo (*map p. 541, B1*)

€ **San Giorgio e il Drago**. Close to the old walls, in the cellars of the convent of St George. The home-made pasta is particularly inviting. Good value for money. Closed Tues. *Piazza San Giorgio 28, T: 095 923972.*

Riposto (*map p. 541, C2*)

€ **Marricriu**. ■ Near the yachting harbour, a great little *trattoria* run by competent and

enthusiastic young people: superb seafood dishes, good local wines, simple Sicilian desserts. *Via Gramsci 160 (corner of Via Dogana), T: 340 9091513.*

Sant'Alfio (*map p. 541, C2*)

€ **Case Perrotta**. This old farm, close to the village, produces award-winning olive oil and is renowned for its excellent food. 12 rooms, some in the farmhouse, some in the old winepress. *Via Andronico 2, T: 095 968928, www.caseperrotta.it.*

Santa Maria La Scala (*outside Acireale*)

€€ **Al Molino**. Fish dishes in the tiny village of Santa Maria La Scala under the Timpa, prepared the moment the boats land. Closed Wed. *Via Molino 106, T: 095 7648116.*

€€ **La Grotta**. This restaurant in a cave is legendary, and gourmets try to keep the secret to themselves. Fantastic fish; raw anchovy salad, fried shrimps, seafood *antipasto*, and lots more, always superb. Closed Tues. *Via Scalo Grande 46, T: 095 7648153.*

Zafferana Etnea (*map p. 541, C2*)

€€ **Parco dei Principi**. Very elegant, member of the Buon Ricordo chain. Closed Tues. *Via delle Ginestre 1, T: 095 7082335.*

€ **La Capannina**. ■ By the Silvestri craters on top of Mt Etna, this little inn was almost swallowed up by lava in 2001. Very good *arancini* (fried rice balls), barbecued sausages, *cannoli* and pistachio cake. Honey, local wine and other souvenirs are sold. *T: 095 6143889.*

LOCAL SPECIALITIES

Acireale Try Condorelli (*Via Scionti 26*) for superb *granita*, almond pastries and home-made nougat; their unique breakfast pastry is called *senzanome alla ricotta*. Pasticceria Bella (*Corso Umberto 66*), which opened in 1914, is the place to buy home-made candied and crystallised fruit. Chiarenza (*Via Vittorio Emanuele 86/88*) is a sculptor with a fascinating souvenir shop. Ask him to show you his *magazzini*, an endless sequence of dusty storerooms packed with dismantled carts, puppets, old furniture and curiosities.

Bronte Caffetteria Luca (*Via Messina 273*) is a historic confectioner's known for pistachio ice-cream. For pistachio delicacies also Gino (*Viale Regina Margherita 46*) and Conti (*Corso Umberto 275*). To simply buy pistachios, go to Marullo (*Via Baracca 59/a*), or order some on-line (*www.marullospa.com*). For the renowned local olive oil, Oleificio Costa (*Via Palermo 122, www.oleificiocosta.com*).

Caltagirone There are some 150 ceramic workshops in town which sell their products. Many of them are around Piazza Umberto and on the Scala (*Info: www.ceramicadicaltagirone.it*). Albanian art historian Harizay Besnik (*Via Gueli 1*) makes excellent replicas of the antique pottery in the museum. Caltagirone's puppet theatre was renowned in the past: Teatro Stabile dei Pupi Siciliani (*Discesa Verdumai i, open daily 10–12.30 & 3.30–7*), displays 70 marionettes, backdrops and costumes, and will put on a show on request.

Castiglione di Sicilia Tenuta di Fessina (*Via Nazionale 22 SS 120, Contrada Rovittello, T: 345 7230176 (Silvia), 348 0115329 (Federico), www.cuntu.it*) is an ancient vineyard of Nerello Mascalese grapes, where Silvia, Roberto and Federico produce excellent Etna Rosso DOC wine.

Catania Markets are open mornings only, 7.30–1. A large daily food market (antiques on Sun) is held in Piazza Carlo Alberto, called 'a Fera d'o Luni, and a general market in the surrounding streets (including Via San Gaetano alle Grotte), now largely taken over by Chinese. In the streets to the southwest of Piazza Duomo and Via Garibaldi (including Via Gisira) there is another vast and colourful daily food market called 'A Pescheria, where fresh fish, meat and other foodstuffs are sold.

Fecarotta (*Via Etnea 162*) for jewellery made with amber from the River Simeto. A wonderful traditional pastry shop is I Dolci di Nonna Vincenza (*Piazza San Placido 7, www. dolcinonnavincenza.it*). They also have an outlet at Catania Airport and the port, and you can order online. Mantegna (*Via Etnea 350*) is a historic coffee house which opened more than 100 years ago: a good place for cakes and pastries, Sicilian breakfast. Also Scardaci has an excellent reputation; about midnight the insomniacs and night-owls line up here for fresh breakfast pastries, the famous *cornetti* (*Via Santa Maddalena 84, also at Via Etnea 158*). At Sa di Sapone (*Viale Africa 31, www. sadisapone.it*) you will find soap and cosmetics hand-made using olive oil, local herbs, fruits and spices, and lava from Mt Etna.

Etna In **Belpasso** visit Bar Condorelli (*Via Vittorio Emanuele 536, www.condorelli.it*) for the world-famous *torroncini*, soft nougat covered with chocolate. At **Linguaglossa**, at Azienda Agricola Gambino (*Contrada Petto Dragone, T: 349 8874223, 348 8220130, www.agricolagambino.it*), you can visit the high-altitude (800m) vineyard and taste the various wines in production; on-line shopping, too. Their Cantari white wine made with black Nerello Mascalese grapes, is delightful, so is the red Alicante, with hints of roses and raspberries, an ideal accompaniment to fish, cheese or lamb. Also very special Etna Rosso and Bianco DOCs, both named Tifeo. One of the oldest and most prestigious wineries of Etna is that of the Barone di Villagrande at **Milo** (*Via del Bosco 25, T: 095 7082175, www.villagrande.it*), where the vineyards on the sunny eastern slopes of the volcano have been carefully groomed since 1727 to produce award-winning DOCs, Etna Rosso and Etna Bianco Superiore. The village of **Passopisciaro** is in the heart of the Etna Rosso district. Antichi Vinai (*Via Castiglione*

49, www.antichivinai.it), for very good local wines, all the Etna DOCs, and their own *spumante*. Their vineyards have been in the family for four generations, since 1877. You will find excellent award-winning Etna Rosso also at Girolamo Russo's vineyards (*Via Regina Margherita 78, www.girolamorusso.it*), or Graci, who has vineyards at altitudes of 600, 1000 and 1100m, producing Etna Rosso and Bianco, and their own red, Quota 600, using only Nerello Mascalese grapes (*Contrada Arcuria, T: 095 386372, 348 7016773, www. graci.eu*). In **Piedimonte Etneo** the Caffè Calì is a historic coffee-house famous throughout Sicily for its *granita*, but also for the superb pastries, *cannoli*, and a remarkable almond cake (*Via Vittorio Emanuele 19*). **Zafferana Etnea** is renowned for its paper-thin cookies made with hazelnuts, pistachios or almonds, called *foglie da té* (tea leaves). You will find them still warm from the oven at Salemi (*Via Eusebio Longo 30*).

Giarre Fabbrica Finocchiaro (*Corso Italia 109/203, www.fabbricafinocchiaro.it*) is a historic Art Nouveau coffee-house and chocolate factory which opened in 1914, the place to stop for a cup of hot chocolate and a slice of cake, listen to music and play draughts or chess, and learn all about chocolate. Giarre was also renowned in the past for its puppet theatre; now arranged with its marionettes at the Pro Loco at Piazza Monsignor Alessi 8, near the War Memorial (*open Mon-Sat 9–1 & 4–8; Sun 10–12.30 & 4–7.30, T: 095 9704257; to see a show, call Sig. Zappalà, T: 336 885062, 347 8572580*).

Militello Val di Catania Snack Poker Bar (*Via Umberto 197*) for Militello's celebrated pastries: the *cassatelline, infasciatelli, totò* and *'nzulli*. The place is very humble-looking: you need to know about it or you would simply pass it by. They have been making these pastries to their own secret recipes for genera-

tions. Another good pastry-shop is Bulla (*Via Principe Branciforte 129*).

Mineo Mineo's historic coffee-house is the Bar Salerno in Piazza Baglio, for fragrant *cannoli di ricotta*; much appreciated by Luigi Capuana.

Raddusa For some delicious organic bread from this superb wheat-growing district, try Biorg (*Via Martiri D'Ungheria 21*).

Randazzo Musumeci (*Piazza Santa Maria 5*) for *biscotti della nonna* (grandma's biscuits), *croccantini alla nocciola* (hazelnut crunchies), *paste di mandorla aromatizzate* (almond biscuits flavoured with lemon, orange or tangerine), and excellent pistachio cakes. Arturo (Chiamatemi pure Maestà; *Via Umberto 73*), is a historic coffee house with a stunning Art Nouveau interior, for fragrant breakfast pastries and hot chocolate.

Vizzini La Spiga d'Oro Terlato (*Via Guzzardi 6, near public gardens*), is the best place for bread, biscuits, and snacks; always crowded.

FESTIVALS & EVENTS

Acireale 20 Jan, colourful processions and fireworks for St Sebastian: the saint is rushed out of the church and down the steps into the crowds, and later in the day is slowly taken back. You will see many people in tears as their saint leaves them for another year. Feb, Carnival, one of the most famous in Italy (*Info: T: 095 893134, www.carnevalediacireale. it*). 26 July, Feast of the patron St Venera, including the procession of the *candelore*, Baroque candlesticks up to 5m high, one for each of the city corporations, and a magnificent firework display.

Acitrezza 24 June, 'U Pisci a Mari, on the feast day of St John the Baptist, the fishermen enact a pantomime from their boats to ensure a good catch for the following year; the most agile swims around the boats pretending to be a swordfish, until someone 'catches' him, and 'spears' him to death (*Info: T: 0957373426*).

Adrano Easter Sun, the *Diavolata*, in the main square, a medieval-origin play celebrating the victory of Christianity over the Devils. Great fun.

Bronte late Sept, pistachio festival (*Info: T: 095 7747213*).

Calatabiano 3rd weekend in May, Feast of St Philip of Syria (*San Filippo Siriaco*), when the heavy statue of the saint is carried down a steep path from his church near the castle, and around the town; very exciting, because he has to race down at breakneck speed.

Caltagirone Easter, Procession of the Dead Christ, followed on Easter Sunday afternoon with 'A *Giunta*, when an enormous *papier mâché* St Peter endeavours to contrive the meeting of the Madonna with her Son, and other processions and events, including an exhibition of terracotta whistles; the Santa Maria del Monte stairway is illuminated with coloured paper lamps, and there is a also a ceramics fair. Last week of May, Feast of the Madonna of Conadomini with a procession of Sicilian carts and decorated tractors, to assure a good harvest, called 'a *Russedda*. The Santa Maria del Monte stairway is completely decorated with vases of flowers, forming a design. 24–25 July, procession of San Giacomo (St James), when the stairway is again illuminated with paper lamps. Christmas-Epiphany, *La Città del Presepe*, exhibitions of terracotta Christmas cribs. Every 3rd Sun of the month, throughout the winter, 'a *Truvatura* (the treasure hunt), with puppet shows, concerts, and antique fairs (*Info: www.comune.caltagirone. ct.it*).

Catania 3–5 Feb and 17 Aug, the Feast of St Agatha, celebrated with traditional processions and magnificent fireworks.

Militello last week in Aug, *Settimana del Barocco*, a celebration of Baroque art. 2nd Sun in Oct, prickly-pear festival.

Mineo Christmas, *Natale nei Vicoli*, a series of displays and tableaux in the little streets of the old centre.

Motta Sant'Anastasia 23–25 Aug, Feast of the patron St Anastasia, with much flag-tossing and fireworks, to celebrate the victory of Count Roger over the Saracens; also pageants in medieval costume to evoke the romantic story of Queen Blanche of Navarre and her would-be lover, Count Bernardo Cabrera.

Raddusa mid-Sept, *Festa del Grano*, a feast celebrating wheat, with parades of traditional wooden carts, Sicilian music and dancing, free tasting of bread and pasta (*Info: www. festadelgrano.it*).

Ramacca April, the town celebrates its famous artichokes, *violetto di Ramacca*, with opportunities for tasting them prepared in many different ways (*Info: T: 335 1531605, www.carciofofest.it*).

Randazzo 15 Aug, Festival of the Madonna.

Sant'Alfio 10 May, Feast of the patron saint.

Trecastagni early May, feast for the three patron saints—*i tre casti agni*—Alfio, Cirino and Filadelfo, culminating on Sun closest to 10 May with parades, Sicilian carts and fireworks, and Sicily's largest garlic market.

Vizzini June, *Sagra della Ricotta*, celebrations and a fair in honour of the local sheep's milk ricotta, rich and creamy. Info: www.sagradellaricotta.it.

Zafferana Etnea Sundays in Oct, autumn festival known as the *Ottobrata*, with local specialities (especially honey) sold in the square, and craftsmen (carpenters, stonemasons and bee-keepers) demonstrating their skills along the main street.

THE PROVINCE OF MESSINA

The province of Messina encompasses two meandering mountain ranges, the Peloritans and the Nebrodi; the famous hilltop town of Taormina; the ancient sanctuary of the Black Madonna of Tindari, and the tiny Aeolian Islands, all of volcanic origin yet each with its own particular character. The city of Messina itself is the main entry point for people arriving in Sicily by train, car or on foot, all via ferry across the straits from Calabria. Most tourists regrettably head on immediately to other destinations, without spending a little time getting to know this interesting city.

MESSINA

Messina (*map p. 536, D2*), on the western shore of the straits bearing its name, extends along the lowest slopes of the Peloritan Mountains above a splendid harbour, one of the deepest and safest in the Mediterranean. With its fine port and ideal position between Europe and Africa, the Straits of Gibraltar and the Bosphorus, Messina was long an important city, a key trading-post from the Bronze Age until the discovery of America, and for some time afterwards. Today the port is always busy with ferries and hydrofoils travelling to and from the mainland; controversial plans for a bridge over the Straits have been shelved. The third largest city in Sicily, Messina was destroyed by an earth-

Detail of the base of the Orion Fountain in Messina: relief representing the River Nile.

quake followed by a tsunami in 1908, when 84,000 people died out of a population of 120,000. It was soon rebuilt, with broad streets planted with trees, and low buildings to minimise the danger from future earthquakes. The centre of Messina now combines sea, sky and hills in a pleasant, open townscape. The prevailing wind is the *maestrale*, which blows from the northwest, making it one of the breeziest places in Sicily.

HISTORY OF MESSINA

Zancle, as Messina was called by the Greeks in allusion to the sickle-shaped peninsula enclosing its harbour, was probably a settlement of the Sicels before being occupied by a colony from Chalcis. In 493 BC it was captured by Anaxilas, tyrant of Rhegium, and renamed Messana, in honour of his native country of Messenia in the Peloponnese. It took part in local wars against Syracuse and then against Athens, and was destroyed by the Carthaginian general Himilco. Rebuilt by Syracuse, it was occupied by the Campanian mercenaries of Agathocles, who called themselves Mamertines. These obtained the alliance of Rome against the Carthaginians and Messina prospered with the fortunes of Rome. Under Byzantium, and later under the Arabs, the surrounding hills were planted with groves of mulberry trees to support the burgeoning silk industry, which brought fame and fortune until the late 19th century when the industry came to a standstill because of a parasite which attacked the silkworms.

Under the Normans the town was renowned for monastic learning and was important as a Crusader port. In September 1190 Richard Coeur de Lion and Philip Augustus of France arrived to spend the winter here before leaving for their Crusade in March 1191. Richard ensconced himself and his troops in the Basilian monastery of San Salvatore, and proceeded to ransack the city as redress for perceived offences to his sister Joanna, widow of William II. The Holy Roman Emperor Henry VI died of dysentery at Messina in 1197. After a heroic and successful resistance to Charles of Anjou in 1282, the city flourished until losing privileges for rebelling against Spanish misrule in 1674.

Much of the city's history has been disastrous: plague in 1743, an earthquake in 1783, naval bombardment in 1848, cholera in 1854, another earthquake in 1894, culminating in the catastrophe of 1908, 7.24 on the Richter scale. The first shock, at 5.20 in the morning of 28th December, lasted only 37 seconds but destroyed almost the entire city, causing the shore to sink more than half a metre. The subsidence caused a violent tsunami which swept the coast, rising to a height of 8m, drowning many as they escaped from their ruined homes. A series of lesser shocks continued almost daily for two months. Reconstruction, though assisted by liberal contributions from all over the world, was by no means complete when the city was again devastated in 1943 by aerial bombardment. In 1955 a preliminary agreement was signed by 'the six' in Messina to found the European Union (EU).

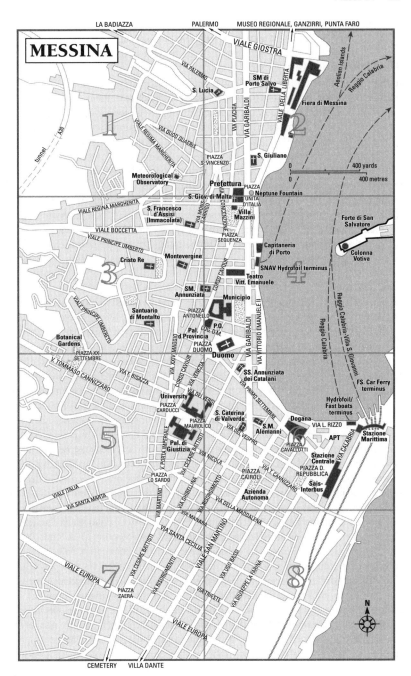

MESSINA

LA BADIAZZA
PALERMO
MUSEO REGIONALE, GANZIRRI, PUNTA FARO

VIALE GIOSTRA

VIA PALERMO

VIA DUOD QUAERIS

VIALE REGINA MARGHERITA

tunnel
A20

S. Lucia

SM di
Porto Salvo

VIA PLACIDA

VIA GARIBALDI

VIALE DELLA LIBERTÀ

Aeolian Islands

Reggio Calabria

Fiera di Messina

1

2

PIAZZA
S. VINCENZO

S. Giuliano

0   400 yards
0   400 metres

Meteorological
Observatory

Prefettura

PIAZZA
Neptune Fountain

S. Giov. di Malta

PIAZZA
UNITÀ
D'ITALIA

VIALE REGINA MARGHERITA

S. Francesco
d'Assisi
(Immacolata)

Villa
Mazzini

Forte di San
Salvatore

VIALE BOCCETTA

VIA MONS. GARIBIO

VIALE PRINCIPE UMBERTO

Cristo Re

Montevergine

Capitaneria
di Porto

Colonna
Votiva

3

SNAV Hydrofoil terminus

Teatro
Vitt. Emanuele

4

VIALE PRINCIPE UMBERTO

SM.
Annunziata

Municipio

CORSO CAVOUR

Santuario
di Montalto

PIAZZA
ANTONELLO

P.O.
LOG. DM.
Pal.
d Provincia

VIA GARIBALDI

Reggio Calabria-Villa S. Giovanni

Reggio Calabria

FS. Car Ferry
terminus

Botanical
Gardens

PIAZZA XX
SETTEMBRE

PIAZZA
DUOMO

Duomo

VIA VITTORIO EMANUELE II

V. TOMMASO CANNIZZARO

VIA F. BISAZZA

CORSO CAVOUR

VIA XXIV MAGGIO

VIA VENEZIA

SS. Annunziata
dei Catalani

University

VIA DEI VERDI

PIAZZA
CARDUCCI

VIA PRIMO SETTEMBRE

S. Caterina
di Valverde

PIAZZA
MAUROLICO

S.M.
Alemanni

Dogana

VIA L. RIZZO

Hydrofoil/
Fast boats
terminus

Stazione
Marittima

Pal. di
Giustizia

V. PORTA IMPERIALE

VIA CESARE BATTISTI

VIA DEL VESPRO

PIAZZA
CAVALLOTTI

APT

VIA CALABRIA

5

VIA NICOLA

PIAZZA
LO SARDO

VIA T. CANNIZZARO

PIAZZA
CAIROLI

Stazione
Centrale

6

VIALE ITALIA

VIA MARTINO

VIA GHIBELLINA

VIA RISORGIMENTO

Azienda
Autonoma

PIAZZA D.
REPUBBLICA

Sais-
Interbus

VIA SANTA MARTA

VIA DELLA MADDALENA

VIA MANARA

VIA SANTA CECILIA

VIALE SAN MARTINO

VIA UGO BASSI

VIA CESARE BATTISTI

VIA RISORGIMENTO

VIA GIUSEPPE LA FARINA

VIALE EUROPA

PIAZZA
ZAERA

VIA TRIESTE

7

8

VIALE EUROPA

N

CEMETERY   VILLA DANTE

EXPLORING MESSINA

The Orion Fountain

In the centre of the city, Piazza Duomo (*map 3–4*) was spaciously laid out in the 18th century. Beside the cathedral is the 1933 free-standing bell-tower and, in front of them, the Orion Fountain, the masterpiece of the Florentine sculptor Giovanni Angelo Montorsoli (1553), and described by Berenson as the most beautiful Renaissance fountain in Europe. In white marble and black lava stone, it was commissioned to celebrate the construction of an aqueduct from the nearby River Camaro, which made running water available to a large part of the city for the first time. Although the people had wanted Michelangelo to design the fountain, the commission went instead to his pupil Montorsoli, who enjoyed his stay in Messina enough to delay his return to Tuscany for more than ten years, and then only on the orders of the pope. The figures around the fountain represent the Nile, Tiber, Ebro and Camaro, and they are shown looking in the direction of their respective rivers. On the top is Orion, mythical founder of the city, with his faithful dog Sirius.

The duomo

Despite successive reconstructions, the duomo (*map 4; open 8–7*) retains much of the appearance of the original medieval church. Originally built by Count Roger, the cathedral was one of the major Norman churches in Sicily. It was consecrated in 1197 in the presence of Emperor Henry VI and Queen Constance, and was first destroyed in 1254 by a fire which broke out during a funeral service for Conrad IV, son of Frederick II, because the mourners had lit too many candles. The new building was shattered by earthquakes in 1783 and 1908 and in 1943 was hit by an incendiary bomb aimed at the port. The fire raged for three days, and many treasures were destroyed, including the mosaics and the frescoes, the royal tombs and choir-stalls. Everything that could be salvaged was carefully replaced in the reconstructed church. A surviving column can be seen outside the building on the north side, with a carved fragment from the church on top, erected as a monument in 1958 to record the 50th anniversary of the disaster. The lower part of the façade preserves much of the original sculpted decoration, including panels in relief with *naif* farming scenes, and three fine doorways, by 14th-, 15th- and 16th-century artists. The beautiful central doorway has a tympanum by Pietro da Bonitate (1468). On the south side is a doorway by Polidoro da Caravaggio and a wall, still intact, with fine Catalan Gothic windows.

Interior of the duomo

The majestic basilican interior, in pink and grey tones, was well restored after the fire. The side altars (copies of originals by Montorsoli), the columns (made of cement), the marble floor and the painted wooden roof are all copies of the originals. On the first south altar is a statue of St John the Baptist by Antonello Gagini (1525). At the end of the aisle is the so-called 'tomb of five archbishops' (14th century), with five Gothic trilobed arches. On the nave pillar in the transept is the fragmented Byzantine-style tomb slab of Archbishop Palmer (d. 1195). From the south aisle is the entrance to the **treasury** (*open April–Oct Mon–Fri 9–1 & 4.30–7, Sat 9–1; Nov–March Mon–Sat 9–1*). Arranged in four rooms and on two floors, it is particularly rich in 17th- and 18th-century artefacts, including church silver made in Messina. Among the most important pieces are a 10th-century lamp in rock crystal, altered in 1250, and a very fine reliquary of the arm of St Martianus, commissioned by Richard Palmer (as the inscription states) when he was bishop of Syracuse. Brought with him when he became archbishop of Messina around 1182, it shows the influence of Islamic and Byzantine goldsmiths' art. The most precious piece in the treasury collection is the golden *manta*, used only on important ceremonial occasions to cover the image of the *Madonna della Lettera*. It was made by a 17th-century Florentine goldsmith. Other works of particular interest include a 13th-century processional Cross, a large, brightly-coloured 17th-century silk embroidery, and a pair of silver candlesticks made in 1701.

Outside the south apse chapel, elaborately decorated in marble, is the damaged tomb of Archbishop De Tabiatis by Goro di Gregorio (1333). The high altar bears a copy of the venerated Byzantine **Madonna della Lettera**, which was destroyed in 1943. The canopy, the stalls, and the bishop's throne have all been reconstructed. In front of the high altar is a lower altar which encloses a silver frontal attributed to the local silversmith Francesco Juvarra (late 17th or early 18th century), depicting the Madonna in the act of consigning a letter to the ambassadors of Messina after hearing of the citizens' conversion by St Paul. The dedication of the church dates back to 1638 and the foundation of the 'Congregation of the Slaves of the Madonna of the Letter', whose seat was the crypt of the church. The mosaic in the central apse has been recomposed. In the north apse chapel is the only original mosaic to have survived *in situ* from the 14th century, showing the Madonna and Child. The monument to Bishop Angelo Paino (1870–1967), who rebuilt the cathedral after the last war, is to the left of the apse.

In the two transepts part of the organ can be seen, manufactured by Tamburini of Crema in 1948; with its 16,000 pipes and 127 registers, it is the largest in Italy and one of the biggest in Europe. In the north transept the tomb effigy of Bishop Antonio La Lignamine is surrounded by twelve fine small panels of the *Passion* sculpted by the Gagini school. Nearby is a 17th-century bust of Archbishop Proto, and part of the tomb of Archbishop Bellorado by Giovanni Battista Mazzola (1513). In the north aisle, beside the doorway, is a 16th-century relief of St Jerome (the exterior of the 15th-century north doorway can be seen here).

The campanile

The campanile (*open Mon–Sat 9–1 & 4.30–7, Sun and holidays 10–1 & 4.30–7, last entry 30mins before closing*) was designed by Francesco Valenti to house a remarkable astronomical clock, the largest of its kind in the world, built by the Strasbourg firm of Josef Ungerer in 1933. At noon the chimes herald an elaborate and very noisy movement of mechanical figures (Dina and Clarenza, the 13th-century heroines who ring the bells, are 3m tall), representing episodes in the city's history, religious festivals, the phases of life and the days of the week, accompanied by the *Ave Maria*. On the right side of the tower are the quadrants showing the planetarium, the phases of the moon, and the perpetual calendar.

South from Piazza Duomo

South along **Corso Cavour** is the University (1927), whose library dates from the university's foundation in 1548, facing the Law Courts (Palazzo di Giustizia; 1928), a monumental Neoclassical building in ochre stone, surmounted by a Roman chariot representing the victorious course of Justice (*map 5*).

Via I Settembre (a stone on the corner records the outbreak of the Sicilian revolt against the Bourbons in 1847) leads southeast from Piazza Duomo towards the railway station. It passes two Baroque corner fountains, which survived the earthquake, near (left) the church of **Santissima Annunziata dei Catalani** (*map 6; Via Garibaldi 111, open 8.30–10.30, closed Sun; T: 090 661691*), with its remarkable exterior. It is a 12th-century Norman church, altered under the Swabians. The apse, transepts and cupola, with beautiful arcading, date from the 12th century, while the three doors at the west end were added in the 13th century. The interior has a brick apse and dome in yellow and white stone, and tall dark grey columns with Corinthian capitals. The windows and nave arches are decorated with red and white stone. The large stoup is made up of two capitals. In Piazza Catalani is a statue of Don Juan of Austria, by Andrea Calamech (1572), which was erected to celebrate the commander's victory over the Turks at Lepanto in 1571. On the morning after the battle, the general personally congratulated the wounded Miguel Cervantes on his devotion to duty.

Just off Via Garibaldi, the long broad thoroughfare which crosses Via I Settembre, are the ruins of **Santa Maria degli Alemanni** (c. 1220), founded by the Teutonic order of Knights, damaged by the 1783 earthquake and since restored. It is one of the few Gothic churches in Sicily, and is thought to have been built by German craftsmen, hence the name 'Alemanni'. On the opposite side of the street, the church of **Santa Caterina di Valverde** contains a beautiful 16th-century painting of *Madonna of Itria between Sts Peter and Paul* by the local artist Antonello Riccio.

Via Garibaldi ends in Piazza Cairoli, the centre of the modern town and the most popular meeting place for the *passeggiata*. Thanks to its fountains and magnificent ficus trees, it is always cool and shady.

Viale San Martino

Viale San Martino (*map 7–8*), one of the main shopping streets, with the tram running down the centre, traverses an area of attractive Art Nouveau-style houses. The avenue is the most beautiful in Messina, with its rows of date palms. It ends at the public gardens of **Villa Dante** beside the monumental cemetery, designed in 1872 by Leone Savoja. The luxuriant garden, built in terraces on the slopes of the hill, has a lovely view of Calabria. The Famedio, or Pantheon, was damaged by the 1908 earthquake, but almost all the smaller family tombs were left intact. In 1940 the British cemetery, founded during the Napoleonic wars, was transferred here (reached by a path on the extreme left side of the cemetery) when its original site near the harbour was needed for defence works.

North from Piazza Duomo

A short way north of the duomo is the circular **Piazza Antonello** (*map 3–4*), dedicated to the famous local painter Antonello da Messina and laid out in 1914–29 with a group of monumental buildings: the Post Office (1915), the administrative seat of the province (1918), the Town Hall (1924) and an arcade (1929) with a café, offices and shops.

In **Via XXIV Maggio** (*map 3*) are the remains of the 18th-century Monte di Pietà (pawnshop), with a beautiful flight of steps, and the **church of Montevergine** with a lovely Baroque interior.

Via Garibaldi runs north–south, parallel to Corso Vittorio Emanuele and the waterfront, with a view of the busy harbour and the sickle-shaped tongue of land protecting it that ends at the Forte di San Salvatore, erected by the Spanish in 1546. On the point of the sickle, at the entrance to the port, can be seen the golden statue of the Madonna, patroness of Messina, on a white pillar 60m high. The opera house, **Teatro Vittorio Emanuele** (*map 4; T: 090 8966215, www.teatrodimessina.it*), on Via Garibaldi, built in 1842, was re-opened in 1985 after repairs; strangely, the earthquake had spared the perimeter walls and only the interior was ruined.

The two parallel streets passing a statue of Ferdinand II, end in Piazza Unità d'Italia, with the **Neptune Fountain** by Montorsoli (*map 2;* 1557; the figures of Neptune and Scylla are 19th-century copies, the originals being kept in the regional museum). Behind is the huge 1920s Prefecture, and nearby the little church of **San Giovanni di Malta** (c. 1590; Camillo Camilliani). Here, in the Cappella Palatina, an exhibition of sacred art (*open Tues–Sat 9–1 & 3–7, Sun 9.30–12.30; closed Mon*) displays embroidered silk vestments, Church silver and paintings. Also facing the piazza is Palazzo Carrozza, built in the 1930s in an eclectic style. There is a garden with pines and ficus trees facing the waterfront, and, behind, the public gardens of **Villa Mazzini**, with beautiful trees and an interesting aquarium with a collection of fish from the Straits (*open Tues–Sun 9–1 & 3–7, closed Sun afternoon and all day Mon; T: 090 48897*).

Viale Boccetta, which was a water-course before the earthquake, leads inland from Piazza Sequenza to the church of San Francesco d'Assisi, better known by the inhabitants as the **Immacolata** (*map 3*). Built in 1252 with a large convent in Sicilian Gothic style, it stood outside the city walls, as was usual with Franciscan foundations. The church can be identified in some of Antonello da Messina's works, as can the Straits of Messina, which often appear in the background.

Along the northern waterfront

Viale della Libertà (*map 2*), which follows the shore in full view of the Calabrian coastline, passes the *passeggiata a mare*, opposite which is the church of San Giuliano, with red domes in eclectic style. The road runs along the coast passing the church of **Gesù e Maria del Buonviaggio**, known as the church of Ringo (an old fishing village close by). Built in 1598 and dedicated to seamen, its façade is adorned with a fine portal, Corinthian capitals and two niches with statues of Christ and the Virgin: both statues have one hand pierced to hold oil lamps to guide passing boats. From here, Viale della Libertà leads to the Museo Regionale (c. 3km from Piazza Duomo; *described below*).

Museo Regionale

Housed in an old silk mill since the 1908 earthquake, this important museum (*beyond map 2; open Mon, Tues, Thur, Fri, Sat 9–2, Sun and holidays 9–1, last tickets 30mins before closing; Tues, Thur and Sat also 3–6 (4–7 in summer; T: 090 361292), closed all day Wed*) was, at the time of writing, in the process of moving into a new purpose-built construction next door, on three floors, thus allowing much more space for the exhibits. At the time of going to press only some paintings could be seen, together with carved and gilded woodwork from churches and monasteries and a fine collection of majolica pharmacy jars. The works are displayed in chronological order.

There are some splendid **paintings by Antonello da Messina**, his school, and Flemish and Spanish artists from the late 15th century. A remarkable work is the luminous polyptych of the *Madonna with Sts Gregory and Benedict* (oil on panel), an ideal synthesis of Flemish and Italian Renaissance styles, painted by Antonello da Messina in 1473 and bearing his signature. Painted for the monastery of St Gregory and much damaged in the earthquake it has since been restored. Also here is a recent acquisition, a tiny panel by Antonello painted on both sides and, among other works, a striking *Pietà* and *Symbols of the Passion*, by an unknown Flemish painter.

Girolamo Alibrandi represents the early 16th century. He was a native artist who admired the work of Leonardo and Raphael, whose influence can be seen in the two panel-paintings of the *Circumcision* and the *Presentation in the Temple* (1519); this latter work is thought to be his finest. Recovered after the earthquake in more than 300 fragments, it has been extensively restored.

Next come works of the 16th–17th centuries, in the Sicilian Mannerist style. But the *Adoration of the Shepherds* (1533) by Polidoro da Caravaggio shows the influence of Raphael, with whom Polidoro studied. A collection of majolica pharmacy vases (mostly from the Casteldurante and Venetian workshops) follows, and carved and gilded wooden furniture from the wealthy monasteries of Messina.

17th-century paintings include the *Madonna Appearing to Sts Francis and Clare* (1604) by Antonio Catalano il Vecchio; *St Francis Receiving the Stigmata* by Filippo Paladini; and *The Madonna of the Letter* (1629) by Antonio Catalano il Giovane.

The museum also possesses **two masterpieces by Caravaggio**, both dramatic late works painted during his stay in Messina in 1608–09: *Nativity* (commissioned by the Senate of Messina for the Capuchin church) and *The Raising of Lazarus*, commissioned by the De Lazzari family for their private chapel in the church of St Camillo (demolished in 1880 and rebuilt on Viale Principe Umberto). Sicilian works of his school displayed here include: Alonso Rodriguez: *Meeting between Sts Peter and Paul*; Mario Minniti: *Miracle of the Widow of Naim*; and a beautiful painting by Carlo Sellitto, *St Lucy*.

Cristo Re and the Botanical Gardens

On the slopes of the hillside above the town stands the church of **Cristo Re** (Christ the King, 1939; *map 3*), which dominates the city with its huge dome. It was designed to be a collective memorial for the victims of the 1908 earthquake and for all those killed in war. To one side stands an old tower called the Torre Guelfonia (part of the old city fortifications) with a great bell (diameter 3m) made from the melted-down enemy guns of the First World War. The interior of the church is richly decorated with fine marble and stuccoes; in the crypt is a sarcophagus on which lies the symbolic marble image of a soldier.

From here Viale Principe Umberto runs south, passing Torre Vittoria and the ruins of the 16th-century Spanish walls, and the striking **sanctuary church of Montalto** (rebuilt in 1930; *map 3*). Its twin bell-towers are a city landmark. The lush **Botanical Gardens** are in Piazza XX Settembre (*map 3–5; open 8.30–12.30, closed Sun and holidays; T: 090 391940*).

THE OUTSKIRTS OF MESSINA: PUNTA FARO & LA BADIAZZA

Punta Faro (14km north; *beyond map 2*), at Cape Peloro, the extreme northeastern tip of Sicily and the nearest point to Calabria, can be reached by the old road lined with a modest row of houses along the sea front, which traverses the ambitiously-named suburbs of Paradiso, Contemplazione, Pace (and Sant'Agata). It is at the mouth of the Straits of Messina, the *Fretum Siculum* of the Romans. This is the site of the legendary whirlpools called Scylla and Charybdis, greatly feared by sailors in ancient times. Further south the Calabrian coast is sometimes, in certain weather conditions, strangely magnified and distorted by a mirage called *Fata Morgana*: what appears to be the city of King Arthur's half-sister, exiled here, floats on the water in the middle of the Straits.

Just short of the cape is the fishing village of **Ganzirri**, on two little lagoons (the Pantano Grande and the Pantano Piccolo), separated from the sea by a dune barrier and fed by artesian water, famous for mussels and other shellfish.

The twin pylons, over 150m high, at **Punta Faro** (*map p. 536, D1–D2*) are an impressive landmark, standing where the strongly contested bridge between Sicily and the mainland may one day be built. Because of the unfavourable economic situation, work on the bridge had been put on hold at the time of writing.

Sword-fishing has taken place off the coast here since ancient times; it was for many years considered one of the sights of Messina. The traditional method of harpooning the fish from characteristic small boats (*luntri*) with tall look-out masts, is still carried out, but most fishermen nowadays use modern equipment and motor-boats called *felucche*. Illegal fishing methods and over-exploitation have decimated the number of fish found in this area.

West to the Badiazza and the Peloritan Mountains

The road is well signposted from the centre of Messina (Colle San Rizzo, Portella Castanea, Santa Maria Dinnamare and Badiazza). Off the SS 113, a very poor road on the river bed (almost impassable in places) leads right (signposted) past Sant'Andrea, a little church built in 1929, and poor houses to the head of the valley. Here, in a group of pine trees, is **La Badiazza** (also called Santa Maria della Scala or Santa Maria della Valle; *map p. 536, D2*). This fine 13th-century church (*although recently restored, it is of-*

ficially closed) belonged to a ruined Cistercian convent and has an interesting exterior with lava-stone decoration.

The main road continues uphill to enter all that remains of the forest which once covered the slopes of the Peloritan Mountains. Thick pinewoods survive here. The road sign indicating Palermo (250km) is a reminder that this was the main road to Palermo before the motorway was built. At **Colle San Rizzo** (460m) is a crossroads. From here a spectacular road (signposted 'Santuario di Maria Santissima di Dinnamare') leads for 9km along the crest of the Peloritan range to a height of 1130m. The first stretch is extremely narrow and dangerous but further on the road improves. The views on either side are breathtaking: on the right Milazzo can be seen and on the left the toe of Italy. The church of **Maria Santissima di Dinnamare**, built in the 18th century, was rebuilt in 1899. The superb panorama, one of the most exceptional in Italy, takes in the whole of Calabria, the port of Messina and the tip of Punta Faro. On the other side the Aeolian Islands, including Stromboli (beyond Milazzo), and Mt Etna, can be seen.

From the Colle San Rizzo crossroads, the road signposted to Castanea leads through fine pinewoods, with wide views down over the port of Messina to the right, and to the left of the Aeolian Islands, and the motorway snaking through the hills. In spring Mt Ciccia (609m) is on the migratory route from Africa to central Europe for thousands of birds, especially honey buzzards.

A winding road leads to the village of **Castanea delle Furie** (*map p. 536, D2*). Castanea, despite the menacing name, has a typical medieval town plan and some lovely old churches. The road continues down to Spartà past olives and pines. As the road nears the sea there is a wonderful view of Stromboli.

TAORMINA & ENVIRONS

Taormina (204m; *map p. 536, C3*) is renowned for its magnificent position above the sea on a spur of Mt Taurus (so-called for its resemblance to a bull when seen from the south), commanding a celebrated view of Etna. Being a particularly deep and solid wedge of limestone, Mt Taurus is not subject to earthquakes, thus preserving the medieval buildings of the little town. With a delightful winter climate, it became a fashionable international resort at the end of the 19th century, and during the 20th century was the most famous holiday destination on the island. The small town, with the elegant Corso off which lead intriguing little stepped streets, is now virtually given over to tourism and can be very crowded from Easter to September. Many of the villas and hotels, built in mock Gothic or eclectic styles at the beginning of the 20th century, are surrounded with verdant gardens. Too much building has been allowed on the hillsides in recent years, although the medieval churches and palaces, the tiny streets and Roman remains, have lost none of their magic.

There are two large car parks, one close to the south gate, Porta Catania. The other, called Lumbi, is convenient for Porta Messina, the north gate. Both, thanks to a tunnel which goes through the mountain, are easily accessible from the motorway exit.

HISTORY OF TAORMINA

Tauromenion for the Greeks, *Tauromenium* for the Romans, Taormina was probably founded by the Sicels before being captured and repopulated by Dionysius of Syracuse in 392, who began the process of turning it into a Greek city. The town was further enlarged in 358 under Andromachus, father of the historian Timaeus, who gathered together the survivors of the destruction of Naxos in 403 BC.

It was favoured by Rome during the early days of occupation, and suffered in the Servile War (135–132 BC) when the city was held by slaves for several months, but forfeited its rights as an allied city by taking sides with Sextus Pompey against Octavian. In 902 it was the last Christian centre to fall to the Arabs, but this did not save it from being attacked again by the Tunisian Caliph al-Muez in 965, when the theatre (which was by then a city district) was destroyed. The caliph, who later founded modern Cairo, rebuilt the town, modestly renaming it Almoezia, as it was known until Count Roger conquered it in 1078. Here the Sicilian Parliament assembled in 1410 to choose a king on the extinction of the line of Peter of Aragon.

Taormina has been visited and described by numerous travellers through the centuries, and the famous view of Etna from the theatre has been painted countless times. John Dryden came here in 1701. John Henry (later Cardinal) Newman stayed in the town as a young man in 1833. In 1847 Edward Lear spent four or five days in what he described as 'Taormina the Magnificent'. Taormina was first connected to Messina by railway in 1866 and a year later the line to Catania was inaugurated. In 1864 the first hotel, the Timeo, was opened in the town, and it became internationally known as a winter resort soon after the first visit of the Kaiser (Wilhelm II) in 1896. The Kaiser returned in 1904 and 1905 with a large retinue, and set the fashion for royal visitors, some of whom came here incognito, using false names. In 1906 Edward VII wintered at the San Domenico Hotel and George V made a private visit in 1924. Before the First World War the town had a considerable Anglo-American, German and Scandinavian colony, including the impoverished Baron Wilhelm von Gloeden (1896–1931), who opened a photographic studio, specialising in mildly erotic child portraits, his atelier becoming one of the sights of the town. The painter Robert Kitson built a villa for himself here where he lived from 1905 onwards. Kitson was concerned about the poverty of the local inhabitants and encouraged Mabel Hill, another English resident, to set up a lace-making school. The Scottish writer Robert Hitchens arrived by car in Taormina in the winter of 1910, the first time a car had reached the town. D.H. Lawrence and his wife Frieda lived here from 1920–23.

The town attracted the attention of Allied aircraft in July 1943, when it temporarily became Field Marshal Kesselring's headquarters. In the '50s and '60s, King Gustav of Sweden regularly spent a winter month in Taormina, delighting in the climate and indulging his passion for archaeology. But what saved Taormina from the post-war economic crisis was its re-invention as a bathing resort, and above all, in 1954, the institution of the June film festival. Famous visitors in this period include Truman Capote—who wrote *Breakfast at Tiffany's* while here—Cecil Beaton, Jean Cocteau, Osbert Sitwell, Salvador Dalí, Winston Churchill, Sibelius, Orson Welles, John Steinbeck, Tennessee Williams, Rita Hayworth, Marlene Dietrich, Greta Garbo and Cary Grant. Elizabeth Taylor and Richard Burton spent at least part of both of their honeymoons in Taormina.

EXPLORING TAORMINA

The main street, Corso Umberto, runs south–north from Porta Catania to Porta Messina, connecting three squares: Piazza Duomo, Piazza IX Aprile and Piazza Vittorio Emanuele. Side streets lead to the Greek Theatre and to the public gardens, and steps and a road go up to the Saracen Fort, the sanctuary church of the Madonna della Roccia, and Castelmola.

Porta Catania
Porta Catania or Porta del Tocco (*map 5*; 1440), has the Aragon family emblem on the outside. The Jewish Ghetto was located by the walls here (the Jews were forced to leave Sicily and all the Spanish possessions in 1492), with narrow alleys and the interesting old **Palazzo Duchi di Santo Stefano** (*open 9–1 & 3–8*). Built in the 14th–15th centuries, the palace formed part of the second ring of city walls, and with its decorative stone work in contrasting colours of black and white, is a masterpiece of Sicilian Gothic architecture. The garden and upper floors have a permanent display of works by the sculptor Giuseppe Mazzullo, born in Graniti, a village near Taormina, while the lower floor (with four cross-vaults) is used for exhibitions and civil-rite weddings. South of the gate, the little 14th-century church of **Sant'Antonio** (Gothic portal) was damaged in an air raid in 1943. The church contains a crib made in 1953, which is modelled on the town. The Art Nouveau **Hotel Excelsior**, built in the 1920s, has a superb vista from the terrace.

The duomo and district
At the south end of Corso Umberto, close to Porta Catania, is the attractive square facing the **duomo** (St Nicholas of Bari; *map 5*), founded in the 13th century, with battlements and two lovely side-portals (15th and 16th century). The façade has a late rose window and portal of 1636. In the interior, with six monolithic antique pink marble columns, are a painting of the *Visitation* by Antonio Giuffrè (1463) and a polyptych, some say the work of Antonello da Messina, others say by Antonello de Saliba (1504), from the former church of San Giovanni, both in the south aisle. In the chapel at the end of the aisle is a delicate tabernacle dated 1648, and an early 16th-century *Madonna and Child* in marble. In the north aisle, first altar, there is a 16th-century panel painting

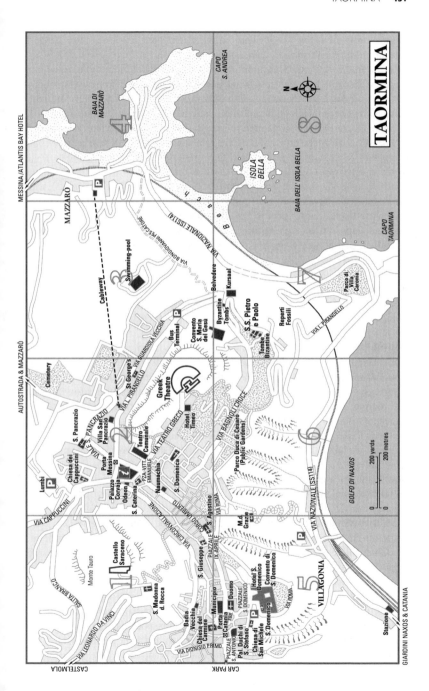

of the *Madonna Enthroned with Saints*, on the second altar, a 16th-century statue of St Agatha and on the third altar, *Adoration of the Magi*.

In the piazza is a charming **fountain** of 1635, a symbol of Taormina. The bizarre figure on the top would appear to be the bust of an angel on the body of a bull (adapted here as a pregnant female centaur with only two legs). Said to have been found in the ruins of the Greek theatre, it is probably a Baroque pastiche.

From Piazza Duomo steps ascend past a small black-and-white Roman mosaic (right; within an enclosure) and (left) the rebuilt church of the **Carmine** with a pretty campanile. More steps lead up to (left) the Porta Cuseni (or Saraceni), the name given to the district just outside the walls. Outside the gate steps (the Salita Castelmola) continue up to Via Dionisio I which leads right to the **Badia Vecchia** (*map 1*), with its large crenellated tower with fine mullioned windows and black and white intarsias. From here Via Leonardo da Vinci leads past a wall in front of cypresses, bougainvillea and plumbago to **Casa Cuseni** (no. 7). The villa was built by Robert Kitson, a painter, in 1907. It later became a *pensione*, run by his niece, Daphne Phelps, author of *A House in Sicily*.

On the opposite side of Piazza Duomo, a street descends to the ex-convent, **Hotel San Domenico** (*map 5*; first opened as a hotel in 1894), which has a late 16th-century cloister. Field Marshal Kesselring set up his headquarters here in July 1943, and many of his staff were killed by an Allied air raid which destroyed the church.

Along Corso Umberto

Corso Umberto is lined with shops selling clothes, shoes, jewellery, local pottery, confectionery and antiques, with medieval doorways, flower-filled balconies and stepped alleyways. Facing the west wall of the cathedral is the pink 18th-century Town Hall (**Municipio**; *map 1*), with its mysterious star of David, perhaps replacing a Jewish merchant's house. This south stretch of the Corso, called Borgo Medioevale, is lined with small medieval palaces, where supposedly Arab influences linger among the 15th-century Catalan Gothic details. Near no. 209 a wide flight of steps leads up to **Palazzo Ciampoli** (1412). At no. 185 is the former church of **San Giovanni** (1533), which is now a club for war veterans and is full of trophies and photographs. The glorious old **Hotel Metropol** at no.154, recently restored, has two columns recuperated from the Roman theatre.

Halfway along, Corso Umberto passes through the **Clock Tower** (?12th century, using blocks of stone cut by the Greeks; notice the beautiful modern mosaic of the Madonna, full of Byzantine symbolism; the gate was restored 1679), and opens into **Piazza IX Aprile** (often called Piazza Panoramica; *map 1–5*), where there is a superb view south across to the sea and Etna. The date refers to 9th April 1860, when the people of Taormina rebelled against the authority of the Bourbons during the Risorgimento: they were among the first in Sicily to do so. Several cafés here have tables outside, including the Mocambo, once one of the most celebrated hotspots in the town, notorious for scandalous brawls and assignations among the rich and famous, now with a mildly decadent atmosphere; Churchill's favourite was the Wunderbar.

On the north side is the former church of **Sant'Agostino** (1448), now the public library, with a Gothic doorway. To the west, approached by a pretty flight of steps, stands the 17th-century church of **San Giuseppe**, with a heavily decorated Rococo stucco interior, much in demand for fashionable weddings, and often used as a film set. Eight paintings of scenes from the life of the Virgin (*Nativity of Christ, Visitation, Annunciation, Marriage of the Virgin, Assumption, Rest on the Flight into Egypt, Presentation in the Temple* and *Adoration of the Magi*), painted for this church by an unknown Flemish artist in the late 17th century, have recently been returned to it after careful restoration; in many of the scenes, the city of Taormina appears in the background, seen from several viewpoints. Steps to the left of the church lead up to the Castello Saraceno (*see p. 442*) and Castelmola (*see p. 445*).

Between nos. 133 and 135, on the left as you head towards Piazza Vittorio Emanuele, is **Vicolo Stretto**, only 52cm wide, one of the narrowest streets in Italy. On the opposite side, near no. 100, steps (Via Naumachia) lead down to the so-called **Naumachia** (left), a long brick wall (122m) with niches (formerly decorated with statues) of late Roman date, now supporting a row of houses. Behind it is a huge cistern (*no admission*). The complex is thought to have been a monumental nymphaeum or part of a gymnasium.

After passing at no. 42 the pretty doorway and tiny rose window of the deconsecrated church of Santa Maria del Piliere, Corso Umberto reaches Piazza Vittorio Emanuele.

Piazza Vittorio Emanuele

Often called Piazza Badia, and the site of the ancient agora and the Roman forum, Piazza Vittorio Emanuele (*map 2*) is now a popular meeting-place, with shady *Ficus benjamin* trees and a taxi-stand. The two coffee-bars are ideal for people-watching and good for a Sicilian breakfast, ice cream, hot chocolate, or aperitifs. The Shaker Bar was the favourite of Tennessee Williams, who was in the habit of ordering a glass of whisky that he replenished from a hip flask, filled at a cheap wine store in the back streets, and sitting for hours here, reading or talking.

The west side of the square is occupied by **Palazzo Corvaja** (early 15th century; the central part is a 10th-century Arab structure), with mullioned windows and a 15th-century side-portal in Catalan Gothic form. The limestone ornamentation with black lava-stone inlay is characteristic of Taormina. Inside the courtyard is a staircase with a very worn relief of *Adam and Eve*. The building houses the tourist information office, where you will find a collection of authentic 19th-century marionettes and two Sicilian carts. The great hall, meeting-place in 1410 of the Sicilian Parliament, and other rooms, now house the **Museo Siciliano di Arte e Tradizioni Popolari** (*open 9–1 & 4–8, closed Mon; T: 0942 610274*), a collection donated by local antique dealer and antiquarian Giovanni Panarello, offering a synthesis of Sicilian handicrafts from the 16th–20th centuries. In the first room are pieces of decorated Sicilian carts, puppets and puppet-show posters, along with a section dedicated to shepherding in the Peloritan Mountains and Calabria: items made of wood and horn (collars for cows and sheep, spoons, bowls, flasks, kegs, walking-sticks and spindles). Engraved with geometric and fertility symbols, the decorations were also the proud stamp of property. The collars of animals never went with their sale. The spindles are usually decorated with a female figure. These, and decorated whalebones for corsets, were love-tokens from the shepherds to their women. There is also a good collection of anthropomorphic pottery from Caltagirone, Collesano, Patti and Seminara (Calabria), especially cache-pots representing human faces. In the second room is a collection of traditional Christmas cribs, made of ivory, coral and mother-of-pearl.

The 17th-century church of **Santa Caterina** has three large white stucco Baroque altars and a (very ruined) panel-painting on the high altar of the *Martyrdom of St Catherine* (16th century), by the native artist Jacopo Vignerio. In the floor of the nave, parts of a Hellenistic building have been revealed. A lovely 15th-century marble statue of St Catherine stands on a plinth with stories of her life and martyrdom. Behind the church are the scant remains of the **Odeon** or Teatrino Romano, incorporating part of the earlier Hellenistic structure. Built in the 1st century AD, it could hold 200 people. Excavations nearby have revealed public baths of the Imperial Roman period and traces of the forum.

The Greek Theatre

From Piazza Vittorio Emanuele, Via Teatro Greco leads east past souvenir shops and (on the right) **Villa Papale** (no. 41), once Palazzo Cacciola and the residence of Florence Trevelyan (*see opposite*). The street ends at a group of cypresses covered with bougainvillea beside the historic **Hotel Timeo** (*map 2*), with a pergola, the first hotel to be opened in the town in 1864. In 1850 the painter W.H. Bartlett had complained that 'anywhere but in Sicily a place like Taormina would be a fortune to the innkeepers, but here is not a single place where a traveller can linger to explore the spot'. Illustrious guests of the hotel have included Kaiser Wilhelm, King George V, Winston Churchill, the writers Thomas Mann, Oscar Wilde, Somerset Maugham and Tennessee Williams (who wrote *A Streetcar named Desire* and *Cat on a Hot Tin Roof* here), Rudolph Nureyev, Bob Dylan and Elton John.

Here also is the entrance to the magnificent **Greek Theatre** (*open 9–1hr before sunset; T: 0942 23220*), famous for its panoramic position, and acclaimed for its acoustic properties. First erected in the Hellenistic period (4th century BC), it was almost entirely rebuilt under the Romans when it was considerably altered (1st–3rd centuries AD). This is the largest ancient theatre in Sicily after that of Syracuse (109m in diameter; orchestra 35m across). The cavea, as was usual, was dug out of the hillside; above the nine wedge-shaped blocks of seats, a portico (partially restored in 1955) ran around the top (a few stumps of the 45 columns in front survive). The scena is well preserved; it must have had a double order of columns, the four now visible were erected during restoration carried out in the 19th century. The outer brick wall is pierced by three arched gates; the inner wall was once cased with marble. The foundations of the proscenium, or stage, remain, together with the parascenia, or wings, and traces of porticoes at the back. The superb view from the top of the cavea inspired Gustav Klimt, Paul Klee and many other artists, including the Hungarian colorist Tivadar Csontváry. Goethe, visiting in 1787, exclaimed: 'Never did any audience, in any theatre, have before it such a

Old aerial photo of the Greek Theatre, before the modern tiers of seating were constructed, clearly showing a number of salient features. The retaining semicircular wall and the buildings of the scena date from the third phase of building (early 2nd century AD). The remains of an underground room in the centre of the orchestra are earlier, from around the turn of the 1st centuries BC and AD.

spectacle.' On a clear day Etna is seen at its most majestic. In the other direction the Aspromonte Mountains of Calabria extend to the northern horizon, and inland the Peloritans stretch behind Castelmola.

The public gardens

By continuing down the steps after the Naumachia, you reach Via Bagnoli Croce and the beautiful public gardens, Parco Duca di Cesarò, among the loveliest in Italy (*map 6*). The gardens are colourful at all times of the year, with many different varieties of flowering plants and a vast array of Mediterranean and exotic trees. They were created in 1899 by Florence Trevelyan Cacciola (1852–1907), whose bust (a copy of her funerary monument) has been placed just inside the main entrance on Via Bagnoli Croce. The daughter of Lord Edward Spencer Trevelyan (cousin of the historian), Florence was lady-in-waiting to Queen Victoria, but she fell from favour and came to Taormina in 1881 with her four dogs, married the wealthy local doctor Salvatore Cacciola in 1890 and dedicated herself to charitable works among the poor of the town, and to her favourite hobbies: landscape gardening and birdwatching. In the heart of the garden, near her monument, is a group of mock Renaissance ruins, delightful Victorian follies which were used by Lady Florence as bird-feeders, with a maze of wooden terraces, antique fragments and lava-stone decoration. In Florence Trevelyan's day the gardens were known, after this construction, as 'The Beehives'. Outside the west entrance, a narrow road with steps descends to the Monte Tauro Hotel past a plaque which records the work of Mabel Hill (see p. 435)

Madonna della Rocca and the Castello Saraceno

Above the town, from the Circonvallazione, a path (signposted) leads up through trees to the tiny church of the **Madonna della Rocca**, carved into the rock. The Crucifix in front of it, which dominates all Taormina, was erected in 1743 by the grateful popula-tion when an epidemic of plague passed them by. Here, at a height of 398m, is the so-called **Castello Saraceno** (map 1; closed), from which there are wonderful views. The castle stands on the remains of the Greek acropolis, and shows signs of construction dating from Byzantine, Arab, Norman and Spanish times; forming part of a defensive system completed by the castles of Castelmola and Calatabiano, it was never captured by the enemy, although rebellious slaves held it for several months during the Servile War, before their commander accepted a bribe and let the Romans in. The slaves were tortured and then thrown from a high precipice. The return can be made by the 738 steps that link the serpentine loops of the Castelmola road.

Outside the centre and down to Mazzarò

Outside Porta Messina, at the lower end of a busy, downward-sloping square, by the beautiful Ashbee Hotel, is the church of **San Pancrazio** (map 2; St Pancras is the patron saint of Taormina), built on the ruins of a 4th-century BC Greek temple to Isis, Zeus and Serapis, still partly visible; the remains of Roman houses can be seen in the mid-dle of the square. Continuing downhill, you reach the Lumbi car park, and then the motorway entrance and the beach of Spisone. By turning right on exiting Porta Messina you are on the old Via Pirandello which winds down the hill past lovely gardens to Capo Taormina. You soon reach on the left the glass cableway station, and then, again on the left, (no. 24), surrounded by a little garden, is the Anglican **St George's church**, built by the British community in 1922, with lava-stone decoration on the exterior. It contains British and American funerary monuments, and memorials to the victims of the two World Wars. On the right is the bus terminal. Via Pirandello proceeds down by a little belvedere with a fine view of Isola Bella and Mazzarò, and then a series of **Byzantine tomb-recesses** in the wall below the former convent of Santa Caterina, and the attractive 1920s Villa Carlotta Hotel. It then passes the tiny 15th-century church of Santi Pietro e Paolo (open only for services), and the ruins of the unfinished Kursaal. By turning left on arriving at Capo Taormina, you reach the beach of Mazzarò and the bottom station of the cableway.

Mazzarò

The fishing-village of Mazzarò (map 4) by Capo Sant'Andrea (St Andrew is patron

Photograph of a young Sicilian boy in the guise of a 'Greek' shepherd, a work by the eccentric pioneer photographer Baron Wilhelm von Gloeden. This sitter at least is clad: Von Gloeden's most famous photographs show children naked, arranged in faintly suggestive postures.

saint of fishermen), with its sandy beach, is well supplied with hotels. A narrow isthmus leads to **Isola Bella** (*map 8; closed*), of great natural beauty, a famous symbol of Taormina. In the 19th century the government sold the island to Florence Trevelyan, who built a house on it. It was acquired by the Sicilian region in 1987, but its destiny is as yet uncertain. The whole bay enjoys protected status as a nature reserve. To the south are the sheer limestone cliffs of **Capo Taormina**, where 35 Roman columns lie submerged: they are unworked quarried stone, probably destined for a temple or the portico of a villa, which must have been lost in a shipwreck. This point is the wide part of the funnel formed by the Straits; the toe of the boot of Italy is 17km away. The beautiful cove just inside the promontory, at the foot of the northern slopes of the mountain of Taormina, looking out over the Straits, is the fashionable little **Spisone beach**, with white sand and crystal turquoise water, the most exclusive place for bathing.

GIARDINI NAXOS

Four kilometres south of Cape Taormina, Giardini Naxos (*map p. 536, C3*) was founded by a group of settlers led by Theocles of Naxos in 734 BC, and was the first Greek colony on Sicily, closely followed by Syracuse and Leontinoi. It flourished, thanks to the strategic position dominating the straits, but in 403 BC Dionysius of Syracuse, while extending his power over the island, sent an army to destroy Naxos, possibly in fear of a revolt because of the inhabitants' good relations with the Sicels. Some of the survivors fled to join the Sicels in what is now Taormina, while the others settled at Francavilla di Sicilia. In the Middle Ages it became a town of fishermen and lemon-growers (*giardini* means citrus groves in Sicilian). From this bay, Garibaldi, with two steamboats and 4,200 men, set out on his victorious campaign against the 30,000 Bourbon troops on the Aspromonte in Calabria (19th August 1860). This place, with a long main street parallel to the sea, was developed in the 1960s into a holiday resort. The wide bay is now lined with hotels, apartments and restaurants from Cape Schisò as far as the railway station of Taormina-Giardini, and new buildings have been erected wherever possible. The point of Cape Schisò, where the Greeks presumably made their landfall, was formed by an ancient lava flow which can still be clearly seen at the water's edge, by the little harbour. From the sea front there is a view of Monte Tauro, with Taormina and Castelmola, and south, a splendid view of Mount Etna.

Museo Archeologico

By the modern harbour wall is the entrance to the excavations of Naxos and the Archaeological Museum (*site and museum open daily 9–1 hr before sunset; T: 0942 51001*). The entrance is through a pretty garden, in which an ancient lava stream is still visible. An old Bourbon fort here has been restored to house the museum, which has a collection displayed chronologically on two floors and is well labelled. Recent finds on the site include pottery of the 8th century BC from the island of Naxos in the Ionian Sea, the first tangible proof that at least some of the first settlers came from there, and gave the name to this first Greek colony on Sicily.

Ground floor: Neolithic and Bronze-Age finds from the Cape including Stentinello ware. A Neolithic village site near Syracuse, Stentinello has given its name to the type of impressed ware which usually features round-based dishes with carefully stamped designs, which are also occasionally decorated to suggest human features, dating from c. 5600–4400 BC. Also here are Iron-Age finds from the necropolis of Mola including geometric-style pottery.

First floor: The main part of the museum displays terracottas and architectural fragments from a sanctuary at Santa Venera (6th century BC) and finds from a tomb nearby of the 3rd century BC, including four pretty vases for perfume and a glass bowl; material found in the area of the ancient city including a fine antefix with polychrome decoration, and Attic pottery; a little altar dating from around 540 BC decorated with sphinxes in relief; a statuette of a goddess (late 5th century BC); a rare marble lamp from the Cyclades found in the sea (late 7th century BC); and some exceptionally fine Greek coins, dating from 410–360 BC, many of them bearing the head of the satyr also known as Marsyas, who after losing a musical contest to which he had incautiously challenged Apollo, was tied to a tree and skinned alive by the god.

Garden: Beyond the lava flow a collection of underwater finds has been arranged in a small fort. It includes anchors (7th–4th century BC) and amphorae dating from various periods.

The excavations

The interesting excavations (well signposted) in the fields to the south are reached from the garden. A path, lined with bougainvillea, leads through the peaceful site of the ancient city. Excavations, which are ongoing, were first carried out here in 1953.

On the right a path leads across a field planted with lemon trees to a stretch of Greek walls. The main area of excavation is about 15mins' walk from the museum in a beautiful orchard planted with a wide variety of exotic trees, including lemons, palms, olives, oranges, eucalyptus and Japanese medlars (loquats), above flowering bougainvillea, hibiscus and jasmine. Prickly pear, agave and oleander plants also flourish here.

There is an impressive stretch of city walls in black lava stone (c. 500m) parallel to a line of eucalyptus trees. The West Gate is raised on two circular terraces. A path leads to the original entrance of the *area sacra*, and other remains from the 7th and 6th centuries, including part of the walls, an altar and a temenos of Aphrodite. A simple temple, constructed towards the end of the 7th century, was built over with a larger temple at the end of the 6th century. Under cover, two kilns are preserved, a circular one for water jars, and a rectangular one for tiles; both were in use during the late 6th and 5th centuries BC. Beyond is the Sea Gate with a fine polygonal lava-stone wall. The high wall, behind a row of cypresses, which blocks the view of the sea, was built during excavation work.

CASTELMOLA

Of probable Sicel origin, now a tiny town with a dwindling population, Castelmola (529m; *map p. 536, C3*) sits on top of a rock with a ruined Byzantine castle, high above Taormina; it forms part of the association of Italy's most beautiful villages. In the postage-stamp-sized square, with a view from the terrace of Etna and the bay of Naxos, the **Caffè San Giorgio** was founded in 1907 and has a famous collection of autographs in dozens of visitors' books, totalling many thousands of signatures. Castelmola is well known for its almond wine, which was invented here at the San Giorgio. Another picturesque café is in Piazza Duomo, the **Caffè Turrisi**, with an interesting collection of another sort, phalluses in every shape, form and material. The façade of the parish church of San Giorgio, reconstructed in Gothic style, opens onto a terrace with another wonderful panorama. The view is still better from Mt Venere or Veneretta (884m), reached by a long footpath from the cemetery of Castelmola.

THE PELORITAN MOUNTAINS

The Peloritan Mountains, in northeastern Sicily, of which the highest peak is the Montagna Grande (1374m), were once thickly forested, but now the slopes are carpeted with wildflowers in the spring, and barren for the rest of the year. Conspicuous features of the landscape are the *fiumare*—wide, flat-bottomed torrent beds filled with gravel, similar to the wadis of the Middle East, and usually waterless. With the autumn rain storms the water descends these channels in spate, carrying a considerable quantity of alluvial matter, and sometimes washing away roads, bridges and even villages.

SOUTHERN FOOTHILLS

Although the mountains are for the most part inaccessible, there are a number of remote little upland villages that can be reached by steep roads from the coast between Taormina and Messina.

Just north of Taormina, above the thriving holiday resort of **Letojanni**, with its sandy beach, bars and restaurants, are **Mongiuffi** and **Melia** (*map p. 536, C3*), characteristic of the hill villages on the southern slopes of the Peloritans. Pilgrimages are organised in summer to several sanctuaries of the Madonna here, following an ancient tradition.

Forza d'Agrò (*map p. 536, D3*) is a charming little medieval town, overlooking the privately-owned Arab-Norman castle on a spur of red Dolomitic limestone, a sacred spot for prehistoric populations, at Cape Sant'Alessio, from which the views extend along the straight coastline towards Messina, across the straits to Calabria and south to Taormina. Above the piazza a lane leads up to circular steps which ascend through a 15th-century Catalan Gothic archway, Arco Durazzesco, in front of the church of the Santa Trinità, with a 15th-century façade and campanile. It stands next to the former 15th-century Augustinian convent, with a cloister. A wide view of the coast can be had from the terrace behind the church. From the other side of the piazza, a narrow road leads through the village past the Baroque Chiesa Madre, with a lovely 16th-century façade, used as a setting in Francis Ford Coppola's *Godfather 2*. Opposite is a charming abandoned old house with pretty balconies. The road continues past old houses covered with flowering plants to the castle which was strengthened at the end of the 16th century by a double circle of walls, and which was used for many years as the cemetery.

Savoca

From the coastal town of Santa Teresa Riva, a byroad runs inland to Savoca (303m; *map p. 536, D3*), a village on a saddle between two hills, belonging to the association of Italy's most beautiful villages. In the Middle Ages this was a city, the most important in the province, controlling more territory and with a larger population than Messina, and rich because of its silk production.

In an old house in Piazza Fossia, at the entrance to the village, is the **Bar Vitelli**, with a flowery veranda, a collection of local artisans' tools, and photographs taken when Francis Ford Coppola shot some scenes of *The Godfather* here in July 1971. Facing the Bar Vitelli is a profile in stainless steel representing Coppola, by the local artist Nino Ucchino (more sculptures by this interesting artist can be seen along the seafront of Santa Teresa di Riva). Walk up the street, keeping left at the junction (fabulous view over mountains and valleys, studded with tiny villages, to Mt Etna), then through the old Porta della Città to the 15th-century church of **San Michele** (small exhibition of photographs regarding the local cult of St Lucy) with its two portals dating from the early 16th century. Near here is the **Museo Comunale Città di Savoca** (*open 9–1 & 4–8, 3–7 in winter; T: 0942 761125*), displaying a collection of furniture, household equipment, folk-medicine charms against illness and the Evil Eye, and information on the local aristocracy. Beyond the church of San Nicolò, usually known as **Santa Lucia** (with a 16th-century bust of St Lucy above the portal), the road continues up to the **Chiesa Madre**, built in the 12th century and restored in the 15th century. From here the remains of the 17th-century church of the **Immacolata** and the ruins of the Arab castle can be seen. The street continues round the mountain, bringing you back to the Bar Vitelli.

Outside the town in the church of the **Cappuccini** are catacombs (*open April–Sept 9–1 & 4–7, Oct–March 9–12 & 3–5, Sun afternoons only, closed Mon*) which once preserved the mummified bodies, fully dressed, of citizens who lived here in the 18th century, but the corpses were vandalised with green paint a few years ago and although now restored, they are in undignified wooden crates.

Casalvecchio Siculo

Casalvecchio Siculo (*map p. 536, D3*) is charmingly situated on the slopes of a hill. This was the Byzantine *Palachorion*, meaning 'ancient outpost'. Next to the 16th-century **Chiesa Madre** (which has a beautiful wooden Baroque ceiling), in the central Piazza Crisafulli, is an interesting little **Museo di Arte Sacra** (*T: 0942 761030 to request visit*), with religious paintings and other works of art, also tools used by farmers and craftsmen, dating from the 12th–20th centuries.

The narrow Via Sant'Onofrio continues through the village; beyond, after c. 700m a very narrow road (in places single-track) leads left and descends through lovely countryside to one of the most complex and interesting Norman constructions in Sicily, the church of **Santissimi Pietro e Paolo d'Agrò** (*open 9–sunset; T: 0942 761008*). On the site of a Basilian monastery built during the Byzantine domination in the 6th century, this imposing and elegant church occupies a beautiful, lonely spot near the Agrò torrent. Begun in 1116, it is extremely well preserved both inside and out. An inscription over the door relates how Gerardo il Franco dedicated it to Sts Peter and Paul for the Basilian monks in 1172; having suffered intense damage from earthquakes and Arab incursions, it was probably also restored at this time. Built of brick and black lavastone, the exterior has splendid polychrome decoration. The Byzantine interior also shows Arab influence in the stalactite vaulting and the tiny domes in the apse and nave. The stucco was removed from the walls in the 20th century to reveal the attractive brickwork. The columns made from Sardinian granite appear to be Roman in origin. It is possible to return to the coast road from here along a very rough road on the gravel bed of the wide torrent (*fiumara*).

Along the coast to Messina

Back on the coast road, a byroad leads inland to **Fiumedinisi** (*map p. 536, D2*), where the duomo, probably of Norman origin, has an interesting interior with monolithic columns made of the local marble, and an unusual raised transept. Here, over the north altar, is a Byzantine-style fresco of the *Madonna and Child*. The Fiumedinisi torrent is one of the most important of these mountains; much of its water is channelled off to supply the needs of Messina. The bed of the torrent is rich in silver ore, exploited until the 18th century for minting coins.

Famous for its thermal baths and mineral springs, **Alì Terme** (*map p. 536, D3*) has been visited since the 18th century for the treatment of various ailments. From here the Calabrian coastline is in full view. A winding road leads up to the picturesque village of Alì, sadly suffering from depopulation. It is formed of two distinct parts, an Islamic settlement on the southern slopes of Mt Santa Lena, and a 16th-century enlargement on the eastern hill, with the Chiesa Madre (1582), dedicated to the patron St Agatha.

Itala (*map p. 536, D2*) is built on the side of a valley with lush vegetation. Above the village a road (very narrow in places) continues uphill and then left past ancient olive trees and lemon groves to the well-preserved church of San Pietro. It is preceded by a delightful little courtyard with a garden and palm trees. The priest who has the key lives in the house by the church. The church was built in 1093 by Count Roger in thanksgiving for the Norman victory over the Arabs and has a handsome exterior with blind arcading and a little dome; the interior also presents a raised transept, like that of the church of Fiumedinisi; among the works of art is a 16th-century painted Crucifix and a 16th-century panel-painting of the *Madonna with Two Saints*.

Scaletta Zanclea has a long narrow main street (still the main coast road); fishingboats are kept in the alleyways which lead down to the sea under the railway line. The street is particularly busy in the mornings when fresh fish is sold from stalls here. In the upper town the remains of the 13th-century Castello Ruffo lie beneath Mt Poverello (1279m), one of the highest peaks of the Peloritans.

Mili San Pietro (*map p. 536, D2*) is in a pretty wooded valley with terraced vineyards and orange groves. On the outskirts of the village (by the school), is the primitive little Norman church of Santa Maria di Mili (*open 9–12 & 4–7*), dating from 1092 and founded together with a small convent of Basilian monks by Count Roger as a burial place for his favourite (though illegitimate) son Jourdain; it can be seen just below the road to the left. Steps descend to the ruins of a house, from which the church can be reached under the arch to the left. It has a very interesting vaulted interior.

THE NORTHERN PELORITANS

The northern coast road (*map p. 536, D2*) follows almost exactly the same route as the Roman consular road, Via Valeria, which once joined Messina to Syracuse (south) and Lilybaeum (north). At sea off Venetico, Agrippa defeated the fleet of Sextus Pompey at the Battle of Naulochos (36 BC). Inland from the attractive coastal town of **Spadafora**, famous for its bricks, a road climbs the mountains to **Roccavaldina**, with the imposing palace of its feudal Barone Valdina in the central Piazza Umberto. On the corner is the famous 16th-century Farmacia (*open Mon–Fri 9.30–1; T: 090 9977741*). The Tuscan-style archway at the entrance to the pharmacy is very rare in Sicily. Inside are 256 16th-century decorated majolica pharmacy jars from the Patanazzi workshop of Urbino, perfectly preserved on their original shelves.

Santa Lucia del Mela

A narrow road leads up to Santa Lucia del Mela (*map p. 536, C2*), clinging to the hillside crowned by the ruins of the Arab-Norman castle. The fine **cathedral** (*if closed ring at Via Cappuccini 3, the priest's house*) in the central square is of medieval origins with a 15th-century portal, and a font dated 1485. The first south altarpiece, the *Martyrdom of St Sebastian* (in poor condition), is attributed to the Zoppo di Gangi; on the second altar is a painting of *St Mark the Evangelist* by Deodato Guinaccia (1581) and a statuette of the *Ecce Homo* attributed to Ignazio Marabitti. In the south transept is a painting of St Blaise by Pietro Novelli. In the chapel to the right of the sanctuary there is a marble statue of St Lucy (1512). The high altarpiece of the *Assumption* is by Fra' Felice da Palermo (1771). In the chapel to the left of the sanctuary is an unusual little sculpted *Last Supper* in the altar frontal, attributed to Valerio Villareale. The altarpiece in the north transept is by Filippo Jannelli (1676), and on the third north altar is an 18th-century Crucifix.

Next to the cathedral is the **Palazzo Vescovile** (Bishop's Palace; *T 090 935008 to request visit*), with a small collection of works of art. Other churches of interest (*open only for services*) include the **Santissima Annunziata**, with a campanile of 1461 and a painting of the *Madonna and Child* of c. 1400, and **Santa Maria di Gesù** (or Sacro Cuore) with a Crucifix by Fra' Umile da Petralia. The road leads up to the **castle**, first built by the Arabs, then restructured by the Normans and by Frederick II of Aragon when he repopulated the town with a colony of Lombards in 1322. All that remains of the old fortress is a triangular-plan tower and a round keep. Now it houses the seminary and the sanctuary of the Madonna della Neve (1673) with a *Madonna and Child* by Antonello Gagini.

The Scifo Forest and Barcellona-Pozzo di Gotto

A narrow mountain road (surfaced as far as Calderado) snakes along a crest into the Peloritan Mountains, from Santa Lucia del Mela as far as Pizzo Croce (1214m). The beautiful **Scifo Forest** here (*map p. 536, D2*), with chestnuts, oaks and ash trees, has recently been preserved with the help of the local division of the WWF, and you may spot the pine marten, especially in spring when they are less shy.

Barcellona-Pozzo di Gotto (*map p. 536, C2*) is a busy agricultural centre, famous for its nurseries of ornamental and flowering plants and fruit trees, mostly citrus. Founded in the 17th century, it has some interesting churches, such as the Chiesa Madre, and the church of San Giovanni, and at the eastern extremity of the town, a well-kept museum of farming tradition, the Museo Etno-Anthropologico 'Nello Cassata' (*Contrada Manno 10; open 9–1 & 4–7, morning only on Mon; T: 090 9761883*), the largest and most complete of its kind in Sicily. Nello Cassata was a 19th-century collector and keen local historian. Allow at least an hour to browse among the 13,000 artefacts, including old vehicles, wine and olive-presses, looms, fascinating old clocks and sundials. There is a coffee-shop on the premises. From Barcellona a steep and narrow road leads up to the thickly-forested **Parco Jalari** (*open 2.30–5.30, closed Mon and Fri; T: 090 9702110*), where the theme is water and stone. There are sculptures, pretty stone buildings and fountains, and from the park there is a fine view of Castroreale.

Castroreale

Perched on a mountain crag like an eagle's nest, Castroreale (394m; *map p. 536, C2*) was once the favourite residence of Frederick II of Aragon, from whose castle it gets its name. Despite damage in the earthquake of 1978, the little town is unusually well preserved. The **Chiesa Madre** contains a *St Catherine* by Antonello Gagini (1534) and a magnificent organ dated 1612, recently restored and in regular use. From Piazza dell'Aquila there is a fine view of the fertile plain. The Corso leads to the church of the **Candelora**, with a Moorish dome and a 17th-century carved and gilded wooden high altarpiece.

In Via Guglielmo Siracusa is the old church of **Santa Maria degli Angeli** (*T: 090 9746514 (Arcipretura) or 090 9746534 (Museo Civico) to request visit*), probably built on the synagogue, which contains a gallery with interesting paintings and two sculptures (*St John the Baptist* by Andrea Calamech, 1568; and a *Madonna* by Antonello Freri, 1510), and a rich collection of Church silver and vestments. Further on, at Piazza Marconi 31, is the fine **Museo Civico** (*open summer 1 June–31 Aug 9–1 & 4–8; winter 9–1 & 3–7; closed Wed pm; T: 090 9746633*), housed in the restored former oratory of San Filippo Neri, with a charming balcony decorated with prancing horses and lions above the doorway. The collection of sculpture and paintings comes from local churches. On the ground floor are Crucifixes, including a painted one dating from the mid–15th century, Antonello de Saliba's *Madonna and Child Enthroned with Angels* (a panel from a dismembered polyptych), and a sarcophagus with the effigy of Geronimo Rosso by Antonello Gagini (1507). On the first floor are vestments, precious books, ceramic tiles, and 18th-century paintings, including works by Fra' Felice da Sambuca. An 18th–19th-century silver Cross is from the Chiesa Madre.

At the end of the street is the church of **Sant'Agata**, with a charming *Annunciation* by Antonello Gagini, dated 1519. At the top of the town a circular tower survives from the ruined **castle**, founded by Frederick II of Aragon in 1324.

Terme Vigliatore to Montalbano Elicona

Back on the coast road, just short of **Terme Vigliatore** (a thermal resort with a spring called Fonte di Venere, used for the treatment of gastrointestinal and liver ailments) at **San Biagio** (Via Nazionale 3; *map p. 536, C2*), are the remains of a large Roman villa (*open 9–5; T: 090 9740488*). Dating from the 1st century AD, the remains of a large peristyle and part of the baths can be seen. Several rooms, protected by a plastic roof, have black and white mosaics, mostly geometric, and one floor is decorated with a lively fishing scene: dolphins, swordfish and other fish still found off the coast here can be made out. The main hall has a fine *opus sectile* pavement.

Inland near the long-drawn-out settlement of **Rodì** and **Milici**, overlooking the Patri river valley, is the site of ancient *Longane*, a Sicel town of some importance, which was no longer inhabited by the 5th century BC. Traces of the walls survive and the foundations of a sacred building.

From Terme Vigliatore a road (SS 185) runs inland across the western side of the Peloritans (rising to a height of 1100m), connecting the Tyrrhenian coast with the Ionian Sea at Giardini Naxos. This quiet and exceptionally scenic road follows the wide Mazzarrà and Novara valleys, with their extensive citrus-fruit plantations.

Novara di Sicilia (*map p. 536, C3*), the ancient *Noae*, refounded by the Normans who populated it with Lombards, is now a quiet little town below the main road. From Largo Bertolami, with a 19th-century bronze statue of *David*, Via Duomo leads down to the 16th-century duomo. In the south aisle is a wooden statue of the *Assumption* by Filippo Colicci. In Via Bellini there is a beautiful little 19th-century opera house.

The fantastic bare horn-shaped **Rocca Novara** (1340m) stands at the end of the Peloritan range. The pass of Sella Mandrazzi beyond is surrounded by thick woods of pine and fir. The view extends to the coastline and the sanctuary of Tindari on its promontory. The scenery is particularly lovely in this area. From here the mountain road descends through deserted pastureland and eventually left through orange groves to Francavilla di Sicilia (*see p 403*). Another very winding minor road leads southwest from Terme Vigliatore to **Montalbano Elicona** (*map p. 536, C3*), a little hill town in a fine position surrounded by woods, with a spectacular, remarkably well-preserved castle (*open April–Oct 9–12 & 3–7, winter mornings only; T: 0941 679012*), built by Frederick II of Aragon in 1302.

MILAZZO

The main port for ferries and hydrofoils to the Aeolian Islands, Milazzo (*map p. 536, C2*) stands on the isthmus of a narrow peninsula on the northeast coast of the island. It is an old city with considerable charm, marred by an oil refinery and power station on the outskirts. Milazzo was the ancient *Mylae*, founded as a sub-colony by Greeks from Zancle (Messina) in 716 BC. Here Gaius Duilius defeated the Carthaginians under Hannibal Gisco in the first major naval battle between Rome and Carthage (260 BC), and here in 1860 Garibaldi successfully assaulted the castle, garrisoned by Bourbon troops, promoting J.W. Peard, a Cornish volunteer, to the rank of colonel on the field. The castle, with its successive and extensive modifications, demonstrates the strategic importance of the town in the past.

EXPLORING MILAZZO

NB: All churches are open for visits from 4.30–8. For info, T: 090 9231292/3.

Piano

The town is divided into the older, higher district, Borgo Antico, and the lower-lying, more modern district, Piano, which is now the centre. The road for the centre passes the port where the boats and hydrofoils for the Aeolian Islands dock. In Via Crispi is the late 19th-century Neoclassical Municipio. On the other side of the building (reached through the courtyard) is Piazza Caio Duilio. Here is the harmonious red façade of the former convent of the Carmelitani (16th century; restored). Next to it is the Baroque façade of the Carmine (1574; rebuilt in 1726–52), and, on the other side of the square, Palazzo Proto, Garibaldi's headquarters for a time in 1860. In Via Pescheria, behind the post office, fresh fish is sold in the mornings from stalls in the street.

The marine parade (Lungomare Garibaldi), planted with trees, is a continuation of Via Crispi along the sea front. The 18th-century church of San Giacomo is well-sited at a fork in the road which leads to the Duomo Nuovo (1937–52), which contains paintings by Antonello de Saliba and Antonio Giuffrè, and sculptures attributed to the Gagini school. Further on, Via Colombo leads away from the sea past two little Art Nouveau villas, Villino Greco and Villa Vaccarino, now surrounded by unattractive buildings.

Borgo Antico

From Piazza Roma, Via Impallomeni leads up towards the castle past the 18th-century Baroque church of San Francesco di Paola, which contains six paintings of miracles of the saint by Letterio Paladino. The **Antiquarium Domenico Ryolo** (*open 9–7, closed Sun and holidays*) houses in six rooms a large collection of material found in the necropoleis surrounding the city. The various burials shed interesting light on life and death in the area from the 8th to the 1st centuries BC, and show the evolution of Greek and Roman influence on the population. Terracotta vases were widely used for burying the dead, who were interred in the foetal position, or cremated. The presence of pottery from all over the Mediterranean demonstrates the role of ancient Mylae, an important harbour at the centre of the trade routes of the time. The old prison for women, built in 1816 and abandoned around 1960, has thus been put to good use.

From here the 17th-century church of the Immacolata and the church of San Rocco with its crenellated top can be seen above on the left. Just short of here, on the right, is the closed church of San Salvatore (18th century) by Giovanni Battista Vaccarini. Picturesque low houses and open-air cafés (in the summer) surround the double walls of the **castle** (*guided tours only, at 9.30, 10.30, 11.30, 5, 6, 7; closed Mon; T: 090 9231292-3*). Built by the Arabs in the 10th–11th centuries on the site of the Greek acropolis, enlarged by Frederick II in 1239, then by the Aragonese in the 14th century, by Charles V in the 16th century, and restored in the 17th century. The Spanish walls date from the 16th century and enclose a large area used for theatrical performances and concerts in the summer. Here are the remains of the Palazzo dei Giurati, used as a prison in the 19th century, and the Duomo Antico, an interesting late 17th-century building attributed to Camillo Camilliani or possibly Natale Masuccio. It was abandoned when the new cathedral was begun in 1937. In the same area a Gothic doorway leads to the oldest structures of the castle: the imposing Arab-Norman keep and a great hall known as the Sala del Parlamento. From the castle, a flight of steps leads to the church of the Rosary, built in the 16th century and restored in the 18th. The convent by the church housed the Inquisition.

Capo Milazzo

The narrow peninsula of Capo Milazzo is simply called *il Capo* by the local people. The road threads its way through olive groves and prickly pears to a point where steps go down to the sanctuary of St Anthony of Padua, a little church (1575) built in a cave where the saint took refuge after a shipwreck in January 1221. A path continues to a lighthouse and down to a stony beach and the crystal-clear sea. It is a beautiful spot, but crowded on summer weekends with bathers. From the cape the view (on a clear day) encompasses all the Aeolian Islands, and also Mount Etna.

CAPO TINDARI TO CAPO D'ORLANDO

On the headland of **Capo Tindari** (*map p. 536, C2*) stands a conspicuous church near the excavations of the ancient city of *Tyndaris* founded in the 4th century BC. The road leads to a car park below the church, a modern sanctuary built in 1957–79, to house a seated Byzantine-style statue of the **Black Madonna**, greatly venerated since the 10th century (pilgrimage on 8th Sept) when it was found in a wooden chest on the beach under the cliff, apparently abandoned by pirates. The life-size statue of the Madonna, her Child and her throne has recently been restored and divested of the white silk robe which covered her for centuries. It is made of a single large block of painted cedar wood from Lebanon and was probably made in the 7th or 8th century, although it is not known where. The well-preserved red and blue colours with which the group is painted symbolise divinity and humanity. The structure of the new church encloses the old 16th-century sanctuary, on the seaward side, with a portal of 1598 (*the custodian has the key*) and an interesting reproduction of the Madonna, allowing a closer look. From the terrace in front of the church there are splendid views of the Aeolian Islands. The currents in the shallows at the foot of the cliffs produce beautiful formations of sand and gravel and areas of temporary marshland that are of great interest to naturalists.

The ruins of *Tyndaris*

From the car park a path and steps lead up to the road which brings you to the entrance to the impressive ruins of ancient *Tyndaris* (*map p. 536, C2; open 9–1hr before sunset; T: 0941 369023*). The ancient city was founded by Dionysius of Syracuse in 396 BC after his victory over the Carthaginians, when he felt the need to have a permanent base on the north coast. To achieve this aim, he forcibly transferred the entire population of Leontinoi there. Tyndaris remained an ally of Syracuse until taken by the Romans in 254 BC. A large part of the city slipped into the sea during an earthquake caused by the eruption of Vesuvius in AD 79, and then by another earthquake in AD 365. Excavations begun in the 19th century by Robert Fagan, then British Consul, were resumed from 1949–64, and are still in progress.

A path leads down through a little garden to the excavations in a grove of olives and pines planted with bougainvillea and prickly pear. The beautiful, peaceful site overlooks fields with olive trees on a cliff directly above the sea. To the right, along the **decumanus maximus**, are the remains of Roman buildings, including a series of tabernae, two private houses (with peristyle and mosaics), and a bath-house with black and white mosaics. At the end of the decumanus is the **Basilica**, once called the Gymnasium, but now thought to have been the magistrates' court, or a monumental entrance to the agora (which is thought to lie under the square in front of the church). The façade, which collapsed in Byzantine times, was restored in 1956. It is an unusual building with barrel vaulting across the main road of the city.

To the left of the entrance is the large **theatre**, a Greek building adapted by the Romans for use by gladiators. A long stretch of the nicely paved decumanus has recently been excavated near the theatre, and the front steps of an extremely large public building have been revealed on the south side. To the north of the decumanus, at the far western end of the site is a large early Imperial brick-built **funerary monument**. The **Greek walls** (3rd century BC), obscured by vegetation on the seaward side, survive in a good state of preservation to the south (beside the approach road below the sanctuary), extending, with interval towers, for several hundred metres on either side of the main gate, which takes the form of a dipylon with a barbican.

The **antiquarium** has a reconstruction of the theatre's monumental stage and backdrop, and finds from the site, including a colossal head of the emperor Augustus (1st century).

Patti

Some 7km west of Tindari, Patti (*map p. 536, C2*) is an important agricultural town on a hill, renowned for its colourful ceramics; as the proverb has it: 'If you want a tasty dish, cook it in a pot from Patti'. Founded in 1094 as a Benedictine monastery by Count Roger, the first king of Sicily, the town grew and became prosperous, especially when it became the seat of a bishopric. It was looted and burned by the pirate Kheir ed-Din Barbarossa in 1554, and more recently, in 1978 the town was severely damaged by an earthquake. The **cathedral**, consecrated on 6th March 1094 and dedicated to the patron saints Bartholomew and Febronia, dominates the city. In the south transept is the Renaissance tomb of Queen Adelaide (d. 1118), third wife of Count Roger and mother of Roger II. She died of leprosy in the local Benedictine monastery, where she had withdrawn after the annulment of her marriage to Baldwin of Jerusalem. He had sought her hand because of the rich dowry she would bring as Count Roger's widow, and once he had secured it, he declared their nuptials null and void. There are some fine paintings over the side altars, including a *Madonna and Child Enthroned* (1531) by Antonello de Saliba, and the *Adoration of the Shepherds* by Willem Borremans.

Next to the cathedral is the **Diocesan Museum** (*Via Cattedrale 7; open 9–1 & 3–7, 4–8 from May–Sept; Sat and Sun mornings only; closed Mon; T: 0941 240866, www.diocesi-patti.it*), with a rich collection of bishop's vestments, missals, silverware, paintings and marble reliefs from local churches.

Marina di Patti

A **collection of the famous local pottery** is displayed at Marina di Patti (*map p. 536, C2*), in the old Villa Pisani (*open 9.30–1 & 2–8, closed Sun and holidays; T: Biblioteca 0941 361663*), with over 650 objects with the typical colours and decorations of Patti, including cooking pots, serving dishes, jugs, and large bowls for washing clothes.

During the construction of the motorway from Messina part of a large **Roman villa** (*open 9–7; T: 0941 361593*) was uncovered here in 1973 (follow the signs for Marina di Patti and the motorway: the entrance to the site is beneath the motorway viaduct). This large villa (4th century AD; about 20,000m square including ancillary buildings) was made up of three main structures, with three different orientations. On the western side there are the remains of walls relating to rooms. The main structures centre on a large peristyle with a pillared portico; on the northeast side part of a bath-house has been brought to light. The villa also contains a few polychrome mosaics with geometric and floral designs as well as hunting scenes. There is a small, recently renovated antiquarium on the site with objects found during the excavation, including coins, carved reliefs, fragments of sculpture and pottery. Although the villa was destroyed by an earthquake, perhaps in the 5th century, the area was inhabited continually at least until the 10th century, and the remains of tombs have also been found.

Gioiosa Marea and Brolo

A seaside resort, **Gioiosa Marea** (*map p. 536, B2*) was built in the 18th century after an earthquake destroyed the old town of Gioiosa Guardia (or Gioiosa Vecchia). The alluring ruins of the old town survive high up (828m) on a hill beyond the motorway. A winding road leads up to them, from where there is a wonderful view of the coast and the Aeolian Islands. Vulcano is only 19km offshore.

Midway between Gioiosa and Capo d'Orlando is the charming medieval village of **Brolo**, with a maze of narrow cobbled streets leading up to the well-kept, photogenic castle (*open May–June 9–1 & 4–8; July–Sept 9–1 & 4–midnight; Oct–April Sat, Sun and holidays only, 9–1 & 3–7; T: 0941 562600*) which houses several interesting exhibits on torture, weapons, coastal defences and watch-towers.

Capo d'Orlando

According to legend, the peaceful resort of Capo d'Orlando (*map p. 536, B2*), with a rocky promontory (noted for its sudden storms) and sandy beaches, was founded by one of the sons of the wind god Aeolus and known as *Agathyrnum*. In 210 BC the Roman governor punished its inhabitants for engaging in local banditry by deporting 4,000 inhabitants, and the town declined until the days of Charlemagne, who refounded it with the name of Orlando, his favourite knight. Frederick II of Aragon was defeated off the headland in 1299 by Roger of Lauria, commanding the allied fleets of Catalonia and Anjou. The promontory is crowned by the ruins of the 14th-century **Castello d'Orlando** and the 16th-century sanctuary church of Maria Santissima, the patron saint. A modern building at Via del Fanciullo 1 houses the **Antiquarium** (*open Tues–Sat 9–1 & 3–7, Sun 4–8; closed Mon; T: 0941 911392*) with archaeological material found in the vicinity, recently returned from the principal museums of the island. On the first floor is the **Pinacoteca Tono Zancanaro** (*open 9–1 & 3–7, closed Sun; T: 0941 912946*), a collection of paintings depicting Capo d'Orlando, all of which were winning entries in an annual competition held since 1955; over 200 artists from all over the world are represented, including Giuseppe Migneco, who first organised the event.

Just outside town to the south, at Contrada Vina 44, is the **Fondazione Famiglia Piccolo di Calanovella** (*open 9–12, Tues–Fri also 3–6; closed Mon; T: 0941 957029*), the house and garden of the Calanovella family, now protected as a foundation instituted by the last descendants. The beautifully-kept rooms and gardens are a poignant testimony to the lives led by these artistic, withdrawn and proudly Sicilian aristocrats in the middle of the 20th century, and to an era that was drawing to a close. Baron Lucio Piccolo, a prize-winning poet, was a cousin of Giuseppe Tomasi di Lampedusa (*see p. 207*), and encouraged him to write his famous novel *The Leopard*, while his sister Agata Giovanna was a keen gardener and botanist, and their brother Casimiro a gifted photographer who also painted watercolours. In the garden is the cemetery of their cats and dogs.

To the east, at **Lido di San Gregorio**, there is a beautiful sandy beach and a little fishing harbour. Nearby is the Villa Bagnoli (*open 9–7, closed Mon; T: 0941 955401*): excavations of a luxurious **Roman villa** built in the late 4th or early 5th century AD, surrounded by a little garden. Eight rooms, some with coloured mosaic floors, have been unearthed, as well as the bath-house.

THE NEBRODI MOUNTAINS

The Parco dei Nebrodi (*map p. 536, A3–B3*) is a protected area of great natural beauty, stretching from the Peloritans in the east to the Madonie Mountains in the west. The mountains have an average height of 1200–1500m and are the largest forested area to survive on the island. The remarkable landscape changes constantly. The wide variety of trees includes oak, elm, beech, holm oak, cork and yew, and is especially fine in the Caronia forest. The forests are home to the porcupine, the wildcat and the pine marten; the last wolves disappeared in the 1920s. At Rocche del Crasto, one of the highest peaks of the park near Alcara Li Fusi, there are golden eagles and griffon vultures, besides the lanner and the peregrine falcons. These mountains have abundant water, with many streams, small lakes and springs. The upland plains provide pastureland for numerous farm animals which roam free, including cows, sheep, goats and black pigs, a breed endemic to Sicily. The San Fratello breed of horses (identified by their characteristic rounded noses) are now protected and allowed to run free in the forest. Renowned ricotta, cheeses and salted hams are made by the local farmers.

Monte Soro (1847m) is the highest peak of the Nebrodi. The Biviere di Cesarò (1200m) is a beautiful natural lake with interesting birdlife (including herons, black-winged stilts and great white herons on migration), and a spectacular view of Etna. Nearby Lago Maulazzo is an artificial lake constructed in the 1980s for irrigation but never put into operation. In this area are numerous Turkey oaks, maple trees, beech woods, and wild mushrooms (especially the delicious *boletus*, known locally as *porcino*, 'little pig'). In spring beautiful wild flowers bloom and the hillsides are covered with broom. The colours in autumn are also spectacular. The small towns and villages each have something particular to offer.

THE EASTERN NEBRODI

An old road leads from Capo d'Orlando across the eastern Nebrodi Mountains to Randazzo below Etna. It passes picturesque **Naso** (*map p. 536, B2*), which has 15th–17th-century tombs in the church of Santa Maria del Gesù. The church contains a monument to Artale Cardona (d. 1477) in Gothic-Renaissance style; the Cardona family were once lords of Naso. Other churches in Naso are the church of the Santissimo Salvatore, the Chiesa Madre and the church of San Cono, which has a 17th-century chapel with inlaid marble walls and the reliquary of St Conus, the patron saint. In the 19th century the town was prosperous enough to build an elegant theatre, the Teatro Alfieri. Lady Gaga's grandfather, a shoemaker, came from Naso.

Around Tortorici and Frazzanò

After about 20km a narrow road branches off to the west, reaching **Tortorici** (*map p. 536, B3*), famous for the medieval painted ceilings in its churches, in particular that of San Francesco d'Assisi. The town was also renowned for its bell foundries. You can visit the Fonderia Trusso (*T: 0941 423111, 328 6590199 to request visit*) in Via Torrente Calcagni, in which the combustion and fusion chambers are still intact. Bells from Tortorici are still ringing in many Italian churches. The road continues back towards the coast, passing **San Salvatore di Fitalia** (*map p. 536, B2*), a tiny village with an interesting Museo delle Tradizioni Religiose (*Via Colonnello Musarra 15; open 10–1, closed Mon; T: 0941 486027*) dedicated to ex-votos, *naïf* pictures, sometimes painted on glass, left in the sanctuaries of the saints or the Madonna as thanksgiving for miraculous recovery from illness, or equally miraculous delivery from situations of great danger.

Floresta (*map p. 536, B3*), with its lovely houses of pale grey stone, slow pace and women embroidering in front of their doors, at a height of 1275m is the highest municipality in Sicily, with winter-sports facilities. The road reaches a summit level of 1,280m before descending in full view of Etna to Randazzo.

From the coastal highway a road climbs from Rocca di Caprileone to the old town of **Capri Leone** and to **Frazzanò** (*map p. 536, B2*), where Count Roger built the Basilian monastery and church of San Filippo di Fragalà (*open Mon–Fri 9–1 & 2.30–6.30; T: 0941 959037, 329 1333928*), with three high apses, a large transept and a polychrome exterior of red bricks and local stone. A seat of learning, the monastery had an important library that was dispersed in 1866. Among the few remnants saved and now in Palermo, is the oldest document yet found in Europe written on paper, an edict sent by Queen Adelaide to the abbot in 1099.

From here the road continues up to the ancient centres of **Longi** and **Galati Mamertino**, which has some notable works of art, including two marble statues of the *Madonna* attributed to the Gagini school in the Chiesa Madre, and a Crucifix by Fra' Umile di Petralia, thought by some to be his finest, in the church of Santa Caterina.

San Marco d'Alunzio

At San Marco d'Alunzio (*map p. 536, B2*), Robert Guiscard built the first **Norman castle** in Sicily in 1061 (it survives in ruins at the top of the hill). The interesting little hill town has 22 churches built of a distinctive local red marble (called *rosso di San Marco*). At the entrance to the town, on a spectacular site overlooking the sea, is the **Temple of Herakles**, dating from the Hellenistic era: on the red marble basement a Norman church (now roofless) was built. Later a Baroque portal and windows were added. Above the road on the right is the **church of the Aracoeli**, with a Baroque portal. The interior, including the columns, has local red marble decorations. On the right side a marble altar has a gilded wooden statue of St Michael Archangel, and another chapel has a fine red marble altarpiece. Via Aluntia continues past (left) the deconsecrated 12th-century church of Santa Maria dei Poveri (used for exhibitions) and then descends past the Town Hall and a fountain. On the left is the **Chiesa Madre** (San Nicolò) built in 1584. It has a very unusual triumphal arch with large marble sculptures and an 18th-century organ. In the north aisle, the fourth chapel has a 16th-century painting of the *Madonna of the Rosary* in a fine frame, and the fifth chapel a wooden 16th-century processional statue of the *Immaculate Virgin*.

A road leads uphill to the left past the tiny church of San Giovanni and then down to the side of the hill where San Giuseppe has a lovely portal. There is a fine view of the sea from here. On the left of the façade is the entrance to the **Diocesan Museum of Sacred Art** (*T: Circolo Anspi Demenna, 329 6084536, 329 6091423 to request visit*). In the vestibule are the original capitals from the portal of the church, as well as vestments and statues. The rest of the collection is arranged in the church, which has a lovely red, grey and blue floor and decorative stuccoes. The collection of miscellaneous objects includes a sculpture of the *Madonna dell'Odigitria* by Giuseppe Li Volsi (1616), statues, reliquaries, and church furniture.

Higher up in the town is the tiny church of **Maria Santissima delle Grazie**, with a delightful carved high altar with a statue of the *Madonna and Child with the Young St*

John, and, on either side, two imposing tombs of the Filangieri family, one with an effigy (1481) and the other in red marble (1600). Opposite, built on the rock, is the church of San Basilio.

A short distance south of San Marco d'Alunzio, by the church of San Teodoro, is the ex-Benedictine monastery or Badia Nica (Via Ferrarolo 96), housing the **Museo della Cultura e delle Arti Figurative Bizantine e Normanne** (*open 9.15–1.15 & 3.15–7.15; T: 0941 797719*), with a collection of frescoes removed from the many churches of the town, and displayed with admirable clarity. Beneath San Teodoro there is a Byzantine chapel with interesting remains of frescoes.

Sant'Agata di Militello and the Nebrodi Park

A seaside resort, from which climbing expeditions may be made in the Nebrodi Mountains Park, **Sant'Agata di Militello** (*map p. 536, B2*) also contains the Palazzo Gentile on Via Cosenz, on the sea front, which houses the Museo Etnoantropologico dei Nebrodi (*open 9–1, closed Sun and holidays; T: 0941 722308, 0941 701000*) with a collection devoted to mountain life, divided into three sections: the role of women and women's work; shepherds; and traditions and religious customs.

Alcara Li Fusi (*map p. 536, B3*) is a little mountain village beneath the Rocche del Crasto mountain (1315m). Excursions into the Nebrodi park can easily be organised from here. The mountain, where golden eagles still nest, can be explored on foot to see the Grotta del Lauro (1060m), one of the most interesting caves in Sicily, with impressive stalagmites and stalactites, an important bat population, and where traces of prehistoric habitation have been found. On one of the mountain peaks, Rocca Traora, there is a flourishing colony of griffon vultures, successfully re-introduced after their accidental extermination in 1966.

A picturesque road leads south from Sant'Agata di Militello through the Nebrodi Mountains past **San Fratello**, a Lombard colony founded by Adelaide, wife of Count Roger; the people still use their ancient Gallic dialect. The old town is built of dark brown stone, with mellow, mossy roof-tiles. Recent archaeological surveys on nearby Mt San Fratello, called Monte Vecchio by the local people, show that the town is of prehistoric origin. It was later the ancient *Apollonia*, and was moved to its present position by order of the queen. On Monte Vecchio is the 12th-century Norman sanctuary church of the three brothers, Sts Alfio, Cirino and Filadelfo, three saints martyred in AD 253. San Fratello is surrounded by forests; close by are two lakes: Maulazzo and Biviere, of great interest to bird-watchers and botanists.

Back on the coast, **Acquedolci** is a coastal resort whose name means 'sweet waters', a reference to the sugar industry founded here by the Arabs, which brought prosperity to the whole area. It also had a tuna fishery and a port for exporting wheat from the interior; now its fortunes are declining. A path leads south up the slopes of Mt Pizzo Castellano (c. 30mins) to the Grotta di San Teodoro (*open 9–1 & 3–6, closed Sun*), where important Palaeolithic burials have been found including one of a woman, about 30 years old and 1.65m tall, who has been named Thea. Numerous fossils attest the presence of elephants and hippos here 150,000 years ago.

THE WESTERN NEBRODI

Caronia (*map p. 536, A3*) lies in a beautiful forest of the same name, Sicily's largest. The picturesque town preserves a privately-owned and still-inhabited Norman castle on the top of the hill, traces of its 14th-century fortifications, and an intact Roman bridge spanning the Caronia torrent. On the outskirts, the site of ancient *Kale Akte* has been identified, founded by Ducetius of the Sicels (*see p. 10*) on his return from exile in 447 BC.

A mountain road leads across the Nebrodi from here to the hill town of **Capizzi** (1100m), one of the highest villages in Sicily. The road joins the beautiful SS 120 south of the Nebrodi from Nicosia to Randazzo. East of Troina the road traverses rugged country with a superb view of Etna, passing below remote **Cesarò** (*map p. 536, B3*), where the remains of its castle can be seen.

On the coast, at the western end of the Nebrodi, is **Santo Stefano di Camastra** (*map p. 536, A3*), once situated further inland on a rise, and destroyed by a landslide in 1682. It is noted for fine ceramics, which are made and sold in potteries on the outskirts (most of which are east of the town on the road towards Messina), and for building materials. Local ware is also sold in numerous shops in the town. In the heart of the attractively designed town (the work of Giuseppe Lanza, Duke of Camastra, in 1693), at Via Palazzo 35, is Palazzo Sergio-Trabia, seat of the Museo della Ceramica (*open 9–1 & 3.30–7.30; call the Municipio to request visit; T: 0921 331110*), with a beautiful collection of the local pottery, with its bright colours and typical designs, including a section devoted to the famous floor-tiles.

A pretty road leads inland through the Nebrodi via **Mistretta**, an attractive old town with some beautiful Baroque and Rococo buildings, on the site of the ancient *Amestratus*. At the entrance to the town is the 16th-century church of San Giovanni, with a fine flight of steps and a portal carved in 1534. The 17th-century Chiesa Madre (St Lucy) has some beautiful statues of the Gagini school and two interesting side portals carved in the 14th and 15th centuries respectively. The carved south portal of the church has been ascribed to Giorgio da Milano (1493). At Mistretta they make unique biscuits of white marzipan called *pasta reale*, which are baked until pale gold in colour. From Mistretta a magnificent old mountain road goes south to Nicosia, in Enna province.

Tusa and ancient *Halaesa*

At the northwestern corner of the province of Messina is Castel di Tusa. A road leads inland above the wide torrent bed of the River Tusa, now usually dry, 21km long, the ancient *Halaesus*, to the pretty little hill town of **Tusa** (*map p. 536, A3*), which has interesting medieval sculptures in the Chiesa Madre. Modern sculptures, works of well-known contemporary artists including Pietro Consagra, Tano Festa and Hidetoshi Nagasawa, have been erected on the riverbed, from the shore to the village of Castel Di Lucio. Called **Fiumara d'Arte**, this constitutes an interesting and much appreciated walk, although the local people were hostile at first, back in the 1980s, and there were attempts to have the works demolished by court order. The latest addition is the dramatic three-sided pyramid of red steel, 30m high, called *Pyramid–38° Parallel*, work of the sculptor Mauro Staccioli; its hollow interior can be visited only one day a year, for the summer solstice on 21st June. The sides of the pyramid are aligned with the three points of Trinacria, the ancient name of Sicily. The sponsor of this huge artistic initiative, Antonio Presti, runs the famous Hotel Atelier sul Mare (*see p. 473*), where the same artists and several others have designed 20 rooms.

Off the road to Tusa, in Contrada Santa Maria delle Palate, is the **site of *Halaesa*** (*open 9–1hr before sunset; T: 0921 334531*) on a hill. A road leads up from the gate on the byroad to the car park beside the restored convent and church and custodian's house. The attractive site, with ancient olives and almond trees, commands a fine view of the pretty Tusa valley, the little towns of Tusa and, on a clear day, the Aeolian Islands. Halaesa was founded in 403 BC by Archonides, dynastic ruler of Herbita, who claimed to be the direct descendant of Ducetius. The site has been extensively excavated in recent years, and a lovely stretch of the paved Hellenistic street leading to the agora has been uncovered. The agora itself (partly protected by a roof) preserves part of its marble wall panelling and brick paving on the west side. The walls of the city (a stretch further uphill is strengthened by buttresses) are well preserved, and the Roman necropolis near the entrance to the site consists of an early Imperial columbarium monument and several further tombs. An excellent new antiquarium (the Giacomo Scibona antiquarium) displays some of the objects found at Halaesa, including two recently-published bronze inscriptions in the shape of a temple façade honouring the local resident Nemenios, several statues and some other inscriptions.

THE AEOLIAN ISLANDS

Lipari, Salina, Vulcano, Stromboli, Filicudi, Alicudi and Panarea, together with some rocky islets, form the archipelago known as the Aeolian Islands (*map p. 536*). The islands are very small but each one has its own identity and its own particular beauty. Their name derives from Aeolus, the mythical guardian of the winds, who inhabited the largest island, Lipari. This volcanic area marks the point where the African plate meets the European, folding over and forcing itself under the opposing plate, in the process of subduction. Two of the islands, Vulcano and Stromboli, are still active. All are protected as a nature reserve, and Lipari's tiny beaches of black volcanic sand have been awarded the EU Blue Banner for quality. On Stromboli the slopes on the opposite side to the lava flows are fertile and cultivated with vineyards. Vulcano smells strongly of sulphur and there is little cultivated land, but it is a magical place where shepherds pasture their sheep and goats. In spring, when the yellow broom is in flower, it is breathtakingly beautiful. Alicudi and Filicudi still show signs of the patient terracing carried out for many centuries to preserve the tiniest drop of water. Salina, with its two extinct volcanic cones, is the greenest and most fertile of the group, with extensive vineyards and forests where every effort is made to prevent summer wildfires. Lipari, the largest of the islands, is ideal for gentle trekking. Panarea is a tiny island full of wild flowers, with pretty houses set in the vegetation. The local style of architecture is perfect for the islands: small cube-like homes made of blocks of lava, plastered on the outside with white pumice, with characteristic little round windows like portholes; a flat roof for drying grapes, figs, pumpkins or tomatoes; a veranda in front, which is the main living area, under a pergola supported by white columns; an open-air oven for baking bread, and a cistern underneath the house for storing every precious drop of rain water. Several prehistoric sites have been excavated on the islands, and the Regional Archaeological Museum housed in the citadel of Lipari is one of the most important collections of its kind in Europe.

Capers grow everywhere on the islands, even on sheer rock faces. Birds on their migratory flights frequently stop to rest on the Aeolians. Some of the rocky islets around the larger islands are important nesting-spots for Eleonora's falcon (*Falco eleonorae*), a small, dark bird of prey, now extremely rare, which lays its eggs late in the spring so that its young can prey on the flocks of migrating birds flying south in late summer. Among the mammals, there are plenty of bats of various species and rabbits. Fish are abundant and varied. Flying fish can often be seen in the summer, and also groups of dolphins, playing together close to shore. The whole archipelago is designated a UNESCO World Heritage Site. It is worth noting that it gets very crowded on Lipari, Panarea and Vulcano in July and August, with day trippers from Calabria and Sicily.

Aeolian landscape: aerial view of the island of Stromboli with the village of San Vincenzo and the Sciara del Fuoco, down which magma pours when the volcano erupts.

HISTORY OF THE AEOLIAN ISLANDS

The islands were important in ancient times because of the abundance of obsidian, a hard volcanic glass used for making tools and exported throughout the Mediterranean. The earliest traces of settlement found belong to the Stentinello culture of the Neolithic Age. In the Middle Bronze Age the islands were on the main trade routes between the Aegean Islands and the Western Mediterranean. The Greeks colonised Lipari in c. 600 BC, and in the following centuries the islands were attacked by the Athenians and the Carthaginians. They fell to Rome in 252 BC. The population dropped in later centuries, because of an increase in the activity of the volcanoes, especially on Lipari. In AD 836 the islands were raided by the Arabs, who destroyed the towns and burnt them, carrying off the inhabitants as slaves and scattering the remains of St Bartholomew. A stone sarcophagus containing the mummified body of a man who had been flayed alive, thought to be Bartholomew, had drifted onto a Lipari beach in the 5th century. From that time nobody returned to live on the islands until Count Roger sent a group of Benedictine monks there in 1083. In spite of the concession of various privileges, it was not easy to attract people to colonise the islands, because of the precarious security situation; an enterprising monk declared that he had miraculously traced all the remains of St Bartholomew, who would again protect the islands. But piracy, notwithstanding the good saint, was a constant threat; when the fearsome pirate Kheir ed-Din Barbarossa attacked Lipari in 1544, burning the city and carrying off the entire population, there was pessimism about the islands ever being inhabited again. But the viceroy Peter of Toledo immediately sent aid, rebuilt the fortifications, confirmed the old privileges and allowed so many new ones that large groups of settlers came from Campania and Calabria. In the 19th century the citadel of Lipari was transformed into a prison, and in 1926 it became a place of isolation for the political opponents of the Fascist regime. Only in 1950 was the citadel opened again to visitors. A heavy blow to the economy came in the late 19th century, when thousands of people emigrated (mostly to Australia), after phylloxera destroyed the grape-vines.

LIPARI

Lipari (37km square), ancient *Meligunis*, the largest island of the group, 40km from Milazzo, is formed of twelve volcanoes, now dormant. About half of the island's 12,000 inhabitants are concentrated in the lively and attractive little town of Lipari, with its acropolis of narrow streets and its low houses, their balconies decorated with plants. The citadel of deep red lava rock commands the shore above the town, and separates the two harbours. On the north side of the acropolis is the port used by hydrofoils and ferries, Marina Lunga or Porto Sottomonastero.

The main road of the town is Corso Vittorio Emanuele. On the far (west) side is the **Palazzo Vescovile** (*map 3*), eventually to be restored as the seat of a Diocesan Museum. Beside it is the **archaeological zone of Contrada Diana** (*map 5*), where two Roman hypogea were found, and where excavations revealed part of the Greek walls of the ancient city (5th–4th centuries BC) and Roman houses. It is now very overgrown and no longer open regularly to the public.

Near Porto Sottomonastero is **Piazza Mazzini** (*map 2–4*), with a garden and some charming houses beside the neo-Gothic Town Hall (Municipio). The 17th-century church of Sant'Antonio (or San Francesco) has pretty marble altars. Steps lead down to the crypt which was the burial-place for the islanders before the cemetery (which can be seen nearby) was opened. The route from Piazza Mazzini to the citadel or acropolis leads through impressive 16th-century Spanish fortifications, with double gates and an entrance tunnel which incorporate Classical fragments.

On the other side of the acropolis, at **Marina Corta** (*map 8*), the fishing-boats dock beside the picturesque church of the Anime del Purgatorio. Another attractive church close by is San Giuseppe, at the top of a ramp. Outside the church, fishermen are often at work mending their nets, their colourful boats pulled up on the quay beside a solitary palm tree, watched over by the statue of the patron St Bartholomew.

Via Garibaldi winds uphill through the town from Marina Corta. It passes a wide, scenic flight of steps constructed at the beginning of the 20th century up to the acropolis, framing the façade of the duomo at the top. The hill itself is a very peaceful spot, verdant with oleanders, prickly pear and ivy.

The acropolis

The **duomo** (*map 6; open 10–12*), more easily reached by using the street from Porto Sottomonastero rather than the long flight of steps from Via Garibaldi, is dedicated to the patron saint Bartholomew, and was first built on this site by Count Roger (c. 1084). Admire the bronze doors with reliefs describing the strange arrival of the saint's body on a beach of Lipari, and some of the miracles he has accomplished for the islanders. The pretty interior, hung with chandeliers, has a vault frescoed in the 18th century. On the side altars are 18th-century reliquary busts in gilded wood. In the north transept is a *Madonna of the Rosary*, attributed to Girolamo Alibrandi, and a statue in silver of St Bartholomew which dates from 1728. The statue, together with an elaborate silver reliquary of a boat, is carried in procession through the streets on 24th August, 16th November, 13th February and 5th March. The Benedictine cloister has been restored. Dating from 1131, with later additions, it has vaulted walks, and columns of different shapes and sizes (some of them Doric, and some re-used from Roman buildings). Several primitive capitals are decorated with animals and birds.

The church of **Maria Santissima delle Grazie**, with a fine restored façade, is reached down a few steps in a little garden. On the other side of the road are public gardens (with fine views) with a large number of Greek and Roman sarcophagi, found in the necropolis of Contrada Diana (late 5th century and 4th century BC), at the foot of the acropolis (now covered by the modern town). There is also an open-air theatre, built in 1978.

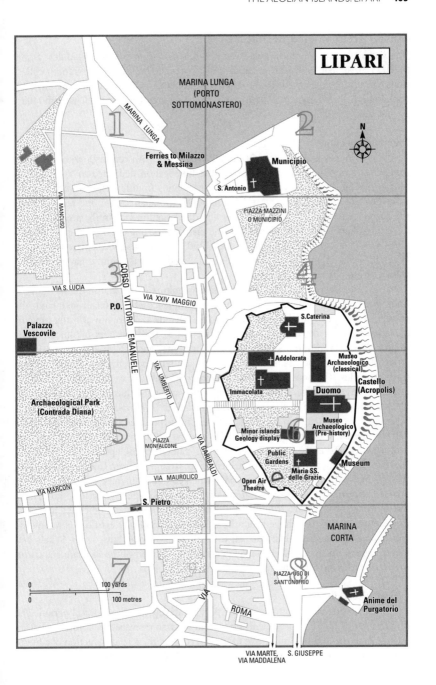

LIPARI

MARINA LUNGA
(PORTO
SOTTOMONASTERO)

N

1

2

Ferries to Milazzo
& Messina

Municipio

S. Antonio

PIAZZA MAZZINI
O MUNICIPIO

VIA MANCUSO

CORSO

VITTORO EMANUELE

3

VIA S. LUCIA

P.O.

VIA XXIV MAGGIO

Palazzo
Vescovile

4

S. Caterina

Museo
Archaeologico
(classical)

Addolorata

VIA UMBERTO I

Immacolata

Castello
(Acropolis)

Duomo

Archaeological Park
(Contrada Diana)

5

PIAZZA
MONFALCONE

6

Minor islands
Geology display

Museo
Archaeologico
(Pre-history)

VIA GARIBALDI

Public
Gardens

Museum

VIA MAUROLICO

Maria SS.
delle Grazie

VIA MARCONI

Open Air
Theatre

S. Pietro

MARINA
CORTA

0   100 yards
0   100 metres

7

8

PIAZZA UGO DI
SANT'ONOFRIO

VIA

ROMA

Anime del
Purgatorio

VIA MARTE,   S. GIUSEPPE
VIA MADDALENA

Museo Archeologico Bernabò Brea

The Archaeological Museum (*map 6; open 9–1.30 & 3–7; until 6 in Nov–March; T: 090 9880174, 090 9880594*) is arranged in several separate buildings. The superb collections, beautifully displayed in chronological sequence (with labels also in English), contain finds from Lipari and other islands in the Aeolian group, as well as from Milazzo and southern Italy.

Prehistory section

Beside the duomo is the former Bishop's Palace (early 18th century), with an attractive portal and balconies, which houses the first section dedicated to Prehistory. A tour begins on the first floor here with Neolithic finds from Lipari, including painted vases, Serra d'Alto-style pottery (resembling southern Italian forms), and red pottery of the Diana style, so called because it was first discovered nearby in the area known as Contrada Diana. Objects found here on the castle hill belonging to the Capo Graziano (1800–1400 BC) and Milazzese (c. 1400–1250 BC) cultures are displayed, showing Greek influences. Notable are the vessels on tall pedestals, thought to have been used from a sitting position on the floor.

The ground floor is dedicated to the Ausonian culture (from southern Italy) and the finds made on the castle hill. Many show the influence of the Italian mainland: the vessels have a great variety of strangely-shaped handles. There are also the remains of a small cooking device, and a large terracotta pot, the repository of almost 100kg of bronze objects from the 9th century BC. There are signs of a violent destruction of Lipari at that time, and the island appears to have remained uninhabited for the next three centuries. The Greek and Roman period on Lipari is covered in Room 10. The large restored Attic vase, used for mixing water and wine, has an exquisite delicate black-figure decoration on the rim showing the *Labours of Herakles* and (inside) a frieze of ships. The couchant lion (c. 575 BC) carved from volcanic rock probably guarded a votive deposit to the wind-god Aeolus. Also here are a Roman statue of a girl of the 2nd century AD, found in the bishop's palace, and a statuette of Asclepius (4th century BC).

A door leads out to the garden which contains sarcophagi from Contrada Diana and the Epigraphic Pavilion (*not always open*), which contains funerary inscriptions of the 5th–1st centuries BC. Opposite, a group of old houses display prehistoric finds from the minor islands: Panarea (from the Calcara and Milazzese sites), Filicudi and Salina. In the entrance are three huge pithoi from Portella on Salina. Next door is a building which houses a geological display on three floors with diagrams, maps, reliefs and models which illustrate volcanic activity and the formation of the Aeolian Islands. In the courtyard is a small collection of inscriptions.

Classical section

On the other side of the cathedral is the pavilion devoted to the Classical period. The displays in this building begin with finds from Milazzo displayed in chronological sequence from the Middle Bronze Age to the 3rd century BC. A reconstruction of a burial site shows the burial pots in the position in which they were found. Another reconstruction, of the Piazza Monfalcone necropolis in Lipari (1125–1050 BC), is followed by the superb collection of terracotta and stone sarcophagi from Lipari, including the stone example found in Contrada Diana, which is perfectly preserved. It is thought to have been made by a sculptor in the 2nd or 1st centuries BC as his own tomb.

On the upper floors are Attic red-figure kraters of the 5th century BC and early Sicilian and Campanian red-figure vases (4th century BC) including a splendid krater with columns (c. 450 BC). Grave goods from a similar period, and Attic pottery decorated on a white ground, are followed by a superb display of theatrical figurines in terracotta. Especially striking are the statuettes of dancers, and Andromeda with her child. A fascinating and unique collection of tragic masks and theatrical terracottas can also be seen here along with some very fine gold jewellery. Further rooms contain brightly-coloured vases by the Lipari Painter, a master who depicted exclusively female figures, and who enjoyed working with different colours, and southern Italian vases including a krater with Dionysus watching a nude acrobat and two actors, and a bronze hydra with a female bust (early 5th century BC). Hellenistic gold jewellery here includes a ring of the 4th century BC with a female nude. The top floor displays the latest finds from the hill showing evidence of the destruction of Lipari in 252 BC, and sporadic finds from the Roman and Norman periods, as well as medieval and Renaissance ceramics.

In the basement, underwater archaeology has provided finds dating from 2000 BC to the 5th century BC, discovered near Capistello (Lipari), and near Filicudi and Panarea, including a magnificent display of amphorae. There are also finds from the wreck of a 17th-century Spanish warship.

Outside, the extensive **excavations** begun in 1950 on the summit of the hill by Luigi Bernabò Brea (*see www.luigibernabobrea.it for more information on this exceptional archaeologist*), have revealed a sequence of levels of occupation, dating from the Neolithic Age when the islands were first inhabited. Because the prevailing winds have consistently brought volcanic dust and sand to settle here, cuttings reveal the history of habitation in remarkable detail. The unique pottery strata (reaching a depth of 9m) make the acropolis the key dating-site for the central Mediterranean. The different levels are well labelled and explained by diagrams. The exterior of the church of Santa Caterina has been restored. Beyond the excavations, the small Baroque churches of the Addolorata and the Immacolata can be seen.

Around the island

A road (26.5km) encircles the island. It leads north from Lipari via the stony beach of Canneto to traverse magnificent white cliffs of pumice, with deep gallery-quarries. The loading jetties protrude into the sea, a brilliant turquoise blue because of the pumice on the seabed. Beyond Porticello the road crosses remarkable red and black veins of obsidian, some of which reach the sea. The beaches are covered with pumice and obsidian, and some of the paths in the villages are cut out of obsidian. A road connects Acquacalda (where there are hot springs in the sea) with Quattropani. At Piano Conte lava-stone battle-axes and Bronze-Age weapons have been found. Near the coast (reached by a byroad) are the hot springs of San Calogero with remains of Roman baths. A tholos has come to light here. The road returns to Lipari past the viewpoint of Quattrocchi with its superb panorama. Monte Sant'Angelo (594m), in the centre of the island, is an extinct stratified volcano of unusual form (superb views).

ALICUDI & FILICUDI

The most westerly island is **Alicudi**, with a particularly far-away, lonely character, one-and-a-half hours' hydrofoil journey from Lipari. Here five square kilometres support a dwindling population of 102, several of whom are originally from Germany. It is a particularly beautiful island, with terraces and attractive local architecture. There are no roads, only steep tracks and steps over the hills, and no public illumination (it has only had electricity since 1990). Several houses can be rented, but it should be borne in mind that there is only one small shop selling basic necessities. Visitors should bring everything else with them, including a torch for getting around after dark, and spare batteries.

The remote and picturesque island of **Filicudi** (9.5km square; pop. 305) lies 19km west of Salina. Anciently called *Phoenicoesa*, it has comfortable accommodation and is a peaceful place to spend a holiday. Two prehistoric villages have been excavated on Capo Graziano; on the point (Montagnola) twelve huts were uncovered showing evidence of rebuilding before their destruction in the Milazzese period, while just inland, three oval huts yielded Bronze-Age vases. Off the cape in 1975 a hoard of Bronze-Age pottery was found on the site of a shipwreck. The picturesque little fishing-harbour of Pecorini is very popular with the rich and famous in the summer. The offshore stacks are a haven for birds, especially Eleonora's falcon.

PANAREA

Panarea (3.5km square; pop. 320) lies to the northeast (15km from Lipari), towards Stromboli. Its natural beauty and the style of the local architecture have been carefully preserved although the hotels and restaurants, popular with famous and wealthy Italians, are more expensive than those on the other islands. Electricity was only brought to the island in 1982. Near the fishing-harbour hot spring water mixes with the sea.

A walk (c. 30mins) leads to a naturally defended promontory on the southern tip of the island. On this superb site the Bronze-Age village of the Milazzese culture (probably inhabited in the 14th century BC), with 23 huts, was excavated in 1948. Mycenaean ceramics and native vases showing Minoan influences were brought to light (now in the archaeological museum on Lipari; *see p. 466*).

At the opposite end of the island, near the last houses on the coast, a path descends to the shore at Calcara where the fumaroles emit sulphurous gases. Nearby are traces of Neolithic pits made from boulders and volcanic clay, probably used for offerings. A Greek wreck was found offshore here in 1980, and from then until 1987 some 600 pieces of ceramics were recovered from its cargo of precious terracotta vases (5th–4th centuries BC), some of which are now exhibited in the Lipari Museum.

In the sea near the island the beautifully coloured rocks of Lisca Bianca and Basiluzzo (with many traces of Roman occupation) provide a foreground to the ever-changing view of Stromboli.

SALINA

Salina (27km square; pop. 2,400), 4km northwest of Lipari, is the highest of the islands and is formed of two twin volcanic cones and the saddle between them. The shape of Monte dei Porri (962m) is one of the most perfect mountain cones in the world. It has been identified with *Anthemoessa*, Homer's island of the Sirens, and was later called *Didyme*. Salina is justly famous for its Malvasia wine (*see box below*). Capers are also grown here in abundance. Its population lives in three municipalities, each formed of several picturesque villages: Santa Marina, Malfa and Leni.

THE SWEET MALVASIA OF SALINA

This exquisite wine was once so much in demand that almost all the available land on the Aeolian Islands, including the tiny islet of Basiluzzo, was dedicated to its production. The industry supported a population (in 1880) of over 32,000 people, while today there are only 15,000 inhabitants in the archipelago. Most of the wine was exported, some of it to England where it was called Malmsey. In 1881 the phylloxera blight destroyed almost all the vines; at least 20,000 islanders emigrated, mostly to Australia.

New incentives for Malvasia came in the 1960s, when a young architect, Carlo Hauner, was invited to spend a few days painting on Salina, and he decided to take up the challenge of re-introducing the production of Malvasia. Hauner is still the name to look for when buying this delectable drink; the winery is now run by his son. Made from white Malvasia grapes (95 percent) and black Corinth (5 percent), after harvesting, the bunches are left to wither in the sun on wicker trays for ten days before being pressed. Sweet but not cloying, it is best drunk chilled as an aperitif. It is thought that the Greeks first planted vines here in the 5th century BC.

On the east coast, near the Santa Marina lighthouse, a Middle Bronze-Age village has been excavated (*not open to the public*), and traces of Roman houses have been found (at the north end of the Lungomare). After the Arab conquest of the Aeolian Islands in 838, the island remained virtually uninhabited until the 16th century. The island was the setting for the Oscar-winning film *Il Postino*, which describes an episode in the life of Pablo Neruda. Among the interesting varieties of bird life that can be spotted on a visit to Salina are flamingoes. They usually pause to rest during their migratory flights on the salt pan of Salina, at Lingua. The kestrel, sparrow hawk and buzzard are birds of prey present as nesting species, both here and on the other islands.

On disembarking from the ferry or hydrofoil at **Santa Marina**, aim straight for the little square, where some of the best fresh-fruit *granita* on the islands can be found. The island is exceptionally green, and very pleasant walks can be taken on the two mountains, the Monte dei Porri (mountain of leeks) and the Fossa delle Felci (glen of the ferns). The latter is partly covered in woods of chestnut. The attractive old houses and the fine scenery have been protected for many years.

STROMBOLI

Stromboli (12.5km square; pop. 410), c. 28km from Lipari, is the best-known island in the archipelago because of its continual volcanic activity. It consists of a single cone (924m); the present active crater is 200m below the summit. It has been abandoned several times after eruptions, but is now again increasing in population and is popular with tourists. Strong activity in December 2002 caused a tsunami, and considerable damage. The inhabitants never refer to their volcano by name, calling it simply *Iddu*, 'Him'. Stromboli provided the setting for a landmark film of Italian cinema history, *Stromboli*, (1949), by Roberto Rossellini, starring his lover Ingrid Bergman. The islands became a popular location for movie-makers. Significant films include *Islands of Fire* (1956) by Vittorio De Seta, *The Adventure* (1960) by Michelangelo Antonioni, *Kaos* (1984) by the Taviani brothers, and *Dear Diary* (1991) by Nanni Moretti. A cinema museum is planned (*www.museodistromboli.it*).

The main village of Stromboli, San Vincenzo, is on the northeast side; ferries and hydrofoils dock at the harbour of Scauri. The boats also call at Ginostra, an attractive small group of houses on a rocky headland on the southwest tip of the island, still using generators for electricity, and completely isolated from the rest of the island. A small dock for ferries and hydrofoils has been built here, in spite of opposition. Ginostra has about 30 permanent inhabitants, of whom ten are originally from Germany.

Eruptions occur on the northwest side of the volcano and are not visible from the villages. The cone should be ascended with a guide (c. 3hrs), because trekking on the volcano is dangerous, but an easy footpath from San Vincenzo ascends as far as the Semaforo (c. 1hr 30mins), from which point the explosions can usually be seen. Small eruptions normally occur at frequent intervals; on days of unusual violence the spectacle (best seen at night from the sea) of the volcanic matter rushing down the Sciara del Fuoco into the sea is particularly impressive. Climbs on the volcano (very strenuous, and particularly exhilarating at night) can be booked (well ahead, places are limited) with Magmatrek (*Via Vittorio Emanuele; T: 090 9865768, www.magmatrek.it*); take a torch, chocolate and water with you.

Off the northeast coast is the striking isolated rock of Strombolicchio, a steep block of basalt (43m) looking like a cathedral in the sea.

VULCANO

Vulcano (21km square; pop. 800) is the most southerly of the islands (separated from the southern tip of Lipari by a channel less than a kilometre wide) and easily reached from the Sicilian mainland or by frequent hydrofoil services from Lipari (and by local boat excursions). It is of outstanding interest because of its geological structure and the spectacular volcanic landscape with black lava rocks on the sea and beaches of black sand. Formed of four volcanoes, the last volcanic eruption of Fossa Grande took place from 1888 to 1890. It has simple houses mostly built in the 20th century in a disorderly way. Deserted out of season, it becomes very crowded in summer. Many northern Italians have their summer houses here. A characteristic of Vulcano is the strong smell of sulphur, especially in the area around the port. The easily accessible deposits of sulphur, alum, boric acid and other minerals were first exploited industrially in the early 19th century; after 1860 the deposits were purchased for extraction by a certain Mr Stevenson, a Scot who had fallen in love with the island. He also planted vineyards and fruit orchards, dug wells, and tried to improve the lot of the islanders. The eruption of 1898 put a violent end to his dreams. His house, near the mud pools, can still be seen.

The boats dock at **Porto di Levante** near the quay used by the hydrofoils. A road with simple shops and a few cafés leads to **Porto di Ponente**, with mud pools on the beach, fed by hot springs. The fine black lava-sand beach nearby, with a number of hotels, is crowded in summer. Caution is advised while swimming, because there are scalding-hot springs in the sea, quite close to the shore.

In the other direction from the port a straight road leads across the plain at the foot of the volcano. A narrow path (signposted; about 1km from the port) leads up across the fine volcanic soil and rocks to the top of the crater (391m), called **Fossa Grande**, in about 2hrs. The route can be damaged and almost impassable after heavy rain, but is normally quite easy (although sturdy shoes are necessary). There is a remarkable view of the inside of the crater, and the rim steams constantly with sulphurous vapours. On a clear day all of the Aeolian Islands can be seen from here. The path can be followed right around the rim in about one hour.

Most of the islanders live in the upland plain of the island known as **Piano**, 7km from the port (reached by a few buses every day). There is a bar, a shop, a church, a couple of restaurants and a school: most of the farms have now been abandoned, and some of the houses are only used in summer. The Piano road passes close to the volcano and at the top of the hill, by the first house on the corner, a byroad leads left. Another turn left leads to the edge of a cliff with a number of caves and a view of the coast. The road continues gently uphill past a road on the left for **Gelso**, with some restaurants open in summer and good sea bathing. Another byroad leads to **Capo Grillo**, which has the best panorama on the island. The Piano road ends in front of the parish church destroyed by an earthquake in 1978 and rebuilt in 1988.

On the northern tip of the island is **Vulcanello**, a volcanic cone which rose out of the sea in 183 BC. Near the Faraglione della Fabbrica, a high rock with alum quarries, are the hot springs of Acqua Bollente and Acqua del Bagno. Between Vulcano and Lipari are some dramatically tall stacks emerging from the sea, including the Pietralunga, a 72-metre-high obelisk of basalt.

PRACTICAL INFORMATION

GETTING AROUND

In Messina luggage can be deposited at the SAIS ticket office in Piazza Repubblica (in front of the station) from Mon–Sat 4.30am–1.30 & 3.30–10.30pm.

• **By air:** There are helicopter services run by **Air Panarea**, Via Isitella, Panarea (*T: 090 9834428, 340 3667214, www.airpanarea.it*), **Icarus Elicotteri** (*Via Siena 16, Villa San Giovanni, T: 0968 53737, www.elicotteri-icarus. it*) and **Dedalus Elicotteri** of Panarea (*T: 090 983333, www.elieolie.it*) connecting the Aeolian Islands with some airports, and offering air-taxi services.

• **By train:** Messina, Giardini and Taormina are on the main line which runs along the coast from Syracuse via Catania to Messina. Milazzo is on the Messina–Palermo line.

• **By bus:** ATM (*www.atmmessina.it*) runs town buses and trams. Useful services are no. 79 from the station–Via I Settembre–Duomo–Corso Cavour and Via Garibaldi to the Regional Museum (continuing to Ganzirri and Punta Faro), no. 28 (Velocittà) from Piazza Cairoli and Via Garibaldi, no. 29 from Piazza Cairoli to the cemetery, and the tram that runs through Messina from the cemetery in the south to the regional museum in the north. **Giuntabus** (*www.giuntabus.com*) from Via Terranova 8 (at the junction with Viale San Martino) run services from Messina to Milazzo in 50mins (connecting with hydrofoils to the Aeolian Islands), also services to/from Catania Airport and Milazzo from May–Sept. **INTERBUS** (*www.interbus.it*) to Taormina (via SS 114) in 90mins, also to Alì Terme, Barcellona, Forza D'Agrò, Giardini Naxos, Santa Teresa di Riva, Scaletta Zanclea and Terme Vigliatore. There are local buses from Santa Teresa di Riva to Savoca and Casalvecchio.

Jonica Trasporti (*www.jonicatrasporti.it*) serves the southern Peloritans, from Messina to Taormina and Roccafiorita. **SAIS Autolinee** (*www.saisautolinee.it*), terminus by the railway station, in Piazza della Repubblica, run coaches from Messina to Castel di Tusa and Palermo in 2hrs 30mins, and Catania (direct via the motorway) in 90mins (continuing to Catania airport). **TAI** (*www.autolineetai.it*) and **Magistro** (*www.autolineemagistro.it*), departing from Via Santa Maria Alemanna in front of the Chamber of Commerce, run weekday-only services to towns in the northern Peloritan and Nebrodi mountains, including Brolo, Capo d'Orlando, Caprileone, Falcone, Galati Mamertino, Longi, Mirto, Naso, Olivarella, Rocca di Caprileone, Tindari and Tortorici.

From **Taormina** (bus station in Via Pirandello) there are buses to Mazzarò, Castelmola, the Alcantara Gorge and the towns on the foothills of Etna, as well as services to Catania (and Catania airport) and Messina.

Aeolian Islands On Lipari buses run by Urso (*www.ursobus.it*), from Marina Lunga to Canneto and to the pumice quarries and Acquacalda; to Quattrocchi, Pianoconte, and Quattropani; also tours of the island in summer. There are a few buses a day from the port on Vulcano to Piano. On Salina buses run by CITIS (*www.trasportisalina.it*), from Santa Marina Salina and Rinella to Leni, Pollara, Malfa and Lingua.

• **By car:** Cars are allowed (not July and Aug) on Lipari, Vulcano, Filicudi and Salina. However, visitors are not advised to take one as distances are short and local transport good. It is a good idea to garage your car at Milazzo; the attendant will pick it up for you and then bring it back on your return. A reliable company is Garage delle Isole (*Via San Paolino 66, T: 090 9288585, 090 9286986, 090 9223256,*

333 1623329; *English spoken; www.garagedell-leisole.it*). On request they can provide shuttle service to/from Catania, Palermo and Trapani airports. Some car-hire services operate on Lipari, Vulcano and Salina. On the other islands small motor vehicles are used to transport luggage, and on Alicudi and Stromboli, mules and donkeys. On Lipari and Vulcano, vespas and bicycles can also be hired.

• **By sea:** Throughout the year ferries, hydrofoils and catamarans run to the Aeolian Islands. The most convenient starting-point is Milazzo. For information, see www.bookingitalia.it.

N.G.I. (Milazzo; *www.ngi-spa.it*) runs car-ferries to Vulcano, Lipari, Salina, Panarea and Stromboli. **Siremar** (*www.siremar.it*) runs car-ferries taking 1hr 45mins to Vulcano, 2hrs to Lipari. **Ustica Lines** (*www.usticalines.it*) run hydrofoils from Milazzo (*Agenzia Catalano, Via dei Mille 32*) to the Aeolian Islands, taking 45mins to Vulcano, 1hr to Lipari.

Ferry and hydrofoil ticket offices on the islands: Some ticket offices on the islands open only 30mins before sailing. All the islands are connected by ferry and hydrofoil services; the ferries are slower, cheaper, more reliable and often less direct. Fishing-boats may be hired on all the islands, and the trip around the coast of the islands is strongly recommended.

WHERE TO STAY

Acquedolci (*map p. 536, B2*)
€ **Villa Nicetta**. Sleeps 15 people in a series of strange but comfortable rooms with private bath, in a very old fortified farmhouse (once the hunting-lodge of Prince Pignatelli)with its own church, close to Acquedolci. Many activities on offer, including horse-riding and trekking in the Nebrodi Mountains park, organic food (bread, pasta and cakes are all home-made); it is possible to take part in har-

vesting, sheep-milking, etc. *Contrada Nicetta, T: 0941 726142, www.villanicetta.it.*
Alì Terme (*map p. 536, D3*)
€ **Liberty B&B**. The roads in this area are a bit hectic, especially in summer, but the town is friendly and the wide beach (shale and sand) is clean. This B&B, in a pretty building in the town centre, has welcoming rooms and the breakfasts are very good. *Via Federico, T: 0942 701009, www.libertybeb.com.*
Capo d'Orlando (*map p. 536, B2*)
€€€ **Sant'Andrea**. New structure just out of town with 25 rooms, good restaurant, car park, pool. *Via Torrente Forno 67/b, T: 0941 914284, www.hotelsantandrea.eu.*
€€ **Il Mulino**. A good hotel on the seafront with 85 rooms and suites, reputable restaurant. *Via Andrea Doria 46, T: 0941 902431, www.hotelilmulino.it.*
€ **Nuovo Hotel Faro**. Good value for money at this little place on the seafront, 20 clean rooms, close to centre, no restaurant, friendly staff. *Via Libertà 7, T: 0941 902466, www. nuovohotelfaro.com.*
Capri Leone (*map p. 536, B2*)
€€ **Antica Filanda**. Small inn with 16 comfortable rooms, air conditioning, pool, panoramic terrace, fantastic restaurant. *Contrada Raviola, T: 0941 919704, www.anticafilanda.net.*
Castel di Tusa (*map p. 536, A3*)
€€€ **Atelier sul Mare**. Close to the sea, 20 of the 40 rooms have been 'created' by famous contemporary artists so you can literally sleep in a work of art. *Via Cesare Battisti 4, T: 0921 334295, www.ateliersulmare.it.*
Castelmola (*map p. 536, C3*)
€€€ **Villa Sonia**. Superb position just beneath the castle, for this old villa. Lovely rooms, most with panoramic balcony. Pool, garden, sauna, gymnasium, tennis. The hotel has an exceptionally good restaurant, worth a visit in its own right. *Via Porta Mola 9, T: 0942 28082, www.hotelvillasonia.com.*

Castroreale (*map p. 536, C2*)

€€€ **Green Manors**. Luxurious old country house surrounded by olive groves, 10 beautiful rooms, all different, pool, good restaurant. *Borgo Porticato, T: 090 9746515, www.greenmanors.it.*

Ganzirri (*map p. 536, D2*)

€€ **Villa Morgana**. A luxurious 1970s villa on one of the Ganzirri lakes, transformed into a lovely small hotel surrounded by a garden, good fitness centre, pool, the 15 rooms are all different. *Via Consolare Pompea 1965, T: 090 325575, www.villamorgana.it.*

Giardini Naxos (*map p. 536, C3*)

€€€ **Hellenia Yachting**. Refined atmosphere, restaurant, private beach and pool. *Via Jannuzzo 41, Località Recanati, T: 0942 51737, www.hotel-hellenia.it.*

€€ **Nike**. ■ Comfortable hotel in a quiet position on a rocky headland, 57 rooms, snack bar and restaurant serving Sicilian dishes, in the garden in summer, private beach (rocks), car park, airport shuttle on request, free bikes. *Via Calcide Eubea 27, T: 0942 51207, 0942 56314, www.hotelnike.it.*

€€ **Palladio**. Colourful, comfortable small hotel in good position on the seafront, no restaurant but nice breakfast on the veranda overlooking the bay. *Via Umberto 470, T: 0942 52267, www.hotelpalladiogiardini.com.*

Longi (*map p. 536, B3*)

€ **La Casetta**. The village of Longi is the ideal base for nature-lovers and especially birdwatchers. This B&B is in the heart of the village, a perfectly-restored stone house built in the 17th century, on three floors, with comfortable rooms and Jacuzzi tubs, marvellous Sicilian breakfasts. *Corso Umberto 50, T: 0941 485068, www.nebrodibandb.it.*

€ **Il Vignale**. In the heart of the Nebrodi Park, ideal for birdwatchers and ramblers, close to the Rocche del Crasto (griffon vultures, golden eagles, pine martens), but only for serious nature-lovers; the building, an ancient silk-mill which sleeps 15, is on the wooded mountainside above the village of Longi, where the owners live, there is no telephone on the premises, self-catering only, the track is difficult after rain. *Contrada Pado, T: 0941 485015, 338 2779383. www.il.vignale.com.*

Messina (*map p. 536, D2*)

€€€ **Grand Hotel Liberty**. One of the oldest (built in 1930) and most prestigious hotels, beautifully restored, central, award-winning for environmentally friendly management, cosy lounge bar, good restaurant. *Via Primo Settembre 15, T: 090 6409436, www.messina-hotel-liberty.com. Map p. 427, 6.*

€ **Sant'Elia**. Small, friendly, old-fashioned, central hotel, no restaurant. *Via I Settembre 67, T: 090 6010082, www.hotelsantelia.com. Map p. 427, 6.*

Milazzo (*map p. 536, C2*)

€€€ **Cassisi**. Aristocratic residence transformed into a charming hotel, comfortable modern interior. *Via Cassisi 5, T: 090 9229099, www.cassisihotel.com.*

€€ **Petit Hotel**. Close to the pier for ferries to the islands, this hotel built entirely to standards respecting the environment (ceiling fans, no air conditioning!) has tiny rooms, a spectacular terrace and serves very good organic breakfasts. *Via dei Mille 37, T: 090 9286784, www.petithotel.it.*

€€ **Garibaldi**. Charming little hotel in the fishermen's quarter, rooms (some with extra-large beds) or apartments with air conditioning, nice buffet breakfasts, shuttle to/from port or railway station on request. *Lungomare Garibaldi 160, T: 090 9240189, www.hotel-garibaldi.net.*

Montalbano Elicona (*map p. 536, C3*)

€ **Paese-albergo**. Ask at the tourist office (*Piazza Maria Provvidenza, T: 0941 679384, 0941 679065*) if you would like to stay in one of the little medieval houses of this beautiful village.

Patti (*map p. 536, C2*)

€€ **La Playa**. On the sea front, surrounded by a garden, with 42 rooms, 26 bungalows and a restaurant, ideal for a seaside holiday. *Via Playa 3, Marina di Patti, T: 0941 361301, www.laplaya-hotel.it.*

€ **Hotel Sacra Famiglia**. In the high part of the town, ex-monastery recently restored and run by the Diocese, with its own church; clean simple rooms, restaurant. Intended for Tindari pilgrims, it's excellent value for money for anyone. *Via Dante Alighieri 1, T: 0941 241622, www.sacrafamiglia.it.*

Savoca (*map p. 536, D3*)

€€€ **Borgo San Rocco**. ◼ Old houses of the fishermen's quarter in this hilltop village, meticulously restored and transformed into a delightful hotel, with 21 rooms and suites, fitness centre, gardens, pool and a good restaurant. *Via San Rocco, T: 0942 761234, www.borgosanrocco.com.*

Taormina (*map p. 536, C3*)

€€€ **Grand Hotel Timeo**. The first hotel to open in Sicily; now a little faded; 70 rooms and suites (some in Villa Flora on the other side of the street), pool, glorious views, good restaurant. *Via Teatro Greco 59, T: 0942 6270200, www.grandhoteltimeo.com. Map p. 437, 2.*

€€€ **San Domenico**. One of Sicily's oldest hotels, a converted 15th-century convent; ambassadors, royalty and ageing film stars stay here. 105 rooms with varying levels of luxury, beautiful gardens, pool. Fraying at the seams a little. *Piazza San Domenico 5, T: 0942 613111, www.amthotels.it. Map p. 437, 5.*

€€€ **El Jebel**. In the medieval quarter close to the duomo, reached by stepped streets just behind the Municipio, a little agility required. Stunning design for the 9 rooms, all different, roof garden, gourmet restaurant with winter garden, fitness centre, highly professional staff. *Salita Ciampoli 9, T: 0942 625494, www.hoteleljebel.com. Map p. 437, 5.*

€€€ **Metropole**. A few defects: some of the 23 rooms and suites have a cramped feel; decidedly overpriced. But this fascinating historic hotel, recently rescued from oblivion, oozes good taste and exclusiveness, has heart-stopping views, is right in the centre of town, and the restaurant is already legendary, including the breakfasts. Pool and fitness centre. *Corso Umberto 154, T: 0942 625417, www.hotelmetropoletaormina.it. Map p. 437, 5.*

€€€ **The Ashbee**. ◼ Historic hotel in a panoramic position just outside Porta Messina, with cool, spacious rooms, good bathrooms, beautiful terraced garden, good restaurant, designed in 1907 for Colonel Shaw-Hellier by Charles Ashbee, exponent of William Morris's Arts and Crafts movement. *Viale San Pancrazio 46, T: 0942 23537, www.theashbeehotel.com. Map p. 437, 2.*

€€€ **Atlantis Bay**. Built for the Hollywood stars arriving for the film festival in the 1950s, a luxurious, delightfully kitsch hotel with a series of terraces descending to sea level at the Bay of the Mermaids, with 85 rooms and suites, fitness centre, seawater pool and a good restaurant. Excellent breakfasts. *Via Nazionale 161, T: 0942 618011, www.atlantisbay.it. Beyond map p. 437, 4.*

€€€ **Imperiale**. Close to the heart of town, 138 beautiful rooms, pool, fitness centre and good restaurant. *Via Circonvallazione 11, T: 0942 625202, www.imperialetaormina.com. Map p. 437, 2.*

€€€ **Villa Angela**. The home of Jim Kerr (Simple Minds); way up above Taormina, on the road to Castelmola, 43 nice rooms, stunning views, pool, tennis, Scottish-style brunches. *Via Leonardo da Vinci, T: 0942 27038, www.hotelvillaangela.com. Map p. 437, 1.*

€€ **Villa Schuler**. ◼ One of the best small hotels in town, opened 1905, with 51 rooms and suites, garden, garage, no restaurant. *Via*

Roma 16, T: 0942 23481, www.hotelvillaschuler. com. Map p. 437, 6.

€€ **Piccolo Giardino**. Tiny hotel with 25 comfortable rooms, nice restaurant, a roof garden, fitness centre and panoramic pool, in the town centre, just above Corso Umberto. *Salita Lucio Denti 4, T: 0942 23463, www.ilpiccologiardino.it. Map p. 437, 2.*

€ **Villa Caterina**. Old villa surrounded by a lovely Mediterranean garden, 11 rooms all with air conditioning. No restaurant. Close to the sea and to the cableway for Taormina, car park. Lots of stairs. *Via Nazionale 155, T: 0942 24709, www.hotelvillacaterina.it. Map p. 437, 4.*

Terme Vigliatore *(map p. 536, C2)*

€ **Grand Hotel Terme Parco Augusto**. For a relaxing break, 90 comfortable rooms, restaurant, spa, and a Maurice Mességué fitness and beauty centre. The baths, first exploited by the Romans, were conceded to the city by Felipe III of Spain in 1643. *Viale delle Terme 85, T: 090 9781078, www.parcoaugusto.com.*

Tortorici *(map p. 536, B3)*

€ **Casa Zia Maria Antonina**. 6 spotless, comfortable rooms in the oldest part of Tortorici, some with shared bathrooms, no breakfast provided but there are plenty of coffee-bars close by, excellent value for money. *Via Roma 54, T: 0941 421028, 349 2708891, www.casaziamariantonina.org.*

Aeolian Islands

NB: Many hotels on the islands close in winter.
Alicudi
€€ **Ericusa**. The only hotel on the island, charmingly rustic, on the beach. 21 air-conditioned rooms. Good restaurant. *Via Regina Elena, T: 090 9889902, www.alicudihotel.it.*

€ **Casa Mulino**. Typical harbourside house. Self-catering rooms. *Via Regina Elena, T: 090 9889681, www.alicudicasamulino.it.*

Filicudi
€€ **La Sirena**. Comfortable rooms furnished

with antiques. Balconies overlooking the sea, which is only a stone's throw away. Excellent restaurant, or self-catering on request. *Via Pecorini Mare, T: 090 9889997, www.pensionelasirena.it.*

€€ **Villa La Rosa**. The rooms open onto personal verandas, Aeolian-style; renowned restaurant, where even the bread is baked every day in a wood-burning oven. *Via Rosa 24, Contrada Rocca di Ciauli, T: 090 9889965, www.villalarosa.it.*

€ **La Canna**. In a breathtaking panoramic position, with 14 rooms, open all year, good restaurant and panoramic pool. Book early; the word is getting around! *Via Rosa 43, Contrada Rocca di Ciauli, T: 090 9889956, www. lacannahotel.it.*

Lipari
€€€ **Villa Meligunis**. Right in the heart of the old city, beautiful rooms, atmosphere, and a rooftop terrace. Good restaurant serving vegetarian dishes on request, scuba-diving, water-skiing and sailing are organised. *Via Marte 7 (two blocks south of Via Roma), T: 090 9812426, www.villameligunis.it. Beyond map p. 465, 8.*

€€ **Villa Liberty**. 12 comfortable rooms, all different, in a pretty Art Nouveau villa surrounded by a lush garden, no restaurant. *Via Isabella Conti Eller Vainicher 20 (west of the Archaeological Park), T: 090 9814270, www. libertyresort.it. Beyond map p. 465, 5.*

€€ **Gattopardo**. A 19th-century villa in a beautiful sub-tropical garden, with 47 rooms in little Aeolian cottages, good restaurant. *Via Diana 67, T: 090 9811035/6, www.gattopardoparkhotel.it. Beyond map p. 465, 5.*

€€ **Giardino sul Mare**. 46 rooms in cottages, beautiful gardens going down to the sea; pool. *Via Maddalena 65, T: 090 9811004, www.giardinosulmare.it. Beyond map p. 465, 8.*

€€ **Casajanca**. Interesting and comfortable little hotel in Canneto village, run by the daughter of a poet. 10 rooms and a verdant patio, close to the sea. *Marina Garibaldi 115, Canneto, T: 090 9880222, www.casajanca.it.*

€ **Oriente**. Very comfortable hotel, albeit rather bizarre, 30 rooms and a garden, no restaurant. *Via Marconi 35, T: 090 9811493, www.hotelorientelipari.it. Map p. 465, 5.*

€ **Enzo il Negro**. ■ Near Marina Corta, a spotlessy clean *pensione* with 8 rooms, all with private bath and air conditioning; there is a beautiful rooftop terrace for breakfasts. Enzo, a popular figure here, can give you lots of help for organising boat trips or even finding an apartment. *Via Garibaldi 29, T: 090 9813163, www.enzoilnegro.com. Map p. 465, 8.*

Panarea

€€€ **Raya**. Perched on a hill dominating the port; exclusive clientele, very expensive. 30 rooms, all with sea view, no TV or telephone, peaceful (but they have a famous discothèque), beautiful thermal pool and fitness centre, good restaurant serving only organic food. *Via San Pietro, Località Costa Galletta, T: 090 983013, www.hotelraya.it.*

€€€ **Hycesia**. Small hotel with 11 rooms, surrounded by a garden, with a wine bar and good restaurant. *Via San Pietro, T: 090 983041, 090 924001, www.hycesia.it.*

€€ **Cincotta**. Right on the brink of the cliff, this was the first hotel to open on the island. Gardens, seawater pool, close to harbour. Closed winter. *Via San Pietro, T: 090 983014/5, www.hotelcincotta.it.*

€€ **Lisca Bianca**. Now a Best Western, small hotel in a panoramic position in front of harbour, all rooms and suites with terrace or patio in true Aeolian Islands style; lush garden, good restaurant. *Via Lani 1, T: 090 983004-5, www.liscabianca.it.*

Salina

€€€ **Capofaro Malvasia**. Splendid hotel consisting of Aeolian cottages immersed in the vineyards belonging to the Tasca d'Almerita family, for a really relaxing holiday.

Good restaurant, excellent breakfasts, pool. *Via Faro 3, T: 090 9844330/1, www.capofaro.it.*

€€€ **Santa Isabel**. Small hotel in a lovely clifftop position, accommodation in 10 comfortable suites, gourmet restaurant (cookery courses available). *Via Scalo 12, Malfa, T: 090 9844018, www.santaisabel.it.*

€€€ **Signum**. ■ A restructured hamlet, Aeolian-style architecture for the 30 cool and welcoming rooms, peaceful position surrounded by vineyards, fitness centre, pool. *Via Scalo 15, Malfa, T: 090 9844222, 090 9844375, www.hotelsignum.it.*

€€€ **L'Ariana**. Strange building on the edge of the cliff, the terrace allows access to the sea. Family-run. Excellent restaurant. *Via Rotabile 11, Rinella, Leni, T: 090 9809075, www.hotelariana.it.*

€€ **Locanda del Postino**. The most romantic and out-of-the-way place to stay on Salina is at the tiny village of Pollara (70 inhabitants), in the house used as a set for Michael Radford's 1994 Oscar-winning film *The Postman*. 10 quiet rooms with private bath, and a colourful, airy restaurant. Open May–Oct. *Via Picone 120, T: 090 9843958, www.lalocandadelpostino.it.*

Stromboli

€€€ **La Sirenetta**. One of the oldest hotels, many say it is still the best. Pool, scuba-diving centre, tennis, water-skiing, windsurfing, sailing. *Via Marina 33, Ficogrande, T: 090 986025, www.lasirenetta.it.*

€€ **Ossidiana**. In the fishermen's quarter of Scari, a short walk from the harbour, all rooms offer panoramic views. Thermal pool and Turkish bath. *Via Marina, T: 090 986006, www.hotelossidiana.it.*

€€ **Il Giardino Segreto**. B&B surrounded by a beautiful garden, with a wide terrace. *Via Francesco Natoli, T: 090 986211, 368 664918, www.giardinosegretobb.it.*

Stromboli (Ginostra)

NB: Ginostra is totally isolated from the rest

of the island and can only be reached by boat, the streets are steep steps, donkeys provide the only means of transport. Bring a torch. A small general store supplies food and other necessities, meat is seldom available in this village.

€ **Locanda L'Incontro**. Tiny inn run by Immacolata Petrusa, a famous cook. *Via Sopra Pertuso, T: 090 9812305, www.ginostraincontro. it. Immacolata can assist in finding rooms or apartments to rent.*

Vulcano
€€€ **Therasia Resort**. Ex Hotel Arcipelago, it is in a quiet position on Vulcanello, with a breathtaking view embracing all seven islands. Very comfortable, 97 spacious rooms, seawater infinity pool and whirlpool, fitness centre with sauna and Turkish bath, two excellent restaurants. *Vulcanello, T: 090 9852555, www.therasiaresort.it.*

€€€ **Les Sables Noirs**. One of the oldest and most prestigious hotels on Vulcano, comfortable rooms, garden, pool, with restaurant on a panoramic terrace facing the beach of black sands. *Porto Ponente, T: 090 9850, www. stelledelsudhotels.com.*

€€€ **Eros**. Small hotel near the hot water springs, 26 rather tiny rooms, restaurant, pool with whirlpool, private beach. *Via Porto Levante 64, T: 090 9853265, www.eroshotel.it.*

WHERE TO EAT

Alì Terme *(map p. 536, D3)*
€€ **L'Oasi**. Friendly *trattoria* serving magnificently cooked fish, freshly caught every day by the local fishermen. Closed Wed. *Via Francesco Crispi 161, T: 0942 716143.*

Capo d'Orlando *(map p. 536, B2)*
€€ **Chocolate**. Restaurant, also bar and coffee shop, relaxed friendly atmosphere, absolutely marvellous fish dishes, a good idea for lunch or dinner. *Piazza Duca degli Abruzzi 3, T: 0941 914190.*

€ **Pasticceria Giulio**. The historic pastry-shop of Capo d'Orlando, just the place for light lunch and fantastic home-made ice cream. *Via Amendola 25, T: 0941 912546.*

Capri Leone *(map p. 536, B2)*
€€€ **Antica Filanda**. Family-run, with a long tradition for excellent and inventive food, making much use of local ham, lamb, kid, various cheeses, and wild fungi from the Nebrodi Mountains, but also foie gras and truffles. Fantastic desserts. Vast wine list. In summer you eat on the terrace looking out towards the Aeolian Islands. Closed Mon. *Contrada Raviola, T: 0941 919704.*

Giardini Naxos *(map p. 536, C3)*
€€€ **Garden da Nino**. Eat right next to the sea, very good seafood (especially the antipasti!), good wine list. Just let Nino take you by the hand. *Via Tysandros 74, T: 0942 51502.*

€€ **'A Putia**. Delightful atmosphere, well-presented Sicilian dishes brought up-to-date with flair, good wine list. For dessert, delicious cinnamon or tangerine jelly. Closed Sun. *Via Umberto 456, T: 0942 52755.*

€ **Angelina**. Airy veranda on the dockside, with a superlative view of Taormina. Very good *spaghetti con le vongole* (clams), or seafood risotto. *T: 0942 51477.*

Messina *(map p. 536, D2)*
€€€ **Le Due Sorelle**. Unusual, imaginative dishes making good use of fish, fresh vegetables, cheese and meat from the Nebrodi Mountains, local wines. Closed midday Sat and Sun. *Piazza Municipio 4, T: 090 44720. Map p. 427, 4.*

€€ **Osteria del Campanile**. This elegant restaurant behind the cathedral serves a wide variety of very good pasta dishes. Closed Sun evening. *Via Loggia dei Mercanti 9, T: 090 711418. Map p. 427, 4.*

€ **Porta Messina**. Simple restaurant serving freshly-cooked food, generous portions, conveniently close to the railway station.

Closed Sat. *Via Calabria 16, T: 090 673831. Map p. 427, 6.*

€ Bar Cardullo. Close to the harbour, excellent food, always crowded. Light lunches or delicious hot snacks, home-made ice cream and cakes. *Via Ugo Bassi 7, T: 090 774413. Map p. 427, 6.*

€ Il Cappero. Excellent lunch stop, for tasty Sicilian 'fast food', and *focacce*, soft bread rolls with various fillings. Closed Sun evening. *Via Manara 85, T: 090 669693. Map p. 427, 7.*

Milazzo *(map p. 536, C2)*

€€€ Al Piccolo Casale. Elegant and fashionable, for excellent fish; also pizzeria, nice desserts, amazing wine list. In summer you eat on the terrace. Closed Mon. *Via R. D'Amico 12, T: 090 9224479.*

€€€ Doppio Gusto. Of course fish is the speciality in this restaurant, with a veranda providing a view of the port; very nice hot and cold *antipasti*; crudités, spaghetti with lobster, home-made desserts, Sicilian wines, all very well presented. Closed Sun. *Via Rizzo 44/45, T: 090 9240045.*

€€ La Casalinga. In a tiny alley, friendly, relaxed atmosphere, generous portions. *Via D'Amico, T: 090 9222697.*

Patti *(map p. 536, C2)*

€ Mare e Monti. Very fresh fish, creative cuisine, also excellent pizza, good service. *Via Colombo 191 (Piazza Amedeo di Savoia), Marina di Patti, T: 0941 362479.*

Taormina *(map p. 536, C3)*

€€€ Duomo. Beautiful setting on a flowery terrace overlooking the cathedral, very high standard Sicilian cuisine; popular with celebrities. Closed Mon in winter. *Vico Ebrei 11, T: 0942 625656. Map p. 437, 5.*

€€ La Botte. Congenial trattoria frequented by musicians performing at the Greek Theatre, or locals like Jim Kerr and Mick Hucknall. Good Sicilian *antipasti*. *Piazzetta San Domenico, T: 0942 24198.Map p. 437, 5.*

€€ La Griglia. The owner, Giorgio, takes good care of his guests. Closed Tues. *Corso Umberto 54, T: 0942 23980. Map p. 437, 1.*

Taormina (Mazzarò)

€€ Il Barcaiolo. ■ Tiny family-run restaurant for delicious fish, especially the local red shrimps caught just a few yards away, accompanied by Sicilian wines. From the road opposite Hotel Villa Esperia you go down 120 steps to the beach. It is very romantic in the evening, but don't forget the midge repellent. Open summer only. *T: 0942 625633. Map p. 437, 4.*

Taormina (Spisone)

€€€ La Capinera. Award-winning chef Pietro D'Agostino prepares his fabulous dishes inspired by tradition, with an innovative twist. Everything is prepared fresh in his kitchen, from the bread to the after-dinner chocolates, and served on the terrace overlooking the sea. Good wine list, also lists for mineral water and beer. Closed Mon. Expensive. *Via Nazionale 177, T: 0942 626247. Beyond map p. 437, 4.*

Aeolian Islands
Alicudi

€€ L'Airone. Overlooking the sea, romantic, for memorable seafood feasts. Alicudi is particularly famous for tattlers, a type of squid. *Via Perciato, T: 090 9889690.*

Filicudi

€€ Da Nino sul Mare. A terrace overlooking the sea; good seafood antipasti, pasta, spaghetti with lobster. Closed winter. *Via Porto, T: 090 9889984.*

Lipari

€€€ Filippino. Well-known restaurant, of the Buon Ricordo chain, opened in 1910. Memorable *ravioli di cernia* (sea-perch ravioli), swordfish soufflé, or lobster Aeolian-style with caper sauce. Closed Mon in winter. *Piazza Mazzini, T: 090 9811002. Map p. 465, 4.*

€€€ **Kasbah Café**. Delightful restaurant with a quiet garden, excellent seafood and pizza, delicious desserts. Closed winter. *Via Maurolico 25, T: 090 9811075. Map p. 465, 5.*

€€ **E' Pulera**. Beautiful setting for this elegant restaurant with a long-standing reputation for excellence. Open May–Oct. *Via Diana, T: 090 9811158. Beyond map p. 465, 5.*

€€ **Caffè La Vela**. ■ For people-watching on the harbour. The owner, Carlo, has won prizes for his superb, deceptively simple salads, and Sicilian breakfast with mulberry *granita* is worth the trip to Lipari. *Marina Corta, T: 090 9880064. Map p. 465, 8.*

Panarea

€€€ **Da Pina**. Pina is an institution, innovative and imaginative. Her *gnocchi di melanzane* (aubergine dumplings) are unique. *Via San Pietro, T: 090 983041.*

€€ **Antonio il Macellaio**. Only grilled meat is served here, for carnivores who have had enough fish. *Via San Pietro, T: 090 983033.*

Salina

€€€ **Porto Bello**. Famous for *spaghetti al fuoco* (fiery spaghetti) and a dessert made of fresh ricotta with honey, pine nuts and currants. Meals are served on the terrace overlooking the harbour. Closed winter. *Via Lungomare, Santa Marina, T: 090 9843125.*

€€€ **Il Delfino**. Run by three sisters, talented chefs, you will find perfect grilled tattlers. Closed winter. *Via Marina Garibaldi 5, Lingua,T: 090 9843024.*

€€ **Franco**. Franco is very proud of his spaghetti with sea urchins, or the unique caper salad. *Via Belvedere, Santa Marina, T: 090 9843287.*

€ **Il Gambero**. For shrimps and grilled squid, or try the *pane cunzato* for lunch. Closed winter. *Via Marina Garibaldi, Lingua, T: 090 9843049.*

Stromboli

€€€ **Da Zurro**. Try the black ravioli filled with fish and ricotta. *Via Picone 18, T: 090 986283.*

€€€ **Punta Lena**. On a panoramic terrace overlooking Strombolicchio; excellent grilled vegetables, sardines with onions, fish is cooked on a hot slab of lava. *Via Marina 8, Ficogrande, T: 090 986204.*

€€ **Ai Geki**. A firm favourite with local people, for creative Aeolian cuisine. Closed lunchtime in summer, open only on request in winter. *Vico Salina 12, T: 090 986213.*

Vulcano

€€ **Cantine Stevenson**. Modern, pleasant atmosphere; interesting cuisine and vast wine-list. *Porto di Levante, T: 090 9853247.*

€€ **Vincenzino**. Restaurant in a good position, with a long-standing reputation, but it has its ups and downs. Spaghetti 'alla Vincenzina' (with shrimps and capers) are excellent. Closed winter. *Via Porto Levante, T: 090 9852016.*

€ **Maria Tindara**. At Piano, in the heart of the island, Maria Tindara is an excellent cook specialising both in grilled meat, such as chicken, kid, or rabbit, or freshly-caught fish; home-made pasta is prepared daily. Call and she will arrange transport at no extra charge. *T: 090 9853004.*

LOCAL SPECIALITIES

Letojanni Niny Bar. Run by the same family for three generations, their speciality is *granita arcobaleno* (rainbow), with alternating layers of fresh fruit *granita*—lemon, peach, mulberry, strawberry and pineapple—in a glass. Top it with whipped cream (*Via Vittorio Emanuele 214, corner of Piazza Durante, T: 0942 36104*).

Messina Irrera (*Piazza Cairoli 12*) is one of the most famous pastry shops in Sicily, founded in 1910 and renowned for its *pignolata messinese*, a confection formed of small pastry balls individually iced with lemon and chocolate, and piled up on a tray to form a cake. Salumeria Francesco Doddis (*Via Garibaldi 317*) for cheese, salami and ham from the Nebrodi Mountains. Salvatore Geraci of the Azienda Agricola Palari (*Villa Geraci, Santo Stefano di Briga, T: 090 630194, www.palari.it*), on the hills overlooking Messina, produces the wonderful DOC Faro and several other excellent wines,

Mistretta Antonino Testa (*Via Libertà 2*) for the local biscuits made of white marzipan.

Novara di Sicilia Coop Cucinotta (*Via Benigno Salvo 3*) is a bakery where you will find the large, round, fragrant loaves of bread for which Novara is famous. The cafés in Novara serve *gelato di cedro*, made with large knobbly lemons with very thick peel and practically no flesh inside. The zest is particularly aromatic.

Patti Decorative ceramic oven-to-table-to-freezer-to dishwasher ware, beautiful designs inspired by nature, with all the light and the energy of Sicily; so delightful they are voraciously and illegally copied by Chinese manufacturers. No cadmium or lead is used in the colours. Caleca (*Contrada Ponte Vecchio, T: 0941 2421, www.caleca.it*).

San Marco d'Alunzio La Tela di Penelope (*Via Aluntina 48, T: 0941 797734, www.teladipenelope.it*) is a delightful shop offering hand-woven linen articles according to the local tradition, decorated with embroidery, lace, macramé or drawn-thread work. Upstairs is a comfortable little B&B.

Santa Lucia del Mela Mamertino DOC is produced by Azienda Agricola Vasari (*Contrada Casale, T: 090 9359956, www.biovinivasari.it*).

Santo Stefano di Camastra La Maga (*Via Nazionale 112/114, T: 0921 331286*) for irresistible pottery and tiles, all hand-made using traditional colours and designs.

Taormina Gladys Art (*Corso Umberto, near Porta Messina*), sells paintings by local art-

ists, perfect souvenirs. Gelatomania (*Corso Umberto 7*), for award-winning ice cream; try their delectable Ferrero Rocher, or in summer, mango flavour, prepared with locally grown fruit.

Tortorici For the exquisite *pasta reale* pastries made with hazelnuts, a good address is Ciancio (*Piazza Mazzini 2, T: 0941 430595*).

Aeolian Islands

Lipari I Gioielli del Mare (*Via Garibaldi 8, Marina Corta, T: 090 9880857, www.igioiellidelmare.com*) is where Francesco Berté creates striking jewels inspired by the sea, using shells, semi-precious stones, and obsidian, the black glass-like volcanic stone. Closed Fri–Sun in winter. Da Giulio (*Via Garibaldi 153*) is a browser's paradise, with antiques, nautical curios and odd bric-à-brac.

Salina Carlo Hauner (*Via Umberto, Lingua, T: 090 9843141, www.hauner.it*) for some Malvasia or Malvasia Passito, or even some capers. Carpe Diem (*Via Risorgimento 28 and 156, Santa Marina*) for excellent capers and other local products. At Lingua, Da Alfredo (opposite the pier in Piazza Marina Garibaldi) serves scrumptious fresh-fruit *granita*: try prickly pear flavour. Closed winter. Cosi Duci (*Via San Lorenzo 9, Malfa, T: 090 9844358; open every day; if closed in winter, they will open if you phone*) is a Salina institution. They sell sweets and jams made with local wild fruits such as pomegranates, mulberries, prickly pears, sorb-apples and arbutus.

FESTIVALS & EVENTS

Acquedolci 14–15 May, *Fiera del Bestiame*, when local farmers meet to trade cattle, horses, pigs and sheep.

Alcara Li Fusi 24 June, *Festa del Muzzuni*—the summer solstice. The *muzzuni* is a large glass bottle, or earthenware jar, one for each of the town districts. On the evening of the 23rd the jars are richly decorated with silk scarves, gold jewellery and ears of wheat, and carried to roadside altars by young, unmarried girls. The altars are draped with brightly coloured *pezzare*, hand-woven rugs. The statue of St John the Baptist is carried in procession through the streets, blessing the *muzzuni*, thus guaranteeing prosperity and fertility to every part of the town. The custom probably goes back to pre-Christian fertility rituals (*Info: www.comune.alcaralifusi.me.it*).

Capo d'Orlando July, International Blues Festival, in the gardens of Villa Piccolo (*Info: www.nebrodieventi.it*).

Castroreale 23–25 Aug, the *Cristo Longo*, a Crucifix on a pole fully as high as the Matrice is carried in procession through the streets.

Messina 30 March, St Eustochia, preceded by a week of concerts and debates. Good Friday, *Le Varette*, traditional religious procession. 3 June, *'A Matri 'a Littra'*, festivities for the feast of the Madonna of the Letter, the patron saint. June, Corpus Domini procession including a ship, the *Vascelluzzo*. 13-14 Aug, traditional processions of the *Giganti* (Giants). 15 Aug, the *Vara* (float with tableau) for the feast of the Assumption.

Novara di Sicilia last week before Lent, *Gara del maiorchino* is a competition between teams of three who each roll a wheel of *maiorchino* cheese down the steep streets (*Info: www.comune.novara-di-sicilia.me.it*).

San Fratello Good Friday, the ancient *Festa dei Giudei* is celebrated; colourfully dressed 'Judaeans', wearing helmets, performing acrobatics and blowing trumpets, try to interrupt the solemn procession for the dead Christ, of course unsuccessfully. 10 May, *Cavalcata*, a procession on horseback to the sanctuary-church (national monument) on the nearby mountain where the three patron saints, Alfio, Cirino and Filadelfo, stopped on their way to matyrdom at Trecastagni or Lentini (c. 350 AD). 1st Sun in Sept, *Mercato-Concorso del Cavallo di San Fratello*, traditional parade and market of the famous San Fratello horses, the only ones in Europe still living wild in their native habitat. 17 Sept, Feast of St Benedict the Moor, with a procession and fireworks.

Taormina June–Sept, *Taormina Arte*, a series of events, starting with the Film Festival, including drama, concerts, and ballet, with top performers (*Info: www.taormina-arte.com*). 20 Sept, feast dedicated to the Madonna della Rocca, when roast kid and lamb is offered to the pilgrims on their way down from the church.

Tindari May–July, the old theatre is used for presenting concerts, plays and operas (*Info: T: 0941 246318, www.teatrodeiduemari.it*).

Tortorici 20 Jan, the annual feast of St Sebastian (here known as *Sammastianuzzu*) involves a dramatic procession of barefooted faithful who carry the heavy stone statue of the saint through the river in full flood.

Aeolian Islands

Lipari 18 July, Our Lady of Portosalvo, a fishermen's celebration. 24 Aug, San Bartolomeo, the patron saint of the islands. July–Aug, *Efesto D'Oro*, screening and prize-giving for films which have been inspired by, or made on, the islands.

Salina 23 July *Madonna del Terzito*, at Leni, very colourful and heartfelt. 20–25 Sept, festival of local products: Salina DOC Fest (*Info: www.salinadocfest.it*).

PRACTICAL INFORMATION

PLANNING YOUR TRIP

When to go

Travelling in Sicily is enjoyable year round, though autumn rainstorms can be very heavy. Winters are mild, but there can be some very cold days. It is usually very hot in July and August (sometimes 40°C or more). The dreaded scirocco, the hot, suffocating wind from Africa, can blow at any time of year. The best time for wildflowers is Feb–March and Feb is also Carnival time. Easter is celebrated with impressive traditional processions in many towns, but in March, April and May school groups descend on historical sites and museums. The best time to visit places such as the Roman villa at Piazza Armerina, or the Greek theatre in Taormina, for example, is at lunchtime. The *maestrale*, the prevailing wind around Messina and the Aeolian Islands, blows from the northwest, and is very strong in winter, often making it difficult for the hydrofoils; sometimes even the ferryboats have problems and the islands can be cut off for several days. Strong winds can also affect communications between Trapani and the Aegadian Islands, and between Porto Empedocle and the Pelagian Islands. In winter, although the days are shorter, there are no crowds, the weather is usually mild with cloudless skies, and there is the incomparable sight of Mt Etna covered in snow. At the end of Oct and early Nov there is much preparation for one of the island's most popular celebrations, the *Festa dei Morti*, All Souls Day (2nd Nov), when everyone takes sheaves of chrysanthemums to the cemeteries and children receive toys, ostensibly from their dead ancestors. Special cakes and sweets are made for the occasion.

Maps

Still a necessary supplement even to the best GPS system. The best are published by the Touring Club Italiano (*www.touringclub.it*). Their *Grande Carta Stradale d'Italia*, on a scale of 1:200,000, is divided into 15 maps covering the regions of Italy, including Sicily (sheet 14). They are also published in a three-volume atlas called the *Atlante Stradale d'Italia*. The one entitled *Sud* covers Sicily. Individual city, province and island maps are available in most local bookshops in Sicily, along with some detailed walking maps for regions of specific interest, such as Mt Etna.

Health and insurance

EU citizens have the right to health services in Italy if they have possession of the free European Health Insurance Card (EHIC). Otherwise you are advised to take out insurance before travelling. Remember to keep all receipts (*ricevute*) and medical reports (*cartella clinica*) to give to your insurer if you need to make a claim. Thefts or damage to property must be reported immediately at the local police station; a copy of the report (*denuncia*) will be needed to claim on your insurance.

Disabled travellers

Sicily is not good for disabled travellers, who will need all their resources of patience and adaptability in order to get around. Although legislation obliges public buildings to provide access and facilities, it will be many years before Sicily catches up with mainland Italy or the rest of Europe. Many churches have imposing flights of steps as their only means of access, not to mention stepped streets and alleys. Toilets in coffee bars or restaurants are often on the first floor, and lifts are rare. In the annual accommodation list published by the local tourist offices, establishments which can offer hospitality to the disabled are indicated. Airports and railway stations now provide assistance and certain trains are equipped to transport wheelchairs. Access for cars with disabled people is allowed to town centres usually closed to traffic, where parking places are reserved for them. For more information, contact the local tourist offices.

GETTING AROUND

By air

Palermo (Falcone Borsellino Airport, www.gesap.it), Catania (Fontanarossa Airport, www.aeroporto.catania.it) and Trapani (Vincenzo Florio Airport, www.aeroportotrapani.com) are served by national and international flights. In addition, Trapani connects Pantelleria and Lampedusa to Sicily and the mainland. New airports are planned for Comiso to serve the Ragusa-Syracuse area, and Racalmuto for Agrigento-Sciacca. In addition to direct international flights, several companies offer one-stop flights via Rome or Milan. Most Italian mainland cities and Sardinia have frequent flights to Sicily.

By sea

Car ferries on the Straits of Messina operate from to and from Villa San Giovanni on the mainland (every 20mins 24hrs a day, no booking necessary), taking about 20mins to reach Messina. There are often queues and delays in the summer. Less frequent ferries and hydrofoils leave from Reggio Calabria, taking 40mins. Ferries and hydrofoils for the offshore islands are dealt with at the end of each relevant chapter.

By rail

Rail services in Sicily lag behind those on the mainland. Rolling stock is outdated while most lines are single track and in some cases are those laid in the 19th century. The journey from Catania to Palermo, c. 200kms, takes less than 3hrs by coach, but 6hrs by train. Recent cutbacks mean that intercity services within the island have been slashed, and it is wise to check the frequency of connections.

The Italian Railway Company, Trenitalia (www.trenitalia.com) runs various categories of trains: ES (Eurostar) are international express trains between major cities (with obligatory seat reservation) with first- and second-class carriages; EC and IC are international and national express trains; Espressi are long-distance trains (both classes), not as fast as the Intercity trains; Diretti, although not stopping at every station, are slower than Espressi; and Inter-regionali and Regionali are local trains stopping at all stations, mostly with second-class carriages only. Many stations are now unmanned: tickets can be purchased in the nearest coffee bar, tobacconist or newsagent. Valid for two months after the day sold, they must be bought before the journey, and date-stamped in the machines you find on the platforms, otherwise the ticket-collector will exact a stiff fine. In Italy fares are still much lower than many other parts of Europe. Children under the age of four travel free, and between the ages of four and 12 travel half price. If you are planning a lengthy journey through Europe starting in Italy, then a Eurodomino pass (www.eurodomino.it) is useful, with a voucher for each country you intend to visit. Also for journeys starting in Italy, the Carta Verde and Carta Verde Railplus allow discounts on tickets.

By bus
Inter-city and inter-village services in Sicily are widespread, punctual (although perhaps infrequent) and fairly comfortable. Services tend to finish in the early evening. Information on the bus companies, with websites, are in each chapter listing. Tickets can sometimes be purchased on board, sometimes at the nearest coffee bar or tobacconist; unfortunately there is no standard system.

By car
The quality of the roads is on the whole quite good. In large towns, traffic is chaotic, the streets congested and parking difficult. Signposting is erratic, and you will often have to stop to ask directions. Motorways (*autostrade*) have green signs, normal roads blue signs. At the entrance to motorways, the two directions are indicated by the name of the town at the end of the road, not by that of the nearest town. They are a fast and convenient way of travelling around, crossing difficult terrain by means of viaducts and tunnels, and in places they are spectacularly beautiful. Most stretches are toll free.

NB: always lock your car when parked, and never leave anything of value inside it. If purchasing fuel or oil at a motorway service station, always check that you have been given the right amount, that the seal on the oil can is intact, and that you have been given the correct change.

ADDITIONAL INFORMATION

Crime and personal security
Pickpocketing is a widespread problem: it is always advisable not to carry valuables and to take special care of handbags or shoulder bags. Snatch thefts, especially by passing scooters, are common. Crimes should be reported immediately to the police or local *carabinieri* office (found in every small town and village).

Emergency numbers
Police: 113 (Polizia di Stato) or 112 (Carabinieri).
Fire and Rescue: 115
Ambulance and First Aid: 118

Opening times

The opening times of museums, churches and archaeological sites are given in the text, though they are subject to change without warning. Churches usually close in the middle of the day, opening again around 4pm. Visitors are expected to dress suitably (no miniskirts, shorts, or bare shoulders), and to avoid eating, drinking, talking loudly or using mobile phones. Photography is always forbidden when Mass is in progress. In Holy Week most of the images are covered and are on no account shown. Many museums and archaeological sites are suffering from staff shortages and are ever more likely to close in the afternoons and on public holidays. If some of the rooms are closed, try asking one of the guards to open them. If they can, they are often happy to help and may be able to arrange for the room to be opened especially for you if you can wait for just a few minutes. Thank them profusely if they are able to arrange this, as it is often done on their own initiative and at their own risk, and such behaviour must be encouraged. Local tourist offices are supposed to have up-to-date information, but this is often not the case.

Telephones and the internet

For all calls in Italy, local and long distance, dial the city code (for instance, 091 for Palermo), then the phone number. For international and intercontinental calls, dial 00 plus the country code, then the city code (for numbers in the UK drop the initial zero) and number. To call Sicily from abroad (not USA) dial 0039, then the city code and number. To call Sicily from the USA dial 011 39, then the city code and number.

Mobile phone coverage has very few gaps on Sicily and the offshore islands; often it is sufficient to move a few metres to get the line back. Most hotels, and many restaurants and coffee bars, offer Wifi. If you have problems, you will find plenty of people ready to help.

Useful websites

General: www.regione.sicilia.it/turismo; www.bestofsicily.com; www.retesicilia.it; www.saporiegustidisicilia.it; www.sicilia.indettaglio.it; www.borghitalia.it (beautiful villages).

News: www.siciliaonline.it; www.balarm.it; www.siciliano.it.

Travel and timetables: www.orariautobus.it (buses) and www.bookingitalia.it (up-to-date info on ferries, timetables, tariffs and buses to and from ports).

Events: www.regione.sicilia.it/eventiturismo.

Food and wines: www.slowfood.com; www.justsicilia.it (to order food products and wine online); www.cookandsicily.com; www.vitevino.it; www.movimentoturismovino.it.

Museums and galleries: www.regione.sicilia.it/beniculturali.

Nature: www.siciliaparchi.com; www.parks.it; www.entefaunasiciliana.it; www.legambientesicilia.it; www.wwfitalia.it/sicilia; www.lipu.it.

Personalised tours: www.si-sicily.it; www.sicilyguides.com; www.sicilytravel.net.

Renting a villa: www.dicasainsicilia.it; www.livesicily.it; www.solosicily.com; www.travelsicilia.com.

ACCOMMODATION

A few places to stay have been suggested in the text, chosen for at least one of these qualities: character; historical interest; location; value for money; and comfort. They range from luxurious, world-famous 5-star hotels, to *relais de charme*, simple inns or B&B accommodation in farms or country houses. They are classified as €€€ (200 euros or over), €€ (100–200 euros) or € (under 100 euros). Prices vary widely according to season and location.

BLUE GUIDES RECOMMENDED

Hotels and restaurants and *trattorie* that are particularly good choices in their category—in terms of excellence, location, charm, value for money or the quality of the experience they provide—carry the Blue Guides Recommended sign: ■. All these establishments have been visited and selected by our authors, editors or contributors as places they have particularly enjoyed and would be happy to recommend to others. To keep our entries up-to-date, reader feedback is essential: please do not hesitate to contact us (www.blueguides.com) with any views, corrections or suggestions.

NB: Continental breakfast is usually included in the room price: by law it is an optional extra. Hotels are now also obliged (for tax purposes) to issue a receipt: in theory guests can be fined for leaving the premises without one.

There is a wide choice of B&B accommodation in Sicily, both in the towns and in the countryside; legislation in Italy has been relaxed, making it much easier for those so inclined to offer rooms to paying guests, who are in turn likely to achieve a much better understanding of the places they visit. Sicilians are extremely hospitable, and their homes are comfortable. Most of the provinces classify this type of accommodation according to the star system: one star means you will have to share the bathroom with the family; three-star establishments can be as good as luxurious small hotels.

There are hundreds of working farms in Sicily which offer rooms (*agriturismo*), highly recommended for travellers with their own transport and families with young children. Terms vary from bed and breakfast to full board or self-contained flats; some farms require a stay of a minimum number of days. Cultural or recreational activities such as horse-riding are sometimes provided; on some farms you can help with the work on a voluntary basis: milking sheep, gathering olives or fruit, harvesting wheat, and so forth. Again, most provinces use the star system to classify the standards.

Country houses are simply houses in the country without a working farm; some of them are aristocratic villas, others are quite basic. They can be recommended to independent travellers who enjoy the countryside.

There is a wide range of rooms and apartments to rent, including villas, farmhouses, beach bungalows and city-centre apartments, readily available for short-term rental. In some towns where the old centres are being abandoned, civic administrations are helping home-owners to restore their properties in order to provide accommodation for tourists in *paese-albergo*. The owners usually live elsewhere. It is an adventurous (and inexpensive) solution for those who want to get a 'feel' for a town. The neighbours will certainly be welcoming. Information from the town councils or from the tourist offices.

Many convents and monasteries have rooms available for visitors in religious institutions. These are very basic, but always with private bath or shower. Sometimes meals can be taken in the refectory. It is not required that guests be Catholic in religion, and it always represents very good value for money.

FOOD & DRINK

Restaurants

A selected choice of restaurants for all pockets is given at the end of each chapter. The choices reflect pleasant personal experience and an endeavour to introduce travellers to the very best local dishes and wines. They are categorised according to the approximate cost of a meal without drinks: €€€ means a fine-dining restaurant, over 40 euros per head (sometimes well over); €€ means a good restaurant, 25–35 euros per head; € means a simple *trattoria* where you will pay 15–30 euros per head.

Mealtimes and tipping

Mealtimes are later than elsewhere in Italy: lunch usually about 1.30pm; dinner at 8.30pm or later. Service charges are included in the bill unless otherwise stated (some places also add a cover charge), so tipping is not an obligation, but always much appreciated. The main meal of the day is lunch, almost invariably consisting of pasta; soup rarely appears on the menu. Restaurant meals are the occasion for dressing up, to look and be looked at, in the comfortable knowledge that each dish you have chosen will be specially prepared, and not warmed up in the microwave. Sicilians rarely ask for the menu, they prefer to accept the advice of the waiter, cook, or restaurant owner, who will describe the delicacies found at the market that morning, and how they will be prepared; eventually suggesting the best wine to accompany each course, or the whole meal.

SICILIAN FOOD

That food, its preparation and consumption should be of such absorbing interest for Sicilians is not so surprising; their cuisine is the sum of many different foreign dominations, each one of which introduced new foods and cooking techniques. Sicilian cooks have an innate sense of colour and design, a strong natural talent and inventiveness, and stubbornly refuse to use anything but the freshest ingredients available; qualities for which they are known and appreciated everywhere. The earliest surviving cookery-book in the world was written in the 4th century BC by Archestratus of Gela, and called the *Hedypatheia* or *On Good Taste*, a long poem listing various foods and drinks, how they should be prepared, and how they should be enjoyed. He enthuses about the flavour of lobsters from Lipari, gilt-head bream from Syracuse, swordfish from Messina, tuna from Tindari, bread, wine and hares, advising cooks to keep condiments to a minimum. His book was translated into Latin and even became the object of the satire of Horatio; some of the recipes were included by the famous gourmet Apicius (1st century AD), in his book *De Re Coquinaria*, or *The Art of Cooking*.

Sicilians have known and used saffron since prehistory; they were the first in Italy to cultivate artichokes, and the first to use rice. The Arabs, in fact, in the 9th century created rice-paddies in the meadows south of Catania, between the Simeto and the San Leonardo rivers, and also introduced citrus, dates, sugar-cane, aubergines, pistachios, a taste for cinnamon, and the use of terracing and irrigation in the countryside. Pasta, in the form of vermicelli, was already being made at Trabia near Palermo in the 12th century, according to Roger II's geographer el-Edrisi, long before Marco Polo brought some back from China, and it was certainly the Sicilians who invented sun-dried tomatoes. Tomatoes, together with chilli pepper and chocolate, had arrived with the Spanish in the 17th century. A hundred years later, the Kingdom of the Two Sicilies, based in Naples, ushered in the demand for the expensive, capricious, but indispensable *monzù*, the French chef, whom aristocratic families of the island deemed a status-symbol. With him came butter, cream, and refined sauces and soups.

Many local writers have described the symphony of colours, aromas and flavours which can be achieved only in Sicily. Federico De Roberto, in his *I Viceré*, opens for us the monastic kitchens of San Benedetto in Catania, Giuseppe Tomasi di Lampedusa in *Il Gattopardo* conjures up the magnificent banquets prepared by the prince's French *monzù*, and Andrea Camilleri evokes Chief Inspector Montalbano's *arancine*, golden-brown rice balls, or his favourite grilled red mullet and baby octopus.

SICILIAN SPECIALITIES

Bread

It was the wheat-fields of Ramacca, in the province of Catania, that inspired Wagner's *Harvesters' Hymn*; the wheat-fields which were the gift of Demeter herself. Sicilian bread varies enormously in shape, size, colour and flavour. There are 72 different specialities. Each family eats an average of almost 100kg of bread a year, and they treat it with almost religious reverence. Often made using the sourdough method and topped with sesame seeds, it is preferably cooked in stone ovens, which are heated by burning olive, almond, oak, lemon or orange wood, or even almond shells, depending on what fuel is more abundant. Some bakers can trace the origin of their sourdough back over 200 years. The basic ingredient is durum-wheat flour, usually a blend of different varieties. At Castelvetrano, for example, the coffee-coloured loaves owe their aroma and rich flavour to the addition of *tumminia* flour, which grows only in a very small area, and is thought to have been first cultivated by the people of Selinunte, while in Lentini they add a little *timilia* wheat. Other localities renowned for the quality of the bread are Monreale,

Favara, Novara di Sicilia, Montalbano Elicona and San Giuseppe Jato. Bread is at the centre of several religious festivities, some probably of pagan origin. At Campofranco, for the feast of St Calogero huge 'bread-men', almost life-size, are paraded around the town with the saint, before kissing him goodbye and being broken up by the priest and divided among the onlookers, while in Agrigento the same saint is pelted with tiny loaves thrown from the balconies as he makes his progress through the streets. 18 March, St Joseph's day, is the occasion for baking particularly fancy loaves to place on the altars set up in the streets of many towns, together with hundreds of different foods which will be presented to the poor; but nowhere is this art expressed better than in Salemi, where the loaves are worked with such intricacy they look like delicate carvings in old ivory.

Olive oil

Sicilian olive oil is excellent. So many different soil types, and slight local variations in climate, mean that several different varieties of olive tree can be cultivated, some of which can be traced back thousands of years, and may be native to the island. Sicily provides only ten percent of the entire national production of oil, but by far the largest quantity of olives for salting and curing, both black and green. The finest groves are probably those of the province of Trapani, around Castelvetrano. Here the trees are pruned to stay very small, and the olives are picked by hand, resulting in perfect oil and sublime pickles. Excellent oil is also produced at Caronia (Messina), Ragalna, Bronte and Mineo (Catania), Syracuse, and Chiaramonte Gulfi (Ragusa), where the precious liquid is the linchpin of the economy, and there is even an olive-oil museum. Nowadays the best oils are protected by the DOP seal (*Denominazione d'Origine di Produzione*), a guarantee of quality similar to that offered to the finest wines.

Confectionery

Sicilian confectionery is a delectable riot of colours, aromas and flavours: there are the simple, fragrant breakfast pastries; crystallised and candied fruits; fruits made of marzipan; nougat; biscuits made with almonds, pistachios or hazelnuts; crunchy *cannoli* filled with sweet ricotta cheese; the elaborate Baroque complexities of the magnificent *cassata siciliana*, filled with ricotta; and the light and delicate *paste di mandorla*, the almond pastries of Acireale. Every town or village has its own speciality, and different sweets are prepared for the main feasts of the year. The abundance of local nuts and fruits, and the introduction of sugar by the Arabs, are at the base of the Sicilian tradition, perfected through the centuries first by the Arab ladies in their harems, preparing sweet delights to offer to guests, and later by the nuns in many convents in Sicily. They achieved such excellence that their exquisite confections were always much in demand, especially at Easter time: the nuns were kept so busy that the bishops were forced to intervene, warning the sisters to abstain from baking, at least during Holy Week, and to dedicate their energies to prayer instead.

Ice cream

Italians eat a lot of ice cream (apparently only Americans and Australians eat more) and

Sicilians even have it for breakfast. It is quite possible that ice cream was invented in Sicily: we know that the Romans brought down snow from Mt Etna during the winter. They stored it in *niviere*, pits dug in cool cellars, covering it with a thick layer of straw or sawdust to keep it fresh until summer. It was then recovered and mixed with wine, honey and spices, and sold as a great luxury to those who could afford it. The Arabs in Sicily took the process one step further, by using sugar instead of honey, and fruit juice instead of wine; they called their confection *sharbat* (hence sherbet; sorbet). But the first confectioner to have the brainwave of adding cream to the mixture was a young late 17th-century Sicilian, Procopio de' Coltelli of Acitrezza. He took his discovery to Paris, to delight Louis XIV; the king gave him the exclusive rights of manufacture. He opened the Café Procope, still in existence, which claims to be the world's first coffee-house, frequented by Voltaire, Benjamin Franklin and much of Parisian society.

In Sicily the manufacture of ice cream is still a point of honour, and there are plenty of pastry shops and coffee bars where you will find ice cream made on the premises. The coveted annual Procopio de' Coltelli award goes to the best ice cream maker on the island. A list of ingredients by the counter is a very good sign of quality. *Gelato* is ice cream made with eggs and milk or cream. *Granita* is fruit juice (or coffee, or ground almonds or pistachios) and sugar, blended and frozen together. *Cremolata* and *sorbetto* are variations on the theme, which sometimes see the addition of egg-whites.

In Sicilian towns from April–Oct the ice cream vendors take up their stands in the early morning, and blow a whistle or ring a bell to announce breakfast. People some-times come down into the street in their pyjamas. Ice cream is usually served in a soft brioche roll, like a sandwich. Granita comes in a plastic cup, into which pieces of brio-che are dunked. You can have several flavours at the same time, and even add a dollop of whipped cream. In city centres people will have their ice-cream breakfast at the cof-fee bar. Wherever it takes place, it is the first moment of social aggregation of the day.

Soft drinks

The thirsty Sicilian asks for *latte di mandorla* (almond milk), made with crushed al-monds and sugar diluted with water and chilled (the best are to be found in Catania and Modica). Very sweet, it is surprisingly refreshing. In town centres, kiosks serve other inexpensive thirst-quenchers: freshly-squeezed lemon juice with soda water and a pinch of salt is one of the most popular (*selz, limone e sale*). Kiosk owners often make their own fluorescent fruit syrups, which are then diluted with soda water. Cheap and popular fizzy drinks, which have been around for generations, are *spuma, gazzosa* and *chinotto*.

Unique culinary delights, province by province

The geography of Sicily varies dramatically and it is only natural that different re-gions should have different specialities. The international Slow Food Foundation has a strong following here and has nominated about 40 Sicilian food products as *presidia*, or worthy of protection. Several risked disappearing altogether, due to globalisation and tough EU laws (the use of time-honoured equipment, and ancient farming methods, are not always compatible with strict modern hygiene standards). Special regional decrees have had to be issued for many of them, underlining their incalculable traditional value, to save them from oblivion.

Palermo

The people of Palermo love to eat simple, cheap snacks in the street, such as boiled octopus, chick-pea fritters or beef spleen sandwiched in crunchy bread rolls, intestines of sheep or kid wound around a piece of cane and grilled. The list is endless. The Palermitans are also the acknowledged masters in the preparation of *pasta con le sarde*, macaroni served with a rich sauce of wild fennel, anchovies, onion, fresh sardines, pine nuts, currants, saffron, almonds and sometimes tomatoes—an addition which is frequently hotly disputed. Pollina and Castelbuono in the Madonie Mountains are the only places in the world where the manna ash trunks are incised to collect the white syrupy sap, which is dried and used for making medicines and sweeteners. Also from the Madonie Mountains comes *provola*, sweet-flavoured sheep's milk cheese, each weighing about 1kg with a little 'neck' to hang it from as it ripens. On the island of Ustica, tiny, dark brown lentils are grown completely without herbicides or fertilisers; donkeys dragging stones are still used for threshing. They are soft, tender and quick to cook. Late-ripening tangerines can be found at Ciaculli, in the Conca d'Oro behind Palermo.

Trapani

The salt-pans of Trapani, so jealously husbanded by Phoenicians and Romans, and profitably used by the Florio family in the 19th century, meant that Trapani's fabulous bluefin tuna could be salted, preserved and exported widely. Red garlic is grown in the salt marshes around Nubia. It has small corms, red skin, and an intense flavour. The island of Pantelleria is famous for its capers: very small and strong-flavoured, they are the flower buds of the plant, gathered just before blossoming. Black bread is baked in stone ovens in Castelvetrano, using the sourdough method and a mixture of two different kinds of durum wheat. Each loaf weighs 1kg. The crust is very dark brown, almost black, the crumb is golden, the flavour is sublime. *Vastedda* cheeses from the Belice Valley are small round cheeses formed in a soup plate (the meaning of the name in Sicilian). They are made only from local sheep's milk, which is kneaded and pulled. Slightly elastic, it has a vague aroma of vanilla. The production is very small (only 15 people make it), and the cheese must be eaten fresh. The winter melons of Trapani are bright yellow, very sweet, and stay ripe until Christmas. Cooks of Trapani are acknowledged masters in the art of preparing durum wheat cous cous served with a rich fish broth; so good that there is even an annual Cous Cous Festival at San Vito Lo Capo, an eagerly-awaited event, when chefs from Trapani and Africa (where cous cous is usually served with meat and vegetables) compete with their culinary miracles to win the coveted award.

Agrigento

Girgentana goats from Agrigento are a highly-prized breed. These attractive animals with their long horns and silky hair are exploited for their milk and their skins. Wild strawberries from Ribera are derived from seedlings brought back to Sicily from the Alps, by soldiers who had fought in the First World War. The island of Lampedusa is famous for its *cernia* (sea-perch or grouper).

Caltanissetta and Enna
Inland, at Caltanissetta and Enna, we find sheep's cheeses: *tuma, primosale* and *pecorino*, often with the addition of black peppercorns or coriander seeds, and even (in the province of Enna) of wild saffron, gathered in spring from the hillside crocuses. Here, too, are the finest beans and pulses, essential ingredients in dishes such as the *zuppa di ceci* (chick-pea potage) or *maccu di fave* (broad beans seasoned with wild fennel). Late peaches from Leonforte are succulent: they ripen from Sept–Nov and each fruit is protected in its own little bag, from birds, insects and hail.

Ragusa and Syracuse
Modicana cattle from Ragusa and Modica graze in the open air, indifferent to the hot climate. The meat is tough but good; the excellent milk is used for making several local cheeses, such as *caciocavallo*. It is pressed into long rectangular shapes whcih are then hung two by two over a beam to mature. The town of Modica has the reputation of producing the best food on the island, both in the restaurants and in the households; chocolate is still prepared according to the Aztec tradition (*see p. 295*). Almond trees are grown everywhere in Sicily, and probably form part of the native flora, but those from Noto and Avola (*Pizzuta d'Avola*) have the finest flavour of all.

Catania
Though the soil is fertile in central Sicily, no area can compare with the hinterland of Catania, where rich volcanic soil and sunshine give an intensity to the fruits and perfumes of its orchards and gardens. This is the secret of the huge success of its ices and sorbets, and its citrus summer salads. In fact, a healthy simplicity informs the food of this area, much of which is based upon the household bread oven: golden pies called *scacciate*, richly-filled *focacce*, vegetables grilled over charcoal, and fish and seafood wrapped in fig or citrus leaves and then roasted over the coals. Sheep's milk ricotta from Vizzini is as rich as double cream. Pistachios were introduced by the Arabs and the nuts now grown at Bronte have a superb flavour and are deep emerald green in colour. Snuff-box peaches from Mt Etna (*pesche tabacchiera*) are small, flat and intensely aromatic. Sicilian blood oranges are protected by the IGP seal (*Indicazione Geografica di Produzione*). There are several different varieties, all limited to the area of Mt Etna and the Plain of Catania, the only place in the world where the colour of the flesh is so intense, almost purple. From the Gulf of Catania come anchovies, *masculini di magghia*, so good that they can be eaten raw; the *magghia* is the fine-meshed net with which they are caught, from small boats. Catania's special pasta dish is *pasta ca' Norma*, spaghetti with a topping of fresh tomato, basil leaves, tasty slices of fried aubergine, and salted ricotta, invented to celebrate Bellini's triumphal inauguration of the Teatro Massimo Bellini opera house.

Messina

The tiny, offshore Aeolian Islands base their cuisine on the intense flavours of the capers (those from Salina are protected) and wild herbs which grow there, such as oregano, thyme, wild fennel, and *nepitella* (calamint); the currants and the Malvasia grapes which they produce; tasty goat's cheese and ricotta; and the cactus fruits and miniature lentils which survive in the dry and rocky environment. The islands and the coastal cities have always prized their abundance of fish, and in Messina the swordfish, intercepted during its periods of migration, is the most famed. *Impanata di pesce spada* from here is a magnificent envelope of delicate short-crust pastry containing swordfish and its accompaniments of tiny *pireddu* tomatoes which have been hung up in the kitchen until they wither like raisins, olives, capers, currants, pine nuts and bits of ripe caciocavallo cheese. In the Nebrodi Mountains an ancient breed of black pig (seen in medieval paintings and probably introduced by the Normans) is allowed to live wild in the woods, eating acorns and beech-nuts. The result is excellent sausage, salami, ham and bacon. In Novara di Sicilia they make *maiorchino*, a round, flat, well-matured sheep's milk cheese, with a dark brown rind that is becoming increasingly rare, as its manufacture is very time-consuming.

Wine

Archaeologists confirm the ancient origin of wine production in Sicily, where the first vines were certainly autochthonous. The Greeks taught the trick of cultivating the vine *ad alberello*, close to the ground, increasing sugar-content and alcohol level; Romans introduced new varieties and new techniques of manufacture. The famous wine of ancient Sicily was Mamertine, said to have been the favourite of Julius Caesar. Even the Arabs, who as Muslims could not drink wine, carefully cultivated and improved the vines, in order to present the grapes as table fruit, and for drying as raisins and sultanas. The heyday of Sicilian wine-making began in the 13th century and lasted some 200 years, a period when Sicilian wines were exported to Rome, Liguria, Venice and Tuscany, playing an important role in shaping the tastes of European palates. Real innovation began in the late 18th century, when the British wine merchant John Woodhouse successfully introduced the Spanish and Portuguese methods of manufacture to Marsala. The late 19th-century phylloxera blight, which destroyed the vineyards, was a setback, followed after the Second World War by a total neglect of quality—the only thing that mattered at the time was quantity.

Thankfully those days are receding, and we are now seeing the dawn of some energetic and exciting new winemaking. Local and foreign investors in Sicilian viticulture are drawing out the virtues of the island's terroir. Although traditional winemaking methods are largely giving way to modern vinification technology, the focus is firmly on getting the best out of indigenous grape varieties. A new generation of producers, in the tradition of Vincenzo Florio's legendary Marsala, and Duke Alliata di Salaparuta with his Corvo, are experimenting with new techniques, new varieties and new blends, while nurturing the native vines at the same time, and are consistently winning major international awards.

Noble grape varieties such as Chardonnay, Sauvignon Blanc, Cabernet Sauvignon, Syrah, Sangiovese and Merlot also flourish in the hot dry sulphurous soil, or in the richness of the black lava; even German varieties from the Rhine Valley thrive in Sicily. The grape harvest begins earlier than anywhere else in the northern hemisphere; on some estates even in August. In one or two places the grapes are gathered in the time-honoured way, at night, when the fruit is cool, so that it doesn't start fermenting too soon.

There are at present 23 DOC wine denominations in Sicily (*Denominazione d'Origine Controllata*) and one DOCG (*Denominazione d'Origine Controllata e Garantita*). Such a long and complete list means that the island is one of the most important oenological areas in Italy (in fact the province of Trapani comes second only to Bordeaux as the largest wine-producing district in Europe). The areas are as follows:

Alcamo, from the gentle hills between Trapani and Palermo;

Cerasuolo di Vittoria, the only Sicilian DOCG, is a characteristically cherry-red wine, pleasantly dry and vaguely aromatic of fruits and flowers;

Contessa Entellina;

Contea di Sclafani;

Delia Nivolelli from the banks of the River Delia ('vineyard' in Arabic), in the territory of Mazara del Vallo, Marsala, Petrosino and Salemi;

Eloro, from the area of Noto, Pachino, Portopalo di Capo Passero, Rosolini and Ispica;

Erice;

Etna, the first to receive the DOC seal in 1968;

Faro, from the hillsides behind Messina;

Malvasia delle Lipari from the Aeolian Islands;

Mamertino di Milazzo from the foothills of the Madonie and Nebrodi Mountains;

Marsala, a DOC since 1984, aged wines of three types, according to colour: Oro (gold), Ambra (amber), and Rubino (ruby). Fine is aged one year, Superiore for two years, Superiore Riserva for four years, Vergine or Soleras for five years. Also, Vergine or Soleras can be Stravecchio or Riserva, aged for ten years;

Menfi;

Monreale;

Moscato di Noto, the *pollium* mentioned by Pliny, produced in the territory of Noto, Rosolini, Pachino and Avola;

Moscato di Siracusa, produced exclusively from the vineyards surrounding Syracuse with a flavour is subtly different from that of Noto;

Moscato di Pantelleria, produced exclusively on the island;

Passito di Pantelleria;

Riesi;

Sambuca Siciliana;

Santa Margherita di Belice;

Salaparuta;

Sciacca;

Vittoria.

GLOSSARY OF SICILIAN ARTISTS

Mainly Sicilian artists are listed here, or lesser-known figures from elsewhere who were active in Sicily or had an influence on Sicilian art.

Alberti, Antonio ('Il Barbalunga', Messina, 1600–49), painter who introduced a new and original style to Sicilian art. In Rome where he studied with Domenichino, who greatly influenced him. His opus consists of numerous altarpieces carried out for the churches of Rome, Messina and Palermo.

Alessi, Giuseppe (Avola, fl. early 18C), priest and architect who worked on the reconstruction of Avola and the surrounding towns after the 1693 earthquake.

Alì, Luciano (Syracuse, 1736–1820), Baroque architect, much in demand after the 1693 earthquake. His masterpiece is Palazzo Beneventano del Bosco in Syracuse, with its lovely courtyard. He was often assisted by his brothers **Antonino** and **Saverio**, master-builders, and by his son **Salvatore** (Syracuse, 1767–?1820), friar, architect and civil engineer, a follower of the teachings of Vitruvius and Palladio.

Alibrandi, Girolamo (Messina, 1470–1524), painter sometimes called the 'Raphael of Messina', follower of Antonello da Messina, who died of the plague after completing relatively few paintings (because he started late), most of which are now in the Regional Museum of his city.

Almeyda, Giuseppe Damiani (Capua, 1834–1911), architect employed as civil engineer by the municipality of Palermo, he received many private commissions to design architectural works, but he was sometimes hindered by his Neapolitan origins, and the final choice often went to his Palermo rival, Ernesto Basile. Fortunately he could count on the friendship of Ignazio Florio, for whom he designed the villa of Favignana. Almeyda's projects are less monumental in character compared with those of Basile, but they give a particular flavour to the *fin de siècle* Palermo, with their elegant, Pompeian-style ornamentation.

Amato, Antonino (Messina, fl. 1697–1717), architect and sculptor; he was often assisted in his projects by his son **Andrea** (Messina, fl. 1720–35). His most important project was the Catania palace of the Prince of Biscari. Andrea was engaged on the construction of the huge Benedictine monastery of San Nicolò l'Arena.

Amato, Giacomo (Palermo, 1643–1732), architect who studied in Rome with Carlo Rainaldi.

Amico, Giovanni Biagio (Trapani, 1684–1754), theologian and self-taught architect who designed many sacred and secular buildings for his city. In 1726 he wrote the influential treatise *L'Architetto Prattico*.

Andrea da Salerno (Andrea Sabatini, Salerno, 1480–1530), one of the finest Renaissance painters of southern Italy.

Antonello da Messina (Messina, c. 1430–79), painter, noted for his superb portraits and sense of perspective. One of the first Italian artists to perfect the technique of oil painting, he exerted considerable influence on Giovanni Bellini. His son **Jacobello** and his nephew **Antonello de Saliba** were also painters.

Archifel, Arcifer or Arichitofel, Vincenzo (?Naples, fl. 1486–1533), goldsmith and sculptor. Arriving in Catania aged 25, he married a local girl and opened his workshop at the Pescheria. The archbishop invited him to make the splendid reliquaries to contain parts of the body of St Agatha, and he spent the rest of his life completing them, together with the huge silver catafalque used for her processions, but also finding the time to carve some statues for several churches in Caltagirone, Mineo and Vizzini. On his death he was honoured by being buried in the church of the Carmine. His son **Antonio** continued his trade, completing all his unfinished works.

Bagnasco, Nicola or Nicolò (Palermo, fl. 18–19C), sculptor and wood-carver, member of a highly acclaimed family of craftsmen.

Baragli, Giacomo (Palermo, 1934–89), sculptor and medal-engraver.

Barisano da Trani (Bari, fl. 1175–85), sculptor and metal worker, who made beautiful bronze doors for the cathedrals of Ravello and Trani in south Italy and Monreale in Sicily; the two latter are signed.

Basile, Ernesto (Palermo, 1857–1932), the most famous *fin de siècle* architect in Palermo, a major exponent of international Modernism and Art Nouveau, and the eternal rival of Almeyda, Basile was particularly influenced by the Arab-Norman architecture of the city in developing his style. He started his career in the studio of his father, **Giovanni Battista Filippo** (Palermo, 1825–91), later inheriting his university post, and he completed the Teatro Massimo opera house, where his long collaboration with painter Ettore De Maria Bergler and furniture-designer Vittorio Ducrot began. His outstanding works in Palermo include the Villino Florio (one of the first examples of Art Nouveau to appear in Italy), and Villa Igiea. He designed several buildings for Messina during the post-earthquake reconstruction, while for Rome he created Palazzo Montecitorio, the seat of Parliament.

Battaglia, Francesco (Catania, 1701–88), architect and sculptor, son-in-law of Andrea Amato, for whom he continued work on the monastery of San Nicolò l'Arena. He was the father of **Antonino** or Antonio (fl. 18–19C), architect and Jesuit priest.

Battaglia, Matteo (Ragusa, fl. 18C), gifted, self-taught painter who worked exclusively in the city of Ragusa.

Benefial, Marco (Rome, 1684–1764), painter who followed the classical tradition of the Bologna artists such as Guercino or Ludovico Carracci.

Berrettaro or Berrettari or Birrittaro, Bartolomeo (Carrara, fl. 1499–1524), sculptor, whose first commissions in Sicily were in Alcamo, where he met (or invited) a fellow-citizen and sculptor from Carrara, **Giuliano Mancino**. Their atelier flourished, and they created sculptures for many towns in Sicily.

Besio, Fra' Giacomo (Genoa, 1612–45), architect who succeeded in blending the Baroque of his native Genoa with elements of the Roman style, expressing in Palermo a new, elegant form of his own.

Bonaiuto, Natale (Syracuse, fl. 1781–94), architect and stucco-moulder who appears to have worked exclusively in his own area.

Bonaiuto Vincenzo (fl. 17C), silversmith who worked in one of the most renowned ateliers of Trapani.

Bongiovanni, Giacomo (Caltagirone, 1772–1859), sculptor and ceramics-moulder, founder together with his nephew Giuseppe Vaccaro (Caltagirone, ?1808–99) of the famous Bongiovanni-Vaccaro atelier which specialised in creating terracotta statuettes for Christmas cribs.

Borremans, Willem (Antwerp, 1672–1744), fresco painter who learned his art in the atelier of Rubens. He decorated many churches as well as villas for the aristocracy. In his later years he was assisted by his son **Luigi** (?Palermo, fl. early 18C), about whom little is known.

Boscarino, Rosario (Modica, fl. 1693–1706), master-builder who often worked together with Mario Spada. After completing the church of St Peter in Modica in 1697, they designed and built the new cathedral of St John the Baptist in Ragusa.

Calamech or Calamecca, Andrea (Carrara, 1524–89), sculptor and architect from a family of artists and marble-traders. He learned his art in Florence, where he perfected his Michelangelesque-Mannerist style.

Camilliani, Camillo (Florence, d.1603), sculptor, son of **Francesco Camilliani or Della Camilla** (Florence, 1530–76), sculptor, a follower of Baccio Bandinelli, Michelangelo's arch rival. Camillo appears to have settled in Sicily, where he carried out several works, and was asked by the Spanish government to work on the watch-towers and coastal defences of the island.

Canzoneri, Michele (Palermo, 1944), abstract sculptor, happiest working with glass.

Caracciolo, Luciano (Syracuse, fl. late 17C–early 18C), little-known architect or master-builder who was engaged in the reconstruction of the city after the 1693 earthquake.

Carasi, Costantino (Noto, fl. early 18C), artist who painted numerous frescoes and altarpieces for the churches of Noto and many other towns in southeast Sicily.

Carnelivari or Carnilivari, Matteo (Noto, fl. late 15C–1506), architect who probably began his activity in Noto and Syracuse. He went to Palermo in 1486 in order to obtain the acquittal of his son Antonio, who had committed murder. Palazzo Abatellis is one of is masterpieces.

Carreca or Carrera, Andrea (Trapani, 1592–1677), painter initially inspired by Novelli, Caravaggio, the Venetian school and Flemish art, he soon developed an inclination for Roman Baroque and Pietro Cortona.

Carrera, Giuseppe (Trapani, fl. 1608–30), painter, whose elder brother **Vito** (Trapani, 1552–1622) was Novelli's maestro. On the death of Vito, Giuseppe completed on his behalf a series of paintings for the royal palace in Palermo, commissioned by the viceroy. He worked for some time in Alcamo.

Caruso, Bruno (Palermo, 1927), painter who lives and works in Rome, first taught by his father, who made him copy the works of the old masters.

Cascio, Lorenzo (Sciacca, 1940, www.cascio.it), painter and sculptor who started modelling clay as a child. He lives and works in Portofino, and is noted for his delicate bronze statuettes and his large paintings with bold designs and jewel-like colours.

Castello, Bernardo (Genoa, 1557–1629), Late-Mannerist painter, a friend of Torquato Tasso, for whom he illustrated the first two editions of *Gerusalemme Liberata*.

Catalano, Antonio ('Il Giovane', Messina, 1585–1666), painter, the son of another painter by the same name called 'L'Antico' or '**Il Vecchio**', who had studied with Barocci. Il Giovane liked painting frescoes besides canvases, but of his vast production very little remains, principally in the Regional Museum of Messina.

Catti, Michele (Palermo, 1855–1914), painter inspired by De Nittis, who after a long period of sunny landscapes, fell into depression, thereafter preferring to depict Palermo in rainy, cold weather.

Cecco di Naro (Naro, nr Agrigento, fl. 1377–80), fresco painter. After carrying out the frescoes for the church of St Catherine and the castle of the Chiaramonte family, he was invited to decorate their home in Palermo, Palazzo Steri, together with Simone da Corleone and Pellegrino Dareno.

Civiletti, Benedetto (Palermo, 1845–99), sculptor whose true-to-life renditions of popular subjects were much in demand. Besides small marble statues, he made many large monuments in bronze, including the figure representing *Tragedy* on the right-hand side of the stairway in front of Palermo's Teatro Massimo.

Conca, Sebastiano ('Il Cavaliere', Gaeta, 1680–1764), painter, one of the most successful artists in Rome during the early 18th century, with a distinctive style that introduced elements of academic Classicism into the grandeur of Late Baroque. He achieved fame for his frescoes. In Rome he opened an art school in Piazza Farnese, where many young Sicilian artists learnt how to paint.

Consagra, Pietro (Mazara del Vallo, 1920–2005), one of Italy's leading abstract sculptors, he dedicated much of his activity to Gibellina and the post-earthquake reconstruction.

Contini, Giovanni Battista (Montalcino, 1641–1723), architect, exponent of latter-day Roman Baroque. A student both of his father Francesco and of Gian Lorenzo Bernini, he later collaborated with Carlo Fontana.

Crescenzio, Antonello ('Antonello da Palermo', Palermo, 1467–1542), painter whose style changed so abruptly half-way through his career that some critics believe there were two artists of the same name, father and son. If he was indeed one person, his first period reveals Spanish and Flemish influences, while the second phase shows the effect of Vincenzo da Pavia and Andrea da Salerno. Existing documents prove that he collaborated with Antonello Gagini.

Cristadoro or Crestadoro, Giuseppe (Palermo, 1711–1808), painter, the son of a goldsmith, who learned his art in the studio of Vito d'Anna, where he was able to examine drawings by Carlo Maratta, Sebastiano Conca and Corrado Giaquinto, and where he made friends with Olivio Sozzi and Pier Paolo Vasta, often collaborating with them.

D'Anna, Vito (Palermo, 1718–69), painter, probably the greatest Sicilian artist of his time. He married the daughter of Olivio Sozzi and used her conspicuous dowry to go to Rome, where he studied with Corrado Giaquinto. Once back in Palermo, he was soon caught up in a vast number of projects, painting frescoes for the most important villas and palaces, and splendid altarpieces for many churches in Sicily.

D'Antoni, Andrea (Palermo, 1811–68), painter, a pupil of the Neoclassicist artist Giuseppe Patania. Sensitive to social problems and politically involved, he took part in the 1848 riots, after which his paintings are exhortations to withstand the bitterness of exile.

D'Asaro, Pietro ('Il Monocolo di Racalmuto', Racalmuto, 1591–1647), late Mannerist painter, his nickname derives from the fact that he had only one eye. His work shows touches of Caravaggio, Filippo Paladino and the two Zoppi di Gangi.

De Lisi, Benedetto (Palermo, 1830–75), sculptor from a family of sculptors. He was often invited to sculpt monuments and portrait busts of illustrious citizens.

Del Piano, Donato (Naples, 1704–85), organ manufacturer who spent most of his life in Sicily, where he arrived together with his brother Giuseppe in 1722 to repair the organ in the cathedral of Syracuse.

De Maria Bergler, Ettore (Naples, 1850–1938), the acknowledged master of interior decoration in the Art Nouveau style, also one of the finest landscape artists of his generation, and a superb portraitist.

Dufourny, Léon (Paris, 1754–1818), architect present in Sicily from 1788–93, spending there the worst years of the French Revolution. On returning to Paris, he became curator of the Louvre.

Dupré, Giovanni (Siena, 1817–82), sculptor. Aged 25, he carved a very realistic marble statue of *Abel Dying* (now in the Hermitage), which caused a scandal for its naturalistic abandoned pose.

Felice da Sambuca, Fra' (Sambuca, 1733–1805), painter and Capuchin monk. He worked with Olivio Sozzi in Palermo, and also with Vito d'Anna. His intensely devotional works adorn many Capuchin convents in Sicily.

Ferraro, Antonino (Giuliana, fl. 1552–98), painter, sculptor and stucco-moulder, talented Mannerist artist. He was often assisted in his work by his son **Orazio** (fl. 1573–1650) and grandson, also **Antonino** (fl. 1651–60).

Ferretti, Mario (Livorno, 1915–74), artist who often designed stained-glass windows, but was happiest sculpting in bronze.

Fiume, Salvatore (Comiso,1915–97), painter, poet, playwright and novelist, noted for his characteristic Metaphysical-style paintings with scenes formed of bright patches of colour, and his bronze statues, often of a humourous nature. He also ventured into the realm of Land Art.

Franzese, Gaetano (Naples, 18C), renowned wood-carver called to Catania in 1766 by the organ manufacturer Donato del Piano to decorate the case of the organ he was completing for the church of San Nicolò l'Arena.

Freri, Antonello (Messina, fl. 1479–1513), sculptor who seems to have followed the Lombard school, with a decorative touch of his own. Most of his surviving works are in the cathedral of Catania and in the Regional Museum of Messina.

Fuga, Ferdinando (Florence, 1699–1782), architect who studied in Rome with Alessandro Specchi and Filippo Juvarra. In Sicily he is remembered for his disastrous interventions in the cathedral of Palermo, which King Ferdinand III of Bourbon had asked him to re-design in 1767. Among other things, he replaced the columns with piers, moved the royal tombs and opened them, dismantled the enormous marble altarpiece (the Gagini's masterpiece) and surmounted the roof with an ungainly dome and a series of small pepper-pot cupolas, in order to change it from a Norman basilica into a Latin-cross building with side aisles and long transepts. But some say it was not entirely his fault; perhaps the king should have let well alone?

Fumagalli, Gaspare (Rome, fl. 1735–85), painter who probably arrived in Sicily in 1730, where he worked with Borremans at the archbishop's palace in Palermo. After a sojourn in Rome, where he admired Maratta's frescoes, he returned to Sicily, working mainly in Gangi and Palermo, sometimes assisted by his three sons, **Eugenio**, **Ermenegildo** and **Epifanio**.

Furetto, Orazio (Palermo, 1714–85), architect chiefly remembered for his design for the charitable institution in Palermo known as the Albergo delle Povere (1746–72).

Gabrieli or Gabrielli, Onofrio ('Onofrio da Messina', Messina, 1616–1706), painter; as a boy he was sent to the atelier of Antonio Alberti, the Barbalunga. Later he went to Rome, where he met Poussin and Pietro Cortona, then to Venice and Padua, where he became art tutor to the children of Count Antonio Maria Borromeo. On returning to Messina in 1650 he began a period of intense activity, painting for many towns and villages, and also working as a civil engineer. His style is reminiscent both of

Alberti and Cortona, but the tenderness of his paintings is all his own.

Gagini family Although originally from Switzerland, they were prominent in Italy as sculptors, metalworkers and also architects (but never officially acknowledged as such), who managed their workshops along medieval lines, frequently collaborating on different tasks. They were active in several parts of Italy from the 15th century until well into the 1800s. Examples of their work can be found in almost every town of any size in Sicily, as well as many villages. **Domenico** (c. 1420–92) was the most outstanding of the early artists, possibly a disciple of Brunelleschi. Born in Bissone (Switzerland), he worked for a time in Genoa, notably in the cathedral, and brought skills perfected in Lombardy to Palermo, where in 1478 he founded the association of marble-workers, and where his son, **Antonello** (1478–1536) was born. Trained in his father's workshops, Antonello became the head of the family in Sicily. He was probably briefly an assistant to Michelangelo in Rome. His best-known works, carefully composed statues of the Madonna, also show the influence of Francesco Laurana. Less well documented is his work as an architect. Another talented member of the family, Antonello's son **Antonino** (fl. 1537–81), continued to maintain the family's virtual monopoly on decorative religious art commissions on the island, although himself with less confident artistic talent. One of Antonello's younger brothers, **Gian Domenico** (c. 1503–c. 1567), was also a sculptor of note, and his son **Antonuzzo** (fl. 1576–c.1606) went on to collaborate with his own offspring, also named **Gian Domenico**, who was probably born in Caltagirone, where Antonuzzo died. **Nibilio** Gagini (fl. 1583–1607) was raised in Palermo, and became a much sought-

after goldsmith and medal-engraver, a craft also practised around the same time by **Giuseppe** (fl. 1575–1610).

Gagliardi, Rosario (Syracuse, ?1690–1762), architect who played a prominent part in the reconstruction of the city of Noto, where the characteristic layout of the new town, and many of the churches and convents, were to his design. He is one of the finest exponents of the Sicilian Baroque, on a par with Vaccarini.

Galimberti, Silvio (Rome, 1869–1956), painter who during his long career mainly painted frescoes in the churches of Rome and the Marche.

Gambara, Antonio (?Palermo, 15C), sculptor and master-builder, responsible for the magnificent south portal of the cathedral of Palermo, partly inspired by the 14th-century west doorway.

Gaspare da Pesaro (?Palermo, 15C), painter and engraver, active mainly in Palermo, he is thought to be the author of the *Triumph of Death* fresco in the Palazzo Abatellis. He had two sons, both artists: **Guglielmo** (Palermo, b.1430), who might have painted the wooden Crucifix in the cathedral of Cefalù, and **Benedetto**.

Gianforma, Giuseppe (Palermo, fl. 1740–70), stucco-moulder. His two sons **Gioacchino** and **Giovanni** were also stucco-moulders. Giovanni was a greater talent than his father; his work recalls that of Giacomo Serpotta..

Giganti or Gigante, Andrea (Trapani, 1731–87), priest and architect originally inspired by the work of Giovanni Biagio Amico. Arriving in Palermo after his studies, he was soon at the centre of attention for the excellence of his work; he proved himself capable of running large building-sites with smooth efficiency, and finishing constructions down to the last tiny decorative detail, on occasion working also as civil engineer. Many sumptuous villas and palaces, such as Villa Valguarnera Gangi in Palermo and Villa Galletti at Bagheria, and numerous fine churches, were designed and completed by Giganti.

Giordano, Luca (Naples, 1634–1705), painter, such a fast worker that he was nicknamed 'Luca Fapresto' (Luca works fast) by his contemporaries. He was apprenticed to Jusepe de Ribera for nine years and frequented the atelier of Pietro da Cortona, before going to Parma to see the works of Correggio and Veronese.

Giorgio di Faccio (Turin, 16C), Mannerist architect summoned to Palermo by the Genoese community to design their church of St George at the Loggia (1576).

Giorgio da Milano (Milan, 15C), sculptor who left his native Lombardy to work in Sicily, one of the first to introduce the Early Renaissance style to the island.

Giovanni di Bartolo (Siena, 14C), sculptor and goldsmith, invited to Catania in 1372 to make the reliquary bust of St Agatha.

Goro di Gregorio (Siena, 1275–1334), sculptor whose father was the assistant of Nicola Pisano, he was summoned to Messina in 1333 to make the tomb of Archbishop Guidotto de' Tabiati in the cathedral.

Graffeo, Nicolò and Giacomo (Termini Imerese, fl. late 15C), painters and miniaturists, brothers, they usually worked together.

Gramignani, Francesco (Palermo, 18C), typesetter and engraver, a student of Olivio Sozzi.

Grano, Antonino or Antonio (Palermo, 1660–1718), painter and engraver. His first task as an apprentice was to restore the frescoes by Pietro Novelli in the church of Casa Professa in Palermo. In 1680 he went to Rome, where he worked with artists following the tradition of Maratta. On returning to

Palermo he found that his conservative style was out of favour.

Greco, Emilio (Catania, 1913–95), sculptor, initially inspired by the medieval master Francesco Laurana. Angered by the indifference with which he was treated in his home town, he left Catania nothing in his will.

Greco, Ignazio (Palermo, 1830–?1910), architect best known for his collaboration with the Whitaker family, for whom he designed Villa Malfitano in Palermo.

Guarino, Francesco (Noto, 18C), modeller of processional statues in *papier mâché* and stucco.

Guccione, Piero (Scicli, b.1935), painter, fascinated by the sea and its myriad colours, his depictions of waves and the water are very impressive.

Guerci, Dario (Ragusa, 19C), painter; from 1856–66 he painted some canvases for the duomo at Ibla.

Guercio, Gaspare (Palermo, 1611–79), architect and sculptor who worked occasionally with Gaspare Serpotta, and designed and built numerous monumental tombs for aristocratic families.

Guttuso, Renato (Bagheria, 1912–87), committed Communist and controversial painter noted for his bold brush strokes and use of colour. His most famous painting is of the Vucciria street-market in Palermo.

Houbraken, Jan van (Flanders, fl. 1636–65), artist versed in the tradition of Flemish still-life painting, who travelled to Messina after a sojourn in Naples, where he appreciated the effect that Caravaggio had on local painters. Nothing survives of the work of his son **Ettore**, who fled Messina for Livorno in 1674 because of the anti-Spanish uprisings together with his son **Nicola** (Messina, 1660–1732), who became a great still-life painter.

Italia, Angelo (Licata,1628–1700), Jesuit

architect who started his career in his home town and in Palma di Montechiaro, where he worked for the Tomasi di Lampedusa family. In Monreale he designed the Cappella del Crocifisso for Archbishop Roano.

Ittar, Stefano (Owrucks, present-day Ukraine, 1724–90), architect who carried out various projects in Catania, including Porta Ferdinandea. His son **Sebastiano** (Catania, 1768–1847), a skilled draughtsman, showed a strong interest in ancient monuments. In 1800 Lord Elgin took him to Greece to draw the ancient monuments for him, photography not having yet been invented (his drawings are now in the British Museum).

Labisi, Paolo (Noto, fl. 1731–90), architect, exponent of Sicilian Baroque style. A student of Rosario Gagliardi, he worked almost exclusively in Noto.

Laurana, Francesco (Vrana, Dalmatia, fl. 1458–1500), sculptor, architect and medal-engraver, who absorbed a variety of influences in France and Naples as well as Sicily, where he worked in the late 1460s and early '70s. In his most famous works, often quiet and austere portraits of women, there is a pursuit of abstract formal perfection that has led to comparisons with Piero della Francesca.

La Valle, Raffaele (Palermo, 16C) and his son **Antonino** (?Cefalù,1572–1645), organ manufacturers. Their instruments had an unmistakable sound and were beautiful to look at. Five of the superb organs built by Antonino still survive.

Leto, Antonino (Monreale, 1844–1913), painter, noted for his landscapes blazing with sunlight. He considered his most important painting to be *La Mattanza, Tuna-Fishing*, which he witnessed in the Florio fishery at Favignana.

Li Volsi family Sculptors, wood-carvers and stucco-moulders, the sons and descendants of **Giuseppe** (?Nicosia, fl. 1607), include **Francesco** (Tusa, fl. 1621–30), and his brother **Giovanni Battista** (Nicosia, fl. 1622–86), who often worked together with his son **Stefano**. Another brother was **Scipione** (Tusa, fl. 1621–30), an excellent sculptor; although he never achieved fame, his work bears comparison to the best production of the Serpotta and Gagini families.

Lojacono, Francesco (Palermo, 1838–1915), influential painter, called the 'thief of the sun' by his contemporaries, for the inimitable way he illuminates his landscapes.

Lo Monaco, Sebastiano (Catania, 1730–75), fresco-painter who studied under Olivio Sozzi.

Lo Verde, Giacomo (Trapani, fl. 1619–45), painter, he studied together with his friend Andrea Carreca under Pietro Novelli.

Mancini or Mancino, Giacomo (?, 16C), sculptor, probably Sicilian.

Mancino, Andrea (Lombardy, fl. 1480–1500), sculptor brought to Sicily by Domenico Gagini, and about whom very little is known.

Mancino, Giuliano *see Berrettaro.*

Manno, Antonio or Antonino (Palermo, 1739–1810) **Vincenzo** and **Francesco** (Palermo, 1752–1831), all painters, were brothers who often worked together. Antonio was a student of Vito d'Anna.

Manzù, Giacomo (Giacomo Manzoni; Bergamo, 1908–91), sculptor and painter. Self-taught, he admired Gothic and Romanesque art, Donatello and Picasso. Bronze and wax were his preferred materials. His lifelong friend was Renato Guttuso, whose tomb he made at Bagheria.

Marabitti, Ignazio (Palermo, 1719–97), sculptor who studied in Rome under Filippo Della Valle. A prolific worker, he prepared statues for several Sicilian towns, especially Palermo, where his most notable works are his graceful fountains.

Mariani, Giuseppe (Pistoia, 1681–1731), architect and painter. In 1700 he went to Rome where he probably worked together with Giacomo Amato, a fellow monk and a Sicilian, who invited him to Palermo. He designed Villa Aragona Cutò in Bagheria, inspired by the 16th-century palaces and villas of Rome.

Martorana, Gioacchino (Palermo, 1735–79), painter, draughtsman and portraitist. In Palermo he had a successful career painting canvases, altarpieces and frescoes for churches and palaces. He died very young of pneumonia, leaving his atelier to two of his sons, **Ermenegildo** (who worked in Syracuse, Piazza Armerina and Palermo), and **Pietro**, expert in watercolour, who married the daughter of Vito d'Anna.

Marvuglia, Giuseppe Venanzio (Palermo, 1729–1814), Neoclassical architect often assisted in his projects (for example the royal hunting-lodge at Ficuzza) by his son **Alessandro Emanuele** (Palermo, 1769–1845) and his brother **Salvatore** (Palermo, 1735–1802).

Master of the Trapani Polyptych (?, 14–15C), painter with a superb technique and an original style who would appear to have carefully studied the works of Tuscan masters. Bright colours, elegant figures and symmetrical settings characterise his work.

Masuccio, Natale (Messina, 1568–1619), Jesuit architect who designed churches exclusively for his Order. He travelled frequently to Rome and Malta, and in 1599 was kidnapped by pirates, who released him without demanding a ransom, interpreted by Masuccio as divine intervention. Bad-tempered and arrogant, after several heated arguments with his superiors he left the Order in 1616.

Matera, Giovanni (Trapani, 1653–1718), wood-carver and clay-modeller, famous for his skill in carving figurines for Christmas cribs. Accused of murder, he found refuge in the convent of Sant'Antonino in Palermo, where he spent the rest of his life.

Matinati, Giovannello ('Giovanni Antonio', Messina, fl. 1509–48), sculptor and engraver renowned for his Crucifixes, showing Christ wearing a gold-trimmed loincloth.

Mazza, Antonio (Noto, 1761–1825), architect and painter who designed and decorated several buildings in his native Noto and also in Scicli.

Mazzola or Mazzolo, Gian Domenico (Carrara, fl. 1544–77), sculptor who arrived in Messina in 1513 with his father **Giovan Battista** (fl. 1513–50) to complete the cathedral sculptures left unfinished on the death of Antonello Gagini. Later Gian Domenico carried out some work for the cathedral of St Agatha in Catania, notably the north door.

Mazzullo, Giuseppe (Graniti, nr Taormina, 1913–88), sculptor, son of a building-site foreman. He was apprenticed to a tailor, where he took an interest in art. His father helped him go to Rome and Perugia, where he studied at the Academy of Fine Arts. In 1939 he opened a studio in Rome, which soon became the haunt of intellectuals and the artistic élite. His taste evolved towards sculpture in stone, preferably granite, while his inspiration derived from the humble lives of fishermen and peasants. In 1980 he settled in Taormina, creating a foundation in his name, for which the city conceded the palace of the dukes of Santo Stefano.

Mendola, Carmelo (Catania, 1895–1976), self-taught sculptor whose preferred medium was bronze.

Messina, Francesco (Linguaglossa, nr. Catania, 1900–95), sculptor. His bronze studies of young girls and dancers are unmistakeable for their graceful abandon; he also liked to portray horses. His study of a fallen stallion caused an outcry in Catania, where it stands in a central square, and the council blacksmith was ordered to provide the animal with a pair of iron knickers to avoid embarrassing the ladies. The story was featured on CNN, and the ridiculous 'panties' were immediately removed.

Messina, Vincenzo (Sambuca di Sicilia, 1670–1757), painter and stucco-moulder, admirer of Giacomo Serpotta. He usually carried out work to the design of other artists. His sons **Giacomo**, **Giovanni** and **Gabriele** also worked in his atelier.

Minniti, Mario (Syracuse, 1577–1640), painter who he went to Rome to seek his fortune, soon becoming a friend and follower of Caravaggio, for whom he also acted as model. When Caravaggio came to Sicily, he was the guest of Minniti.

Montalbano, Leonardo (Sambuca, fl. 1606–53), silversmith who made at least two masterpieces, the *Sfera d'Oro* (Abatellis gallery, Palermo), and the *Corona della Visitazione* for the statue of the Madonna in Enna, now in the Alessi Museum.

Montorsoli, Fra' Giovanni Angelo (Montorsoli, nr Florence, 1507–63), sculptor, engraver and architect, who learnt his art in the atelier of Michelangelo. In 1547 he was called to Messina by the city senate to design a fountain in order to celebrate a rational new water-supply system; the resulting Orion Fountain is considered one of the loveliest in Italy.

Moschetti, Giulio (Ascoli Piceno, 1847–1909), sculptor who settled in Catania when he was invited to make the fountain in front of the railway station. He also carried out some of the sculptures of musicians on the façade of the opera house, and the Fountain of Diana in Syracuse. Cement was his favourite material. His son **Mario** (Rome, 1879–1960), also a sculptor, helped his father with some of his later projects.

Musarra, Giuliano (Palermo, fl. 1591), craftsman who specialised in making bronze gates for chapels.

Napoli, Tommaso Maria (Palermo, 1655–1723), Domincan friar, mathematician and architect, an expert in fortifications and military architecture. He designed Palermo's first Baroque square, Piazza San Domenico, and two of the most elegant houses in Bagheria, Villa Valguarnera and Villa Palagonia, with its famous grotesque statues.

Nicolò da Mineo (Mineo, 1542–1625), sculptor who worked almost exclusively with the Gagini family.

Nicolò da Pettineo (Pettineo, fl. 15–16C), painter who excelled in frescoes and panel-paintings.

Niger or Nigro, Bernardino (Modica, fl. 1513–88), painter. The fact that he always signed and dated his paintings helps trace his artistic career through the provinces of Ragusa and Catania. His later pictures show the influence of Polidoro da Caravaggio.

Nolfo, Antonio (Trapani, 1696–1784), sculptor and modeller of statuary groups for the procession of the *Misteri*, in particular that of the Confraternity of Bakers, representing *The Coronation with the Crown of Thorns*. His three sons **Domenico**, **Francesco** and **Antonio** continued the work of his atelier.

Novelli, Antonio ('Pietro Antonio', Monreale, 1568–1625), a gifted painter, well known and much sought-after in his day. His fame has been overshadowed by that of his far greater son Pietro (*see below*). Between 1614 and 1616 he was commissioned to paint 40 altarpieces on slate, showing the Madonna and Child. Similar yet not quite identical, five of these paintings survive, at Piana degli Albanesi, Sclafani Bagni, Caltanissetta, Cerami and Licata.

Novelli, Pietro ('Il Monrealese'; Monreale, 1603–47), painter and architect; one of Sicily's finest artists, who perfected his chiaroscuro in Naples under Jusepe de Ribera and was fascinated by Van Dyck during that artist's visit to Palermo. Recognisable by his stylish beard and moustache, he often appears in his own works. He eventually became court painter to Philip IV of Spain, but he offended the king and fled to Ragusa in Sicily, where the monks gave him refuge. His daughter **Rosalia** (Palermo, 1628–?88) was a gifted artist, two of whose works can be seen in the Casa Professa church in Palermo: *St Agatha Professing her Faith in front of Quintianus*, and *The Immaculate Virgin with St Francesco Borgia*.

Padula, Pietro (Naples, fl. 1773–76), sculptor and wood-carver, famed for his Christmas cribs peopled with realistic shepherds, craftsmen, washerwomen and peasants.

Paladini, Filippo ('Il Paladino'; Casi, nr. Rufina,1544–1615), Mannerist painter, he arrived in Sicily from Malta in 1601, at the invitation of Counter-Reformation religious orders. His cool, elegant colour schemes and careful positioning of figures owes much to his Tuscan origins. He was tutor to the two Zoppi di Gangi, and his later works show the influence of Caravaggio.

Palma, Andrea (Trapani, 1644–1730), architect and painter who helped introduce the Neoclassical style to Palermo. His grandson **Nicolò** (Trapani, 1694–1779) was also a successful architect who designed many aristocratic palaces in Palermo and designed the Villa Giulia public gardens.

Pampillonia, Giuseppe or Baldassarre (Palermo, 1646–1741), sculptor particularly skilled in inlaid marble decoration. He worked for Angelo Italia at the cathedral of Monreale. One of his finest achievements is the altar of the Madonna in the sanctuary of Gibilmanna.

Paradiso, Angelo (Acireale, 19–20C), blacksmith renowned for his beautiful iron gates; he was considered to be the finest craftsman in a city famous for its wrought-iron work.

Patania, Giuseppe (Palermo, 1780–1852), versatile painter especially noted for his portraits.

Patricolo, Giuseppe (Palermo, 1834–1905), architect and painter, member of an illustrious family of artists.

Pennino, Giacomo (Palermo, 18C), sculptor, a student of Giacomo Serpotta; it is reported that he died at the age of 104. His son **Filippo** (Palermo, 1733–94), also a sculptor, studied with Marabitti.

Piero or Pietro da Bonitate (Bonate Sotto, nr Bergamo, fl. 1466–1501), sculptor who served his apprenticeship with Francesco Laurana, becoming his partner until Laurana went to Naples in 1471. They opened an atelier in Sciacca, but were forced to close it because of local hostility. In Palermo they made the arch for the Mastrantonio Chapel in the church of St Francis, thus introducing the Renaissance into Sicilian sculpture and architecture.

Pirandello, Fausto (Rome, 1899–1975), painter. Son of the famous writer, he lived from an early age in Paris, with a circle of friends including Picasso, Severini, Tozzi, De Chirico and De Pisis; he was also strongly influenced by Modigliani, Marini, Manzù and Moore.

Platania, Giacinto (Acireale, 1612–97), one of the greatest painters of his age. He liked to include realistic details in his paintings, and to use as a background the city of Acireale or its surroundings. He worked almost exclusively for the religious authorities, and his canvases and frescoes can be found in many churches of Acireale and eastern Sicily. Something of an engineer, during the eruption of Mt Etna in 1669, together with some friends he tried to divert the lava stream (it was the first-ever attempt to do this) that was heading for Catania, by building dykes. His efforts were unsuccessful because landowners objected to having their vineyards and orange groves submerged with rock.

Poidomani, Gaspare (Comiso, fl. 1517), architect or master-builder responsible for the splendid apse of the church of St Francis in Comiso.

Polidoro da Caravaggio (Polidoro Caldara, Caravaggio, nr Bergamo, ?1495–1546), painter who found employment as a painter in Raphael's atelier. After the Sack of Rome in 1527, he worked in Naples and Messina, where he was murdered by his servant on the eve of his planned return to Rome.

Provenzano, Domenico (Palma di Montechiaro, 1736–94), fresco-painter, The son of a carpenter, he trained in Palermo under arch-rivals Gaspare Serenario and Vito d'Anna, eventually showing more of the influence of the latter.

Quartararo, Riccardo (Sciacca, 1443–1506), painter with a complex personality who worked in Naples, central Italy, and perhaps Valencia, areas that strongly influenced his art, which also shows Flemish touches.

Quattrocchi, Filippo (Gangi, 1734–1818), sculptor in wood. Although he served his apprenticeship in Palermo, he returned to Gangi where he spent the rest of his life, sculpting groups for the churches of his home town and other villages of the Madonie. His son **Francesco** (Palermo, 1779–1861) followed in his father's footsteps, although he used marble and stucco for his sculptures, besides wood.

Ragusa, Giovanni Battista (Palermo, fl.

1713–1797), sculptor; at the start of his career he divided his time between Palermo and Rome, where he had fallen under the spell of Bernini. He spent most of the rest of his life carving statues for the cathedral and several other churches in Palermo.

Ragusa, Vincenzo (Palermo, 1841–1927), sculptor and painter of humble origins (his parents were servants in an aristocratic household). As a boy he signed up with the 'Thousand' for the Battle of Milazzo. Aged 24 he commenced his artistic career. For many years he was director of the department of sculpture at the Academy of Fine Arts of Palermo, and in 1892 he won the competition for the bronze monument to Giuseppe Garibaldi which now stands in Via Libertà.

Randazzo, Filippo ('Il Monocolo di Nicosia', Nicosia, 1695–1748), painter with only one eye, who after an apprenticeship in Palermo was sent to study at the school of Sebastiano Conca in Rome. His style was found pleasing, and he had a long and successful career painting frescoes and altarpieces. His son **Mariano** was also a minor painter.

Ribera, Jusepe de ('Lo Spagnoletto'; Jativa, Spain, 1588–1652), painter and etcher. He went to Naples as court painter for the viceroy of Spain. Impressed by Caravaggio, in his turn he impressed Pietro Novelli.

Ricca, Michele (Palermo, 1590–1654), silversmith, a prestigious exponent of the Palermo-style Baroque.

Riccio, Antonello (Messina, fl. 16C), painter, perhaps a disciple of Polidoro da Caravaggio, and son of **Mariano** (Messina, 1510– ?), with whom he is often confused. Mariano was a fine artist whose works are distinguished by the skilful drawing.

Riolo, Vincenzo (Palermo, 1772–1837), Neoclassical painter who studied with Antonio Manno before going to Rome. Returning to Palermo in 1799, his popularity soon eclipsed that of his contemporaries, for example Giuseppe Velasco (Velasquez), and he was much in demand by the élite to decorate their palaces and villas. He died together with his eldest son Antonio during the 1837 cholera epidemic.

Rizzo, Pietro (Palermo, fl. 1590–1628), silversmith who probably learnt his craft in the atelier of Nibilio Gagini. He was invited to make the silver reliquary statue of St Lucy for the duomo of Syracuse, before working almost exclusively for the monastery of San Martino delle Scale, near Monreale.

Rizzo, Pippo or Filippo (Corleone, 1897–1964), painter, the most important Sicilian exponent of Futurism.

Roberto di Oderisio (Naples, c. 1335–82), painter, one of the greatest exponents of Neapolitan art, often called the Giotto of Naples.

Rosa, Salvator (Naples, 1615–73), Baroque painter, etcher, musician and poet, one of the most unconventional and rebellious artists of his city. He studied under Jusepe de Ribera. Orphaned at 17, with his mother and five siblings to support, he apprenticed himself to Aniello Falcone, working with him on enormous battle scenes. After a spell in Rome he returned to Naples, painting romantic landscapes full of wild rocks and vegetation, peopled with bandits, seamen, shepherds and peasants, his finest work.

Rossi, Epifanio (?Caltagirone 17C), elegant painter who appears to have worked exclusively in Caltagirone.

Rossi, Mariano (Mariano Russo, Sciacca, 1731–1807), painter described by Berenson as anti/Baroque. Much liked by the Bourbons, he followed them to Sicily in 1798 when they were fleeing the Napoleonic troops, but refused to join them in Caserta

in 1806, preferring to stay in Rome, where he died in solitude after refusing to paint for the new masters, the French.

Rutelli, Mario (Palermo, 1859–1941), member of a family of talented sculptors, wood- and stone-carvers and stucco-moulders.

Ruzzolone, Pietro (Palermo, fl. 1484–1526), highly esteemed painter, sometimes compared with Raphael, noted for his remarkable Crucifixes.

Sada, Carlo (Bellagio, nr Como, 1809–73), architect. After the success of the Massimo Bellini opera house in Catania, he spent the rest of his life in the city, as the most fashionable architect in town.

Salerno, Giuseppe *see Zoppo di Gangi.*

Sarzana, Nicolò (Palermo, 1700–86), ceramicist who made majolica floors for palaces and churches, possibly including that of San Benedetto in Caccamo.

Savoja, Leone (Messina, 1814–85), architect. His most remarkable achievement was Messina's monumental cemetery, in a splendid position overlooking the Straits.

Scilla, Agostino (Messina, 1629–1700), painter; in 1670 he published a controversial argument for the organic origin of fossils, an important contribution to palaeontology.

Scipione di Blasi (Naples, 16C), silversmith who brought a new Mannerism to Sicily, influencing a generation of the Gagini family.

Scipione di Guido (Naples, fl. 1587–1604), wood-carver who was invited to Catania to decorate the choir-stalls in the cathedral. Before returning to Naples he carried out work in Caltagirone and Enna.

Sciuti, Giuseppe (Zafferana Etnea, nr. Catania, 1834–1911), painter who loved portraying historical events by using huge canvases, a rich colour palette, an eye for drama, and careful attention to detail. His liking for large surfaces led to him being invited to paint frescoes in many churches and villas. His dramatic works have been compared to blockbuster films à la Cecil B. De Mille, and undoubtedly, if he had been born a few years later, he would have found in Hollywood the fame which eluded him all his life.

Serassi (Bergamo, 1720–1895), as **Fratelli Serassi**, organ manufacturers, the family dominated their field for six generations.

Serenario or Serenari, Gaspare or Gasparo (Palermo, 1694 or 1707–59), painter who worked for a time in the atelier of Borremans (the artist who would appear to have most strongly influenced him), before going to Rome in 1730 to join the group of Sebastiano Conca. On his return to Palermo he worked there with amazing energy.

Serpotta, Giacomo (Palermo, 1656–1732), sculptor and stucco-moulder, son of **Gaspare** (Palermo, d. 1669). Giacomo took the art of moulding to its highest levels; he is credited with ushering in the Rococo style. The name Serpotta means snake or lizard; the sculptor often included either reptile in his works as a trademark. He was sometimes assisted by his brother **Giuseppe** (Palermo, 1653–1719) and his talented son **Procopio** (Palermo, 1679–1755). Serpotta's secret, by means of which his stuccoes acquired the glossy appearance of carved stone, was to add marble dust to his paste.

Simone da Corleone (Corleone, nr Palermo, fl. 1377–88), painter whose only known surviving work is the ceiling of the Steri palace in Palermo, which he decorated with Arab motifs together with Cecco di Naro and Pellegrino Dareno.

Sinatra, Vincenzo (Noto, 1707–65), builder and architect who began as a stonemason. He married the niece of Rosario Gagliardi, and took over the atelier when Gagliardi was paralysed by a stroke.

Siragusa, Federico (?Milazzo, fl. late 18C–early 19C), sculptor. Little is known about him. Nunzio Morello was his student.

Smiriglio, Mariano (Palermo, 1561–1636), architect and painter, his maestro was Paladini. Chief Architect for the senate, he also worked for the theatre and planned religious processions.

Sogliani, Giovanni Antonio (Florence, 1492–1544), a painter who learned his art in the atelier of Lorenzo di Credi. His restrained Mannerist style, free of formal exaggerations, delighted those religious orders devoted to poverty, and earned him many commissions from monasteries and confraternities.

Sozzi, Olivio (Catania, 1690–1765), painter; after marrying a wealthy woman, he used her dowry to put himself through his studies, working in Rome under Sebastiano Conca and the fresco painter Corrado Giaquinto, as his son-in-law Vito D'Anna would later do. His style is largely Roman Classicist. On returning to Sicily he worked in Catania and Palermo. His body is preserved in a glass case in the church of Santa Maria Maggiore at Ispica, where you can also see some of his finest frescoes.

Spada or Spata, Mario see *Rosario Boscarino*.

Stom, Matthias (or Stomer; Amersfoort, Holland, c. 1600–?50), painter. He began his career in Rome, about 1630, probably attracted there by the works of Caravaggio. After a long stay in Naples, in 1641 he came to Sicily, and lived in Palermo for the rest of his life. Theatrical and unconventional, most of his vast production of paintings were carried out for wealthy private families rather than for churches and convents.

Tancredi, Filippo (Messina, 1655–1722), influential painter who studied under Maratta in Rome. Noted for his precise draughtsmanship and skilful use of colour.

Tartaglio, Giacomo (Trapani, fl. 1729), sculptor, one of a group of artists who modelled figures for the annual Easter procession of the *Misteri*.

Tassara, Giovanni Battista (Genoa, 1841–1916), sculptor and soldier for Garibaldi, who took part in the 1860 expedition of the Thousand at Marsala. Born into a family of fishermen, he made his way to Florence where he befriended Giovanni Dupré and perfected his technique as a sculptor. In 1876 he won the competition for the tomb of Vincenzo Bellini in the cathedral of Catania, and in 1890 Ernesto Basile asked him to carve the bronze reliefs for the monument to the Thousand at Pianto Romano near Calatafimi. During the First World War he served as a nurse in the military hospital of Genoa, where he died in 1916.

Tedeschi, Gregorio (Florence, fl. 1609–50), sculptor who lived most of his life in Sicily. He created some of the allegorical figures (1629) for Piazza Vigliena in Palermo, where he also carved the statue of St Rosalia sleeping (1650) for her sanctuary on Monte Pellegrino, which fascinated Goethe.

Tipa, Andrea (Trapani, fl. 1725–76), sculptor, chief member of a family of sculptors who brought new life to the art in Trapani in the mid-18th century.

Tomaselli, Onofrio (Bagheria, 1886–1956), painter, particularly sensitive to the plight of the poor, especially the children working in the sulphur mines. Renato Guttuso decided to become a painter after viewing one of his canvases, the *Carusi nelle Zolfare* (now in Palermo's Gallery of Modern Art).

Tommaso de Vigilia (?Palermo, fl. 1444–97), painter, particularly active in western Sicily. He was perhaps an assistant of Gaspare da Pesaro, perhaps the Master of the Triumph of Death.

Tuccari, Giovanni (Messina, 1667–1743), Baroque-style painter who used a restricted palette enlivened by sudden flashes of colour.

Umile da Petralia, Fra' (Giovanni Francesco Pintorno; Petralia Soprana, c. 1580–1639), wood-carver. To escape an arranged marriage, he became a Franciscan friar, and devoted his life to fasting, prayer, and carving and painting Crucifixes, 32 of which are still extant. He always shows Christ with a triple crown of thorns, one of which is piercing His left eyebrow (the artist suffered all his life from a similar pain). The face of Christ has three expressions, depending from which angle it is viewed: suffering, smiling, and dying.

Vaccarini, Giovambattista or Giovanni Battista (Palermo, 1702–67), the greatest 18th-century Sicilian architect. Born into a poor family, his parents asked the priest who christened him to act as his godfather, which he did with zeal: the boy became a priest himself before his 23rd birthday. An earthquake in 1726 called into action all the priests who could design to assist in rebuilding, and Giovambattista's talents were revealed. Self-taught, he was inspired by the Renaissance and Baroque art that he found in books and drawings. Having followed his godfather to Catania, where he had been appointed archbishop, Vaccarini took part in the massive reconstruction of the city after the earthquake of 1693. After completing a difficult commission for King Charles of Bourbon, the grateful king awarded Vaccarini a rich pension; he lived the remaining ten years of his life as a wealthy abbot.

Vaccaro, Giuseppe, Francesco and Mario (Caltagirone, 19C), brothers, painters, ceramicists and moulders, famous for their terracotta Christmas-crib statuettes.

Vasta, Pier Paolo (Acireale, 1697–1760), painter, noted for his soft pastel colours.

He was particularly happy when painting women, and Biblical episodes featuring heroines.

Vazano or Bazano, Gaspare *see Zoppo di Gangi.*

Velasco or Velasquez, Giuseppe (Palermo, 1750–1827), very popular painter; after following the taste for Baroque art, he developed Neoclassical tendencies.

Vermexio, Andrea (Spain, fl. 1594–1643), architect and master-builder who settled in Syracuse, where he carried out several commissions in the Late Renaissance style, including the archbishop's palace with its hanging garden. His two sons **Giovanni** (Syracuse, fl. 1618–48), who designed the city hall, and **Francesco** were also architects. They often applied a carved lizard (an allusion to the family nickname) as a signature on the façade of their buildings.

Villareale, Valerio (Palermo, 1773–1854), Neoclassical sculptor, who studied in Rome from 1797 at the school created by Antonio Canova. Several works of art in Sicily, previously attributed to a youthful Canova, are now thought to be by Villareale. His particular skill was in carving portrait-busts and celebratory reliefs.

Vincenzo da Pavia or Vincenzo degli Azani da Pavia (Pavia, fl. 1495–1557), painter who spent the last part of his life in Palermo, and was one of the principal exponents in Sicily of the style of Raphael and Perugino.

Vitaliano, Gioacchino (Palermo, 1669–1739), sculptor who liked working to the design of other artists, such as Antonio Grano or Paolo Amato, with whom he created his masterpiece, the Garraffo Fountain in Piazza Marina, Palermo. He married Teresa, sister of Giacomo Serpotta. His brother **Giacomo** and his son **Vincenzo** (Palermo, fl. 1743–53) were also sculptors.

Ximenes, Ettore (Palermo, 1855–1926) eclectic sculptor who studied with Nunzio Morello before going to Naples in order to attend the Academy of Fine Arts. He became famous abroad, especially after winning the competition organised by the city of Kiev for a new monument to Tsar Alexander II, to replace that destroyed during the Russian Revolution.

Zoppo di Gangi two painters went under the name of Zoppo di Gangi ('Cripple of Gangi'): **Giuseppe Salerno** (1570–1632) and **Gaspare Vazano or Bazano** (1555–1630), both born in the town of Gangi. Known to have been friends and colleagues, their working relationship remains obscure. It is possible that they were both prepared to adopt the same signature, common practice among the decorators of the time. Gaspare Vazano, the senior of the pair, is less widely known and seems to have preferred working in fresco. The majority of works attributed to the Zoppo di Gangi are by Giuseppe Salerno, the younger and perhaps the more talented of the two. His work demonstrates the influence of Raphael and also, very markedly, and typically for the time, that of Spanish art. His masterpiece, the *Last Judgement*, adorns the church of St Nicholas of Bari in Gangi. Closely based on Michelangelo's work of the same name in the Sistine Chapel, the painting even includes a possible self-portrait of Salerno on Bartholomew's flayed skin. Such direct quotation of the master's work in Rome would have lent authority to the painting, and this kind of direct 'borrowing' was not unusual in the 17th century. Works by both Zoppi can be seen in many of the small towns and villages of the area, especially in Isnello and Polizzi Generosa, besides Gangi.

GLOSSARY OF SPECIAL TERMS

Abacus, flat stone in the upper part of a capital

Acrolith, extremity of a statue (hand, foot, head) made of stone or other durable material, while the body of the statue would have been of wood

Acroterion, an ornamental feature on the corner or highest point of a pediment

Adyton, inner sanctum of a temple, with no natural light

Aedicule, small opening framed by two columns and a pediment, originally used in classical architecture

Agora, public square or market-place

Ambo (pl. *ambones*) pulpit in a Christian basilica; two pulpits on opposite sides of a church, from which the gospel and epistle were read

Amphiprostyle, temple with colonnades at both ends

Amphora, antique vase, usually of large dimensions, for oil and other liquids

Antefix, ornament placed at the lower corner of the tiled roof of a temple to conceal the space between the tiles and the cornice

Antis, *in antis* describes the portico of a temple when the side-walls (antae) are prolonged to end in a pilaster flush with the columns of the portico

Architrave, lowest part of the entablature, horizontal frame above a door

Archivolt, moulded architrave carried round an arch

Arcosolium (pl. arcosolia), tomb where the sarcophagus is in an arched recess

Atlantes (or telamones) male figures used as supporting columns

Atrium, forecourt, usually of a Byzantine church or a classical Roman house

Badia (*abbazia*), abbey

Baglio (pl. *bagli*), from the medieval word *Ballium* meaning a large fortified building. It is now usually used to describe the warehouse of a wine distillery

Baldachin, canopy supported by columns, usually over an altar

Basilica, originally a Roman building used for public administration; in Christian architecture, an aisled church with a clerestory and apse, and no transepts

Borgo, a suburb; street leading away from the centre of a town

Bottega, the studio of an artist; the pupils who worked under his direction

Bouleuterion, council chamber

Bozzetto, sketch, often used to describe a small model for a piece of sculpture

Bucchero, Etruscan black terracotta ware

Caldarium (or calidarium) room for hot or vapour baths in a Roman bath

Campanile, bell-tower, often detached from the building to which it belongs

Camposanto, cemetery

Capital, the top of a column

Cardo (pl. cardines), the main north–south street of a Roman town, at right-angles to the decumanus

Caryatid, female figure used as a supporting column

Cavea, the part of a theatre or amphitheatre occupied by the row of seats

Cella, sanctuary of a temple, usually in the centre of the building

Chiaroscuro, distribution of light and shade, apart from colour, in a painting

Chiesa Madre or **Chiesa Matrice**, parish church

Chryselephantine, overlaid with gold and ivory

Chthonic, dwelling in or under the ground

Ciborium, casket or tabernacle containing the Host

Cipollino, onion-marble; a greyish marble with streaks of white or green

Cippus, sepulchral monument in the form of an altar

Cista, casket, usually of bronze and cylindrical in shape, to hold jewels, toilet articles, etc., and decorated with mythological subjects

Console, ornamental bracket

Crenellations, battlements

Crepidoma, stepped platform on which an ancient temple stood

Cuneus, wedge-shaped block of seats in an antique theatre

Cyclopean, the term applied to walls of unmortared masonry, older than the Etruscan civilisation, and attributed by the ancients to the giant Cyclopes

Decumanus, the main east–west street of a Roman town

Diorite, a type of greenish coloured rock

Dioscuri, name given to Castor and Pollux, twin sons of Zeus

Dipteral, temple surrounded by a double peristyle

Diptych, painting or ivory tablet in two sections

Dipylon, monumental gateway between two supporting piers or pylons

Distyle, of a temple, having two columns in front

Dithyrambic, pertaining to an ecstatic hymn of ancient Greece, especially one dedicated to Dionysus

Duomo, cathedral

Ekklesiasterion, council house for the assembly of the citizens of a town

Emporium, commercial centre of an ancient city, where imported goods were traded

Entablature, the part above the capital (consisting of architrave, frieze and cornice) of a classical building

Entasis, the difference in the diameter of a column at its top, middle and base.

Ephebos, Greek youth under training (military or university)

Epigraph, inscription, especially on coins or sculpture.

Exedra, semicircular recess

Ex-voto, tablet or small painting expressing gratitude to a saint

Fiumare, wide flat-bottomed torrent-bed filled with gravel, usually waterless

Forum, open space in a town serving as a market or meeting-place

Fresco (*affresco*), painting executed on wet plaster. On the wall beneath the sinopia is sketched, and the *cartone* is transferred onto the fresh plaster (*intonaco*) before the fresco is begun, either by pricking the outline with small holes over which a powder is dusted, or by means of a stylus which leaves an incised line on the wet plaster. In recent years many frescoes have been detached from the walls on which they were executed

Frigidarium, room for cold baths in a Roman bath

Fumarole, volcanic spurt of vapour (usually sulphurous) emerging from the ground

Gigantomachia, a contest of gods and giants, a popular motif for relief carvings on temple exteriors

Graffiti, design on a wall made with an iron tool on a prepared surface, the design showing in white. Also used loosely to describe scratched designs or words on walls

Greek cross, cross with arms of equal length

Hellenistic, the period from Alexander the Great to Augustus (c. 325–31 BC)

Herm (pl. *hermae*), quadrangular pillar decreasing in girth towards the ground, surmounted by a bust

Hexastyle, temple with a portico of six columns at the end

Hypogeum, subterranean excavation for the interment of the dead (usually Etruscan)

Intarsia, inlay of wood, marble, or metal

Kore, maiden

Kouros (pl. kouroi), boy; in statuary, an Archaic male standing figure

Krater, antique mixing-bowl, conical in shape with rounded base

Kufic, early decorative, angular form of the Arabic alphabet

Kylix, wide shallow vase with two handles and short stem

Latomiae, the limestone quarries of Siracusa, later used as prisons, and now tropical gardens

Lekythos, container for storing oil, ointment or perfume

Loculus, one of many small cavities, especially in a catacomb or necropolis.

Loggia, covered gallery or balcony, usually preceding a larger building

Lunette, semicircular space in a vault or ceiling, often decorated with a painting or a relief

Mandorla, in art, an almond-shaped aureole around a holy figure

Mascaron, caricatured human face or mask used as architectural decoration

Marmi mischi, inlay decoration of various polychrome marbles and *pietre dure*, used in church interiors in the 17th and 18th century

Medallion, large medal, or a circular ornament

Megalith, a huge stone (often used as a monument)

Megaron, an oblong hall (usually in a Mycenaean palace)

Metope, panel between two triglyphs on the frieze of a temple

Monolith, single stone (usually a column)

Muqarna, stalactite moulding characteristic of Islamic architecture

Narthex, vestibule of a Christian basilica

Naumachia, mock naval combat for which the arena of an amphitheatre was flooded

Nymphaeum, a sort of summer-house in the gardens of baths, palaces, etc., originally a temple of the Nymphs, and decorated with statues of those goddesses

Octastyle, a portico with eight columns

Odeon, a concert hall, usually in the shape of a Greek theatre, but roofed

Ogee (arch.), arch shaped in a double curve, convex above and concave below

Oinochoe, wine-jug usually of elongated shape for dipping wine out of a krater

Opisthodomos, the enclosed rear part of a temple

Opus sectile, mosaic or paving of thin slabs of coloured marble cut in geometrical shapes

Ossuary, deposit of or receptacle for the bones of the dead

Palazzo, any dignified and important building

Pantocrator, the Almighty

Pax, sacred object used by a priest for the blessing of peace, and offered for the kiss of the faithful, usually circular, engraved, enamelled or painted in a rich gold or silver frame

Pediment, gable above the portico of a classical building

Pendentive, concave spandrel beneath a dome

Peripteral, temple surrounded by a colonnade

Peristyle, a columned portico surrounding a court or temple

Pietà, group of the Virgin mourning the dead Christ

Piscina, Roman tank; a basin for an officiating priest to wash his hands before Mass

Pithos, large pottery vessel

Podium, a continuous base or plinth supporting columns, and the lowest row of seats in the cavea of a theatre or amphitheatre

Polyptych, painting or tablet in more than three sections

Predella, small painting attached below a large altarpiece

Presepio, literally, crib or manger. A group of statuary of which the central subject is the Infant Jesus in the manger

Pronaos, porch in front of the cella of a temple

Propylon, **propylaea**. Entrance gate to a temenos; in plural form when there is more than one door

Prostyle, edifice with columns on the front only

Pulvin, cushion stone between the capital and the impost block

Punic, pertaining to the Carthaginians

Putto, figure of a child sculpted or painted, usually nude

Quadriga, four-horsed chariot

Quadriporticus, courtyard surrounded on each side by a portico

Rhyton, drinking-horn usually ending in an animal's head

Sinopia, a reddish brown pigment used to mark the first outline of a fresco

Situla, a small pail for water for ritual use

Squinch, arched space at the angle of a tower

Stamnos, big-bellied vase with two small handles at the sides, closed by a lid

Stele (pl. stelae), upright stone bearing a monumental inscription

Stereobate, basement of a temple or other building

Stilted arch, round arch that rises vertically before it springs

Stoa, a covered, free-standing colonnaded portico, often with shops

Stoup, vessel for Holy Water, usually near the west door of a church

Stucco, plasterwork

Stylobate, basement of a columned temple or other building

Taberna (pl. tabernae) shop in an ancient town

Tablinum, reception room in a Roman house with one side opening onto the central courtyard

Telamon (pl. telamones), see Atlantes

Temenos, a sacred enclosure

Tepidarium, room for warm baths in a Roman bath

Tessera, a small cube of stone, terracotta, marble, glass, etc., used in mosaic work

Tetrastyle, having four columns at the end

Thermae, originally simply baths, later elaborate buildings fitted with libraries, assembly rooms, gymnasia, circuses, etc

Tholos, a circular building

Tondo, round painting or bas-relief

Transenna, open grille or screen, usually of marble, in an early Christian church

Triclinium, dining-room and reception room of a Roman house

Triglyph, blocks with vertical grooves on either side of a metope on the frieze of a temple

Trinacria, the ancient name for Sicily derived from its triangular shape; also the symbol of Sicily: three legs with a head (of Apollo or the Medusa) in the centre

Triptych, painting or tablet in three sections

Tympanum, area above a doorway or the space enclosed by a pediment

Tyrant, in ancient times, the head of a city state, who ruled autocratically (though not necessarily tyrannically)

Villa, country house with its garden

Xystus, an exercise court or covered running track

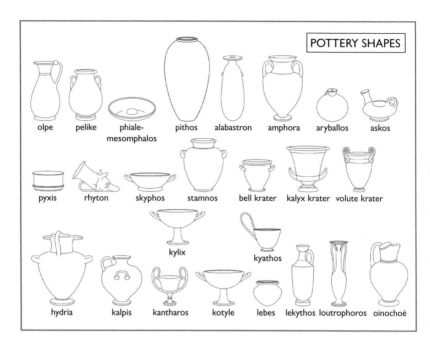

POTTERY SHAPES

olpe   pelike   phiale-mesomphalos   pithos   alabastron   amphora   aryballos   askos

pyxis   rhyton   skyphos   stamnos   bell krater   kalyx krater   volute krater

kylix   kyathos

hydria   kalpis   kantharos   kotyle   lebes   lekythos   loutrophoros   oinochoë

TEMPLE DESIGN

Early temple. This example is distyle in antis, meaning that the entrance has two columns nestling between the projecting piers (antae) of the side walls. The inner chamber (naos) is preceded by an antechamber (pronaos).

More complex temple design, again with two columns in antis, but this time also amphiprostyle, meaning that each end has a colonnaded porch (prostyle). The temple and its porches are built onto a crepidoma, a stepped platform.

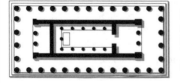

Peripteral temple, with peristyle (colonnade surrounding the naos). Access to the inner chamber (the naos) is through the pronaos (antechamber). The room at the back (with no access to the naos) is the opisthodomos.

THE CLASSICAL ORDERS

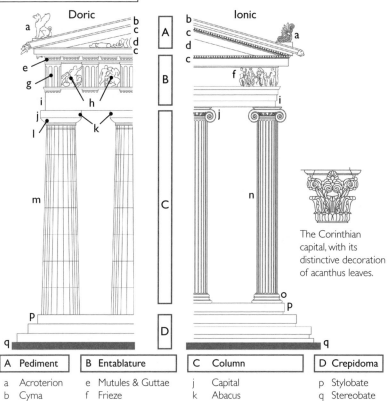

The Corinthian capital, with its distinctive decoration of acanthus leaves.

A	Pediment	B	Entablature	C	Column	D	Crepidoma
a	Acroterion	e	Mutules & Guttae	j	Capital	p	Stylobate
b	Cyma	f	Frieze	k	Abacus	q	Stereobate
c	Cornice	g	Triglyph	l	Echinus		
d	Tympanum	h	Metopes	m/n	Shaft: (m) flutes meet in sharp ridges		
		i	Architrave		(arrises); (n) flutes lie between flat ridges		
					(fillets)		
				o	Base		

ANCIENT THEATRE DESIGN

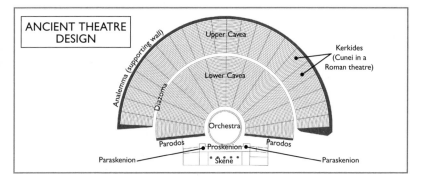

INDEX

Explanatory or more detailed references, or references to places where an artist's work is best represented, are given in bold. Numbers in italics are picture references. Dates are given for all artists, architects and sculptors. Many artists also have entries in the glossary beginning on p. 496.

Alvino, Giuseppe (il Sozzo; 1550–1611) 49

Amato, Andrea (active 1720–35) 383, 413

Amato, Antonino (father of Andrea; active 1697–1717) 383, 386

Amato, Giacomo (1643–1732) 15, 42, 44, 49

Amato, Paolo (1634–1714) 24, 29, 44, 54, 104, 165

Ambrogio da Como (15C) 90

Ameselon, ancient city 273

Amestratus, ancient town 460

Amico, Giovanni Biagio (1684–1754) 51, 52, 121, 122, 123, 130, 142, 216

Anapo valley 360

Andrault, Michel (b. 1926) 338

Andrea da Salerno (Andrea Sabatini; 1480–1530) 48

Andromachus, ruler of Taormina 435

Angell, Samuel 155

Angevins 14, 69, 279

Antonello da Messina (c. 1430–79) 15, **48**, **92**, *93*, 327, 328, 432, 436

Antonello de Saliba (1466–1535) 92, 391, 436, 450, 452, 455

Antonio da Messina (18C) 105

Arabs **13**, 19, 23, 153, 218, 232, 235, 240, 253, 271, 285, 299, 321, 347, 356, 408, 416, 426, 435, 459

Aragona 212

Aragonese 14

Aragonese tombs 381

Archifel, Vincenzo (active 1486–1533) 411

Archimedes 11, 125, 329, **330**

Archonides 461

Arethusa, nymph 327

Asinaro, river 354

Assoro 271

Athens, Athenians 10, 127, 136, 138, 320, 342, 346, 369, 384, 463

Attilius Regulus, consul 218

Augusta 367

Augustus, emperor 274, 377 (*see also* Octavian)

Aulenti, Gae (b. 1927) 92

Ausonians 9

Avola 353

Avola Antica 353

B

Badiazza, La 433

Bagheria 79

Bagnasco, Nicola (18–19C) 101, 272

Balate, Mt 233

Balla, Giacomo (1871–1958) 124

Baragli, Giacomo (1934–89) 150

Barbarossa, Kheir ed-Din 454, 463

Barcellona-Pozzo di Gotto 450

Barisano da Trani (active 1175–85) 72

Baroque architecture 296

Barrafranca 263

Bartholomew, St 463, 464

Bartlett, W.H. (1809–54) 440

Basile, Ernesto (1857–1932) 16, 61, 65, 139, 152, 200, 216, 249

Basile, Giovanni Battista (father of Ernesto; 1825–91) 61, 405, 412

Battaglia, Antonino (son of Francesco; 18–19C) 385

Battaglia, Francesco (1701–88) 380, 383, 390, 410, 411

Battaglia, Matteo (18C) 290, 291

Bedell Smith, general 347

Belice Valley 163

Belisarius, Byzantine general 13

Bellini, Vincenzo 382, 383, 386; (monument to) 389; (tomb of) 381

Belmonte Mezzagno 103

Belpasso 399

Benedetto, Silvio (b. 1938) 218

Benefial, Marco (1684–1764) 78

Bentivegna, Filippo (d. 1967) 205

Berenson, Bernard 301, 428

Bernini, Gian Lorenzo (1598–1680) 247

Berrettaro, Bartolomeo (active 1499–1524) 83, 124, 141, 142, 150, 153, 205, 295

Besio, Giacomo (1612–45) 25

Biancavilla 399

Biangiardi, Francesco (19C) 229

Bisacquino 105

Biviere di Cesarò 457

Biviere di Gela 240

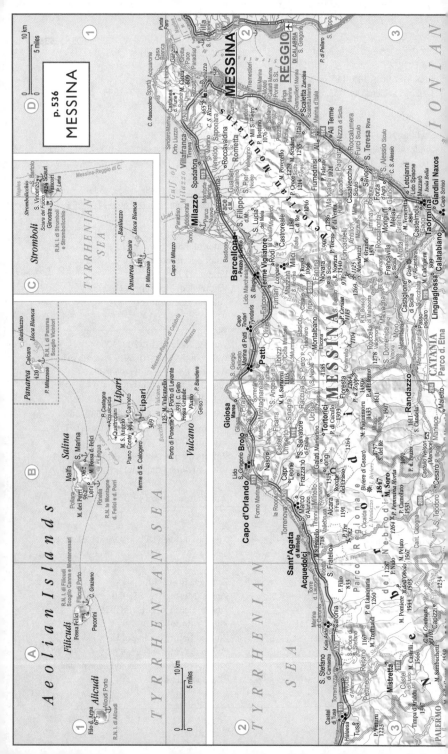

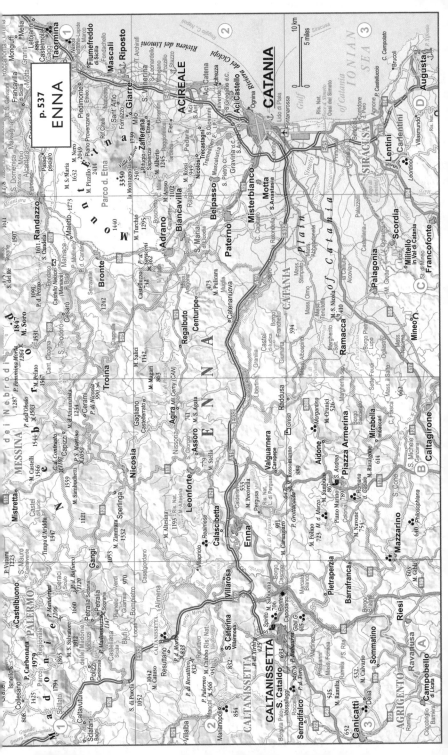

RAGUSA & SYRACUSE

p. 538

0   10 km

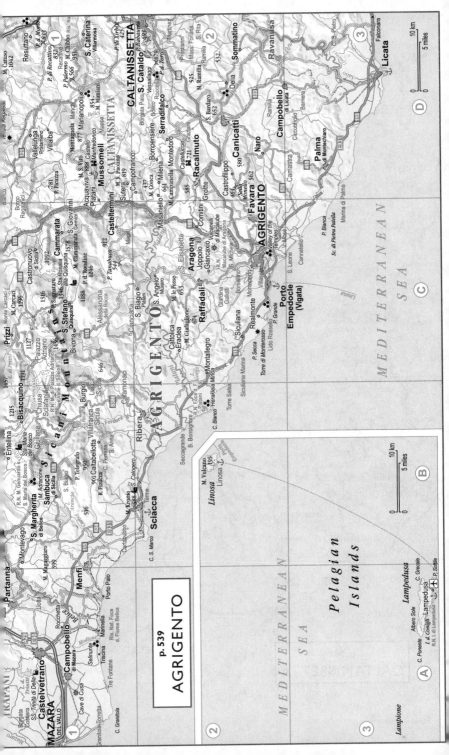

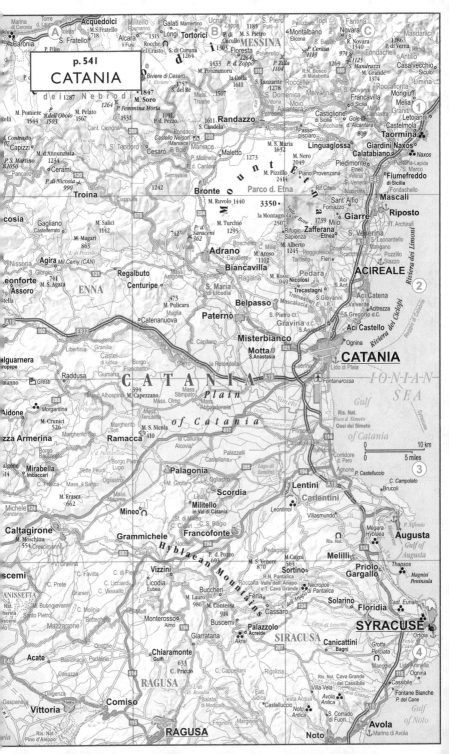

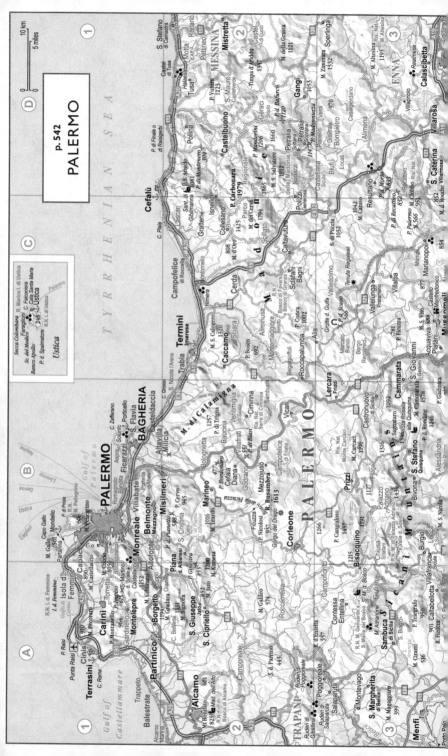

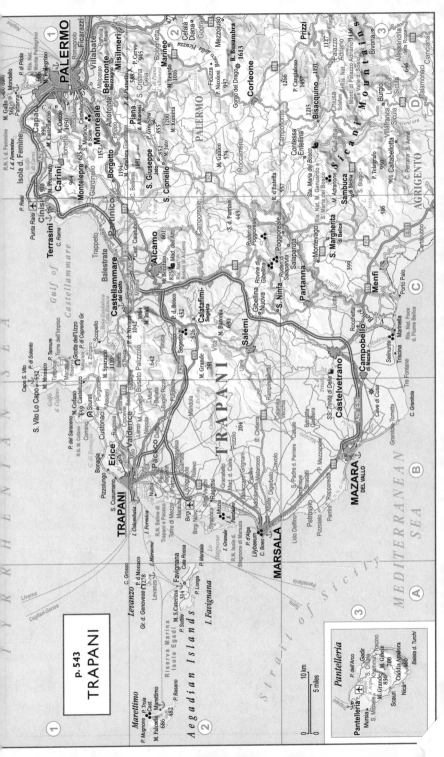